Literature Connections to World History, K-6

Literature Connections to World History, K-6

Resources to Enhance and Entice

Lynda G. Adamson

1998
Libraries Unlimited, Inc.
Englewood, Colorado

For Frank

LIBRARIES UNLIMITED, INC.
P.O. Box 6633
Englewood, CO 80155-6633
1-800-237-6124
www.lu.com

Production Editor: Stephen Haenel
Bibliography Copy Editor: Aviva Rothschild
Bibliography Proofreader: Ann Marie Damian
Layout and Design: Michael Florman

Library of Congress Cataloging-in-Publication Data

Adamson, Lynda G.
    Literature connections to world history, K-6 : resources to
enhance and entice / Lynda G. Adamson.
    xii, 326 p. 19x26 cm.
    Includes bibliographical references and indexes.
    ISBN 1-56308-504-6
    1. Literature and history--Juvenile literature--Bibliography.
2. World history--Juvenile literature--Bibliography. 3. World
history--CD-ROM--Catalogs. 4. World history--Juvenile films--
Catalogs. I. Title.
Z1037.A1A28 1997
[PN50]
016.809'93358--dc21   97-35952
                                                              CIP

Contents

Preface

Studies show that people must respond emotionally to something if they are to remember it. If young readers travel with Rifka in her escape from the pogroms in her beloved Russian village to Ellis Island in Hesse's *Letters from Rifka*, or share Rachel's surprise over losing the right to ride her bicycle in Holland during 1940 in Vos's *Hide and Seek*, they see that some governments have mistreated children because of their parents' religions. By becoming angry at the situations in which Rifka and Rachel find themselves, these readers remember the time and the place of the incidents. Their responses might lead them to read further in additional sources about Hitler's mistreatment of other groups, such as the gypsies and the disabled. Or they might want to know about the immigrants who entered the United States through Ellis Island, and learn what fears they had when they arrived, often unable to speak English or sick from a long sea journey in steerage class. These vicarious experiences could even help readers empathize more readily with the difficulties of contemporary refugees.

If a young reader becomes interested in a topic, a character, or a time period, and asks for books or multimedia about them, the adult consulted needs rapid retrieval capabilities. I have attempted to fulfill that need. This resource connects historical fiction, biography, history trade books, CD-ROMs, and videotapes for individual grade levels within specific time periods and geographic areas. Those books, CD-ROMs, and videotapes included have received at least one favorable review, are well written, or fit a category for which few resources are available. Some of the books and videotapes are award winners, and I have listed known awards won at the end of the annotations. Some of the books are out-of-print but are still available in many libraries. Reprints of them, especially award winners, frequently become available in paperback or under the imprint of another publisher.

When I first began this project, my purpose was to link "good reads" in historical fiction, biography, and history trade books. That focus has continued throughout the creation of this annotated bibliography. I did not anticipate finding as many entries as appear in this resource, but writing style in both biography and history trade books has improved. For that reason, I have listed biographies about the same person by several different authors. I have not made a choice as to which is the best, because each has a different focus. Authors of biography as literature try to make their subjects come alive, and the authors here have achieved this goal. The annotations in the final section attempt to include different facts about the biographical subjects instead of trying to identify the sometimes elusive differences among the authors' writing styles and themes.

History trade books differ from history textbooks because their authors rarely use passive voice, and they rely heavily on diaries, letters, documents, and other references that tell about the people who lived during the time. Thus, young readers might respond more often to these books than to history textbooks filled with dull dates and incident inventories. Some of the history trade books included have more illustrations than text, but they can be valuable for enticing slow or unwilling readers to look for other books. These information books bridge the distance between unillustrated books and videotapes.

The multimedia category covers CD-ROMs and videotapes. Because videotapes seem more accessible for the classroom, or even for home use, I have omitted laser discs and filmstrips. Because computer use is increasing both in the home and in the schools, I have included favorably reviewed CD-ROMs or those on specific topics that will help readers find further information. Some of the more recent CD-ROMs have stunning pictures, excellent biographical information, and other attractions that may lead a viewer to books.

Because readers become interested in a variety of topics for many different reasons, the books in the historical fiction category listed in a specific grade level may or may not deal with the same persons as in the biographies, cover the variety of time periods in the history trade titles, or fulfill the traditional definition of "historical fiction." A specific correspondence of titles seems unnecessary. Hitler may not be named in Vos's *Hide and Seek*, but his presence permeates the book. The same reader might want more information about other people who worked under Hitler's influence. The book lists, along with the annotations, will reveal other resources on these subjects. Additionally, I have broadened the definition of historical fiction to include books outside most young readers' memories rather than books whose authors are writing about time periods prior to two or more generations. Children and young adults today do not know the importance of the fall of the Berlin Wall, and many do not understand that Bosnia is an area of the world. Thus I have included some books that might loosely be termed historical fiction or contemporary realistic fiction because they will give readers an insight into a time separate from their own.

While doing the research for this reference, I realized that it should include as many good books or videotapes published since 1990 as possible, as well as some highly regarded works from prior years. I hope that adults will find most of the recommended books on library shelves or can order them from a publisher. I have tried to include a wide range of titles so that the researcher will have choices if the first title selected from this resource is not readily available. My goal is for young readers to have emotional responses to the people who have made history so that they, as future world citizens, can better understand themselves and the times in which they live.

During this period of intensive work, two people have made this book possible. Elena Rodriguez at Gunston Middle School in Arlington, Virginia, allowed me to raid her library shelves for many days. Without her excellent collection, I would not have been able to easily locate many of the books that I have included. The other indispensable helper was my husband, who edited text. Additionally, the editorial staff at Libraries Unlimited, especially Stephen Haenel, has offered advice and aid in an effort to make this resource available.

Introduction

This resource divides naturally into two main sections. The first part lists authors and book titles in the categories of historical fiction, biography, collective biography, history trade book, CD-ROM, and videotape within specific regions and time periods according to grade levels. The second part contains annotated bibliographies of titles listed in the first part: books, CD-ROMs, and videotapes. The books, videotapes, and CD-ROMs merit inclusion because they have received favorable reviews, are well written, or are one of the few titles available on a particular subject; thus, the annotations are descriptive rather than evaluative.

Chapter divisions in the first section are by chronological time periods or areas of the world. In each chapter, works appropriate for a particular grade level appear under that grade-level heading in their specific category of historical fiction, biography (including collective biography), history, and multimedia (CD-ROMs and videotapes). Books are alphabetized according to the author's last name so that the researcher can easily locate the annotation in the second section of the resource. CD-ROMs and videotapes are alphabetized by title.

Some titles in the first part appear several different times. For example, when a title about the Middle Ages is suitable for grades four through six, the title appears under each grade level of four, five, and six in the chapter covering the medieval period (A.D. 476-1491). Other titles appear in different chapters because their settings, either fiction or fact, occur in more than one place or involve more than one nation. For example, battles fought in the Pacific during World War II have the Pacific Islands as their settings, but Europeans and Americans as their participants.

I based grade-level choices on recommended grade levels in review sources or publisher catalogs. In some cases, when the grade levels seemed unusually low or high, I adjusted them after evaluating the text and the subject matter. For example, few fifth graders would probably be interested in Queen Victoria, but a high school student who is curious about motivations in women who have led their countries could be very interested. I adjusted that grade level upward so that the biography on Queen Victoria appears in *Literature Connections to World History, 7-12: Resources to Enhance and Entice*. Several biographies on Marie Curie describe her long searches through pitchblende for the elements she needed to continue her work. Concrete scientific results seem more accessible to the younger reader than political discussions.

The chapter divisions correspond as nearly as possible to major historical events in Europe and the British Isles, such as the era of the Roman Empire. The chapters based on geographical areas loosely link countries within a particular part of the world—Israel with Arab countries and the Pacific Islands with Australia. Identifying a book's country of origin in these chapters may be difficult merely by reading the title, so researchers will have to rely on the annotations in the second part for more specific information.

The annotations include such information as author, title, publisher, price, ISBN, paper imprint, and grade levels. The book prices are accurate at printing, based on publishers' catalogs and such library buying sources as *Books in Print* and Baker and Taylor. I have made a similar attempt to include sources for books and their paper imprints, if available. The range of grade levels appears at the end of each bibliographic entry.

For easiest access to this resource, researchers should find the time period or geographic area of interest in the table of contents. Grade levels under the chapter listings will tell where to locate the book and multimedia categories. In the grade-level listings, researchers should select titles. Then they should go to the appropriate section of the second part of the book.

Researchers unsure of the dates of a particular historical event might want to skim the listings for the sixth-grade level, as that level has more entries with titles referring to historical events than the other levels. After finding the correct time period or geographical area, the researcher can then refer to the appropriate grade level to see if a book or multimedia source is available. If it is not, the researcher may be able to choose an appropriate title from the next highest or lowest grade-level categories. Another point of access for readers is the subject index.

Prehistory and the Ancient World to 54 B.C.

GRADES KINDERGARTEN THROUGH TWO

Historical Fiction

Nolan. *Wolf Child*

Stoltz. *Zekmet the Stone Carver*

Walsh. *Pepi and the Secret Names*

Biography

Lasker. *The Great Alexander the Great*

Collective Biography

Marzollo. *My First Book of Biographies*

History

Aliki. *Mummies Made in Egypt*

Delafosse. *Pyramids*

Gibbons. *Beacons of Light: Lighthouses*

Jacobsen. *Egypt*

MacDonald. *I Wonder Why Greeks Built Temples*

GRADE THREE

Historical Fiction

Bunting. *I Am the Mummy Heb-Nefert*

Nolan. *Wolf Child*

Pryor. *Seth of the Lion People*

Rubalcaba. *A Place in the Sun*

Sabuda. *Tutankhamen's Gift*

Stoltz. *Zekmet the Stone Carver*

Turner. *Time of the Bison*

Walsh. *Pepi and the Secret Names*

Biography

Ash. *Alexander the Great*

Lasker. *The Great Alexander the Great*

Collective Biography

Marzollo. *My First Book of Biographies*

History

Aliki. *Mummies Made in Egypt*

Arnold. *Stone Age Farmers Beside the Sea: Scotland's Prehistoric Village*

Brierley. *Explorers of the Ancient World*

Briquebec. *The Ancient World*

Burns. *The Mail*

Chrisp. *The Farmer Through History*

Chrisp. *The Soldier Through History*

Cohen. *Ancient Egypt*

Cohen. *Ancient Greece*

Colville. *Prehistoric Peoples*

Gibbons. *Beacons of Light: Lighthouses*

Golden. *The Passover Journey*

Gravett. *Arms and Armor*

Guiberson. *Lighthouses*

Harris. *Life in Ancient Egypt*

Haslam. *Ancient Egypt*

Humble. *Ships*
Jackson. *The Winter Solstice*
Jacobsen. *Egypt*
Jessop. *Big Buildings of the Ancient World*
King. *Seven Ancient Wonders of the World*
Knight. *The Olympic Games*
Krupp. *Let's Go Traveling*
Lessum. *The Ice Man*

MacDonald. *I Wonder Why Greeks Built Temples*
Maestro. *The Story of Money*
Martell. *What Do We Know About the Celts?*
Mason. *If You Were There in Biblical Times*
Moss. *Forts and Castles*
Pearson. *Everyday Life in Ancient Greece*

Pearson. *What Do We Know About the Greeks?*
Rees. *The Ancient Egyptians*
Rees. *The Ancient Greeks*
Tanaka. *I Was There: Discovering the Iceman*
Wilson. *Visual Timeline of Transportation*

Multimedia

Video

The Mystery of the Cave Paintings

GRADE FOUR

Historical Fiction

Bellairs. *The Trolley to Yesterday*
Bunting. *I Am the Mummy Heb-Nefert*
Cowley. *Dar and the Spear-thrower*

Mann. *The Great Pyramid*
Nolan. *Wolf Child*
Pryor. *Seth of the Lion People*
Rubalcaba. *A Place in the Sun*
Sabuda. *Tutankhamen's Gift*

Stoltz. *Zekmet the Stone Carver*
Turner. *Time of the Bison*
Walsh. *Pepi and the Secret Names*

Biography

Ash. *Alexander the Great*
Green. *Alexander the Great*
Lafferty. *Archimedes*

Lasker. *The Great Alexander the Great*

Parker. *Aristotle and Scientific Thought*

Collective Biography

Clements. *The Picture History of Great Inventors*

Jacobs. *Great Lives: World Religions*

History

Aliki. *Mummies Made in Egypt*
Arnold. *Stone Age Farmers Beside the Sea: Scotland's Prehistoric Village*
Balkwill. *Food and Feasts in Ancient Egypt*
Berrill. *Mummies, Masks, & Mourners*
Brierley. *Explorers of the Ancient World*
Briquebec. *The Ancient World*
Burns. *The Mail*
Burns. *Money*
Chrisp. *The Farmer Through History*
Chrisp. *The Soldier Through History*
Clare. *Pyramids of Ancient Egypt*
Cohen. *Ancient Egypt*
Cohen. *Ancient Greece*

Colville. *Prehistoric Peoples*
Coolidge. *The Golden Days of Greece*
Coote. *The Egyptians*
Corbishley. *Secret Cities*
Dawson. *Food and Feasts in Ancient Greece*
Deem. *How to Make a Mummy Talk*
Descamps-Lequime. *The Ancient Greeks*
Duggleby. *Impossible Quests*
Eschle. *The Curse of Tutankhamen*
Freeman. *The Ancient Greeks*
Gay. *Science in Ancient Greece*
Getz. *Frozen Man*
Gibbons. *Beacons of Light: Lighthouses*
Giblin. *Be Seated: A Book About Chairs*
Golden. *The Passover Journey*

Grant. *The Egyptians*
Gravett. *Arms and Armor*
Guiberson. *Lighthouses*
Harris. *Life in Ancient Egypt*
Harris. *Mummies*
Hart. *Ancient Egypt*
Haslam. *Ancient Egypt*
Humble. *Ships*
Jackson. *The Winter Solstice*
Jacobsen. *Egypt*
Jessop. *Big Buildings of the Ancient World*
Kent. *A Slice Through a City*
Kerr. *Keeping Clean*
King. *Seven Ancient Wonders of the World*
Knight. *The Olympic Games*
Krupp. *Let's Go Traveling*
Landau. *The Curse of Tutankhamen*
Lessum. *The Ice Man*

MacDonald. *First Facts About the Ancient Greeks*
MacDonald. *A Greek Temple*
MacDonald. *I Wonder Why Greeks Built Temples*
Maestro. *The Story of Money*
Martell. *Over 6,000 Years Ago*
Martell. *What Do We Know About the Celts?*
Mason. *If You Were There in Biblical Times*
Matthews. *The First People*
Matthews. *The First Settlements*
Millard. *Pyramids*
Moss. *Forts and Castles*
Oliphant. *The Earliest Civilizations*
Pearson. *Everyday Life in Ancient Greece*

Pearson. *What Do We Know About the Greeks?*
Poulton. *Life in the Time of Pericles and the Ancient Greeks*
Powell. *The Greek News*
Putnam. *Mummy*
Rees. *The Ancient Egyptians*
Rees. *The Ancient Greeks*
Reeves. *Into the Mummy's Tomb*
Ross. *Conquerors & Explorers*
Ryan. *Explorers and Mapmakers*
Sattler. *Hominids*
Simon. *Explorers of the Ancient World*
Steedman. *The Egyptian News*

Steele. *The Egyptians and the Valley of the Kings*
Steele. *I Wonder Why Pyramids Were Built*
Stones and Bones: How Archaeologists Trace Human Origins
Tanaka. *I Was There: Discovering the Iceman*
Ventura. *Clothing*
Ventura. *Food*
Wilcox. *Mummies and Their Mysteries*
Williams. *The Greeks*
Wilson. *Visual Timeline of Transportation*
Woolf. *Picture This: A First Introduction to Paintings*
Wright. *Egyptians*

Multimedia

CD-ROM

Teach Your Kids World History

Video

Egypt: Children of the Nile
Egypt: The Nile River Kingdom

The Mystery of the Cave Paintings
The Mystery of the Pyramids

Who Built the Pyramids?

GRADE FIVE

Historical Fiction

Bellairs. *The Trolley to Yesterday*
Brennan. *Shiva: An Adventure of the Ice Age*
Bunting. *I Am the Mummy Heb-Nefert*
Cowley. *Dar and the Spear-thrower*

Furlong. *Juniper*
Lewis. *The Ship That Flew*
Mann. *The Great Pyramid*
McGowen. *The Time of the Forest*
McGraw. *The Golden Goblet*
McGraw. *Mara, Daughter of the Nile*

Nolan. *Wolf Child*
Pryor. *Seth of the Lion People*
Rubalcaba. *A Place in the Sun*
Sabuda. *Tutankhamen's Gift*
Sutcliff. *Warrior Scarlet*
Turner. *Time of the Bison*
Walsh. *Pepi and the Secret Names*

Biography

Ash. *Alexander the Great*
Green. *Alexander the Great*
Green. *Tutankhamun*

King. *Pericles*
Lafferty. *Archimedes*
Llywelyn. *Xerxes*

Parker. *Aristotle and Scientific Thought*
Wepman. *Alexander the Great*

Collective Biography

Clements. *The Picture History of Great Inventors*
Hazell. *Heroines: Great Women Through the Ages*

Jacobs. *Great Lives: World Religions*
Wilkinson. *Generals Who Changed the World*

History

Aliki. *Mummies Made in Egypt*

Arnold. *Stone Age Farmers Beside the Sea: Scotland's Prehistoric Village*

Avi-Yonah. *Piece By Piece! Mosaics of the Ancient World*

Balkwill. *Food and Feasts in Ancient Egypt*

Berrill. *Mummies, Masks, & Mourners*

Brierley. *Explorers of the Ancient World*

Briquebec. *The Ancient World*

Burns. *The Mail*

Burns. *Money*

Burrell. *The Greeks*

Capek. *Murals*

Chaikin. *Menorahs, Mezuzas, and Other Jewish Symbols*

Chaikin. *A Nightmare in History*

Charley. *Tombs and Treasures*

Chrisp. *The Farmer Through History*

Chrisp. *The Soldier Through History*

Clare. *Pyramids of Ancient Egypt*

Cohen. *Ancient Egypt*

Cohen. *Ancient Greece*

Colville. *Prehistoric Peoples*

Coolidge. *The Golden Days of Greece*

Cooper. *The Dead Sea Scrolls*

Coote. *The Egyptians*

Corbishley. *Secret Cities*

Crosher. *Ancient Egypt*

Davies. *Transport*

Dawson. *Food and Feasts in Ancient Greece*

Deem. *How to Make a Mummy Talk*

Descamps-Lequime. *The Ancient Greeks*

Duggleby. *Impossible Quests*

Eschle. *The Curse of Tutankhamen*

Freeman. *The Ancient Greeks*

Gay. *Science in Ancient Greece*

Getz. *Frozen Man*

Giblin. *Be Seated: A Book About Chairs*

Giblin. *The Riddle of the Rosetta Stone*

Giblin. *When Plague Strikes*

Golden. *The Passover Journey*

Gonen. *Charge! Weapons and Warfare in Ancient Times*

Gonen. *Fired Up: Making Pottery*

Grant. *The Egyptians*

Gravett. *Arms and Armor*

Guiberson. *Lighthouses*

Harris. *Life in Ancient Egypt*

Harris. *Mummies*

Hart. *Ancient Egypt*

Haslam. *Ancient Egypt*

Hirsch. *Taxation*

Humble. *Ships*

Jessop. *Big Buildings of the Ancient World*

Kent. *A Slice Through a City*

Kerr. *Keeping Clean*

King. *Seven Ancient Wonders of the World*

Koenig. *The Ancient Egyptians*

Knight. *The Olympic Games*

Krupp. *Let's Go Traveling*

Landau. *The Curse of Tutankhamen*

Lessum. *The Ice Man*

Loverance. *Ancient Greece*

MacDonald. *First Facts About the Ancient Greeks*

MacDonald. *A Greek Temple*

Maestro. *The Story of Money*

Marston. *The Ancient Egyptians*

Martell. *The Celts*

Martell. *Kingfisher: From the Ice Age to the Roman Empire*

Martell. *Over 6,000 Years Ago*

Martell. *What Do We Know About the Celts?*

Mason. *If You Were There in Biblical Times*

Matthews. *The First People*

Matthews. *The First Settlements*

McNeill. *Ancient Egyptian People*

McNeill. *Ancient Egyptian Places*

Millard. *Pyramids*

Morley. *Clothes*

Moss. *Forts and Castles*

Moss. *Science in Ancient Mesopotamia*

Odijk. *The Phoenicians*

Odijk. *The Sumerians*

Oliphant. *The Earliest Civilizations*

Pearson. *Everyday Life in Ancient Greece*

Pearson. *What Do We Know About the Greeks?*

Platt. *Pirate*

Platt. *The Smithsonian Visual Timeline of Inventions*

Poulton. *Life in the Time of Pericles and the Ancient Greeks*

Powell. *The Greek News*

Putnam. *Mummy*

Reeves. *Into the Mummy's Tomb*

Ross. *Conquerors & Explorers*

Ryan. *Explorers and Mapmakers*

Sattler. *Hominids*

Schomp. *The Ancient Greeks*

Simon. *Explorers of the Ancient World*

Steedman. *The Egyptian News*

Steele. *The Egyptians and the Valley of the Kings*

Steele. *I Wonder Why Pyramids Were Built*

Steele. *Kidnapping*

Steele. *Smuggling*

Steele. *Thermopylae*

Stones and Bones: How Archaeologists Trace Human Origins

Street Smart! Cities of the Ancient World

Tanaka. *I Was There: Discovering the Iceman*

Turvey. *Inventions: Inventors and Ingenious Ideas*

Ventura. *Clothing*

Ventura. *Food*

Wilcox. *Mummies and Their Mysteries*

Wilkinson. *The Mediterranean*

Williams. *The Greeks*

Wilson. *Visual Timeline of Transportation*

Wood. *Ancient Wonders*

Woods. *Science in Ancient Egypt*

Woolf. *Picture This: A First Introduction to Paintings*

Wright. *Egyptians*

Multimedia —————————————————————————————

CD-ROM

*Eyewitness Encyclopedia of
Science*

*Teach Your Kids World
History*

Video

*Ancient Egypt: The Gift of the
Nile (3000 BC-30 BC)*
The British Way of Life
Egypt: Children of the Nile

*Egypt: The Nile River
Kingdom*
*The Mystery of the Cave
Paintings*

The Mystery of the Pyramids
Who Built the Pyramids?

GRADE SIX

Historical Fiction —————————————————————

Brennan. *Shiva: An
Adventure of the Ice Age*
Carter. *His Majesty, Queen
Hatshepsut*
Cowley. *Dar and the
Spear-thrower*
Furlong. *Juniper*

Furlong. *Wise Child*
Lewis. *The Ship That Flew*
Mann. *The Great Pyramid*
McGowen. *The Time of the
Forest*
McGraw. *The Golden Goblet*

McGraw. *Mara, Daughter of
the Nile*
Pryor. *Seth of the Lion People*
Rubalcaba. *A Place in the Sun*
Service. *The Reluctant God*
Sutcliff. *Warrior Scarlet*
Treece. *Men of the Hills*

Biography ——————————————————————————————

Ash. *Alexander the Great*
Green. *Alexander the Great*
Green. *Tutankhamun*
King. *Pericles*

Lafferty. *Archimedes*
Lasky. *The Librarian Who
Measured the Earth*
Llywelyn. *Xerxes*

Parker. *Aristotle and
Scientific Thought*
Wepman. *Alexander the Great*

Collective Biography

Clements. *The Picture
History of Great Inventors*
Cohen. *Prophets of Doom*

Hazell. *Heroines: Great
Women Through the Ages*
Jacobs. *Great Lives: World
Religions*

Scheller. *Amazing
Archaeologists*
Wilkinson. *Generals Who
Changed the World*

History ———————————————————————————————

Aliki. *Mummies Made in
Egypt*
Avi-Yonah. *Piece By Piece!
Mosaics of the Ancient
World*
Balkwill. *Food and Feasts in
Ancient Egypt*
Berrill. *Mummies, Masks, &
Mourners*
Brierley. *Explorers of the
Ancient World*
Briquebec. *The Ancient World*
Burns. *Money*
Burrell. *The Greeks*
Capek. *Murals*
Chaikin. *Menorahs, Mezuzas,
and Other Jewish Symbols*
Chaikin. *A Nightmare in
History*
Charley. *Tombs and Treasures*
Clare. *Ancient Greece*
Clare. *Pyramids of Ancient
Egypt*

Clements. *An Illustrated
History of the World*
Cohen. *Ancient Egypt*
Cohen. *Ancient Greece*
Coolidge. *The Golden Days
of Greece*
Cooper. *The Dead Sea
Scrolls*
Coote. *The Egyptians*
Corbishley. *Secret Cities*
Crosher. *Ancient Egypt*
Davies. *Transport*
Dawson. *Food and Feasts in
Ancient Greece*
*Dazzling! Jewelry of the
Ancient World*
Deem. *How to Make a
Mummy Talk*
Descamps-Lequime. *The
Ancient Greeks*
Duggleby. *Impossible Quests*
Eschle. *The Curse of
Tutankhamen*

Freeman. *The Ancient Greeks*
Gay. *Science in Ancient
Greece*
Getz. *Frozen Man*
Giblin. *Be Seated: A Book
About Chairs*
Giblin. *The Riddle of the
Rosetta Stone*
Giblin. *When Plague Strikes*
Golden. *The Passover Journey*
Gonen. *Charge! Weapons
and Warfare in Ancient
Times*
Gonen. *Fired Up: Making
Pottery*
Grant. *The Egyptians*
Gravett. *Arms and Armor*
Guiberson. *Lighthouses*
Harris. *Ancient Egypt*
Harris. *Life in Ancient Egypt*
Harris. *Mummies*
Hart. *Ancient Egypt*
Haslam. *Ancient Egypt*

Hirsch. *Taxation*
Humble. *Ships*
Hunter. *First Civilizations*
Jessop. *Big Buildings of the Ancient World*
Kent. *A Slice Through a City*
Kerr. *Keeping Clean*
King. *Seven Ancient Wonders of the World*
Koenig. *The Ancient Egyptians*
Landau. *The Curse of Tutankhamen*
Lessum. *The Ice Man*
Loverance. *Ancient Greece*
MacDonald. *Cities*
MacDonald. *First Facts About the Ancient Greeks*
MacDonald. *A Greek Temple*
Marston. *The Ancient Egyptians*
Martell. *The Celts*
Martell. *Kingfisher: From the Ice Age to the Roman Empire*
Martell. *Over 6,000 Years Ago*
Martell. *What Do We Know About the Celts?*
Mason. *If You Were There in Biblical Times*
Matthews. *The First People*
Matthews. *The First Settlements*
McNeill. *Ancient Egyptian People*
McNeill. *Ancient Egyptian Places*
Millard. *Pyramids*
Morley. *Clothes*

Moss. *Forts and Castles*
Moss. *Science in Ancient Mesopotamia*
Odijk. *The Phoenicians*
Odijk. *The Sumerians*
Oliphant. *The Earliest Civilizations*
O'Neal. *Pyramids*
Pearson. *Ancient Greece*
Pearson. *Everyday Life in Ancient Greece*
Pearson. *What Do We Know About the Greeks?*
Platt. *Pirate*
Platt. *The Smithsonian Visual Timeline of Inventions*
Poulton. *Life in the Time of Pericles and the Ancient Greeks*
Powell. *Ancient Greece*
Powell. *The Greek News*
Putnam. *Mummy*
Reeves. *Into the Mummy's Tomb*
Rogerson. *Cultural Atlas of the Bible*
Ross. *Conquerors & Explorers*
Ryan. *Explorers and Mapmakers*
Sattler. *Hominids*
Schomp. *The Ancient Greeks*
Scrawl! *Writing in Ancient Times*
Simon. *Explorers of the Ancient World*
Singer. *Structures that Changed the Way the World Looked*

Smith. *Egypt of the Pharaohs*
Sold! *The Origins of Money and Trade*
Steedman. *The Egyptian News*
Steele. *The Egyptians and the Valley of the Kings*
Steele. *I Wonder Why Pyramids Were Built*
Steele. *Kidnapping*
Steele. *Smuggling*
Steele. *Thermopylae*
Stones and Bones: *How Archaeologists Trace Human Origins*
Street Smart! *Cities of the Ancient World*
Time-Life. *What Life Was Like on the Banks of the Nile*
Turvey. *Inventions: Inventors and Ingenious Ideas*
Ventura. *Clothing*
Ventura. *Food*
Warburton. *The Beginning of Writing*
Wilcox. *Mummies and Their Mysteries*
Wilkinson. *The Lands of the Bible*
Wilkinson. *The Mediterranean*
Williams. *Forts and Castles*
Williams. *The Greeks*
Wood. *Ancient Wonders*
Woods. *Science in Ancient Egypt*
Woolf. *Picture This: A First Introduction to Paintings*
Wright. *Egyptians*

Multimedia

CD-ROM

Exploring Ancient Cities
Eyewitness Encyclopedia of Science

History Through Art: Ancient Greece
Le Louvre: The Palace & Its Paintings

Teach Your Kids World History

Video

Ancient Egypt: The Gift of the Nile (3000 BC-30 BC)
The Beginning Is in the End
The British Way of Life
Egypt: Children of the Nile

Egypt: The Nile River Kingdom
The End Is the Beginning
The Mystery of the Cave Paintings

The Mystery of the Pyramids
On the Town
Safekeeping
Who Built the Pyramids?

Roman Empire to A.D. 476

GRADES KINDERGARTEN THROUGH TWO

Biography

DePaola. *Patrick*

Collective Biography

Marzollo. *My First Book of Biographies*

History

Ballard. *The Lost Wreck of the Isis*
MacDonald. *I Wonder Why Romans Wore Togas*

Rockwell. *Romulus and Remus*
Ventura. *Venice: Birth of a City*

GRADE THREE

Biography

DePaola. *Patrick*

Dunlop. *Tales of St. Patrick*

Collective Biography

Marzollo. *My First Book of Biographies*

Steele. *Pirates*

History

Ballard. *The Lost Wreck of the Isis*
Brierley. *Explorers of the Ancient World*
Burns. *The Mail*
Chrisp. *The Farmer Through History*
Chrisp. *The Soldier Through History*

Coote. *The Sailor Through History*
Corbishley. *What Do We Know About the Romans?*
Gravett. *Arms and Armor*
Humble. *Ships*
Jackson. *The Winter Solstice*
Jessop. *Big Buildings of the Ancient World*

MacDonald. *I Wonder Why Romans Wore Togas*
Maestro. *The Story of Money*
Moss. *Forts and Castles*
Mulvihill. *Roman Forts*
Ventura. *Venice: Birth of a City*
Wilson. *Visual Timeline of Transportation*

GRADE FOUR

Biography

Dunlop. *Tales of St. Patrick*
Green. *Cleopatra*

Green. *Herod the Great*
Green. *Julius Caesar*

Collective Biography

Clements. *The Picture History of Great Inventors*

Jacobs. *Great Lives: World Religions*

Steele. *Pirates*

History

Ballard. *The Lost Wreck of the Isis*
Bisel. *The Secrets of Vesuvius*
Brierley. *Explorers of the Ancient World*
Burke. *Food and Fasting*
Burns. *The Mail*
Burns. *Money*
Bursell. *Haunted Houses*
Chrisp. *The Farmer Through History*
Chrisp. *The Soldier Through History*
Compton. *Marriage Customs*
Coote. *The Sailor Through History*
Corbishley. *Everyday Life in Roman Times*
Corbishley. *Rome and the Ancient World*
Corbishley. *What Do We Know About the Romans?*

Giblin. *Be Seated: A Book About Chairs*
Gravett. *Arms and Armor*
Haywood. *The Romans*
Hicks. *The Romans*
Howarth. *Roman People*
Howarth. *Roman Places*
Humble. *Ships*
James. *Ancient Rome*
Jackson. *The Winter Solstice*
Jessop. *Big Buildings of the Ancient World*
Kent. *A Slice Through a City*
Kerr. *Keeping Clean*
MacDonald. *I Wonder Why Romans Wore Togas*
Maestro. *The Story of Money*
Morley. *A Roman Villa*
Moss. *Forts and Castles*
Mulvihill. *Roman Forts*
Pirotta. *Rome*

Poulton. *Life in the Time of Augustus and the Ancient Romans*
Prior. *Initiation Customs*
Prior. *Pilgrimages and Journeys*
Putnam. *Mummy*
Ross. *Bandits & Outlaws*
Rowland-Warne. *Costume*
Rushton. *Birth Customs*
Rushton. *Death Customs*
Schneider. *Between the Dragon and the Eagle*
Steele. *The Romans and Pompeii*
Ventura. *Clothing*
Ventura. *Food*
Whittock. *The Roman Empire*
Wilson. *Visual Timeline of Transportation*
Woolf. *Picture This: A First Introduction to Paintings*

Multimedia

CD-ROM

Teach Your Kids World History

Video

Turkey: Between Europe and Asia

GRADE FIVE

Biography

Bruns. *Julius Caesar*
Dunlop. *Tales of St. Patrick*
Green. *Cleopatra*
Green. *Herod the Great*
Green. *Julius Caesar*

Hoobler. *Cleopatra*
Kittredge. *Marc Antony*
Simms. *St. Patrick: The Real Story of Patrick*
Stanley. *Cleopatra*

Várdy. *Attila*
Walworth. *Augustus Caesar*
Walworth. *Constantine*

Collective Bibliography

Clements. *The Picture History of Great Inventors*
Jacobs. *Great Lives: World Religions*
Steele. *Pirates*

Wilkinson. *Generals Who Changed the World*
Wilkinson. *People Who Changed the World*

Wilkinson. *Statesmen Who Changed the World*

History

Avi-Yonah. *Piece By Piece! Mosaics of the Ancient World*

Ballard. *The Lost Wreck of the Isis*
Baxter. *Invaders and Settlers*
Baxter. *Romans*

Biel. *Pompeii*
Bisel. *The Secrets of Vesuvius*
Brierley. *Explorers of the Ancient World*

Burke. *Food and Fasting*
Burns. *The Mail*
Burns. *Money*
Bursell. *Haunted Houses*
Chaikin. *Menorahs, Mezuzas, and Other Jewish Symbols*
Charley. *Tombs and Treasures*
Chrisp. *The Farmer Through History*
Chrisp. *The Soldier Through History*
Compton. *Marriage Customs*
Connolly. *Tiberius Claudius Maximus: The Calvaryman*
Connolly. *Tiberius Claudius Maximus: The Legionary*
Coote. *The Sailor Through History*
Corbishley. *Everyday Life in Roman Times*
Corbishley. *Rome and the Ancient World*
Corbishley. *What Do We Know About the Romans?*
Davies. *Transport*
Giblin. *Be Seated: A Book About Chairs*

Giblin. *The Truth About Unicorns*
Gravett. *Arms and Armor*
Guittard. *The Romans*
Harris. *Science in Ancient Rome*
Haywood. *The Romans*
Hicks. *The Romans*
Hirsch. *Taxation*
Howarth. *Roman People*
Howarth. *Roman Places*
Humble. *Ships*
James. *Ancient Rome*
Jessop. *Big Buildings of the Ancient World*
Kent. *A Slice Through a City*
Kerr. *Keeping Clean*
Langley. *The Roman News*
MacDonald. *Cities*
Maestro. *The Story of Money*
Morley. *Clothes*
Morley. *A Roman Villa*
Moss. *Forts and Castles*
Mulvihill. *Roman Forts*
Nardo. *The Age of Augustus*
Odijk. *The Romans*
Pirotta. *Rome*
Platt. *Pirate*

Platt. *The Smithsonian Visual Timeline of Inventions*
Poulton. *Life in the Time of Augustus and the Ancient Romans*
Prior. *Initiation Customs*
Prior. *Pilgrimages and Journeys*
Putnam. *Mummy*
Ross. *Bandits & Outlaws*
Rowland-Warne. *Costume*
Rushton. *Birth Customs*
Rushton. *Death Customs*
Schneider. *Between the Dragon and the Eagle*
Steele. *Kidnapping*
Steele. *The Romans and Pompeii*
Turvey. *Inventions: Inventors and Ingenious Ideas*
Ventura. *Clothing*
Ventura. *Food*
Watkins. *Gladiator*
Whittock. *The Roman Empire*
Wilkinson. *The Mediterranean*
Wilson. *Visual Timeline of Transportation*
Woolf. *Picture This: A First Introduction to Paintings*

Multimedia

CD-ROM

Teach Your Kids World History

Video

The British Way of Life

Turkey: Between Europe and Asia

GRADE SIX

Biography

Bruns. *Julius Caesar*
Dunlop. *Tales of St. Patrick*
Green. *Cleopatra*
Green. *Herod the Great*
Green. *Julius Caesar*

Hoobler. *Cleopatra*
Kittredge. *Marc Antony*
Simms. *St. Patrick: The Real Story of Patrick*
Stanley. *Cleopatra*

Várdy. *Attila*
Walworth. *Augustus Caesar*
Walworth. *Constantine*

Collective Biography

Clements. *The Picture History of Great Inventors*
Hoobler. *Italian Portraits*
Jacobs. *Great Lives: World Religions*

Wilkinson. *Generals Who Changed the World*
Wilkinson. *People Who Changed the World*

Wilkinson. *Statesmen Who Changed the World*

History

Avi-Yonah. *Piece By Piece! Mosaics of the Ancient World*

Ballard. *The Lost Wreck of the Isis*
Baxter. *Invaders and Settlers*
Baxter. *Romans*

Biel. *Pompeii*
Bisel. *The Secrets of Vesuvius*
Brierley. *Explorers of the Ancient World*

Burke. *Food and Fasting*
Burns. *Money*
Bursell. *Haunted Houses*
Chaikin. *Menorahs, Mezuzas, and Other Jewish Symbols*
Charley. *Tombs and Treasures*
Clare. *Classical Rome*
Clements. *An Illustrated History of the World*
Compton. *Marriage Customs*
Connolly. *Pompeii*
Connolly. *The Roman Fort*
Connolly. *Tiberius Claudius Maximus: The Calvaryman*
Connolly. *Tiberius Claudius Maximus: The Legionary*
Corbishley. *Ancient Rome*
Corbishley. *Everyday Life in Roman Times*
Corbishley. *Rome and the Ancient World*
Corbishley. *Secret Cities*
Corbishley. *What Do We Know About the Romans?*
Cush. *Disasters That Shook the World*
Davies. *Transport*
Dazzling!: Jewelry of the Ancient World
Giblin. *Be Seated: A Book About Chairs*

Giblin. *The Truth About Unicorns*
Gravett. *Arms and Armor*
Guittard. *The Romans*
Harris. *Science in Ancient Rome*
Haywood. *The Romans*
Hicks. *The Romans*
Hirsch. *Taxation*
Howarth. *Roman People*
Howarth. *Roman Places*
Humble. *Ships*
James. *Ancient Rome*
Jessop. *Big Buildings of the Ancient World*
Kent. *A Slice Through a City*
Kerr. *Keeping Clean*
Langley. *The Roman News*
MacDonald. *Cities*
MacDonald. *A Roman Fort*
Morley. *Clothes*
Morley. *A Roman Villa*
Moss. *Forts and Castles*
Nardo. *The Age of Augustus*
Odijk. *The Romans*
Pirotta. *Rome*
Platt. *Pirate*
Platt. *The Smithsonian Visual Timeline of Inventions*
Poulton. *Life in the Time of Augustus and the Ancient Romans*

Prior. *Initiation Customs*
Prior. *Pilgrimages and Journeys*
Putnam. *Mummy*
Ridd. *Julius Caesar in Gaul and Britain*
Ross. *Bandits & Outlaws*
Rowland-Warne. *Costume*
Rushton. *Birth Customs*
Rushton. *Death Customs*
Schneider. *Between the Dragon and the Eagle*
Singer. *Structures that Changed the Way the World Looked*
Steele. *Kidnapping*
Steele. *The Romans and Pompeii*
Turvey. *Inventions: Inventors and Ingenious Ideas*
Ventura. *Clothing*
Ventura. *Food*
Watkins. *Gladiator*
Whittock. *The Roman Empire*
Wilkinson. *The Mediterranean*
Williams. *Forts and Castles*
Woolf. *Picture This: A First Introduction to Paintings*

Multimedia

CD-ROM

Le Louvre: The Palace & Its Paintings

Teach Your Kids World History

Video

The British Way of Life

Turkey: Between Europe and Asia

Ukraine: Kiev and Lvov

Europe and the British Isles, A.D. 476–1289

GRADES KINDERGARTEN THROUGH TWO

Historical Fiction

Carrick. *Harald and the Giant Knight*
Carrick. *Harald and the Great Stag*

Garfield. *The Saracen Maid*
Hunt. *Leif's Saga*
Lattimore. *The Sailor Who Captured the Sea*

Rumford. *The Cloudmakers*
Skurzynski. *The Minstrel in the Tower*

Biography

Collective Biography

Marzollo. *My First Book of Biographies*

History

Aliki. *A Medieval Feast*
Clements. *The Truth About Castles*

Gibbons. *Knights in Shining Armor*
Lasker. *A Tournament of Knights*

Littlefield. *Colors of Germany*
Triggs. *Viking Warriors*

Multimedia

Video

Marco Polo

GRADE THREE

Historical Fiction

Carrick. *Harald and the Giant Knight*
Carrick. *Harald and the Great Stag*
Garfield. *The Saracen Maid*

Hunt. *Leif's Saga*
Lattimore. *The Sailor Who Captured the Sea*
Manson. *Two Travelers*

Needham. *The Time Trekkers Visit the Middle Ages*
Rumford. *The Cloudmakers*
Skurzynski. *The Minstrel in the Tower*

Biography

Humble. *The Age of Lief Eriksson*

San Souci. *Young Arthur*

Collective Biography

Marzollo. *My First Book of Biographies*

Steele. *Pirates*

History

Aliki. *A Medieval Feast*
Burns. *The Mail*

Chrisp. *The Farmer Through History*

Chrisp. *The Soldier Through History*

Clements. *The Truth About Castles*
Coote. *The Sailor Through History*
Gibbons. *Knights in Shining Armor*
Gravett. *Arms and Armor*
Humble. *Ships*

Jessop. *Big Buildings of the Ancient World*
Lasker. *A Tournament of Knights*
Littlefield. *Colors of Germany*
Macaulay. *Cathedral*
Maestro. *The Story of Money*
Mason. *If You Were There in Medieval Times*
Moss. *Forts and Castles*

Oakes. *The Middle Ages*
Pruneti. *Viking Explorers*
Ross. *Knights*
Steele. *Castles*
Triggs. *Viking Warriors*
Wilkinson. *Amazing Buildings*
Wilson. *Visual Timeline of Transportation*

Multimedia

Video

Marco Polo

GRADE FOUR

Historical Fiction

Bulla. *The Sword in the Tree*
Garfield. *The Saracen Maid*
Hunt. *Leif's Saga*

Manson. *Two Travelers*
Needham. *The Time Trekkers Visit the Middle Ages*

Rumford. *The Cloudmakers*
Skurzynski. *The Minstrel in the Tower*

Biography

Humble. *The Age of Lief Eriksson*

San Souci. *Young Arthur*

Collective Biography

Clements. *The Picture History of Great Inventors*

Jacobs. *Great Lives: World Religions*

Steele. *Pirates*

History

Aliki. *A Medieval Feast*
Burke. *Food and Fasting*
Burns. *The Mail*
Burns. *Money*
Bursell. *Haunted Houses*
Chrisp. *The Farmer Through History*
Chrisp. *The Normans*
Chrisp. *The Soldier Through History*
Clements. *The Truth About Castles*
Compton. *Marriage Customs*
Coote. *The Anglo-Saxons*
Coote. *The Sailor Through History*
Dawson. *Food and Feasts in the Middle Ages*
Fradon. *Harald the Herald*
Fradon. *The King's Fool*
Gravett. *Arms and Armor*
Gravett. *Castle*
Gravett. *Knight*
Gregory. *The Dark Ages*
Hook. *The Vikings*

Howarth. *Medieval People*
Howarth. *Medieval Places*
Humble. *Ships*
Husain. *What Do We Know About Islam?*
Jessop. *Big Buildings of the Ancient World*
Kerr. *Keeping Clean*
Macaulay. *Cathedral*
MacDonald. *The Middle Ages*
Maestro. *The Story of Money*
Margeson. *Viking*
Martell. *Food and Feasts with the Vikings*
Martell. *The Vikings and Jorvik*
Martell. *What Do We Know About the Vikings?*
Mason. *If You Were There in Medieval Times*
Moss. *Forts and Castles*
Oakes. *The Middle Ages*
Pirotta. *Rome*
Prior. *Initiation Customs*

Prior. *Pilgrimages and Journeys*
Pruneti. *Viking Explorers*
Rowland-Warne. *Costume*
Ross. *Knights*
Roth. *Marco Polo*
Rushton. *Birth Customs*
Rushton. *Death Customs*
Speed. *Life in the Time of Harald Hardrada and the Vikings*
Steele. *Castles*
Steele. *I Wonder Why Castles Had Moats*
Steffens. *The Children's Crusade*
Triggs. *Viking Warriors*
Ventura. *Clothing*
Ventura. *Food*
Wilkinson. *Amazing Buildings*
Wilson. *Visual Timeline of Transportation*
Woolf. *Picture This: A First Introduction to Paintings*

Multimedia

CD-ROM

Teach Your Kids World History

Video

Turkey: Between Europe and Asia

GRADE FIVE

Historical Fiction

Bulla. *The Sword in the Tree*
Hendry. *Quest for a Maid*
Lewis. *The Ship That Flew*
Manson. *Two Travelers*
Skurzynski. *What Happened in Hamelin*
Snyder. *Song of the Gargoyle*
Sutcliff. *The Witch's Brat*

Biography

Banfield. *Charlemagne*
Doherty. *King Arthur*
Dramer. *Kublai Khan: Mongol Emperor*
Humble. *The Age of Lief Eriksson*
Humphrey. *Genghis Khan*
Kaplan. *Eleanor of Aquitaine*
Koslow. *El Cid*
San Souci. *Young Arthur*

Collective Biography

Clements. *The Picture History of Great Inventors*
Hazell. *Heroines: Great Women Through the Ages*
Jacobs. *Great Lives: World Religions*
Steele. *Pirates*
Wilkinson. *Generals Who Changed the World*
Wilkinson. *People Who Changed the World*
Wilkinson. *Statesmen Who Changed the World*

History

Aliki. *A Medieval Feast*
Baxter. *Invaders and Settlers*
Burke. *Food and Fasting*
Burns. *The Mail*
Burns. *Money*
Bursell. *Haunted Houses*
Chaikin. *Menorahs, Mezuzas, and Other Jewish Symbols*
Charley. *Tombs and Treasures*
Child. *The Crusades*
Chrisp. *The Farmer Through History*
Chrisp. *The Normans*
Chrisp. *The Soldier Through History*
Clements. *The Truth About Castles*
Compton. *Marriage Customs*
Coote. *The Anglo-Saxons*
Coote. *The Sailor Through History*
Corbishley. *The Medieval World*
Davies. *Transport*
Dawson. *Food and Feasts in the Middle Ages*
Fradon. *Harald the Herald*
Fradon. *The King's Fool*
Gravett. *Arms and Armor*
Gravett. *Castle*
Gravett. *Knight*
Gregory. *The Dark Ages*
Hook. *The Vikings*
Howarth. *Medieval People*
Howarth. *Medieval Places*
Humble. *Ships*
Husain. *What Do We Know About Islam?*
Jessop. *Big Buildings of the Ancient World*
Kerr. *Keeping Clean*
Langley. *Medieval Life*
Macaulay. *Cathedral*
MacDonald. *Cities*
MacDonald. *A Medieval Castle*
MacDonald. *A Medieval Cathedral*
MacDonald. *The Middle Ages*
Maestro. *The Story of Money*
Margeson. *Viking*
Martell. *Food and Feasts with the Vikings*
Martell. *The Vikings and Jorvik*
Martell. *What Do We Know About The Vikings?*
Mason. *If You Were There in Medieval Times*
Morley. *Clothes*
Moss. *Forts and Castles*
Oakes. *The Middle Ages*
Pearson. *The Vikings*
Perdrizet. *The Cathedral Builders*
Pernoud. *A Day with a Medieval Troubadour*
Pernoud. *A Day with a Miller*
Pernoud. *A Day with a Noblewoman*
Pernoud. *A Day with a Stonecutter*
Pirotta. *Rome*
Platt. *Pirate*
Prior. *Initiation Customs*
Prior. *Pilgrimages and Journeys*
Pruneti. *Viking Explorers*
Rowland-Warne. *Costume*
Ross. *Knights*
Roth. *Marco Polo*
Rushton. *Birth Customs*
Rushton. *Death Customs*

Sauvain. *Hastings*
Seymour-Jones. *Refugees*
Speed. *Life in the Time of
    Harald Hardrada and the
    Vikings*
Steele. *Castles*
Steele. *Censorship*

Steele. *I Wonder Why Castles
    Had Moats*
Steele. *Kidnapping*
Steffens. *The Children's
    Crusade*
Stefoff. *The Viking Explorers*
Turvey. *Inventions: Inventors
    and Ingenious Ideas*

Ventura. *Clothing*
Ventura. *Food*
Wilkinson. *Amazing Buildings*
Wilkinson. *The Mediterranean*
Wilson. *Visual Timeline of
    Transportation*
Woolf. *Picture This: A First
    Introduction to Paintings*

Multimedia

CD-ROM

*Eyewitness Encyclopedia of
    Science*

*Teach Your Kids World
    History*

Video

*The British Way of Life
Cathedrals with a Project*

*Medieval Times: Life in the
    Middle Ages (1000-1450
    AD)*

*Middle Ages School Kit
Turkey: Between Europe and
    Asia*

GRADE SIX

Historical Fiction

Alder. *The King's Shadow*
Anderson. *The Druid's Gift*
Bulla. *The Sword in the Tree*
Goodman. *The Winter Hare*
Hendry. *Quest for a Maid*
Konigsburg. *A Proud Taste
    for Scarlet and Miniver*

Lewis. *The Ship That Flew*
Llywelyn. *Brian Boru:
    Emperor of the Irish*
Manson. *Two Travelers*
Skurzynski. *What Happened
    in Hamelin*
Snyder. *Song of the Gargoyle*

Sutcliff. *The Shining
    Company*
Sutcliff. *The Witch's Brat*
Treece. *The Road to
    Miklagard*

Biography

Banfield. *Charlemagne*
Biel. *Charlemagne*
Doherty. *King Arthur*
Dramer. *Kublai Khan:
    Mongol Emperor*

Humble. *The Age of Lief
    Eriksson*
Humphrey. *Genghis Khan*
Kaplan. *Eleanor of Aquitaine*
Koslow. *El Cid*

McCaughrean. *El Cid*
O'Neal. *King Arthur:
    Opposing Viewpoints*
San Souci. *Young Arthur*

Collective Biography

Clements. *The Picture
    History of Great Inventors*
Cohen. *Real Vampires*
Hazell. *Heroines: Great
    Women Through the Ages*
Hoobler. *French Portraits*

Hoobler. *Italian Portraits*
Hoobler. *Russian Portraits*
Jacobs. *Great Lives: World
    Religions*
Wilkinson. *Generals Who
    Changed the World*

Wilkinson. *People Who
    Changed the World*
Wilkinson. *Statesmen Who
    Changed the World*

History

Baxter. *Invaders and Settlers*
Biel. *The Crusades*
Burke. *Food and Fasting*
Burns. *Money*
Bursell. *Haunted Houses*
Chaikin. *Menorahs, Mezuzas,
    and Other Jewish Symbols*
Charley. *Tombs and Treasures*
Child. *The Crusades*
Child. *The Rise of Islam*
Chrisp. *The Normans*
Clare. *The Vikings*

Clements. *An Illustrated
    History of the World*
Compton. *Marriage Customs*
Coote. *The Anglo-Saxons*
Corbishley. *The Medieval
    World*
Corbishley. *The Middle Ages*
Cush. *Disasters that Shook
    the World*
Davies. *Transport*
Dawson. *Food and Feasts in
    the Middle Ages*

Fradon. *Harald the Herald*
Fradon. *The King's Fool*
Gravett. *Arms and Armor*
Gravett. *Castle*
Gravett. *Knight*
Gregory. *The Dark Ages*
Hook. *The Vikings*
Howarth. *Medieval People*
Howarth. *Medieval Places*
Humble. *Ships*
Husain. *What Do We Know
    About Islam?*

Jessop. *Big Buildings of the Ancient World*
Kerr. *Keeping Clean*
Langley. *Medieval Life*
Macaulay. *Cathedral*
MacDonald. *Cities*
MacDonald. *A Medieval Castle*
MacDonald. *A Medieval Cathedral*
MacDonald. *The Middle Ages*
Margeson. *Viking*
Martell. *Food and Feasts with the Vikings*
Martell. *The Vikings and Jorvik*
Martell. *What Do We Know About the Vikings?*
Mason. *If You Were There in Medieval Times*
Morley. *Clothes*
Moss. *Forts and Castles*
Oakes. *The Middle Ages*

Pearson. *The Vikings*
Perdrizet. *The Cathedral Builders*
Pernoud. *A Day with a Medieval Troubadour*
Pernoud. *A Day with a Miller*
Pernoud. *A Day with a Noblewoman*
Pernoud. *A Day with a Stonecutter*
Pirotta. *Rome*
Platt. *Pirate*
Prior. *Initiation Customs*
Prior. *Pilgrimages and Journeys*
Pruneti. *Viking Explorers*
Rowland-Warne. *Costume*
Ross. *Knights*
Roth. *Marco Polo*
Rushton. *Birth Customs*
Rushton. *Death Customs*
Sauvain. *Hastings*
Seymour-Jones. *Refugees*

Singer. *Structures that Changed the Way the World Looked*
Speed. *Life in the Time of Harald Hardrada and the Vikings*
Steele. *Castles*
Steele. *Censorship*
Steele. *I Wonder Why Castles Had Moats*
Steele. *Kidnapping*
Steffens. *The Children's Crusade*
Stefoff. *The Viking Explorers*
Turvey. *Inventions: Inventors and Ingenious Ideas*
Ventura. *Clothing*
Ventura. *Food*
Wilkinson. *Amazing Buildings*
Wilkinson. *The Mediterranean*
Williams. *Forts and Castles*
Woolf. *Picture This: A First Introduction to Paintings*

Multimedia

CD-ROM

Art & Music: The Medieval Era

Eyewitness Encyclopedia of Science

Teach Your Kids World History

Video

The British Way of Life
Cathedrals with a Project
England's Historic Treasures

Medieval Times: Life in the Middle Ages (1000-1450 AD)
Medieval Women
Middle Ages School Kit

Turkey: Between Europe and Asia
The Vikings: Seafarers and Explorers

Europe and the British Isles, 1290–1491

GRADES KINDERGARTEN THROUGH TWO

Historical Fiction

Kirwan. *Juliet: A Dream Takes Flight*

Kirwan. *Juliet: Rescue at Marlehead Manor, England, 1340*

Wooding. *The Painter's Cat*

Biography

Burch. *Fine Print: Johann Gutenberg*

Kramer. *Theodoric's Rainbow*
Venezia. *Botticelli*

Wildsmith. *Saint Francis*

Collective Biography

Marzollo. *My First Book of Biographies*

History

Falwell. *The Letter Jesters*
Krensky. *Breaking into Print*

Littlefield. *Colors of Germany*

Ventura. *Venice: Birth of a City*

GRADE THREE

Historical Fiction

De Angeli. *The Door in the Wall*
Kirwan. *Juliet: A Dream Takes Flight*

Kirwan. *Juliet: Rescue at Marlehead Manor, England, 1340*

Morrison. *Antonio's Apprenticeship*
Wooding. *The Painter's Cat*

Biography

Bender. *Waiting for Filippo*
Burch. *Fine Print: Johann Gutenberg*

Graves. *Marco Polo*
Humble. *The Travels of Marco Polo*

Kramer. *Theodoric's Rainbow*
Venezia. *Botticelli*
Wildsmith. *Saint Francis*

Collective Biography

Marzollo. *My First Book of Biographies*

History

Burns. *The Mail*
Chrisp. *The Farmer Through History*
Chrisp. *The Soldier Through History*
Coote. *The Sailor Through History*

Denny. *A Taste of France*
Falwell. *The Letter Jesters*
Gravett. *Arms and Armor*
Gravett. *The Knight's Handbook: How to Become a Champion in Shining Armor*

Krensky. *Breaking into Print*
Littlefield. *Colors of Germany*
Maestro. *The Story of Money*
Willard. *Gutenberg's Gift*
Wilson. *Visual Timeline of Transportation*
Ventura. *Venice: Birth of a City*

GRADE FOUR

Historical Fiction

Bellairs. *The Trolley to Yesterday*
De Angeli. *The Door in the Wall*
Kirwan. *Juliet: A Dream Takes Flight*

Kirwan. *Juliet: Rescue at Marlehead Manor, England, 1340*
Morrison. *Antonio's Apprenticeship*
Vining. *Adam of the Road*

Wooding. *The Painter's Cat*
Woodruff. *The Disappearing Bike Shop*

Biography

Bender. *Waiting for Filippo*
Burch. *Isabella of Castile*
Codye. *Queen Isabella I*
Corrain. *Giotto and Medieval Art*

Fisher. *Prince Henry the Navigator*
Graves. *Marco Polo*
Greene. *Marco Polo*
Humble. *The Travels of Marco Polo*

Kramer. *Theodoric's Rainbow*
Noonan. *Marco Polo*
Stanley. *Leonardo Da Vinci*
Wildsmith. *Saint Francis*

Collective Biography

Clements. *The Picture History of Great Inventors*

Fritz. *Around the World in a Hundred Years*

Jacobs. *Great Lives: World Religions*

History

Burns. *The Mail*
Burns. *Money*
Chrisp. *The Farmer Through History*
Chrisp. *The Soldier Through History*
Coote. *The Sailor Through History*
Denny. *A Taste of France*
Falwell. *The Letter Jesters*

Giblin. *Chimney Sweeps*
Gravett. *Arms and Armor*
Gravett. *The Knight's Handbook*
Howarth. *Renaissance People*
Howarth. *Renaissance Places*
Kerr. *Keeping Clean*
Krensky. *Breaking into Print*
Lampton. *Epidemic*
Maestro. *The Story of Money*

Pirotta. *Rome*
Ross. *Bandits & Outlaws*
Ventura. *Clothing*
Ventura. *Food*
Willard. *Gutenberg's Gift*
Wilson. *Visual Timeline of Transportation*
Woolf. *Picture This: A First Introduction to Paintings*

Multimedia

CD-ROM

Teach Your Kids World History

GRADE FIVE

Historical Fiction

Bellairs. *The Trolley to Yesterday*
Cushman. *The Midwife's Apprentice*
De Angeli. *The Door in the Wall*
Harnett. *The Sign of the Green Falcon*

Harnett. *The Writing on the Hearth*
Kirwan. *Juliet: A Dream Takes Flight*
Kirwan. *Juliet: Rescue at Marlehead Manor, England, 1340*
Lewis. *The Ship That Flew*

Morrison. *Antonio's Apprenticeship*
Phillips. *The Peace Child*
Vining. *Adam of the Road*
Woodruff. *The Disappearing Bike Shop*

Biography

Banfield. *Joan of Arc*
Bender. *Waiting for Filippo*
Burch. *Isabella of Castile*

Ceserani. *Marco Polo*
Codye. *Queen Isabella I*

Corrain. *Giotto and Medieval Art*
Dana. *Young Joan*

Fisher. *Prince Henry the Navigator*
Graves. *Marco Polo*

Greene. *Marco Polo*
Humble. *The Travels of Marco Polo*

Kent. *Marco Polo*
Noonan. *Marco Polo*
Stanley. *Leonardo Da Vinci*

Collective Biography

Clements. *The Picture History of Great Inventors*
Fritz. *Around the World in a Hundred Years*
Hazell. *Heroes: Great Men Through the Ages*

Hazell. *Heroines: Great Women Through the Ages*
Jacobs. *Great Lives: World Religions*
Wilkinson. *People Who Changed the World*

Wilkinson. *Scientists Who Changed the World*
Wilkinson. *Statesmen Who Changed the World*

History

Armenia
Biel. *The Black Death*
Burns. *The Mail*
Burns. *Money*
Capek. *Artistic Trickery: Trompe L'oeil Art*
Chrisp. *The Farmer Through History*
Chrisp. *The Soldier Through History*
Coote. *The Sailor Through History*
Corzine. *The Black Death*
Davies. *Transport*
Denny. *A Taste of France*
Giblin. *Chimney Sweeps*
Gravett. *Arms and Armor*

Gravett. *The Knight's Handbook*
Gravett. *The World of the Medieval Knight*
Howarth. *Renaissance People*
Howarth. *Renaissance Places*
Kerr. *Keeping Clean*
Krensky. *Breaking into Print*
Lampton. *Epidemic*
Macaulay. *Castle*
MacDonald. *Cities*
Maestro. *The Story of Money*
Morley. *Clothes*
Nicolle. *Medieval Knights*
Pirotta. *Rome*
Platt. *Pirate*

Platt. *The Smithsonian Visual Timeline of Inventions*
Ross. *Bandits & Outlaws*
Steele. *Censorship*
Steele. *Kidnapping*
Turvey. *Inventions: Inventors and Ingenious Ideas*
Ventura. *Clothing*
Ventura. *Food*
Wilkinson. *The Mediterranean*
Willard. *Gutenberg's Gift*
Wilson. *Visual Timeline of Transportation*
Woolf. *Picture This: A First Introduction to Paintings*

Multimedia

CD-ROM

Castle Explorer

Eyewitness Encyclopedia of Science

Teach Your Kids World History

Video

The British Way of Life

Medieval Times: Life in the Middle Ages (1000-1450 AD)

Turkey: Between Europe and Asia

GRADE SIX

Historical Fiction

Bellairs. *The Trolley to Yesterday*
Cushman. *The Midwife's Apprentice*
De Angeli. *The Door in the Wall*
Harnett. *The Sign of the Green Falcon*

Harnett. *The Writing on the Hearth*
Kirwan. *Juliet: A Dream Takes Flight*
Lewis. *The Ship That Flew*
Llorente. *The Apprentice*
McCaughrean. *A Little Lower Than the Angels*

Phillips. *The Peace Child*
Temple. *The Beduins' Gazelle*
Vining. *Adam of the Road*
Woodruff. *The Disappearing Bike Shop*

Biography

Banfield. *Joan of Arc*
Bender. *Waiting for Filippo*
Burch. *Isabella of Castile*

Ceserani. *Marco Polo*
Codye. *Queen Isabella I*

Corrain. *Giotto and Medieval Art*
Dana. *Young Joan*

Fisher. *Gutenberg*
Fisher. *Prince Henry the
    Navigator*
Fisher. *William Tell*

Graves. *Marco Polo*
Greene. *Marco Polo*
Humble. *The Travels of
    Marco Polo*

Kent. *Marco Polo*
Noonan. *Marco Polo*
Stanley. *Leonardo Da Vinci*

Collective Biography

Clements. *The Picture
    History of Great Inventors*
Cohen. *Real Vampires*
Fritz. *Around the World in a
    Hundred Years*
Hazell. *Heroes: Great Men
    Through the Ages*

Hazell. *Heroines: Great
    Women Through the Ages*
Hoobler. *French Portraits*
Hoobler. *Italian Portraits*
Hoobler. *Russian Portraits*
Jacobs. *Great Lives: World
    Religions*

Wilkinson. *People Who
    Changed the World*
Wilkinson. *Scientists Who
    Changed the World*
Wilkinson. *Statesmen Who
    Changed the World*

History

Armenia
Beckett. *The Duke and the
    Peasant*
Biel. *The Black Death*
Burns. *Money*
Capek. *Artistic Trickery:
    Trompe L'oeil Art*
Child. *The Rise of Islam*
Clare. *Fourteenth-Century
    Towns*
Clements. *An Illustrated
    History of the World*
Corzine. *The Black Death*
Davies. *Transport*
Denny. *A Taste of France*
Giblin. *Chimney Sweeps*
Gravett. *Arms and Armor*

Gravett. *The Knight's
    Handbook*
Gravett. *The World of the
    Medieval Knight*
Howarth. *Renaissance People*
Howarth. *Renaissance Places*
Kerr. *Keeping Clean*
Krensky. *Breaking into Print*
Lampton. *Epidemic*
Langley. *The Industrial
    Revolution*
Macaulay. *Castle*
MacDonald. *Cities*
Morley. *Clothes*
Nicolle. *Medieval Knights*
Pirotta. *Rome*
Platt. *Pirate*

Platt. *The Smithsonian Visual
    Timeline of Inventions*
Ross. *Bandits & Outlaws*
Steele. *Censorship*
Steele. *Kidnapping*
Stein. *Witches: Opposing
    Viewpoints*
Turvey. *Inventions: Inventors
    and Ingenious Ideas*
Ventura. *Clothing*
Ventura. *Food*
Wilkinson. *The
    Mediterranean*
Willard. *Gutenberg's Gift*
Wood. *The Renaissance*
Woolf. *Picture This: A First
    Introduction to Paintings*

Multimedia

CD-ROM

Art & Music: The Renaissance
Castle Explorer
*Eyewitness Encyclopedia of
    Science*

Great Artists
*History Through Art:
    Renaissance*

*Le Louvre: The Palace & Its
    Paintings*
*Teach Your Kids World
    History*

Video

The British Way of Life

*Medieval Times: Life in the
    Middle Ages (1000-1450
    AD)*

Poland: A Proud Heritage

Europe and the British Isles, 1492–1649

GRADES KINDERGARTEN THROUGH TWO

Historical Fiction

Bulla. *A Lion to Guard Us*

Foreman. *The Boy Who Sailed with Columbus*

Biography

Asimov. *Christopher Columbus*
Asimov. *Ferdinand Magellan*
Fischetto. *Michel the Angel*

Galli. *Mona Lisa*
Gleiter. *Christopher Columbus*
Provenson. *Leonardo da Vinci*

Venezia. *Da Vinci*
Venezia. *Michelangelo*
Venezia. *Pieter Bruegel*
Venezia. *Rembrandt*

Collective Biography

Marzollo. *My First Book of Biographies*

History

Gibbons. *Pirates: Robbers of the High Seas*

Littlefield. *Colors of Germany*

Maestro. *The Discovery of the Americas*

Multimedia

Video

Children's Heroes from Christian History

Galileo

GRADE THREE

Historical Fiction

Birchman. *A Tale of Tulips, a Tale of Onions*
Bulla. *A Lion to Guard Us*

Conrad. *Pedro's Journal*
Foreman. *The Boy Who Sailed with Columbus*

Schlein. *I Sailed with Columbus*

Biography

Adler. *Christopher Columbus*
Anderson. *Christopher Columbus*
Ash. *Vasco Núñez De Balboa*
Asimov. *Christopher Columbus*
Asimov. *Ferdinand Magellan*
Blassingame. *Ponce de León*
Carson. *Hernando De Soto*

Dyson. *Westward with Columbus*
Fischetto. *Michel the Angel*
Fritz. *Where Do You Think You're Going, Christopher Columbus?*
Galli. *Mona Lisa*
Gleiter. *Christopher Columbus*
Kent. *Christopher Columbus*

Pinguilly. *Da Vinci*
Richmond. *Introducing Michelangelo*
Stein. *Christopher Columbus*
Venezia. *Da Vinci*
Venezia. *Michelangelo*
Venezia. *Pieter Bruegel*
Venezia. *Rembrandt*
Ventura. *Michelangelo's World*

Collective Biography

Marzollo. *My First Book of Biographies*

Steele. *Pirates*

History ────────────────────────────

Burns. *The Mail*
Carrion. *The Empire of the Czars*
Chrisp. *The Farmer Through History*
Chrisp. *The Soldier Through History*
Coote. *The Sailor Through History*
Denny. *A Taste of Britain*

Fisher. *The Tower of London*
Goodall. *Great Days of a Country House*
Jessop. *Big Buildings of the Ancient World*
Kramer. *Exploration and Empire: Science*
Lincoln. *The Pirate's Handbook*
Littlefield. *Colors of Germany*

MacDonald. *Exploring the World*
Maestro. *The Discovery of the Americas*
Maestro. *The Story of Money*
Morley. *Exploring North America*
Wilkinson. *Amazing Buildings*
Wilson. *Visual Timeline of Transportation*

Multimedia ────────────────────────────

Video

Children's Heroes from Christian History

Galileo

┌─────────────────────┐
│   **GRADE FOUR**   │
└─────────────────────┘

Historical Fiction ────────────────────────────

Birchman. *A Tale of Tulips, a Tale of Onions*
Bulla. *A Lion to Guard Us*
Conrad. *Pedro's Journal*
Foreman. *The Boy Who Sailed with Columbus*

Morris. *The Dangerous Voyage*
Morrison. *Neptune's Fountain: A Young Sculptor in Renaissance Italy*

O'Dell. *The Hawk That Dare Not Hunt by Day*
Trease. *A Flight of Angels*

Biography ────────────────────────────

Adler. *Christopher Columbus*
Anderson. *Christopher Columbus*
Alper. *Forgotten Voyager: Amerigo Vespucci*
Ash. *Vasco Núñez De Balboa*
Asimov. *Christopher Columbus*
Asimov. *Ferdinand Magellan*
Blassingame. *Ponce de León*
Burch. *Isabella of Castile*
Carson. *Hernando De Soto*
Chrisman. *Hernando de Soto*

Codye. *Queen Isabella I*
Dyson. *Westward with Columbus*
Fradin. *Amerigo Vespucci*
Jacobs. *Magellan*
Kent. *Christopher Columbus*
Langley. *Discovering the New World: Christopher Columbus*
Macht. *Christopher Columbus*
McTavish. *Galileo*
Noonan. *Ferdinand Magellan*

Parker. *Galileo and the Universe*
Pinguilly. *Da Vinci*
Richmond. *Introducing Michelangelo*
Romei. *Leonardo da Vinci*
Roop. *I, Columbus: My Journal—1492-3*
Stanley. *Leonardo Da Vinci*
Stein. *Christopher Columbus*
Ventura. *Michelangelo's World*
Yount. *William Harvey*

Collective Biography

Steele. *Pirates*

History ────────────────────────────

Balkwill. *Food and Feasts in Tudor Times*
Burns. *The Mail*
Burns. *Money*
Carrion. *The Empire of the Czars*
Chrisp. *The Farmer Through History*

Chrisp. *The Search for the East*
Chrisp. *The Soldier Through History*
Chrisp. *Voyages to the New World*
Coote. *The First Voyage Around the World*

Coote. *The Sailor Through History*
Denny. *A Taste of Britain*
Fisher. *The Tower of London*
Giblin. *Be Seated: A Book About Chairs*
Giblin. *Chimney Sweeps*

Goodall. *Great Days of a Country House*
Guiberson. *Lighthouses*
Jessop. *Big Buildings of the Ancient World*
Kerr. *Keeping Clean*
Kramer. *Exploration and Empire: Science*
Lincoln. *The Pirate's Handbook*

MacDonald. *Exploring the World*
Maestro. *The Discovery of the Americas*
Maestro. *The Story of Money*
Martell. *The Age of Discovery*
Morley. *Exploring North America*
Ross. *Conquerors & Explorers*
Rowland-Warne. *Costume*

Ryan. *Explorers and Mapmakers*
Ventura. *Clothing*
Ventura. *Food*
Ventura. *1492*
Wilkinson. *Amazing Buildings*
Wilson. *Visual Timeline of Transportation*
Woolf. *Picture This: A First Introduction to Paintings*

Multimedia

CD-ROM

Teach Your Kids World History

Video

Children's Heroes from Christian History

Galileo: The Solar System

GRADE FIVE

Historical Fiction

Beatty. *Master Rosalind*
Birchman. *A Tale of Tulips, a Tale of Onions*
Bulla. *A Lion to Guard Us*
Conrad. *Pedro's Journal*
Harnett. *The Merchant's Mark*
Harnett. *Stars of Fortune*

Hunter. *The Spanish Letters*
Kisling. *The Fool's War*
Litowinsky. *The High Voyage*
Morris. *The Dangerous Voyage*
Morrison. *Neptune's Fountain: A Young*

Sculptor in Renaissance Italy
O'Dell. *The Hawk That Dare Not Hunt by Day*
Stolz. *Bartholomew Fair*
Trease. *A Flight of Angels*

Biography

Adler. *Christopher Columbus*
Anderson. *Christopher Columbus*
Alper. *Forgotten Voyager: Amerigo Vespucci*
Ash. *Vasco Núñez De Balboa*
Asimov. *Christopher Columbus*
Asimov. *Ferdinand Magellan*
Bard. *Sir Francis Drake and the Struggle for an Ocean Empire*
Bernhard. *Pizarro, Orellana, and the Exploration of the Amazon*
Blassingame. *Ponce de León*
Burch. *Isabella of Castile*
Bush. *Elizabeth I*
Carson. *Hernando De Soto*
Chrisman. *Hernando de Soto*
Codye. *Queen Isabella I*
Dodge. *Christopher Columbus and the First Voyages*

Dolan. *Juan Ponce de León*
Dwyer. *Henry VIII*
Dyson. *Westward with Columbus*
Fradin. *Amerigo Vespucci*
Fritz. *Where Do You Think You're Going, Christopher Columbus?*
Jacobs. *Magellan*
Kent. *Christopher Columbus*
Langley. *Discovering the New World: Christopher Columbus*
Levinson. *Christopher Columbus*
Macht. *Christopher Columbus*
Mason. *Leonardo Da Vinci: An Introduction*
Mason. *Michelangelo: An Introduction*
McTavish. *Galileo*
Muhlberger. *What Makes a Bruegel a Bruegel?*

Muhlberger. *What Makes a Leonardo a Leonardo?*
Noonan. *Ferdinand Magellan*
Parker. *Galileo and the Universe*
Pinguilly. *Da Vinci*
Richmond. *Introducing Michelangelo*
Romei. *Leonardo da Vinci*
Roop. *I, Columbus: My Journal—1492-3*
Stanley. *Leonardo Da Vinci*
Stein. *Christopher Columbus*
Sterckx. *Brueghel: A Gift for Telling Stories*
Twist. *Christopher Columbus*
Ventura. *Michelangelo's World*
Whitman. *Hernando de Soto*
Yount. *William Harvey*
Yue. *Christopher Columbus*

Collective Biography

Clements. *The Picture History of Great Inventors*
Fritz. *Around the World in a Hundred Years*
Glubok. *Great Lives: Painting*
Hazell. *Heroes: Great Men Through the Ages*
Hazell. *Heroines: Great Women Through the Ages*

Jacobs. *Great Lives: World Religions*
Krull. *Lives of the Artists*
Krull. *Lives of the Musicians*
Krull. *Lives of the Writers*
Maestro. *Exploration and Conquest After Columbus*
Steele. *Pirates*

Wilkinson. *Generals Who Changed the World*
Wilkinson. *People Who Changed the World*
Wilkinson. *Scientists Who Changed the World*
Wilkinson. *Statesmen Who Changed the World*

History

Balkwill. *Food and Feasts in Tudor Times*
Burns. *The Mail*
Burns. *Money*
Carrion. *The Empire of the Czars*
Chrisp. *The Farmer Through History*
Chrisp. *The Search for the East*
Chrisp. *The Soldier Through History*
Chrisp. *Voyages to the New World*
Coote. *The First Voyage Around the World*
Coote. *The Sailor Through History*
Corzine. *The Black Death*
Davies. *Transport*
Denny. *A Taste of Britain*
Fisher. *The Tower of London*
Giblin. *Be Seated: A Book About Chairs*
Giblin. *Chimney Sweeps*

Goodall. *Great Days of a Country House*
Guiberson. *Lighthouses*
Jessop. *Big Buildings of the Ancient World*
Kerr. *Keeping Clean*
Kramer. *Exploration and Empire: Science*
Lincoln. *The Pirate's Handbook*
Macaulay. *Ship*
MacDonald. *Cities*
MacDonald. *Exploring the World*
Maestro. *The Discovery of the Americas*
Maestro. *The Story of Money*
Marrin. *The Sea Rovers*
Martell. *The Age of Discovery*
Maurer. *Airborne*
Morley. *Clothes*
Morley. *Exploring North America*
Perl. *From Top Hats to Baseball Caps, from Bustles to Blue Jeans*

Platt. *Pirate*
Platt. *The Smithsonian Visual Timeline of Inventions*
Ross. *Conquerors & Explorers*
Rowland-Warne. *Costume*
Ryan. *Explorers and Mapmakers*
Steele. *Kidnapping*
Steele. *Smuggling*
Van der Linde. *The White Stallions*
Ventura. *Clothing*
Ventura. *Food*
Ventura. *1492*
Wilkinson. *Amazing Buildings*
Williams. *The Age of Discovery*
Wilson. *Visual Timeline of Transportation*
Woolf. *Picture This: A First Introduction to Paintings*

Multimedia

CD-ROM

Eyewitness Encyclopedia of Science

Teach Your Kids World History

Video

The British Way of Life

Galileo: The Solar System

GRADE SIX

Historical Fiction

Beatty. *Master Rosalind*
Conrad. *Pedro's Journal*
Graham. *A Boy and His Bear*
Harnett. *The Merchant's Mark*
Harnett. *Stars of Fortune*
Haugaard. *A Messenger for Parliament*
Hunter. *The Spanish Letters*

Hunter. *The 13th Member*
Kisling. *The Fool's War*
Litowinsky. *The High Voyage*
Matas. *The Burning Time*
Morris. *The Dangerous Voyage*
Morrison. *Neptune's Fountain: A Young Sculptor in Renaissance Italy*

O'Dell. *The Hawk That Dare Not Hunt by Day*
Pope. *The Perilous Gard*
Schlein. *I Sailed with Columbus*
Stolz. *Bartholomew Fair*
Trease. *A Flight of Angels*

Biography

Alper. *Forgotten Voyager: Amerigo Vespucci*
Ash. *Vasco Núñez De Balboa*
Bard. *Sir Francis Drake and the Struggle for an Ocean Empire*
Bernhard. *Pizarro, Orellana, and the Exploration of the Amazon*
Blassingame. *Ponce de León*
Burch. *Isabella of Castile*
Bush. *Elizabeth I*
Carson. *Hernando De Soto*
Chrisman. *Hernando de Soto*
Codye. *Queen Isabella I*
Dodge. *Christopher Columbus and the First Voyages*
Dolan. *Juan Ponce de León*
Dwyer. *Henry VIII*
Dyson. *Westward with Columbus*
Fisher. *Galileo*
Fradin. *Amerigo Vespucci*

Fritz. *Where Do You Think You're Going, Christopher Columbus?*
Jacobs. *Magellan*
Kent. *Christopher Columbus*
Langley. *Discovering the New World: Christopher Columbus*
Levinson. *Christopher Columbus*
Macht. *Christopher Columbus*
Marrin. *The Sea King: Sir Francis Drake*
Mason. *Leonardo Da Vinci: An Introduction*
Mason. *Michelangelo: An Introduction*
McCully. *The Pirate Queen*
McTavish. *Galileo*
Meltzer. *Columbus and the World Around Him*
Muhlberger. *What Makes a Bruegel a Bruegel?*

Muhlberger. *What Makes a Leonardo a Leonardo?*
Noonan. *Ferdinand Magellan*
Parker. *Galileo and the Universe*
Pelta. *Discovering Christopher Columbus*
Pinguilly. *Da Vinci*
Richmond. *Introducing Michelangelo*
Romei. *Leonardo da Vinci*
Roop. *I, Columbus: My Journal—1492-3*
Stanley. *Leonardo Da Vinci*
Sterckx. *Brueghel: A Gift For Telling Stories*
Sturgis. *Introducing Rembrandt*
Twist. *Christopher Columbus*
Ventura. *Michelangelo's World*
Whitman. *Hernando de Soto*
Yount. *William Harvey*
Yue. *Christopher Columbus*

Collective Biography

Anderson. *Explorers Who Found New Worlds*
Clements. *The Picture History of Great Inventors*
Cohen. *Real Vampires*
Fritz. *Around the World in a Hundred Years*
Glubok. *Great Lives: Painting*
Hazell. *Heroes: Great Men Through the Ages*

Hazell. *Heroines: Great Women Through the Ages*
Hoobler. *French Portraits*
Hoobler. *Italian Portraits*
Hoobler. *Russian Portraits*
Jacobs. *Great Lives: World Religions*
Krull. *Lives of the Artists*
Krull. *Lives of the Musicians*
Krull. *Lives of the Writers*

Maestro. *Exploration and Conquest After Columbus*
Wilkinson. *Generals Who Changed the World*
Wilkinson. *People Who Changed the World*
Wilkinson. *Scientists Who Changed the World*
Wilkinson. *Statesmen Who Changed the World*

History

Balkwill. *Food and Feasts in Tudor Times*
Burns. *Money*
Carrion. *The Empire of the Czars*
Child. *The Rise of Islam*
Chrisp. *The Search for the East*
Chrisp. *Voyages to the New World*
Clements. *An Illustrated History of the World*
Coote. *The First Voyage Around the World*
Corzine. *The Black Death*
Davies. *Transport*
Denny. *A Taste of Britain*
Fisher. *The Tower of London*
Garfunkel. *On Wings of Joy: Ballet*
Giblin. *Be Seated: A Book About Chairs*
Giblin. *Chimney Sweeps*

Guiberson. *Lighthouses*
Jessop. *Big Buildings of the Ancient World*
Kerr. *Keeping Clean*
Kramer. *Exploration and Empire: Science*
Lincoln. *The Pirate's Handbook*
Macaulay. *Ship*
MacDonald. *Cities*
MacDonald. *Exploring the World*
Marrin. *The Sea Rovers*
Martell. *The Age of Discovery*
Maurer. *Airborne*
Morley. *Clothes*
Morley. *Exploring North America*
Perl. *From Top Hats to Baseball Caps, from Bustles to Blue Jeans*
Platt. *Pirate*

Platt. *The Smithsonian Visual Timeline of Inventions*
Ross. *Conquerors & Explorers*
Rowland-Warne. *Costume*
Ryan. *Explorers and Mapmakers*
Steele. *Kidnapping*
Steele. *Smuggling*
Stein. *Witches: Opposing Viewpoints*
Van der Linde. *The White Stallions*
Ventura. *Clothing*
Ventura. *Food*
Ventura. *1492*
Wilkinson. *Amazing Buildings*
Williams. *The Age of Discovery*
Wood. *The Renaissance*
Woolf. *Picture This: A First Introduction to Paintings*
Yancey. *Life in the Elizabethan Theater*

Multimedia ——

CD-ROM

Art & Music: The Baroque
*Art & Music: The Eighteenth
Century*
Art & Music: The Renaissance
*Eyewitness Encyclopedia of
Science*

Great Artists
History Through Art: Baroque
*History Through Art:
Renaissance*
*Le Louvre: The Palace & Its
Paintings*

Stowaway!
*Teach Your Kids World
History*

Video

The British Way of Life
Galileo: The Solar System
*Martin Luther: Beginning of
the Reformation*

*Martin Luther: Translating
the Bible*
Poland: A Proud Heritage

*This Just In . . . Columbus
Has Landed*

Europe and the British Isles, 1650–1788

GRADES KINDERGARTEN THROUGH TWO

Historical Fiction

Armstrong. *Little Salt Lick and the Sun King*

Bunting. *Market Day*

Kudlinsky. *Marie: An Invitation to Dance in Paris*

Biography

Brighton. *Mozart*
Isadora. *Young Mozart*

Weil. *Wolferl: Wolfgang Amadeus Mozart, 1756-1762*

Collective Biography

Marzollo. *My First Book of Biographies*

History

Aliki. *The King's Day; Louis XIV of France*

Gibbons. *Pirates: Robbers of the High Seas*

Littlefield. *Colors of Germany*

Multimedia

Video

Children's Heroes from Christian History

Galileo

GRADE THREE

Historical Fiction

Armstrong. *Little Salt Lick and the Sun King*

Kudlinsky. *Marie: An Invitation to Dance in Paris*
Speir. *Father, May I Come?*

Yolen. *The Ballad of the Pirate Queens*

Biography

Brighton. *Mozart*
Fritz. *Can't You Make Them Behave, King George?*
Isadora. *Young Mozart*
Kent. *James Cook*

Parker. *Isaac Newton and Gravity*
Switzer. *The Magic of Mozart*
Venezia. *Wolfgang Amadeus Mozart*

Vernon. *Introducing Bach*
Weil. *Wolferl: Wolfgang Amadeus Mozart, 1756-1762*

Collective Biography

Marzollo. *My First Book of Biographies*

Steele. *Pirates*

History

Aliki. *The King's Day; Louis XIV of France*
Burns. *The Mail*
Chrisp. *The Farmer Through History*
Chrisp. *The Soldier Through History*

Coote. *The Sailor Through History*
Goodall. *Great Days of a Country House*
Kramer. *Exploration and Empire: Science*
Lincoln. *The Pirate's Handbook*

Littlefield. *Colors of Germany*
Maestro. *The Story of Money*
Morley. *Exploring North America*
Moss. *Forts and Castles*
Wilkinson. *Amazing Buildings*
Wilson. *Visual Timeline of Transportation*

Multimedia

Video

Children's Heroes from Christian History

Galileo

GRADE FOUR

Historical Fiction

Anderson. *Children of Summer*
Armstrong. *Little Salt Lick and the Sun King*
Haugaard. *A Boy's Will*

Hautzig. *Riches*
Kudlinsky. *Marie: An Invitation to Dance in Paris*
Morrison. *Neptune's Fountain: A Young*

Sculptor in Renaissance Italy
Speir. *Father, May I Come?*
Yolen. *The Ballad of the Pirate Queens*

Biography

Anderson. *Carl Linnaeus: Father of Classification*
Brighton. *Mozart*
Fritz. *Can't You Make Them Behave, King George?*
Greene. *Wolfgang Amadeus Mozart*
Hargrove. *René-Robert Cavelier Sieur de La Salle*

Kent. *James Cook*
Langley. *Exploring the Pacific: The Expeditions of James Cook*
Noonan. *Captain Cook*
Parker. *Isaac Newton and Gravity*
Switzer. *The Magic of Mozart*

Venezia. *Wolfgang Amadeus Mozart*
Vernon. *Introducing Bach*
Yount. *Antoni Van Leeuwenhoek: First to See Microscopic Life*

Collective Biography

Clements. *The Picture History of Great Inventors*
Fritz. *Around the World in a Hundred Years*

Jacobs. *Great Lives: World Religions*
Krull. *Lives of the Artists*
Krull. *Lives of the Musicians*

Krull. *Lives of the Writers*
Steele. *Pirates*

History

Aliki. *The King's Day; Louis XIV of France*
Burns. *The Mail*
Burns. *Money*
Chrisp. *The Farmer Through History*
Chrisp. *The Soldier Through History*
Clare. *Industrial Revolution*
Coote. *The Sailor Through History*
Giblin. *Be Seated: A Book About Chairs*

Giblin. *Chimney Sweeps*
Goodall. *Great Days of a Country House*
Kerr. *Keeping Clean*
Kramer. *Exploration and Empire: Science*
Lampton. *Epidemic*
Lincoln. *The Pirate's Handbook*
Maestro. *The Story of Money*
Morley. *Exploring North America*
Moss. *Forts and Castles*

Reynoldson. *Conflict and Change*
Ross. *Conquerors & Explorers*
Rowland-Warne. *Costume*
Ventura. *Clothing*
Ventura. *Food*
Wilkinson. *Amazing Buildings*
Wilson. *Visual Timeline of Transportation*
Woolf. *Picture This: A First Introduction to Paintings*

Multimedia ───────────────────────────────

CD-ROM

Your Kids World History

Video

*Children's Heroes from
  Christian History*

Galileo: The Solar System

GRADE FIVE

Historical Fiction ───────────────────────────────

Anderson. *Children of
  Summer*
Calvert. *Hadder MacColl*
Garfield. *Devil-in-the-Fog*
Garfield. *Footsteps*
Garfield. *Young Nick and Jubilee*
Greene. *One Foot Ashore*
Greene. *Out of Many Waters*
Harnett. *The Cargo of the
  Madalena*

Harnett. *The Great House*
Haugaard. *A Boy's Will*
Hautzig. *Riches*
Hersom. *The Half Child*
Hunter. *The Lothian Run*
Kudlinsky. *Marie: An
  Invitation to Dance in Paris*
Malterre. *The Last Wolf of
  Ireland*
McGraw. *Master Cornhill*

Morrison. *Neptune's
  Fountain: A Young
  Sculptor in Renaissance
  Italy*
Speir. *Father, May I Come?*
Wulffson. *The Upside-Down
  Ship*
Yolen. *The Ballad of the
  Pirate Queens*

Biography ───────────────────────────────

Anderson. *Carl Linnaeus:
  Father of Classification*
Anderson. *Isaac Newton: The
  Greatest Scientist of All Time*
Blakely. *Wolfgang Amadeus
  Mozart*
Blumberg. *The Remarkable
  Voyages of Captain Cook*
Dolan. *Junípero Serra*
Downing. *Mozart Tonight*

Fritz. *Can't You Make Them
  Behave, King George?*
Greene. *Wolfgang Amadeus
  Mozart*
Hargrove. *René-Robert
  Cavelier Sieur de La Salle*
Kent. *James Cook*
Langley. *Exploring the
  Pacific: The Expeditions of
  James Cook*
McTavish. *Isaac Newton*

Noonan. *Captain Cook*
Parker. *Isaac Newton and
  Gravity*
Switzer. *The Magic of Mozart*
Twist. *James Cook*
Vernon. *Introducing Bach*
Vernon. *Introducing Mozart*
Yount. *Antoni Van
  Leeuwenhoek: First to See
  Microscopic Life*

Collective Biography ───────────────────────────────

Clements. *The Picture
  History of Great Inventors*
Fritz. *Around the World in a
  Hundred Years*
Glubok. *Great Lives: Painting*

Jacobs. *Great Lives: World
  Religions*
Krull. *Lives of the Artists*
Krull. *Lives of the Musicians*
Krull. *Lives of the Writers*
Steele. *Pirates*

Wilkinson. *Generals Who
  Changed the World*
Wilkinson. *People Who
  Changed the World*
Wilkinson. *Statesmen Who
  Changed the World*

History ───────────────────────────────

Aliki. *The King's Day; Louis
  XIV of France*
Biel. *The Black Death*
Burns. *The Mail*
Burns. *Money*
Chrisp. *The Farmer Through
  History*
Chrisp. *The Soldier Through
  History*
Clare. *Industrial Revolution*
Coote. *The Sailor Through
  History*
Davies. *Transport*

Garfunkel. *On Wings of Joy:
  Ballet*
Giblin. *Be Seated: A Book
  About Chairs*
Giblin. *Chimney Sweeps*
Giblin. *When Plague Strikes*
Goodall. *Great Days of a
  Country House*
Greene. *Child Labor*
Kerr. *Keeping Clean*
Kramer. *Exploration and
  Empire: Science*
Lampton. *Epidemic*

Lincoln. *The Pirate's
  Handbook*
MacDonald. *Cities*
Maestro. *The Story of Money*
Marrin. *The Sea Rovers*
Maurer. *Airborne*
Morley. *Clothes*
Morley. *Exploring North
  America*
Moss. *Forts and Castles*
Perl. *From Top Hats to
  Baseball Caps, from
  Bustles to Blue Jeans*
Platt. *Pirate*

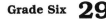

Platt. *The Smithsonian Visual Timeline of Inventions*
Reynoldson. *Conflict and Change*
Ross. *Conquerors & Explorers*

Rowland-Warne. *Costume*
Steele. *Kidnapping*
Steele. *Smuggling*
Ventura. *Clothing*
Ventura. *Food*
Wilkinson. *Amazing Buildings*

Williams. *The Age of Discovery*
Wilson. *Visual Timeline of Transportation*
Woolf. *Picture This: A First Introduction to Paintings*

Multimedia

CD-ROM

Encyclopedia of Science

Teach Your Kids World History

Video

The British Way of Life

Galileo: The Solar Sytem

GRADE SIX

Historical Fiction

Anderson. *Children of Summer*
Calvert. *Hadder MacColl*
Garfield. *Black Jack*
Garfield. *The December Rose*
Garfield. *Devil-in-the-Fog*
Garfield. *The Empty Sleeve*
Garfield. *Footsteps*
Garfield. *Jack Holborn*
Garfield. *The Night of the Comet*
Garfield. *Smith*
Garfield. *Young Nick and Jubilee*

Greene. *One Foot Ashore*
Greene. *Out of Many Waters*
Harnett. *The Cargo of the Madalena*
Harnett. *The Great House*
Haugaard. *A Boy's Will*
Hautzig. *Riches*
Hersom. *The Half Child*
Hunter. *The Ghosts of Glencoe*
Hunter. *The Lothian Run*
Kudlinsky. *Marie: An Invitation to Dance in Paris*

Malterre. *The Last Wolf of Ireland*
McGraw. *Master Cornhill*
Morrison. *Neptune's Fountain: A Young Sculptor in Renaissance Italy*
Speir. *Father, May I Come?*
Sutcliff. *Flame-Colored Taffeta*
Wulffson. *The Upside-Down Ship*
Yolen. *The Ballad of the Pirate Queens*

Biography

Anderson. *Carl Linnaeus: Father of Classification*
Anderson. *Isaac Newton: The Greatest Scientist of All Time*
Blakely. *Wolfgang Amadeus Mozart*
Blumberg. *The Remarkable Voyages of Captain Cook*
Dolan. *Junípero Serra*
Downing. *Mozart Tonight*

Fritz. *Can't You Make Them Behave, King George?*
Greene. *Wolfgang Amadeus Mozart*
Hargrove. *René-Robert Cavelier Sieur de La Salle*
Kent. *James Cook*
Langley. *Exploring the Pacific: The Expeditions of James Cook*
McTavish. *Isaac Newton*

Noonan. *Captain Cook*
Parker. *Isaac Newton and Gravity*
Switzer. *The Magic of Mozart*
Twist. *James Cook*
Vernon. *Introducing Bach*
Vernon. *Introducing Mozart*
Yount. *Antoni Van Leeuwenhoek: First to See Microscopic Life*

Collective Biography

Anderson. *Explorers Who Found New Worlds*
Clements. *The Picture History of Great Inventors*
Cohen. *Real Vampires*
Fritz. *Around the World in a Hundred Years*
Glubok. *Great Lives: Painting*

Hoobler. *French Portraits*
Hoobler. *Italian Portraits*
Hoobler. *Russian Portraits*
Jacobs. *Great Lives: World Religions*
Krull. *Lives of the Artists*
Krull. *Lives of the Musicians*
Krull. *Lives of the Writers*

Wilkinson. *Generals Who Changed the World*
Wilkinson. *People Who Changed the World*
Wilkinson. *Scientists Who Changed the World*
Wilkinson. *Statesmen Who Changed the World*

History

Aliki. *The King's Day; Louis XIV of France*
Biel. *The Black Death*
Burns. *Money*
Child. *The Rise of Islam*
Clare. *Industrial Revolution*
Clements. *An Illustrated History of the World*
Davies. *Transport*
Garfunkel. *On Wings of Joy: Ballet*
Giblin. *Be Seated: A Book About Chairs*
Giblin. *Chimney Sweeps*
Giblin. *When Plague Strikes*
Greene. *Child Labor*
Kerr. *Keeping Clean*

Kramer. *Exploration and Empire: Science*
Lampton. *Epidemic*
Lincoln. *The Pirate's Handbook*
MacDonald. *Cities*
Marrin. *The Sea Rovers*
Maurer. *Airborne*
Morley. *Clothes*
Morley. *Exploring North America*
Moss. *Forts and Castles*
Perl. *From Top Hats to Baseball Caps, from Bustles to Blue Jeans*
Platt. *Pirate*
Platt. *The Smithsonian Visual Timeline of Inventions*

Reynoldson. *Conflict and Change*
Ross. *Conquerors & Explorers*
Rowland-Warne. *Costume*
Steele. *Kidnapping*
Steele. *Smuggling*
Stein. *Witches: Opposing Viewpoints*
Ventura. *Clothing*
Ventura. *Food*
Wilkinson. *Amazing Buildings*
Williams. *The Age of Discovery*
Woolf. *Picture This: A First Introduction to Paintings*

Multimedia

CD-ROM

Art & Music: The Baroque
Art & Music: The Eighteenth Century
Art & Music: The Renaissance
Eyewitness Encyclopedia of Science

Great Artists
History Through Art: Baroque
History Through Art: Renaissance
Le Louvre: The Palace & Its Paintings

Stowaway!
Teach Your Kids World History

Video

The British Way of Life
Galileo: The Solar System

Poland: A Proud Heritage

Europe and the British Isles, 1789–1859

GRADES KINDERGARTEN THROUGH TWO

Historical Fiction

Winter. *Klara's New World*

Biography

Adler. *A Picture Book of Louis Braille*
Brighton. *The Brontes*

Brighton. *My Napoleon*
Fradin. *Louis Braille: The Blind Boy Who Wanted to Read*

Venezia. *Francisco Goya*

Collective Biography

Marzollo. *My First Book of Biographies*

History

Littlefield. *Colors of Germany*

Multimedia

Video

Children's Heroes from Christian History

GRADE THREE

Historical Fiction

Nichol. *Beethoven Lives Upstairs*

Winter. *Klara's New World*

Biography

Adler. *A Picture Book of Louis Braille*
Allman. *Her Piano Sang: A Story About Clara Schumann*
Bedard. *Glass Town*
Birch. *Louis Braille*
Brighton. *The Brontes*
Brighton. *My Napoleon*

Fradin. *Louis Braille: The Blind Boy Who Wanted to Read*
Freedman. *Louis Braille*
Kamen. *Edward Lear*
Parker. *Louis Pasteur and Germs*
Parsons. *Pierre Auguste Renoir*

Venezia. *Francisco Goya*
Venezia. *Ludwig van Beethoven*
Venezia. *Wolfgang Amadeus Mozart*
Vernon. *Introducing Beethoven*

Collective Biography

Marzollo. *My First Book of Biographies*

History

Bowler. *Trains*
Burns. *The Mail*
Carrion. *The Empire of the Czars*

Chrisp. *The Farmer Through History*

Chrisp. *The Soldier Through History*
English. *Transportation*

Fix. *Not So Very Long Ago:
Life in a Country Village*
Gibbons. *Beacons of Light:
Lighthouses*
Goodall. *Great Days of a
Country House*

Harris. *Mummies*
Humble. *Ships*
Kerr. *Keeping Clean*
Lincoln. *The Pirate's Handbook*
Littlefield. *Colors of Germany*
Maestro. *The Story of Money*

Mulvihill. *The French Revolution*
Wilkinson. *Amazing Buildings*
Wilson. *Visual Timeline of
Transportation*

Multimedia

Video

*Children's Heroes from
Christian History*

GRADE FOUR

Historical Fiction

Nichol. *Beethoven Lives Upstairs*

Winter. *Klara's New World*

Biography

Allman. *Her Piano Sang: A
Story About Clara Schumann*
Anderson. *Charles Darwin:
Naturalist*
Bedard. *Glass Town*
Birch. *Louis Braille*
Brighton. *The Brontes*
Brighton. *My Napoleon*
Bryant. *Louis Braille:
Teacher of the Blind*

Collins. *Tales for Hard
Times: Charles Dickens*
Fradin. *Louis Braille: The Blind
Boy Who Wanted to Read*
Freedman. *Louis Braille*
Kamen. *Edward Lear*
Larroche. *Corot from A to Z*
Loewen. *Beethoven*

O'Connor. *The World at His
Fingertips: A Story About
Louis Braille*
Parsons. *Pierre Auguste Renoir*
Venezia. *Ludwig van Beethoven*
Venezia. *Wolfgang Amadeus
Mozart*
Vernon. *Introducing
Beethoven*

Collective Biography

Clements. *The Picture
History of Great Inventors*

Jacobs. *Great Lives: World
Religions*
Krull. *Lives of the Artists*

Krull. *Lives of the Musicians*
Krull. *Lives of the Writers*

History

Biesty. *Man-of-War*
Bowler. *Trains*
Burns. *The Mail*
Burns. *Money*
Carrion. *The Empire of the Czars*
Chrisp. *The Farmer Through
History*
Chrisp. *The Soldier Through
History*
English. *Transportation*
Fix. *Not So Very Long Ago:
Life in a Country Village*
Giblin. *Be Seated: A Book
About Chairs*

Giblin. *Chimney Sweeps*
Gilbert. *The French Revolution*
Gibbons. *Beacons of Light:
Lighthouses*
Goodall. *Great Days of a
Country House*
Harris. *Mummies*
Humble. *Ships*
Kerr. *Keeping Clean*
Lincoln. *The Pirate's Handbook*
Maestro. *The Story of Money*
Mulvihill. *The French
Revolution*

Platt. *The Smithsonian Visual
Timeline of Inventions*
Pollard. *The Nineteenth Century*
Reynoldson. *Conflict and
Change*
Rowland-Warne. *Costume*
Ventura. *Clothing*
Ventura. *Food*
Wilkinson. *Amazing Buildings*
Wilson. *Visual Timeline of
Transportation*
Woolf. *Picture This: A First
Introduction to Paintings*

Multimedia

CD-ROM

*Teach Your Kids World
History*

Video

*Charles Darwin: Species
Evolution*

*Children's Heroes from
Christian History*

GRADE FIVE

Historical Fiction

Avi. *Beyond the Western Sea, Book One: The Escape from Home*
Avi. *Beyond the Western Sea, Book Two: Lord Kirkle's Money*
Cameron. *The Court of the Stone Children*
Conlon-McKenna. *Under the Hawthorn Tree*
Conlon-McKenna. *Wildflower Girl*
Mooney. *The Stove Haunting*
Morpurgo. *Twist of Gold*
Nichol. *Beethoven Lives Upstairs*
Paton Walsh. *A Chance Child*
Schur. *The Circlemaker*
Winter. *Klara's New World*

Biography

Allman. *Her Piano Sang: A Story About Clara Schumann*
Anderson. *Charles Darwin: Naturalist*
Bedard. *Glass Town*
Brophy. *John Ericsson and the Inventions of War*
Bryant. *Louis Braille: Teacher of the Blind*
Collins. *Tales for Hard Times: Charles Dickens*
Evans. *Charles Darwin: Revolutionary Biologist*
Freedman. *Louis Braille*
Gaines. *Alexander von Humboldt*
Hyndley. *The Voyage of the Beagle (Darwin)*
Kamen. *Edward Lear*
Kamen. *Hidden Music: Fanny Mendelssohn*
Larroche. *Corot from A to Z*
Loewen. *Beethoven*
O'Connor. *The World at His Fingertips: A Story About Louis Braille*
Parker. *Charles Darwin and Evolution*
Parsons. *Pierre Auguste Renoir*
Twist. *Charles Darwin*
Ventura. *Darwin*
Vernon. *Introducing Beethoven*

Collective Biography

Clements. *The Picture History of Great Inventors*
Glubok. *Great Lives: Painting*
Jacobs. *Great Lives: World Religions*
Krull. *Lives of the Artists*
Krull. *Lives of the Musicians*
Krull. *Lives of the Writers*
Weitzman. *Great Lives: Human Culture*
Wilkinson. *People Who Changed the World*
Wilkinson. *Scientists Who Changed the World*
Wilkinson. *Statesmen Who Changed the World*

History

Balkwill. *Trafalgar*
Biesty. *Man-of-War*
Bowler. *Trains*
Burns. *The Mail*
Burns. *Money*
Carrion. *The Empire of the Czars*
Chrisp. *The Farmer Through History*
Chrisp. *The Soldier Through History*
Davies. *Transport*
English. *Transportation*
Fix. *Not So Very Long Ago: Life in a Country Village*
Garfunkel. *On Wings of Joy: Ballet*
Giblin. *Be Seated: A Book About Chairs*
Giblin. *Chimney Sweeps*
Gilbert. *The French Revolution*
Goodall. *Great Days of a Country House*
Harris. *Mummies*
Humble. *Ships*
Kerr. *Keeping Clean*
Lincoln. *The Pirate's Handbook*
Maestro. *The Story of Money*
Morley. *Clothes*
Mulvihill. *The French Revolution*
Perl. *Why We Dress the Way We Do*
Platt. *The Smithsonian Visual Timeline of Inventions*
Pollard. *The Nineteenth Century*
Reynoldson. *Conflict and Change*
Rowland-Warne. *Costume*
Sauvain. *Waterloo*
Steele. *Kidnapping*
Van der Linde. *The White Stallions*
Ventura. *Clothing*
Ventura. *Food*
Wilkinson. *Amazing Buildings*
Wilson. *Visual Timeline of Transportation*
Woolf. *Picture This: A First Introduction to Paintings*

Multimedia

CD-ROM

Air and Space Smithsonian Dreams of Flight
Eyewitness Encyclopedia of Science
Teach Your Kids World History

Video

The British Way of Life
Charles Darwin: Species Evolution
The German Way of Life

GRADE SIX

Historical Fiction

Avi. *Beyond the Western Sea, Book One: The Escape from Home*
Avi. *Beyond the Western Sea, Book Two: Lord Kirkle's Money*
Cameron. *The Court of the Stone Children*
Clements. *The Treasure of Plunderell Manor*
Conlon-McKenna. *Fields of Home*
Conlon-McKenna. *Under the Hawthorn Tree*
Conlon-McKenna. *Wildflower Girl*
Matas. *Sworn Enemies*
Mooney. *The Stove Haunting*
Morpurgo. *Twist of Gold*
Overton. *The Ship from Simnel Street*
Paton Walsh. *A Chance Child*
Schur. *The Circlemaker*
Winter. *Klara's New World*

Biography

Allman. *Her Piano Sang: A Story About Clara Schumann*
Altman. *Mr. Darwin's Voyage*
Anderson. *Charles Darwin: Naturalist*
Bedard. *Glass Town*
Birch. *Louis Braille*
Bryant. *Louis Braille: Teacher of the Blind*
Carroll. *Napoleon Bonaparte*
Chiflet. *Victoria and Her Times*
Collins. *Tales for Hard Times: Charles Dickens*
Croll. *Redouté*
Davidson. *Louis Braille*
Evans. *Charles Darwin: Revolutionary Biologist*
Freedman. *Louis Braille*
Gaines. *Alexander von Humboldt*
Guzzetti. *A Family Called Bronte*
Hyndley. *The Voyage of the Beagle (Darwin)*
Kamen. *Edward Lear*
Kamen. *Hidden Music: Fanny Mendelssohn*
Larroche. *Corot from A to Z*
Loewen. *Beethoven*
O'Connor. *The World at His Fingertips: A Story About Louis Braille*
Parker. *Charles Darwin and Evolution*
Twist. *Charles Darwin*
Ventura. *Darwin*
Vernon. *Introducing Beethoven*

Collective Biography

Aaseng. *Genetics*
Aaseng. *You Are the General II: 1800-1899*
Anderson. *Explorers Who Found New Worlds*
Clements. *The Picture History of Great Inventors*
Glubok. *Great Lives: Painting*
Hoobler. *French Portraits*
Hoobler. *Italian Portraits*
Hoobler. *Russian Portraits*
Italia. *Courageous Crimefighters*
Jacobs. *Great Lives: World Religions*
Krull. *Lives of the Artists*
Krull. *Lives of the Musicians*
Krull. *Lives of the Writers*
Weitzman. *Great Lives: Human Culture*
Wilkinson. *People Who Changed the World*
Wilkinson. *Scientists Who Changed the World*
Wilkinson. *Statesmen Who Changed the World*

History

Anderson. *Battles that Changed the Modern World*
Balkwill. *Trafalgar*
Biesty. *Man-of-War*
Bowler. *Trains*
Burns. *Money*
Carrion. *The Empire of the Czars*
Clements. *An Illustrated History of the World*
Coote. *The Sailor Through History*
Cush. *Disasters that Shook the World*
Davies. *Transport*
English. *Transportation*
Fix. *Not So Very Long Ago: Life in a Country Village*
Garfunkel. *On Wings of Joy: Ballet*
Giblin. *Be Seated: A Book About Chairs*
Giblin. *Chimney Sweeps*
Gilbert. *The French Revolution*
Harris. *Mummies*
Humble. *Ships*
Kerr. *Keeping Clean*
Lincoln. *The Pirate's Handbook*
Markham. *Inventions that Changed Modern Life*
Morley. *Clothes*
Moscinski. *Tracing Our Irish Roots*
Mulvihill. *The French Revolution*
Perl. *Why We Dress the Way We Do*
Pietrusza. *The Battle of Waterloo*
Platt. *The Smithsonian Visual Timeline of Inventions*
Pollard. *The Nineteenth Century*
Reynoldson. *Conflict and Change*
Rowland-Warne. *Costume*
Sauvain. *Waterloo*
Steele. *Kidnapping*
Stein. *Witches: Opposing Viewpoints*

Van der Linde. *The White
Stallions*
Ventura. *Clothing*

Ventura. *Food*
Warburton. *Railroads:
Bridging the Continents*

Wilkinson. *Amazing Buildings*
Woolf. *Picture This: A First
Introduction to Paintings*

Multimedia

CD-ROM

*Air and Space Smithsonian
Dreams of Flight*
Art & Music: Impressionism
Art & Music: Romanticism
Exploring the Titanic

*Eyewitness Encyclopedia of
Science*
Great Artists
*History Through Art:
Pre-Modern Era*

*Le Louvre: The Palace & Its
Paintings*
*Teach Your Kids World
History*

Video

The British Way of Life
*Charles Darwin: Species
Evolution*

The French Revolution
The German Way of Life
Poland: A Proud Heritage

Sight by Touch

Europe and the British Isles, 1860–1918

GRADES KINDERGARTEN THROUGH TWO

Historical Fiction

Goode. *Mama's Perfect Present*

Levitin. *A Piece of Home*

Littlesugar. *Marie in Fourth Position*

McCully. *Mirette on the Highwire*

McCully. *Starring Mirette & Bellini*

Spyri. *Heidi*

Biography

Fradin. *Maria de Sautuola: Discoverer of the Bulls in the Cave*

Gherman. *The Mysterious Rays of Dr. Röntgen*

Greene. *Albert Schweitzer*

Greene. *Robert Louis Stevenson*

Greene. *Rudyard Kipling*

Provenson. *The Glorious Flight: Louis Blériot*

Say. *El Chino*

Venezia. *Henri Toulouse-Lautrec*

Venezia. *Monet*

Venezia. *Peter Tchaikovsky*

Venezia. *Vincent van Gogh*

Collective Biography

Marzollo. *My First Book of Biographies*

History

Donnelly. *Titanic: Lost and Found*

Littlefield. *Colors of Germany*

Micklethwait. *A Child's Book of Art*

Moser. *Fly: A Brief History of Flight*

Multimedia

Video

Children's Heroes from Christian History

GRADE THREE

Historical Fiction

Goode. *Mama's Perfect Present*

Green. *Marie: Mystery at the Paris Ballet, Paris, 1775*

Levitin. *A Piece of Home*

Littlesugar. *Marie in Fourth Position*

McCully. *Mirette on the Highwire*

McCully. *Starring Mirette & Bellini*

Spyri. *Heidi*

Biography

Allman. *Her Piano Sang: A Story About Clara Schumann*

Birch. *Marie Curie*

Colver. *Florence Nightingale: War Nurse*

Fradin. *Maria de Sautuola: Discoverer of the Bulls in the Cave*

Gherman. *The Mysterious Rays of Dr. Röntgen*
Gherman. *Robert Louis Stevenson*
Greene. *Albert Schweitzer*
Greene. *Robert Louis Stevenson*
Greene. *Rudyard Kipling*
Grosjean. *Rousseau: Still Voyages*
Meadows. *Pablo Picasso*

Parker. *Marie Curie and Radium*
Parsons. *Pierre Auguste Renoir*
Pierre. *Good Day, Mister Gauguin*
Provenson. *The Glorious Flight: Louis Blériot*
Say. *El Chino*
Tames. *Florence Nightingale*
Tames. *Marie Curie*

Tolan. *Florence Nightingale*
Turner. *Rosa Bonheur*
Venezia. *Henri Toulouse-Lautrec*
Venezia. *Monet*
Venezia. *Peter Tchaikovsky*
Venezia. *Pierre Auguste Renoir*
Venezia. *Vincent van Gogh*

Collective Biography

Marzollo. *My First Book of Biographies*

History

Carrion. *The Empire of the Czars*
Chrisp. *The Farmer Through History*
Chrisp. *The Soldier Through History*
Donnelly. *Titanic: Lost and Found*
English. *Transportation*

Goodall. *Great Days of a Country House*
Greenberg. *An American Family*
Humble. *Ships*
Kent. *The Titanic*
Knight. *The Olympic Games*
Lincoln. *The Pirate's Handbook*
Littlefield. *Colors of Germany*

Maestro. *The Story of Money*
Micklethwait. *A Child's Book of Art*
Moser. *Fly: A Brief History of Flight*
Munro. *Aircraft*
Wilkinson. *Amazing Buildings*
Wilson. *Visual Timeline of Transportation*

Multimedia

Video

Children's Heroes from Christian History

GRADE FOUR

Historical Fiction

McCully. *Mirette on the Highwire*

McCully. *Starring Mirette & Bellini*
Morpurgo. *Butterfly Lion*

Woodruff. *The Orphan of Ellis Island*

Biography

Allman. *Her Piano Sang: A Story About Clara Schumann*
Angel. *Louis Pasteur*
Birch. *Marie Curie*
Colver. *Florence Nightingale: War Nurse*
Fradin. *Maria de Sautuola: Discoverer of the Bulls in the Cave*
Gherman. *The Mysterious Rays of Dr. Röntgen*
Gherman. *Robert Louis Stevenson*
Greene. *Marie Curie*
Grosjean. *Rousseau: Still Voyages*

Kamen. *Kipling*
Larroche. *Corot from A to Z*
Loumaye. *Degas*
Loumaye. *Van Gogh*
Lucas. *Vincent Van Gogh*
Meadows. *Pablo Picasso*
Newfield. *The Life of Louis Pasteur*
Parker. *Louis Pasteur and Germs*
Parker. *Marie Curie and Radium*
Parsons. *Pierre Auguste Renoir*
Pflaum. *Marie Curie and Her Daughter*

Pierre. *Good Day, Mister Gauguin*
Poynter. *Marie Curie*
Resnick. *Lenin: Founder of the Soviet Union*
Robles. *Albert Schweitzer*
Say. *El Chino*
Tames. *Florence Nightingale*
Tames. *Marie Curie*
Tolan. *Florence Nightingale*
Turner. *Rosa Bonheur*
Twist. *Stanley and Livingstone*
Venezia. *Peter Tchaikovsky*
Venezia. *Pierre Auguste Renoir*

Collective Biography

Clements. *The Picture History of Great Inventors*

Jacobs. *Great Lives: World Religions*

Krull. *Lives of the Artists*

Krull. *Lives of the Musicians*

Krull. *Lives of the Writers*

History

Ballard. *Exploring the Titanic*
Berliner. *Before the Wright Brothers*
Burns. *Money*
Carrion. *The Empire of the Czars*
Cavan. *The Irish-American Experience*
Chrisp. *The Farmer Through History*
Chrisp. *The Soldier Through History*
Chrisp. *The Whalers*
Cohen. *The Alaska Purchase*
English. *Transportation*
Gay. *World War I*

Giblin. *Be Seated: A Book About Chairs*
Giblin. *Chimney Sweeps*
Goodall. *Great Days of a Country House*
Hoare. *The Modern World*
Humble. *Ships*
Kent. *The Titanic*
Kerr. *Keeping Clean*
Knight. *The Olympic Games*
Lincoln. *The Pirate's Handbook*
Maestro. *The Story of Money*
Moser. *Fly: A Brief History of Flight*
Munro. *Aircraft*

Pollard. *The Nineteenth Century*
Pollard. *The Red Cross and the Red Crescent*
Reynoldson. *Conflict and Change*
Rowland-Warne. *Costume The Story of Flight*
Ventura. *Clothing*
Ventura. *Food*
Wilkinson. *Amazing Buildings*
Wilson. *Visual Timeline of Transportation*
Woolf. *Picture This: A First Introduction to Paintings*

Multimedia

CD-ROM

Teach Your Kids World History

Video

Children's Heroes from Christian History

GRADE FIVE

Historical Fiction

Green. *Marie: Mystery at the Paris Ballet, Paris, 1775*

Morpurgo. *Butterfly Lion*

Woodruff. *The Orphan of Ellis Island*

Biography

Aller. *J.M. Barrie*
Allman. *Her Piano Sang: A Story About Clara Schumann*
Angel. *Louis Pasteur*
Birch. *Marie Curie*
Bjork. *Linnea in Monet's Garden*
Colver. *Florence Nightingale: War Nurse*
Dommermuth-Costa. *Agatha Christie: Writer of Mystery*
Fisher. *Marie Curie*
Gherman. *Robert Louis Stevenson*
Greene. *Marie Curie*
Grosjean. *Rousseau: Still Voyages*
Hart. *Toulouse-Lautrec*

Jacobs. *Nansen's Arctic Adventures*
Kamen. *Kipling*
Larroche. *Corot from A to Z*
Levine. *Anna Pavlova*
Loumaye. *Degas*
Loumaye. *Van Gogh*
Lucas. *Vincent Van Gogh*
Martin. *H. G. Wells*
Mason. *Cézanne: An Introduction*
Mason. *Monet: An Introduction*
Mason. *Van Gogh: An Introduction*
Meadows. *Pablo Picasso*
Montgomery. *Marie Curie*
Morgan. *Guglielmo Marconi*
Morgan. *Louis Pasteur*

Muhlberger. *What Makes a Degas a Degas?*
Muhlberger. *What Makes a Goya a Goya?*
Muhlberger. *What Makes a Monet a Monet?*
Newfield. *The Life of Louis Pasteur*
O'Connor. *A Story About Maria Montessori*
Parker. *Louis Pasteur and Germs*
Parker. *Marie Curie and Radium*
Parsons. *Pierre Auguste Renoir*
Pflaum. *Marie Curie and Her Daughter*

Pierre. *Good Day, Mister Gauguin*
Poynter. *Marie Curie*
Resnick. *Lenin: Founder of the Soviet Union*

Robles. *Albert Schweitzer*
Say. *El Chino*
Tames. *Florence Nightingale*
Tames. *Marie Curie*
Tolan. *Florence Nightingale*

Turner. *Rosa Bonheur*
Twist. *Stanley and Livingstone*

Collective Biography

Clements. *The Picture History of Great Inventors*
Glubok. *Great Lives: Painting*
Jacobs. *Great Lives: World Religions*
Krull. *Lives of the Artists*

Krull. *Lives of the Musicians*
Krull. *Lives of the Writers*
Weitzman. *Great Lives: Human Culture*
Wilkinson. *People Who Changed the World*

Wilkinson. *Scientists Who Changed the World*
Wilkinson. *Statesmen Who Changed the World*

History

Armenia
Ballard. *Exploring the Titanic*
Berliner. *Before the Wright Brothers*
Brown. *Conflict in Europe and the Great Depression*
Burns. *Money*
Carrion. *The Empire of the Czars*
Cavan. *The Irish-American Experience*
Chrisp. *The Farmer Through History*
Chrisp. *The Soldier Through History*
Chrisp. *The Whalers*
Clare. *First World War*
Cohen. *The Alaska Purchase*
Cosner. *War Nurses*
Davies. *Transport*
English. *Transportation*
Gay. *World War I*
Giblin. *Be Seated: A Book About Chairs*

Giblin. *Chimney Sweeps*
Goodall. *Great Days of a Country House*
Granfield. *In Flanders Fields: The Story of the Poem by John McCrae*
Greenberg. *An Armenian Family*
Hoare. *The Modern World*
Humble. *Ships*
Kent. *The Titanic*
Kerr. *Keeping Clean*
Knight. *The Olympic Games*
Lincoln. *The Pirate's Handbook*
MacDonald. *A 19th Century Railway Station*
Maestro. *The Story of Money*
Maurer. *Airborne*
Morley. *Clothes*
Moser. *Fly: A Brief History of Flight*
Munro. *Aircraft*

Perl. *Why We Dress the Way We Do*
Platt. *The Smithsonian Visual Timeline of Inventions*
Pollard. *The Nineteenth Century*
Pollard. *The Red Cross and the Red Crescent*
Reynoldson. *Conflict and Change*
Rowland-Warne. *Costume*
Stacey. *The Titanic*
The Story of Flight
Steele. *Kidnapping*
Van der Linde. *The White Stallions*
Ventura. *Clothing*
Ventura. *Food*
Wilkinson. *Amazing Buildings*
Wilson. *Visual Timeline of Transportation*
Woolf. *Picture This: A First Introduction to Paintings*

Multimedia

CD-ROM

Air and Space Smithsonian Dreams of Flight

Eyewitness Encyclopedia of Science

Teach Your Kids World History

Video

The British Way of Life

The German Way of Life

GRADE SIX

Historical Fiction

Anderson. *Black Water*
Avery. *Maria Escapes*
Avery. *Maria's Italian Spring*
Bunting. *SOS Titanic*
Burks. *Soldier Boy*
Burton. *The Henchmans at Home*

Cole. *The Dragon in the Cliff*
Dalokay. *Sister Shako and Kolo the Goat*
Doherty. *Street Child*
Foreman. *War Game*
Geras. *Voyage*
Hooper. *The Violin Man*

Lasky. *The Night Journey*
MacGrory. *The Secret of the Ruby Ring*
Mayerson. *The Cat Who Escaped from Steerage*
McCutcheon. *Summer of the Zeppelin*

Morpurgo. *Butterfly Lion*
Morpurgo. *Why the Whales Came*
Newman. *The Case of the Baker Street Irregular*
Newman. *The Case of the Etruscan Treasure*
Newman. *The Case of the Frightened Friend*
Newman. *The Case of the Indian Curse*
Newman. *The Case of the Somerville Secret*

Newman. *The Case of the Threatened King*
Newman. *The Case of the Vanishing Corpse*
Newman. *The Case of the Watching Boy*
O'Hara. *The Hiring Fair*
Pitt. *Beyond the High White Wall*
Posell. *Homecoming*
Pullman. *Spring-Heeled Jack*
Ross. *Sarah, Also Known as Hannah*

Segal. *The Place Where Nobody Stopped*
Shiefman. *Good-bye to the Trees*
Smucker. *Incredible Jumbo*
Wallace. *Cousins in the Castle*
Williams. *Titanic Crossing*
Woodruff. *The Orphan of Ellis Island*
Yarbro. *Floating Illusions*
Zei. *The Sound of Dragon's Feet*

Biography

Aller. *J.M. Barrie*
Allman. *Her Piano Sang: A Story About Clara Schumann*
Birch. *Marie Curie*
Angel. *Louis Pasteur*
Bjork. *Linnea in Monet's Garden*
Carpenter. *Robert Louis Stevenson: Finding Treasure Island*
Chiflet. *Victoria and Her Times*
Colver. *Florence Nightingale: War Nurse*
Dommermuth-Costa. *Agatha Christie: Writer of Mystery*
Fisher. *Marie Curie*
Gherman. *Robert Louis Stevenson*
Greene. *Marie Curie*
Grosjean. *Rousseau: Still Voyages*
Hart. *Toulouse-Lautrec*

Jacobs. *Nansen's Arctic Adventures*
Kamen. *Kipling*
Larroche. *Corot from A to Z*
Levine. *Anna Pavlova*
Loumaye. *Degas*
Loumaye. *Van Gogh*
Lucas. *Vincent Van Gogh*
Martin. *H. G. Wells*
Mason. *Cézanne: An Introduction*
Mason. *Monet: An Introduction*
Mason. *Van Gogh: An Introduction*
Montgomery. *Marie Curie*
Morgan. *Guglielmo Marconi*
Morgan. *Louis Pasteur*
Muhlberger. *What Makes a Degas a Degas?*
Muhlberger. *What Makes a Goya a Goya?*
Muhlberger. *What Makes a Monet a Monet?*

Newfield. *The Life of Louis Pasteur*
O'Connor. *A Story About Maria Montessori*
Parker. *Louis Pasteur and Germs*
Parker. *Marie Curie and Radium*
Pflaum. *Marie Curie and Her Daughter*
Pierre. *Good Day, Mister Gauguin*
Poynter. *Marie Curie*
Resnick. *Lenin: Founder of the Soviet Union*
Robles. *Albert Schweitzer*
Tames. *Florence Nightingale*
Tames. *Marie Curie*
Tanaka. *Anastasia's Album*
Tolan. *Florence Nightingale*
Turner. *Rosa Bonheur*
Twist. *Stanley and Livingstone*
Yount. *Louis Pasteur*

Collective Biography

Aaseng. *Genetics*
Aaseng. *You Are the General II: 1800-1899*
Anderson. *Explorers Who Found New Worlds*
Clements. *The Picture History of Great Inventors*
Glubok. *Great Lives: Painting*
Hoobler. *French Portraits*

Hoobler. *Italian Portraits*
Hoobler. *Russian Portraits*
Italia. *Courageous Crimefighters*
Jacobs. *Great Lives: World Religions*
Krull. *Lives of the Artists*
Krull. *Lives of the Musicians*
Krull. *Lives of the Writers*

Weitzman. *Great Lives: Human Culture*
Wilkinson. *People Who Changed the World*
Wilkinson. *Scientists Who Changed the World*
Wilkinson. *Statesmen Who Changed the World*

History

Anderson. *Battles That Changed the Modern World*
Armenia
Ballard. *Exploring the Titanic*
Berliner. *Before the Wright Brothers*
Brown. *Conflict in Europe and the Great Depression*
Burns. *Money*

Carrion. *The Empire of the Czars*
Cavan. *The Irish-American Experience*
Chrisp. *The Whalers*
Clare. *First World War*
Clements. *An Illustrated History of the World*
Cohen. *The Alaska Purchase*

Coote. *The Sailor Through History*
Cosner. *War Nurses*
Cush. *Disasters That Shook the World*
Davies. *Transport*
English. *Transportation*
Gallant. *The Day the Sky Split Apart*

Garfunkel. *On Wings of Joy:
Ballet*
Gay. *World War I*
Giblin. *Be Seated: A Book
About Chairs*
Giblin. *Chimney Sweeps*
Granfield. *In Flanders Fields:
The Story of the Poem by
John McCrae*
Hoare. *The Modern World*
Humble. *Ships*
Kent. *World War I*
Kerr. *Keeping Clean*
Lincoln. *The Pirate's
Handbook*
MacDonald. *A 19th Century
Railway Station*

Markham. *Inventions That
Changed Modern Life*
Maurer. *Airborne*
Morley. *Clothes*
Moser. *Fly: A Brief History of
Flight*
Munro. *Aircraft*
Perl. *Why We Dress the Way
We Do*
Platt. *The Smithsonian Visual
Timeline of Inventions*
Pollard. *The Nineteenth
Century*
Pollard. *The Red Cross and
the Red Crescent*
Reynoldson. *Conflict and
Change*
Rowland-Warne. *Costume*

Singer. *Structures That
Changed the Way the
World Looked*
Stacey. *The Titanic*
The Story of Flight
Steele. *Kidnapping*
Stein. *Witches: Opposing
Viewpoints*
Van der Linde. *The White
Stallions*
Ventura. *Clothing*
Ventura. *Food*
Warburton. *Railroads:
Bridging the Continents*
Wilkinson. *Amazing Buildings*
Woolf. *Picture This: A First
Introduction to Paintings*

Multimedia

CD-ROM

*Air and Space Smithsonian
Dreams of Flight*
Art & Music: Impressionism
Art & Music: Romanticism
Exploring the Titanic

*Eyewitness Encyclopedia of
Science*
Great Artists
*History Through Art:
Pre-Modern Era*

*Le Louvre: The Palace & Its
Paintings*
*Teach Your Kids World
History*

Video

The British Way of Life
England's Historic Treasures
The German Way of Life

Linnea in Monet's Garden
Poland: A Proud Heritage
Tsiolkovski: The Space Age

Europe and the British Isles, 1919–1945

GRADES KINDERGARTEN THROUGH TWO

Historical Fiction

Adler. *The Number on My Grandfather's Arm*
Cech. *My Grandmother's Journey*
Feder. *The Feather-Bed Journey*
Hoestlandt. *Star of Fear, Star of Hope*
Marton. *You Can Go Home Again*
McCully. *The Amazing Felix*
Mellecker. *Randolph's Dream*
Nerlove. *Flowers on the Wall*
Oppenheim. *The Lily Cupboard*
Ringgold. *Bonjour, Lonnie*
Sim. *In My Pocket*

Biography

Adler. *Hilde and Eli*
Adler. *A Picture Book of Anne Frank*
Greene. *Albert Schweitzer*
Hurwitz. *Anne Frank*
Venezia. *Picasso*
Venezia. *Salvador Dali*

Collective Biography

Marzollo. *My First Book of Biographies*

History

Bresnick-Perry. *Leaving for America*
Littlefield. *Colors of Germany*

GRADE THREE

Historical Fiction

Adler. *The Number on My Grandfather's Arm*
Bawden. *Henry*
Bawden. *The Peppermint Pig*
Cech. *My Grandmother's Journey*
Hoestlandt. *Star of Fear, Star of Hope*
Holm. *North to Freedom*
Levitin. *Journey to America*
Marton. *You Can Go Home Again*
McCully. *The Amazing Felix*
McSwigan. *Snow Treasure*
Mellecker. *Randolph's Dream*
Nerlove. *Flowers on the Wall*
Oppenheim. *The Lily Cupboard*
Ringgold. *Bonjour, Lonnie*
Sim. *In My Pocket*
Turnbull. *No Friend of Mine*
Vos. *Anna Is Still Here*

Biography

Adler. *Hilde and Eli*
Adler. *A Picture Book of Anne Frank*
Birch. *Marie Curie*
Brown. *Anne Frank*
Dahl. *Boy: Tales of Childhood*
Daniel. *Raoul Wallenberg*
Greene. *Albert Schweitzer*
Hunter. *Einstein*
Hurwitz. *Anne Frank*
Lantier. *Albert Schweitzer*
Mochizuki. *Passage to Freedom: The Sugihara Story*
Parker. *Guglielmo Marconi and Radio*
Reef. *Albert Einstein*
Venezia. *Picasso*
Venezia. *Salvador Dali*

Collective Biography
Marzollo. *My First Book of Biographies*

History
Adler. *Child of the Warsaw Ghetto*
Bresnick-Perry. *Leaving for America*
English. *Transportation*
Fluek. *Passover as I Remember It*

Foreman. *War Boy*
Golden. *The Passover Journey*
Humble. *Ships*
Humble. *U-Boat*
Leitner. *The Big Lie*
Littlefield. *The Colors of Germany*

Maestro. *The Story of Money*
Munro. *Aircraft*
Wilkinson. *Amazing Buildings*
Wilson. *Visual Timeline of Transportation*

Multimedia

Video
Nightmare: The Immigration of Joachim and Rachel

GRADE FOUR

Historical Fiction
Adler. *The Number on My Grandfather's Arm*
Bawden. *Carrie's War*
Bawden. *Henry*
Bawden. *The Peppermint Pig*
Douglas. *The Broken Mirror*
Heuck. *The Hideout*
Hoestlandt. *Star of Fear, Star of Hope*
Holm. *North to Freedom*

Howard. *A Different Kind of Courage*
Kemp. *The Well*
Kerr. *When Hitler Stole Pink Rabbit*
Levitin. *Journey to America*
Lowry. *Number the Stars*
Matas. *Daniel's Story*
McCully. *The Amazing Felix*
McSwigan. *Snow Treasure*

Prince. *How's Business*
Ringgold. *Bonjour, Lonnie*
Shemin. *The Little Riders*
Turnbull. *No Friend of Mine*
Vos. *Anna Is Still Here*
Vos. *Dancing on the Bridge at Avignon*
Vos. *Hide and Seek*
Zei. *Petro's War*

Biography
Adler. *Hilde and Eli*
Adler. *A Picture Book of Anne Frank*
Birch. *Marie Curie*
Besson. *October 45*
Brown. *Anne Frank*
Cech. *Jacques-Henri Lartigue*
Dahl. *Boy: Tales of Childhood*
Daniel. *Raoul Wallenberg*

Davidson. *Hillary and Tenzing*
Heslewood. *Introducing Picasso*
Hunter. *Einstein*
Hurwitz. *Anne Frank*
Kamen. *Kipling*
Lantier. *Albert Schweitzer*
Loumaye. *Chagall*
Meadows. *Pablo Picasso*

Mochizuki. *Passage to Freedom: The Sugihara Story*
Parker. *Guglielmo Marconi and Radio*
Pflaum. *Marie Curie and Her Daughter*
Poynter. *Marie Curie*
Reef. *Albert Einstein*

Collective Biography
Clements. *The Picture History of Great Inventors*

Jacobs. *Great Lives: World Religions*
Krull. *Lives of the Artists*

Krull. *Lives of the Musicians*
Krull. *Lives of the Writers*

History
Adler. *Child of the Warsaw Ghetto*
Ballard. *Exploring The Bismarck*
Black. *Battle of the Atlantic*
Black. *Battle of the Bulge*
Black. *Russia at War*

Borden. *The Little Ships: The Heroic Rescue at Dunkirk in World War II*
Burns. *Money*
Emmerich. *My Childhood in Nazi Germany*
English. *Transportation*

Fluek. *Passover as I Remember It*
Foreman. *War Boy*
Gay. *World War II*
Golden. *The Passover Journey*
Greenfeld. *The Hidden Children*
Hoare. *The Modern World*

Humble. *Ships*
Humble. *U-Boat*
Humble. *A World War Two Submarine*
Kerr. *Keeping Clean*
Leitner. *The Big Lie*

Maestro. *The Story of Money*
Munro. *Aircraft*
Pfeifer. *The 761st Tank Battalion*
Resnick. *The Holocaust*
Ventura. *Clothing*

Ventura. *Food*
Wilkinson. *Amazing Buildings*
Wilson. *Visual Timeline of Transportation*
Woolf. *Picture This: A First Introduction to Paintings*

Multimedia

CD-ROM

Teach Your Kids World History

Video

Albert Einstein: The Education of a Genius

Children Remember the Holocaust
The Life of Anne Frank

Nightmare: The Immigration of Joachim and Rachel

GRADE FIVE

Historical Fiction

Anderson. *Searching for Shona*
Bawden. *Carrie's War*
Bawden. *Henry*
Bawden. *The Peppermint Pig*
Bishop. *Twenty and Ten*
Bunting. *Spying on Miss Muller*
Burgess. *An Angel for May*
Cooper. *Dawn of Fear*
Dillon. *Children of Bach*
Douglas. *The Broken Mirror*
Härtling. *Crutches*
Heneghan. *Wish Me Luck*
Hesse. *Letters from Rifka*
Heuck. *The Hideout*

Hoestlandt. *Star of Fear, Star of Hope*
Holm. *North to Freedom*
Howard. *A Different Kind of Courage*
Kemp. *The Well*
Kerr. *When Hitler Stole Pink Rabbit*
Kordon. *Brothers Like Friends*
Levitin. *Journey to America*
Lowry. *Number the Stars*
Marvin. *Bridge to Freedom*
Matas. *Daniel's Story*
McSwigan. *Snow Treasure*
Morpurgo. *Waiting for Anya*
Nivola. *Elisabeth*

Orlev. *The Island on Bird Street*
Prince. *How's Business*
Rees. *The Exeter Blitz*
Reiss. *The Upstairs Room*
Richter. *Friedrich*
Roth-Hano. *Touch Wood*
Shemin. *The Little Riders*
Turnbull. *No Friend of Mine*
Turnbull. *Room for a Stranger*
Turnbull. *Speedwell*
Vos. *Anna Is Still Here*
Vos. *Dancing on the Bridge at Avignon*
Vos. *Hide and Seek*
Zei. *Petro's War*
Zei. *Wildcat Under Glass*

Biography

Amdur. *Anne Frank*
Amdur. *Chaim Weizmann*
Baillet. *Matisse*
Birch. *Marie Curie*
Besson. *October 45*
Brown. *Anne Frank*
Cech. *Jacques-Henri Lartigue*
Dahl. *Boy: Tales of Childhood*
Daniel. *Raoul Wallenberg*
Davidson. *Hillary and Tenzing*
Dommermuth-Costa. *Nikola Tesla*
Driemen. *Winston Churchill*
Drucker. *Kindersport*
Dunn. *Marie Curie*

Heslewood. *Introducing Picasso*
Hunter. *Einstein*
Hurwitz. *Anne Frank*
Ireland. *Albert Einstein*
Kamen. *Kipling*
Lantier. *Albert Schweitzer*
Loumaye. *Chagall*
Mason. *Matisse: An Introduction*
Mason. *Picasso: An Introduction*
McPherson. *Ordinary Genius: Albert Einstein*
Meadows. *Pablo Picasso*

Mochizuki. *Passage to Freedom: The Sugihara Story*
Muhlberger. *What Makes a Picasso a Picasso?*
Parker. *Guglielmo Marconi and Radio*
Pflaum. *Marie Curie and Her Daughter*
Poynter. *Marie Curie*
Reef. *Albert Einstein*
Ross. *Miró*
Swisher. *Pablo Picasso*
Verhoeven. *Anne Frank: Beyond the Diary*
Whitelaw. *Joseph Stalin*

Collective Biography

Clements. *The Picture History of Great Inventors*
Glubok. *Great Lives: Painting*
Hazell. *Heroines: Great Women Through the Ages*
Jacobs. *Great Lives: World Religions*

Krull. *Lives of the Artists*
Krull. *Lives of the Musicians*
Krull. *Lives of the Writers*
Weitzman. *Great Lives: Human Culture*
Wilkinson. *People Who Changed the World*

Wilkinson. *Scientists Who Changed the World*
Wilkinson. *Statesmen Who Changed the World*

History

Adler. *Child of the Warsaw Ghetto*
Adler. *We Remember the Holocaust*
Ballard. *Exploring the Bismarck*
Black. *Battle of Britain*
Black. *Battle of the Atlantic*
Black. *Battle of the Bulge*
Black. *Blitzkrieg*
Black. *Bombing Fortress Europe*
Black. *D-Day*
Black. *Desert Warfare*
Black. *Flattops at War*
Black. *Invasion of Italy*
Black. *Russia at War*
Black. *Victory in Europe*
Black. *War Behind the Lines*
Borden. *The Little Ships: The Heroic Rescue at Dunkirk in World War II*
Brown. *Conflict in Europe and the Great Depression*
Burns. *Money*
Cavan. *The Irish-American Experience*

Chaikin. *A Nightmare in History*
Cosner. *War Nurses*
Cross. *Children and War*
Cross. *Technology of War*
Emmerich. *My Childhood in Nazi Germany*
English. *Transportation*
Estonia
Fluek. *Passover as I Remember It*
Foreman. *War Boy*
Friedman. *The Other Victims*
Gay. *World War II*
Giblin. *When Plague Strikes*
Golden. *The Passover Journey*
Greene. *Child Labor*
Greenberg. *An Armenian Family*
Greenfeld. *The Hidden Children*
Haas. *Tracking the Holocaust*
Hoare. *The Modern World*
Humble. *Ships*
Humble. *U-Boat*
Humble. *A World War Two Submarine*
Kerr. *Keeping Clean*
Leitner. *The Big Lie*

Maestro. *The Story of Money*
Marrin. *The Airman's War: World War II in the Sky*
Marrin. *The Secret Armies: Spies, Counterspies, and Saboteurs in World War II*
Marx. *Echoes of World War II*
Morley. *Clothes*
Munro. *Aircraft*
Perl. *Why We Dress the Way We Do*
Pfeifer. *The 761st Tank Battalion*
Platt. *The Smithsonian Visual Timeline of Inventions*
Resnick. *The Holocaust*
Reynoldson. *Women and War*
Rogasky. *Smoke and Ashes*
Sauvain. *El Alamein*
Steins. *The Allies Against the Axis*
Ventura. *Clothing*
Ventura. *Food*
Wilkinson. *Amazing Buildings*
Wilson. *Visual Timeline of Transportation*
Woolf. *Picture This: A First Introduction to Paintings*

Multimedia

CD-ROM

Eyewitness Encyclopedia of Science

Teach Your Kids World History

Video

Albert Einstein: The Education of a Genius
The British Way of Life

Children Remember the Holocaust
The German Way of Life
Hiroshima Maiden

The Life of Anne Frank
Nightmare: The Immigration of Joachim and Rachel

$$\boxed{\textbf{GRADE SIX}}$$

Historical Fiction

Anderson. *Paper Faces*
Anderson. *Searching for Shona*
Atlan. *The Passersby*
Bawden. *Carrie's War*
Bawden. *Henry*

Bawden. *The Peppermint Pig*
Bergman. *Along the Tracks*
Bishop. *Twenty and Ten*
Booth. *War Dog*
Bunting. *Spying on Miss Muller*

Burgess. *An Angel for May*
Cooper. *Dawn of Fear*
Dillon. *Children of Bach*
Douglas. *The Broken Mirror*
Gallaz. *Rose Blanche*

Gardam. *A Long Way from Verona*
Härtling. *Crutches*
Haugaard. *Chase Me, Catch Nobody*
Heneghan. *Wish Me Luck*
Hesse. *Letters from Rifka*
Heuck. *The Hideout*
Holm. *North to Freedom*
Holman. *The Wild Children*
Howard. *A Different Kind of Courage*
Kemp. *The Well*
Kerr. *When Hitler Stole Pink Rabbit*
Kordon. *Brothers Like Friends*

Levitin. *Journey to America*
Lowry. *Number the Stars*
Marvin. *Bridge to Freedom*
Matas. *Daniel's Story*
McSwigan. *Snow Treasure*
Morpurgo. *Waiting for Anya*
Nivola. *Elisabeth*
Orgel. *The Devil in Vienna*
Orlev. *The Island on Bird Street*
Paton Walsh. *Fireweed*
Pelgrom. *The Winter When Time Was Frozen*
Prince. *How's Business*
Rees. *The Exeter Blitz*
Reiss. *The Upstairs Room*
Richter. *Friedrich*

Roth-Hano. *Touch Wood*
Shemin. *The Little Riders*
Treseder. *Hear O Israel*
Turnbull. *No Friend of Mine*
Turnbull. *Room for a Stranger*
Turnbull. *Speedwell*
Vos. *Anna Is Still Here*
Vos. *Dancing on the Bridge at Avignon*
Vos. *Hide and Seek*
Westall. *The Kingdom by the Sea*
Westall. *The Promise*
Zei. *Petro's War*
Zei. *Wildcat Under Glass*

Biography

Amdur. *Anne Frank*
Amdur. *Chaim Weizmann*
Ayer. *Adolf Hitler*
Baillet. *Matisse*
Birch. *Marie Curie*
Bernheim. *Father of the Orphans: Janusz Korczak*
Besson. *October 45*
Bradley. *Hitler and the Third Reich*
Brown. *Anne Frank*
Cech. *Jacques-Henri Lartigue*
Dahl. *Boy: Tales of Childhood*
Dahl. *My Year*
Daniel. *Raoul Wallenberg*
Davidson. *Hillary and Tenzing*
Dommermuth-Costa. *Nikola Tesla*
Driemen. *Winston Churchill*
Drucker. *Kindersport*

Dunn. *Marie Curie*
Frank. *The Diary of a Young Girl*
Gold. *Memories of Anne Frank*
Goldenstern. *Albert Einstein*
Gourley. *Beryl Markham: Never Turn Back*
Hargrove. *Pablo Casals*
Heslewood. *Introducing Picasso*
Hunter. *Einstein*
Ireland. *Albert Einstein*
Kamen. *Kipling*
Lantier. *Albert Schweitzer*
Linnéa. *Raoul Wallenberg*
Loumaye. *Chagall*
Mason. *Matisse: An Introduction*
Mason. *Picasso: An Introduction*

McPherson. *Ordinary Genius: Albert Einstein*
Meadows. *Pablo Picasso*
Mochizuki. *Passage to Freedom: The Sugihara Story*
Muhlberger. *What Makes a Picasso a Picasso?*
Parker. *Guglielmo Marconi and Radio*
Pflaum. *Marie Curie and her Daughter*
Poynter. *Marie Curie*
Reef. *Albert Einstein*
Ross. *Miró*
Swisher. *Pablo Picasso*
Tames. *Anne Frank: 1929-1945*
Verhoeven. *Anne Frank: Beyond the Diary*
Whitelaw. *Joseph Stalin*

Collective Biography

Aaseng. *Genetics*
Anderson. *Explorers Who Found New Worlds*
Clements. *The Picture History of Great Inventors*
Glubok. *Great Lives: Painting*
Hazell. *Heroines: Great Women Through the Ages*
Hoobler. *French Portraits*

Hoobler. *Italian Portraits*
Hoobler. *Russian Portraits*
Italia. *Courageous Crimefighters*
Jacobs. *Great Lives: World Religions*
Krull. *Lives of the Artists*
Krull. *Lives of the Musicians*
Krull. *Lives of the Writers*

Weitzman. *Great Lives: Human Culture*
Wilkinson. *People Who Changed the World*
Wilkinson. *Scientists Who Changed the World*
Wilkinson. *Statesmen Who Changed the World*

History

Aaseng. *Paris*
Adler. *Child of the Warsaw Ghetto*
Adler. *We Remember the Holocaust*
Anderson. *Battles That Changed the Modern World*
Ayer. *Berlin*

Ballard. *Exploring the Bismarck*
Black. *Battle of Britain*
Black. *Battle of the Atlantic*
Black. *Battle of the Bulge*
Black. *Blitzkrieg*
Black. *Bombing Fortress Europe*
Black. *D-Day*

Black. *Desert Warfare*
Black. *Flattops at War*
Black. *Invasion of Italy*
Black. *Russia at War*
Black. *Victory in Europe*
Black. *War Behind the Lines*
Boas. *We Are Witnesses*

Borden. *The Little Ships: The Heroic Rescue at Dunkirk in World War II*
Brown. *Conflict in Europe and the Great Depression*
Burns. *Money*
Carroll. *The Battle of Stalingrad*
Cavan. *The Irish-American Experience*
Chaikin. *A Nightmare in History*
Cosner. *War Nurses*
Cross. *Children and War*
Cross. *Technology of War*
Emmerich. *My Childhood in Nazi Germany*
English. *Transportation Estonia*
Fluek. *Passover as I Remember It*
Foreman. *War Boy*
Friedman. *Escape or Die*
Friedman. *The Other Victims*
Garfunkel. *On Wings of Joy: Ballet*
Gay. *World War II*

Giblin. *When Plague Strikes*
Golden. *The Passover Journey*
Greenberg. *An Armenian Family*
Greene. *Child Labor*
Greenfeld. *The Hidden Children*
Haas. *Tracking the Holocaust*
Handler. *Young People Speak: Surviving the Holocaust in Hungary*
Hanmer. *Leningrad*
Hoare. *The Modern World*
Humble. *A World War Two Submarine*
Humble. *Ships*
Kerr. *Keeping Clean*
Leitner. *Isabella: From Auschwitz to Freedom*
Leitner. *The Big Lie*
Marrin. *The Airman's War: World War II in the Sky*
Marrin. *The Secret Armies: Spies, Counterspies, and Saboteurs in World War II*
Marx. *Echoes of World War II*
Morley. *Clothes*

Munro. *Aircraft*
Perl. *Why We Dress the Way We Do*
Pfeifer. *The 761st Tank Battalion*
Platt. *The Smithsonian Visual Timeline of Inventions*
Resnick. *The Holocaust*
Reynoldson. *Women and War*
Rogasky. *Smoke and Ashes*
Rosenberg. *Hiding to Survive*
Sauvain. *El Alamein*
Sherrow. *Amsterdam*
Sloan. *Bismarck!*
Stein. *World War II in Europe*
Steins. *The Allies Against the Axis*
Strahinich. *The Holocaust: Understanding and Remembering*
Ventura. *Clothing*
Ventura. *Food*
Wilkinson. *Amazing Buildings*
Woolf. *Picture This: A First Introduction to Paintings*

Multimedia

CD-ROM

Art & Music: Surrealism
Art & Music: The Twentieth Century

Eyewitness Encyclopedia of Science
History Through Art: 20th Century

Lest We Forget: A History of the Holocaust
Teach Your Kids World History

Video

Albert Einstein: The Education of a Genius
Barefoot Gen
The British Way of Life
Child in Two Worlds
Children Remember the Holocaust

Diamonds in the Snow
The German Way of Life
Hiroshima Maiden
The Life of Anne Frank
Nightmare: The Immigration of Joachim and Rachel
Poland: A Proud Heritage

Tsiolkovski: The Space Age
Ukraine: Kiev and Lvov
We Must Never Forget: The Story of the Holocaust

Europe and the British Isles, 1946 to the Present

GRADES KINDERGARTEN THROUGH TWO

Historical Fiction
Adler. *One Yellow Daffodil*   Ringgold. *Bonjour, Lonnie*   Zeifert. *A New Coat for Anna*

Biography

Collective Biography
Marzollo. *My First Book of Biographies*

History
Adler. *A Picture Book of Jewish Holidays*
Cashman. *Jewish Days and Holidays*

Falwell. *The Letter Jesters*
Littlefield. *Colors of Germany*
MacMillan. *Jewish Holidays in the Spring*

Streisguth. *A Ticket to France*
Streisguth. *A Ticket to Russia*

GRADE THREE

Historical Fiction
Adler. *One Yellow Daffodil*
Hill. *The Glass Angels*

Mooney. *The Voices of Silence*
Ringgold. *Bonjour, Lonnie*

Speir. *Father, May I Come?*
Zeifert. *A New Coat for Anna*

Biography
Angel. *Lech Walesa*
Bennett. *Mikhail Gorbachev*
Fraser. *On Top of the World*
Gray. *Bob Geldof*

Greene. *Albert Schweitzer*
Heslewood. *Introducing Picasso*
Hunter. *Einstein*

Hurwitz. *Astrid Lindgren*
Meadows. *Pablo Picasso*
Venezia. *Picasso*
Venezia. *Salvador Dali*

Collective Biography
Marzollo. *My First Book of Biographies*

Steele. *Pirates*

History
Adler. *A Picture Book of Jewish Holidays*
Archibald. *A Sudanese Family*
Berg. *An Eritrean Family*
Cashman. *Jewish Days and Holidays*
Chicoine. *A Liberian Family*
Denny. *A Taste of Britain*
Denny. *A Taste of France*
Falwell. *The Letter Jesters*
Graham. *Spacecraft*

Greenberg. *An Armenian Family*
Jessop. *Big Buildings of the Ancient World*
Knight. *The Olympic Games*
Krensky. *Breaking into Print*
Leder. *A Russian Jewish Family*
Littlefield. *Colors of Germany*
MacMillan. *Jewish Holidays in the Spring*

Maestro. *The Story of Money*
Moscinski. *Tracing Our Irish Roots*
Silverman. *A Bosnian Family*
Streisguth. *A Ticket to France*
Streisguth. *A Ticket to Russia*
Wilkinson. *Amazing Buildings*
Wilson. *Visual Timeline of Transportation*

GRADE FOUR

Historical Fiction

Hill. *The Glass Angels*
Kossman. *Behind the Border*
Mooney. *The Voices of Silence*
Ringgold. *Bonjour, Lonnie*
Roper. *In Caverns of Blue Ice*
Rowlands. *Milk and Honey*
Speir. *Father, May I Come?*

Biography

Angel. *Lech Walesa*
Ayer. *Boris Yeltsin*
Bennett. *Mikhail Gorbachev*
Cech. *Jacques-Henri Lartigue*
Fraser. *On Top of the World*
Fromer. *Jane Goodall: Living with the Chimps*
Gray. *Bob Geldof*
Heslewood. *Introducing Picasso*
Hunter. *Einstein*
Hurwitz. *Astrid Lindgren*
Lazo. *Elie Wiesel*
Lazo. *Lech Walesa*
Meadows. *Pablo Picasso*

Collective Biography

Jacobs. *Great Lives: World Religions*
Krull. *Lives of the Artists*
Krull. *Lives of the Musicians*
Steele. *Pirates*
Wilkinson. *Scientists Who Changed the World*

History

Archibald. *A Sudanese Family*
Berg. *An Eritrean Family*
Bradley. *Kazakhstan*
Bursell. *Haunted Houses*
Cashman. *Jewish Days and Holidays*
Chicoine. *A Liberian Family*
Clark. *The Commonwealth of Independent States*
Denny. *A Taste of Britain*
Denny. *A Taste of France*
Falwell. *The Letter Jesters*
Flint. *The Baltic States*
Flint. *The Russian Federation*
Giblin. *Be Seated: A Book About Chairs*
Gosnell. *Belarus, Ukraine, and Moldova*
Graham. *Spacecraft*
Greenberg. *An Armenian Family*
Jessop. *Big Buildings of the Ancient World*
Knight. *The Olympic Games*
Krensky. *Breaking into Print*
Leder. *A Russian Jewish Family*
MacMillan. *Jewish Holidays in the Spring*
Maestro. *The Story of Money*
Meltzer. *Gold*
Moscinski. *Tracing Our Irish Roots*
Roberts. *Georgia, Armenia, and Azerbaijan*
Ross. *Conquerors & Explorers*
Silverman. *A Bosnian Family*
Streisguth. *A Ticket to France*
Streisguth. *A Ticket to Russia*
Thomas. *The Central Asian States*
Wilkinson. *Amazing Buildings*
Wilkinson. *Building*
Wilson. *Visual Timeline of Transportation*
Woolf. *Picture This: A First Introduction to Paintings*

Multimedia

CD-ROM

Teach Your Kids World History

Video

Albert Einstein: The Education of a Genius
The Baltic States: Finding Independence

GRADE FIVE

Historical Fiction

Elmer. *Touch the Sky*
Goodman. *Songs from Home*
Hill. *The Glass Angels*
Kossman. *Behind the Border*
Layton. *The Swap*
Mead. *Adem's Cross*
Mooney. *The Voices of Silence*
Morpurgo. *Mr. Nobody's Eyes*
Reiss. *The Journey Back*
Roper. *In Caverns of Blue Ice*
Rowlands. *Milk and Honey*
Speir. *Father, May I Come?*
Szablya. *The Fall of the Red Star*

Biography

Angel. *Lech Walesa*
Auerbach. *Queen Elizabeth II*
Ayer. *Boris Yeltsin*
Bennett. *Mikhail Gorbachev*
Cech. *Jacques-Henri Lartigue*
Craig. *Lech Wal esa and His Poland*
Ebon. *Nikita Khrushchev*
Fraser. *On Top of the World*
Fromer. *Jane Goodall: Living with the Chimps*

Gray. *Bob Geldof*
Heslewood. *Introducing Picasso*
Hunter. *Einstein*
Hurwitz. *Astrid Lindgren*
Kaye. *Lech Walesa*
Kristy. *George Balanchine*
Lazo. *Elie Wiesel*
Lazo. *Lech Walesa*
Lorbiecki. *From My Palace of Leaves in Sarajevo*

Mason. *Picasso: An Introduction*
Meadows. *Pablo Picasso*
Muhlberger. *What Makes a Picasso a Picasso?*
Perl. *Isaac Bashevis Singer*
Ross. *Miró*
Stewart. *Sir Edmund Hillary*
Twist. *Gagarin and Armstrong*

Collective Biography

Blue. *People of Peace*
Jacobs. *Great Lives: World Religions*

Krull. *Lives of the Artists*
Krull. *Lives of the Musicians*
Steele. *Pirates*

Wilkinson. *Scientists Who Changed the World*

History

Archibald. *A Sudanese Family*
Azerbaijan
Bachrach. *Tell Them We Remember*
Belarus
Berg. *An Eritrean Family*
Bortz. *Catastrophe!*
Bradley. *Kazakhstan*
Bursell. *Haunted Houses*
Capek. *Artistic Trickery: Trompe L'oeil Art*
Chaikin. *A Nightmare in History*
Chicoine. *A Liberian Family*
Clark. *The Commonwealth of Independent States*
Cross. *Aftermath of War*
Cumming. *Russia*
Deltenre. *Russia*
Denny. *A Taste of Britain*
Denny. *A Taste of France*
Estonia
Flint. *The Baltic States*
Flint. *The Russian Federation*
Georgia
Giblin. *Be Seated: A Book About Chairs*
Giblin. *When Plague Strikes*
Gosnell. *Belarus, Ukraine, and Moldova*

Graham. *Spacecraft*
Greenberg. *An Armenian Family*
Jessop. *Big Buildings of the Ancient World*
Kazakhstan
King. *The Gulf War*
Knight. *The Olympic Games*
Krensky. *Breaking into Print*
Kyrgyzstan
Latvia
Leder. *A Russian Jewish Family*
Lithuania
Lynch. *Great Buildings*
MacMillan. *Jewish Holidays in the Spring*
Maestro. *The Story of Money*
Meltzer. *Gold*
Moldova
Morley. *Clothes*
Moscinski. *Tracing Our Irish Roots*
Nardo. *Chernobyl*
Perl. *From Top Hats to Baseball Caps, from Bustles to Blue Jeans*
Platt. *The Smithsonian Visual Timeline of Inventions*

Roberts. *Georgia, Armenia, and Azerbaijan*
Russia
Ross. *Conquerors & Explorers*
Seymour-Jones. *Refugees*
Silverman. *A Bosnian Family*
Steele. *Censorship*
Steele. *Smuggling*
Streisguth. *A Ticket to France*
Streisguth. *A Ticket to Russia*
Strom. *Searching for the Gypsies*
Sunk! Exploring Underwater Archaeology
Tajikistan
Thomas. *The Central Asian States*
Turkmenistan
Turvey. *Inventions: Inventors and Ingenious Ideas*
Ukraine
Uzbekistan
Westerfeld. *The Berlin Airlift*
Wilkinson. *Amazing Buildings*
Wilkinson. *Building*
Wilson. *Visual Timeline of Transportation*
Woolf. *Picture This: A First Introduction to Paintings*

Multimedia

CD-ROM

Eyewitness Encyclopedia of Science

Teach Your Kids World History

Video

Albert Einstein: The Education of a Genius

The Baltic States: Finding Independence
The British Way of Life

Germany: From Partition to Reunification, 1945-1990

GRADE SIX

Historical Fiction

De Treviño. *Turi's Poppa*
Elmer. *Touch the Sky*
Fenton. *The Morning of the Gods*
Goodman. *Songs from Home*
Hill. *The Glass Angels*
Kossman. *Behind the Border*
Layton. *The Swap*

Lorbiecki. *From My Palace of Leaves in Sarajevo*
Matas. *After the War*
Mead. *Adem's Cross*
Mooney. *The Voices of Silence*
Morpurgo. *Mr. Nobody's Eyes*

Morpurgo. *The War of Jenkins' Ear*
Reiss. *The Journey Back*
Roper. *In Caverns of Blue Ice*
Rosen. *Andi's War*
Rowlands. *Milk and Honey*
Speir. *Father, May I Come?*
Szablya. *The Fall of the Red Star*

Biography

Angel. *Lech Walesa*
Auerbach. *Queen Elizabeth II*
Ayer. *Boris Yeltsin*
Bennett. *Mikhail Gorbachev*
Cech. *Jacques-Henri Lartigue*
Craig. *Lech Wal esa and His Poland*
Ebon. *Nikita Khrushchev*
Foster. *Margaret Thatcher*
Fraser. *On Top of the World*
Fromer. *Jane Goodall: Living with the Chimps*

Gourley. *Beryl Markham: Never Turn Back*
Gray. *Bob Geldof*
Heslewood. *Introducing Picasso*
Hughes. *Madam Prime Minister: Margaret Thatcher*
Hunter. *Einstein*
Hurwitz. *Astrid Lindgren*
Kaye. *Lech Walesa*
Kristy. *George Balanchine*
Lazo. *Elie Wiesel*
Lazo. *Lech Walesa*

Martin. *The Beatles*
Mason. *Picasso: An Introduction*
Muhlberger. *What Makes a Picasso a Picasso?*
Newton. *James Watson & Francis Crick*
Perl. *Isaac Bashevis Singer*
Ross. *Miró*
Steele. *Thor Heyerdahl*
Stewart. *Sir Edmund Hillary*
Twist. *Gagarin and Armstrong*

Collective Biography

Aaseng. *Genetics*
Aaseng. *You Are the General*
Blue. *People of Peace*
Cohen. *Prophets of Doom*
Hoobler. *French Portraits*

Hoobler. *Russian Portraits*
Italia. *Courageous Crimefighters*
Jacobs. *Great Lives: World Religions*

Krull. *Lives of the Artists*
Krull. *Lives of the Musicians*
Wilkinson. *Scientists Who Changed the World*

History

Azerbaijan
Anderson. *Battles that Changed the Modern World*
Archibald. *A Sudanese Family*
Bachrach. *Tell Them We Remember*
Belarus
Berg. *An Eritrean Family*
Bortz. *Catastrophe!*
Bradley. *Kazakhstan*
Bursell. *Haunted Houses*
Capek. *Artistic Trickery: Trompe L'oeil Art*
Chaikin. *A Nightmare in History*
Chicoine. *A Liberian Family*
Clark. *The Commonwealth of Independent States*
Cross. *Aftermath of War*
Cumming. *Russia*
Cush. *Disasters that Shook the World*
Deltenre. *Russia*
Denny. *A Taste of Britain*
Denny. *A Taste of France*

Estonia
Flint. *The Baltic States*
Flint. *The Russian Federation*
Garfunkel. *On Wings of Joy: Ballet*
Georgia
Giblin. *Be Seated: A Book About Chairs*
Giblin. *When Plague Strikes*
Gosnell. *Belarus, Ukraine, and Moldova*
Graham. *Spacecraft*
Harbor. *Conflict in Eastern Europe*
Jessop. *Big Buildings of the Ancient World*
Kazakhstan
King. *The Gulf War*
Koral. *An Album of War Refugees*
Krensky. *Breaking into Print*
Kyrgyzstan
Latvia
Leder. *A Russian Jewish Family*
Lithuania

Lynch. *Great Buildings*
Meltzer. *Gold*
Moldova
Morley. *Clothes*
Moscinski. *Tracing Our Irish Roots*
Nardo. *Chernobyl*
Perl. *From Top Hats to Baseball Caps, from Bustles to Blue Jeans*
Platt. *The Smithsonian Visual Timeline of Inventions*
Roberts. *Georgia, Armenia, and Azerbaijan*
Ross. *Conquerors & Explorers*
Russia
Seymour-Jones. *Refugees*
Silverman. *A Bosnian Family*
Steele. *Censorship*
Steele. *Smuggling*
Strahinich. *The Holocaust: Understanding and Remembering*

Strom. *Searching for the Gypsies*
Sunk! Exploring Underwater Archaeology
Tajikistan
Thomas. *The Central Asian States*

Turkmenistan
Turvey. *Inventions: Inventors and Ingenious Ideas*
Ukraine
Uzbekistan
Westerfeld. *The Berlin Airlift*

Wilkinson. *Amazing Buildings*
Wilkinson. *Building*
Woolf. *Picture This: A First Introduction to Paintings*

Multimedia

CD-ROM

Art & Music: The Twentieth Century

Eyewitness Encyclopedia of Science

Teach Your Kids World History
The Way Things Work

Video

Albert Einstein: The Education of a Genius

The Baltic States: Finding Independence
The British Way of Life

Germany: From Partition to Reunification, 1945-1990
Ukraine: Kiev and Lvov

Africa and South Africa

Before 1900

GRADES KINDERGARTEN THROUGH THREE

Historical Fiction

Johnson. *Now Let Me Fly*

Thomas. *Kai: A Mission for Her Village*

Biography

Wisniewski. *Sundiata*

History

Gibbons. *Pirates: Robbers of the High Seas*
Hetfield. *The Asante of West Africa*

Hetfield. *Maasai*
Hetfield. *The Yoruba of West Africa*
Medearis. *Our People*

Peffer-Engels. *The Benin Kingdom of West Africa*

Multimedia

Video

Children's Heroes from Christian History

GRADES FOUR, FIVE, AND SIX

Historical Fiction

Hansen. *The Captive*
Rupert. *The African Mask*

Thomas. *Kai: A Mission for Her Village*

Biography

Wisniewski. *Sundiata*

Collective Biography

Hoobler. *African Portraits*

History

Bangura. *Kipsigis*
Barboza. *Door of No Return: Gorée Island*
Bianchi. *The Nubians*
Corbishley. *Secret Cities*
De Bruycker. *Africa*
Ibazebo. *Exploration into Africa*

Jenkins. *Ancient Egypt, Ethiopia, and Nubia*
Koslow. *Ancient Ghana*
Koslow. *Asante*
Koslow. *Centuries of Greatness: West African Kingdoms*
Koslow. *Yorubaland*

Lincoln. *The Pirate's Handbook*
Mann. *Egypt, Kush, Aksum: Northeast Africa*
Mann. *Oyo, Benin, Ashanti: The Guinea Coast*
Mann. *Zeni, Buganda: East Africa*

Millar. *The Kingdom of Benin West Africa*
Murray. *Africa*
Parris. *Rendille*

Reynoldson. *Conflict and Change*
Ricciuti. *Somalia*
Street Smart! Cities of the Ancient World

Sullivan. *Slave Ship*
Wangari. *Ameru*
Wilkinson. *The Magical East*

Multimedia

CD-ROM

Teach Your Kids World History

Video

Abubakari: The Explorer King of Mali
Africa

Africa: History and Culture
Children's Heroes from Christian History

Ghana
The Roots of African Civilization

After 1900

GRADES KINDERGARTEN THROUGH THREE

Biography

Cooper. *Mandela: From the Life of the South African Statesman*

Daniel. *Nelson Mandela*
Feinberg. *Nelson Mandela*
Holland. *Nelson Mandela*

Tames. *Nelson Mandela*
Roberts. *Nelson Mandela*

History

Hetfield. *The Asante of West Africa*
Hetfield. *Maasai*

Hetfield. *The Yoruba of West Africa*
Medearis. *Our People*

Peffer-Engels. *The Benin Kingdom of West Africa*

GRADES FOUR, FIVE, AND SIX

Historical Fiction

Case. *92 Queens Road*
Farmer. *A Girl Named Disaster*

Gordon. *The Middle of Somewhere*
Morpurgo. *Butterfly Lion*

Sacks. *Beyond Safe Boundaries*

Biography

Bentley. *Archbishop Tutu of South Africa*
Daniel. *Nelson Mandela*
Denenberg. *Nelson Mandela*

Feinberg. *Nelson Mandela*
Hughes. *Nelson Mandela*
Kellner. *Kwame Nkrumah*
Lantier. *Desmond Tutu*

Roberts. *Nelson Mandela*
Tames. *Nelson Mandela*
Wepman. *Jomo Kenyatta*

Collective Biography

Hazell. *Heroes: Great Men Through the Ages*

Hoobler. *African Portraits*

History

Berg. *An Eritrean Family*
Halliburton. *Africa's Struggle for Independence*
Lynch. *Great Buildings*
Medearis. *Come This Far to Freedom: History of African Americans*

Meltzer. *Gold*
Millar. *The Kingdom of Benin West Africa*
Murray. *Africa*
Parris. *Rendille*
Reynoldson. *Conflict and Change*

Ricciuti. *Somalia*
Schur. *Day of Delight: A Jewish Sabbath in Ethiopia*
Schur. *When I Left My Village*
Swinimer. *Pokot*
Wangari. *Ameru*

Multimedia

CD-ROM

*Teach Your Kids World
    History*

Video

Africa   *Africa: Land and People*

Australia, New Zealand, Pacific Islands, and Antartica

GRADES KINDERGARTEN THROUGH TWO

History

Olawsky. *Colors of Australia*

GRADE THREE

Historical Fiction

Hill. *The Burnt Stick*

Biography

Birch. *Father Damien*

Crofford. *Healing Warrior: Sister Elizabeth Kenney*

History

Lincoln. *The Pirate's Handbook*

Margolies. *Warriors, Wigmen, and the Crocodile People: Papua New Guinea*

Olawsky. *Colors of Australia*

GRADE FOUR

Historical Fiction

Baylis-White. *Sheltering Rebecca*

Hill. *The Burnt Stick*

Mayne. *Low Tide*

Biography

Birch. *Father Damien*

Crofford. *Healing Warrior: Sister Elizabeth Kenney*

McCurdy. *Trapped by the Ice*

History

Lincoln. *The Pirate's Handbook*

MacDonald. *Maori*

Margolies. *Warriors, Wigmen, and the Crocodile People: Papua New Guinea*

Multimedia

CD-ROM

Teach Your Kids World History

GRADE FIVE

Historical Fiction

Baylis-White. *Sheltering Rebecca*
Beatty. *Jonathan Down Under*
Disher. *The Bamboo Flute*
French. *Somewhere Around the Corner*

Gee. *The Fire-Raiser*
Hill. *The Burnt Stick*
Klein. *All in the Blue Unclouded Weather*
Klein. *Dresses of Red and Gold*

Klein. *The Sky in Silver Lace*
Mayne. *Low Tide*
Pople. *The Other Side of the Family*
Sperry. *Call It Courage*

Biography

Birch. *Father Damien*
Chua-eoan. *Corazon Aquino*

Crofford. *Healing Warrior: Sister Elizabeth Kenney*

Gaffney. *Edmund Hillary*
McCurdy. *Trapped by the Ice*

History

Bandon. *Filipino Americans*
Black. *Bataan and Corregidor*
Black. *Guadalcanal*
Black. *Island Hopping in the Pacific*
Black. *Iwo Jima and Okinawa*

Black. *Pearl Harbor!*
Lincoln. *The Pirate's Handbook*
Liptak. *Endangered Peoples*
Lynch. *Great Buildings*
MacDonald. *Maori*

Margolies. *Warriors, Wigmen, and the Crocodile People: Papua New Guinea*
Nardo. *Krakatoa*

Multimedia

CD-ROM

Teach Your Kids World History

GRADE SIX

Historical Fiction

Baylis-White. *Sheltering Rebecca*
Beatty. *Jonathan Down Under*
Disher. *The Bamboo Flute*
Duder. *Alex in Rome*
Dunlop. *The Poetry Girl*
French. *Somewhere Around the Corner*

Gee. *The Champion*
Gee. *The Fire-Raiser*
Griese. *The Wind Is Not a River*
Klein. *All in the Blue Unclouded Weather*
Klein. *Dresses of Red and Gold*

Klein. *The Sky in Silver Lace*
Mayne. *Low Tide*
Pople. *The Other Side of the Family*
Sperry. *Call It Courage*
Wheatley. *My Place*

Biography

Birch. *Father Damien*
Chua-eoan. *Corazon Aquino*

Gaffney. *Edmund Hillary*
McCurdy. *Trapped by the Ice*

History

Bandon. *Filipino Americans*
Black. *Bataan and Corregidor*
Black. *Guadalcanal*
Black. *Island Hopping in the Pacific*

Black. *Iwo Jima and Okinawa*
Black. *Pearl Harbor!*
Lincoln. *The Pirate's Handbook*
Liptak. *Endangered Peoples*

Lynch. *Great Buildings*
MacDonald. *Maori*
Nardo. *Krakatoa*

Multimedia

CD-ROM

Teach Your Kids World History

Canada

GRADES KINDERGARTEN THROUGH TWO

Historical Fiction
Conrad. *Call Me Ahnighito*

Biography
Asimov. *Henry Hudson*

Collective Biography
Marzollo. *My First Book of Biographies*

History
Gibbons. *The Great St. Lawrence Seaway*

GRADE THREE

Historical Fiction

Griese. *At the Mouth of the Luckiest River*

Kinsey-Warnock. *Wilderness Cat*

Kogawa. *Naomi's Road*

Biography
Asimov. *Henry Hudson*

Collective Biography
Marzollo. *My First Book of Biographies*

History

Gibbons. *The Great St. Lawrence Seaway*
Hancock. *Nunavut*

Jackson. *Newfoundland and Labrador*
Richardson. *Saskatchewan*

Thompson. *Nova Scotia*
Yates. *Alberta*

GRADE FOUR

Historical Fiction

Anderson. *Pioneer Settlers in New France*
Ellis. *Next-Door Neighbors*

Griese. *At the Mouth of the Luckiest River*
Kogawa. *Naomi's Road*

Little. *From Anna*
Pearson. *The Sky Is Falling*
Turner. *The Haunted Igloo*

Biography

Asimov. *Henry Hudson* Jacobs. *Champlain*

History

Alexander. *Inuit*
Beattie. *Buried in Ice*
Berrill. *Mummies, Masks, &*
Mourners
Chrisp. *The Search for a*
Northern Route

Gibbons. *The Great St.*
Lawrence Seaway
Hancock. *Nunavut*
Harris. *Mummies*
Jackson. *Newfoundland and*
Labrador

Richardson. *Saskatchewan*
Thompson. *Nova Scotia*
Yates. *Alberta*

Multimedia

CD-ROM

Canadian Treasures *Teach Your Kids World*
History

Video

Michael Arvaarluk Kusugak

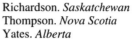

GRADE FIVE

Historical Fiction

Anderson. *Pioneer Settlers in*
New France
Durbin. *The Broken Blade*
Dubois. *Abenaki Captive*
Ellis. *Next-Door Neighbors*
Garrigue. *The Eternal*
Spring of Mr. Ito
Griese. *At the Mouth of the*
Luckiest River

Harris. *Raven's Cry*
Kogawa. *Naomi's Road*
Levin. *Brother Moose*
Lunn. *Shadow in Hawthorn*
Bay
Little. *From Anna*
Marko. *Away to Fundy Bay*
Pearson. *The Lights Go On*
Again

Pearson. *Looking at the Moon*
Pearson. *The Sky Is Falling*
Reed. *The Kraken*
Rice. *The Year the Wolves*
Came
Roe. *Circle of Light*
Sterling. *My Name Is*
Seepeetza
Turner. *The Haunted Igloo*

Biography

Asimov. *Henry Hudson* Jacobs. *Champlain* Xydes. *Alexander Mackenzie*

Collective Biography

Cohen. *The Ghosts of War* Wilkinson. *Generals Who*
Changed the World

History

Alexander. *Inuit*
Beattie. *Buried in Ice*
Berrill. *Mummies, Masks, &*
Mourners
Bonvillain. *The Haidas*
Brown. *The Search for the*
Northwest Passage
Chrisp. *The Search for a*
Northern Route

Gibbons. *The Great St.*
Lawrence Seaway
Granfield. *In Flanders Fields:*
The Story of the Poem by
John McCrae
Hancock. *Nunavut*
Harris. *Mummies*
Jackson. *Newfoundland and*
Labrador
Lynch. *Great Buildings*

Osborn. *The Peoples of the*
Arctic
Richardson. *Saskatchewan*
Thompson. *Nova Scotia*
West. *Braving the North*
Atlantic: Vikings, the
Cabots, and Jacques
Cartier
Wood. *Ancient America*
Yates. *Alberta*

Multimedia

CD-ROM

Adventure Canada
Canadian Treasures

Teach Your Kids World
History

Video

Canada: People and Places

Canada's Maple Tree: The Story of the Country's Emblem

Michael Arvaarluk Kusugak Rendezvous Canada, 1606

GRADE SIX

Historical Fiction

Anderson. *Pioneer Settlers in New France*
Boraks-Nemetz. *The Old Brown Suitcase*
Doyle. *Uncle Ronald*
Durbin. *The Broken Blade*
Dubois. *Abenaki Captive*
Ellis. *Next-Door Neighbors*
Garrigue. *The Eternal Spring of Mr. Ito*
Harris. *Raven's Cry*

Holeman. *Promise Song*
Hudson. *Dawn Rider*
Hudson. *Sweetgrass*
Katz. *Out of the Dark*
Kogawa. *Naomi's Road*
Levin. *Brother Moose*
Little. *From Anna*
Lunn. *Shadow in Hawthorn Bay*
Marko. *Away to Fundy Bay*

Pearson. *The Lights Go On Again*
Pearson. *Looking at the Moon*
Pearson. *The Sky Is Falling*
Reed. *The Kraken*
Rice. *The Year the Wolves Came*
Roe. *Circle of Light*
Sterling. *My Name Is Seepeetza*
Turner. *The Haunted Igloo*

Biography

Jacobs. *Champlain*

Xydes. *Alexander Mackenzie*

Collective Biography

Cohen. *The Ghosts of War*

Italia. *Courageous Crimefighters*

Wilkinson. *Generals Who Changed the World*

History

Alexander. *Inuit*
Beattie. *Buried in Ice*
Berrill. *Mummies, Masks, & Mourners*
Bonvillain. *The Haidas*
Brown. *The Search for the Northwest Passage*
Chrisp. *The Search for a Northern Route*
Gibbons. *The Great St. Lawrence Seaway*

Gorrell. *North Star to Freedom*
Granfield. *In Flanders Fields: The Story of the Poem by John McCrae*
Hancock. *Nunavut*
Harris. *Mummies*
Jackson. *Newfoundland and Labrador*
Liptak. *Endangered Peoples*
Lynch. *Great Buildings*

Minks. *The French and Indian War*
Osborn. *The Peoples of the Arctic*
Richardson. *Saskatchewan*
Thompson. *Nova Scotia*
West. *Braving the North Atlantic: Vikings, the Cabots, and Jacques Cartier*
Wood. *Ancient America*
Yates. *Alberta*

Multimedia

CD-ROM

Adventure Canada
Canadian Treasures

One Tribe

Teach Your Kids World History

Video

Canada: People and Places

Canada's Maple Tree: The Story of the Country's Emblem

The Canadian Way of Life
Michael Arvaarluk Kusugak
Rendezvous Canada, 1606

China

GRADES KINDERGARTEN THROUGH TWO

Historical Fiction

Hong. *The Empress and the Silkworm*

Lattimore. *The Dragon's Robe*
Và. *A Letter to the King*

Yolen. *The Seeing Stick*

Biography

Collective Biography

Marzollo. *My First Book of Biographies*

History

MacMillan. *Chinese New Year*

Multimedia

Video

Look and Do: China Parts 1 and 2

Marco Polo

GRADE THREE

Historical Fiction

Hong. *The Empress and the Silkworm*

Lattimore. *The Dragon's Robe*
Russell. *First Apple*

Và. *A Letter to the King*
Yolen. *The Seeing Stick*

Biography

Collective Biography

Marzollo. *My First Book of Biographies*

Steele. *Pirates*

History

Denny. *A Taste of China*
Gravett. *Arms and Armor*

Jessop. *Big Buildings of the Ancient World*

MacMillan. *Chinese New Year*
Wilkinson. *Amazing Buildings*

Multimedia

Video

China—Festival Celebration of Ancient Traditions

Look and Do: China Parts 1 and 2

Marco Polo

GRADE FOUR

Historical Fiction

Hong. *The Empress and the Silkworm*

Russell. *First Apple*
Russell. *Lichee Tree*

Biography

Foster. *Nien Cheng*

Collective Biography

Jacobs. *Great Lives: World Religions*

Steele. *Pirates*

History

Ashabranner. *Land of Yesterday . . . Chinese Central Asia*
Berrill. *Mummies, Masks, & Mourners*
Burke. *Food and Fasting*
Compton. *Marriage Customs*
Cotterell. *Ancient China*

Daley. *The Chinese Americans*
Denny. *A Taste of China*
Gravett. *Arms and Armor*
Harris. *Mummies*
Jessop. *Big Buildings of the Ancient World*
MacMillan. *Chinese New Year*
Major. *The Silk Route*

Martell. *The Ancient Chinese*
Prior. *Initiation Customs*
Prior. *Pilgrimages and Journeys*
Reynoldson. *Conflict and Change*
Rushton. *Birth Customs*
Rushton. *Death Customs*
Waterlow. *The Ancient Chinese*
Wilkinson. *Amazing Buildings*

Multimedia

CD-ROM

Teach Your Kids World History

Video

China: A History
China—Festival Celebration of Ancient Traditions

Look and Do: China Parts 1 and 2

Marco Polo

GRADE FIVE

Historical Fiction

Chang. *In the Eye of War*
DeJong. *The House of Sixty Fathers*

Russell. *First Apple*
Russell. *Lichee Tree*

Vander Els. *The Bomber's Moon*
Vander Els. *Leaving Point*

Biography

Foster. *Nien Cheng*

Collective Biography

Hazell. *Heroines: Great Women Through the Ages*
Jacobs. *Great Lives: World Religions*
Steele. *Pirates*

Wilkinson. *Generals Who Changed the World*
Wilkinson. *People Who Changed the World*

Wilkinson. *Scientists Who Changed the World*
Wilkinson. *Statesmen Who Changed the World*

History

Ashabranner. *Land of Yesterday . . . Chinese Central Asia*
Bandon. *Chinese Americans*

Berrill. *Mummies, Masks, & Mourners*
Beshore. *Science in Ancient China*

Burke. *Food and Fasting*
Compton. *Marriage Customs*
Cotterell. *Ancient China*
Daley. *The Chinese Americans*

Dauber. *China*
Davies. *Transport*
Denny. *A Taste of China*
Gravett. *Arms and Armor*
Harris. *Mummies*
Jessop. *Big Buildings of the Ancient World*

Lazo. *The Terra Cotta Army of Emperor Qin*
Lynch. *Great Buildings*
MacMillan. *Chinese New Year*
Major. *The Silk Route*
Martell. *The Ancient Chinese*
Odijk. *The Chinese*
Prior. *Initiation Customs*

Prior. *Pilgrimages and Journeys*
Reynoldson. *Conflict and Change*
Rushton. *Birth Customs*
Rushton. *Death Customs*
Steele. *Smuggling*
Waterlow. *The Ancient Chinese*
Wilkinson. *Amazing Buildings*

Multimedia

CD-ROM

Teach Your Kids World History

Video

China: A History

China—Festival Celebration of Ancient Traditions

GRADE SIX

Historical Fiction

Bosse. *The Examination*
Chang. *In the Eye of War*
DeJong. *The House of Sixty Fathers*

Russell. *First Apple*
Russell. *Lichee Tree*
Vander Els. *The Bomber's Moon*

Vander Els. *Leaving Point*

Biography

Foster. *Nien Cheng*

Jiang. *Red Scarf Girl: A Memoir of the Cultural Revolution*

Collective Biography

Cohen. *Real Vampires*
Hazell. *Heroines: Great Women Through the Ages*
Hoobler. *Chinese Portraits*
Jacobs. *Great Lives: World Religions*

Wilkinson. *Generals Who Changed the World*
Wilkinson. *People Who Changed the World*

Wilkinson. *Scientists Who Changed the World*
Wilkinson. *Statesmen Who Changed the World*

History

Ashabranner. *Land of Yesterday . . . Discovering Chinese Central Asia*
Bandon. *Chinese Americans*
Berrill. *Mummies, Masks, & Mourners*
Beshore. *Science in Ancient China*
Burke. *Food and Fasting*
Compton. *Marriage Customs*
Corbishley. *Secret Cities*
Cotterell. *Ancient China*
Daley. *The Chinese Americans*
Dauber. *China*
Davies. *Transport*
Denny. *A Taste of China*

Gravett. *Arms and Armor*
Harris. *Mummies*
Jessop. *Big Buildings of the Ancient World*
Lazo. *The Terra Cotta Army of Emperor Qin*
Lynch. *Great Buildings*
Major. *The Silk Route*
Martell. *The Ancient Chinese*
McNeese. *The Great Wall of China*
Michaelson. *Ancient China*
Millar. *China's Tang Dynasty*
Odijk. *The Chinese*
Prior. *Initiation Customs*
Prior. *Pilgrimages and Journeys*

Reynoldson. *Conflict and Change*
Rushton. *Birth Customs*
Rushton. *Death Customs*
Singer. *Structures That Changed the Way the World Looked*
Steele. *Smuggling*
Warburton. *The Beginning of Writing*
Waterlow. *The Ancient Chinese*
Wilkinson. *Amazing Buildings*
Wilkinson. *The Magical East*
Williams. *Ancient China*
Williams. *Forts and Castles*

Multimedia ———————————————————————————————

CD-ROM

*Teach Your Kids World
  History*

Video

China: A History
*China: From President Sun to
  Chairman Mao*

China: The Ancient Land
China: The Fifth Millennium

*China—Festival Celebration
  of Ancient Tradition*

India, Tibet, and Burma

GRADES KINDERGARTEN THROUGH TWO

Historical Fiction
Baillie. *Rebel*

Biography
Giff. *Mother Teresa*   Roth. *Buddha*

Collective Biography
Marzollo. *My First Book of
Biographies*

GRADE THREE

Historical Fiction
Baillie. *Rebel*

Biography
Birch. *Mahatma Gandhi*   Jacobs. *Mother Teresa*   Ullstein. *Mother Teresa*
Demi. *Buddha*   Roth. *Buddha*
Giff. *Mother Teresa*   Tames. *Mother Teresa*

Collective Biography
Marzollo. *My First Book of
Biographies*

History
Chicoine. *A Tibetan Family*   Landau. *Yeti: Abominable*   Rushton. *Death Customs*
Dhanjal. *Amritsar*   *Snowman*
Jessop. *Big Buildings of the*   Moss. *Forts and Castles*
   Ancient World   Rushton. *Birth Customs*

GRADE FOUR

Historical Fiction
Baillie. *Rebel*

Biography
Birch. *Mahatma Gandhi*   Jacobs. *Mother Teresa*   Tames. *Mother Teresa*
Demi. *Buddha*   Lazo. *Mahatma Gandhi*   Ullstein. *Mother Teresa*
Giff. *Mother Teresa*   Lazo. *Mother Teresa*

Collective Biography

Jacobs. *Great Lives: World Religions*

History

Burke. *Food and Fasting*
Cervera. *The Mughal Empire*
Chicoine. *A Tibetan Family*
Compton. *Marriage Customs*
Dhanjal. *Amritsar*
Ganeri. *Benares*

Ganeri. *Exploration into India*
Ganeri. *India: Things to Make*
Jessop. *Big Buildings of the Ancient World*
Landau. *Yeti: Abominable Snowman*

MacMillan. *Diwali: Hindu Festival of Lights*
Moss. *Forts and Castles*
Prior. *Initiation Customs*
Prior. *Pilgrimages and Journeys*

Multimedia

CD-ROM

Teach Your Kids World History

GRADE FIVE

Historical Fiction

Morpurgo. *King of the Cloud Forests*

Biography

Birch. *Mahatma Gandhi*
Bush. *Mohandas K. Gandhi*
Butler. *Indira Gandhi*
Clucas. *Mother Teresa*
Demi. *Buddha*
Faber. *Mahatma Gandhi*

Giff. *Mother Teresa*
Jacobs. *Mother Teresa*
Lazo. *Mahatma Gandhi*
Lazo. *Mother Teresa*
Perez. *The Dalai Lama*

Stewart. *Aung San Suu Kyi: Fearless Voice of Burma*
Stewart. *The 14th Dalai Lama*
Tames. *Mother Teresa*
Ullstein. *Mother Teresa*

Collective Biography

Blue. *People of Peace*
Hazell. *Heroes: Great Men Through the Ages*

Jacobs. *Great Lives: World Religions*

Wilkinson. *Generals Who Changed the World*

History

Bandon. *Asian Indian Americans*
Black. *Jungle Warfare*
Braquet. *India*
Burke. *Food and Fasting*
Cervera. *The Mughal Empire*
Charley. *Tombs and Treasures*
Chicoine. *A Tibetan Family*
Compton. *Marriage Customs*
De Bruycker. *Tibet*

Dhanjal. *Amritsar*
Ganeri. *Benares*
Ganeri. *Exploration into India*
Ganeri. *India: Things to Make*
Jessop. *Big Buildings of the Ancient World*
Kendra. *Tibetans*
Landau. *Yeti: Abominable Snowman*
Lynch. *Great Buildings*

MacMillan. *Diwali: Hindu Festival of Lights*
Moss. *Forts and Castles*
Prior. *Initiation Customs*
Prior. *Pilgrimages and Journeys*
Rushton. *Birth Customs*
Rushton. *Death Customs*

Multimedia

CD-ROM

Teach Your Kids World History

GRADE SIX

Historical Fiction

Bosse. *Tusk and Stone*

Morpurgo. *King of the Cloud Forests*

Biography

Birch. *Mahatma Gandhi*
Bush. *Mohandas K. Gandhi*
Butler. *Indira Gandhi*
Clucas. *Mother Teresa*
Faber. *Mahatma Gandhi*
Giff. *Mother Teresa*

Lazo. *Mahatma Gandhi*
Lazo. *Mother Teresa*
Perez. *The Dalai Lama*
Severance. *Gandhi, Great Soul*

Stewart. *Aung San Suu Kyi: Fearless Voice of Burma*
Stewart. *The 14th Dalai Lama*
Tames. *Mother Teresa*
Ullstein. *Mother Teresa*

Collective Biography

Blue. *People of Peace*
Hazell. *Heroes: Great Men Through the Ages*

Jacobs. *Great Lives: World Religions*

Wilkinson. *Generals Who Changed the World*

History

Bandon. *Asian Indian Americans*
Black. *Jungle Warfare*
Braquet. *India*
Burke. *Food and Fasting*
Cervera. *The Mughal Empire*
Charley. *Tombs and Treasures*
Chicoine. *A Tibetan Family*
Compton. *Marriage Customs*
Cush. *Disasters That Shook the World*

De Bruycker. *Tibet*
Dhanjal. *Amritsar*
Ganeri. *Benares*
Ganeri. *Exploration into India*
Ganeri. *India: Things to Make*
Jessop. *Big Buildings of the Ancient World*
Kendra. *Tibetans*
Landau. *Yeti: Abominable Snowman*
Lynch. *Great Buildings*

MacMillan. *Diwali: Hindu Festival of Lights*
Moss. *Forts and Castles*
Prior. *Initiation Customs*
Prior. *Pilgrimages and Journeys*
Rushton. *Birth Customs*
Rushton. *Death Customs*

Multimedia

CD-ROM

Teach Your Kids World History

Israel and the Arab Countries

GRADES KINDERGARTEN THROUGH TWO

Biography ───────────────────────────────

Collective Biography

Marzollo. *My First Book of Biographies*

History ───────────────────────────────

Adler. *A Picture Book of Israel*

Adler. *A Picture Book of Jewish Holidays*

Cashman. *Jewish Days and Holidays*

MacMillan. *Ramadan and Id Al-Fitr*

Multimedia ───────────────────────────────

Video

Christmas

GRADE THREE

Biography ───────────────────────────────

Adler. *Our Golda Meir*

Gurko. *Theodor Herzl: The Road to Israel*

Collective Biography

Marzollo. *My First Book of Biographies*

History ───────────────────────────────

Adler. *A Picture Book of Israel*

Adler. *A Picture Book of Jewish Holidays*

Cashman. *Jewish Days and Holidays*

MacMillan. *Ramadan and Id Al-Fitr*

Moss. *Forts and Castles*

O'Connor. *A Kurdish Family*

Pimlott. *Middle East: A Background for Conflicts*

Multimedia ───────────────────────────────

Video

Christmas

GRADE FOUR

Historical Fiction
Orlev. *Lydia, Queen of Palestine*

Biography
Adler. *Our Golda Meir*

Gurko. *Theodor Herzl: The Road to Israel*

Collective Biography
Jacobs. *Great Lives: World Religions*

History
Adler. *A Picture Book of Israel*
Cashman. *Jewish Days and Holidays*
Gay. *Persian Gulf War*
Husain. *What Do We Know About Islam?*

Long. *The Middle East in Search of Peace*
MacMillan. *Ramadan and Id Al-Fitr*
Moktefi. *The Arabs in the Golden Age*
Moss. *Forts and Castles*

O'Connor. *A Kurdish Family*
Pimlott. *Middle East: A Background for Conflicts*
Pirotta. *Jerusalem*
Pollard. *The Red Cross and the Red Crescent*

Multimedia

CD-ROM
Teach Your Kids World History

Video
Israel

Middle East: History and Culture

GRADE FIVE

Historical Fiction
Bergman. *The Boy from over There*

Orlev. *Lydia, Queen of Palestine*

Semel. *Flying Lessons*

Biography
Adler. *Our Golda Meir*
Amdur. *Chaim Weizmann*
Claypool. *Saddam Hussein*
Cockcroft. *Mohammed Reza Pahlavi: Shah of Iran*

Cytron. *Myriam Mendilow: Mother of Jerusalem*
Finkelstein. *Theodor Herzl: Architect of a Nation*
Gordon. *Ayatollah Khomeini*

Gordon. *The Gemayels*
Gurko. *Theodor Herzl: The Road to Israel*
McAuley. *Golda Meir*

Collective Biography
Jacobs. *Great Lives: World Religions*

Weitzman. *Great Lives: Human Culture*

History
Ayoub. *Al Umm El Madayan*
Beshore. *Science in Early Islamic Culture*
Cooper. *The Dead Sea Scrolls*
De Bruycker. *Egypt and the Middle East*

Gay. *Persian Gulf War*
Husain. *Mecca*
Husain. *What Do We Know About Islam?*
King. *The Gulf War*
King. *Kurds*

Long. *The Middle East in Search of Peace*
MacDonald. *A 16th Century Mosque*
MacMillan. *Ramadan and Id Al-Fitr*

Moktefi. *The Arabs in the Golden Age*
Morrison. *Middle East*
Moss. *Forts and Castles*

O'Connor. *A Kurdish Family*
Pimlott. *Middle East: A Background for Conflicts*
Pirotta. *Jerusalem*

Pollard. *The Red Cross and the Red Crescent*
Stein. *The Iran Hostage Crisis*

Multimedia

CD-ROM

Teach Your Kids World History

Video

The Arab World
Israel

Middle East: History and Culture

GRADE SIX

Historical Fiction

Almagor. *Under the Domim Tree*
Bergman. *The Boy from over There*

Orlev. *The Lady with the Hat*
Orlev. *Lydia, Queen of Palestine*
Semel. *Becoming Gershona*

Semel. *Flying Lessons*

Biography

Adler. *Our Golda Meir*
Amdur. *Chaim Weizmann*
Claypool. *Saddam Hussein*
Cockcroft. *Mohammed Reza Pahlavi: Shah of Iran*

Cytron. *Myriam Mendilow: Mother of Jerusalem*
Ferber. *Yasir Arafat*
Finkelstein. *Theodor Herzl: Architect of a Nation*

Gordon. *Ayatollah Khomeini*
Gordon. *The Gemayels*
Gurko. *Theodor Herzl: The Road to Israel*
McAuley. *Golda Meir*

Collective Biography

Jacobs. *Great Lives*: *World Religions*

Weitzman. *Great Lives: Human Culture*

History

Ayoub. *Al Umm El Madayan*
Beshore. *Science in Early Islamic Culture*
Cooper. *The Dead Sea Scrolls*
Corzine. *The Palestinian-Israeli Accord*
Cush. *Disasters that Shook the World*
De Bruycker. *Egypt and the Middle East*
Gay. *Persian Gulf War*

Husain. *Mecca*
Husain. *What Do We Know About Islam?*
King. *The Gulf War*
King. *Kurds*
Long. *The Middle East in Search of Peace*
MacDonald. *A 16th Century Mosque*
Moktefi. *The Arabs in the Golden Age*

Morrison. *Middle East*
Moss. *Forts and Castles*
O'Connor. *A Kurdish Family*
Pirotta. *Jerusalem*
Pollard. *The Red Cross and the Red Crescent*
Singer. *Structures That Changed the Way the World Looked*
Stein. *The Iran Hostage Crisis*

Multimedia

CD-ROM

Jerusalem: Interactive Pilgrimage to the Holy City

Teach Your Kids World History

Video

The Arab World
Israel

Jordan, the Desert Kingdom

Middle East: History and Culture

Japan

GRADES KINDERGARTEN THROUGH TWO

Historical Fiction

Coerr. *Sadko*

Little. *Yoshiko and the Foreigner*

Say. *Grandfather's Journey*

Biography

Spivak. *Grass Sandals*

Collective Biography

Marzollo. *My First Book of Biographies*

History

Littlefield. *Colors of Japan*

Streisguth. *A Ticket to Japan*

GRADE THREE

Historical Fiction

Coerr. *Sadko*

Little. *Yoshiko and the Foreigner*

Say. *Grandfather's Journey*

Biography

Kodama. *Shin's Tricycle*

Morimoto. *My Hiroshima*

Spivak. *Grass Sandals*

Collective Biography

Marzollo. *My First Book of Biographies*

History

Gravett. *Arms and Armor*
Littlefield. *Colors of Japan*

Streisguth. *A Ticket to Japan*
Wilkinson. *Amazing Buildings*

GRADE FOUR

Historical Fiction

Coerr. *Mieko and the Fifth Treasure*
Coerr. *Sadako and the Thousand Paper Cranes*

Crofford. *Born in the Year of Courage*
Little. *Yoshiko and the Foreigner*

Maruki. *Hiroshima, No Pika*

Biography ————————————————————————————————

Kodama. *Shin's Tricycle*   Morimoto. *My Hiroshima*   Spivak. *Grass Sandals*

Collective Biography

Krull. *Lives of the Writers*

History ————————————————————————————————

Doran. *The Japanese*   Martell. *The Age of Discovery*   Streisguth. *Japan*
Gravett. *Arms and Armor*   Reynoldson. *Conflict and*   Wilkinson. *Amazing Buildings*
Lynch. *Great Buildings*   *Change*   Wilkinson. *The Magical East*

Multimedia ————————————————————————————————

CD-ROM

*Teach Your Kids World
    History*

Video

Growing Up in Japan

GRADE FIVE

Historical Fiction ————————————————————————————————

Coerr. *Mieko and the Fifth*   Crofford. *Born in the Year of*   Maruki. *Hiroshima, No Pika*
    Treasure   *Courage*   Paterson. *Of Nightingales*
Coerr. *Sadako and the*   Little. *Yoshiko and the*   *That Weep*
    Thousand Paper Cranes   *Foreigner*

Biography ————————————————————————————————

Kodama. *Shin's Tricycle*   Morimoto. *My Hiroshima*

Collective Biography

Cohen. *The Ghosts of War*   Krull. *Lives of the Writers*
Hazell. *Heroines: Great*   Wilkinson. *Generals Who*
    Women Through the Ages   *Changed the World*

History ————————————————————————————————

Black. *Hiroshima and the*   Lynch. *Great Buildings*   Reynoldson. *Conflict and*
    Atomic Bomb   MacDonald. *A Samurai Castle*   *Change*
Cross. *Technology of War*   Martell. *The Age of Discovery*   Streisguth. *Japan*
Doran. *The Japanese*   Odijk. *The Japanese*   Wilkinson. *Amazing Buildings*
Gravett. *Arms and Armor*   Wilkinson. *The Magical East*

Multimedia ————————————————————————————————

CD-ROM

*Teach Your Kids World
    History*

Video

Growing Up in Japan

GRADE SIX

Historical Fiction

Coerr. *Mieko and the Fifth Treasure*
Coerr. *Sadako and the Thousand Paper Cranes*

Crofford. *Born in the Year of Courage*
Haugaard. *The Boy and the Samurai*

Haugaard. *The Revenge of the Forty-Seven Samurai*
Maruki. *Hiroshima, No Pika*
Paterson. *Of Nightingales That Weep*

Biography

Morimoto. *My Hiroshima*

Collective Biography

Cohen. *The Ghosts of War*
Hazell. *Heroines: Great Women Through the Ages*

Hoobler. *Japanese Portraits*
Krull. *Lives of the Writers*

Wilkinson. *Generals Who Changed the World*

History

Black. *Hiroshima and the Atomic Bomb*
Cross. *Technology of War*
Doran. *The Japanese*
Gravett. *Arms and Armor*
Hoobler. *Showa: The Age of Hirohito*

Langone. *In the Shogun's Shadow*
Lynch. *Great Buildings*
MacDonald. *A Samurai Castle*
Martell. *The Age of Discovery*
Nardo. *Traditional Japan*
Newton. *Tokyo*

Odijk. *The Japanese*
Reynoldson. *Conflict and Change*
Wilkinson. *Amazing Buildings*
Wilkinson. *The Magical East*
Williams. *Forts and Castles*

Multimedia

CD-ROM

Teach Your Kids World History

Video

Growing Up in Japan
Japan: Japan Today

Japan: Nation Reborn
Japan: The Sacred Islands

Vietnam, Korea, Cambodia, and Thailand

GRADES KINDERGARTEN THROUGH TWO

Historical Fiction

Breckler. *Sweet Dried Apples: A Vietnamese Wartime Childhood*

Shea. *The Whispering Cloth*

Biography

Collective Biography

Marzollo. *My First Book of Biographies*

History

MacMillan. *Tet: Vietnamese New Year*

GRADE THREE

Historical Fiction

Baillie. *Little Brother*

Breckler. *Sweet Dried Apples: A Vietnamese Wartime Childhood*

Shea. *The Whispering Cloth*

Biography

Collective Biography

Marzollo. *My First Book of Biographies*

History

Gogol. *A Mien Family*

MacMillan. *Tet: Vietnamese New Year*

Murphy. *A Hmong Family*

GRADE FOUR

Historical Fiction

Baillie. *Little Brother*
Breckler. *Sweet Dried Apples: A Vietnamese Wartime Childhood*
Cha. *Dia's Story Cloth*

Fritsch. *A Part of the Ribbon: A Time Travel Adventure Through the History of Korea*

Giles. *Breath of the Dragon*
Neuberger. *The Girl-Son*

Biography

Huynh Quang Nhuong. *The Land I Lost*

History

Gay. *Korean War*
Gay. *Vietnam War*
Gogol. *A Mien Family*

MacMillan. *Tet: Vietnamese New Year*
Murphy. *A Hmong Family*

Smith. *The Korean War*
Wilkinson. *The Magical East*

Multimedia

CD-ROM

Teach Your Kids World History

Video

Korea/Vietnam

GRADE FIVE

Historical Fiction

Baillie. *Little Brother*
Cha. *Dia's Story Cloth*
Choi. *Year of Impossible Goodbyes*

Fritsch. *A Part of the Ribbon: A Time Travel Adventure Through the History of Korea*
Giles. *Breath of the Dragon*

Neuberger. *The Girl-Son*
Pettit. *My Name Is San Ho*
Watkins. *My Brother, My Sister, and I*

Biography

Huynh Quang Nhuong. *The Land I Lost*

Kuckreja. *Prince Norodom Sihanouk*

Lloyd. *Ho Chi Minh*

History

Balaban. *Vietnam*
Bandon. *Korean Americans*
Bandon. *Vietnamese Americans*
Cosner. *War Nurses*
Gay. *Korean War*
Gay. *Vietnam War*

Gibson. *The War in Vietnam*
Gogol. *A Mien Family*
Lynch. *Great Buildings*
MacMillan. *Tet: Vietnamese New Year*
Murphy. *A Hmong Family*

Nickelson. *Vietnam*
Smith. *The Korean War*
Wilkinson. *The Magical East*

Multimedia

CD-ROM

Teach Your Kids World History

GRADE SIX

Historical Fiction

Baillie. *Little Brother*
Cha. *Dia's Story Cloth*
Choi. *Echoes of the White Giraffe*
Choi. *Year of Impossible Goodbyes*

Fritsch. *A Part of the Ribbon: A Time Travel Adventure Through the History of Korea*
Giles. *Breath of the Dragon*

Ho. *The Clay Marble*
Neuberger. *The Girl-Son*
Pettit. *My Name Is San Ho*
Watkins. *My Brother, My Sister, and I*

Biography

Huynh Quang Nhuong. *The Land I Lost*

Kuckreja. *Prince Norodom Sihanouk*

Lloyd. *Ho Chi Minh*

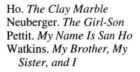

Collective Biography

Scheller. *Amazing
Archaeologists*

History

Balaban. *Vietnam*	Gibson. *The War in Vietnam*	Singer. *Structures That*
Bandon. *Korean Americans*	Gogol. *A Mien Family*	*Changed the Way the*
Bandon. *Vietnamese Americans*	Lynch. *Great Buildings*	*World Looked*
Cosner. *War Nurses*	Murphy. *A Hmong Family*	Smith. *The Korean War*
Gay. *Korean War*	Nash. *North Korea*	Stein. *The Korean War*
Gay. *Vietnam War*	Nickelson. *Vietnam*	Wilkinson. *The Magical East*

Multimedia

CD-ROM

*Teach Your Kids World
History*

South and Central America and the Caribbean

GRADES KINDERGARTEN THROUGH TWO

Historical Fiction
Alphin. *A Bear for Miguel*

Pico. *The Red Comb*

Biography
Adler. *A Picture Book of Simón Bolívar*
Fernandez. *José De San Martín*
Holland. *Diego Rivera*

Martinez. *Sor Juana*
Palacios. *!Viva Mexico!: Benito Juarez and Cinco de Mayo*
Venezia. *Diego Rivera*

Winter. *Diego*

Collective Biography
Marzollo. *My First Book of Biographies*

History
Olawsky. *Colors of Mexico*

Streisguth. *A Ticket to Mexico*

GRADE THREE

Historical Fiction
Alphin. *A Bear for Miguel*

Dorris. *Morning Girl*

Pico. *The Red Comb*

Biography
Adler. *A Picture Book of Simón Bolívar*
De Varona. *Benito Juarez*
De Varona. *Miguel Hidalgo y Costilla*
De Varona. *Simon Bolivar*
Fernandez. *José De San Martín*

Holland. *Diego Rivera*
Jacobs. *Coronado*
Jacobs. *Cortés*
Iverson. *Carlos Montezuma*
Martinez. *Sor Juana*
Myers. *Toussaint L'Ouverture*
Neimark. *Diego Rivera*

Palacios. *!Viva Mexico!: Benito Juarez and Cinco de Mayo*
Stein. *Francisco de Coronado*
Turner. *Frida Kahlo*
Venezia. *Diego Rivera*
Winter. *Diego*

Collective Biography
Marzollo. *My First Book of Biographies*

Steele. *Pirates*

History
Chrisp. *The Farmer Through History*
Chrisp. *The Soldier Through History*
Greenberg. *A Haitian Family*

Hoyt-Goldsmith. *Day of the Dead*
Lasky. *Days of the Dead*
Malone. *A Guatemalan Family*

Malone. *A Nicaraguan Family*
Olawsky. *Colors of Mexico*
Sherrow. *The Maya Indians*
Streisguth. *Mexico*

┌─────────────────┐
│   **GRADE FOUR**   │
└─────────────────┘

Historical Fiction

Dorris. *Morning Girl*
Finley. *Soaring Eagle*

Head. *Culebra Cut*
Pico. *The Red Comb*

Stanley. *Elena*

Biography

Adler. *A Picture Book of Simón Bolívar*
Arnold. *Alicia Alonso*
Brill. *Journey for Peace: The Story of Rigoberta Menchú*
Burch. *Chico Mendes*
Chrisman. *Hernando de Soto*
Chrisman. *Luis Muñoz Marín*
De Varona. *Benito Juarez*
De Varona. *Bernardo de Gálvez*
De Varona. *Miguel Hidalgo y Costilla*
De Varona. *Simon Bolivar*
DeStefano. *Chico Mendes*

Fernandez. *José De San Martín*
Gleiter. *Benito Juárez*
Gleiter. *Diego Rivera*
Gleiter. *José Martí*
Gleiter. *Junípero Serra*
Gleiter. *Miguel Hidalgo y Costilla*
Gleiter. *Simón Bolívar*
Greene. *Símon Bolívar*
Hargrove. *Diego Rivera*
Jacobs. *Coronado*
Jacobs. *Cortés*
Jacobs. *Pizarro*
Iverson. *Carlos Montezuma*
Lazo. *Rigoberta Menchú*
Martinez. *Sor Juana*

Myers. *Toussaint L'Ouverture*
Neimark. *Diego Rivera*
Palacios. *!Viva Mexico!: Benito Juarez and Cinco de Mayo*
Stein. *Francisco de Coronado*
Sumption. *Carlos Finlay*
Thompson. *Pedro Menéndez de Avilés*
Thompson. *Sor Juana Inés de la Cruz*
Turner. *Frida Kahlo*
Winter. *Diego*

Collective Biography

Steele. *Pirates*

History

Arnold. *City of the Gods: Mexico's Teotihuacán*
Burrell. *Life in the Time of Moctezuma and the Aztecs*
Carter. *The Spanish-American War*
Chrisp. *The Farmer Through History*
Chrisp. *The Incas*
Chrisp. *The Maya*
Chrisp. *The Soldier Through History*
Chrisp. *The Spanish Conquests in the New World*

Cordoba. *Pre-Columbian Peoples of North America*
Dawson. *Food and Feasts with the Aztecs*
Fisher. *Pyramid of the Sun, Pyramid of the Moon*
Gay. *Spanish American War*
Greenberg. *A Haitian Family*
Halliburton. *The West Indian-American Experience*
Harris. *Mummies*
Hicks. *The Aztecs*
Hoyt-Goldsmith. *Day of the Dead*

Lankford. *Quinceañera*
Lasky. *Days of the Dead*
Malone. *A Guatemalan Family*
Malone. *A Nicaraguan Family*
Martell. *The Age of Discovery*
Mathews. *The Sad Night; The Story of an Aztec Victory*
Putnam. *Mummy*
Ross. *Bandits & Outlaws*
Sherrow. *The Maya Indians*
Steele. *The Aztec News*
Streisguth. *Mexico*
Wood. *The Aztecs*

Multimedia

CD-ROM

Teach Your Kids World History

Video

The Art and Architecture of the Maya
Central Americans

Christopher Columbus
Estevanico and the Seven Cities of Gold

The Maya
Mexico: The Heritage
Peru's Treasure Tombs

GRADE FIVE

Historical Fiction

Baker. *Walk the World's Rim*
De Treviño. *Leona*
Dorris. *Morning Girl*
Finley. *Soaring Eagle*

Garland. *Cabin 102*
Head. *Culebra Cut*
Howard. *When Daylight Comes*

O'Dell. *My Name Is Not Angelica*
Slaughter. *The Dirty War*
Stanley. *Elena*

Biography

Appel. *José Martí*
Arnold. *Alicia Alonso*
Bernier-Grand. *Don Luis Muñoz Marín*
Braun. *A Weekend with Diego Rivera*
Brill. *Journey for Peace: The Story of Rigoberta Menchú*
Burch. *Chico Mendes*
Chrisman. *Hernando de Soto*
Chrisman. *Luis Muñoz Marín*
Cockcroft. *Daniel Ortega*
Cockcroft. *Diego Rivera*
de Ruiz. *To Fly with the Swallows*
De Varona. *Benito Juarez*
De Varona. *Bernardo de Gálvez*

De Varona. *Miguel Hidalgo y Costilla*
De Varona. *Simon Bolivar*
DeStefano. *Chico Mendes*
Garza. *Frida Kahlo*
Gleiter. *Benito Juárez*
Gleiter. *Diego Rivera*
Gleiter. *José Martí*
Gleiter. *Junípero Serra*
Gleiter. *Miguel Hidalgo y Costilla*
Gleiter. *Simón Bolívar*
Goodnough. *Jose Marti*
Greene. *Símon Bolívar*
Hargrove. *Diego Rivera*
Jacobs. *Coronado*
Jacobs. *Cortés*
Jacobs. *Pizarro*

Hoobler. *Toussaint L'Ouverture*
Iverson. *Carlos Montezuma*
Kellner. *Ernesto Che Guevara*
Lazo. *Rigoberta Menchú*
Myers. *Toussaint L'Ouverture*
Neimark. *Diego Rivera*
Palacios. *!Viva Mexico!: Benito Juarez and Cinco de Mayo*
Stein. *Francisco de Coronado*
Sumption. *Carlos Finlay*
Thompson. *Pedro Menéndez de Avilés*
Thompson. *Sor Juana Inés de la Cruz*
Turner. *Frida Kahlo*
West. *José Martí*

Collective Biography

Blue. *People of Peace*
Hazell. *Heroes: Great Men Through the Ages*

Hazell. *Heroines: Great Women Through the Ages*
Steele. *Pirates*

Wilkinson. *People Who Changed the World*
Wilkinson. *Statesmen Who Changed the World*

History

Anthony. *West Indies*
Arnold. *City of the Gods: Mexico's Teotihuacán*
Bandon. *Dominican Americans*
Bandon. *Mexican Americans*
Bandon. *West Indian Americans*
Bierhorst. *The Hungry Woman: The Aztecs*
Blair. *The Land and People of Bolivia*
Burrell. *Life in the Time of Moctezuma and the Aztecs*
Capek. *Murals*
Carter. *The Spanish-American War*
Charley. *Tombs and Treasures*
Chrisp. *The Farmer Through History*
Chrisp. *The Incas*
Chrisp. *The Maya*
Chrisp. *The Soldier Through History*

Chrisp. *The Spanish Conquests in the New World*
Cordoba. *Pre-Columbian Peoples of North America*
Dawson. *Food and Feasts with the Aztecs*
Deltenre. *Peru and the Andean Countries*
Dolan. *Panama and the United States*
Fisher. *Pyramid of the Sun, Pyramid of the Moon*
Gay. *Spanish American War*
Greenberg. *A Haitian Family*
Halliburton. *The West Indian-American Experience*
Harris. *Mummies*
Hicks. *The Aztecs*
Hoyt-Goldsmith. *Day of the Dead*
Jacobs. *The Tainos*
Jacobs. *War with Mexico*

Lankford. *Quinceañera*
Lasky. *Days of the Dead*
Malone. *A Guatemalan Family*
Malone. *A Nicaraguan Family*
Marrin. *Aztecs and Spaniards*
Martell. *The Age of Discovery*
Mathews. *The Sad Night; The Story of an Aztec Victory*
Noblet. *The Amazon and the Americas*
Odijk. *The Aztecs*
Odijk. *The Mayas*
Putnam. *Mummy*
Ross. *Bandits & Outlaws*
Sherrow. *The Maya Indians*
Steele. *The Aztec News*
Stein. *The Aztec Empire*
Streisguth. *Mexico*
Wood. *The Aztecs*

Multimedia

CD-ROM

*Teach Your Kids World
  History*

Video

*Art and Architecture of
  Precolumbian Mexico*
Central America
Central Americans
Christopher Columbus

The Columbian Way of Life
*Estevanico and the Seven
  Cities of Gold*
The Maya
Mexico: The Heritage

Mexico: The People of the Sun
*Middle America: Mexico to
  Venezuela and the
  Caribbean Islands*
Peru's Treasure Tombs

GRADE SIX

Historical Fiction

Baker. *Walk the World's Rim*
De Treviño. *El Güero*
De Treviño. *Leona*
Dorris. *Morning Girl*
Finley. *Soaring Eagle*

Garland. *Cabin 102*
Head. *Culebra Cut*
Howard. *When Daylight
  Comes*

O'Dell. *My Name Is Not
  Angelica*
Slaughter. *The Dirty War*
Stanley. *Elena*
Taylor. *The Cay*

Biography

Appel. *José Martí*
Arnold. *Alicia Alonso*
Bernier-Grand. *Don Luis
  Muñoz Marín*
Braun. *A Weekend with Diego
  Rivera*
Brill. *Journey for Peace: The
  Story of Rigoberta Menchú*
Burch. *Chico Mendes*
Chrisman. *Hernando de Soto*
Chrisman. *Luis Muñoz Marín*
Cockcroft. *Daniel Ortega*
Cockcroft. *Diego Rivera*
Cruz. *Frida Kahlo: Portrait
  of a Mexican Painter*
de Ruiz. *To Fly with the
  Swallows*

de Varona. *Bernardo de
  Gálvez*
DeStefano. *Chico Mendes*
Garza. *Frida Kahlo*
Gleiter. *Benito Juárez*
Gleiter. *Diego Rivera*
Gleiter. *José Martí*
Gleiter. *Junípero Serra*
Gleiter. *Miguel Hidalgo y
  Costilla*
Gleiter. *Simón Bolívar*
Gonzales. *Diego Rivera: His
  Art, His Life*
Goodnough. *Jose Marti*
Greene. *Símon Bolívar*
Hargrove. *Diego Rivera*
Jacobs. *Coronado*

Jacobs. *Cortés*
Jacobs. *Pizarro*
Hoobler. *Toussaint
  L'Ouverture*
Kellner. *Ernesto Che Guevara*
Lazo. *Rigoberta Menchú*
Myers. *Toussaint L'Ouverture*
Neimark. *Diego Rivera*
Stein. *Francisco de Coronado*
Stein. *Hernando Cortés*
Sumption. *Carlos Finlay*
Thompson. *Pedro Menéndez
  de Avilés*
Thompson. *Sor Juana Inés de
  la Cruz*
Turner. *Frida Kahlo*
West. *José Martí*

Collective Biography

Blue. *People of Peace*
Hazell. *Heroes: Great Men
  Through the Ages*
Hazell. *Heroines: Great
  Women Through the Ages*

Hoobler. *Mexican Portraits*
Hoobler. *South American
  Portraits*
Scheller. *Amazing
  Archaeologists*

Wilkinson. *People Who
  Changed the World*
Wilkinson. *Statesmen Who
  Changed the World*

History

Anthony. *West Indies*
Arnold. *City of the Gods:
  Mexico's Teotihuacán*
Bandon. *Dominican
  Americans*
Bandon. *Mexican Americans*
Bandon. *West Indian
  Americans*
Bierhorst. *The Hungry
  Woman: The Aztecs*

Blair. *The Land and People of
  Bolivia*
Burrell. *Life in the Time of
  Moctezuma and the Aztecs*
Capek. *Murals*
Carter. *The
  Spanish-American War*
Charley. *Tombs and Treasures*
Chrisp. *The Incas*
Chrisp. *The Maya*

Chrisp. *The Spanish
  Conquests in the New
  World*
Corbishley. *Secret Cities*
Cordoba. *Pre-Columbian
  Peoples of North America*
Dawson. *Food and Feasts
  with the Aztecs*
Deltenre. *Peru and the
  Andean Countries*

Dolan. *Panama and the United States*
Fisher. *Pyramid of the Sun, Pyramid of the Moon*
Galvin. *The Maya of Central America*
Gay. *Spanish American War*
Greenberg. *A Haitian Family*
Halliburton. *The West Indian-American Experience*
Harris. *Mummies*
Hicks. *The Aztecs*
Hoyt-Goldsmith. *Day of the Dead*
Jacobs. *The Tainos*
Jacobs. *War with Mexico*
Koral. *An Album of War Refugees*

Lankford. *Quinceañera*
Lasky. *Days of the Dead*
Liptak. *Endangered Peoples*
Malone. *A Guatemalan Family*
Malone. *A Nicaraguan Family*
Marrin. *Aztecs and Spaniards*
Martell. *The Age of Discovery*
Mathews. *The Sad Night; The Story of an Aztec Victory*
Meyer. *The Mystery of the Ancient Maya*
Noblet. *The Amazon and the Americas*
Odijk. *The Aztecs*
Odijk. *The Mayas*
Putnam. *Mummy*
Rice. *The Cuban Revolution*
Ross. *Bandits & Outlaws*

Sherrow. *The Maya Indians*
Steele. *The Aztec News*
Steele. *The Incas and Machu Picchu*
Stein. *The Aztec Empire*
Street Smart! Cities of the Ancient World
Thompson. *Aztecs: Facts, Things to Make*
Ventura. *1492*
Warburton. *Aztec Civilization*
Warburton. *The Beginning of Writing*
Wood. *Ancient America*
Wood. *The Aztecs*
Wood. *The Incas*

Multimedia

CD-ROM

Exploring Ancient Cities
Maya Quest

One Tribe

Teach Your Kids World History

Video

Art and Architecture of Precolumbian Mexico
The Art and Architecture of the Maya
Central America
Central Americans
Christopher Columbus
The Columbian Way of Life

Estevanico and the Seven Cities of Gold
The Maya
The Mayans and Aztecs
Mexico: The Heritage
Mexico: The People of the Sun

Middle America: Mexico to Venezuela and the Caribbean Islands
The Moon Woman's Sisters Highland Guatemala Maya Weaving
Mystery of the Maya
Peru's Treasure Tombs

Books: An Annotated Bibliography

1. Aaseng, Nathan. **Genetics: Unlocking the Secrets of Life**. Minneapolis, MN: Oliver Press, 1996. 144p. $14.95. ISBN 1-881508-27-7. 6 up

The study of genetics has been a science for only 100 years. Not until the work of Charles Darwin in the nineteenth century and his publication of *The Origin of Species* was an explanation for heredity given other than what Aristotle had posited during the fifth century B.C. The text looks at the nineteenth- and twentieth-century figures who developed the theories behind this science. They include Gregor Mendel and the discovery of dominant and recessive traits, Thomas Hunt Morgan and the chromosome, Oswald Avery and the transforming principle, James Watson and Francis Crick with their work on the double helix of DNA, and Har Gobind Khorana and synthetic genes. Nobel Prize Winners, Glossary, Bibliography, and Index.

2. Aaseng, Nathan. **Paris**. New York: New Discovery, 1992. 96p. $14.95. ISBN 0-02-700010-9. (Cities at War). 6-9

In World War II, German troops entered Paris, France, and occupied the city from 1940 to 1944. Although no fighting occurred in the city, Nazi soldiers abused people, persecuted the city's Jews, and enforced curfews. The French had mixed feelings about their own conduct because of collaboration with the Germans during the war in order to save themselves. Photographs, Notes, Further Reading, and Index.

3. Aaseng, Nathan. **You Are the General**. Minneapolis, MN: Oliver Press, 1994. 160p. $14.95. ISBN 1-881508-11-0. (Great Decisions). 6 up

The text presents the decisions that several twentieth-century generals had to make in the middle of battle. Readers can decide what they would do in the same situation. What they decide will help them understand those who had to make real and life-threatening decisions in the past. Generals include those from the Kaiser's army in August 1914, the German Reich in the summer of 1940, the Imperial Japanese Navy in June 1942, the Allied Forces in June 1944, the United Nations Forces in July 1950, the Vietnamese Communist Forces in July 1967, and the Coalition Forces of Operation Desert Storm in February 1991. Source Notes, Bibliography, and Index.

4. Aaseng, Nathan. **You Are the General II: 1800-1899**. Minneapolis, MN: Oliver Press, 1995. 160p. $14.95. ISBN 1-881508-25-0. (Great Decisions). 6 up

Battles are carefully created patterns of military strategy to gain territory, erode an enemy army's morale, and win a broader war. The text presents eight battles and the generals who fought them. The battles are the British Army at New Orleans in 1815, the Prussian Army at Waterloo in 1815, the U.S. Army in Mexico in August of 1847, the Allied Army in Crimea in September 1854, the Army of Northern Virginia at Chancellorsville in May 1863, the U.S. Army at Little Bighorn in June 1876, and the Boer Army in Natal in December 1899. Source Notes, Bibliography, and Index.

5. Ackerman, Karen. **The Night Crossing**. New York: Knopf, 1994. 56p. $14. ISBN 0-679-83169-X. 3-4

In 1938, Clara and her family escape over the mountains into Switzerland from Germany as Nazi hostility rises. The family takes with them two silver candlesticks, which become symbols of their freedom after many other family members die in the ensuing Holocaust, and Clara's two dolls, which had belonged to her grandmother. To get the candlesticks across the border, Clara inserts them inside her dolls.

6. Adler, David. **Child of the Warsaw Ghetto**. Karen Ritz, illustrator. New York: Holiday House, 1995. Unpaged. $15.95. ISBN 0-8234-1160-5. 3-6

As a young boy growing up in Poland, Froim must deal with his father's death and his mother's inability to support the family. He and his brothers enter an orphans' home, but in 1938 the Nazis begin to persecute the Jews. When he is twelve, Froim is locked with other Jews inside the Warsaw, Poland, ghetto; however, because he does not look Jewish, he is able to sneak outside to buy bread for his mother and the orphans' home. Eventually he and his family are transported to the camps. Froim survives several camps and is still alive in Dachau when the Allies free the prisoners at the end of World War II. This account of the war is based on the story of Froim Baum, who told it to the author. *Notable Children's Trade Books in the Field of Social Studies.*

7.   Adler, David. **One Yellow Daffodil**. Lloyd Bloom, illustrator. San Diego, CA: Gulliver, Harcourt Brace, 1995. Unpaged. $16. ISBN 0-15-200537-4. K-3

When children come into Mr. Kaplan's shop to buy flowers for *Shabbat* and then for Hanukkah, they invite him to dinner on the first night of the celebration. He does not want to come, but he does, and he begins to remember his childhood in Poland when he lost almost everything during World War II. He remembers seeing a yellow daffodil outside the concentration camp and thinking that if the flower could live, so could he. What he did not lose was a box with his menorah in it, and he gives the menorah to the children. *Notable Children's Trade Books in the Field of Social Studies.*

8.   Adler, David A. **Christopher Columbus: Great Explorer**. Lyle Miller, illustrator. New York: Holiday House, 1991. 48p. $14.95. ISBN 0-8234-0895-7. (First Biography). 3-5

Born into a wool weaver's family in the city-state of Genoa (before Italy was founded) in 1451, Columbus (1451-1506) read of Marco Polo's travels during 1271 to 1274 across Asia, and decided that he wanted to find China. In 1484, Columbus first attempted to get provisions for a journey to Japan, which he thought was 2,400 miles away (it was actually four times further). Adler relates the types of people Columbus hired for the voyage and notes that the date of departure—August 3, 1492—was one day after Ferdinand and Isabella's proclamation that all unconverted Jews had to leave Spain. The pen-and-ink sketches show scenes as they might have been. The text recounts the tragedy that Columbus's arrival was for the people in the New World, who caught new diseases or were enslaved by the Spaniards, as well as the tribulations Columbus faced on his subsequent voyages. Index.

9.   Adler, David A. **Hilde and Eli, Children of the Holocaust**. Karen Ritz, illustrator. New York: Holiday House, 1994. Unpaged. $15.95. ISBN 0-8234-1091-9. K-4

This book tells the story of two children who perished in the Holocaust during World War II. They were Hilde Rosenzweig (1923-1941), who was gassed in a boxcar, and Eli Lax (1932-1944), who was murdered at Auschwitz after being taken from his Carpathian home. *Notable Children's Trade Books in the Field of Social Studies.*

10.   Adler, David A. **The Number on My Grandfather's Arm**. New York: UAHC Press, 1987. 28p. $9.95. ISBN 0-8074-0328-8. 2-4

A young girl asks her grandfather about the number tattooed across his forearm. He tells her his story of World War II, not in graphic detail, but so that she can understand that he had a terrible time and almost lost his life during his imprisonment in Auschwitz, a concentration camp.

11.   Adler, David A. **Our Golda: The Story of Golda Meir**. Donna Ruff, illustrator. New York: Viking, 1984. 52p. $4.99pa. ISBN 0-14-032104-7pa. 3-7

Golda Meir (1898-1978) lived in Kiev, Russia, outside the Pale of Settlement where only skilled Jews, like her carpenter father, were allowed. At five, Golda had to return to the Pale when her father left for America. In Pinsk, amid the Cossacks and pogroms, they heard talk of a Jewish homeland. Meir's family went to Milwaukee to join her father, and she left for Denver to live with her sister before she and her husband went to Palestine in the 1920s. Meir spoke to crowds about Jewish causes from the time she was 11, and during the rest of her life she led others in the fight for Israel. In 1956, she became Israel's Foreign Minister, and then Prime Minister in 1969. Before her death in 1978, she met with Anwar Sadat in one of many attempts to find peace between the Arabs and the Jews.

12.   Adler, David A. **A Picture Book of Anne Frank**. Karen Ritz, illustrator. New York: Holiday House, 1993. Unpaged. $15.95; $6.95pa. ISBN 0-8234-1003-X; 0-8234-1078-1pa. (Picture Book Biography). 2-4

By 1929, when Anne Frank was born, her family had lived in Frankfurt, Germany, for hundreds of years. When Hitler came to power during the 1930s, her Jewish family left for Amsterdam, where they hoped to escape persecution. Their lives were fairly normal—Anne even starred in plays at her Montessori school—until the Nazis entered Holland. In 1942, when her sister was ordered to go to a work camp, the family went into hiding on the top floor of a warehouse beside an Amsterdam canal. It was here that Anne wrote her diary. Nazis discovered the family in 1944, and Anne was sent first to Auschwitz and then to Bergen-Belsen, where she died at the age of fifteen, two months before the war ended in 1945. Hitler murdered 6 million Jews; of 120,000 Jews in Holland in 1940, only 14,000 survived. The thoughtful illustrations come from photographs. Author's Notes. *Notable Children's Trade Books in the Field of Social Studies.*

13. Adler, David A. **A Picture Book of Florence Nightingale**. Alexandra and John Wallner, illustrators. New York: Holiday House, 1992. Unpaged. $14.95; $6.95pa.. ISBN 0-8234-9065-1; 0-8234-1284-9pa. K-3

Florence Nightingale (1820-1910) was a nineteenth-century upper-class English woman who followed her calling to work in hospitals and improve the conditions for treating the sick.

14. Adler, David A. **A Picture Book of Israel**. New York: Holiday House, 1984. 40p. $10.95. ISBN 0-8234-0513-3. 2-4

A combination of historical and contemporary photographs aids the text in this brief overview of Israel's history, which includes the centuries before Israel became a state and the people who live there—Jew, Arab, and Christian. A *sabra* (native of Israel) and a *halutzin* (immigrant) show the composition of the Jewish population.

15. Adler, David A. **A Picture Book of Jewish Holidays**. Linda Heller, illustrator. New York: Holiday House, 1981. 32p. $14.95; $5.95pa. ISBN 0-8234-0396-3; 0-8234-0756-Xpa. K-3

This book introduces terms and explanations for important holidays in the Jewish tradition for people of all religions. They include the Sabbath, Rosh Hashanah, Yom Kippur, Sukkot, Simhat Torah, Hanukkah, Tu bi-Shevat, Purim, Passover, Yom Ha-Azma'ut, Tishah Bov, and others. Glossary.

16. Adler, David A. **A Picture Book of Louis Braille**. John and Alexandra Wallner, illustrators. New York: Holiday House, 1997. Unpaged. $16.95. ISBN 0-8234-1291-1. 1-3

Louis Braille (1809-1852) developed the system for reading that the blind now use. The text looks at his life as a young student and teacher and his contributions to the blind community. Important Dates.

17. Adler, David A. **A Picture Book of Simón Bolívar**. Robert Casilla, illustrator. New York: Holiday House, 1992. Unpaged. $15.95. ISBN 0-8234-0927-9. (Picture Book Biography). 2-4

The thirteen colonies received independence from England under the Treaty of Versailles in 1783, the year Simón Bolívar was born in the Spanish colony of Venezuela. Only those born in Spain could rule, and although his family had come from Spain, they had been born in South America and were called *creoles*. Creoles, Indians, blacks, and slaves had few, if any, rights. When Bolívar was nineteen, he traveled and saw what was happening in Europe, but not until 1811, when Napoleon invaded Spain, did he decide to free Venezuela. After setbacks and more battles, he became *El liberador*, the man who freed South America from Spain in 1824. Important Dates.

18. Adler, David A. **Remember Betsy Floss: And Other Colonial Riddles**. John Wallner, illustrator. New York: Holiday House, 1987. 64p. $12.95. ISBN 0-8234-0664-4. 2-6

Although the text is a collection of riddles with illustrations of people who lived during colonial times, it gives solid history underneath the humor. It is an entertaining view of the times, and to understand the riddles, one must know something of the history itself. *International Reading Association Children's Choices.*

19. Adler, David A. **We Remember the Holocaust**. New York: Henry Holt, 1989. 144p. $18.95; $9.95pa. ISBN 0-8050-0434-3; 0-805-3715-2pa. 6 up

Interviews with Holocaust survivors recount the horrors of Hitler from the time he came to power, through *Kristallnacht* on November 9, 1938, to the Polish killing of Jews in 1947, after the war ended. Millions of people were exterminated for no reason except that they had Jewish blood. The guilt of those who survived, as well as their need to keep the traditions of their forebears alive, permeate this book. Photographs of people and places enhance the impact of these accounts of heinous crimes. Bibliography, Chronology, Glossary, Index, and Suggested Reading.

20. Alder, Elizabeth. **The King's Shadow**. New York: Farrar, Straus & Giroux, 1995. 257p. $17. ISBN 0-374-34182-6. 6-9

Evyn, a young Welsh serf, wants to be a traveling storyteller. But ruffians destroy his dream by killing his parents and cutting out his tongue before his uncle sells him into slavery. Although he cannot speak to the people with whom he works, he learns to read and write, and eventually he begins to serve Harold Godwinson, the charismatic man who becomes the King of England. Evyn loves Harold as a father and stays by him until his death at the Battle of Hastings in 1066, when William defeats Harold and becomes king. Harold's widow takes Evyn home and nurses him back to health so that Evyn can write about his former master, the king whose shadow he had been. *American Library Association Best Books for Young Adults.*

21. Alexander, Bryan, and Cherry Alexander. **Inuit**. Austin, TX: Raintree/Steck-Vaughn, 1993. 48p. $15.96. ISBN 0-8114-2301-8. (Threatened Cultures). 4-9

The Inuit (Eskimos) from Arctic Canada and Greenland have many traditions, but they must strive to preserve their way of life and maintain their cultural identity in the modern world. Bibliography and Index.

22. Aliki, author/illustrator. **The King's Day: Louis XIV of France.** New York: Crowell, 1989. Unpaged. $14.95. ISBN 0-690-04588-3. 2-6

The ritual of Louis XIV's day—*lever, petit couverte*, exercise, *apartement*, and *coucher*—must have exhausted his servants and courtiers. Because he became king at age five in 1643, he likely saw himself as the most important man alive. Aliki's illustrations and brief text reveal the king's vanity, appetite, and control over his subjects. Chronology and Definitions.

23. Aliki, author/illustrator. **A Medieval Feast**. New York: Harper Trophy, 1986. 32p. $5.95pa. ISBN 0-06-556050-9pa. 1-5

When the king decides to visit Camdenton Manor with all of his retinue, the manor fold have to prepare food. The text looks at the types of food that were served and the customs for serving it. *Notable Trade Books in the Field of Social Studies, Booklist Children's Editor's Choices,* and *School Library Journal Best Book.*

24. Aliki, author/illustrator. **Mummies Made in Egypt**. New York: Harper Trophy, 1985. 32p. $5.95pa. ISBN 0-06-446011-8pa. 2-6

The text describes various rituals of Egyptian life, the preparation of the dead, the belief in the afterlife, and the gods and goddesses of the dead. *Notable Children's Trade Books in the Field of Social Studies* and *IRA Children's Choices.*

25. Aller, Susan Bivin. **J.M. Barrie: The Magic Behind Peter Pan**. Minneapolis, MN: Lerner, 1994. 128p. $22.95. ISBN 0-8225-4918-2. (Lerner Biographies). 5 up

The author of *Peter Pan*, James Matthew Barrie (1860-1937), was a journalist before his story about a boy who refused to grow up made him famous. Bibliography and Index.

26. Allman, Barbara. **Her Piano Sang: A Story About Clara Schumann**. Shelly O. Haas, illustrator. Minneapolis, MN: Carolrhoda, 1996. 64p. $18.95. ISBN 1-57505-012-9. (Creative Minds). 3-7

Clara Schumann (1819-1896) made her professional debut as a pianist when she was only nine years old. Her father demanded much of her, and when she married Robert Schumann after a long courtship, it was against her father's wishes. She raised her family as Robert developed mental illness, but she continued to compose and perform. She pursued a career that had been open only to men and succeeded. Illustrations highlight the text. Index.

27. Almagor, Gila. **Under the Domim Tree**. Hillel Schenker, translator. New York: Simon & Schuster, 1995. 164p. $15. ISBN 0-671-89020-4. 6-10

After World War II, in 1953, Aviya, Yola, and Mira live at Udim, a youth village on Israel's coast. They all have survived the Holocaust. Each eventually tells of personal tragedy, while they all hope that a family member will someday appear. Mira cannot remember her family, and when two people take her to court because they say she is their child, the others realize that adults may take advantage of all of them. Not until the trial in the courtroom can Mira remember her repressed past in Poland and her name. She escapes the clutches of the two impostors who want her reparation money.

28. Almedingen, E. M. **Katia**. Victor Ambrus, illustrator. New York: Farrar, Straus & Giroux, 1967. 207p. $3.95. ISBN 9-99750-148-9. 6-9

As a girl of five, Katia goes to live with her cousin after her mother's death. During the six years she lives with her cousin (1836-1842), she learns to speak French, German, and English along with her Russian while she studies many other subjects. Her most important lesson is learning that she must respect other humans, regardless of class. When Katia returns to her father's house, finding that her stepmother accepts and likes her is a surprise.

29. Alper, Ann Fitzpatrick. **Forgotten Voyager: The Story of Amerigo Vespucci**. Minneapolis, MN: Carolrhoda, 1991. 80p. $11.95. ISBN 0-87614-442-3. 4-8

This biography of Amerigo Vespucci (1451-1512) discusses his discoveries and explorations for Spain. In 1499, he sailed to the West Indies and discovered the mouth of the Amazon. Later (1501) he sailed along the northern coast of South America and proved that the land was one continent. Bibliography and Index.

30. Alphin, Elaine Marie. **A Bear for Miguel**. Joan Sandin, illustrator. New York: HarperCollins, 1996. 64p. $14.95. ISBN 0-06-024521-2. (An I Can Read Book). 1-3

In the 1980s, María's father cannot work because the guerillas will punish him if he works in El Salvador's government factory, and the government will punish him if he works for the guerillas. He has to trade family items for food, and María goes with him to the market. After her father goes away, she finds people who want to trade food for her stuffed bear, her favorite thing. Since they want to give the bear to their wounded son, she decides that she must help both her family and the child. Glossary.

31. Altman, Linda Jacobs. **Mr. Darwin's Voyage**. New York: Dillon Press, 1995. 160p. $13.95; $7.95pa. ISBN 0-87518-609-2; 0-382-24962-3pa. (People in Focus). 6-9

Charles Darwin (1809-1882) expected to become a country parson, but on his way to divinity school, Captain Robert FitzRoy, of the survey ship HMS *Beagle,* offered to take him on a voyage around the globe as its resident naturalist. He went through the rain forests of Brazil, the wastelands of Tierra del Fuego, and the Galápagos Islands. His research showed that slow change over time had formed the earth and the species on it, including humans. He thought the theory good for a scientist, but his own humanity inherently rejected it. Photographs and reproductions enhance the text. Selected Bibliography, Notes, and Index.

32. Amdur, Richard. **Anne Frank**. New York: Chelsea House, 1993. 111p. $18.95; $7.95pa. ISBN 0-7910-1641-2; 0-7910-1645-5pa. (Library of Biography). 5 up

This story traces the life of the young Jewish girl, Anne Frank (1929-1945), whose diary tells of the years during which she and her family hid from the Nazis in an Amsterdam attic. Bibliography and Index.

33. Amdur, Richard. **Chaim Weizmann**. New York: Chelsea House, 1988. 112p. $18.95. ISBN 0-87754-446-8. (World Leaders Past and Present). 5 up

Chaim Weizmann (1874-1952), born in czarist Russia, grew up to become the president of Israel. As a student he became interested in Zionism and the movement for the Jews to establish their own country in Palestine. Weizmann, a scientist by profession, helped England in World War I and convinced Britain to support the idea of a new Jewish nation. For twenty years, he served as president of the World Zionist Organization and raised funds for this endeavor. He tried to found a country peacefully but was unable to resolve conflicts between militant Zionists and Palestinian Arabs. When Israel became a reality after World War II, Weizmann served as its first president. Photographs enhance the text. Chronology, Further Reading, and Index.

34. Anderson, Dale. **Battles That Changed the Modern World**. Austin, TX: Raintree/Steck-Vaughn, 1994. 48p. $15.96. ISBN 0-8114-4928-9. (20 Events Series). 6 up

Since the beginning of the nineteenth century, twenty battles have had a great impact on the world. In two-page spreads, Anderson presents the important aspects of these battles. They are Waterloo (1812), Antietam (1862), Gettysburg (1863), Sedan (1870), Little Bighorn (1875), Tsushima Strait (1905), the Marne (1914), Guernica (1937), Nanking (1937), Britain (1940), El Alamein (1942), Midway (1942), Stalingrad (1941-1943), Normandy (1944), the Chinese Civil War (1947-1949), Inchon (1950), Dien Bien Phu (1954), the Six-Day War (1967), the Tet Offensive (1968), and Desert Storm (1991). Glossary, Suggested Readings, and Index.

35. Anderson, Dale. **Explorers Who Found New Worlds**. Austin, TX: Raintree/Steck-Vaughn, 1994. 48p. $15.96. ISBN 0-8114-4931-9. (20 Events Series). 6 up

Anderson identifies twenty explorers who have found places that changed the lives of people throughout the world and presents profiles of them in two-page spreads. The explorers discussed here start with Marco Polo (Venice) in the thirteenth century. In the fifteenth century, Christopher Columbus (Portugal) and Vasco da Gama (Portugal) set forth. Their work continued in the sixteenth century with Vasco Nuñez de Balboa (Spain), Ferdinand Magellan (Portugal), Francisco Vasquez de Coronado (Spain), and Jacques Cartier (France). In the seventeenth century, Henry Hudson (England), Louis Jolliet and Jacques Marquette (France), and René-Robert Cavelier, Sieur de La Salle (France) explored North America. The eighteenth-century explorers were Vitus Bering (Denmark), James Cook (England), and Alexander Mackenzie (Scotland). The nineteenth century began with Americans Meriwether Lewis and William Clark, and continued with David Livingstone (Scotland), Richard Francis Burton and John Hanning Speke (England), John McDouall Stuart (Scotland and Australia), Sven Hedin (Sweden), and Robert Peary (America). The twentieth century boasts Roald Amundsen (Norway). Glossary, Suggested Readings, and Index.

36. Anderson, Joan. **Christopher Columbus: From Vision to Voyage**. George Ancona, photographs. New York: Dial, 1991. Unpaged. $14.95. ISBN 0-8037-1041-0. 3-5

Anderson concludes, after studying Christopher Columbus (1451-1506), that although he was ordinary in many respects, he had imagination, curiosity, energy, courage, and the willingness to take risks. The text looks at portions of his life, including his famous voyages. Photographs of persons in period dress add authenticity. Map, Characters, and Places.

37. Anderson, Joan. **Pioneer Settlers in New France**. George Ancona, photographs. New York: Lodestar, Dutton, 1990. 60p. $15.95. ISBN 0-525-67291-5. 4-7

Jean François lives with his aunt and uncle in Louisbourg, Nova Scotia, in 1763. An orphaned French noble, he prefers sailing to working in his uncle's store. One day he slips away with a peasant fisherman's son to enjoy an afternoon on the sea. But the French and the British have recently declared war, and he jeopardizes his freedom by being in unsafe waters.

38. Anderson, Margaret. **The Druid's Gift**. New York: Knopf, 1989. 211p. $12.95. ISBN 0-394-91936-X. 6-9

Three historical periods (the age of the Vikings, the eighteenth century, and the twentieth century) fuse in this historical fantasy set on Hirta, an island off the coast of Scotland. Caitlin—or Cathan, or Catie, or Catriona—uses her ability to see into the future as a basis for urging the druids to forgo their Samhain human sacrifices and form a truce with the villagers who need their blessings. She finds that changing centuries of ritual needs a supernatural force.

39. Anderson, Margaret. **Searching for Shona**. New York: Knopf, 1979. 159p. $6.95; $3.95pa. ISBN 0-394-93724-4; 0-394-82587-Xpa. 5-8

Marjorie's wealthy uncle leaves her at the Edinburgh, Scotland, train station in 1939, on the first leg in her journey to Canada as a war evacuee. She meets a girl whom she had known at the orphanage. The two girls decide to trade places, so Shona goes to Marjorie's relatives in Canada and Marjorie takes Shona's place. After the war, when Shona returns to Edinburgh and her parents appear, she does not want to return to her real identity. Marjorie continues living happily as Shona with Shona's family.

40. Anderson, Margaret J. **Carl Linnaeus: Father of Classification**. Springfield, NJ: Enslow, 1997. 128p. $18.95. ISBN 0-89490-786-7. (Great Minds of Science). 4-8

Carl von Linne (1707-1778), a Swedish botanist, invented the binomial nomenclature for classifying plants and animals. Photographs of places where he lived and worked illustrate the text, which includes much about him and his scientific expeditions. Chronology, Further Reading, Glossary, and Index.

41. Anderson, Margaret J. **Charles Darwin: Naturalist**. Springfield, NJ: Enslow, 1994. 128p. $17.95. ISBN 0-89490-476-0. (Great Minds of Science). 4-7

Charles Darwin (1809-1882) shared his birth date with Abraham Lincoln, but rather than trying to stop a civil war, he almost caused one when he published *The Origin of Species* in 1859. His book claimed that, over time, small differences among similar plants and animals can cause new species to evolve. He did much of his research on a five-year trip around the world on the HMS *Beagle*. His three main ideas were that plants and animals have more offspring than needed; that, overall, numbers of each kind of plant and animal remain stable; and that all offspring are not alike. The offspring survive based on natural selection. People who believed that all species had been created and "fixed" by God were horrified by this theory. Notes, Chronology, Glossary, Further Reading, and Index.

42. Anderson, Margaret Jean. **Isaac Newton: The Greatest Scientist of All Time**. Springfield, NJ: Enslow, 1996. 128p. $18.95. ISBN 0-89490-681-X. (Great Minds of Science). 5-8

Isaac Newton (1642-1727) made enormous scientific advances, but they did not keep him from skipping meals or holding grudges against his colleagues. The text places Newton within the context of his times and shows the relationship of his life to his work. Photographs, Reproductions, Further Reading, Glossary, Notes, and Index.

43. Anderson, Rachel. **Black Water**. New York: Henry Holt, 1995. 168p. $14.95. ISBN 0-8050-3847-7. New York: Paper Star, 1996. 168p. $4.95pa. ISBN 0-698-11421-3pa. 6-10

People think that Albert is freaky or mad because of his lapses of consciousness. His mother searches frantically for a cure, but when she fails, Albert has to rely on his own resources as he copes with his epilepsy in Victorian England. On a train he meets Edward Lear, also a victim of epilepsy, and Lear gives Albert a curious recipe for the malady after Albert has a seizure. The objectivity and humor of this book make an intriguing story.

44. Anderson, Rachel. **Paper Faces**. New York: Henry Holt, 1993. 150p. $14.95. ISBN 0-8050-2527-8. 6-8

World War II in London is difficult for Dot and her mother, but the end of the war and the changes it brings, especially the anticipated arrival of a father she has never known, are almost overwhelming.

45. Angel, Ann, and Beverley Birch. **Louis Pasteur: Leading the Way to a Healthier World**. Milwaukee, WI: Gareth Stevens, 1992. 68p. $16.95. ISBN 0-8368-0625-5. (People Who Made a Difference). 3-6

Louis Pasteur (1822-1895) found that germs or microbes, visible only with a microscope, were the cause of liquids becoming sour and other problems. He found that heating the substances could kill the microbes. He was curious about science and loved to teach what he knew to others. He spent his life trying to find cures for some diseases and successfully created a vaccine against rabies. Two of his own children died from typhoid. Organizations, Books, List of New Words, Important Dates, and Index.

46. Angel, Ann, and Mary Craig. **Lech Walesa: Champion of Freedom for Poland**. Milwaukee, WI: Gareth Stevens, 1992. 68p. $16.95. ISBN 0-8368-0628-X. (People Who Made a Difference). 3-6

In 1939, Hitler wanted the lands of Poland but not its people; the Nazis both committed and encouraged the murders of Polish citizens. One in five Poles were killed, including Lech Walesa's father, who died in 1945 when Lech was two. After the German defeat, Stalin and his Communists marched into Poland. The Poles revolted in 1956 but were defeated. After school and training, Walesa went to Gdansk and became a ship's electrician. There the working conditions appalled him. He supported student protests in 1968, but other workers accepted the government's view that the students were lazy and undisciplined. In 1970, the government raised food prices but not wages. The ship workers went on a strike, but some were killed in Gdansk and many were massacred in another town. Walesa was eventually fired three times because of his activism. Among those who joined in the cry for freedom was the Cardinal of Krakow, Karol Wojtyla, later Pope John Paul II. In 1980, the strike reached its height, with the government making agreements but reneging soon after the workers returned. Walesa was imprisoned, but was later freed because the government said he was no longer important. The world and the workers disagreed; he received the Nobel Peace Prize in 1983, and in 1990, after the communist government failed, the people elected Walesa president. Organizations, Books, List of New Words, Important Dates, and Index.

47. Anthony, Suzanne. **West Indies**. New York: Chelsea House, 1989. 127p. $15.95. ISBN 1-55546-793-8. 5 up

This general overview of the West Indies introduces the Greater and Lesser Antilles. The Great Antilles islands include Cuba, Jamaica, the Dominican Republic, Haiti, and Puerto Rico; the Lesser Antilles contains the rest of the islands loosely associated with Columbus's arrival. These islands are also famous for such figures as Henry Morgan, a buccaneer made governor of Port Royal, Jamaica, around 1675; Toussaint Louverture, who led the slave revolt on Haiti in 1804; and Joséphine de Beauharnais, wife of Napoléon Bonaparte. Clearly, tourism helps these islands to overcome poverty and the legacies of some of their former rulers—England, Spain, France, and the Netherlands—although they are basically united in a common Creole bond. Facts at a Glance, History at a Glance, Glossary, Index, and Map.

48. Appel, Todd M. **José Martí**. New York: Chelsea House, 1992. 110p. $18.95. ISBN 0-7910-1246-8. (Hispanics of Achievement). 5 up

In Cuba, José Martí (1853-1895) is one of the most revered figures. He was a communicator, an organizer, a political theorist, and a guerrilla fighter. When he was sixteen, the Spanish imprisoned him for organizing against them and exiled him to Spain, where he studied at Madrid's Central University. He returned to Cuba and led an insurrection in 1878. Again he was exiled, this time to the United States, where he spent fifteen years working for Cuban independence. In 1892, he founded the Cuban Revolutionary Party and went to Cuba to fight the Second War of Independence. He died before his party won. Photographs enhance the text. Chronology, Further Reading, and Index.

49. Archibald, Erica. **A Sudanese Family**. Minneapolis, MN: Lerner, 1997. 64p. $21.50. ISBN 0-8225-3428-2. (Journey Between Two Worlds). 3-6

Although not a history book, this text includes the history of the Sudanese people as a background for understanding why families from the Sudan have had to leave their homes. Photographs and personal experiences explain the social and religious traditions of Sudan and how the people have had to adapt to a new culture to survive as refugees. Further Reading.

50. **Armenia**. Minneapolis, MN: Lerner, 1993. 56p. $19.95. ISBN 0-8225-2806-1. (Then and Now). 5-9

Timur and the Mongolian hordes came into Armenia in the late 1300s and massacred much of the population. Other countries have done the same throughout the centuries. This text discusses these massacres and other problems the country faces as it tries to succeed since becoming independent in 1991. Photographs and maps enhance additional information about economics, geography, politics, and ethnography. Glossary and Index.

51. Armstrong, Jennifer. **Little Salt Lick and the Sun King**. Jon Goodell, illustrator. New York: Crown, 1994. Unpaged. $15. ISBN 0-517-59620-2. K-4

During the reign of Louis XIV of France (1638-1715), the Second Assistant Rotisserie Turner at the court rises to the position of First Assistant Bearer of the King's Dog and all of the responsibilities that it entails.

52. Arnold, Caroline. **City of the Gods: Mexico's Ancient City of Teotihuacán**. Richard Hewitt, illustrator. New York: Clarion, 1994. 48p. $14.95. ISBN 0-395-66584-1. 4-6

For 800 years, Teotihuacán was the most important city in Central America (contemporary Mexico), but it was abandoned between A.D. 700 and 900. The text discusses the finds at the ruins of this once-powerful city and tries to describe the people who lived there, their buildings, their trade, and the reasons they fell from power. It stresses the city's importance as a ceremonial center for its inhabitants' religion, which included worship of the pyramid, the sun, the moon, and the feathered serpent. Glossary and Index.

53. Arnold, Caroline. **Stone Age Farmers Beside the Sea: Scotland's Prehistoric Village Arnold of Skara Brae**. New York: Clarion, 1997. 48p. $15.95. ISBN 0-395-77601-5. 3-5

Skara Brae, in northern Scotland's Orkney Islands, predates the Egyptian pyramids, having been inhabited from 3100 to 2500 B.C. and buried under sand until 150 years ago. Arnold describes the construction of the stone houses, the daily life of the people, and how archaeologists have uncovered the site. Glossary and Index.

54. Arnold, Sandra Martín. **Alicia Alonso: First Lady of the Ballet**. New York: Walker, 1993. 100p. $14.95. ISBN 0-8027-8242-6. 4 up

Alicia Alonso (b. 1917), although plagued by serious eyesight problems, was, from 1941 to 1960, one of the principal stars of the American Ballet Theatre. She was particularly famous in the role of Giselle. In 1948, she formed the Ballet Alicia Alonso (renamed Ballet de Cuba in 1955 and the Ballet Nacional de Cuba in 1959). Her school has been admired for the quality of its training. Bibliography and Index.

55. Ash, Maureen. **Alexander the Great: Ancient Empire Builder**. Chicago: Childrens Press, 1991. 128p. $28.20. ISBN 0-516-03063-9. (The World's Great Explorers). 3 up

Photographs, reproductions, maps, and text tell the story of Alexander the Great (356-323 B.C.), the general who directed the Macedonian expansion. The chapters look at his background, his father, Philip of Macedonia, his subjugation of the Grecian states, and the invasion of Persia. They also discuss Darius, Issus, the siege of Tyre, and conquests on Alexander's way to Egypt and India. Appendices, Timeline, Glossary, and Bibliography.

56. Ash, Maureen. **Vasco Núñez de Balboa**. Chicago: Childrens Press, 1990. 126p. $28.20. ISBN 0-516-03057-4. (The World's Great Explorers). 3 up

Beautiful color photographs and reproductions illustrate this introduction to Balboa (1475-1519), the Spaniard who discovered the Pacific Ocean. Balboa had trained to be a soldier, but the advent of peace led him to search for other ways to gain fame. He became an explorer and left for the New World when he was twenty-six. The text looks at his conflicts with other leaders at Dárien and how he tried to defend his purpose before they executed him. Timeline, Glossary, Bibliography, and Index.

57. Ashabranner, Brent. **Land of Yesterday, Land of Tomorrow: Discovering Chinese Central Asia**. Paul, David, and Peter Conklin, photographs. New York: Cobblehill/Dutton, 1992. 84p. $16. ISBN 0-525-65086-5. 4-7

Although Ashabranner is the author, the text concerns a trip that the photographers took into China's Xinjiang Province, which was open to foreigners between 1984 and 1990. The main city of Kashgar lies on the trade route of the ancient Silk Road, where Marco Polo visited in the thirteenth century. The basically non-Chinese population of this area continues to live as it has for many years. Especially interesting are photographs of *buz kashi*, a polo match, and the bazaars. Bibliography and Index.

58. Asimov, Isaac. **Christopher Columbus: Navigator to the New World**. Minneapolis, MN: Gareth Stevens, 1991. 48p. $14.95. ISBN 0-8368-0556-9. (Isaac Asimov's Pioneers of Exploration). 2-5

Christopher Columbus surprised many when he succeeded at finding land across the ocean in 1492. Even when his crew threatened to mutiny, he held steadfast in his quest. The text discusses the controversy surrounding Columbus, including his treatment of the natives he found on America's shores, along with his contemporary legacy. Chronology, Glossary, Books to Read, Places to Write, and Index.

59. Asimov, Isaac. **Ferdinand Magellan: Opening the Door to World Exploration**. Minneapolis, MN: Gareth Stevens, 1991. 48p. $14.95. ISBN 0-8368-0560-7. (Isaac Asimov's Pioneers of Exploration). 2-5

In 1519, Magellan left Spain on a quest to find a passage through the Americas that Columbus might have missed. He was trying to provide Spain with a route to the Far East. After mutiny and misery, Magellan sailed around South America and across the Pacific. Although he died before returning home, his ship was the first to sail around the world. Chronology, Glossary, More to Read, Places to Write, Other Activities, and Index.

60. Asimov, Isaac, and Elizabeth Kaplan. **Henry Hudson: Arctic Explorer and North American Adventurer**. Minneapolis, MN: Gareth Stevens, 1991. 48p. $14.95. ISBN 0-8368-0558-5. (Isaac Asimov's Pioneers of Exploration). 2-5

Henry Hudson (d. 1611) searched for a short route from Europe to the Orient, but he never found it. His sailors mutinied, and he disappeared. Hudson, an expert navigator, explored the Arctic regions north of Russia and the eastern coast of North America, and was the first European to enter the body of water now known as Hudson Bay. Chronology, Glossary, Things to Read, Places to Write, Other Activities, and Index.

61. Atlan, Liliane. **The Passersby**. Rochelle Owens, translator; Lisa Desimini, illustrator. New York: Henry Holt, 1993. 80p. $13.95. ISBN 0-8050-3054-9. 6-8

No, anorectic after World War II, has to learn to understand why a human should want to live. She interacts with members of her family, but her adopted brother, an Auschwitz survivor, finally helps her realize that she has qualities to help others.

62. Auerbach, Susan. **Queen Elizabeth II**. Vero Beach, FL: Rourke, 1993. 112p. $16.95. ISBN 0-86625-481-1. (World Leaders). 5-8

Queen Elizabeth II (b. 1926) became queen of England in 1953 after the death of her father. She has ruled for the latter half of the twentieth century. The text looks at her life and the influences on her decisions as the titular head of England. Photographs and reproductions enhance the text. Time Line, Glossary, Bibliography, Media Resources, and Index.

63. Avery, Gillian. **Maria Escapes**. Scott Snow, illustrator. New York: Simon & Schuster, 1992. 258p. $15. ISBN 0-671-77074-8. 4-8

Maria, an orphan bundled off to boarding school in 1875, hates the people and the lessons and runs away. She goes to her uncle in Oxford, England, who decides to let her stay when he hears that she wants to study Latin and Greek and be an Oxford professor. She and the three boys next door work with a tutor, and Maria is learning to do her own research in the Oxford Bodleian Library when she becomes interested in the story of a local boy from the seventeenth century. Although the four neighbors get into trouble, Maria's uncle remains kindly and helpful.

64. Avery, Gillian. **Maria's Italian Spring**. Scott Snow, illustrator. New York: Simon & Schuster, 1993. 265p. $15. ISBN 0-671-79582-1. 4-8

Maria's uncle, from *Maria Escapes*, dies in 1877. Maria's only remaining relative lives in Italy, and because Maria likes Greek and Latin, the relative takes her back to Italy. Maria hates having to visit all the famous buildings and museums because she is unable to speak Italian. She pretends to be ill. Instead, she sneaks out of the house to visit with an English girl nearby. With her newfound friend, Maria explores the town as she would like to see it.

65. Avi. **Beyond the Western Sea, Book One: The Escape from Home**. New York: Jackson, Orchard, 1996. 304p. $18.95. ISBN 0-531-09513-4. 5-8

Patrick and his sister, Maura, have to escape from Ireland in 1851 after their landlord destroys their hovel. Also trying to catch the *Robert Peel* from Liverpool, England, on January 24 is Laurence, age eleven, the son of an English lord; Laurence is running away from abuse and his own guilt. The three have various difficulties getting to the ship because of people who wish to keep them off it; the novel spans the five days before they finally get on board and start their trip. *Booklist Starred Review, Bulletin Blue Ribbon Book,* and *American Library Association Best Books for Young Adults.*

66. Avi. **Beyond the Western Sea, Book Two: Lord Kirkle's Money**. New York: Jackson, Orchard, 1996. 380p. $18.95. ISBN 0-531-09520-7. 5-8

Patrick O'Connell and his sister Maura, along with their friends Mr. Horatio Drabble and Laurence Kirkle, sail on the *Robert Peel* from England to Boston in 1851. After arrival, they all go to Lowell, Massachusetts, where they find out that the O'Connell father has died. The characters must endure prejudice and hardship, but they eventually overcome the evil forces that would ruin their lives.

67. Avi-Yonah, Michael. **Piece by Piece! Mosaics of the Ancient World**. Minneapolis, MN: Runestone Press, 1993. 64p. $22.95. ISBN 0-8225-3204-2. (Buried Worlds). 5 up

Mosaics reveal what the people who made them wanted to show. The subject might be a story from the classical world, an illustration of a myth, or merely a pleasing picture. This book follows archaeologists' investigations of ancient mosaics, which have told them about the Greek, Roman, and Byzantine worlds. Glossary and Index.

68. Ayer, Eleanor. **Berlin**. New York: New Discovery, 1992. 96p. $14.95. ISBN 0-02-707800-0. (Cities at War). 6 up

The text looks at the effects of World War II on the people who lived in Berlin. Eyewitnesses, diaries, and other primary sources tell about the rise of Nazism, what having a bomb drop in the street outside was like, what the victims of the Holocaust looked like, how the Holocaust victims were treated, and the response to Hitler's fall. Documentary photographs accentuate the text. Bibliography and Index.

69.   Ayer, Eleanor H. **Boris Yeltsin: Man of the People**. New York: Macmillan, 1992. 144p. $13.95. ISBN 0-87518543-6. (People in Focus). 4-7

Born in 1931, Boris Nikolayevich Yeltsin went from his childhood on a collective farm, through his education as a civil engineer, to his election as the first president of Russia after it became a republic in 1991. He has had the difficult task of trying to turn the country from a socialist economy into a capitalist economy.

70.   Ayoub, Abderrahman, ed. **Al Umm El Madayan: An Islamic City Through the Ages**. Kathleen Leverich, translator; Francesco Corni, illustrator. Boston: Houghton Mifflin, 1994. 61p. $16.95. ISBN 0-395-65967-1. 5 up

Accompanied by detailed drawings and text, this story traces a fictional city in North Africa from its Islamic beginnings. It shows the social life and customs as they have developed and as they are practiced today. Index.

71.   **Azerbaijan**. Minneapolis, MN: Lerner, 1993. 56p. $19.95. ISBN 0-8225-2810-X. (Then and Now). 5-9

With its history linked to that of Armenia and Persia, Azerbaijan has been subsumed by the Persians, Mongols, and the Communists. This text discusses these and other problems for the country in its struggle since becoming independent in 1991. Photographs and maps enhance additional information about economics, geography, politics, and ethnography. Glossary and Index.

72. Bachrach, Susan D. **Tell Them We Remember: The Story of the Holocaust**. Boston: Little, Brown, 1994. 109p. $19.95. ISBN 0-316-07484-5. 5-9

Bachrach uses the same format that the United States Holocaust Museum uses for visitors. She starts with a series of photographs of children and traces their experiences throughout the Holocaust—where they went and, in some cases, where they died. The other photographs also come from the museum's collection. The text follows the chronology of the Holocaust, beginning with life before the Holocaust and Hitler's rise to power in 1933, and follows the survivors through the Nuremberg Trials in 1945 and 1946. Chronology, Suggestions for Further Reading, Glossary, and Index.

73. Baillet, Yolande. **Matisse: Painter of the Essential**. John Goodman, translator; Bernadette Theulet-Luzie, illustrator. New York: Chelsea House, 1995. 53p. $14.95. ISBN 0-7910-2812-7. (Art for Children). 5-9

Henri Matisse (1869-1954) was a French painter whose use of pure colors and simple shapes on canvas and in collage have delighted his viewers. Reproductions enhance the text.

74. Baillie, Allan. **Little Brother**. New York: Viking, 1992. 144p. $14. ISBN 0-670-84381-4. 3-7

Vithy and his brother, Mang, try to cross the Cambodian border into Thailand after escaping from the Big Paddy where they had been held for nearly a year following the Vietnamese war. Although they manage to evade the Khmer Rouge soldiers, they are separated, and Vithy must travel alone. He has to cross jungles, mountains, and landscape where enemies hide throughout, and where the rules that he has known throughout his life no longer exist. He eventually realizes that he must trust someone to help him escape and search for his brother, because he can do neither alone. People help him get to Australia, and there he finds what he was looking for.

75. Baillie, Allan. **Rebel**. Di Wu, illustrator. New York: Ticknor & Fields, 1994. 32p. $13.95. ISBN 0-395-69250-4. 1-4

When the general comes to the small Burmese town (probably in the 1970s) and destroys the playground with his tanks, he tells the people that they must do everything he demands. He will make all the laws and tell the townspeople when to plant rice. When a sandal flies out of a school window and knocks off the general's hat, he demands that everyone come out of the school, because he expects to arrest the child wearing one thong. What he does not expect is that everyone, including the teacher, will come out barefoot. After his troops laugh at him, the general supposedly leaves. (A similar incident supposedly occurred in Rangoon.)

76. Baker, Betty. **Walk the World's Rim**. New York: HarperCollins, 1965. 80p. $14.89. ISBN 0-06-020381-1. 5-9

Of 600 men who sailed from Cuba to Florida in 1527, only 4 survived. One, the black slave Esteban, encourages a young Indian, Chako, to go with him to Mexico. While their leaders petition for money to go to the seven cities of Cíbola, they wait separately in the city; Chako is disturbed that Esteban has not come to tell him what will happen. When Cortez tells Chako to feed his horse, Chako finds Esteban, the slave, confined to the stables. Although taught not to respect slaves, Chako soon realizes that Esteban tells the truth, and when the Cíbolans murder Esteban, Chako dejectedly returns to his Florida home.

77. Balaban, John. **Vietnam: The Land We Never Knew**. Geoffrey Clifford, photographer. San Francisco: Chronicle, 1989. 144p. $29.95. ISBN 0-87701-597-X. 5-7

A land of rice and monsoons; of four religions—Taoism, Buddhism, Confucianism, and now Christianity; and of numerous foreign invasions during its 3,000-year history, Vietnam has kept its traditions. Beautiful photographs of everyday life enhance the text of this book One sees the country's natural beauty, the people, the government, the remnants of war, and the hope for the future.

78. Balkwill, Richard. **Food and Feasts in Ancient Egypt**. New York: New Discovery, Silver Burdett, 1994. 32p. $14.95. ISBN 0-02-726323-1. 4-6

The text looks at the ways the Egyptians grew and prepared food by focusing on the crops in the countryside and the types of food needed to be shipped to the cities. If one traveled, one had to eat, and the text covers food in taverns or inns and for armies. Additional information about cooking utensils and recipes from the Egyptians give a good sense of the times. Photographs and reproductions enhance the text. Glossary, Further Reading, and Index.

79. Balkwill, Richard. **Food and Feasts in Tudor Times**. New York: New Discovery, Silver Burdett, 1995. 32p. $14.95. ISBN 0-02-726319-3. 4-6

The text looks at the ways the Tudors grew and prepared food from 1485 to 1558 by focusing on the crops in the countryside and the types of food needed to be shipped to the cities and suburbs. If one traveled, one had to eat, and the text covers food in taverns and inns and for armies. Additional information about cooking utensils and recipes from the Tudor period give a good sense of the times. Photographs and reproductions enhance the text. Glossary, Further Reading, and Index.

80. Balkwill, Richard. **Trafalgar**. Fred Anderson, illustrator. New York: New Discovery, 1993. 32p. $13.95. ISBN 0-02-726326-6. (Great Battles and Sieges). 5 up

Sixteen miles west of Cape Trafalgar, near Cadiz, Spain, on Monday, October 21, 1805, twenty-seven ships of the British Royal Navy met a combined French and Spanish fleet of thirty-three ships. Seventeen thousand British sailors and more than 2,000 guns served under Admiral Lord Nelson from his flagship, the HMS *Victory*. The French and Spanish fleet had more men and more guns, but after a five-hour battle in which 5,000 men died, the British won, without losing any ships, whereas the French and Spanish lost nineteen. Discussion follows on Horatio Nelson, Napoleon, the ships, the sailor's life, fighting at sea, the preparation for the battle, and the events after Trafalgar. Glossary and Index.

81. Ballard, Robert D. **Exploring the Bismarck**. New York: Scholastic, 1991. 64p. $15.95. ISBN 0-590-44268-6. (Time Quest). 3-8

Robert Ballard and his assistants recovered the shipwreck of the German battleship *Bismarck* in 1989. Photographs of the ship complement the story of the battle during which it sank in World War II. Recommended Further Reading. *American Library Association Recommended Book for the Reluctant Young Reader* and *Outstanding Science Trade Books for Children*.

82. Ballard, Robert D. **Exploring the Titanic**. Ken Marschall, illustrator. New York: Madison, Scholastic, 1988. 96p. $14.95; $6.95pa. ISBN 0-590-41953-6; 0-590-41952-8pa. 4-7

Dr. Robert Ballard became fascinated with the story of the *Titanic*. When the tiny submarine *Alvin*'s tether was extended to 13,000 feet, Ballard realized that he could reach the wreck two and one-half miles under the sea. In July 1986, he saw the ship that had last been above the water on April 14, 1912. On that night, only 705 of the 1,500 people on board the magnificent ship reached the safety of a rescue vessel, the *Carpathia*, after an iceberg tore through the hull. Ballard returned to the Titanic eight times, going inside and reliving the scene based on what he had read or heard from survivors of that doomed voyage. Further Reading, Glossary, and *Titanic* Timeline. *American Library Association Best Books for Young Adults*, *School Library Journal Best Books of the Year*, and *Horn Book Fanfare*.

83. Ballard, Robert D., with Rich Archbold. **The Lost Wreck of the Isis**. Ken Marshall and Wesley Lowe, illustrators. New York: Scholastic, 1990. 63p. $15.95; $6.95pa. ISBN 0-590-43852-2; 0-590-43853-0pa. (Time Quest). 2-8

When Ballard located the wreck of the *Isis* off the coast of Italy, he found artifacts of the Roman world. The text describing the "find" alternates with a story set at the time when the *Isis* actually sailed so that the reader can connect more readily with the people who might have been on the *Isis* and what they would have transported. The book is, therefore, both historical fiction and information. It gives excellent insight as to how modern tools (underwater vehicles, cameras, and computers) can find ancient ones. Glossary and Recommended Further Reading. *Outstanding Science Trade Books for Children*.

84. Bandon, Alexandra. **Asian Indian Americans**. New York: New Discovery, Silver Burdett, 1994. 112p. $14.95. ISBN 0-02-768144-0. (Footsteps to America). 5-8

Bandon examines the lives of Asian Indian Americans after they began to arrive in America around 1965. For them to leave their country was a major decision; therefore, Bandon tries to identify what in the history of the country would have precipitated such a move. Using personal narratives as a basis, she shows what the journey to America was like, what life in America has been like for those who came, the prejudice they faced, and the opportunities they found. For Further Reading and Index.

85. Bandon, Alexandra. **Chinese Americans**. New York: New Discovery, Silver Burdett, 1994. 112p. $14.95. ISBN 0-02-768149-1. (Footsteps to America). 5-8

Bandon examines the lives of Chinese Americans. For them to leave their country was a major decision; therefore, Bandon tries to identify what in the history of the country would have precipitated such a move. Using personal narratives as a basis, she shows what the journey to America was like, what life in America has been like for those who came, the prejudice they faced, and the opportunities they found. For Further Reading and Index.

86. Bandon, Alexandra. **Dominican Americans**. New York: New Discovery, Silver Burdett, 1994. 112p. $14.95. ISBN 0-02-768152-1. (Footsteps to America). 5-8

Bandon examines the lives of Dominican Americans after they began to arrive in America around 1965. For them to leave their country was a major decision, so Bandon tries to identify what in the history of their country would have precipitated such a move. Using personal narratives as a basis, she shows what the journey to America was like, what life in America has been like for those who came, the prejudice they faced, and the opportunities they found. For Further Reading and Index.

87. Bandon, Alexandra. **Filipino Americans**. New York: New Discovery, Macmillan, 1993. 112p. $14.95. ISBN 0-02-768143-2. (Footsteps to America). 5-8

Bandon examines the lives of Filipino Americans. For them to leave their country was a major decision; therefore, Bandon tries to identify what in the history of their country would have precipitated such a move. Using personal narratives as a basis, she shows what the journey to America was like, what life in America has been like for those who came, the prejudice they faced, and the opportunities they found. For Further Reading and Index.

88. Bandon, Alexandra. **Korean Americans**. New York: New Discovery, Silver Burdett, 1994. 111p. $14.95. ISBN 0-02-768147-5. (Footsteps to America). 5-8

Bandon examines the lives of Korean Americans. For them to leave their country was a major decision; therefore, Bandon tries to identify what in the history of their country would have precipitated such a move. Using personal narratives as a basis, she shows what the journey to America was like, what life in America has been like for those who came, the prejudice they faced, and the opportunities they found. For Further Reading and Index.

89. Bandon, Alexandra. **Mexican Americans**. New York: New Discovery, Macmillan, 1993. 110p. $14.95. ISBN 0-02-768412-4. (Footsteps to America). 5-8

Bandon examines the lives of Mexican Americans. For them to leave their country was a major decision; therefore, Bandon tries to identify what in the history of their country would have precipitated such a move. Using personal narratives as a basis, she shows what the journey to America was like, what life in America has been like for those who came, the prejudice they faced, and the opportunities they found. For Further Reading and Index.

90. Bandon, Alexandra. **Vietnamese Americans**. New York: New Discovery, Silver Burdett, 1994. 112p. $14.95. ISBN 0-02-768146-7. (Footsteps to America). 5-8

Bandon examines the lives of Vietnamese Americans. For them to leave their country was a major decision; therefore, Bandon tries to identify what in the history of their country would have precipitated such a move. Using personal narratives as a basis, she shows what the journey to America was like, what life in America has been like for those who came, the prejudice they faced, and the opportunities they found. For Further Reading and Index.

91. Bandon, Alexandra. **West Indian Americans**. New York: New Discovery, Silver Burdett, 1994. 112p. $14.95. ISBN 0-02-768148-3. (Footsteps to America). 5-8

In this text, Bandon examines the lives of West Indian Americans. For them to decide to leave their country was a major decision; therefore, Bandon tries to identify what in the history of their country would have precipitated such a move. Using personal narratives as a basis, she shows what the journey to America was like, what life in America has been like for those who have come, the prejudices they faced, and the opportunities they found. For Further Reading and Index.

92. Banfield, Susan. **Charlemagne**. New York: Chelsea House, 1986. 112p. $18.95. ISBN 0-87754-592-8. (World Leaders Past and Present). 5 up

Charlemagne (742-814) came to the Frankish throne in 771 and fought savage Christian crusades against the Germans and the Moorish infidels in Spain. His politics and his religious zeal gained him a coronation as Emperor of the West in 800. As a lawmaker, a warrior, and a lover of learning, he helped revive Europe during his rule in the Carolingian Renaissance. He became the first great monarch of medieval Europe. Reproductions and maps enhance the text. Chronology, Further Reading, and Index.

93. Banfield, Susan. **Joan of Arc**. New York: Chelsea House, 1985. 112p. $18.95. ISBN 0-87754-556-1. (World Leaders Past and Present). 5 up

With little formal education, Joan of Arc (1412-1431) helped the French overcome the English occupation. She heard voices from St. Michael, St. Catherine, and St. Margaret, which convinced her that she had to help France. She persuaded the Dauphin Charles to give her an army, and in 1429, she led the French to victory at Orléans. She was eventually captured, imprisoned, tried, and executed. The Catholic Church declared her a saint in 1920, and her bravery is still legend. Photographs and reproductions enhance the text. Chronology, Further Reading, and Index.

94. Bangura, Abdul Karim. **Kipsigis**. New York: Rosen, 1995. 64p. $15.95. ISBN 0-8239-1765-7. (Heritage Library of African Peoples). 5-8

The Kipsigis, now in the western portion of Kenya, migrated from Egypt through the Sudan. Their proud history shows that they were able to govern themselves with equality. Topics discussed in addition to general history are the organization of their society, initiation, marriage and family, European contact and rule, and a view of their future. Photographs, boxed information, and maps enhance the text. Glossary, Further Reading, and Index.

95. Barboza, Steven. **Door of No Return: The Legend of Gorée Island**. New York: Cobblehill, Dutton, 1994. 42p. $14.99. ISBN 0-525-65188-8. 5 up

As early as 1433, Africans captured other Africans and sold them to Portuguese traders. They assembled the captured slaves on Gorée Island, two miles west of Dakar, Senegal. According to records in Lisbon, 3,589 slaves arrived there between 1486 and 1493. In 1619, a Dutch ship sailed into Jamestown, Virginia, with 20 slaves. Many Africans also owned slaves, and by the late 1800s slaves comprised two-thirds of many African societies. On Gorée, the wealthy kept slave houses. Anne Pepin, a *signare* who acted as the wife of the French governor of Senegal (although unmarried to him), had more than 35 slaves. The island today is a place of pilgrimage for Americans wanting to see where their ancestors started their long journey to servitude. Index.

96. Bard, Roberta. **Sir Francis Drake and the Struggle for an Ocean Empire**. New York: Chelsea House, 1992. 128p. $19.95. ISBN 0-7910-1302-2. (World Explorers). 5 up

Francis Drake (1540?-1596), the son of Protestants who had fled from Catholic persecution in 1549, began working aboard ship when he was still a teenager. He traveled to the Caribbean and the Spanish West Indies several times before he returned to raid Spanish treasure. He became the first Englishman to circumnavigate the globe, was elected to the House of Commons, attacked Spain in Cadiz harbor, battled the Spanish Armada, and died at sea. Photographs and reproductions enhance the text. Glossary, Bibliography, and Index.

97. Bawden, Nina. **Carrie's War**. Colleen Browning, illustrator. 1973. New York: HarperCollins, 1992. 160p. $14.89. ISBN 0-397-31450-7. 4-7

Evacuated from London in 1939, an eleven-year-old girl and her younger brother stay in a small Welsh town. They and another evacuee befriend a young boy who is unable to speak clearly and are, in turn, protected by the woman caring for him. As she returns to her family, Carrie sees that their house is afire, but she has no way to contact them. She thinks that her misbehavior prior to her departure caused the fire. Carrie's son finds out thirty years later that she had nothing to do with the fire, but her guilt and fears have controlled her life. *Carnegie Commendation* and *Phoenix Award*.

98. Bawden, Nina. **Henry**. Joyce Powzyk, illustrator. New York: Lothrop, Lee & Shepard, 1988. 119p. $15. ISBN 0-688-07894-X; New York: Yearling, Dell, 1990. 119p. $3.25pa. ISBN 0-440-40309-Xpa. 3-7

The first-person female narrator, her mother, and two brothers evacuate to Wales from England during World War II while her father fights. They find and tend a baby squirrel whom they name Henry. Soon she and the two boys are slightly jealous of the attention their mother gives to Henry. They try to adjust during the long separation by focusing on their schoolwork, the people who own the farm on which they live, and the farm animals. They realize that their mother is trying to cope with the absence of their father, but all of them have a similar problem. *Parenting's Reading Magic Award* and *American Library Association Notable Books for Children*.

99. Bawden, Nina. **The Peppermint Pig**. 1975. New York: H. G. Hall, 1987. 160p. $12.95pa. ISBN 0-440-40122-4pa. 3-6

In 1901, Poll's father takes the blame for a robbery he did not commit in order to keep a man from finding out that his son committed it. Poll and her mother and siblings go to live with an aunt while her father goes to the United States to work with his brother. They buy a runt pig which they later must slaughter, and they face other difficult situations as well. As she reaches maturity, Poll learns that much indecision and uncertainty fills life. *Guardian Award* and *Yorkshire Post Award*.

100. Baxter, Nicola. **Invaders and Settlers: Facts—Things to Make—Activities**. New York: Franklin Watts, 1994. 32p. $18.50. ISBN 0-531-14338-4. (Craft Topics). 5-8

The text covers the Romans, Britain, Anglo-Saxons, Alfred, later British kings, and William the Conqueror. Accompanying the illustrations and history are ideas for crafts. For example, coupled with the discussion of the Roman invasion of Britain are directions to create a Celtic shield. Glossary, Resources, and Index.

101. Baxter, Nicola. **Romans: Facts—Things to Make—Activities**. Nigel Longden, illustrator. New York: Franklin Watts, 1992. 32p. $18.50. ISBN 0-531-14143-8. (Craft Topics). 5-8

In addition to describing the daily life of Romans, the text gives ideas for making items that help in the comprehension of how something might have been done. Patterns and suggestions for materials to make a Roman villa, a mosaic, a victor's wreath, a theater mask, a writing tablet, a tunic and toga, and a statue are included. Glossary, Resources, and Index.

102. Baylis-White, Mary. **Sheltering Rebecca**. New York: Lodestar, 1991. 99p. $14.95. ISBN 0-525-67349-0. 4-6

Clarissa, grade six, asks her grandparents to help with a history project, so they tell her about their lives during 1937 to 1945 before they married and moved from England to Australia. Her grandmother had a German-Jewish refugee, Rebecca, as her friend. When Rebecca arrived, she could speak no English. As she learned, she shared her worries with Sally (Clarissa's grandmother) about her parents and her brother. After the war ended and Rebecca's brother, Helmut, came to England from a concentration camp, he met Sally. They married and became Clarissa's grandparents.

103. Beattie, Owen, and John Geiger. **Buried in Ice: The Mystery of a Lost Arctic Expedition**. Janet Wilson, illustrator. New York: Scholastic, Madison Press, 1992. 64p. $15.95. ISBN 0-590-43848-4. (Time Quest). 4 up

In 1845, Sir John Franklin led an expedition of 128 men to find the Northwest Passage between the Atlantic and Pacific Oceans. No one returned. In 1984, Owen Beattie, an archaeologist, found three graves of crewmen on a remote island in the Canadian Arctic, which have given insight into the voyage and its failure. The results of the find are reported, with photographs of the scene. Glossary, The Search for the Northwest Passage History, and Recommended Further Reading. *Notable Children's Trade Books in the Field of Social Studies, American Library Association Best Books for Young Adults, American Library Association Quick Picks for Reluctant Young Adult Readers,* and *Outstanding Science Trade Books for Children.*

104. Beatty, John, and Patricia Beatty. **Master Rosalind**. New York: Morrow, 1974. 221p. $11.25. ISBN 0-688-21819-9. 5-9

Rosalind, age twelve in 1598, dresses as a boy and walks to Oxford, England, to borrow a valuable book from her grandfather's friend. A man who knows the value of the book pretends to be crazy and kidnaps her. When she shows no talent for helping the man and his accomplice steal, they release her. Instead of returning home, she spends a year traveling with Shakespeare's players. After various events, someone finds out that she is not male, but in the interim she has received an inheritance and can return to her grandfather without ignominy.

105. 176. Beatty, Patricia. **Jonathan Down Under**. New York: Morrow, 1982. 219p. $10.25. ISBN 0-688-01467-4. 5-9

Jonathan Cole's father, crazy for gold in 1851, goes to Australia after little success in California and takes Jonathan with him. After Jonathan recovers from "sandy blight," a disease during which he stayed inside for several months and had his eyes scraped daily to keep him from going blind, he hears that his father's partner has left with their gold. Then a mine cave-in kills his father. Jonathan begins working for an Irish woman who has come to Australia to escape the potato famine, but she soon dies. When he helps others find gold, they give him money to return home because he is interested in neither gold nor Australia.

106. Beckett, Wendy. **The Duke and the Peasant**: Life in the Middle Ages. New York: Prestel, 1997. 30p. $14. ISBN 0-7913-1813-6. (Adventures in Art). 5-9

Paintings from the late medieval period recreate the lives of dukes and courtiers as well as of the peasants. Index.

107. Bedard, Michael. **Glass Town: The Secret World of the Brontë Children**. Laura Fernandez and Rick Jacobson, illustrators. New York: Atheneum, 1997. 38p. $16. ISBN 0-689-81185-3. 3-6

The Brontë sisters, Charlotte, Emily, and Anne, lived in their Victorian England home and, as children, wrote more than 100 miniature books and magazines before they began their adult novels, which made them famous.

108. **Belarus**. Minneapolis, MN: Lerner, 1993. 56p. $19.95. ISBN 0-8225-2811-8. (Then and Now). 5-9

Known as "White Russia," Belarus lies east of Poland, south of Latvia and Lithuania, and north of Ukraine. Originally inhabited by the Slavs, the country is trying to succeed after becoming independent in 1991. Photographs and maps enhance additional information about economics, geography, politics, and ethnography. Glossary and Index.

109. Bellairs, John. **The Trolley to Yesterday**. New York: Dial, 1989. 183p. $12.95. ISBN 0-8037-0582-4. 4-6

In this historical fantasy, Johnny, thirteen, and his friend join Professor Childermass on a trolley to Egypt in 14 B.C. and to Constantinople, arriving in 1453. In Turkey, they try to keep people from dying during the invasion, but are unsuccessful. When they return to the 1950s, they themselves are relieved to be alive.

110. Bender, Michael, author/illustrator. **Waiting for Filippo: The Life of Renaissance Architect Filippo Brunelleschi**. San Francisco: Chronicle, 1996. Unpaged. $19.95. ISBN 0-8118-0181-0. 3-7

This book details the life of Filippo Brunelleschi (1377-1446) of Florence, Italy, with pop-ups of some of the buildings he designed. *Parents Choice Honor Book.*

111.   Bennett, Russell, and Anna Sproule. **Mikhail Gorbachev: Changing the World Order**. Milwaukee, WI: Gareth Stevens, 1992. 68p. $16.95. ISBN 0-8368-0619-0. (People Who Made a Difference). 3-6

In 1985, Gorbachev (b. 1931) became the Soviet leader and changed the leadership style of the country. He favored *glasnost* (openness) and *perestroika* (rebuilding) to keeping secrets and tearing down. His policies led to the independence of the countries in the former Soviet Union after the destruction of the Berlin Wall in 1989. The text looks at his life and his rise to power. Organizations, Books, List of New Words, Important Dates, and Index.

112.   Bentley, Judith. **Archbishop Tutu of South Africa**. Springfield, NJ: Enslow, 1988. 96p. $16.95. ISBN 0-89490-180-X. 5-7

This book predates changes in South Africa to abolish apartheid, but it gives good background about this severe problem. In introducing Tutu's parents, the author presents historical information about their tribes, the Xhosa and the Tswana, and their encounters with the Boers. Tutu's educated father taught school and paid for Tutu (b. 1931) to attend mission schools, whereas white children were able to attend segregated public schools for free. Tutu gained admittance to medical school, but the family did not have enough money to pay for it. Instead, he began teaching. When he was twenty-five, however, his school closed, and he decided to become an Anglican priest, because a clergyman who opposed apartheid had treated him and his people with respect. As a black adult, Tutu had to carry a pass, and he as well as Nelson Mandela, who spoke for the African National Congress, were against such laws. In 1960, initial black protests against the white government caused deaths and shocked the world. Tutu soon qualified to attend King's College in England, and the government finally gave him permission to leave for four years. The taste of freedom made him refuse to accept his prior status, and he returned to England to work for the World Council of Churches. He received the Nobel Peace Prize for his efforts against apartheid, but not until the 1990s did apartheid end. Further Reading and Index.

113.   Berg, Lois Anne. **An Eritrean Family**. Minneapolis, MN: Lerner, 1996. 64p. $16.13; $8.95pa. ISBN 0-8225-3405-3; 0-8225-9755-1pa. (Journey Between Two Worlds). 5-7

Although not a history book, the text includes the history of the people of Eritrea as a background for understanding why families from Eritrea have had to leave Ethiopia. Photographs and personal experiences explain Eritrean social and religious traditions and how the people have had to adapt to a new culture to survive as refugees from a home they loved. Further Reading.

114.   Bergman, Tamar. **Along the Tracks**. Michael Swirsky, translator. Boston: Houghton Mifflin, 1991. 245p. $14.95. ISBN 0-395-55328-8. 6-10

Yankele is seven when World War II begins, and his family journeys from Lodz, Poland, toward the Urals in Russia. His father joins the Russian army. As Yankele and his mother travel by train, Yankele gets off during a bombing raid but does not get back on before the train leaves. Thus Yankele begins four years of wandering through Uzbekistan, surviving starvation and incarceration with petty theft and careful hiding. He eventually finds his mother and, miraculously, his father, who had been missing in action, alive in Poland. *Bulletin Blue Ribbon Book.*

115.   Bergman, Tamar. **The Boy from Over There**. Hillel Halkin, translator. Boston: Houghton Mifflin, 1988. 181p. $12.95. ISBN 0-395-43077-1. 5-8

When Rami's father brings an orphaned Jewish refugee from Poland to the kibbutz after World War II, some of the people welcome the newcomer and some do not. The boy has to learn to deal with his mother's death, and Rina, his best friend, has to cope with the loss of her father. After they accept the fact that they cannot bring back their parents, they begin to look forward to their life in the Jordan Valley after Israel's recognition as a country in 1948.

116.   Berliner, Don. **Before the Wright Brothers**. Minneapolis, MN: Lerner, 1990. 72p. $19.95. ISBN 0-8225-1588-1. 4-6

After discussing several theories about flying that have developed through the centuries, Berliner notes that the air screw principle, used by the Chinese in making toys as early as 400 B.C., and propeller-driven windmills in the Middle Ages were what finally worked rather than the ornithopter (flapping wings) approach. Without the many inventors before them, the Wright brothers probably could not have piloted their plane in 1903. Men upon whom they relied included George Cayley, who in the late eighteenth and early nineteenth centuries originated the airplane. Others after him were William Henson, John Stringfellow, Felix du Temple, Alexander Mozhaiski, Hiram Maxim, Clement Ader, Otto Lilienthal, Octave Chanute, Augustus Herring, Gustave Whitehead, Karl Jatho, and Samuel Langley. For Further Reading and Index.

117.   Bernhard, Brendan. **Pizarro, Orellana, and the Exploration of the Amazon**. New York: Chelsea House, 1991. 110p. $18.95; $7.95pa. ISBN 0-7910-1305-7; 0-7910-1529-7pa. (World Explorers). 5 up

Francisco de Orellana (d. c. 1546) and Francisco Pizarro (c. 1475-1541) journeyed through the Amazon Basin in the early sixteenth century. The text also discusses the Inca and the Spanish conquest of South America. Bibliography and Index.

118. Bernheim, Mark. **Father of the Orphans: The Story of Janusz Korczak**. New York: Lodestar, 1988. 139p. $14.95. ISBN 0-525-67265-6. 6-9

As a child in Poland, Korczak (born Henryk Goldszmit) was intensely lonely because his parents would not allow him to play with children below their social class. His father then went insane, adding to Korczak's alienation. After Korczak became a doctor, he devoted his time to orphans. He followed many of them to Treblinka in World War II, where they all died. Photographs, Bibliography, and Index.

119. Bernier-Grand, Carmen T. **Poet and Politician of Puerto Rico: Don Luis Muñoz Marín**. New York: Orchard, 1995. 118p. $15.95. ISBN 0-531-06887-0. 5-8

Don Luis Muñoz Marín (1898-1980), educated in the United States, wanted to be a poet. But his father's commitment to improving Puerto Rico influenced him so that he too became a politician. After the Liberal Party expelled him, he founded the Popular Democratic Party based on enhancing the lives of ordinary Puerto Rican families. He used aid from the United States to improve Puerto Rican facilities in Operation Bootstrap with his governing principle being "Give a man a fish, and he will have a single meal. Teach him to fish and he can eat the rest of his life." Later Muñoz Marín became the first governor of Puerto Rico in its new status as a commonwealth. Photographs enhance the text. Afterword, Appendix, Sources and Other Information, and Index.

120. Berrill, Margaret. **Mummies, Masks, & Mourners**. Chris Molan, illustrator. New York: Lodestar, Dutton, 1990. 48p. $14.95. ISBN 0-525-67282-6. (Time Detectives). 4-7

The "grave goods" that archaeologists find buried with the dead often reveal something about the culture and its burial customs. Berrill presents an unusual group of "finds." First are two Stone Age excavations: Çatal Hüyük in Turkey, found in 1958, and Haddenham, near Ely in England, the oldest wooden building ever discovered. From investigations of the pyramids in Egypt come mummies searching for the Field of Reeds. Recent excavations reveal Sumerians in 2500 B.C. Other places excavated include the Siberian Altai horsemen from 400 B.C.; the Lindow Man, who died 2,000 years ago and was recently discovered in a peat bog; the Lady Dai from the Han Dynasty in China, buried 2,100 years previously; Roman memorials in Ephesus; Basket Makers in the American Southwest at Four Corners; Hopewell mounds in the Ohio/Tennessee area; Viking Ship burials; Qilakitsoq of the Inuits, buried in 1475 and found in Greenland; and the Kalabar Ijaw funeral screens from Africa. Fact boxes give additional information about each burial place and its culture. Drawings and photographs, one of a piece of 2,000-year-old preserved tattooed skin, augment the text. Glossary and Index.

121. Beshore, George. **Science in Ancient China**. New York: Franklin Watts, 1988. 95p. $16.60. ISBN 0-531-10596-2. (First Book). 5-8

An introduction to China and its science precedes chapters on different developments from this culture. They include scanning the heavens, basic science and mathematics, healing and herbal medicine, finding food for the people, roads and canals, tools and technology, and contemporary debt to the culture for its discoveries. Photographs and drawings enhance the text. Glossary, Further Reading, and Index.

122. Beshore, George. **Science in Early Islamic Culture**. New York: Franklin Watts, 1988. 70p. $16.60. ISBN 0-531-10596-2. (First Book). 5-8

An introduction to early Islamic culture and its science precedes chapters on different developments. They include mathematics, astronomy, the study of optics or light and vision, alchemy, and contemporary debt to the culture for its discoveries. Drawings and Reproductions supplement the text. Glossary, Further Reading, and Index.

123. Besson, Jean-Louis, author/illustrator. **October 45: Childhood Memories of the War**. Carol Volk, translator. San Diego, CA: Creative Editions, Harcourt Brace, 1995. 94p. $22. ISBN 0-15-200955-8. 4-8

Jean-Louis Besson, age seven, and his family take a vacation to Normandy in 1939, which the Germans interrupt with the beginning of World War II. The family moves to a small Brittany village from Paris to avoid anticipated bombing and returns during the occupation, during which they face food shortages, rationing, hiding in subway stations during air raids, and the deportation of Jewish friends. To hear about the outside world, they have to secretly listen to British broadcasts. Because his family did not experience the horrors of the war that many faced, Besson's viewpoint in this story is that of a young boy whose main concern is the unpleasant and uncomfortable train ride to Brittany. Each page indicates a month and a year as he tells of the lovely German uniforms and the American ballpoint pens, along with other observations during the period. *Prix Octognone, International Center of Children's Literature, France.*

124. Bianchi, Robert Steven. **The Nubians: People of the Ancient Nile**. Brookfield, CT: Millbrook Press, 1994. 63p. $15.90. ISBN 1-56294-356-1. 5-8

The Nubian civilization developed in southern Egypt about 10,000 years ago, along the banks of the Nile River between the modern cities of Aswan, Egypt, and Khartoum, Sudan, while the pharaohs were building their pyramids to the north. The Egyptians often mentioned the Nubians, but the Nubian written language,

Meroitic, did not develop until 250 B.C. They did carve pictures in sandstone, and archaeologists study these along with artifacts discovered in the area to find other clues about the civilization. Important Dates in the History of Ancient Nubia, Find Out More, and Index.

125. Biel, Timothy L. **Charlemagne**. San Diego, CA: Lucent, 1997. 127p. $17.96. ISBN 1-56006-074-3 (The Importance Of). 6 up

Primary and secondary sources help tell the history of the Frankish kingdom and reveal Charlemagne (768-814) and his achievements. The text explores both the negative and positive aspects of Charlemagne's character but clearly asserts his influence on the future of Europe.

126. Biel, Timothy L. **Pompeii**. San Diego, CA: Lucent, 1989. 64p. $12.95. ISBN 1-56006-000-X. (World Disasters). 5-8

In A.D. 79, Vesuvius erupted and destroyed the ancient city of Pompeii, south of Rome, Italy. Seventeen hundred years later, archaeologists uncovered many of its secrets and exposed the life of the people in the Roman Empire, in general and specifically on that day. Bibliography and Index.

127. Biel, Timothy Levi. **The Black Death**. Maurie Manning and Michael Spackman, illustrators. San Diego, CA: Lucent, 1989. 64p. $12.95. ISBN 1-56006-001-8. 5-7

The title fails to reveal the myriad details included in this book about life in England during the Middle Ages around 1347. Important terms appear in bold type for easy identification of information about the feudal system, the church hierarchy, the growth of cities, the plague itself, and its treatment. Documents from the years 1347 to 1350 chronicle the spread of the plague from the Tatars to Messina, Italy, and up to England via Europe; eventually, the Black Death killed 25 million of the 60 million living in Europe, taking more lives than both World Wars I and II combined. Plague outbreaks continued every decade or so, including a serious outbreak in England during 1665. Not until 1894 did a Swiss scientist, investigating an outbreak in Hong Kong, connect the disease to rats. Glossary, Further Reading, Other Works Consulted, and Index.

128. Biel, Timothy Levi. **The Crusades**. San Diego, CA: Lucent, 1995. 128p. $14.95. ISBN 1-56006-245-2. (World History). 6 up

The text gives a thorough treatment of the crusades, starting with a chronology of the most important dates beginning in 1027 and continuing through 1270. It looks at the different classes of people who went on the journeys and the roles of leaders, including Pope Leo IX, Urban II, Godfrey of Bouillon, Bernard of Clairvaux, King Louis VII, Eleanor of Aquitaine, and Richard the Lionheart. Photographs and reproductions enhance the text. Glossary, Further Reading, Primary Sources, and Index.

129. Bierhorst, John, ed. **The Hungry Woman: Myths and Legends of the Aztecs**. New York: Morrow, 1984. 148p. $11.95; $9pa. ISBN 0-688-02766-0; 0-688-12301-5pa. 5-10

Aztec legends began with the Toltec civilization in its capital, Tula, center of the arts and sciences, which flourished from 150 B.C. through A.D. 850 as Teotihuacán. When the city fell, northern tribes intermarried, and they all became known as Aztecs. Eventually Mexicans founded their capital on the remaining, though undesirable, land, but their armies gained a reputation for fierceness. Thus, by 1440, Mexico, Texcoco, and Tlacopan had formed an alliance. The empire took shape under the fourth ruler, Itzcoatl, and reached its zenith under the ninth ruler, Montezuma II. In the myths two important spirits, Quetzalcoatl (creator) and Tezcatlipoca (destroyer) oppose each other. Because the bearded Quetzalcoatl was supposed to return in the year 1 Reed (Aztec calendar), Montezuma greeted the bearded Cortés in 1519 as if a returning god. Two other important figures in the legends are Tonantzin (Our Mother), identified now with the Lady of Mercy at Guadalupe, and *la llorona*, the weeping woman who lures men to their deaths after she murdered her children. In the stories, separating history from legend is often impossible. Guide to Terms and References.

130. Biesty, Stephen, and Richard Platt. **Man-of-War**. Boston: Dorling Kindersley, Houghton Mifflin, 1993. 27p. $16.95. ISBN 1-56458-321-X. (Cross-sections). 4 up

This British warship from the time of Napoleon was a complex building. Detailed illustrations give the cross-sections of the ship. Among the topics covered, along with appropriate pictures, are health, leisure, discipline, navigating, work, cooking and eating, battle stations, sleeping, officers, and admiral's privileges. Glossary and Index.

131. Bingham, Mindy. **Berta Benz and the Motorwagen: The Story of the First Automobile Journey**. Itoko Maeno, illustrator. San Francisco: Advocacy Press, 1989. 48p. $14.95. ISBN 0-911655-38-7. 3-5

In 1888, a German housewife and her two sons steal away from home in one of the motorcars that Karl Benz invented. A local law restricts the use of the invention, so Benz cannot prove how useful it could be. His wife purchases fuel at pharmacies, but the cross-country trip is successful in showing the value of the invention.

132. Birch, Beverley. **Louis Braille**. Milwaukee, WI: Gareth Stevens, 1989. 68p. $16.95. ISBN 0-8368-0097-4. (People Who Have Helped the World). 3-6

In 1812, when he was only three, Louis Braille stuck an awl in his eye. An ensuing infection spread to his other eye, and he lost the sight in both. Persons seeing his intelligence encouraged his family to send him to school in Paris. There, when only fourteen, he built on the work of another and devised a simple system of raised letters that blind students could rapidly learn. He was a teacher, a musician, and a loyal friend throughout the government intrigues of Napoleon and those who followed, until his untimely death of tuberculosis at the age of forty-three.

133. Birch, Beverley. **Marie Curie: Pioneer in the Study of Radiation**. Milwaukee, WI: Gareth Stevens, 1990. 68p. $16.95. ISBN 0-8368-0388-4. (People Who Made a Difference). 3-6

Marie Curie (1867-1934) had to leave Poland to finish her education. In Paris, at the Sorbonne, she met and married Pierre Curie, and their research led to the discovery of two new elements, polonium and radium. She won two Nobel Prizes for her work, created a portable x-ray machine to take to the battle front during World War I to quickly locate shrapnel in soldiers' bodies, and died from an unknown disease eventually identified as radiation poisoning. For More Information, Glossary, Chronology, and Index.

134. Birch, Beverley, and Pam Brown. **Father Damien: Missionary to a Forgotten People**. Milwaukee, WI: Gareth Stevens, 1990. 68p. $16.95. ISBN 0-8368-0389-2. (People Who Made a Difference). 3-6

Josef de Veuster-Wouters (1840-1885), born in Belgium, decided to become a priest. He went to Molokai, a leper colony in the Pacific Islands, where he stayed to help the people trapped by a disease that had no cure. He established laws and decency in the colony, to which people were exiled against their will, and eventually contracted the disease himself. Photographs show leprosy's terrible effect. Organizations, Books, Glossary, Chronology, and Index.

135. Birch, Beverley, and Michael Nicholson. **Mahatma Gandhi: Champion of Human Rights**. Milwaukee, WI: Gareth Stevens, 1990. 68p. $16.95. ISBN 0-8368-0390-6. (People Who Made a Difference). 3-6

Mohandas Gandhi was born in 1869 into the *Vaisya* caste, below the *Brahmins* (priests) and the *Kshatriyas* (soldiers or rulers), but above the *Sudra* (workers) and those in no caste (the "untouchables") in India. As a young lawyer, trained in England, Gandhi faced discrimination in South Africa because his skin was brown. He stayed in South Africa for twenty-one years, helping the blacks use unarmed protests or *satyagraha* against their country's unfair laws. Although most of Gandhi's ideas centered on the *Bhagavad Gita* (the Hindu religious work), he borrowed tenets from other religions such as Christianity (in particular Jesus' Sermon on the Mount.) Strict Hindus hated him. He believed in *samakhava* (not being upset by pain or pleasure), *aparigraha* (rejecting money and possessions), *ahimsa* (nonviolence to all living things), and meditation. When he returned to India, people called him "Mahatma," or "great soul." After the British massacred Indians in 1919, Gandhi began working to peacefully overthrow the British government. Although not with the peace that Gandhi had envisioned, India gained independence on August 15, 1947. The next year, a fellow Hindu assassinated Gandhi. Organizations, Books, List of New Words, Important Dates, and Index.

136. Birchman, David Francis. **A Tale of Tulips, a Tale of Onions**. Jonathan Hunt, illustrator. New York: Four Winds, 1994. Unpaged. $15.95. ISBN 0-02-710112-6. 3-5

While they enjoy tulips in seventeenth-century Holland, the gardener Ed Vard Grooter's love of tulips and sea captain Drooter Van Zooter's love of onions almost causes a major conflict.

137. Bisel, Sara C. **The Secrets of Vesuvius: Exploring the Mysteries of an Ancient Buried City**. New York: Scholastic, 1990. 64p. $6.95pa. ISBN 0-590-43851-4pa. (Time Quest Book). 4-7

Alternating chapters of historical fiction and of history present the story of an archaeologist who, in 1982, first began exhuming the bones of people buried in Herculaneum by the sixty-five feet of volcanic material blown from Mount Vesuvius in A.D. 79. Pliny recorded his view of the volcano from twenty miles across the bay, and his uncle, who had tried to get closer, died in it. At Pompeii, on the other side of the mountain, twelve feet of ash and pumice buried the inhabitants. Bisel's careful assessment of the bones and the artifacts surrounding them weave an interesting story of what the life of a slave girl serving in a wealthy family might have been—including her sore gums with two recently pulled teeth. Glossary, Recommended Further Reading, and pictures of the Buried Town through the Ages. *Outstanding Science Trade Books for Children.*

138. Bishop, Claire Huchet. **Twenty and Ten**. William Pène du Bois, illustrator. 1952. New York: Peter Smith, 1984. 76p. $17.75. ISBN 0-8446-6168-6. New York: Puffin, Penguin, 1991. 76p. $3.99pa. ISBN 0-14-031076-2pa. 5-9

During World War II in France, Janet and twenty of her classmates are evacuated to the countryside with the Catholic sister who teaches them. When ten Jewish children arrive and hide in a nearby cave, all risk their lives by denying any knowledge of the children to the Nazis who come questioning. They continue to feed the children as long as needed. *Child Study Children's Book Committee at Bank Street College Award.*

139. Bjork, Christine, and Lena Anderson, author/illustrators. **Linnea in Monet's Garden**. Joan Sandin, translator. Stockholm, Sweden: R&S and New York: Farrar, Straus & Giroux, 1987. 53p. $15. ISBN 91-29-58314-4. 4-7

Linnea and her friend, Mr. Bloom, go from Sweden to Paris to visit the Marmottan Museum where many of Monet's paintings hang. Then they go to Giverny, his garden outside of Paris. There Linnea sees some of the lovely scenes Monet painted. The text also includes information about Monet's life as an Impressionist painter (1840-1926). What Happened When.

140. Black, Wallace B., and Jean F. Blashfield. **Bataan and Corregidor**. New York: Crestwood House, 1991. 48p. $12.95. ISBN 0-89686-557-6. (World War II 50th Anniversary). 5-8

After the attack on Pearl Harbor, the Japanese went to the Philippines. Japanese air attacks led the United States to use Corregidor in Manila Bay as the command post while Bataan, part of the island of Luzon across from Manila, was the stronghold for troops to hold off the invading Japanese. The Battle of Bataan under General MacArthur failed, and on April 9, 1942, the Allies surrendered it to the Japanese. Then Corregidor was surrendered on May 6, 1942. Black-and-white photographs supplement the text. Glossary and Index.

141. Black, Wallace B., and Jean F. Blashfield. **Battle of Britain**. New York: Crestwood House, 1991. 48p. $12.95. ISBN 0-89686-553-3. (World War II 50th Anniversary). 5-8

When the German *Luftwaffe* bombed Great Britain for three months in 1940, it fortunately made some errors. A Channel battle ensued from July 10 until August 12. Then the Eagle Attack occurred from August 13 to September 6, followed by the Blitz from September 7 to 30. The courage of both the British public and the British flyers contributed to the *Luftwaffe*'s failure to achieve its goals. Black-and-white photographs highlight the text. Glossary and Index.

142. Black, Wallace B., and Jean F. Blashfield. **Battle of the Atlantic**. New York: Crestwood House, 1991. 48p. $12.95. ISBN 0-89686-558-4. (World War II 50th Anniversary). 4-9

This account of the Battle of the Atlantic tells of the struggle that the Allied forces had in trying to keep the North Atlantic free of German U-boats, or submarines, during World War II. On September 3, 1939, when the Germans torpedoed the *Athenia*, a British ocean liner with 1,300 passengers, they claimed that they thought it was an armed merchant ship. Photos and diagrams show the blitzkrieg at sea. U-boats and bombers, along with convoys to Russia, appeared before the U.S. Navy joined the battle, and the Allies fought back. Although U-boats were discovered off the coast of New York, antisubmarine warfare helped control them. Black-and-white photographs augment the text. Closer Look at German U-Boats and Allied Ships and Planes, Glossary, and Index.

143. Black, Wallace B., and Jean F. Blashfield. **Battle of the Bulge**. New York: Crestwood House, 1992. 48p. $12.95. ISBN 0-89686-568-1. (World War II 50th Anniversary). 5-8

The road to Ardennes started in 1944. The Watch on the Rhine was Hitler's plan to divide the American and British attack before the Battle of the Bulge, December 16, 1944. He failed, but with Bastogne under siege, the German commander asked for an Allied surrender. The Allied commander, McAuliffe, replied, "Nuts!" On December 26, General Patton broke through the German lines and stopped the siege. Nordwind and Bodenplatte were two plans of the German offense that failed, and the Germans withdrew by January 22, 1945. The Bridge at Remagen was where the Allies crossed into German territory on March 7, 1945. Black-and-white photographs highlight the text. Glossary and Index.

144. Black, Wallace B., and Jean F. Blashfield. **Blitzkrieg**. New York: Crestwood House, 1991. 48p. $12.95. ISBN 0-89686-552-5. (World War II 50th Anniversary). 5-8

In 1939, the Germans attacked Poland. In the "lightning war" of the *Blitzkrieg,* they used tanks to swoop across the countryside with aircraft and artillery supporting them. Names such as *Panzer* (tanks), *Luftwaffe* (air force), *Wehrmacht* (German army), and *Stuka* (dive bombers) became common words. Two days later, on September 3, 1939, England and France declared war on Germany, because they had promised to support Poland. War in Scandinavia followed, first against the Soviets and then against the Germans. The battle for France began when the Germans invaded Holland in 1940. People were rescued from France through Dunkirk on May 26, after the Germans arrived on May 19; France surrendered on June 6, 1940. Black-and-white photographs supplement the text. Glossary and Index.

145. Black, Wallace B., and Jean F. Blashfield. **Bombing Fortress Europe**. New York: Crestwood House, 1992. 48p. $12.95. ISBN 0-89686-562-2. (World War II 50th Anniversary). 5 up

Hitler's "Fortress Europe" was to take back lands Germany had lost during World War I, such as the Saar (the Rhineland bordering France and Memel on Germany's northern border) and Poland. By the end of 1940, Hitler controlled all of central and most of western Europe. Great Britain's only recourse was to bomb the Fortress, beginning in 1941; thus the Eighth Air Force was born. After four disastrous missions, the Ploesti raid, Operation Pointblank, Schweinfurt, and Regensburg, Britain began preparations for D-Day and the Battle for Berlin. Black-and-white photographs augment the text. Glossary and Index.

146.   Black, Wallace B., and Jean F. Blashfield. **D-Day**. New York: Crestwood House, 1992. 48p. $12.95. ISBN 0-89686-566-6. (World War II 50th Anniversary). 5 up

In planning for D-Day, the Allies decided to invade the Normandy beaches to retake France. Operation Neptune called for naval operations to land on the Normandy beaches while protected from the air by the Allied forces. The Germans delayed in their pursuit, and the June 6, 1944, Allied invasion was successful. Black-and-white photographs supplement the text. Glossary and Index.

147.   Black, Wallace B., and Jean F. Blashfield. **Desert Warfare**. New York: Crestwood House, 1992. 48p. $12.95. ISBN 0-89686-561-4. (World War II 50th Anniversary). 5 up

Italy had a disaster in Africa when the British took control of East Africa in February 1941. The German army, with Rommel, the Desert Fox, in charge, came to rescue the Italian forces. The British retreated to El Alamein, 240 miles from Egypt, but Montgomery took charge and defeated Rommel. The Allied Operation Torch invasion led to the race for Tunis. Next was the Battle of Kasserine Pass, which the British won because the Germans could not agree on the best plan of attack. Victory at Hill 609 prepared the way for the May 13, 1943, invasion of Italy. Black-and-white photographs supplement the text. Glossary and Index.

148.   Black, Wallace B., and Jean F. Blashfield. **Flattops at War**. New York: Crestwood House, 1992. 48p. $12.95. ISBN 0-89686-559-2. (World War II 50th Anniversary). 5 up

After Pearl Harbor, the Battle of Coral Sea took place in February 1942. The Battle of Midway followed in June 1942. In these battles, the flattops (aircraft carriers) were most important. They continued to escort U-boats and participated in the Marianas "Turkey Shoot," June 19-21, 1944. Photographs of the war with flattops and planes of the U.S. Navy correlate with the text. Glossary and Index.

149.   Black, Wallace B., and Jean F. Blashfield. **Guadalcanal**. New York: Crestwood House, 1992. 48p. $12.95. ISBN 0-89686-560-6. (World War II 50th Anniversary). 5 up

The Japanese attacked Midway Island on June 4, 1942. Following the attack, the Allies decided to invade Guadalcanal in August. Land battles ensued, as did sea battles, culminating with the Battle of the Solomon Islands on November 12, 1942. The Air Force helped, and the Japanese finally withdrew from Guadalcanal in February 1943. Black-and-white photographs augment the text. Index.

150.   Black, Wallace B., and Jean F. Blashfield. **Hiroshima and the Atomic Bomb**. New York: Crestwood House, 1993. 48p. $12.95. ISBN 0-89686-571-1. (World War II 50th Anniversary). 5 up

In 1942, the Manhattan Project in Los Alamos and uranium manufacturing at Oak Ridge, Tennessee, simultaneously allowed the creation of the atomic bomb. After Iwo Jima and Okinawa, the Allies firebombed Tokyo in March 1945. Although the Japanese were starving, they kept fighting. The *Enola Gay* dropped "Little Boy," the first atomic bomb ordered by President Truman, on August 6, 1945, at 8:16 A.M. After the second bomb ("Fat Man") on Nagasaki three days later, Japan surrendered. Black-and-white photographs supplement the text. Glossary and Index.

151.   Black, Wallace B., and Jean F. Blashfield. **Invasion of Italy**. New York: Crestwood House, 1992. 48p. $12.95. ISBN 0-89686-565-7. (World War II 50th Anniversary). 5 up

In 1943, Operation Husky marked the invasion of Sicily to gain control of the Mediterranean Sea. The Allied forces landed there on July 10, 1943, under British Field Marshal Sir Harold Alexander, and Italy surrendered on September 1. Then the Allies invaded southern Italy. The Italian fleet surrendered, and the Germans retreated toward Rome. The Allies became temporarily trapped at Anzio because of misunderstandings and delays. The Battle for Monte Cassino occurred in late 1944, and Rome finally fell on June 4, 1944. The Germans made their new line 150 miles north of Rome before they surrendered Italy on April 29, 1945, after Mussolini's assassination. Black-and-white photographs augment the text. Glossary and Index.

152.   Black, Wallace B., and Jean F. Blashfield. **Island Hopping in the Pacific**. New York: Crestwood House, 1992. 48p. $12.95. ISBN 0-89686-567-3. (World War II 50th Anniversary). 5 up

Japan threatened Australia in 1942, and the first encounter with naval forces occurred at the Battle of the Coral Sea. The strategy of island-hopping began from Guadalcanal and Papua, New Guinea. The Japanese had Rabaul, a fortress on the island of New Britain, that the Allies decided to capture after taking the Solomons and New Guinea. In 1944, the Allies' target date for retaking Philippines and Formosa (Taiwan) was February 1945, but they succeeded by June 1944. General MacArthur returned to the Philippines in October 1944 and plotted to take Iwo Jima. Black-and-white photographs augment the text. Glossary and Index.

153. Black, Wallace B., and Jean F. Blashfield. **Iwo Jima and Okinawa**. New York: Crestwood House, 1993. 48p. $12.95. ISBN 0-89686-569-X. (World War II 50th Anniversary). 5 up

The battles of Coral Sea and Midway occurred in 1945 before the Marines began landing on Iwo Jima beaches. They captured Mount Suribachi on February 23, 1945. Then they continued until victory on June 20 with Operation Iceberg. The Allied forces needed Okinawa for a base from which to launch other attacks on the Japanese. Black-and-white photographs highlight the text. Glossary and Index.

154. Black, Wallace B., and Jean F. Blashfield. **Jungle Warfare**. New York: Crestwood House, 1992. 48p. $12.95. ISBN 0-89686-563-0. (World War II 50th Anniversary). 5 up

In January 1942, Japan invaded Burma. The Allied commanders Vinegar Joe Stillwell, Chiang Kai-Shek, and Claire Chennault of the Flying Tigers in France, disagreed about approaches to the difficult jungle terrain. Then Wingate's Chindit Raiders, British guerrilla forces, completed daring missions so that Wingate earned the label of "half genius and half mad." Merrill's Marauders were America's jungle fighters. Also in this area were the U.S. Air Force and the OSS, forerunner of the CIA. The last campaigns in the China-India-Burma area occurred in 1945. Black-and-white photographs supplement the text. Glossary and Index.

155. Black, Wallace B., and Jean F. Blashfield. **Pearl Harbor!** New York: Crestwood House, 1991. 48p. $12.95. ISBN 0-89686-555-X. (World War II 50th Anniversary). 5-8

In 1941, when the Japanese bombed the Pacific fleet at Pearl Harbor, America was ill-prepared for combat but still declared war on Japan. This account discusses the Japanese strategy and tactics and why the American forces were surprised by the attack. Black-and-white photographs complement the text. Glossary and Index.

156. Black, Wallace B., and Jean F. Blashfield. **Russia at War**. New York: Crestwood House, 1991. 48p. $12.95. ISBN 0-89686-556-8. (World War II 50th Anniversary). 4-8

The Germans attacked Russia on June 22, 1941, although Joseph Stalin and Adolf Hitler were supposedly friends. The major points of engagement included Barbarossa, where the Germans invaded; the Siege of Leningrad, which lasted 900 days; Operation Typhoon, during which Moscow awaited attack; the Battle of Stalingrad; and the beginning of the end at Kursk. Other information on partisans and guerrilla warfare also appears. Glossary and Index.

157. Black, Wallace B., and Jean F. Blashfield. **Victory in Europe**. New York: Crestwood House, 1992. 48p. $12.95. ISBN 0-89686-570-3. (World War II 50th Anniversary). 5 up

The text gives an overview of World War II in Europe, the trek eastward from the Rhine, the Russian thousand-mile front, Germany surrounded, the Battle of Berlin in 1945, and the unconditional German surrender on May 7, 1945. The book also covers the Holocaust, starting with *Kristallnacht* (Crystal Night), as it looks at the cost of the war to all. Capsule biographies of Allied leaders end the information. Black-and-white photographs supplement the text. Glossary and Index.

158. Black, Wallace B., and Jean F. Blashfield. **War Behind the Lines**. New York: Crestwood House, 1992. 48p. $12.95. ISBN 0-89686-564-9. (World War II 50th Anniversary). 5 up

During World War II, battles behind the lines helped win the war. The text looks at the British Secret Services, the OSS of the Americans, the organization of the Resistance against the Nazis, the *Maquis* or Resistance heroes, women and the underground war, the Resistance in Norway, *Chetniks* (Yugoslavians) and Partisans (Communists against Hitler in other countries), and Russian Partisans. Heroes of the Resistance include Major General William Donovan, Marshal Tito, and General Charles de Gaulle. Glossary and Index.

159. Blair, David Nelson. **The Land and People of Bolivia**. New York: Lippincott, 1990. 208p. $15.89. ISBN 0-397-32383-2. (Portraits of the Nations). 5-8

A combination of current information and historical background shows that Bolivia was an important site of the Tiahuanaco culture between 400 B.C. and A.D. 1200 on Lake Titicaca. The Incas rose to power in the area by the 1520s, with an empire of 6 million people stretching over 2,500 miles. The Spanish explorers Cortés and later Pizarro arrived and conquered the Incas. Simon Bolívar freed the Bolivians from Spanish rule by 1825. In 1952, the Chaco War erupted, with workers challenging their employers. By 1979, Bolivia had a female president, Lydia Tejada. Further Reading, Filmography, Diskography, and Index.

160. Blakely, Roger K. **Wolfgang Amadeus Mozart**. San Diego, CA: Lucent, 1993. 112p. $16.95. ISBN 1-56006-028-X. (The Importance Of). 5-8

Wolfgang Amadeus Mozart (1756-1791) rarely used his middle name, preferring Amadée or no middle name. Sometimes he composed as he played; other times he seemed to be merely writing down the music that was all in his head. Mozart produced music both for his own pleasure and for money. His music reflected his era, and he wrote sacred music as well as the orderly secular music expected during the Enlightenment. He enjoyed parties and had a sense of humor, but he realized the gift of each day and the burden of bringing renown to Austria, his country, through his music. Notes, Glossary, For Further Reading, Works Consulted, and Index.

161. Blassingame, Wyatt. **Ponce de León**. Russ Hoover, illustrator. New York: Chelsea Juniors, 1991. 100p. $14.95. ISBN 0-7910-1493-2. (Discovery Biography). 3-7

Juan Ponce de León (1474-1521) learned to be a soldier as a boy so that he could fight the Moors in Spain. He decided to join Columbus's second voyage, and he and his family spent the rest of his life in the New World. He is still credited with discovering Florida, although John Cabot may have been there fifteen years previously, or the Norsemen 500 years before.

162. Blue, Rose, and Corrine Naden. **People of Peace**. Brookfield, CT: Millbrook Press, 1994. 80p. $18.90. ISBN 1-56294-409-6. 5-8

Because some people refused to compromise with the status quo and instead worked for peace, they made the world better than before. Some of these people won the Nobel Peace Prize for their efforts, but they have all saved lives. The people presented here are Andrew Carnegie (United States, 1835-1919), Jane Addams (United States, 1860-1935), Woodrow Wilson (United States, 1856-1924), Mohandas Gandhi (India, 1869-1948), Ralph Bunche (United States, 1904-1971), Dag Hammarskjöld (Sweden, 1905-1961), Jimmy Carter (United States, b. 1924), Desmond Tutu (South Africa, b. 1931), Oscar Arias Sanchez (Costa Rica, b. 1941), Betty Williams (Northern Ireland, b. 1943), and Mairead Corrigan Maguire (Northern Ireland, b. 1944). Conclusion, For Further Reading, and Index.

163. Blumberg, Rhoda. **The Remarkable Voyages of Captain Cook**. New York: Bradbury, 1991. 137p. $18.95. ISBN 0-02-711682-4. 6 up

James Cook (1728-1779) took three voyages around the world. Possible riches in the southern continents lured him to take the first two; on the third he was searching for the Northwest Passage between the Atlantic and the Pacific Oceans. He traveled from the heat of Tahiti to the cold of Antarctica and to other places around the globe. He stayed in Hawaii on his last voyage, departed with gifts, and returned after a storm. The Hawaiians were unhappy to see him return, and they killed him. Photographs augment the text. Notes, Bibliography, and Index. *Bulletin Blue Ribbon Book.*

164. Boas, Jacob, ed. **We Are Witnesses: Five Diaries of Teenagers Who Died in the Holocaust**. New York: Edge, Henry Holt, 1995. 196p. $15.95. ISBN 0-8050-3702-0. 6 up

Teenagers who did not survive the World War II Holocaust wrote the diaries presented in this book. They are David Rubinowicz in Poland, Yitzhak Rudashevski in Lithuania, Moshe Ze'ev Flinker in Belgium, Éva Heyman in Hungary, and Anne Frank in Holland. The diaries all give insight into the fears and hopes that these young people had during their short lives. Notes and Index. *American Library Association Notable Books for Young Adults* and *Notable Children's Trade Books in the Field of Social Studies.*

165. Bonvillain, Nancy. **The Haidas: People of the Northwest Coast**. Brookfield, CT: Millbrook Press, 1994. 64p. $15.90. ISBN 1-56294-491-6. (Native Americans). 5-8

The Haida ancestors settled on the Queen Charlotte Islands in British Columbia, Canada, c. 1000. Many died in Alaska after 1750 from smallpox. Part of their culture was the celebration of potlatches and ceremonial dances that Canada outlawed in 1884. In the twentieth century, the Haidas joined with the Tlingits to file a land claim against the United States in Alaska, which they won. As they have become integrated into Alaskan and Canadian life, they have tried to preserve their identity through their traditions and artifacts. Important Dates, Glossary, Bibliography, and Index.

166. Booth, Martin. **War Dog: A Novel**. New York: Simon & Schuster, 1997. 133p. $15. ISBN 0-689-81380-5. 6-9

The owner of the black Labrador Jet has trained him to poach. After her owner is arrested, she begins to serve the British army in World War II by finding wounded soldiers and casualties in bombed cities. When she accompanies the military to Italy, she encounters her original owner.

167. Boraks-Nemetz, Lillian. **The Old Brown Suitcase: A Teenager's Story of War and Peace**. Port Angeles, WA: Ben-Simon, 1994. 148p. $9.50pa. ISBN 0-914539-10-8pa. 6-10

In alternating chapters, the reader follows Slava's story as a child in the Warsaw ghetto and as a teenager safe in Canada. By starting with the Canadian segment, the author alleviates the reader's fear that Slava might die in World War II's Nazi camps. Slava's parents change her name to Elizabeth, but unfeeling, wealthy children who have no idea what she has endured still persecute her for being Jewish and for being unable to speak English well. Her father, trained to be a lawyer, finally buys a delicatessen, but never enjoys the work. Slava remembers her little sister who did not survive the war, but one boy is kind to her, and she soon realizes that she cares for him more than just as a friend. *Sheila A. Egoff Children's Book Prize.*

168.   Borden, Louise. **The Little Ships: The Heroic Rescue at Dunkirk in World War II**. Michael Foreman, illustrator. New York: Simon & Schuster, Margaret K. McElderry, 1997. 32p. $15. ISBN 0-689-80827-5. 3-5

A young English girl who sails on her father's fishing boat, one of 861 small ships, to help rescue the soldiers at Dunkirk in May of 1940 during World War II tells the story in verse. Her brother John who waits to be rescued from behind the lines that she sees onshore stays in her mind as her father navigates their boat through the harbor while German planes bomb from overhead.

169.   Bortz, Fred. **Catastrophe!: Great Engineering Failure—and Success**. New York: W. H. Freeman, 1995. 80p. $19.95; $13.95pa. ISBN 0-7167-6538-1; 0-7167-6539-Xpa. (Scientific American's Mystery of Science). 5-9

Six engineering debacles have changed the lives of people who experienced them and lived as well as the families of those who died. The six discussed in the text are the collapse of the Kansas City Hyatt skywalk in 1980; the Tacoma Narrows Bridge in 1940; the crash of Eastern Airlines Flight 401 in Florida in 1972; the U.S. Space Shuttle *Challenger* disaster in 1986; nuclear power plant accidents (Three-Mile Island in 1979 and Chernobyl in 1986); and "The Great Northeast Blackout" of 1965. By explaining the science behind each disaster, the text shows how inadequate planning caused the problems and how engineers have corrected them. Photographs and Index.

170.   Bosse, Malcolm. **The Examination**. New York: Farrar, Straus & Giroux, 1994. 296p. $17. ISBN 0-374-32234-1. 6-10

Around 1448, in China, Hong Chen decides to sell his prized fighting crickets to finance his brother's trip to Beijing for the government examinations that can earn his brother fame and lifelong wealth. Troubles and tests of varied kinds—rains, famine, locusts, and pirates—occur during the journey to Beijing. They eventually arrive, and Hong delivers a mysterious letter, which he has carried throughout the trip, to a barber. Hong finds that he has his own "exam" in Beijing while his brother exhibits his knowledge of and belief in Confucius. Both succeed, with Chen being welcomed inside the Forbidden City and Hong finding his future.

171.   Bosse, Malcolm. **Tusk and Stone**. Emeryville, CA: Front Street, 1995. 244p. $15.95. ISBN 1-886910-01-4. 6-10

As Arjun travels across India in the seventh century, bandits attack the caravan, kill people, kidnap his sister, and drug him before selling him into the army. Arjun humbly begins to rebuild his life, saying that he will serve those well who bought his soldiering. He rises in the military to become an elephant handler and then a mounted soldier. His Brahmin pride wins over his concept of karma when he is a warrior and faces a rival who almost destroys him. Then he must again rebuild his life, this time as a stonecutter and carver. In that profession, he becomes introspective about his spiritual beliefs.

172.   Bowler, Mike. **Trains**. Steve Herridge, Paul Higgens, and Martin Woodward, illustrators. Austin, TX: Raintree/Steck-Vaughn, 1995. 32p. $13.98. ISBN 0-8114-6192-0. (Pointers). 3-7

The first locomotive ran along tracks in 1804. Two-page spreads of text and illustration present the history of trains. Topics and trains discussed are early railroads (c. 1825), the first inter-city railroad (1829), American locomotives (mid-nineteenth century), long-distance express trains (c. 1900), express steam trains, the largest steam engine, long-distance diesels, diesel-electric trains, high-speed diesels, subways, and the fastest trains currently in use. Glossary and Index.

173.   Bradley, Catherine. **Hitler and the Third Reich**. New York: Franklin Watts, Gloucester, 1990. 62p. $13.95. ISBN 0-531-17228-7. (World War II Biographies). 6 up

Although Adolf Hitler (1889-1945) created many myths about his childhood to support his rise to greatness, he was particularly ordinary. When he served in the army during World War I, he was not promoted because his superiors did not think he had leadership qualities. This nondescript beginning to the career of a man who almost controlled the world twenty years later indicates that Hitler was very good at covering his real intentions until horrendous economic times allowed him to begin his program to "purify" Germany. Photographs, Chronology, Glossary, Further Reading, and Index.

174.   Bradley, Catherine. **Kazakhstan**. Brookfield, CT: Millbrook Press, 1992. 32p. $15.90. ISBN 1-56294-308-1. (Former Soviet States). 4-7

The text discusses the cultural background, politics, economics, and history of the former Soviet republic of Kazakhstan. Rock pictures, stone tools, and cave paintings dated as 40,000 years old have been found in the area. Kazakhstan's current peoples are mainly Muslim, though some follow Sufism. Glossary and Index.

175.   Braquet, Anne, and Martine Noblet. **India**. Maureen Walker, translator. Hauppauge, NY: Barron's, 1994. 77p. $11.95; $6.95pa. ISBN 0-8120-6427-5; 0-8120-1866-4pa. (Tintin's Travel Diaries). 5 up

The text asks thirty questions about India, covering a variety of topics such as whether the term "Hindu" or "Indian" is correct, the definition of "untouchable," why monsoons are both good and bad, why cows are sacred to Hindus, cremation, the maharajas, and who was Gandhi. Illustrations and photographs complement the simple question text on the lefthand pages and the more thorough and scholarly answer on the righthand pages. Glossary, Chronological Chart, Map, Bibliography, and Index.

176. Braun, Barbara. **A Weekend with Diego Rivera**. New York: Rizzoli, 1994. 63p. $19.95. ISBN 0-8478-1749-0. (Weekend with the Artist). 5-8

Diego Rivera (1886-1957) tells about his life and career as if the reader were talking with him. He says that he tells the story of Mexico in his work—its history, its Revolution, its Indian past, and its popular traditions. Because of his devotion, Mexico considers Rivera one of its three greatest painters. He has been collecting pre-Columbian artifacts since his return to Mexico in 1920, after spending fourteen years in Paris where he knew Picasso, Modigliani, Mondrian, and Delaunay. Pictures of his paintings decorate the pages of his story. Where to See Rivera, Important Dates in Rivera's Life, and List of Illustrations.

177. Breckler, Rosemary. **Sweet Dried Apples: A Vietnamese Wartime Childhood**. Deborah Kogan Ray, illustrator. Boston: Houghton Mifflin, 1996. 32p. $15.95. ISBN 0-395-73570-X. 2-4

Ong Noi, the young girl protagonist's grandfather, treats his Vietnamese villagers by camouflaging bitter herbs with expensive apples to heal them. But he saves no medicine for himself, and after the enemy napalms the village, he dies. The girl, her brother, and her mother leave on a boat for the United States while their father fights in the war. She says she will some day return to honor her grandfather.

178. Brennan, J. H. **Shiva: An Adventure of the Ice Age**. New York: Lippincott, 1990. 184p. $13.95. ISBN 0-397-32453-7. 5-8

Shiva, age eleven, has survived as an orphan and as a left-handed member of her Ice Age tribe. When she finds a circle of stones and the skull of a saber-toothed tiger, magical items in the eyes of her tribe, the tribe gains respect for her. She warns the tribe to stay away from the ogres, a different species, in order to protect the ogres who once saved her life.

179. Bresnick-Perry, Roslyn. **Leaving for America**. Mira Reisberg, illustrator. Chicago: Childrens Press, 1992. 28p. $13.95. ISBN 0-829239-105-7. 1-3

The author left her home of Wysokie-Litewskie, Belarus, to come to America when she was very young because of Russian persecution of Jews. She recalls her days there before she and her mother had to leave relatives to join her father in the United States.

180. Brierley, Anthony. **Explorers of the Ancient World**. New York: Peter Bedrick, 1996. 48p. $18.95. ISBN 0-87226-485-8. (Voyages of Discovery). 3-6

The text recreates several trips such as an Egyptian trade expedition to the country of Punt through the Red Sea and a Phoenician journey around Africa. The detailed illustrations expand the text and include cross sections of ships as well as maps. Glossary and Index.

181. Brighton, Catherine, author/illustrator. **The Brontes: Scenes from the Childhood of Charlotte, Branwell, Emily and Anne**. San Francisco: Chronicle, 1994. Unpaged. $11.95. ISBN 0-8118-0608-1. 2-4

From the first-person point of view, Charlotte tells her story of family life with her aloof father after her mother's death. On the Haworth moors of England, Emily has a hawk, Branwell has his toy soldiers, and Anne has a dog. These "pets" help them create a fantasy life with adventures about which Emily and Charlotte write tiny books before they begin their lengthy adult novels. Epilogue.

182. Brighton, Catherine, author/illustrator. **Mozart: Scenes from the Childhood of a Great Composer**. New York: Doubleday, 1990. Unpaged. $14.95. ISBN 0-385-41537-0. K-4

Nannerl, Mozart's sister, tells about her younger brother's early years. The book presents double-spread pages depicting various episodes of their lives. Her brother Wolfgang (1756-1791), at the age of six, appeared before the Empress Maria Theresa and performed blindfolded for the King of France. Nannerl also elaborates on some of his other precocious performances.

183. Brighton, Catherine, author/illustrator. **My Napoleon**. Brookfield, CT: Millbrook Press, 1997. 32p. $16.95. 32p. ISBN 0-7613-0106-2. 2-4

Betsy Balcombe was a child when Napoleon (1769-1821) lived in her home during his exile on St. Helena. She wrote about him in a journal, and Brighton uses the journal as her source for the story. Betsy seems to have a rapport with Napoleon after she overcomes her fear of him and his status as "V.I.P.N." or "Very Important Prisoner, Napoleon," and he takes her for carriage rides and gives her enough candy to make her sick. When her family leaves for England, Betsy regrets parting from him.

184. Brill, Marlene Targ. **Journey for Peace: The Story of Rigoberta Menchú**. Rubén De Anda, illustrator. New York: Lodestar, 1996. 64p. $14.99. ISBN 0-525-67524-8. 4-7

Rigoberta Menchú believed her father's political stance, and after he was murdered, she became a leader of the Mayan people as they struggled against an oppressive government. In 1992, she received the Nobel Peace Prize for her efforts. The text draws on information in Menchú's biography, information from United Nations' publications, and interviews with people in the international peace movement. Her life is a testimony of what one human can do for others.

185. Briquebec, John. **The Ancient World: From the Earliest Civilizations to the Roman Empire**. New York: Warwick Press, Franklin Watts, 1990. 48p. $19.86. ISBN 0-531-19073-0. (Historical Atlas). 3-8

In looking at civilizations known to exist before the establishment of the Roman Empire, the text gives information about historical and social events from prehistoric peoples up through the fall of the Roman Empire. Index.

186. Brophy, Ann. **John Ericsson and the Inventions of War**. Englewood Cliffs, NJ: Silver Burdett, 1991. 126p. $12.95; $7.95pa. ISBN 0-382-09943-5; 0-382-24052-9pa. (The History of the Civil War). 5 up

John Ericsson (1803-1889) was a Swedish-born inventor who spent time in England, where he designed one of the world's first steam locomotives, before he arrived in the United States. He neglected to get patents on many of his inventions, but he made a major contribution to the Union forces during the Civil War. He created a propeller for moving ships and built the ironclad warship, the *Monitor*. In a famous naval duel, the *Monitor* engaged the Confederate ship, the *Merrimack,* and Ericsson's creation was strong enough to win. Photographs and drawings highlight the text. Timetables, Suggested Reading, Selected Sources, and Index.

187. Brown, Gene. **Anne Frank: Child of the Holocaust**. New York: Blackbirch Press, Rosen, 1991. 64p. $14.95. ISBN 1-56711030-4. (Library of Famous Women). 3-6

The text presents Anne Frank (1929-1945) as a normal young girl who talks in class, even as it explains why her story is important. Half of the book describes her life while hiding during the Nazi occupation of Amsterdam. It is based on Frank's diary, which was discovered after she died in a Nazi concentration camp. Bibliography and Index.

188. Brown, Gene. **Conflict in Europe and the Great Depression: World War I (1914-1940)**. New York: Twenty-First Century, 1994. 64p. $15.98. ISBN 0-8050-2585-5. (First Person American). 5-9

Brown posits that the time between World Wars I and II was when modern America was born. He discusses the rugged individualism that characterized many Americans at the time, but notes that the government became a major force in everyday lives during and after the Great Depression of the 1930s. Most Americans were moving to cities, and mass media were growing in importance. From being a nation of ballplayers and performers, Americans became watchers. Among persons presented are John Reed, Gordon Parks, Al Capone, Marcus Garvey, and Lillian Gish. Photographs enhance the text. Timeline, For Further Reading, and Index.

189. Brown, Warren. **The Search for the Northwest Passage**. New York: Chelsea House, 1991. 111p. $18.95. ISBN 0-7910-1297-2. (World Explorers). 5 up

From approximately 1497, with John Cabot, until 1850, with Sir John Franklin, men searched for a passage along the top of the North American continent between Europe and China. The text includes personal accounts of these searches along with maps and color photographs. Bibliography and Index.

190. Bruns, Roger. **Julius Caesar**. New York: Chelsea House, 1987. 112p. $18.95. ISBN 1-87754-514-6. (World Leaders Past and Present). 5 up

Julius Caesar (b. 100 B.C.) spent his life working toward the highest position in Rome, first as an emerging politician who appealed directly to the people in 59 B.C. and later as part of a governing triumvirate with Pompey and Crassus. With the Gauls, from 58 to 51 B.C., he used brutality to gain what he wanted. In 49 B.C., he declared war on an elite group of conservative senators and wrested power from them. On the Ides of March, 44 B.C., he went to the Roman Senate, where his men stabbed him to death because they thought he wanted too much power. Yet he brought glory to Rome, along with elaborate celebrations of it and many reforms. Photographs and reproductions enhance the text. Chronology, Further Reading, and Index.

191. Bryant, Jennifer Fisher. **Louis Braille: Teacher of the Blind**. New York: Chelsea House, 1994. 111p. $18.95; $7.95pa. ISBN 0-7910-2077-0; 0-7910-2090-8pa. (Great Achievers: Lives of the Physically Challenged). 4-8

Louis Braille (1809-1852) spent many years at the Royal Institute for Blind Youth in Paris. After becoming blind as a youth, he developed his "braille" touch system for reading when he was fifteen, but political disagreements kept those who could promote it from accepting it for many years. Drawings, reproductions, and historical photographs complement the text. Bibliography and Index.

192. Bulla, Clyde Robert. **A Lion to Guard Us**. Michele Chessare, illustrator. New York: HarperCollins, 1981. 118p. $14.89. ISBN 0-690-04097-0. 2-5

In 1609, Amanda, Meg, and Jemmy sail from England to meet their father in Jamestown. Although their ship is wrecked in Bermuda, they survive. During their struggle, they keep a door knocker shaped like a lion from their old home, and it gives them hope that their father still protects them. They eventually reunite with him in Jamestown. *Notable Children's Trade Books in the Field of Social Studies.*

193. Bulla, Clyde Robert. **The Sword in the Tree**. Paul Galdone, illustrator. 1956. New York: HarperCollins, 1974. 128p. $14.89. ISBN 0-690-79909-8. 4-6

Shan's Uncle Lionel reappears at Weldon Castle after many years, and disposes of Shan's father so that he may take the family inheritance. Shan and his mother escape and search for King Arthur at Camelot with the help of herdsmen. When they return to the castle with Sir Gareth, he challenges Lionel for the castle and wins. When they discover Shan's father in the dungeon, instead of dead, they realize that Shan's courage has reunited the family.

194. Bunting, Eve. **I Am the Mummy Heb-Nefert**. David Christiana, illustrator. San Diego, CA: Harcourt Brace, 1997. 32p. $15. ISBN 0-15-200479-3. 3-6

Heb-Nefert lives leisurely with her royal husband on the banks of the Nile. Bunting pretends that Heb-Nefert recalls these pleasant days as she lies as a mummy encased in museum glass. Her story tells of ancient Egypt and its customs.

195. Bunting, Eve. **Market Day**. Holly Berry, illustrator. New York: HarperCollins, 1996. 32p. $14.95. ISBN 0-06-025364-9. K-2

Tess, age seven, and her friend Wee Boy, of the same age, although slightly retarded, enjoy the monthly market in their Irish town. They carefully choose how to spend their money and do so in unusual ways.

196. Bunting, Eve. **SOS Titanic**. San Diego, CA: Harcourt Brace, 1996. 256p. $12; $6pa. ISBN 0-15-200271-5; 0-15-201305-9pa. 6-9

Barry, an upper-class Irish boy of fifteen, prepares to join his parents in America after living with his grandparents while his parents worked in China. On board the ship are Frank and Jonnie, who blame Barry's grandfather for forcing their departure from Ireland via steerage. Frank threatens Barry for having a relationship with Frank's sister. After the *Titanic*'s collision with an iceberg on April 14, 1912, Barry tries to save Frank; he cannot, but he does save Frank's sister. The *Carpathia* rescues both of them the following morning.

197. Bunting, Eve. **Spying on Miss Müller**. New York: Clarion, 1995. 181p. $13.95. ISBN 0-395-69172-9. 5-7

Jessie and her friends in her Belfast, Ireland, school think their German teacher, Miss Müller, is wonderful. After World War II begins, they change their minds and start rumors. When they see her climb the stairs to the roof one night, they wonder if she is a spy. Jessie wants to prove her teacher's innocence, so she begins watching her. What she discovers is a tryst between Miss Müller and Mr. Bolton, the Latin teacher. But another friend, Greta, is angry that her father has been killed, and she exposes the lovers. Because teachers cannot be married, Miss Müller is fired, and Mr. Bolton joins the army. Jessie hopes they will be happy, but she doubts that they will see each other again.

198. Burch, Joann J. **Chico Mendes: Defender of the Rain Forest**. Brookfield, CT: Millbrook Press, 1994. 48p. $13.90. ISBN 1-56294-413-4. (Gateway Greens). 4-6

Francisco "Chico" Mendes Filho (d. 1988) tried to secure fair treatment for rubber tappers in the Amazon rain forests. His concern for the deforestation led to his murder in 1988. Bibliography and Index.

199. Burch, Joann J. **Isabella of Castile: Queen on Horseback**. New York: Franklin Watts, 1991. 63p. $18.43. ISBN 0-531-20033-7. (First Books). 4-8

When Isabella I (1451-1504) was Queen of Spain, ruling with her husband Ferdinand from 1479 until 1504, she rode through the countryside on horseback garnering support for their works. Her horsewomanship helped to bring political and religious unity to their kingdom. Its prosperity allowed her to support Columbus in his quest for the Indies. Bibliography and Index.

200. Burch, Joann Johansen. **Fine Print: A Story About Johann Gutenberg**. Kent Alan Aldrich, illustrator. Minneapolis, MN: Carolrhoda, 1991. 64p. $17.50; $5.95pa. ISBN 0-87614-682-5; 0-87614-565-9pa. K-3

Because information about Gutenberg's (1397?-1468) life is very limited, the text discusses the times during which he lived in Mainz, based on chronicles and the status of books before his invention of moveable type. His family was very wealthy; his father owned three homes and several books, very expensive items before his son's invention. Gutenberg became a stonecutter and polisher, but he experimented with metal letters to see if he could make them print. When his invention was ready, he spent several years trying to print the

Bible, but he would reject a page if just one letter was blurred. One of his investors sued him, and Gutenberg had to give the creditor all his printing equipment to pay back the loan. He received no credit during his time for the first printing of the Bible, but history has called that book the Gutenberg Bible. His invention changed the world. Sources and For Further Reading.

201. Burgess, Melvin. **An Angel for May**. New York: Simon & Schuster, 1995. 154p. $15. ISBN 0-671-89004-2. 5-7

In this historical fantasy, Tam roams around a ruined farm in the English countryside after his parents divorce, and the dog of a homeless woman he sees there leads him through the fireplace into the time of World War II, when the farm is thriving. Mr. Nutter, the owner, wants Tam to stay and be friends with May, a traumatized girl who refuses to eat or sleep indoors. When Tam returns to the present, he sees that a fire will destroy the farm and Mr. Nutter, and he tries to find a way to go back in time again to warn them.

202. Burke, Deirdre. **Food and Fasting**. New York: Thomson Learning, 1993. 32p. $13.95. ISBN 1-56847-034-7. (Comparing Religions). 4-8

Six major religions—Buddhism, Christianity, Hinduism, Judaism, Islam, and Sikhism—have rules about what some foods mean and which foods they may eat. The text looks at what they eat, how they eat it, what and when they cannot eat, what foods appear at religious festivals, and what foods (e.g., bread and wine) appear in places of worship. Photographs enhance the information. Glossary, Books to Read, and Index.

203. Burks, Brian. **Soldier Boy**. San Diego, CA: Harcourt Brace, 1997. 154p. $12. ISBN 0-15-201218-4. 6-9

When Johnny "The Kid" McBane flees from his Chicago boxing promoter, he enlists in the cavalry after lying about his age. When he arrives at Custer's Seventh Cavalry at Fort Lincoln, he prepares to fight the Indians in the spring. The story mainly describes the escapades in camp before Johnny dies in battle at the end of the book.

204. Burns, Peggy. **The Mail**. New York: Thomson Learning, 1995. 32p. $13.95. ISBN 1-56847-249-8. (Stepping Through History). 3-5

In the past, people wrote letters on wax, clay, bronze tablets, or papyrus. Sometimes a messenger memorized the words and delivered them verbally. Around 500 B.C., Cyrus created the longest postal route in ancient times so that he could send his decrees across the kingdom. Romans had postal routes, but they were discontinued after Rome fell. In the eleventh century, monasteries began messenger services. Other ancient cultures had their own systems. Topics include mailboxes, stamps, the Pony Express, international mail, and mail sorting. Time Line, Books to Read, Places to Visit, Further Information, Glossary, and Index.

205. Burns, Peggy. **Money**. New York: Thomson Learning, 1995. 32p. $13.95. ISBN 1-56847-248-X. (Stepping Through History). 4-6

The text looks at money by discussing barter and trade, the history of coins and paper money, banks and credit cards, and currency exchange between countries. Chronology, Glossary, Bibliography, and Index.

206. Burrell, Roy. **The Greeks**. Peter Connolly, illustrator. New York: Oxford University Press, 1990. 112p. $16.95. ISBN 0-19-917161-0. 5-7

This overview of the ancient Greeks presents their life, culture, and customs, with an emphasis on their military strategies, especially the armies and navies of Alexander the Great. By having the narrator converse with someone living at the time, Burrell gives a sense of immediacy to the information. Illustrations highlight the text. Chronology.

207. Burrell, Roy. **Life in the Time of Moctezuma and the Aztecs**. Angus McBride, illustrator. Austin, TX: Raintree/Steck-Vaughn, 1993. 63p. $16.98. ISBN 0-8114-3351-X. (Life in the Time Of). 4-8

During the early 1500s, Moctezuma ruled the Aztecs in Tenochtitlán. The text presents the people who supported and fought for him, how they did it, religious rituals, women and girls and their maturation customs, life in the town and countryside, crafts and trades, and myths. But Cortés arrived with his soldiers and destroyed the Aztec civilization by 1521. Each chapter covers a specific topic, using illustrations to clarify. Glossary and Index.

208. Bursell, Susan. **Haunted Houses**. San Diego, CA: Lucent, 1994. 48p. $16.95. ISBN 1-56006-153-7. (Exploring the Unknown). 4-6

Reports of haunted houses have appeared throughout history. Glamis Castle in County Angus, Scotland, supposedly harbors the ghost of Malcolm II from the tenth century. The Roman historian Pliny the Younger reported that Athenodorus, in the first century A.D., was concerned about the haunting of his house in Athens. Other reports of haunted houses and boats are myriad, but people have differing views about their validity. Parapsychologists who study the paranormal or the unusual also disagree as to whether spirits exist and can manifest themselves so that humans can perceive them. Not all parapsychologists are spiritualists; certainly those who are not want scientific evidence for these accounts. Glossary, For Further Reading, Works Consulted, and Index.

209.   Burton, Hester. **The Henchmans at Home**. New York: Crowell, 1972. $4.50. 182p. ISBN 0-690-37706-1. 6-10

In English Victorian society of the 1890s, Rob, Ellen, and William mature over a period of eleven years. They experience various events, observe prejudice, and find that their beliefs change when they look at situations from new perspectives. What they realize most is that each has to accept the individuality of the other and that their parents have reasons for the decisions they make.

210.   Bush, Catherine. **Elizabeth I**. New York: Chelsea House, 1988. 112p. $18.95. ISBN 0-87754-579-0. (World Leaders Past and Present). 5 up

The unwanted daughter of Henry VIII, Elizabeth I (1533-1603) grew up without her mother, Anne Boleyn, whom Henry had executed. Elizabeth had a lonely childhood while watching her half-sister Mary misrule England. Elizabeth acceded to the throne in 1558, where she showed her political skill and united her country. She was a scholar, a believer in religious tolerance, and a patron of the arts. She refused to allow anyone to gain power over her, and her country flourished while she ruled. Photographs and reproductions enhance the text. Chronology, Further Reading, and Index.

211.   Bush, Catherine. **Mohandas K. Gandhi: Indian Nationalist Leader**. New York: Chelsea House, 1985. 112p. $18.95. ISBN 0-87754-555-3. (World Leaders Past and Present). 5 up

For two generations, Gandhi (1869-1948) was the conscience of India. He returned to India, after being educated in England and working in South Africa, to forward the cause of independence from Britain through nonviolent means. He succeeded, but one of his own countrymen assassinated him. Photographs and reproductions enhance the text. Chronology, Further Reading, and Index.

212.   Butler, Francelia. **Indira Gandhi**. New York: Chelsea House, 1986. 116p. $18.95. ISBN 0-87754-596-0. (World Leaders Past and Present). 5 up

Indira Gandhi (1917-1984) became prime minister of India after Jawaharlal Nehru, her father, and Mohandas Gandhi. She fought for economic progress and social reform in India, the country with the second largest population in the world. She believed in democracy, but she also used dictatorial tactics if nothing else worked. She suspended civil rights during a "state of emergency" between 1975 and 1977, but she was overwhelmingly reelected in 1980. The text looks at her life and the forces that shaped it, including the constant support for Indian independence from Britain that she heard at home as a child. Photographs enhance the text. Chronology, Further Reading, and Index.

©

213. Calvert, Patricia. **Hadder MacColl.** New York: Scribners, 1985. 160p. $12.95. ISBN 0-684-18447-8. 5-9

In 1745, Hadder MacColl looks forward to her brother's return from the university at Edinburgh, Scotland. Disappointed that he brings a friend home with him, and concerned that he no longer wants the clans to fight each other, she discounts him when he refuses to kill a mountain lion that is threatening their dogs. But he has to fight at Culloden to help restore the Jacobites to Scotland's throne, and at his death, Hadder realizes that she and her father are the ones with misplaced values. After her father's death, others help Hadder in her decision to emigrate to America.

214. Cameron, Eleanor. **The Court of the Stone Children.** 1973. Magnolia, MA: Peter Smith, 1983. 208p. $18.05. ISBN 0-8446-6757-9. New York: Puffin, 1992. $4.99pa. ISBN 0-14-034289-3pa. 4 up

Nina wants to become a museum curator because she finds solace in San Francisco's French Museum, a place where Chagall's painting *Time Is a River Without Banks* greets her. In this historical fantasy, Nina meets Dominique, a figure in an early-nineteenth-century painting. Dominique says that she dreamed about Nina as a girl and wants Nina to help her find out what happened to her father. Nina solves the puzzle by guessing about a painting and shows Dominique that her father was innocent of charges made against him by Napoleon's army. *American Book Award.*

215. Capek, Michael. **Artistic Trickery: The Tradition of the Trompe L'oeil Art.** Minneapolis, MN: Lerner, 1995. Unpaged. $21.50. ISBN 0-8225-2064-8. (Art Beyond Borders). 5 up

Trompe l'oeil paintings trick the viewer so that the eye thinks it is seeing something that it really is not. *Trompe l'oeil* is not realism, because realism tries to represent objects truthfully; instead, *trompe l'oeil* is a visual game. The text looks at several contemporary artists who make *trompe l'oeil* paintings and discusses the subjects that have intrigued artists through the years. These themes include damaged goods, money and stamps, food, people, animals and insects, slates and letter racks, doors, landscapes, and murals. The earliest illustration comes from 1475, and other illustrations cover each century since. Glossary and Index. *IRA Children's Choices.*

216. Capek, Michael. **Murals: Cave, Cathedral, to Street.** Minneapolis, MN: Lerner, 1996. 72p. $17.21. ISBN 0-8225-2065-6. (American Pastfinder). 5 up

The text looks at murals, huge drawings that decorate caves, walls, ceilings, and the sides of buildings. In an unusual order, the text looks at contemporary murals first and goes backward in history; the last chapter examines cave paintings. Among the topics are contemporary community murals, historical murals in the United States, Mexican murals, Italian Renaissance murals, early Christian murals, murals of ancient Rome and Egypt, and cave paintings. Glossary, For Further Reading, and Index.

217. Carpenter, Angelica S., and Jean Shirley. **Robert Louis Stevenson: Finding Treasure Island.** Minneapolis, MN: Lerner, 1997. 144p. $17.95. ISBN 0-8225-4955-7. 6-9

Robert Louis Stevenson (1850-1894) grew up in Scotland, but traveled in France and the United States. At thirty-seven, he traveled in the South Seas with his family and eventually settled on the Samoan island of Upolu. These experiences served as the settings for his novels, including *Treasure Island*. Bibliography and Index.

218. Carrick, Donald, author/illustrator. **Harald and the Giant Knight.** New York: Clarion, 1982. 32p. $15.95. ISBN 0-89919-060-X. 1-3

The baron's knights decide to use Harald's family's land to practice their jousting. The family fears that it will lose the animals and fruit trees already on the land and has to delay planting the crops because the knights will destroy them. When Harald watches the thoughtless knights, he no longer admires them. He suggests that his father weave a giant knight to scare them after they become drunk one night. His plan succeeds.

219. Carrick, Donald, author/illustrator. **Harald and the Great Stag.** New York: Clarion, 1988. 32p. $15.95. ISBN 0-89919-514-8. Boston: Houghton Mifflin, 1990. $4.95pa. ISBN 0-395-52596-9pa. K-3

Harald sees the Great Stag, which the baron is trying to kill in the England of medieval times, and he decides to save it. He scatters the stag's droppings in patterns that confuse the hunting dogs, and an old hunter who agrees with his tactics saves him from discovery. Harald learns that no living thing should have to endure the fear of being hunted.

220.   Carrion, Esther. **The Empire of the Czars**. Chicago: Childrens Press, 1994. 34p. $20. ISBN 0-516-08319-0. (The World Heritage). 3 up

Russia is so diverse that one must look at many facets to get a glimpse into its history and its people. In the sixth and seventh centuries, Kiev was founded, and from this city grew the current country. Muscovy became heir to Kiev's power in the fourteenth and fifteenth centuries. Sites shown in photographs include St. Petersburg, Moscow's Kremlin and Red Square, Petcherskaya Lavra of Kiev, Kizhi Pogost, and the historic city of Itchan Kala in the heart of Asia. Glossary and Index.

221.   Carroll, Bob. **The Battle of Stalingrad**. San Diego, CA: Lucent, 1997. 95p. $19.95. ISBN 1-56006-452-8. (Battles of World War II). 6-10

The German Sixth Army held the Russian defenders from the end of August 1942 until the end of January 1943 at the city of Stalingrad. Carroll notes that this battle was one of the important turning points in the war and proves his point by expounding upon the battle of "wills" between the two dictators, Stalin and Hitler. Boxed text and archival photographs augment the information. Bibliography, Chronology, Further Reading, and Index.

222.   Carroll, Bob. **Napoleon Bonaparte**. San Diego, CA: Lucent, 1994. 112p. $16.95. ISBN 1-56006-021-2. (The Importance of). 6-9

Napoleon Bonaparte (1769-1821) rose to become the greatest military leader of France and perhaps of the world. After the French Revolution, he used the concepts of equality, liberty, and brotherhood as the basis for the *Code Napoleon* (the basis of law in France and much of Europe today); centralized the government (a model for dictatorships everywhere); and pursued foreign policy that led to the creation of modern Italy, Germany, and Poland, and the expansion of the United States into a powerful nation. At the same time, he killed millions of people and enriched France by stealing treasures from other countries (such as da Vinci's *Mona Lisa*, which hangs in the Louvre rather than in Italy). He preached freedom but enslaved many. In 1799, at thirty-five, he had himself designated the "First Consul for Life"; in 1804, he crowned himself emperor of France. When his beloved wife Josephine did not bear him an heir, he divorced her and married Marie Louise of Austria. Napoleon II was born in 1811, but Napoleon I continued to visit Josephine. His conquest of Egypt made him feel equal to Alexander the Great and Julius Caesar; it was in Egypt that his men found the Rosetta Stone. Eventually he lost power and was exiled to Elba. But he came back, started amassing an army, and fought Wellington at the Battle of Waterloo in 1815, suffering a stunning loss. His final exile was to the isolated St. Helene where he died, perhaps poisoned by arsenic. Notes, For Further Reading, Additional Works Consulted, and Index.

223.   Carson, Robert. **Hernando de Soto**. Chicago: Childrens Press, 1991. 128p. $26.60. ISBN 0-516-03065-5. (The World's Great Explorers). 3-6

Hernando de Soto (1500-1542) learned to be a warrior before joining Pizarro's expedition to Peru. Happy with the wealth he received there, he returned to Florida, at Charles I's request, to gain control of the land and its wealth. He and his explorers cut through the American south on their search for gold, but found only the Mississippi River. They took anything they could find to satisfy their greed. Timeline, Glossary, Bibliography, and Index.

224.   Carter, Alden R. **The Mexican War: Manifest Destiny**. New York: Franklin Watts, 1992. 63p. $12.40. ISBN 0-531-20081-7. (First Books). 4-8

With a general focus on military and political strategies, the text gives the history of the Mexican War, which lasted from 1846 to 1848. It discusses events, personalities, and the aftermath of the war as well. Reproductions enhance the text. Bibliography and Index.

225.   Carter, Alden R. **The Spanish-American War: Imperial Ambitions**. New York: Franklin Watts, 1992. 64p. $12.40. ISBN 0-531-20078-7. (First Books). 4-8

The text tells of the ten-week war in 1898 between the United States and Spain over the liberation of Cuba. Theodore Roosevelt and his Rough Riders gained stature when the fight ended the Spanish colonial empire, and other countries recognized the United States as a world power. Bibliography and Index.

226.   Carter, Dorothy S. **His Majesty, Queen Hatshepsut**. Michele Chessare, illustrator. Philadelphia: Lippincott, 1987. 248p. $13.95. ISBN 0-397-32178-3. 6-9

Having to share the reign with her young half-nephew annoys Hatshepsut, so she maneuvers to declare herself the only ruler of Egypt by saying that her father told her in a dream that she was the Pharaoh. She rules for twenty-two years, surviving the schemes of the priesthood to kill her until an advisor serves her poisoned wine. Although fictionalized, this book is based on facts about Hatshepsut, the woman who ruled in Egypt from 1503 B.C. to 1482 B.C. She advanced the civilization by renovating portions of Karnak and building the beautiful temple of Dayr al-Bahrī on the Nile near Thebes. By the time of her death, a viper had bitten and killed her daughter and her confidant had been murdered. Carter supposes that Hatshepsut was tired of fighting her subordinates when her own life ended.

227.   Case, Dianne. **92 Queens Road**. New York: Farrar, Straus & Giroux, 1994. 155p. $16. ISBN 0-374-35518-5. 4-6

Katie, six, narrates a story about her life in South Africa during the apartheid regime of the 1960s. She becomes aware that her skin color keeps her from doing some things and going some places in Cape Town, where she and her family live, and that her being illegitimate stops her in other ways. Her uncle, however, is light-skinned and declared legally "white," a situation that makes him reluctant to associate with the family. Katie's aunt has a miscarriage after a racially motivated incident on a bus, and she and her husband decide that going to Canada is the only hope they have for a normal life. The story tells about Katie's daily life as the family copes with their situation.

228.   Cashman, Greer, and Alona Frankel. **Jewish Days and Holidays**. New York: Modan-Adama, 1986. 64p. $12.95. ISBN 0-915361-58-2. K-4

With Jewish history integrated into the definitions, the authors present Rosh Hashanah, Yom Kippur, Sukkot, Simchat Torah, Chanukah, Purim, Pesach, Yom-Ha-Atzmaut, Shavuot, Tisha B'Av, and Shabbat. Sidebars contain simple illustrations and further clarifications.

229.   Cavan, Seamus. **The Irish-American Experience**. Brookfield, CT: Millbrook Press, 1993. 64p. $14.90. ISBN 1-56294-218-2. 5-7

The text presents the history of Ireland with an emphasis on the last two centuries, when the Irish suffered the potato famine, and many had to leave Ireland in order to survive. Among the topics included are the Irish at sea on the way to America, tenement life in America, and the way that men started to take leadership roles in politics. Photographs, Bibliography, Notes, and Index. *Child Study Association Children's Books of the Year.*

230.   Cech, John. **Jacques-Henri Lartigue: Boy with a Camera**. New York: Four Winds, 1994. 32p. $15.95. ISBN 0-02-718136-7. 4-9

From the age of seven in 1902, when he received his first camera, Jacques-Henri Lartigue (1894-1986) knew how to capture the best moment to record on his film. He kept a diary throughout his life, and his reasons for and responses to the photographs in the text are featured. Among the many unique images he caught was one of a pilot at the takeoff of an attempt to cross the English Channel from England to France.

231.   Cech, John. **My Grandmother's Journey**. Sharon McGinley-Nally, illustrator. New York: Bradbury, 1991. 32p. $14.95. ISBN 0-02-718135-9. K-3

Korie's grandmother tells her about surviving the Russian Revolution and World War II as part of a bedtime story. She tells Korie that she saw gypsies twice. The first time, a gypsy helped her get rid of her headaches; the second time, the gypsy told her that one day she would want bread and be happy just to be alive. Soon after, the Russian civil war began, and the gypsy's fortune-telling came true. Korie's grandmother survived that war, Stalin's purges, and the Nazis of World War II before she came to America.

232.   Cervera, Isabel. **The Mughal Empire**. Chicago: Childrens Press, 1994. 34p. $20. ISBN 0-516-08392-9. (The World Heritage). 4-7

In 1526, Zahir ud-din, nicknamed Babur (Persian for "panther"), conquered the sultanate of Dehli, India, after a battle at Panipat. His empire became known as the Mughal (Persian for "Mongol") Empire. The Mughals governed for more than 300 years and tried to unify Hindus and Muslims. Two of Babur's successors were Akbar (1556-1605) and Shah Jahan (1627-1658). These two built the greatest works of Indo-Islamic architecture: the Red Fort of Agra, Fatehpur Sikri, the Shalimar Gardens and Fortress of Lahore (Pakistan), and the Taj Mahal. Photographs of these sites complement the text. Glossary and Index.

233.   Ceserani, Gian Paolo. **Marco Polo**. New York: Philomel, 1982. 33p. $9.95. ISBN 0-399-20843-7. 5-8

Marco Polo (1254-1323?), a thirteenth-century Venetian merchant, traveled to Asia and lived for a while in the court of Kublai Khan. His account of his travels influenced many explorers, notably Christopher Columbus. Maps complement the text.

234.   Cha, Dia. **Dia's Story Cloth**. Chue Cha and Nhia Thao Cha, illustrators. Denver, CO: Lee & Low, Denver Museum of Natural History, 1996. 24p. $14.95. ISBN 1-880000-34-2. 4-6

While the author's aunt and uncle stayed in a Thai refugee camp, they created a *pa'ndau* embroidered cloth, which illustrates this text about the Hmong migration from ancient China. The migration continued through Laos, which Cha's people had to leave in the 1960s because of the war; Cha's father joined the loyalists before disappearing. Then they went to Cambodia and over the Mekong River into Thailand as a way to escape the Communist invasions. Cha's family made this journey, and her experiences highlight the history created in the *pa'ndau*. Bibliography.

235. Chaikin, Miriam. **Menorahs, Mezuzas, and Other Jewish Symbols**. Erika Weihs, illustrator. New York: Clarion, 1990. 102p. $15.95. ISBN 0-899-19856-2. 5-8

Starting with the rise of a new tribe in the Middle East around 1800 B.C.E. (Before the Christian Era) and Abraham and Sarah's belief that one God rules all, Chaikin traces Jewish symbols through history. Abraham's circumcision of himself and his followers was the first symbolic act of these Jews. Chaikin covers symbolic acts and ideas; symbolic garments and dress; symbols in Jewish worship; symbols of the state of Israel; and home, number, and holiday symbols. The information will be of special aid to non-Jewish readers who need explanations of terms. Notes, Bibliography, and Index.

236. Chaikin, Miriam. **A Nightmare in History**. New York: Clarion, 1987. 128p. $15.95. ISBN 0-89919-461-3. New York: Clarion, 1992. 128p. $7.95pa. ISBN 0-395-61579-8pa. 5 up

The Nazis murdered 6 of 9 million Jews who lived in Europe before World War II. They also murdered 5 million more people—Gypsies, Russians, Poles, Slavs, and others. Chaikin traces Judaism from Abraham and Sarah through the centuries in Europe and relates how various "hate" groups formed, eventually leading to *pogroms* and then to Hitler's atrocities. She says that the book is to keep people from forgetting. She includes many facts about the Warsaw Ghetto, Auschwitz-Birkenau, and the help that non-Jews gave to fight against the inhumanity of Hitler's "final solution." Photographs clarify the facts related. Books about the Holocaust and Index.

237. Chandler, David P. **The Land and People of Cambodia**. New York: HarperCollins, 1991. 210p. $17.95. ISBN 0-06-021129-6. (Portraits of Nations). 6-12

After placing Cambodia in modern times, much of the text covers its history. Although somewhat laborious to read, this book offers information not readily available about this particular country. The first historical mention of Cambodia occurred around 200 B.C. Jayavarman, who reigned from 802 to 834, founded Angkor. He and the twenty-five other Angkorean kings ruled until approximately 1300. King Suryavarman II built Angkor, the largest religious building in the world, in the twelfth century. Beginning in the fifteenth century, the Thais invaded Angkor, and the capital shifted southward to Phnom Penh. In 1863, France proclaimed a protectorate over Cambodia and made a treaty with King Norodom. The protectorate lasted until 1953. Other leaders included the Communist Saloth Sar, who took the name Pol Pot; his government, the Democratic Kampuchea (D.K.) Regime, murdered over a million Cambodians from 1976 to 1978, often by starving or overworking them. In 1979, the Vietnamese Communists invaded and Pol Pot fled. In 1989, the People's Republic of Kampuchea (P.D.K.) changed its name to State of Cambodia. Photographs, maps, and drawings augment the text. Bibliography, Filmography, Discography, and Index.

238. Chang, Margaret, and Raymond Chang. **In the Eye of War**. New York: Margaret K. McElderry, 1990. 198p. $14.95. ISBN 0-689-50503-5. 5-7

During Shao-Shao's tenth year, 1945, until the war ends, his family continues its routine in Shanghai, with his father working for Chiang Kai-shek's Nationalist Underground and the man across the courtyard helping the Japanese invaders. Little by little, Shao-Shao understands why his father wants him to excel at his schoolwork and why he does not like the children to keep pets. The concern of the various generations of the family for each other allows them to continue their traditions, including celebration of the New Year, though not as elaborately as in the past.

239. Charbonneau, Claudette, and Patricia Slade Lander. **The Land and People of Norway**. New York: HarperCollins, 1992. 240p. $17.89. ISBN 0-06-02058-30. (Portraits of the Nations). 6-10

The text gives a good background of the history of Norway, from the age of the Vikings (793-1066), to the kingdoms and saga kings, through nationhood and World Wars I and II. The democratic traditions underlying the country's history help clarify the development of its literature, art, music, sports, and family life, as well as its reasons for celebrating certain holidays. Bibliography, Filmography, and Index.

240. Charley, Catherine. **Tombs and Treasures**. New York: Viking, 1995. 48p. $15.99. ISBN 0-670-85899-4. (See Through History). 5-7

Some of the world's greatest archaeological discoveries have included pyramids, hidden burial mounds, sunken treasure ships, mausoleums, and cities of gold. See-through cutaways of an ancient Sumerian "death pit," the tomb of Philip of Macedonia, the grave of a Moche warrior-priest, and the *Mary Rose* (a warship of Tudor England) highlight the text. Topics on two-page spreads cover Tutankhamen (1323 B.C.), the cemetery at Ur (c. 2,500 B.C.), the Etruscans (c. 600-500 B.C.), Scythian tombs (c. 500 B.C.), the first mausoleum (353 B.C.), Philip of Macedonia (336 B.C.), the Jade prince (113 B.C.), Pompeii (A.D. 79), lords of Sipán (A.D. 300), the terra cotta Chinese army (210 B.C.), the tomb of Pacal (A.D. 683), Sutton Hoo (A.D. 625), Tamerlane (A.D. 1405), El Dorado (A.D. 1544), the *Mary Rose* (A.D. 1545), and the Taj Mahal (A.D. 1632). Key Dates, Glossary, and Index. *Notable Children's Trade Books in the Field of Social Studies.*

241. Chicoine, Stephen. **A Liberian Family**. Minneapolis, MN: Lerner, 1997. 64p. $21.50. ISBN 0-8225-3411-8. (Journey Between Two Worlds). 3-6

Although not a history book, the text includes the history of Liberia as a background for understanding why families from Liberia have had to leave their homes. Photographs and personal experiences explain Liberian social and religious traditions and how the people have had to adapt to a new culture in order to survive as refugees from a land they loved. Further Reading.

242. Chicoine, Stephen. **A Tibetan Family**. Minneapolis, MN: Lerner, 1997. 56p. $16.95. ISBN 0-8225-3408-8. (Journey Between Two Worlds). 3-6

The text shares the history of the Tibetans and the Chinese occupation of their country as a background for understanding the reasons that Tibetan families have become refugees. Photographs and personal experiences explain the Tibetan social, political, and religious traditions that the family has had to leave. Further Reading.

243. Chiflet, Jean-Loup, and Alain Beaulet. **Victoria and Her Times**. George Wen, translator. New York: Henry Holt, 1996. $19.95. ISBN 0-8050-5084-1. (Who, What, When, Where, Why). 6 up

Using double-page spreads, the text describes the life of Queen Victoria (1819-1901) and her era. A variety of topics including information on Sherlock Holmes and Victoria's handwriting enliven the information. Index.

244. Child, John. **The Crusades**. Nigel Kelly, illustrator. New York: Peter Bedrick, 1996. 64p. $17.95. ISBN 0-87226-119-0. 5 up

The Crusades began in 1095 when Pope Urban II called for the first one; they did not end until the fall of Acre, the last Crusader stronghold, in 1291. Among those closely associated with the Crusades are Richard the Lionheart, Saladin, Eleanor of Acquitaine, and Saint Louis IX, King of France. Understanding the Crusades helps to interpret the continuing conflict between Christian Europe and America and Islam. Index.

245. Child, John. **The Rise of Islam**. New York: Peter Bedrick, 1995. 64p. $16.95. ISBN 0-87226-116-6. (Biographical History). 6-9

The text presents a history of Islam from the birth of Muhammad in 570 to the present. It describes the spread of the religion and its culture in the Middle East, Asia, and Europe. In two-page chapters covering a variety of topics, Child uses quotes from Islamic leaders, the Koran, and scholarly texts important to the faith. He also notes the contributions throughout history to science, literature, art, and politics from people of Islamic heritage. Index.

246. Choi, Sook Nyul. **Echoes of the White Giraffe**. Boston: Houghton Mifflin, 1993. 137p. $13.95. ISBN 0-395-64721-5. New York: Yearling, 1995. 137p. $3.50pa. ISBN 0-440-40970-5pa. 6-9

Sookan, age fifteen, her mother, and her brother leave their Korean home in 1952 to seek refuge in Pusan. In this sequel to *The Year of Impossible Goodbyes*, they live in a shack near other refugee huts on a mountain covered with slick mud. Sookan makes friends with a young man but cannot pursue the relationship because her culture forbids such liaisons. She knows that when she leaves for America, after passing her exams and winning a scholarship, she will see him no more. Among the characters in the story, one refugee stands outside his hut near the top of the mountain each day and yells "Good morning"; his attitude delights Sookan. Near the end of the story, she finally reunites with the older brothers whom she and the others have longed to find. *American Library Association Notable Books for Children*.

247. Choi, Sook Nyul. **The Year of Impossible Goodbyes**. Boston: Houghton Mifflin, 1991. 171p. $15.95. ISBN 0-395-57419-6. New York: Yearling, 1993. $3.99pa. ISBN 0-440-40759-1pa. 5-9

Sookan, who is ten years old in 1945 when World War II ends, faces the Russian invasion after the Japanese leave North Korea. She, her mother, and her brother are separated from her father and three older brothers. The Russians capture people trying to escape across the Thirty-Eighth Parallel and detain her mother, but Sookan and her brother successfully escape to the south. The story tells about the Japanese occupation and what the soldiers did to the people, including their taking girls from work in the knitting factories to the war front to become prostitutes. *Bulletin Blue Ribbon Book* and *School Library Journal Best Book*.

248. Chrisman, Abbott. **Hernando de Soto**. Rick Whipple, illustrator. Austin, TX: Raintree/Steck-Vaughn, 1993. 32p. $13.98; $5.95pa. ISBN 0-8172-2903-5; 0-8114-6753-8pa. (Hispanic Stories). 4-7

Hernado de Soto (1500-1542) left Spain when he was fourteen to serve as a page to Don Pedro Arias de Ávila, known as Pedrarias. There de Soto met Balboa, who taught him the art of soldiering and helped him train to become a knight by the age of seventeen. He lost a battle against Cortés, a countryman he foolishly trusted, and watched Pisarro kill the Incan Atahualpa. De Soto returned to Spain and married, but he came back to the New World and explored the Mississippi before he died of malaria. Glossary. English and Spanish text.

249. Chrisman, Abbott. **Luis Muñoz Marín**. Dennis Matz, illustrator. Austin, TX: Raintree/Steck-Vaughn, 1993. 32p. $13.98; $5.95pa. ISBN 0-8114-8477-7; 0-8114-6760-0pa. (Hispanic Stories). 4-7

Luis Muñoz Marín (1898-1980), educated in the United States, wanted to be a writer, but his father's desire to see life in Puerto Rico improve became a family concern. In 1938, Muñoz Marín started a new political party in Puerto Rico and got people to support him. In 1947, the people elected him the first governor when Puerto Rico became a commonwealth. After a time in office, Muñoz Marín resigned, saying that he had helped them start and that they must continue without him. Glossary. English and Spanish text.

250. Chrisp, Peter. **The Farmer Through History**. Tony Smith, illustrator. New York: Thomson Learning, 1993. 48p. $15.95. ISBN 1-56847-011-8. (Journey Through History). 3-5

Photographs, reproductions, and drawings show farmers through history as the text covers the change in society from the hunter-gatherer to the farmer. The periods examined are a farmer in Jericho (8000-6000 B.C.), an Egyptian peasant farmer (3100-2150 B.C.), a Roman slave farmer (300 B.C.-A.D. 300), a Mayan maize farmer (300-900), a Chinese rice farmer (960-1279); an English serf (1100-1400), a yam farmer of Benin (1400-1700), an improving farmer of Britain (1730-1830), a Soviet collective farmer (1928-1990), and a modern Western farmer (1990-). Glossary, Further Reading, Timeline, and Index.

251. Chrisp, Peter. **The Incas**. New York: Thompson Learning, 1994. 32p. $14.95. ISBN 1-56847-171-8. (Look into the Past). 4-6

The Incas flourished along the west coast of South America, high in the Andes mountains, until the Spanish conquest in the sixteenth century destroyed them. The text describes their beliefs, their celebrations, their rulers, their methods of overcoming the enemy, their arts and crafts, their family life, and their clothing. Photographs highlight the text. Glossary, Important Dates, Books to Read, and Index.

252. Chrisp, Peter. **The Maya**. New York: Thomson Learning, 1994. 32p. $14.95. ISBN 1-56847-170-X. (Look into the Past). 4-6

The Mayan civilization in Mexico and Central America flourished between A.D. 300 and 800. As artists and craftspeople, the Maya built pyramids and palaces. They had skills in astronomy and mathematics and developed a complex writing system for books and stone carvings. Although the cities disappeared, over 4 million Maya live in Mexico, Guatemala, Belize, and Honduras. Photographs of Mayan ruins complement the text, which discusses gods, rulers, human sacrifice, and daily farming life. No one knows what destroyed this civilization, although speculations include famine and war. Glossary, Important Dates, Pronunciation, Books to Read, and Index.

253. Chrisp, Peter. **The Normans**. New York: Thompson Learning, 1994. 32p. $14.95. ISBN 1-56847-174-2. (Look into the Past). 4-6

The Normans, descendants of the Vikings, were fierce fighters who lived in northern France and conquered England in 1066. The text, supported with color illustrations, recounts their daily life by examining the wars they fought, their travels, their religion, their politics, and their achievements in the arts. Glossary, Important Dates, Books to Read, and Index.

254. Chrisp, Peter. **The Search for a Northern Route**. New York: Thomson Learning, 1994. 48p. $14.95. ISBN 1-56847-122-X. (Exploration & Encounters). 4-6

The idea of a western route to China (Cathay) fascinated explorers from Europe. Records indicate that Christopher Columbus, in 1492, was the first to attempt finding it. Other explorers from Europe followed him: Willem Barents from Holland; Giovanni de Verrazano and Jacques Cartier in the name of France; Gaspar Core Real of Portugal; and Sir Walter Raleigh, John Cabot, Sir Hugh Willoughby, and Martin Frobisher under the British flag. Rather than a way to China, they found places such as Lapland, Russia, and the Arctic and peoples such as the Inuit in North America and Canada. Quotes from sixteenth-century contemporaries complement the text. Glossary, Books to Read, and Index.

255. Chrisp, Peter. **The Search for the East**. New York: Thomson Learning, 1993. 48p. $14.95. ISBN 1-56847-120-3. (Exploration & Encounters). 4-6

Illustrations, first hand accounts, and original maps take the reader along the spice routes that enticed explorers in the fifteenth and sixteenth centuries. Additional information about Europe during these times gives an understanding of Portugal's role in exploration, the influence of Henry the Navigator, and the lure of gold. Glossary, Books to Read, and Index.

256.   Chrisp, Peter. **The Soldier Through History**. Tony Smith, illustrator. New York: Thomson Learning, 1993. 48p. $15.95. ISBN 1-56847-010-X. (Journey Through History). 3-5

With emphasis on ground soldiers, military tactics, and weaponry, the text looks at Greek hoplites from 500-300 B.C., Roman soldiers, knight crusaders, Mongol horsemen, Aztecs, Prussians, and tank fighters in the Gulf War. Maps, illustrations, and sidebars complement the text. Further Reading, Glossary, and Index.

257.   Chrisp, Peter. **The Spanish Conquests in the New World**. New York: Thomson Learning, 1993. 48p. $14.95. ISBN 1-56847-123-8. (Exploration & Encounters). 4-6

The text, using original maps and firsthand accounts, presents a history of the Spanish exploration and conquests in America. It emphasizes Cortés and Pizarro, whose search for gold made them ruthless toward Montezuma and Atahuallpa. Chrisp explains Aztec religious practices without moralizing and goes beyond the better-known stories of the explorers. Glossary, Books to Read, and Index.

258.   Chrisp, Peter. **Voyages to the New World**. New York: Thomson Learning, 1993. 48p. $14.95. ISBN 1-56847-123-8. (Exploration & Encounters). 4-6

In the general background about the explorers who found the New World and exploited it, Chrisp gives information about the fifteenth and sixteenth centuries in Europe, especially Portugal and Spain. With firsthand accounts and original maps, he tries to show how the New World appeared to the first Europeans who saw it five centuries ago. Glossary, Books to Read, and Index.

259.   Chrisp, Peter. **The Whalers**. New York: Thomson Learning, 1995. 47p. $15.95. ISBN 1-56847-421-0. (Remarkable World). 4-6

The text traces the history of whaling, beginning with the Inuits and the Basques. It describes the ships, men, and equipment, including the harpoon cannon (invented in 1868), and the early attempts to curb whaling before its end in 1986. Photographs, drawings, and diagrams augment the text.

260.   Chua-eoan, Howard. **Corazon Aquino**. New York: Chelsea House, 1988. 112p. $18.95; $7.95pa. ISBN 1-55546-825-X; 0-7910-0553-4pa. (World Leaders Past and Present). 5 up

Although very intelligent, Corazon Aquino (b. 1933) spent her early married life as a typical Filipino housewife, raising her family and watching television. In 1986, her life changed. Her husband, a member of the opposition political party against Marcos, was murdered when he returned from the United States. The Catholic Church backed Aquino and her honesty, helping her to overthrow Marcos. In 1986, Marcos defeated her, but the military began to change its support, and its members later ousted Marcos, giving Aquino control of the government. Her help brought democracy to the Philippines. Photographs highlight the text. Chronology, Further Reading, and Index.

261.   Clare, John D. **First World War**. San Diego, CA: Gulliver, Harcourt Brace, 1995. 64p. $16.95. ISBN 0-15-200087-9. (Living History). 5-8

Both real and reenactment photographs augment the text, giving an overview of World War I from its beginning, when Archduke Ferdinand and his wife Sophie were murdered in Sarajevo on June 28, 1914, until its end, on November 11, 1918. The text establishes a sense of the war by discussing why men joined the armed forces, life in the trenches, the use of gas and tanks, the fight from the air and the sea, shortages that occurred, women in the war, and the Treaty of Versailles in 1919. A concluding essay explores the ways that people today benefit from knowing what happened during that time. Index. *Notable Children's Trade Books in the Field of Social Studies.*

262.   Clare, John D., ed. **Ancient Greece**. San Diego, CA: Gulliver, Harcourt Brace, 1994. 64p. $16.95. ISBN 0-15-200516-1. (Living History). 6-9

Complemented with posed photographs depicting Greece, the text looks at life in Greece from about 800 B.C. until 146 B.C. Short discussions of various topics present the Greek world, farming in Attica, Sparta, gods and goddesses, heroes, the Olympic games, Greek colonies, Marathon, Thermopylae and Salamis, Athenian democracy and empire, art and architecture, theater, knowledge and philosophy, doctors and medicine, rituals of men, craftspeople and traders, the agora, old age and death, plague and war, Philip and Alexander, Alexandria, and the rise of Rome, as well as women's roles during the period. A concluding essay explores the ways in which people today benefit from knowing what happened during that time period. Index. *Notable Children's Trade Books in the Field of Social Studies.*

263.   Clare, John D., ed. **Classical Rome**. San Diego, CA: Gulliver, Harcourt Brace, 1993. 64p. $16.95. ISBN 0-15-200513-7. (Living History). 6-10

Complemented with posed photographs, the text presents the beginning and development of Rome in two-page coverage of topics. It shows everyday life, politics and government, and the achievements of Rome's architects and engineers. Index.

264. Clare, John D., ed. **Fourteenth-Century Towns**. San Diego, CA: Gulliver, Harcourt Brace, 1993. 64p. $16.95. ISBN 0-15-200515-3. (Living History). 6-10

The two-page topic spreads include photographs of persons in settings that recreate the Middle Ages. An overview of the time precedes discussions of everyday life, food, the role of the church, commerce, guilds and apprenticeships, contrasts between rich and poor, plague and famine, and social customs. A concluding essay explores the ways in which people today benefit from knowing what happened during that time period. Index.

265. Clare, John D., ed. **Industrial Revolution**. San Diego, CA: Gulliver, Harcourt Brace, 1994. 64p. $16.95. ISBN 0-15-200514-5. (Living History). 4-8

Complemented with posed photographs depicting the Industrial Revolution in Europe and America, along with photographs and prints of works created throughout the time, this text looks at the changes in life from 1712 until the end of the nineteenth century. Short discussions of various topics chronologically present the preceding economic system, trade and growth, the rise of the first factories, coal, the first railways, machines, changes in city life, iron and steel, bridges and tunnels, the men with the money, the second revolution and the attempt to gain power as a result, unions and politics, laws, medicine and health, education, philanthropy, and women's roles. A concluding essay explores the ways in which people today benefit from knowing what happened during that time period. Index. *Notable Children's Trade Books in the Field of Social Studies.*

266. Clare, John D., ed. **Pyramids of Ancient Egypt**. Charles Best, illustrator. San Diego, CA: Gulliver, Harcourt Brace, 1992. 64p. $16.95. ISBN 0-15-200509-9. (Living History). 4-6

About 2555 B.C., when the Pharaoh Chephren decided that he wanted a pyramid, his subjects had to build it. The text, with photographs of living history scenes, describes the daily life of the people, including clothing, makeup, home life, religious practices, burial rituals, and the work involved in building the pyramids. Chronology and Index.

267. Clare, John D., ed. **The Vikings**. San Diego, CA: Gulliver, Harcourt Brace, 1996. 64p. $9pa. ISBN 0-15-201309-1pa. (Living History). 6-10

Complemented with posed photographs depicting Viking times and prints of works created during the Viking period, the text looks at Viking life, including religion, peoples, clothes, homes, and customs, as well as how Viking families spent the long Scandinavian winters. A concluding essay explores the ways in which people today benefit from knowing what happened during that time period. Index. *Notable Children's Trade Books in the Field of Social Studies.*

268. Clark, Mary Jane Behrends. **The Commonwealth of Independent States**. Brookfield, CT: Millbrook Press, 1992. 64p. $16.40. ISBN 1-56294-081-3. (Headliners). 4-8

Eleven countries that were once part of the Soviet Union declared their independence in 1991. Their backgrounds indicate that, in addition to their common problem of surviving through the reign of Stalin and the Communist regime, they have had and will have diverse problems as part of a loosely federated commonwealth. The text discusses the countries, histories. and peoples of Russia, Ukraine, Belarus, Moldova, Armenia, Azerbaijan, Uzbekistan, Kazakhstan, Turkmenistan, Kyrgyzstan, and Tajikistan. Chronology, For Further Reading, and Index. *Society of School Librarians International Best.*

269. Claypool, Jane. **Saddam Hussein**. Vero Beach, FL: Rourke, 1993. 110p. $22.60. ISBN 0-86625-477-3. (World Leaders). 5-9

Saddam Hussein (b. 1937) fought a war with the United States in 1991 and lost. To place him within his world, the text gives an overview of Islam (beginning with Mohammed) as it discusses the resurgence of Iraq, the rise of Arab nationalism, the assassinations associated with the Arab nations, Saddam's exile in Egypt, his battle with the Kurds on the Turkish border, and the war with the United States over Kuwait. Photographs, Sunni and Shiite: The Two Main Branches of Islam, Time Line, Glossary, Bibliography, Media Resources, and Index.

270. Clements, Bruce. **The Treasure of Plunderell Manor**. New York: Farrar, Straus & Giroux, 1987. 180p. $12.95. ISBN 0-374-37746-4. 6-9

Laurel, age fourteen, abandoned in England as a baby, becomes maid to mistress Alice at Plunderell Manor in 1853. Orphaned Alice lives in the house with her aunt and uncle, who have locked her in a tower room and would like for her to disappear before she turns eighteen and inherits her fortune. Laurel helps Alice solve the riddle that reveals where her parents hid the family treasure; in the process, she saves Alice's life. Laurel, however, decides that she would rather go to America than be wealthy in a society she does not like.

271. Clements, Gillian, author/illustrator. **An Illustrated History of the World: How We Got to Where We Are**. New York: Farrar, Straus & Giroux, 1992. 62p. $16. ISBN 0-374-33258-4. 6-8

Clements presents single- and double-spread cartoon segments that cover the events in a period of world history, beginning with theories about the origin of the universe. She continues into the 1970s and ends with a timeline noting different epochs of history. Chronology.

272. Clements, Gillian. **The Picture History of Great Inventors**. New York: Knopf, 1994. 77p. $13pa. ISBN 0-679-84787-1pa. 4-6

Pages cover 60 major inventors, from Archimedes (287-212 B.C.) through inventors in Alexandria during the first century A.D., to the medieval period with Gutenberg and da Vinci, and into the twentieth century. Illustrations of each inventor's contributions enhance the text. Glossary and Index.

273. Clements, Gillian, author/illustrator. **The Truth About Castles**. Minneapolis, MN: Carolrhoda, 1990. 40p. $18.95; $6.95pa. ISBN 0-87614-401-6; 0-87614-552-7pa. 2-5

This cartoon-illustrated presentation of castles will require some guidance for younger readers, because of the pictorial and textual allusions, and may be less interesting to older readers who think they have outgrown books with many pictures. However, much information about castles appears, including their construction, celebrations in them, concentric configurations, their defense and attack, castles in decline, and ten famous European castles. Glossary and Index.

274. Clucas, Joan Graff. **Mother Teresa**. New York: Chelsea House, 1988. 112p. $18.95; $7.95pa. lSBN 1-55546-855-1; 0-7910-0602-6pa. (World Leaders Past and Present). 5 up

Mother Teresa (1910-1997) grew up in Skopje, then Yugoslavia. When she was eighteen, she joined the Loreto order of missionary nuns in India and took her final vows nine years later. After nine more years passed, she began work with the destitute by establishing her own order, the Missionaries of Charity. In Calcutta, she founded shelters for the homeless, the sick, and the dying. In 1965, she began her world travels to establish other centers like the one in Calcutta. By 1969, she had started the International Association of Co-Workers of Mother Teresa, an organization for lay supporters to work with her programs. In 1979, she received the Nobel Peace Prize. Photographs enhance the text. Chronology, Further Reading, and Index.

275. Cockcroft, James. **Diego Rivera**. New York: Chelsea House, 1991. 120p. $18.95; $7.95pa. ISBN 0-7910-1252-2; 0-7910-1279-4pa. (Hispanics of Achievement). 5 up

Diego Rivera (1886-1957) studied art in Europe, but decided not to paint in the European tradition. He worked to develop a uniquely Mexican—and uniquely Rivera—style. After living in Paris for ten years, he returned to Mexico and began painting frescoes and murals. In his work, he treated religious subjects irreverently. Because he condemned social injustice and wanted to celebrate the spirit of the ordinary person, he experimented with communism. His leftist politics, as well as his lifestyle, threatened the wealthy, but he refused to let their opinions rule his life. Photographs and reproductions enhance the text. Chronology, Further Reading, and Index.

276. Cockcroft, James D. **Daniel Ortega**. New York: Chelsea House, 1991. 112p. $18.95. ISBN 1-55546-846-2. (World Leaders Past and Present). 5 up

While in prison for eight years, Daniel Ortega (b. 1945) organized his fellow inmates to overthrow the oppressive Somoza regime in Nicaragua once they were released. They succeeded in 1979 and installed a provisional government on the Day of Joy. One year later, the United States backed rebels who launched an attack against the new Sandinista government. In 1984, the people elected Ortega president, but the fighting, backed with U.S. money, continued for ten more years. In 1990, elections named a new president. Ortega's subversive activities during the 1960s allowed the more democratic government to become a reality in the 1990s. Photographs enhance the text. Chronology, Further Reading, and Index.

277. Cockcroft, James D. **Mohammed Reza Pahlavi: Shah of Iran**. New York: Chelsea House, 1988. 112p. $18.95. ISBN 1-55546-847-0. (World Leaders Past and Present). 5 up

Mohammed Reza Pahlavi (1919-1980) became the Shah of Iran in 1940 and led his country for thirty-seven years in a tyrannical reign. He quelled an uprising in 1953, but the Islamic clergy, under the leadership of the Ayatollah Khomeini, forced him out in 1979 after he murdered unarmed protesters in the streets during 1978. Some historians see him as one of the most brutal leaders in history; others think that his leadership introduced modern technology into Iran. Photographs enhance the text. Chronology, Further Reading, and Index.

278. Codye, Corinn. **Luis W. Alvarez**. Bob Masheris, illustrator. Austin, TX: Raintree/Steck-Vaughn, 1993. 32p. $13.98; $5.95pa. ISBN 0-8114-8467-X; 0-8114-6750-3pa. (Hispanic Stories). 4-7

Luis Alvarez (1911-1988) grew up in California, where he started his scientific career as a youngster by building a radio. He became especially interested in physics, and when the atom bomb fell on Hiroshima in 1945, he and a team of men flew around the area to measure its impact. Later, he and colleagues built a hydrogen bubble chamber in which they discovered many new atomic particles. His work won him the Nobel Prize in Physics in 1968. A new interest in his later life was geology. He and his son studied rocks and hypothesized that a meteor crashing into the Earth had destroyed the dinosaurs because they identified iridium that would not otherwise have been found in Earth's rocks. Glossary.

279. Codye, Corinn. **Queen Isabella I**. Rick Whipple, illustrator. Austin, TX: Raintree/Steck-Vaughn, 1993. 32p. $13.98; $5.95pa. ISBN 0-8172-3380-6; 0-8114-6758-9pa. (Hispanic Stories). 4-7

Isabella (1451-1504), daughter of the king and queen of Castile, near Ávila in Spain, never expected to be queen because her brother was next in the line of succession. Her brother, however, was not a good king, and Castilian nobles urged her to assume the throne. To keep from war, she suggested that Henry be king but that he designate her as his heir. She married Ferdinand, crown prince of Aragón, because she wanted Spain united as a Catholic country. All of her decisions worked to this end, including the one that provided Columbus with money to go to the New World; he had to promise that he would take the Catholic religion to those he met. The Inquisition occurred under her reign, but many speculate that she was unaware of the horrors inflicted by the priests on Muslims, Jews, and alleged heretics. Glossary.

280. Coerr, Eleanor. **Mieko and the Fifth Treasure**. New York: Putnam, 1993. 79p. $13.95. ISBN 0-399-22434-3. 4-7

Meiko, age ten, has four tangible treasures—a sable brush, an inkstick, an inkstone, and a roll of rice paper. She remembers her art teacher telling her, before the bomb dropped on Nagasaki, Japan, in 1945, that she had a fifth treasure—beauty in her heart. But the bomb hurt her hand, and she can no longer paint as she did before. In her new school near her grandparents' farm, she feels isolated, and the children tease her about her scar. She must search deeply to regain the fifth treasure.

281. Coerr, Eleanor. **Sadako**. Ed Young, illustrator. New York: Putnam, 1993. 48p. $17.95. ISBN 0-399-21771-1. K-3

When Sadako was two, the atomic bomb dropped on her home in Hiroshima. At twelve, she developed leukemia. When a friend tells her that the gods will cure a sick person who folds 1,000 paper cranes, she starts folding. She never completes the thousand, but her classmates finish them after she dies. The illustrations and text make this version of *Sadako and the Thousand Paper Cranes* (1977) more appropriate for younger readers.

282. Coerr, Eleanor. **Sadako and the Thousand Paper Cranes**. New York: Putnam, 1977. 64p. $14.95. ISBN 0-399-20520-9. New York: Yearling, 1979. 64p. $15.95 ISBN 0-440-47465-5pa. 4-6

Sadako survived the bombing at Hiroshima for ten years after World War II. She loved to run and was a racer in her junior high school before she contracted the atomic bomb disease, leukemia. In the hospital, she began making paper cranes for good luck; before her death, she completed 664. Her classmates made the rest of the 1,000 cranes to be buried with her. They also published her letters.

283. Cohen, Daniel. **The Alaska Purchase**. Brookfield, CT: Millbrook Press, 1996. 64p. $15.90. ISBN 1-56294-528-9. (Spotlight on American History). 4-8

In 1867, the United States bought from Russia the land that became the 49th state, Alaska. The text looks at the events from 1728 through 1864 that led to the completion of the purchase. Other topics cover the discovery of Alaska, the sea-otter trade, the land of Alaska under Russian rule, the American takeover of the land, and what happened to Alaska after its purchase. Primary sources help to tell Alaska's story along with photographs and reproductions. Chronology, Bibliography, Further Reading, and Index.

284. Cohen, Daniel. **Ancient Egypt**. Gary A. Lippincott, illustrator. New York: Doubleday, 1990. 45p. $10.95. ISBN 0-385-24586-6. 3-6

The text covers 3,000 years of Egyptian history to 332 B.C., with two-page discussions of topics such as mummies, pyramids, religion, daily life, customs, hieroglyphics, warfare, tombs, and major archaeologists and their finds. Chronology and Index.

285. Cohen, Daniel. **Ancient Greece**. James Seward, illustrator. New York: Doubleday, 1990. 45p. $10.95. ISBN 0-385-26064-4. 3-6

The text focuses on the personalities and historical events that shaped the civilization of ancient Greece. Included are the stories of Troy, Knossos, and Atlantis, along with the discoveries of Schliemann, Evans, and others that give credence to the legends. Rituals such as that of Dionysius and the achievements of Alexander the Great through 146 B.C. form a background for the descriptions of daily life. Index.

286.   Cohen, Daniel. **The Ghost of Elvis: And Other Celebrity Spirits**. New York: Putnam, 1994. 100p. $14.95. ISBN 0-399-22611-7. 3-5

The text entertains with selections about the various speculations that exist concerning the ghosts of Elvis, Edgar Allan Poe, and other celebrities.

287.   Cohen, Daniel. **The Ghosts of War**. New York: Putnam, 1990. 95p. $13.95. ISBN 0-399-22200-6. New York: Minstrel, 1993. 95p. $2.99pa. ISBN 0-671-74086-5pa. 5-8

Reports of ghosts near battlefields have occurred in all times. The text recounts samurai ghosts from 1180 to 1185, the angel of Mons in 1914, a Polish mercenary of the Revolutionary War, Steven Decatur's ghost after 1820 in Washington, D.C., and Lieutenant Muir in Canada in 1812. Other ghosts also appear in these thirteen ghost tales, which Cohen says are "true" to the people who related them. Whether the stories can be verified is perhaps not as important as the concepts of realism and the history they impart.

288.   449.   Cohen, Daniel. **Prophets of Doom**. Brookfield, CT: Millbrook Press, 1992. 144p. $15.90. ISBN 1-56294-068-6. 6-9

Taking a skeptical view that anyone can accurately predict the future, the text covers the Millerites, Jehovah's Witnesses, the Greek oracles, the Cumaean Sybil, Mother Shipton, the Bible, Nostradamus, and Edgar Cayce. By noting various prophecies and their failures, Cohen supports his thesis. Bibliography and Index.

289.   Cohen, Daniel. **Real Vampires**. New York: Cobblehill, Dutton, 1995. 114p. $13.99. ISBN 0-525-65189-6. 6-8

Cohen presents vampires in various time periods throughout the world. He includes a German vampire from the early eighteenth century, Hungarian vampires in 1715 and 1725, Chinese and Russian vampires from various centuries, and English vampires since the twelfth century, including nineteenth-century vampires in Oxford and at Highgate. Selected Bibliography.

290.   Cole, Sheila. **The Dragon in the Cliff: A Novel Based on the Life of Mary Anning**. T. C. Farrow, illustrator. New York: Lothrop, Lee & Shepard, 1991. 211p. $12.95. ISBN 0-688-10196-8. 5-7

Mary Anning, age seven, begins climbing the cliffs surrounding the beaches of Lyme Regis, England, to find fossils that her father can clean and sell to tourists. In 1910, her father dies and Mary works to support her family. In 1812, she discovers a fossil ichthyosaurus, or "crocodile," as she called it, that measures seventeen feet. She makes other discoveries, but because women of that time were not archaeologists and never wrote scientific papers, no one mentions her work. Although poor and uneducated, she is very intelligent and teaches herself about her discoveries.

291.   Collier, Mary Jo, and Peter Collier. **The King's Giraffe**. Stephane Poulin, illustrator. New York: Simon & Schuster, 1996. 40p. $16. ISBN 0-689-80679-5. 1-5

After King Charles of France sent a printing press to the Egyptian pasha, Mehemet Ali, in 1826, the pasha wanted to send a return gift. He decides to send his favorite giraffe. The story tells of the giraffe's journey through France and its welcome in Marseilles and Aix-en-Provence on the way to Paris. The people enjoy seeing the animal, and the king welcomes it with pleasure.

292.   Collins, David R. **Tales for Hard Times: A Story About Charles Dickens**. David Mataya, illustrator. Minneapolis, MN: Carolrhoda, 1990. 64p. $9.95. ISBN 0-87614-433-4. (Creative Minds). 4-8

Writing about times in the nineteenth century, Charles Dickens (1812-1870) drew on his own poverty-stricken past, and delighted his audiences around the world. Drawings complement the text. Bibliography.

293.   Colver, Anne. **Florence Nightingale: War Nurse**. New York: Chelsea House, 1992. 80p. $14.95. ISBN 0-7910-1466-5. (Discovery Biography). 3-7

Florence Nightingale (1820-1910) enjoyed playing "nurse" as a child and graduated to tending animals before she began nursing humans in her village. Her wealthy family disapproved of her career choice, but she refused to give up her work for marriage. She became skilled enough that the British government sent her to help in the Crimean War. In England, she became a heroine, and returned to found the Nightingale School for training nurses.

294.   Compton, Anita. **Marriage Customs**. New York: Thomson Learning, 1993. 32p. $13.95. ISBN 1-56847-033-9. (Comparing Religions). 4-8

Six major religions—Buddhism, Christianity, Hinduism, Judaism, Islam, and Sikhism—have specific ceremonies for marriage. Some have signed contracts and ways of affirming the promises connected to the marriage. In all, marriage has its basis in the family's life. Photographs enhance the information. Glossary, Books to Read, and Index.

295. Conlon-McKenna, Marita. **Fields of Home**. New York: Holiday House, 1997. 189p. $15.95. ISBN 0-8234-1295-4. 5-7

The third and final segment of the O'Driscoll family trilogy following *Under the Hawthorn Tree* (1990) and *Wildflower Girl* (1992) occurs twelve years after the Irish potato famine almost destroyed the children. Eily remains in Ireland on a tenant farm with her husband and children, Michael trains to be a horseman, and Peggy continues to work as a housemaid in Boston. All have serious problems to face and difficult decisions to make while they remain concerned about each member of their family.

296. Conlon-McKenna, Marita. **Under the Hawthorn Tree**. Donald Teskey, illustrator. New York: Holiday House, 1990. 153p. $13.95. ISBN 0-8234-0838-8. 5 up

During the Irish famine of the 1840s, twelve-year-old Eily looks after her younger siblings, Michael and Peggy, while their mother goes to find their father, who is working on the roads. While the children's mother is gone, the bailiff repossesses the house, and the children have to find some way to survive without going to the workhouse. Remembering their mother's story of her childhood, the children walk to the far-off town where two aunts may still live. They succeed after having seen many whom they consider even worse off than they during this terrible time. *IRA Teachers' Award.*

297. Conlon-McKenna, Marita. **Wildflower Girl**. New York: Holiday House, 1992. 173p. $14.95. ISBN 0-8234-0988-0. 5-7

In this sequel to *Under the Hawthorn Tree*, Peggy, the youngest in her family at thirteen, decides to leave Ireland and her siblings to go to America. After suffering through forty days in steerage class on a ship crossing the Atlantic, she reaches Boston. She first works for an alcoholic who beats her. She finds another position with a wealthy family where the work is hard but fair. Her relationship with her fellow workers makes her feel as if she has some family around her again.

298. Connolly, Peter, author/illustrator. **Pompeii**. New York: Oxford University Press, 1990. 77p. $19.95; $11.95pa. ISBN 0-19-917159-9; 0-19-917158-0pa. 6-8

The text describes the eruption of Mt. Vesuvius, the volcano that destroyed Pompeii in A.D. 79, by examining the excavation finds at the site. Connolly includes detailed drawings recreating the scenes that might have been caught in the lava on that day. Maps, Glossary, and Index.

299. Connolly, Peter, author/illustrator. **The Roman Fort**. New York: Oxford, 1991. 32p. $19.95. ISBN 0-19-917108-4. (Rebuilding the Past). 6-10

Topographical maps and drawings clearly show the aspects of a Roman fort along Hadrian's Wall in England on the northwest frontier in A.D. 43. The fort is Vindolanda, where the Batavians and Tungrians fought with the Romans. Among the topics presented are the division of soldiers into cohorts and centuries, the headquarters, morning reports, the day's work, toilets, water and waste, baths, the village around the fort, and death and burial practices. Index.

300. Connolly, Peter. **Tiberius Claudius Maximus: The Cavalryman**. New York: Oxford University Press, 1989. 32p. $12.95. ISBN 0-19-917106-8. 5-9

A Roman soldier who served over thirty years for the Emperor Trajan in the Seventh Legion, Tiberius Claudius Maximus lived from approximately A.D. 70. His story appears on his tombstone, discovered in northern Greece in 1965. He captured Decebalus, the Dacian leader who lived in Romania beyond the Danube. This text presents the second part of his career as he returned to Tapae, helped bring about the fall of Sarmizegethusa, and was rewarded for his bravery and his devotion to duty as a member of the cavalry. Photographs, Illustrations, and Index.

301. Connolly, Peter. **Tiberius Claudius Maximus: The Legionary**. New York: Oxford University Press, 1989. 32p. $12.95. ISBN 0-19-917105-X. 5-9

A Roman soldier who served over thirty years for the Emperor Trajan in the Seventh Legion, Tiberius Claudius Maximus lived from approximately A.D. 70. His story appears on his tombstone, discovered in northern Greece in 1965. He captured Decebalus, the Dacian leader who lived in Romania beyond the Danube. Topics in this text discuss the first part of his career and include his life as a soldier, from his sore feet through weapons training to bridging the Danube. The text also looks at the camp in enemy territory, the armor and weapons used, and the battle itself. Photographs, Illustrations, and Index.

302. Conrad, Pam. **Call Me Ahnighito**. Richard Egielski, illustrator. New York: Laura Geringer, HarperCollins, 1995. Unpaged. $14.95. ISBN 0-06-023322-2. 1-2

The meteorite Ahnighito talks of its experiences in Greenland. It is picked up and eventually moved by boat to Brooklyn Naval Yard in 1897. Seven years later, it is moved to the American Museum of Natural History in New York City, where everyone knows its name.

303. Conrad, Pam. **Pedro's Journal: A Voyage with Christopher Columbus.** Peter Koeppen, illustrator. Honesdale, PA: Caroline House, 1991. 81p. $13.95. ISBN 1-878093-17-7. New York: Scholastic, 1992. 81p. $2.95pa. ISBN 0-590-46206-7pa. 3-7

Pedro accompanies Christopher Columbus on the *Santa Maria* in 1492 because he can read and write. He records the crew's frustration, Columbus's responses to events, their encounters with the natives, and the fierceness of storms on their return to Spain.

304. Coolidge, Olivia. **The Golden Days of Greece.** Enrico Arno, illustrator. 1968. New York: HarperCollins, 1990. 224p. $14.89. ISBN 0-690-04795-0. 4-7

First the Achaeans and then the Dorians arrived in the land that became Greece. Coolidge gives a solid overview of Greek history, beginning with Heinrich Schliemann's discovery of the treasures of Troy and Agamemnon's gold at Mycenae, which seem to verify Homer's stories in *The Iliad*. The other chapters include the origins of the Olympic games, Aristodemos the Spartan, the Persians' attack and the ensuing Greek victories, Pericles, Socrates, Plato, Philip, and Alexander. Greek Words and Proper Names and Index.

305. Cooper, Floyd, author/illustrator. **Mandela: From the Life of the South African Statesman.** New York: Philomel, 1996. Unpaged. $15.95. ISBN 0-399-22942-6. 1-4

In this biography of Mandela, Cooper uses "wind" to symbolize the strength that Mandela found from various lessons in his life including the timelessness of African traditions, which helped him become a leader for South Africa. It recalls his youth in his royal family, his school life, he and his partner being the first blacks to open a law office in Johannesburg, his family, his two marriages, and his time in prison. Bibliography.

305a. Cooper, Ilene. **The Dead Sea Scrolls.** John Thompson, illustrator. New York: William Morrow, 1997. 64p. $15. ISBN 0-688-14300-8. 5-9

In 1947, a young boy found some crumbling scrolls in a cave near the Dead Sea. What the scrolls contained has caused controversy since the boy sold them. Cooper tells of the quest to own the scrolls, the rivalry among biblical scholars to interpret them, and the coincidences and scientific advances that have shown their age and importance. Index.

306. Cooper, Susan. **Dawn of Fear.** Margery Gill, illustrator. 1970. New York: Aladdin, 1989. $3.95pa. ISBN 0-689-71327-4pa. 5 up

Derek lives with his family outside London during World War II, and they have to go to the local shelters almost every night during air raids. When a bomb hits his friend's house one night and kills his friend, the war takes on a different meaning. Derek has to adjust to the huge hole in his own life.

307. Coote, Roger. **The Anglo-Saxons.** New York: Thompson Learning, 1994. 32p. $14.95. ISBN 1-56847-062-2. (Look into the Past). 4-6

Anglo-Saxon legends, such as those about Robin Hood and King Arthur, have been cornerstones of western lore. They came from the Anglo-Saxon culture that matured in England during the early Middle Ages. The text, with photographs of artifacts and books, reveals concepts such as the Anglo-Saxons' love of war, their family life, their religious beliefs, their daily lives, and their clothing. Glossary, Important Dates, Books to Read, and Index.

308. Coote, Roger. **The Egyptians.** New York: Thompson Learning, 1993. 32p. $14.95. ISBN 1-56847-061-4. (Look into the Past). 4-6

Photographs of archaeological sites and illustrations of the culture complement a text that discusses Egyptian hieroglyphics, clothing and jewelry, farming and food, stonecutting, politics, and religious beliefs. Glossary, Important Dates, Books to Read, and Index.

309. Coote, Roger. **The First Voyage Around the World.** Tony Smith, illustrator. New York: Bookwright, Franklin Watts, 1990. 32p. $17. ISBN 0-531-18302-5. (Great Journeys). 4-7

Because Charles I of Spain wanted to capture some of the lucrative spice trade, he agreed to finance the Portuguese Magellan's attempt to sail west to the Spice Islands and the Philippines beginning in 1519. Magellan faced a mutiny when at first he was unable to find a passage through South America, but he quelled it. Then he did find the opening, and he and his men eventually saw land and the Philippines in 1521. Upon his arrival, Magellan became the first man to sail around the world. His zeal to convert the islanders to Christianity did not thrill them, and they murdered him. Only 18 of the 277 men who had left Spain with him in 1519 returned (with all their booty) in 1522, nearly three years later. Photographs of maps and appropriate paintings highlight the text. Glossary, Books to Read, and Index.

310. Coote, Roger. **The Sailor Through History.** Tony Smith, illustrator. New York: Thomson Learning, 1993. 48p. $16.95. ISBN 1-56847-012-6. (Journey Through History). 3-5

Four-page chapters present details about a Polynesian mariner, a Roman oarsman, a Viking raider, a sixteenth-century Portuguese explorer, the crew on the Armada, and the Mayflower voyage. Types of ships that the sailors worked on include sails, steamers, liners, U-boats, and supertankers. Drawings, photographs, and information boxes enliven the text. Bibliography and Index.

311. Corbishley, Mike. **Ancient Rome**. New York: Facts on File, 1989. 96p. $17.95. ISBN 0-8160-1970-3. (Cultural Atlas for Young People). 6-9

The text describes all areas of the Roman Empire: Rome itself, other areas of Italy, Africa, Spain, Gaul, Greece, Britain, and Asia Minor. Sidebars and beautiful color illustrations reveal the Rome of the Caesars, the Greek influence on poets and dramatists, and other aspects of daily life during Roman times. Bibliography, Chronology, Glossary, Gazetteer, and Index.

312. Corbishley, Mike. **Everyday Life in Roman Times**. Peter Kesteven, illustrator. New York: Franklin Watts, 1994. 32p. $18. ISBN 0-531-14288-4. (Clues to the Past). 4-8

The Roman civilization and the daily lives of its people are the subjects of this book. The text reveals the strictly observed social strata and the customs of the times; illustrations show examples of the buildings, the dress, the foods, and the items people used for various activities. Index.

313. Corbishley, Mike. **Growing Up in Ancient Rome**. Chris Molan, illustrator. Mahwah, NJ: Troll, 1994. 32p. $11.89; $3.95pa. ISBN 0-8167-2721-X; 0-8167-2722-8pa. (Growing Up In). 3-5

The text describes daily life in ancient Rome, including family life, entertainment, schools, and religion. Illustrations show the buildings in which these activities occurred and the utensils or special clothing needed for them. Index.

314. Corbishley, Mike. **The Medieval World: From the Fall of Rome to the Discovery of America**. New York: Peter Bedrick, 1993. 64p. $18.95. ISBN 0-87226-362-2. (Timelink). 5 up

The text surveys the known world between A.D. 450 and 1500. In detailed time charts, one sees what was happening simultaneously in Africa, Europe, Asia, and the Americas. Among the topics presented are Buddhism, Islam, the Vikings, the Crusades, the plague, and medieval towns. Photographs, maps, and charts highlight the text. Glossary and Index.

315. Corbishley, Mike. **The Middle Ages**. New York: Facts on File, 1990. 96p. $17.95. ISBN 0-8160-1973-8. (Cultural Atlas for Young People). 6-9

Beginning with an overview of medieval Europe, the text then covers the barbarians, Crusades, and empires of the time. Sidebars include information on topics such as stained glass design and the Bayeux Tapestry, which illustrates William's landing in England in 1066. The second section covers the history of each region of Europe, including Scandinavia and Russia. Informative color illustrations augment the text. Bibliography, Chronology, Glossary, Gazetteer, and Index.

316. Corbishley, Mike. **Rome and the Ancient World**. New York: Facts on File, 1993. 78p. $17.95. ISBN 0-8160-2786-2. (Illustrated History of the World). 4-7

The first section of text covers the rise of Rome, the Empire, and everyday life in the Empire. The second segment looks at the world outside the Empire. In this world is ancient China, ancient India, the Kushars, the Parthian and Sassanian Empires, and Africa's Nok, Axum, and Petra. Beautiful illustrations highlight the text. Glossary, Further Reading, and Index.

317. Corbishley, Mike. **Secret Cities**. Roger Walker, illustrator. New York: Lodestar, 1989. 47p. $14.95. ISBN 0-525-67275-3. (Time Detectives). 4-7

Covering a span of 8,000 years, the text speculates about the lives in cities that have been excavated or restored. The cities covered (with approximate dates) are Skara Brae in Scotland (3000 B.C.), Biskupin in Poland (750 B.C.), Jorvik in England (A.D. 800), Çatal Hüyük in Turkey (6500 B.C.), the Pyramid of Khufu in Egypt (2700 B.C.), Knossos in Greece (1500 B.C.), Pompeii and Herculaneum in Italy (A.D. 100), Mohenjo-Daro in China (A.D. 1400), Great Zimbabwe in Zimbabwe (A.D. 1400), Ch'in Shi-huang-ti in China (200 B.C.), Mesa Verde in the United States (A.D. 1200), Machu Picchu in Peru (A.D. 1400), and Williamsburg in the United States (A.D. 1800). Glossary and Index.

318. Corbishley, Mike. **What Do We Know About the Romans?** New York: Peter Bedrick, 1992. 45p. $16.95. ISBN 0-87226-352-5. (What Do We Know About . . .?). 3-7

In an attempt to give a sense of Roman life, the text covers school, work, food, family, clothes, gods, medicine, government, the arts, inventions, travel, and military obligations. Illustrations complement the text. Index.

319. Cordoba, Maria. **Pre-Columbian Peoples of North America**. Chicago: Childrens Press, 1994. 34p. $20. ISBN 0-516-08393-7. (The World Heritage). 4-7

Photographs clearly augment the text in this discussion of the people who lived in North America before Columbus arrived. The main sites presented in Canada are Bison Cliff, where bison jumped; Anthony Island, where the Haida Indians built totem poles; and L'Anse aux Meadows National Historic Park, which holds definitive proof that the Vikings settled in America before Columbus. Two sites in the United States are Mesa Verde National Park, home to the Anasazi nearly 700 years ago, and Cahokia Mounds Historic Site, where remains of mounds that denoted the Mississippian culture are found. Glossary and Index.

320. Corrain, Lucia. **Giotto and Medieval Art: The Lives and Works of the Medieval Artists**. Sergio Ricciardi and Andrea Ricciardi, illustrators. New York: Peter Bedrick, 1995. 64p. $19.95. ISBN 0-87226-315-0. 4 up

As painter, architect, and engineer, Giotto (1267-1337) was the most influential artist of medieval Europe. The text recounts his life, his techniques, and his masterpiece frescoes, wood-panel paintings, and mosaics. Included in the text are many reproductions of his work and pictures of the times. Index.

321. Corzine, Phyllis. **The Black Death**. San Diego, CA: Lucent, 1996. 112p. $16.95. ISBN 1-56006-299-1. (World History). 5-8

In the fourteenth century, the bubonic plague permeated Europe, killing millions. This text discusses its spread from Asia on ships trading throughout the known world. Overpopulation and lack of sanitation in Europe incited it. Changes resulted from the rapid decrease in population such as the breakdown of the feudal system, revised attitudes toward religion, and different farming methods. Photographs, maps, and reproductions augment the text. Bibliography, Chronology, Further Reading, and Index.

321a. Corzine, Phyllis. **The Palestinian-Israeli Accord**. San Diego, CA: Lucent, 1996. 112p. $16.95. ISBN 1-56006-181-2. (Overview). 6-10

Corzine looks at the history preceeding the contemporary Palestinian-Israeli accord. She describes the creation of the state of Israel, a perceived opportunistic role played by the British, and the various wars that resulted from the creation of the new state. The history ends in mid-1996 and gives a good background for the long-standing conflict. Bibliography, Further Reading, Glossary, and Index.

322. Cosner, Shaaron. **War Nurses**. New York: Walker, 1988. 106p. $16.95. ISBN 0-8027-6826-1. 5-9

The text includes chapters on war nurses and their activities in the Civil War, the Crimean War, the Spanish-American War, World Wars I and II, the Korean War, and the Vietnam War. Letters and stories about the various personalities, among them Clara Barton and Florence Nightingale, show what the nurses had to face in their quest to help the wounded. Among the other topics included are a brief history of war weapons, the wounds from each, and the medical developments that evolved from these types of wounds. These nurses were clearly war veterans, a status for which nurses have had to petition. Index.

323. Cotterell, Arthur. **Ancient China**. Allen Hills and Geoff Brightling, illustrators. New York: Knopf, 1994. 63p. $16. ISBN 0-679-96167-4. (Eyewitness). 4-7

China is the world's oldest civilization and was controlled under one empire from 221 B.C. until A.D. 1912. The first great dynasty lasted from 1650 to 1027 B.C. The dynasties include the Shang, Zhon, Qin, Han, Sui, Tang, Song, Yuan, Ming, Quing, and then the People's Republic in 1949. The text, with photographic highlights, covers the health, farm life, waterways, cities, homes, foods, clothes, and beliefs of the Chinese people. Index.

324. Coville, Bruce. **Prehistoric Peoples**. Michael McDermott, illustrator. New York: Doubleday, 1990. 45p. $11.95. ISBN 0-385-24923-3. 3-5

In short chapters, the author discusses the theory of human evolution with supporting facts from fossils found by anthropologists in such sites as Olduvai Gorge, Africa, and Shanidar Cave, Iraq. Carbon-14 dating and DNA testing have aided the search for human beginnings, with the most important find up until 1990 being Lucy, in 1974. Coville comments that scientists must continually rethink their theories as they make new discoveries. The Lascaux Cave paintings discovered in 1940 allowed new understanding of the sophistication of the Cro-Magnons; other sites revealed that the earliest hominids were vegetarians but that *Homo habilis* hominids in the Ice Age were hunters. The Tasaday tribe discovered in the Philippines and the !Kung bushmen in Africa give insight as to what life might have been like during the Stone Age. Coville indicates that "prehistory" covers people through the beginning of Sumer, when the first extant clay tablets were found. Illustrations of fossils and of the possible progress of hominids—*Dryopithecus*, *Sivapithecus* (upright), *Australopithecus*, *Homo habilis*, *Homo erectus*, Neanderthal, Cro-Magnon, modern human—show resemblances. Index.

325. Cowley, Marjorie. **Dar and the Spear-thrower**. New York: Clarion, 1994. 118p. $13.95. ISBN 0-395-68132-4. 4-7

Around 15,000 years ago in France, during the Cro-Magnon period, Dar, age thirteen, undergoes his clan's initiation into manhood. He hears about a spear-thrower, a device that will enable him to throw with greater power and therefore be the warrior his tribe expects, and he goes on a dangerous journey in search of the item. What he finds is much more than he could have imagined.

326. Craig, Mary. **Lech Walesa and His Poland.** New York: Continuum, 1987. 326p. $18.95. ISBN 0-826-40390-5. 5-10

Although circumstances have changed in Poland, with Walesa actually becoming its leader, since Craig wrote the book, the text tells about the twentieth-century trials of Poland under communism and Gomuka. The book is half-biography, half-history, in its telling. Walesa, an intelligent man who passed exams to enter technological school, did not have enough money to attend, but he refused to complain about his fate and became a skilled worker instead. His decisions in his dealings with both the communists and his friends show his strong morality. When he won the Nobel Peace Prize in 1983 for his work in organizing the Solidarity movement in Poland, many felt that he represented all Poles trying to lift themselves out of an untenable situation. Bibliography and Index.

327. Crofford, Emily. **Born in the Year of Courage**. Minneapolis, MN: Carolrhoda, 1992. 160p. $19.95. ISBN 0-87614-679-5. (Adventures in Time). 4-7

In 1841, Manjiro, age fifteen, finds himself shipwrecked. An American whaling ship rescues him, and he is surprised to find that the Americans are not all barbarians as his Japanese heritage has taught him. He decides to work toward opening trade between the two countries by taking a whaling boat back to Japan to begin his work.

328. Crofford, Emily. **Healing Warrior: A Story About Sister Elizabeth Kenny**. Steve Michaels, illustrator. Minneapolis, MN: Carolrhoda, 1989. 64p. $17.50. ISBN 0-87614-382-6. (Creative Minds). 3-5

While living with her family in New South Wales, Australia, Elizabeth Kenny (1880-1952) broke her wrist. The doctor told her about welding bones to muscles, and she decided to help her frail brother build his muscles. She succeeded, and this experience led to her decision to help other people. The personal cost of this decision included not marrying someone she loved, because he forbade her to nurse other people. In the Australian bush, Kenny treated the frightening infantile paralysis with heat and moisture followed by exercise. Her patients recovered, whereas others whose physicians put their limbs in casts did not. She served in World War I in Europe, earning the Australian military rank of "sister," the equivalent of first lieutenant. When she came to America, many doctors refused to try her methods of treatment for polio, but the Mayo Clinic doctors did, and they achieved dramatic results during the 1941 spread of the disease. Her work earned her the title of "mother of modern physical rehabilitation." Sources.

329. Croll, Carolyn. **Redouté: The Man Who Painted Flowers**. New York: Philomel, 1996. 40p. $15.95. ISBN 0-399-22606-0. 3-5

With both biography and French history, Croll tells the story of Redouté, an artist born in Belgium who went to Paris during the French Revolution and stayed to console the Empress Josephine.

330. Crosher, Judith. **Ancient Egypt**. New York: Viking, 1993. 48p. $14.99. ISBN 0-670-84755-0. (See Through History). 5-8

Around 3000 B.C., the Egyptians expanded along the Nile and became the first unified nation. Egypt developed a complex civilization, culminating with the construction of the vast pyramids for their dead rulers. See-through cutaways of a town house, the palace of Akhenaten, the tomb of Sennedjem, and the temple of Khons augment the text. Two-page topical spreads include information on the Nile, the God-King of Egypt, medicine and the law, women, childhood, the home, writing and calculation, arts and crafts, fashion, the palace, peasant farmers, trade and tribute, education, tombs, pyramids, gods and goddesses, death and the afterlife, temples, war, and the last days of the civilization. Key Dates, Glossary, and Index.

331. Cross, Robin. **Aftermath of War.** New York: Thomson Learning, 1994. 48p. $14.95. ISBN 1-56847-178-5. (World War II). 5-7

Many books cover World War II, but this book looks at what happened after the war's end. It reports on the Nuremberg trials of Nazi war criminals, the division of Germany and the Berlin airlift, the contrast in power between the United States and Britain, the beginning of the "cold war," and Japanese factories' shift from producing war goods to making peacetime items. An interesting aspect of the year immediately after the war is the forces of nature: In 1946-1947, Britain had the coldest winter in fifty-three years, with snows melting to flood the island in the spring and the following summer producing a drought. Such natural trials following those inflicted by humans must have been especially frustrating. Glossary, Books to Read, Chronology, and Index.

332. Cross, Robin. **Children and War**. New York: Thomson Learning, 1994. 48p. $14.95. ISBN 1-56847-180-7. (World War II). 5-7

By using the experiences of young people during the war, Cross presents a view of World War II. His subjects include a Polish boy imprisoned by Soviet police, a French girl who fought in the Resistance, a messenger boy in Britain during bombing attacks, a child from Hiroshima, and an American who had no direct contact except through newsreels. Further Reading, Glossary, and Index.

333. Cross, Robin. **Technology of War**. New York: Thomson Learning, 1994. 48p. $14.95. ISBN 1-56847-177-7. (World War II). 5-7

Many weapons used in World War II had been introduced in World War I, with the submarine almost winning both wars for Germany. Between 1918 and 1939, radio communications improved, and the civil aviation industry expanded. Cathode ray tubes appeared, vital for radar screens, and research into the nature of the atom progressed. In 1936-1939, the Soviet Union, Germany, and Japan tested their new weapons, fighter planes, dive bombers, and tanks. The ultimate weapon became the atom bomb that the Americans developed. Glossary, Books to Read, Chronology, and Index.

334. Cruz, Barbara C. **Frida Kahlo: Portrait of a Mexican Painter**. Springfield, NJ: Enslow, 1996. 112p. $18.95. ISBN 0-89490-765-4. 6-9

As a Mexican painter, Frida Kahlo (1907-1954) gained much of her reputation after her death. The text looks at her devotion to her art and also at her more intense commitment to her husband, Diego Rivera. It also discusses her political beliefs and her pride in her Mexican heritage. Further Reading and Index.

335. Cumming, David. **Russia**. New York: Thomson Learning, 1995. 48p. $15.95. ISBN 1-56847-240-4. (Modern Industrial World). 5-8

As the text discusses the current situation in Russia, it also includes Russian history. To understand the Russia of today, one must know the culture and economics of its past. Photographs, tables, and sidebars relay additional information. Glossary, Further Information, and Index.

336. Cush, Cathie. **Artists Who Created Great Works**. Austin, TX: Raintree/Steck-Vaughn, 1995. 48p. $15.96. ISBN 0-8114-4993-5. (20 Events Series). 6 up

In two-page spreads, Cush creates a minihistory of art by presenting profiles on twenty artists spanning from Leonardo Da Vinci (Italy, 1452-1519) to Salvador Dali (Spain, 1904-1989). Photographs of famous paintings accompany the text. Other artists included are Albrecht Dürer (Germany, 1471-1528), Michelangelo Buonarroti (Italy, 1475-1564), Gian Lorenzo Bernini (Italy, 1598-1680), Rembrandt van Rijn (Netherlands, 1606-1669), Christopher Wren (England, 1632-1723), Francisco Goya (Spain, 1746-1828), Joseph M. W. Turner (England, 1775-1851), Eugène Delacroix (France, 1798-1863), Auguste Rodin (France, 1840-1917), Claude Monet (France, 1840-1926), Henri Matisse (France, 1869-1954), Pablo Picasso (Spain, 1881-1973), Diego Rivera (Mexico, 1886-1957), Ludwig Mies van der Rohe (Germany, 1886-1969), Georgia O'Keeffe (United States, 1887-1986), Alexander Calder (United States, 1898-1976), Henry Moore (England, 1898-1986), and Ansel Adams (United States, 1902-1984). Glossary, Suggested Readings, and Index.

337. Cush, Cathie. **Disasters That Shook the World**. Austin, TX: Raintree/Steck-Vaughn, 1994. 48p. $15.96. ISBN 0-8114-4929-7. (20 Events Series). 6 up

Some of the major changes in perception that have occurred in the world have come as a result of a disaster. In two-page spreads, Cush discusses twenty situations that were never expected to happen. They are the explosion of Vesuvius (A.D. 79 in Pompeii, Italy), the Black Death (fourteenth-century Europe), the destruction of the Native Americans (fifteenth through nineteenth centuries), the Great London Fire (1666), the Irish Potato Famine (1845-1849), the Great Chicago Fire (1871), Krakatoa's eruption (Indonesia, 1883), the San Francisco earthquake (1906), the Titanic sinking (1912), the world flu epidemic (1917-1919), the Bangladesh cyclone (1970), famine in Ethiopia and Somalia (1984-1985; 1992), the AIDS epidemic (1980s), the Bhopal chemical disaster (India, 1984), the *Challenger* explosion (United States, 1986), the Chernobyl nuclear meltdown (Russia, 1986), the *Exxon Valdez* oil spill (1989), the death of the Aral Sea (between Kazakhstan and Uzbekistan, 1960-1990), the Gulf War oil disaster (Kuwait, 1991), and hurricanes Andrew (Atlantic, 1992) and Iniki (Hawaii, 1992). Glossary, Suggested Readings, and Index.

338. Cush, Cathie. **Women Who Achieved Greatness**. Austin, TX: Raintree/Steck-Vaughn, 1995. 48p. $15.96. ISBN 0-8114-4938-6. (20 Events Series). 6 up

Women have achieved greatness in a variety of ways, and some, though not all, have received recognition for it. In two-page spreads, Cush profiles some of these women. The women included are Maria Montessori (Italy, 1870-1952), Helen Keller (1880-1968) and Annie Sullivan (d. 1936), Eleanor Roosevelt (1884-1962), Amelia Earhart (1899-1937), Golda Meir (Israel, 1898-1978), Margaret Mead (1901-1978), Barbara McClintock (1902-1992), Marian Anderson (1900-1993), Margaret Bourke-White (1906-1971), Rachel Carson (1907-1964), Mother Teresa (Albania and India, b. 1910), Indira Gandhi (India, 1917-1984), Katharine Meyer Graham (b. 1917), Maya Angelou (b. 1928), Violeta Chamorro (Nicaragua, b. 1929), Jane Goodall (England, b. 1934), Barbara Jordan (1936-1996), Aung San Suu Kyi (Burma, b. 1944), Wilma Mankiller (b. 1945), and Oprah Winfrey (b. 1954). Glossary, Suggested Readings, and Index.

339.   Cushman, Karen. **The Midwife's Apprentice**. New York: Clarion, 1995. 122p. $10.95. ISBN 0-395-69229-6. New York: Trophy, 1995. 122p. $4.50pa. ISBN 0-06-440640-Xpa. 5-9

After the midwife finds Brat, aged twelve or thirteen, hiding in a dung heap, she calls the girl Beetle and gives her a job as midwife's assistant. As Beetle becomes more confident and more articulate, she renames herself Alyce, and soon realizes that midwifery is the profession for her. In the twelfth century, she works to become more proficient as she copes with those around her. *American Library Association Notable Books for Children, American Library Association Notable Books for Young Adults, Booklist Books for Youth Editors' Choices, American Booksellers' Pick of the Lists, Horn Book Fanfare Honor List, School Library Journal Best Book,* and *Newbery Medal.*

340.   Cytron, Barry, and Phyllis Cytron. **Myriam Mendilow: Mother of Jerusalem**. Minneapolis, MN: Lerner, 1994. 128p. $22.95. ISBN 0-8225-4919-0. 5 up

Myriam Mendilow (1909-1989) grew up in a Jewish home with a mother who did not believe that the old ways were the best. Mendilow became a teacher, and one of her skills was seeing when others needed something; she always tried to find what that something was to improve their lives. She saw that the elderly of Jerusalem had no money, no friends, and no esteem. She created places for them to go where they could make crafts for sale and feel as if they were contributing to life instead of merely existing. Epilogue, Source Notes, and Index.

$\boxed{\text{D}}$

341.   Dahl, Roald. **Boy: Tales of Childhood**. New York: Farrar, Straus & Giroux, 1984. 160p. $16. ISBN 0-374-37374-4. 3 up

Dahl lived his early childhood in Wales and England, son of a Norwegian mother and a father who had gone to Wales to start a business supplying ships. His father's early death, soon after Dahl's sister died at age seven, did not seem to cause economic distress, because Dahl's mother was able to give the family whatever it needed, including private school (public, in England) education. Dahl's stories of childhood during the 1920s in England show children fascinated with the local store's candy, hiding a dead mouse in one of the candy jars, and admiring the stunning ride of an older boy on his bicycle. Dahl spent summers in Norway and vividly remembers the summer when a doctor removed his adenoids without using anesthesia. His nose was almost severed in a motor car accident, with his mother driving. While he was in school, the Cadbury candy factory sent bars of unmarked candy for the boys to test. Dahl's mother offered him education at Oxford or Cambridge, but with his application for and receipt of a coveted position with Shell Oil, he ends this book.

342.   Dahl, Roald. **My Year**. Quentin Blake, illustrator. New York: Viking, 1994. 63p. $14.99. ISBN 0-670-85397-6. 4-6

When Roald Dahl was growing up in the 1920s, he lived in England. The text follows a generic year in his life, beginning in January and ending in December. Through his well-crafted words and many concrete details, one gets a sense of what life was like for a young boy living in England during that time.

343.   Daley, William. **The Chinese Americans**. New York: Chelsea House, 1995. 93p. $19.95; $8.95pa. ISBN 0-7910-3357-0; 0-7910-3379-1pa. (The Peoples of North America). 4-7

The immigration of Chinese into the United States began to rise when the first Opium War between China and England (1839-1842) gave Hong Kong to England in the Treaty of Nanking and opened four other Chinese ports. The corrupt Manchu (Ch'ing Dynasty) rulers imposed higher taxes, causing the people to revolt in 1850 under the leadership of Hung Hsiu-ch'uan, a convert to Christianity, in the Taiping "Great Peace" Rebellion. But the Taipings were defeated in 1864. A second Opium War fought at the same time, from 1856 to 1860, caused even more turmoil. By 1848, only seven Chinese were recorded as living in San Francisco, but by 1851 the gold rush had attracted 25,000. The Chinese immigrants were prevented from voting, holding public office, and practicing certain trades. For these reasons, they started laundries and worked to build the railroads across the United States. Immigration laws tightened in 1882, keeping out many women who had stayed behind to look after their husbands' parents. In the twentieth century, other problems in China caused emigration. Sun Yat-Sen ruled from 1866 to 1925, when the Japanese began to trouble the Chinese. In 1949, Mao Zedong declared victory over Chiang and established his brand of Communism. Chinese Americans developed the Bing cherry and were the first to hatch eggs with artificial heat. They have cultural depth through their religions—Confucianism, Taoism, and Buddhism—and their artists and inventors, such as Wang, Yo-Yo Ma, Maya Lin, Maxine Hong Kingston, Lawrence Yep, and David Hwang. Selected References and Index.

344.   Dalokay, Vedat. **Sister Shako and Kolo the Goat: Memories of My Childhood in Turkey**. Güner Ener, translator. New York: Lothrop, Lee & Shepard, 1994. 96p. $13. ISBN 0-688-13271-5. 5-8

In this tale, Dalokay remembers an old woman from his childhood whose family had been murdered during a vendetta. She kept a white goat, Kolo, in his father's old stable. Sister Shako saw signs and omens in the goat's positions, such as raised ears indicating a wolf or a gendarme's arrival. Sister Shako's understanding of nature, close relationship to the goat, and wise advice to Dalokay show the tendencies of rural Turkish people before television infiltrated the land. When Sister Shako died, he knew that she was part of the earth, or, as she said, "I shall enter the blood of whoever drinks Kolo's milk." *Mildred L. Batchelder Honor Book.*

345.   Dana, Barbara. **Young Joan**. New York: Zolotow, HarperCollins, 1991. 384p. $17.95. ISBN 0-06-021422-8. 5-9

Joan of Arc (1412?-1431) supposedly heard her name being spoken aloud in a garden where no other human was present. After a time, she allowed herself to think that she might be the maid of whom Merlin had spoken, the one who would help France. The text looks at Joan of Arc's early life, seeing her as a mystic in her time rather than someone who was either hysterical or a feminist. Joan's favorite activity was praying, and although she enjoyed her family and her pets, God was the center of her life. With this focus, she convinced the Dauphin that she could save France—and she did. Bibliography and Index. *Bulletin Blue Ribbon Book.*

346. Daniel, Jamie, Michael Nicholson, and David Winner. **Raoul Wallenberg: One Man Against Nazi Terror**. Milwaukee, WI: Gareth Stevens, 1992. 68p. $16.95. ISBN 0-8368-0629-8. (People Who Made a Difference). 3-6

Raoul Wallenberg (1912-1945?) was born a Swede and studied architecture in the United States. When he returned to Sweden, he used his knowledge of five languages to go into international business. Eventually the Swedish government asked him to go to Hungary to help the Jews in World War II. He created false passports, which the Hungarians thought were legal, and gave them to as many Jews as he could. Some think that he saved more than 100,000 Jews before the war ended in 1945. But when the Russians arrived in Hungary, Wallenberg disappeared. Although the Russians claimed not to know his whereabouts, people think that they imprisoned or killed him. Organizations, Books, List of New Words, Important Dates, and Index.

347. Daniel, Jamie, and Benjamin Pogrund. **Nelson Mandela: Speaking Out for Freedom in South Africa**. Milwaukee, WI: Gareth Stevens, 1992. 68p. $16.95. ISBN 0-8368-0621-2. (People Who Made a Difference). 3-6

Nelson Mandela (b. 1918) grew up in South Africa where, as a black man, he had few rights, even though he was the son of a chief of the Tembu tribe. He went to college and received legal training and worked to change the situation in South Africa for his people. In 1962, the government sent him to prison, where he stayed for twenty-seven years, until 1990 when he was seventy-one years old. He had refused to leave the prison until the government granted concessions to his people. To Find Out More, List of New Words, Important Dates, and Index.

348. Dauber, Maximilien, and Martine Noblet. **China**. Maureen Walker, translator. Hauppauge, NY: Barron's, 1994. 77p. $11.95; $6.95pa. ISBN 0-8120-6426-7; 0-8120-1865-6pa. (Tintin's Travel Diaries). 5 up

The text asks thirty questions about China, covering a variety of topics such as what the Chinese used to build their houses, what are the "ten thousand small trades," what is the silk road, what are the powers of the dragon, and who was Mao. Illustrations and photographs complement the simple text on the lefthand pages and the more scholarly answers on the righthand pages. Glossary, Chronological Chart, Map, Bibliography, and Index.

349. Davidson, Bob. **Hillary and Tenzing Climb Everest**. New York: Dillon Press, Macmillan, 1993. 32p. $13.95. ISBN 0-87518-534-7. (Great Twentieth Century Expeditions). 4-7

Many failed attempts to climb Mount Everest occurred in the 1920s and 1930s before Sir Edmund Hillary and Norkey Tenzing decided to attack Everest from the south. They eventually succeeded in 1953. The text details the plans for the ascent, the icefall they encountered, and the "roof of the world," which they finally reached. Also included are descriptions of later expeditions and the North face climb of Ronald Messner in 1980. Photographs and drawings enhance the text. Glossary and Index.

350. Davidson, Margaret. **Louis Braille**. New York: Scholastic, 1991. 80p. $2.99pa. ISBN 0-590-44350-Xpa. 2-5

Louis Braille (1809-1853) lost his sight at the age of three. He was a musician and educator, but most importantly, he invented a system of writing for visually impaired people in 1829, called the Braille system. Although initially blocked by people who thought they knew more than he did about teaching the blind to read, his system became accepted and is still in use.

351. Davies, Eryl. **Transport: On Land, Road and Rail**. New York: Franklin Watts, 1992. 47p. $7.95pa. ISBN 0-531-15741-5pa. (Timelines). 5-8

Illustrations interspersed with text show a history of transport. The text covers the first wheels, Roman roads, ancient China, Vikings, medieval Europe, animal power, coaches, steam pioneers, the railroad age, pedal power, the first motorcycles, automobiles, underground trains, streetcars, delivery modes, racing cars, and the future in transportation. Timeline, Glossary, and Index.

352. Dawson, Imogen. **Food and Feasts in Ancient Greece**. New York: New Discovery, Silver Burdett, 1995. 32p. $14.95. ISBN 0-02-726329-0. (Food & Feasts). 4-7

The text looks at the ways food was grown and prepared by people living in ancient Greece from approximately 2500 B.C. to 30 B.C. by focusing on the crops in the countryside and the types of food that had to be shipped to the cities and suburbs. Food from the sea was important in ancient Greece as well. If one traveled, one had to eat, so the text covers food in taverns and inns and aboard ship. Additional information about cooking utensils and recipes from ancient Greece gives a good sense of the times. Photographs and reproductions highlight the text. Glossary, Further Reading, and Index.

353. Dawson, Imogen. **Food and Feasts in the Middle Ages**. New York: New Discovery, 1994. 32p. $14.95. ISBN 0-02-726324-X. (Food & Feasts). 4-7

The text looks at the ways food was grown and prepared during the Middle Ages, from the end of the Roman Empire until approximately A.D. 1500, by focusing on the crops in the countryside and the types of food that had to be shipped to the cities and suburbs. If one traveled, one had to eat, so the text covers food in taverns, inns, and aboard ship. Additional information about cooking utensils and recipes from the medieval period gives a good sense of the times. Photographs and reproductions enhance the text. Glossary, Further Reading, and Index.

354.   Dawson, Imogen. **Food and Feasts with the Aztecs**. New York: New Discovery, Silver Burdett, 1995. 32p. $14.95. ISBN 0-02-726318-5. (Food & Feasts). 4-7

The text looks at the ways Aztecs grew and prepared food, from approximately A.D. 1300 to 1500, by focusing on the crops in the countryside and the types of food that had to be shipped to the cities. If one traveled, one had to eat, so the text covers food offered in taverns and inns and served to the armies. Additional information about cooking utensils and recipes gives a good sense of the times. Photographs and reproductions enhance the text. Glossary, Further Reading, and Index.

355.   **Dazzling!: Jewelry of the Ancient World**. Minneapolis, MN: Runestone Press, 1995. 64p. $22.95. ISBN 0-8225-3203-4. (Buried Worlds). 6 up

Archaeologists have discovered jewelry, made from precious and semiprecious stones, gold, silver, and other metals, in ancient grave sites. Some of these important finds reveal the Ur in Mesopotamia since 2500 B.C.; the Egyptians since 3100 B.C.; the Chinese since 2000 B.C.; Taxila in ancient Pakistan since the first century B.C.; Southeast Asia since 2000 B.C.; Priam of Troy's treasure of 1400 B.C., discovered by Schliemann in the nineteenth century; the Minoan peoples since 1800 B.C.; the Celts since 700 B.C.; the Romans; and the American peoples. Photographs of finds reveal the styles indigenous to these different sites and cultures. Pronunciation Guide, Glossary, and Index.

356.   De Angeli, Marguerite, author/illustrator. **The Door in the Wall: A Story of Medieval London**. 1949. Magnolia, MA: Peter Smith, 1996. 111p. $17.75. ISBN 0-8446-6834-6. New York: Dell, 1990. 111p. $3.99pa. ISBN 0-440-40283-2pa. 3-7

In 1325, Robin becomes ill after his parents have left to serve King Edward III and his queen. A monk takes him to a hospice for his long recovery, patiently teaching him to carve, to write, to read, to play music, and to swim to strengthen his arms. They travel to another area to await Robin's parents, but soon after they arrive at the castle, the Welsh attack it. Robin's ability to swim allows him to go for reinforcements, and ultimately the castle defenders defeat the Welsh soldiers. When his parents and King Edward III return, Edward knights Robin for his bravery. Robin has learned from the monk that one must do one's best with what one has. *Newbery Medal.*

357.   De Bruycker, Daniel, and Maximilien Dauber. **Africa**. Maureen Walker, translator. Hauppauge, NY: Barron's, 1994. 77p. $11.95; $6.95pa. ISBN 0-8120-6425-9; 0-8120-1864-8pa. (Tintin's Travel Diaries). 5 up

The text asks thirty questions about Africa, covering a variety of topics such as the origin of the continent's name, the first explorers, the slavers, and where King Solomon's mines were located. Illustrations and photographs complement the simple text on the lefthand pages and the more scholarly answers on the righthand pages. Glossary, Chronological Chart, Map, Bibliography, and Index.

358.   De Bruycker, Daniel, and Maximilien Dauber. **Egypt and the Middle East**. Maureen Walker, translator. Hauppauge, NY: Barron's, 1995. 77p. $11.95; $6.95pa. ISBN 0-8120-6488-7; 0-8120-9159-0pa. (Tintin's Travel Diaries). 5 up

The text asks thirty questions about Egypt and the Middle East, covering a variety of topics such as what the function of a pyramid was, who the pharaohs were, which queens were famous, who invented writing, and who the Phoenicians were. Illustrations and photographs complement the simple text on the lefthand pages and the more scholarly answers on the righthand pages. Glossary, Chronological Chart, Map, Bibliography, and Index.

359.   De Bruycker, Daniel, and Maximilien Dauber. **Scotland**. Maureen Walker, translator. Hauppauge, NY: Barron's, 1995. 77p. $11.95; $6.95.pa. ISBN 0-8120-6503-4; 0-8120-9238-4pa. (Tintin's Travel Diaries). 5 up

The text asks thirty questions about Scotland, covering a variety of topics such as what the longest wall in Europe is, how clan members recognize each other, what games they play, and what bagpipes are. Illustrations and photographs complement the simple text on the lefthand pages and the more scholarly answers on the righthand pages. Glossary, Chronological Chart, Map, Bibliography, and Index.

360.   De Bruycker, Daniel, and Maximilien Dauber. **Tibet**. Hauppauge, NY: Barron's, 1995. 80p. $11.95; $6.95pa. ISBN 0-8120-6504-2; 0-8120-9237-6pa. (Tintin's Travel Diaries). 5 up

Tibet, at the "top of the world," is home to the Dalai Lama, the *yak,* and the *yeti* or "abominable snowman." The text combines facts about Tibet, set in large type, with separate segments on facing pages incorporating history and anecdotes relating to the facts. Illustrating these two-page spreads are a combination of the cartoon figure Tintin and photographs of the landscape and the people. Glossary, Chronological Chart, Map, Index, and Bibliography for Readers from 7 to 77.

361. de Ruiz, Dana Catharine. **To Fly with the Swallows: A Story of Old California**. Debbe Heller, illustrator. Austin, TX: Raintree/Steck-Vaughn, 1993. 53p. $15.49; $5.95pa. ISBN 0-8114-7234-5; 0-8114-8074-7pa. (Stories of America—Personal Challenge). 5-9

In 1806, Concha, 15, lived with her family in San Francisco, where her father was commander of the presidio defending Spain's New World empire on the northern border of Alta California. Nikolai Petrovich Rezanov arrived from St. Petersburg requesting supplies for his ship. He stayed long enough for Concha and him to want to marry, but Rezanov was not Catholic. He left, as requested, to get the permission of the czar, the King of Spain, and the pope in Italy. Concha waited, but after five years she received word of his death. She never married but spent her life dedicated to Saint Francis and helping those who needed her in childbirth, sickness, and death. At 60, she became California's first nun in Santa Catalina. Epilogue, Afterword, and Notes.

362. de Treviño, Elizabeth. **El Güero: A True Adventure Story**. Leslie W. Bowman, illustrator. New York: Farrar, Straus & Giroux, 1989. 112p. $12.95. ISBN 0-374-31995-2. 6-9

After a military coup deposes the government of Lerdo de Tejada, El Güero's father is sent into exile from Mexico to the outpost of Ensenada during the late nineteenth century. There his father, a judge, tries to establish a justice system, but the military commander puts him in jail. El Güero and two friends travel across the desert to Baja California to tell the *commandante* of his father's difficulties. His effort gets his father released and the power-hungry Captain Alanis arrested.

363. de Treviño, Elizabeth. **Turi's Poppa**. New York: Farrar, Straus & Giroux, 1968. 160p. $3.95. ISBN 0-374-37887-8. 6-9

When Turi is eight, World War II ends, and he and his father walk from Budapest to Cremona, Italy, the site of his father's new job as the Violin Institute director. To get the job, though, Turi's father has to prove that he is an exceptional violin maker, by making a violin that will please a violinist used to a Stradivari. Turi seems to have swapped roles with his father, because he has to keep encouraging his father, in whom he has total faith and confidence that he will be successful in his endeavor. *Boston Globe—Horn Book Award*.

364. de Treviño, Elizabeth Borton. **Leona: A Love Story**. New York: Farrar, Straus & Giroux, 1994. 142p. $15. ISBN 0-374-34382-9. 5-8

Before Leona Vicario became the wife of the Mexican patriot, Andres Quintana Roo, she was honored by her government after Mexico's War for Independence in the 1800s. Her guardian, loyal to the Spanish crown, would not let her leave the house when he realized that she was in love with Roo. She escaped and traveled, with great risk and difficulty, to join Roo and the Insurgent cause, because she wanted to fight for the Criollos, for the abolition of slavery, and for the suppression of the Inquisition. Through it all, she had a debilitating illness.

365. De Varona, Frank. **Benito Juarez: President of Mexico**. Brookfield, CT: Millbrook Press, 1993. 32p. $13.90; $4.95pa. ISBN 1-56294-279-4; 1-56294-862-8pa. (Hispanic Heritage). 3-5

Benito Juarez (1806-1872) was a Zapotec Indian who officially became the president of Mexico in 1861. He instituted many reforms and led his country in a war of independence against Spain from 1861 through 1867. Bibliography and Index.

366. De Varona, Frank. **Bernardo de Gálvez**. Tom Redman, illustrator. Austin, TX: Raintree/Steck-Vaughn, 1993. 32p. $13.98; $5.95pa. ISBN 0-8172-3379-2; 0-8114-6756-2pa. (Hispanic Stories). 4-7

As a Spanish soldier, Bernardo de Gálvez (1746-1786) was assigned first to duty in Mexico, where he fought the Apaches, and then the Louisiana Territory, where he fought France. He ordered the British to leave the territory and gave Americans freedom to use it. His greatest victory was in Pensacola (now Florida) in 1781, when he defeated the British. Glossary. English and Spanish text.

367. De Varona, Frank. **Miguel Hidalgo y Costilla: Father of Mexican Independence**. Brookfield, CT: Millbrook Press, 1993. 32p. $13.90; $4.95pa. ISBN 1-56294-370-7; 1-56294-863-6pa. (Hispanic Heritage). 2-4

Miguel Hidalgo y Costilla (1753-1811) became an activist who worked to free Mexico from Spanish rule. Lacking military skills, he failed to defeat the Spanish, but the war continued ten years after he was tried and shot for treason, and ended with a Mexican victory. Important Events, Find Out More, and Index.

368. De Varona, Frank. **Simón Bolívar: Latin American Liberator**. Brookfield, CT: Millbrook Press, 1993. 32p. $13.90; $4.95pa. ISBN 1-56294-278-6; 1-56294-812-1pa. (Hispanic Heritage). 3-5

Simón Bolívar (1783-1830) was born to a wealthy family in Venezuela. After spending time in Spain, he returned to Venezuela to become the revolutionary leader of Spanish-held Latin America during the Wars of Independence from 1806 until 1830. Bibliography and Index.

369. Deem, James M. **How to Make a Mummy Talk**. True Kelley, illustrator. Boston: Houghton Mifflin, 1995. 184p. $14.95. ISBN 0-395-62427-4. 4-8

Entertaining illustrations and boxed questions guide the reader through this text about mummies. With the premise that mummies "talk" through what archaeologists discover about them, Deem explores fact and myth about how mummies were and are made, what mummies "say," and where to find them. Some of the more famous mummies discussed are the 5,000-year-old Iceman of Europe; Elmer McCurdy, an Oklahoma outlaw; mummies from California; a Bigfoot mummy from Minnesota; and an Egyptian mummy. Bibliography and Index.

370. DeJong, Meindert. **The House of Sixty Fathers**. Maurice Sendak, illustrator. 1956. New York: HarperCollins, 1990. 189p. $14.89; $4.50pa. ISBN 0-06-021481-3; 0-06-440200-2pa. 5-8

The sampan on which Tien Pao is sleeping washes downriver from Hengyang where his parents work at the American airfield. When he comes ashore, he and his pig begin the long walk back to the area through the Japanese-occupied territory of China. When an American airman crashes his plane nearby, Tien Pao helps him, and the Americans in turn look after him. All sixty of the airmen in the area want to adopt him, but he wants to find his family. *Newbery Honor Book, American Library Association Notable Books for Children, International Board of Books for Young People,* and *Child Study Association Children's Book Award.*

371. Delafosse, Claude, and Philippe Biard, authors/illustrators. **Pyramids**. New York: Cartwheel, Scholastic, 1995. Unpaged. $11.95. ISBN 0-590-42786-5. (A First Discovery Book). K-2

The text gives a simple explanation of how the pyramids in Egypt were built and what mummies are; it also names the seven wonders of the ancient world. Acetate-overlay illustrations help clarify the information.

372. Deltenre, Chantal, and Martine Noblet. **Peru and the Andean Countries**. Maureen Walker, translator. Hauppauge, NY: Barron's, 1995. 77p. $11.95; $6.95pa. ISBN 0-8120-6490-9; 0-8120-9161-2pa. (Tintin's Travel Diaries). 5 up

The text asks thirty questions about Peru and the Andean countries, covering a variety of topics such as the mystery of the Nazca, the origin of the Indians, where Machu Picchu is, how the Incas traveled and wrote, and where the giant statues on Easter Island might have come from. Illustrations and photographs complement the simple text on the lefthand pages and the more scholarly answers on the righthand pages. Glossary, Chronological Chart, Map, Bibliography, and Index.

373. Deltenre, Chantal, and Martine Noblet. **Russia**. Maureen Walker, translator. Hauppauge, NY: Barron's, 1995. 77p. $11.95; $6.95pa. ISBN 0-8120-6491-7; 0-8120-9162-2pa. (Tintin's Travel Diaries). 5 up

The text asks thirty questions about Russia, covering a variety of topics such as who the horsemen of the steppes were, what an icon is, the origin of the Russians, who the great Russian novelists were, and what happened at Chernobyl. Illustrations and photographs complement the simple text on the lefthand pages and the more scholarly answers on the righthand pages. Glossary, Chronological Chart, Map, Bibliography, and Index.

374. Demi, author/illustrator. **Buddha**. New York: Henry Holt, 1996. 42p. $18.95. ISBN 0-8050-4203-2. 3-5

This text presents the eighty-year life of Buddha Siddhartha, along with abstract tenets such as the Eightfold Path and Four Noble Truths in the Buddhist faith. As a youth, Siddhartha was sheltered, but when he learned about suffering, he wanted to end it. The illustrations help clarify the text.

375. Demi, author/illustrator. **Chingis Khan**. New York: Henry Holt, 1991. Unpaged. $19.95. ISBN 0-8050-1708-9. 2-4

Chingis Khan (1162-1227) became head of the Yakka Mongols when he was only nine, but most of the tribe deserted him because he was so young. When his brother stole fish meant for the tribe, Chingis killed him because a lack of food meant that the tribe would die. As Chingis grew, he used his brain to become a great leader, uniting the feuding tribes into one group. He pursued absolute supremacy in China and Persia and amassed the greatest land empire in history. *Bulletin Blue Ribbon Book.*

376. Denenberg, Barry. **Nelson Mandela: "No Easy Walk to Freedom."** New York: Scholastic, 1991. 164p. $12.95; $3.50pa. ISBN 0-590-44163-9; 0-590-44154-Xpa. 5-8

Denenberg divides this biography of Mandela into three parts: "Roots," "Afrikaners and Apartheid," and "The Struggle." Within these parts, he includes information about Africa, about the Boers and the British, and about the various groups and events that led to Mandela's imprisonment. In 1980, after the Soweto uprising, the white citizens realized that they must either "adapt or die." When they finally seemed to adapt, Mandela was freed from prison after twenty-seven years. Chronology, Bibliography, and Index.

377. Denny, Roz. **A Taste of Britain**. New York: Thomson Learning, 1994. 48p. $14.95. ISBN 1-56847-184-X. (Food Around the World). 3-7

Through a mixture of contemporary and historical information, the reader learns about food in Britain both today and back to the times of Henry VIII. Recipes that have appeared on British tables through the centuries supplement the text. Glossary, Books to Read, and Index.

378. Denny, Roz. **A Taste of China**. New York: Thomson Learning, 1994. 48p. $14.95. ISBN 1-56847-183-1. (Food Around the World). 3-7

In addition to learning about Chinese cooking and food, the reader finds out about Chinese history and food that children have eaten in China through the centuries. Bibliography and Index.

379. Denny, Roz. **A Taste of France**. New York: Thomson Learning, 1994. 48p. $14.95. ISBN 1-56847-163-7. (Food Around the World). 3-5

Through a mixture of contemporary and historical information, the reader learns about food in France of both today and yesteryear. The text harks back to the time when Marie de Médicis came to France to marry Henri IV, bringing with her Italian cooks whose food delighted the French. Glossary, Further Information, and Index.

380. DePaola, Tomie, author/illustrator. **Bonjour, Mr. Satie**. New York: Putnam, 1991. 32p. $15.95. ISBN 0-399-21782-7. K-3

Mr. Satie, the traveling cat in this historical fantasy, returns to visit his niece and nephew and tell about his adventures in Paris. While there, he had a chance to judge the paintings of two artists, Pablo (Picasso) and Henri (Matisse), when he visited Gertrude (Stein) and Alice (B. Toklas). The text reflects Stein's attempt to write like a Cubist paints. Among the other guests Mr. Satie meets are James Joyce, Ezra Pound, Josephine Baker, and Ernest Hemingway. *Bulletin Blue Ribbon Book*.

381. DePaola, Tomie. **Patrick: Patron Saint of Ireland**. New York: Holiday House, 1992. Unpaged. $15.95. ISBN 0-8234-0924-4. K-3

Although Patrick (d. 461) was born into a noble British family, bandits captured him, took him to Ireland, and sold him as a slave. He worked for six years as a shepherd until he heard a voice telling him to return to "his own country." He left, but then heard other voices, and went back to establish the first church in Ireland. He converted thousands to the Christian faith, risking his life many times in the process. The text also includes some of the legends that have developed around Patrick's deeds.

382. Descamps-Lequime, Sophie, and Denise Vernerey. **The Ancient Greeks: In the Land of the Gods**. Mary Kae LaRose, translator; Veronique Ageorges, illustrator. Brookfield, CT: Millbrook Press, 1992. 64p. $16.40. ISBN 1-56294-069-4. (Peoples of the Past). 5-8

The Greeks, unusually curious about themselves and their world, had a sense of adventure and a desire to know the truth. Evidence of Greek achievement has survived through the centuries. The text looks at the ancient Greek world, growing up in Greece, Greek styles of dress and ways of life, the rights of the citizen, wars, Panhellenic games, Greek theater, and religion. The Family of Gods, Find Out More, Glossary, and Index.

383. DeStefano, Susan. **Chico Mendes: Fight for the Forest**. Larry Raymond, illustrator. New York: Twenty-First Century, 1992. 76p. $14.98. ISBN 0-8050-2501-4. (Earth Keepers). 4-7

Chico Mendes (d. 1988) was a rubber tapper in the Amazon rain forest who tried to stop the destruction of the forest. For his concerns, he was murdered. The text also looks at the history of the rain forest and its ecological importance to the rest of the world. Glossary and Index.

384. Dhanjal, Beryl. **Amritsar**. New York: Dillon Press, Silver Burdett, 1994. 46p. $13.95. ISBN 0-87518-571-1. (Holy Cities). 3-6

The most sacred of Sikh cities is Amritsar in Punjab ("five waters"), in northwestern India. Built in the 1570s by Guru Ram Das, the fourth of ten gurus who developed Sikhism, Amritsar rises into the Himalaya and Karakoran Mountains. The text discusses Sikhism's main temple, Harmandir, and its sacred book, *Guru Granth Sahib*. Additional information covers the legends and three main festivals of Vaisakhi, Hola Mohalla (Holi), and Diwali. Sikhs also participate in service and have an impressive architectural and artistic heritage. Important Events, Further Reading, and Index.

385. Di Franco, J. Philip. **The Italian Americans**. New York: Chelsea House, 1988. 94p. $18.95; $7.95pa. ISBN 0-87754-886-2; 0-7910-0268-3pa. (Peoples of North America). 5 up

Although this book professes to discuss only Italian Americans, it recounts a brief history of Italy through its revolutions and the Italian unification movement, *Risorgimento*, led by Guiseppe Mazzini, G. Garibaldi, and Camillo Benso di Cavour. In the nineteenth century, however, the greed of the wealthy led to a difficult life for many southern Italians. The northern Italians emigrated first, with the southern Italians following them. The peak immigration years were 1900 to 1914, when more than 2 million Italians arrived in the United States. Not all of them remained, but by 1980, 12 million Italians had settled in the United States. Among those who influenced American life was Filippo Mazzei, a physician philosopher whom Thomas Jefferson translated and whose words closely resembled the Bill of Rights. In 1832, Lorenzo de Ponte brought opera to America. Wine growers from Italy established the Swiss Colony winery, and fruit growers began the Del Monte company. Famous Italian Americans include Fiorello La Guardia, Geraldine Ferraro, Mario Cuomo, Mother Cabrini (America's first saint), Joe DiMaggio, Mario Lanza, Frank Sinatra, Marconi, Fermi, Toscanini, Anne Bancroft, and Lee Iacocca. Selected References and Index.

386. Dick, Lois Hoadley. **False Coin, True Coin**. Greenville, SC: Bob Jones University Press, 1993. 172p. $6.49pa. ISBN 0-89084-664-2pa. (Light Line). 6-10

Cissy Nidd's father, the Bedford jailer, also trafficks in counterfeit coins in London around 1660 during the Stuart reign. Cissy meets John Bunyan, a Dissenter against the monarchy's state religion who has been jailed, and he helps her to see that life offers more than drudgery and deceit. She suffers, but because she has been kind to others, they in turn try to help her through her trials.

387. Dillon, Eilís. **Children of Bach**. New York: Scribners, 1992. 164p. $13.95. ISBN 0-684-19440-6. 5-8

When four children return to their Budapest, Hungary, home one afternoon at the beginning of World War II, a neighbor, Mrs. Nagy, tells them that Nazi soldiers have taken away their musician parents and their aunt. Their aunt returns. She, the children, and Mrs. Nagy, who is part Jewish, then hide in a van behind furniture for a trip into Italy to find their cousin in the mountains. There they may play their music without worry, but Mrs. Nagy continues her irritating habits. Although the children are safe, they have to face the possibility that they will never see their parents again.

388. Dionetti, Michelle. **Painting the Wind: A Story of Vincent van Gogh**. Boston: Little, Brown, 1996. Unpaged. $15.95. ISBN 0-316-18602-3. 1-5

They call him "Fou Rou" or "Red Fool" for painting outside regardless of the weather, but Vincent van Gogh's neighbors are somewhat afraid of him, except for Claudine. She loves his paintings with their vivid colors and imaginative lines. When the townspeople of Arles ask the magistrate to ban Vincent from the town, Claudine must decide how she should help him.

389. Disher, Garry. **The Bamboo Flute**. New York: Ticknor & Fields, 1993. 96p. $10.95. ISBN 0-395-66595-7. 5-8

During the Depression of 1932 in Australia, Paul wants his family to return to the music that they loved before the economic troubles. His parents warn him to stay away from the men called swagmen, who roam about seeking food or work, but when he meets Eric the Red, who plays a flute and steals sheep, Paul learns how to bring music back into his family's life. With Eric's help, Paul makes his own flute from bamboo.

390. Dodge, Stephen. **Christopher Columbus and the First Voyages to the New World**. New York: Chelsea House, 1990. 128p. $19.95. ISBN 0-7910-1299-9. (World Explorers). 5 up

Columbus departed on August 2, 1492, from Genoa, and arrived in San Salvador two months later. The text describes his life, this voyage, and Columbus's three additional voyages before his death. Photographs and reproductions enhance the text. Chronology, Further Reading, and Index.

391. Doherty, Berlie. **Street Child**. New York: Orchard, 1994. 149p. $14.95. ISBN 0-531-06864-1. 5-8

The opening chapter helps the reader cope with the pain of Jim Jarvis's story, because the reader learns immediately that Jim does find protection in the end. Around 1886 in London, Jim's mother dies after getting her daughters positions as maids, but Jim has to go to the workhouse, a horrible place from which he escapes. He helps his mother's friend until her grandfather sells him to a man who nearly works him to death. Then he meets Dr. Barnardo, who wants to help him and the other homeless boys on the street.

392. Doherty, Paul C. **King Arthur**. New York: Chelsea House, 1987. 115p. $18.95. ISBN 0-87754-506-5. (World Leaders Past and Present). 5 up

Whether Arthur was a tribal leader or a great king in British history, the many legends about his life leave no doubt that someone of great influence once reigned in the British Isles. The text looks at the archaeological research that seems to prove Arthur's existence, as well as legends about his reign during the Anglo-Saxon period of A.D. 449 to 1066. Photographs and reproductions enhance the text. Further Reading, Chronology, and Index.

393. Dolan, Edward F. **Panama and the United States: Their Canal, Their Stormy Years**. New York: Franklin Watts, 1990. 160p. $19.86. ISBN 0-531-10911-9. 5 up

When Columbus arrived in what is now Panama on his fourth voyage in 1503, probably 750,000 people, from the Cuna tribe and others, lived there. But Balboa arrived first, in 1501. Not until 1513 did Balboa cross Panama to see the great body of water on the other side, the Pacific. Balboa realized that a waterway would make the journey much easier; thus, the idea of a canal began very early in Panama's recorded history. From 1799 to 1804, Alexander von Humbolt surveyed the area and found nine reasonable routes to cut across land to the Pacific. Because of battles, treaties, and misfortune, the United States was not free to complete the canal until the beginning of the twentieth century. The man who made it most possible was William Crawford Gorgas; he discovered that mosquitoes caused malaria and yellow fever and saved the lives of many workers. On August 15, 1913, the canal opened. A further series of treaties and disagreements between Panama and the United States have peppered the canal's history. Finally, Torrijos made an agreement with President Carter to take possession of the canal on December 31, 1999. Panama's new ruler at Torrijos's death, Noriega, did nothing to further good relationships. Photographs show the progress of the canal's construction. Source Notes, Bibliography, and Index.

394.   Dolan, Sean. **Juan Ponce de León**. New York: Chelsea House, 1995. 110p. $18.95. ISBN 0-7910-2023-1. (Hispanics of Achievement). 5 up

While searching for the fountain of youth, Juan Ponce de León (1474-1521) became the first European to reach the area he later named Florida. When he came to the New World with Columbus, on Columbus's second voyage in 1493, de León decided to settle in Hispaniola with his family, where he ruled as the military commander and deputy governor. He began exploring Puerto Rico (Borinquén) and became its governor in 1508. He always wanted more wealth than he had, and when he heard of a place that sounded as if it had money, he went. In Florida, the Calusa Indians fought with and killed him. Engravings and reproductions enhance the text. Chronology, Further Reading, and Index.

395.   Dolan, Sean. **Junípero Serra**. New York: Chelsea House, 1991. 110p. $18.95; $7.95pa. ISBN 0-7910-1255-7; 0-7910-1282-4pa. (Hispanics of Achievement). 5 up

Miguel José Serra (1713-1784), born in Majorca, began his religious training at fifteen. He became a Franciscan and in 1748 left his home and family to become a missionary in the New World. He served the Spanish missions built by the conquerors trying to convert Indians to Catholicism by either persuasion or force. In 1769, he joined the expeditions exploring California and established the string of missions that still stand today from San Diego to San Francisco. In 1988, the church began the process of making him a saint, although Native Americans accuse him of trying to destroy their culture. Engravings and reproductions enhance the text. Chronology, Further Reading, and Index.

396.   Dommermuth-Costa, Carol. **Agatha Christie: Writer of Mystery**. Minneapolis, MN: Lerner, 1997. 112p. $17.21. ISBN 0-8225-4954-9. (Biographies). 5-9

Dame Agatha Christie (1890-1976), the "First Lady of Crime," had the support of family and servants before she married a World War I pilot who left her for another woman. She had begun to write detective fiction, and her second marriage to an archaeologist, Max Mallowan, was successful along with her creations Hercule Poirot and Miss Marple. Photographs highlight the text. Bibliography and Index.

397.   Dommermuth-Costa, Carol. **Nikola Tesla: A Spark of Genius**. Minneapolis, MN: Lerner, 1994. 144p. $17.21. ISBN 0-8225-4920-4. 5-9

Nikola Tesla (1856-1943), born in Croatia, was the true inventor of radio. He developed the technology that harnessed alternating-current electricity. He was a friend to George Westinghouse and a rival of Thomas Edison. He became a millionaire whose fortune evaporated when he bought equipment that burned up. Marconi rather than Tesla received credit for inventing the radio, and Tesla claimed that Marconi was using seventeen of Tesla's patents. Since Tesla's death, scientists have continued to discover the scope of his achievements and to establish awards in his name in the field of electricity. Sources, Bibliography, and Index.

398.   Donnelly, Judy. **Titanic: Lost and Found**. Keith Kohler, illustrator. New York: Random House, 1987. 47p. $5.99; $2.95pa. ISBN 0-394-98669-5; 0-394-88669-0pa. 1-3

The *Titanic* sank in 1912. In 1987, an expedition led by Robert Ballard discovered its remains. The text tells of these two events.

399.   Doran, Clare. **The Japanese**. New York: Thompson Learning, 1995. 32p. $14.95. ISBN 1-56847-173-4. (Look into the Past). 4-6

Photographs of artifacts complement the text, which gives details of life in Japan's Edo period from 1600 to 1868. Highlighted are samurai soldiers, warlords, workers, and artists, but information is also presented about the average citizen. Glossary, Important Dates, Books to Read, and Index.

400.   Dorris, Michael. **Morning Girl**. New York: Hyperion, 1992. 74p. $12.95; $3.50pa. ISBN 1-56282-285-3; 1-56282-661-1pa. 3-7

In 1492, Morning Girl and Star Boy live with their parents on a Bahamian island. Their world changes when Columbus finds them and imposes new concepts of culture on their society. *Scott O'Dell Award.*

401. Douglas, Kirk. **The Broken Mirror**. New York: Simon & Schuster, 1997. 88p. $13. ISBN 0-689-81493-3. 4-7

Moishe's mother thinks that the Nazi "hooligans" will disappear, and his father moves the family to a farm in Germany during 1939. A worker reveals them to the Nazis, and they go to a concentration camp with Moishe being the only one to survive. He claims Catholicism and ends up in an American orphanage before declaring his Jewishness.

402. Downing, Julie, author/illustrator. **Mozart Tonight**. New York: Bradbury, 1991. Unpaged. $15.95. ISBN 0-02-732881-3. New York: Aladdin, 1994. Unpaged. $5.95pa. ISBN 0-689-71808-Xpa. 1-5

Wolfgang Amadeus Mozart (1756-1791) had written over 600 pieces of music by the time he died, after beginning to compose at the age of five. He wrote his first symphony when he was eight and his first opera at twelve. The text uses a first-person point of view to have the young Mozart tell the story of his life, from his love of Salzburg as a child until the success of his opera *Don Giovanni*.

403. Doyle, Brian. **Uncle Ronald**. Buffalo, NY: Firefly Books, 1997. 144p. $16.95. ISBN 0-88899-266-1. 6-8

Mickey McGuire, 112, recalls his life in Ottawa in 1895 when he began bed-wetting at age twelve. His mother sent him to his uncle's farm, and Uncle Ronald is the opposite of Mickey's abusive father. His mother follows after his father beats her severely, and the two expect him to follow. The story includes a conflict between the area and the federal troops over the collection of back taxes as well.

404. Dramer, Kim. **Kublai Khan: Mongol Emperor**. New York: Chelsea House, 1990. 112p. $18.95; $7.95pa. ISBN 0-7910-0697-2; 1-55546-812-8pa. (World Leaders Past and Present). 5 up

Grandson of Genghis the Conqueror, Kublai Khan (1215-1294) was the emperor of China and its states and the head of the Mongol army. He greeted and supposedly welcomed Marco Polo to his court in 1275, urging Polo to stay for many years. Kublai was at times a patron of the arts and sciences and generally the fair and wise ruler of a group of nomadic farmers. The Mongols, a nomadic culture, were military giants who conquered territory from the western area of Russia to Indochina, though they failed against Japan and Java (Indonesia), and Kublai's army protected merchants traveling on the great Silk Route. But his love of luxury eventually bankrupted his court, and after his death the dynasty deteriorated. Marco Polo wrote about Kublai Khan when he returned from his travels. Photographs and reproductions enhance the text. Chronology, Further Reading, and Index.

405. Driemen, J. E. **Winston Churchill: An Unbreakable Spirit**. New York: Dillon Press, 1990. 128p. $13.95. ISBN 0-87518-434-0. (People in Focus). 5 up

Sir Winston Churchill (1874-1965) grew up in an upper-class British family but had to overcome his poor school record with action. His many achievements prepared him for his position as Britain's prime minister during World War II, when Hitler threatened the country. Churchill said that he had nothing to offer but "blood, toil, tears, and sweat." People often remember him with his fingers formed in the "V for Victory" sign. Appendix, Selected Bibliography, and Index

406. Drucker, Olga Levy. **Kindersport**. New York: Henry Holt, 1992. 145p. $14.95. ISBN 0-8050-1711-9. 5-8

Born in Germany in 1927, Ollie Levy enjoyed the life of a publisher's daughter. The German government had honored her father's service in World War I, but in 1938, on *Kristallnacht*, he and the family realized that their Jewish origin would allow them no future honor. Ollie's parents sent her to England on a children's train with other Jewish children. She lived there for six years, enduring a different kind of prejudice, but was able to reunite with her parents in the United States in 1945. This autobiographical story depicts life for a young girl exiled from her family and her home during World War II.

407. Dubois, Muriel L. **Abenaki Captive**. Minneapolis, MN: Carolrhoda, 1994. 180p. $14.96. ISBN 0-87614-753-8. 5-8

In 1752, the St. Francis Abenaki of eastern Canada capture John Stark and his friend, Amos Eastman, while killing a third person who was with them. Because whites had killed a young Abenaki man, Ogistin's brother, Ogistin at first hates Stark, but the other Abenakis like him. Stark stays with the tribe for some time before he decides to leave. Differences between the beliefs of the Abenaki and the Europeans become clear when Ogistin depends on his guardian spirit, a lynx. What also becomes clear are the divisions between settlers at the time: the hostilities between the Catholics and the Protestants and between the French and the English.

408. Duder, Tessa. **Alex in Rome**. Boston: Houghton Mifflin, 1992. 166p. $12.95. ISBN 0-395-62879-2. 6 up

Swimming for New Zealand in the 1960 Olympic games in Rome, Alex, age sixteen, wins a bronze medal. During the games, she meets an "Italian" who finally admits that he is really from New Zealand and is in Italy to study opera. Alex's experiences, both in the pool and out of it, give her added insight into the confusing world of international cultures. *New Zealand's AIM Children's Book Award* and *Esther Glen Medal* (New Zealand).

409. Duggleby, John. **Impossible Quests**. Allan Eitzen, illustrator. New York: Crestwood House, 1990. 48p. $10.95. ISBN 0-89686-509-6. (Incredible History). 4 up

Various quests have attempted to prove the existence of Bigfoot in the Pacific Northwest of the United States and Canada, the Loch Ness Monster in Scotland, Noah's Ark in Turkey, Atlantis in the Mediterranean, and the lost continent of gold in the South Pacific. The text discusses these quests and illustrates them with black-and-white drawings. Bibliography and Index.

410. Dunlop, Betty. **The Poetry Girl**. Boston: Houghton Mifflin, 1989. 209p. $13.95. ISBN 0-395-49679-9. 6-8

Natalia, age twelve, moves with her Russian parents to another town in New Zealand during 1946. Her father, suicidal and harsh, argues with her mother constantly. Natalia feels alone and is often absent from school. Classmates and teachers seem to persecute her, and her only outlet is the poetry she writes for herself. Her brother tells her two years later that she is growing up, and she decides that she will try to fulfill her own needs.

411. Dunlop, Eileen. **Tales of St. Patrick**. New York: Holiday House, 1996. 125p. $15.95. ISBN 0-8234-1218-0. 3-6

Saint Patrick, born in a Roman villa in western England during the fifth century, was sold into slavery by Irish raiders, and spent six years as a shepherd before God called him to convert the Irish to Christianity. The text looks at the legends surrounding Patrick and the few facts known about his life to emphasize the charisma through which he attracted others to his beliefs.

412. Dunn, Andrew. **Marie Curie**. New York: Gloucester, 1991. 48p. $17.71. ISBN 0-531-18375-0. (Pioneers of Science). 5 up

Marie Curie's (1867-1934) work led to an understanding of the atom. Radioactivity is helpful in medicine and in industry; it gives power in nuclear reactors, but it can cause the destruction of humans if misused. Photographs, Date Chart, Glossary, and Index.

413. Durbin, William. **The Broken Blade**. New York: Delacorte, 1997. 160p. $14.95. ISBN 0-385-32224-0. 5-8

Pierre, thirteen, has to go to work for his father's company in 1800 when his father injuries himself in a wood-chopping accident in Canada. He becomes a voyager, a French-Canadian canoeman. On his first canoe trip to Grand Portage, he ages in many ways and becomes a man. While he has to deal with an unsavory character and mourn the drowning of one of the crew, he also sees the natural beauty of his environment.

414. Dwyer, Frank. **Henry VIII**. New York: Chelsea House, 1987. 112p. $18.95. ISBN 0-87754-530-8. (World Leaders Past and Present). 5 up

Called "Great Henry" when he came to the English throne in 1509, Henry VIII (1491-1547) had many positive qualities. In the 1530s, when a desire for church reform arose, Henry declared himself as the Supreme Head of the Church. He ordered the dissolution of monasteries, levied heavy taxes, suppressed opposition, and demanded that all pledge loyalty to him. By the time he died, he had had six wives (some of whom he had executed), beheaded his able minister Thomas More, expanded the power of Parliament, and used up most of his country's funds. But the overall result of his reign was the creation of England as a nation; Henry was the link between medieval and modern England. Reproductions enhance the text. Chronology, Further Reading, and Index.

415. Dyson, John. **Westward with Columbus**. Ken Marschall and Peter Christopher, illustrators. New York: Scholastic, 1991. 64p. $15.95. ISBN 0-590-43846-8. (Time Quest). 3-7

When Christopher Columbus (1451-1506) discovered the New World, he might have taken a more southerly route than previously thought. One scholar, Luís Miguel Coin, took the journey and believes that Columbus had a secret map. Living history photographs illustrate the fifteenth century, and a parallel fiction story about Pedro, a deckhand on the *Santa Maria*, relates the conditions on board the ship. Bibliography and Glossary. *Notable Children's Trade Book in the Field of Social Studies.*

E

416. Ebon, Martin. **Nikita Khrushchev**. New York: Chelsea House, 1990. 112p. $18.95. ISBN 0-87754-562-6. (World Leaders Past and Present). 5 up

In 1956, Nikita Khrushchev (1894-1971) denounced the crimes of the Soviet leader Joseph Stalin. These statements began the relaxation of political repression in the U.S.S.R. Although born a peasant, Khrushchev rose within the Communist party after joining in 1918, because he was a skillful organizer. In 1961, he almost caused a nuclear war by refusing the demands of the United States to remove missiles he had ordered installed in Cuba. By the time he lost power in 1964, he had begun establishing relations with the western world. Photographs enhance the text. Chronology, Further Reading, and Index.

417. Ellis, Sarah. **Next-Door Neighbors**. New York: Macmillan, 1990. 154p. $13.95. ISBN 0-689-50495-0. 4-7

In 1957, Peggy, age twelve, and her family move to Vancouver where her father is a minister. She finally makes friends with George, a young Russian immigrant, and Sing, Mrs. Manning's gardener and houseboy. They help her overcome her shyness, and she learns that the device of pretending to be a puppet is one way to meet new people. *School Library Journal Best Book.*

418. Elmer, Robert. **Touch the Sky**. Minneapolis, MN: Bethany, 1997. 172p. $5.99pa. ISBN 1-55661-661-9pa. (The Young Underground Book). 5-8

Danish twins Peter and Elise and their Jewish friend Henrik hear about a plan to blow up a ship taking Jewish refugees to Palestine in 1946. They encounter a series of adventures as they try to stop a Syrian from carrying out the plan.

419. Emmerich, Elsbeth. **My Childhood in Nazi Germany**. New York: Bookwright Press, Franklin Watts, 1992. 96p. $19.86. ISBN 0-531-18429-3. 4-6

Elsbeth Emmerich was five when World War II started in Germany. She tells how she and her family coped with the constant moving and the bombings raging around them after her father, a soldier, died in the war. She hated to give the Nazi salute. The Gestapo took away her grandfather, and her mother was chastised for not being a Party member. When the war ended, she and others were surprised to find that the Americans were not monsters.

420. English, June. **Transportation: Automobiles to Zeppelins**. New York: Scholastic, 1995. 154p. $16.95. ISBN 0-590-27550-X. 3-6

The text covers each topic in a double-page spread with a picture, diagrams, general information, notes on historic interest, and photographs. Among the items are balloons, bridges, engines, tunnels, submersibles, bicycles, snowmobiles, and zeppelins. Glossary and Index.

421. Eschle, Lou. **The Curse of Tutankhamen**. San Diego, CA: Lucent, 1994. 48p. $18.95. ISBN 1-56006-152-9. (Exploring the Unknown). 4-6

In 1922, Howard Carter found an unopened tomb in Egypt. Carter immediately contacted his patron, Lord Carnarvon, and asked him to hurry to Egypt for the opening. Within a few weeks, Carnarvon died of a fever. He was not the first to die after being present at the opening of an Egyptian tomb. Giovanni Gelzoni mysteriously died in 1823 after discovering Seti I's tomb in 1817. Dr. Theodor Bilharz, who performed autopsies on mummies, died unexpectedly in 1862. By 1929, seven years after Carter opened Tutankhamen's tomb, twenty-two people who had been involved with the opening had died; thirteen of them had been present at the opening of the inner chamber. Two theories as to why such coincidences have occurred are especially interesting. The modern world knows very little about the Egyptians, because most of their writings were destroyed in the library fire at Alexandria, but scientists think that they may have known quite a bit about poisons and fungi. They could have coated the tombs with such a substance, which could still be potent after thousands of years, so that whoever unsealed the grave would suffer intensely. Glossary, For Further Reading, Works Consulted, and Index.

422. **Estonia**. Minneapolis, MN: Lerner, 1992. 56p. $19.95. ISBN 0-8225-2803-7. (Then and Now). 5-9

The text covers the history, economics, geography, politics, ethnography, and possible future of Estonia, a Baltic country, which the Soviet Union annexed in 1940 and which gained freedom in 1991. Maps and photographs complement the text. Glossary and Index.

423. Evans, J. Edward. **Charles Darwin: Revolutionary Biologist**. Minneapolis, MN: Lerner, 1993. 112p. $21.50. ISBN 0-8225-4914-X. 5 up

When Charles Darwin (1809-1882) left the Galápagos Islands, he realized that he had been making serious mistakes in his categorization of plants and animals. He began to ask why some species inhabited some islands and not others, and why different species appeared on the same island. His reformulation of questions led to his major work, *The Origin of Species*, published many years later in 1859. His work shocked many, but others recognized it as a major contribution about the beginnings of life. Bibliography and Index. *Outstanding Science Trade Book for Children* and *John S. Burroughs Nature Book for Young Readers.*

424. Faber, Doris, and Harold Faber. **Mahatma Gandhi**. New York: Julian Messner, 1986. 122p. $10.98. ISBN 0-671-60176-8. 5 up

Mahatma, the name given to Mohandas Gandhi (1869-1948), means "Great Soul." He was warm, unassuming, and sometimes comic. He also wrote his own autobiography when he was fifty, in which he set forth his philosophical and religious beliefs. The Fabers have used this autobiography to give insights into various situations in Gandhi's life. A husband at the age thirteen, he was surprised to find that his preoccupation with his young wife was detracting from his concentration in other areas. Another time he became physically ill after eating meat, a practice that his religion forbade. Other pieces of information reveal the character of this man who helped India to gain its freedom from Britain in 1947 through mainly nonviolent means. Source Note, Suggested Further Readings, and Index.

425. Falwell, Cathryn, author/illustrator. **The Letter Jesters**. New York: Ticknor & Fields, 1994. Unpaged. $14.95. ISBN 0-395-66898-0. 2-4

With the characters of two jesters and their dog, Falwell tells the story of typography. Included are different styles of typeface and why or where certain letter designs originated. Since Gutenberg invented the printing press, printing and type fonts have affected humans in subtle but meaningful ways.

426. Farmer, Nancy. **A Girl Named Disaster**. New York: Jackson, Orchard, 1996. 309p. $19.95. ISBN 0-531-09539-8. 6-9

With her grandmother's blessing, Nhamo, eleven, escapes from a horrible marriage in Mozambique during 1981 to her father's family in Zimbabwe. A two-day journey extends to a year when the boat goes astray. Baboons look after her on an island for a while, and when she finally reaches Zimbabwe, she lives with scientists and learns to survive in civilization before she finds her father's family. The background gives information on the Shona and on South Africa in this unusual novel. *American Library Association Notable Books for Children*, *American Library Association Best Books for Young Adults, School Library Journal Best Book,* and *Newbery Honor Book.*

427. Feder, Paula Kurzband. **The Feather-Bed Journey**. Stacey Schuett, illustrator. Niles, IL: Albert Whitman, 1995. 32p. $15.95. ISBN 0-8075-2330-5. K-2

Rachel likes the story that her grandmother tells about a feather pillow ripping open and all the feathers flying in the wind. Her grandmother also tells Rachel about hiding from the Nazis for two years during World War II in a Christian family's basement, until a neighbor saw her and she had to go live with other Jews in the woods. A farmer sent Rachel's grandmother the feather bed that she had left behind in the ghetto, but she found that it had shrunk to a feather pillow because it had partially burned; this pillow is the basis of the story.

428. Feinberg, Brian. **Nelson Mandela and the Quest for Freedom**. New York: Chelsea Juniors, 1992. 80p. $14.95. ISBN 0-7910-1569-6. (Junior World Biographies). 3-7

The text relates Nelson Mandela's story of fighting to win equal rights for blacks in South Africa. He spent twenty-seven years in prison because he believed that people should be free regardless of color. Chronology, Further Reading, Glossary, and Index.

429. Fenton, Edward. **The Morning of the Gods**. New York: Delacorte, 1987. 184p. $14.95. ISBN 0-385-29550-2. 6-8

In 1974, Carla, age twelve, comes to a small Greek village to stay with her great-aunt Tiggie (Antigone) and great-uncle Theo, the people who had raised her orphan mother. With her mother recently dead in a car accident, Carla absorbs all of the atmosphere about which her mother had told her. She finds that life in the village is more complex than she had imagined when comments about the political situation let her know that all is not well with the Greek junta. While she is there, she helps to save a poet, a national hero, from the military, and she learns about Greek Orthodoxy, including the Easter rituals.

430. Ferber, Elizabeth. **Yasir Arafat: A Life of War and Peace**. Brookfield, CT: Millbrook Press, 1995. 144p. $17.40. ISBN 1-56294-585-8. 6 up

Although Yasir Arafat claims to have been born in Jerusalem in 1929, many persons suspect that he was born in Cairo, Egypt, where his family was living at the time. His mother died when he was a boy, and then a favorite uncle, who led the Muslim Brotherhood for young Palestinian boys, was murdered. Arafat's father probably ordered the assassinations. In the 1950s, Arafat emerged as a leader of the Muslim Brotherhood and then of his own group, the *Fatah*. In 1969, he took over the leadership of the Palestinian Liberation Organization (PLO). The text tries to reveal the man known as Arafat with accompanying photographs. Chronology, Bibliography, and Index.

431. Fernandez, José. **José de San Martín: Latin America's Quiet Hero**. Brookfield, CT: Millbrook Press, 1994. 32p. $13.90. ISBN 1-56294-383-9. (Hispanic Heritage). 2-4

José de San Martín (1778-1850) lived among Guarani Indians in Argentina until he was three years old. He was sent to school in Spain and joined the army there when he finished, but when he returned to Argentina, in 1812, he joined its fight for independence. Over the course of nine years, his regiment, the Granaderos, fought twenty major battles for Latin American independence. When he met Simón Bolívar, he realized that Bolívar would have to complete the job of freeing Latin America alone, because the two men were too different from each other. The Argentineans were furious at him for leaving the army and refused to take him back. He went first to Belgium and then to France, where he died; his last wish was to be buried in Argentina. Today he is revered for his part in the liberation of Latin America. Important Dates in the Life of, Find Out More, and Index.

432. Finkelstein, Norman. **Theodor Herzl: Architect of a Nation**. Minneapolis, MN: Lerner, 1992. 128p. $22.95. ISBN 0-8225-4913-1. 5-9

Although Theodor Herzl (b. 1860) died in 1904, he was reburied with honors in Israel on August 17, 1949. He had worked on the possibility of a homeland for the Jews during most of his lifetime in Austria, almost fifty years before the state was founded. He was a journalist and playwright who believed that the only way to escape the torment of anti-Semitism was to have a place for Jews to live together in Israel. He worked tirelessly with Jewish leaders to establish a base for a new nation. He helped with the First Zionist Congress, which met in 1897. Notes, Glossary, and Index.

433. Finley, Mary Peace. **Soaring Eagle**. New York: Simon & Schuster, 1993. 166p. $14. ISBN 0-671-75598-6. 4-9

Julio Montoya wonders who his family is, because he is blond-haired and green-eyed in Mexico during 1845. When Julio's father returns to Taos, the two go on the trail to Bent's Fort. After Apaches kill his father, Julio must survive a snowstorm, a wolf attack, and then snowblindness. Cheyenne Indians find him, nurse him back to health, and claim him as one of their own. While wondering about his childhood, Julio adapts to this new tribe and earns his own name, Soaring Eagle. He never answers his questions, but he finds surrogate family support.

434. Fischetto, Laura. **Michel the Angel**. Letizia Galli, illustrator. New York: Doubleday, 1993. 32p. $15.95. ISBN 0-385-30844-2. K-3

Using "angel" as a thematic device, Fischetto tells the story of Michelangelo Buonnaroti (1475-1564)—first his childhood, then his apprenticeship, and finally his exceptional career as a painter and sculptor. She tries to reveal the individual artist instead of merely detailing Michelangelo's works of art.

435. Fisher, Leonard, author/illustrator. **The Wailing Wall**. New York: Macmillan, 1989. 32p. $14.95. ISBN 0-02-735310-9. 2-4

The Wailing Wall in Jerusalem, a 4,000-year-old, crumbling section of the Second Temple wall, is a sacred site for Jews because it was once also the site of the First Tabernacle and the First Temple. The text gives a chronology of the Wall and discusses historical events that have affected who has permission to pray at the site. Symbols on each page represent the dominance of the Jews, the Babylonians, the Persians, the Greeks, the Romans, the Christians, and the Muslims. A brief afterword comments on the controversial politics of the area.

436. Fisher, Leonard Everett, author/illustrator. **Galileo**. New York: Macmillan, 1992. Unpaged. $15.95. ISBN 0-02-735235-8. 3-5

At age twenty, Galileo (1564-1642) discovered the law of the pendulum and began to experiment with floating and falling objects. After he had experimented with motion, constructed the first thermoscope (to measure heat), a telescope, and a microscope, he began to support the Copernican idea that the earth was not the center of the universe. His book, *The Starry Messenger*, published in 1610, described the craters and mountains he had seen on earth's moon, as well as the moons circling Jupiter. He began selling his spyglasses over Europe, but many would not believe his ideas, and the Church began warning him to change his statements about the earth. He would not, so the Inquisition imprisoned him in his own house. He continued working, and now he is called the father of modern science.

437. Fisher, Leonard Everett, author/illustrator. **Gutenberg**. New York: Macmillan, 1993. Unpaged. $14.95. ISBN 0-02-735238-2. 3-5

Johann Gutenberg (1394?-1468) grew up in Mainz, Germany, where his first job was cutting and polishing gemstones. In 1436, after moving to Strasbourg, records show that he started to experiment casting type in metal for printing. When his business nearly bankrupted him, he returned to Mainz so that he could collect his inheritance; officials in Mainz would not pay him as long as he lived in Strasbourg. He borrowed money to set up his printing shop, but lost the business to the lender in a lawsuit, and the lender and a partner claimed credit for the first Gutenberg Bible. Gutenberg had to start again, and the second time he was successful. His invention changed the world. By 1500, over 1,000 printing presses were already in existence.

438. Fisher, Leonard Everett, author/illustrator. **Marie Curie**. New York: Macmillan, 1994. Unpaged. $14.95. ISBN 0-02-735375-3. 3-5

Fisher's black-and-white paintings illustrate this biography of Marya (Marie) Sklodowska Curie (1867-1934), born in Warsaw, Poland. Marie's kindness in supporting her sister's Paris education before she went to the Sorbonne herself was somewhat rewarded with her two Nobel Prizes, one for physics and one for chemistry; her great love for her fellow scientist and husband Pierre; and her election as the only woman into the French Academy of Medicine. The Curies discovered polonium and radium after coining the term *radioactivity*. Fisher mentions her death as the result of radiation poisoning only in the chronology, not the text. More about Marie Curie.

439. Fisher, Leonard Everett, author/illustrator. **Prince Henry the Navigator**. New York: Macmillan, 1990. Unpaged. $15.95. ISBN 0-027-35231-5. 4-6

Although the Moors were driven from Spain and Portugal in 1249, after having arrived in 711, they continued to attack Portuguese ships from the Moorish stronghold in Ceuta, Morocco. In 1415, King John I and his sons, including Prince Henry (b. 1394), who was twenty-one, defeated the Moors in a war for Portugal. Henry wanted to find India and Prester John, rumored to be a white Christian king ruling a rich African or Asian kingdom. In the navigation school Henry established to find the way to India, his scholars used the circular astrolabe, triangular quadrant, and the compass. He sent ships as far as Madeira and the Azores, and further south than they had previously sailed. His captains, who were required to keep logs, brought back gold and then slaves to finance the trips. Although Henry eventually tried to stop the slavery trade, some continued behind his back. Henry died in 1460, and others discovered the route that he had been pursuing.

440. Fisher, Leonard Everett, author/illustrator. **Pyramid of the Sun, Pyramid of the Moon**. New York: Macmillan, 1988. 32p. $13.95. ISBN 0-02-735300-1. 4-6

The text, with illustrations, tells the history of the Teotihuacán pyramids in the Valley of Mexico. Symbols of the cultures accompany discussions of the Toltecs, Chichimecs, and Aztecs, who lived and worshipped in the area. Although the text discusses human sacrifice and the Spanish destruction of Montezuma's city of Tenochtitlán, it does not emphasize the violence.

441. Fisher, Leonard Everett, author/illustrator. **The Tower of London**. New York: Macmillan, 1987. 32p. $13.95. ISBN 0-02-735370-2. 3-6

The text discusses the history of the Tower of London from its construction in 1078 until today. It functioned as the place of death for such people as Anne Boleyn, Henry VIII's second wife, and Sir Thomas More, when he refused to support Henry VIII's divorce from Catherine. Today it houses the crown jewels and many examples of armor from battles in which the English participated.

442. Fisher, Leonard Everett. **William Tell**. New York: Farrar, Straus & Giroux, 1996. Unpaged. $16. ISBN 0-374-38436-3. 3-5

Hermann Gessler, governor for King Albert of Hapsburg in 1307, demanded that the citizens of Aldorf kneel before his hat, placed in the town square. Three people forgot to do so and were imprisoned. William Tell and his son, however, refused. Gessler was furious and demanded that Tell, a superb hunter, either split an apple set on his son's head or go to prison. Tell succeeded; the next week, he shot Gessler so that the town would also be free.

443. Fix, Philippe, author/illustrator. **Not So Very Long Ago: Life in a Small Country Village**. New York: Dutton, 1994. Unpaged. $15.99. ISBN 0-525-44594-3. 3-6

Set in the early nineteenth century, this story recounts daily life in a country village and its yearly fair. Peddlers, tinkers, and gypsies (basket weavers) travel between town and country. In the town, boys and girls go to separate schools, with boys leaving at twelve to work for and with their fathers. Choices of jobs include tailor, weaver, village glassblower or glazier, potter, apothecary, village store owner, clog maker, cobbler, or craftsman. In the country, boys might become shepherds, millers, mattress makers, or ragpickers. Regardless of trade, all eagerly anticipate the fair with its entertainment and new goods for sale.

444. Flint, David. **The Baltic States**. Brookfield, CT: Millbrook Press, 1992. 32p. $15.90. ISBN 1-56294-310-3. (Former Soviet States). 4-7

The text discusses the cultural background, politics, economics, and histories of the former Soviet republics of Estonia, Lithuania, and Latvia. These states, annexed to the Soviet Union in 1940, have had a long history of invasion because of their arable lands and desirable locations. Glossary and Index.

445. Flint, David. **The Russian Federation**. Brookfield, CT: Millbrook Press, 1992. 32p. $15.90. ISBN 1-56294-305-7. (Former Soviet States). 4-7

The text discusses the cultural background, politics, economics, and history of the former Soviet republic of Russia. In this country, by the fifth century A.D., Slavic tribes had begun migrating from the west. In the ninth century, the Scandinavian chieftains founded the first Russian state, centered in Novgorod and Kiev. In the thirteenth century, the Mongols overran the country. It recovered under the grand dukes and princes of Muscovy, or Moscow, and by 1480 it had freed itself from the Mongols. Ivan the Terrible became the first formally proclaimed Tsar (1547). Peter the Great (1682-1725) extended the domain and, in 1721, founded the Russian Empire. After the rule of Communism in the twentieth century, Russia declared freedom. Glossary and Index.

446. Fluek, Toby Knobel, author/illustrator. **Passover as I Remember It**. New York: Knopf, 1994. Unpaged. $15. ISBN 0-679-83876-7. 3-6

When the author was a young girl growing up in Chernytsia (L'vivs'ka oblast', Ukraine), before the Nazis destroyed it, the community prepared for Passover beginning in the autumn when her father harvested and stored his wheat. New clothes, food made kosher, and other activities contributed to this holy celebration.

447. Foreman, Michael, author/illustrator. **War Boy: A Country Childhood**. New York: Arcade, 1989. Unpaged. $16.95. ISBN 1-55970-049-1. 3-7

Foreman opens this memoir of childhood on April 21, 1941, when bombers strafed his Pakefield village home on the east coast of England. The Germans ignited the church in order to have enough light to find the nearby Lowestoft Airbase, but a huge mist suddenly rolled in from the sea and obscured the fire. He recounts life in the village, where his mother owned a small store during World War II and where soldiers came to drink tea and escape the pervasive fear. Watercolor illustrations augment the poignant text.

448. Foreman, Michael, author/illustrator. **War Game**. New York: Arcade, 1994. 72p. $16.95. ISBN 1-55970-242-7. 5-8

Will, an avid soccer player, has to go to the front lines of World War I, in the French trenches, for Britain in 1914. The daily routine is boring and frightening; war is not the glamorous calling that posters and appeals to serve would have potential soldiers believe. At Christmas, Will participates in a spontaneous carol-fest and soccer game between the German and English troops. But after Christmas, a new group of Germans fills the trenches, and Will dies.

449. Foreman, Michael, and Richard Seaver. **The Boy Who Sailed with Columbus**. New York: Arcade, 1992. 71p. $16.95. ISBN 1-55970-178-1. 1-4

In 1492, Leif, age twelve, sails to the New World with Columbus. He decides to stay in the New World, but a tribe captures him and keeps him with them because of his blond hair (inherited from his deceased Viking father). By age seventeen, Leif has learned the tribe's ways and become its medicine man. In this capacity, he travels throughout their land telling their stories and helping them recover from diseases.

450. Foster, Leila Merrell. **Margaret Thatcher: First Woman Prime Minister of Great Britain**. Chicago: Childrens Press, 1990. 120p. $18.60. ISBN 0-516-03269-0. (People of Distinction). 6 up

The text begins with the race for Margaret Thatcher (b. 1925) to take leadership of the Conservative Party in Parliament in 1975. A discussion of the opposition and the way ballots were counted gives an unexpected suspense to the process which one knows Thatcher won. The remainder of the text looks at her childhood, her choice of career, her family, her race for Parliament, her service as Leader of the Opposition and as Prime Minister during the Falklands War, as well as the difficulties of getting reelected. Notes, Time Line, and Index.

451. Foster, Leila Merrell. **Nien Cheng: Courage in China**. Chicago: Childrens Press, 1992. 111p. $19.30; $5.95pa. ISBN 0-516-03279-8; 0-516-43279-6pa. (People of Distinction). 4-7

Nien Cheng (b. 1915) faced the Red Guards, a group of teenagers and young people organized by Mao Zedong to raid the wealthy after 1966. They destroyed her belongings and then harassed and imprisoned her for seven years, a period she wrote about in *Life and Death in Shanghai*. This text presents some information about her youth but concentrates mostly on her experiences after the Red Guard became a force in China. Photographs, Time Line, and Index.

452. Fradin, Dennis. **Amerigo Vespucci**. New York: Franklin Watts, 1991. 64p. $18.43. ISBN 0-531-20035-3. (First Books). 4-6

Amerigo Vespucci (1451-1512), Florentine explorer, claimed that he had discovered America in 1491, before Columbus. Among his credits are two continents named after him and the discovery of the Amazon River, Venezuela, and Brazil. Bibliography and Index.

453.	Fradin, Dennis. **Louis Braille: The Blind Boy Who Wanted to Read**. Robert Sauber, illustrator. Parsippany, NJ: Silver Burdett Press, 1997. 32p. $15.95; $5.95pa. ISBN 0-382-39468-2; 0-382-39469-0pa. (Remarkable Children). 2-4

Louis Braille (1809-1852) became blind when he was only three years old. He wanted to read but found that reading systems for the blind were cumbersome. He invented his own system at fifteen, and after many years, educators of the blind accepted it. Fradin bases his material on primary sources.

453a.	Fradin, Dennis. **Maria de Sautuola: Discoverer of the Bulls in the Cave**. Ed Martinez, illustrator. Parsippany, NJ: Silver Burdett Press, 1997. 32p. $15.95; $5.95pa. ISBN 0-382-39470-4; 0-382-39471-2pa. (Remarkable Children). 2-4

In 1879, a young girl of eight, Maria de Sautuola, went into a cave in Spain. Inside she found prehistoric cave paintings, the first ones ever known in modern times. Fradin recreates that time in this biographical sketch of her experience. Fradin bases his material on primary sources.

454.	Fradin, Dennis Brindell. **The Nina, the Pinta, and the Santa Maria**. New York: Franklin Watts, 1991. 64p. $19.90. ISBN 0-531-20034-5. (First Books). 4-6

The fleet of three ships that Christopher Columbus took on his voyage to the New World cost him much bargaining time before he was able to leave Portugal. Although one of the ships sank, Columbus was an excellent seaman. Unfortunately, he was a poor administrator and had problems with his crew. Additionally, he probably was the first to begin using Native Americans as slaves. Bibliography and Index.

455.	Fradon, Dana, author/illustrator. **Harald the Herald: A Book About Heraldry**. New York: Dutton, 1990. Unpaged. $14.95. ISBN 0-525-44634-6. 4-7

With clear explanations of terms used in heraldry during the medieval period (from 1066 until 1485), the text shows the duties of heralds, which were to develop, record, and monitor the symbols on coats of arms. The fictional Miss Quincy and her class incorporate the information.

456.	Fradon, Dana, author/illustrator. **The King's Fool: A Book About Medieval and Renaissance Fools**. New York: Dutton, 1993. Unpaged. $14.99. ISBN 0-525-45074-2. 4-6

Cartoon illustrations help to reveal the role of fools or jesters in medieval and Renaissance society. Footnotes define unusual terms such as "hey nonny nonny"; a jester doll, come to life, tells about his role and some of the well-known sixteenth-century jesters such as Will Sommers and Querno.

457.	Frank, Anne. **The Diary of a Young Girl**. B. M. Mooyaart-Doubleday, translator. 1952. New York: Doubleday, 1996. 308p. $25. ISBN 0-385-47378-8. 6 up

Anne Frank (1929-1945) and her family lived a normal life in Holland during the 1930s until Hitler came to power in Germany. Her businessman father looked after the family, but when the Nazis entered Holland and occupied it, the Franks had to hide in the abandoned half of an old office; Anne was then thirteen. Others came to join them, and soon eight people shared two tiny rooms. No one could leave nor be seen from the outside. The few people who knew where they were had to get food to them without being detected. The diary reveals Anne Frank's thoughts and feelings as she copes with this inhumane constraint on her life. *American Library Association Notable Books for Young Adults*.

458.	Fraser, Mary Ann, author/illustrator. **On Top of the World: The Conquest of Mount Everest**. New York: Henry Holt, 1991. Unpaged. $14.95. ISBN 0-8050-1578-7. 3-6

On May 29, 1953, Edmund Hillary and Tenzing Norgay became the first men to reach the top of the highest mountain in the world. The text looks at their triumph by tracing their journey in detail. It mentions those who tried but never completed the quest to climb to the top of Mount Everest. Glossary.

459.	Freedman, Russell. **Louis Braille**. Kate Kiesler, illustrator. New York: Clarion, 1997. $15.95. ISBN 0-395-77516-7. 3-6

Louis Braille (1809-1852) struggled to communicate after he became blind, and he developed his alphabet. Freedman's rendering is lively and informative about the difficulties that Braille faced. Index.

460.	Freeman, Charles. **The Ancient Greeks**. New York: Oxford University Press, 1996. 46p. $9.95. ISBN 0-19-521238-X. (Spotlights). 4-6

The double-page spread text examines the Greeks with topics including the cultural and social life, government, religion, and warfare. Architecture and artifacts related to the topics from museums or historical sites enhance the material. Since the overview has little depth, it is merely an introduction to the Greeks.

461. French, Jackie. **Somewhere Around the Corner**. New York: Henry Holt, 1995. 230p. $14.95. ISBN 0-8050-3889-2. 5-8

In this historical fantasy, Barbara tries to escape a political demonstration in contemporary Australia by imagining that she is "around the corner." She finds herself in a Depression demonstration during 1932 instead. A young man takes her to Poverty Gully, a "susso camp" where the unemployed live. She becomes friends with several people who help her cope with the situation and with whom she can share dancing and building a school. When she tells stories about "around the corner," the adults listen more closely than the young people. Barbara eventually returns to the present, where she discovers that she can have the best of both past and present.

462. Friedman, Ina. **Escape or Die**. 1982. Cambridge, MA: Yellow Moon, 1991. 146p. $10.95pa. ISBN 0-938756-34-6pa. 6 up

Thirty-five million people died in World War II. Six million Jews died in the death camps, but five million non-Jews also met death there. The text looks at survivors, twelve men and women from Africa, Asia, Europe, and North and South America, who under the age of twenty, had both courage and luck. Some of them had never before told their stories of escaping form Germany, Austria, Czechoslovakia, Poland, Holland, Belgium, Ukraine, France, and Hungary. Glossary and Index.

463. Friedman, Ina R. **The Other Victims: First-Person Stories of Non-Jews Persecuted by the Nazis**. Boston: Houghton Mifflin, 1990. 180p. $14.95; $5.95pa. ISBN 0-395-50212-8; 0-395-74515-2pa. 5-9

In addition to the millions of Jews persecuted in World War II's Holocaust, 5 million Christians were also deliberately murdered. They included gypsies, blacks, many Slavs, homosexuals, ministers, and Jehovah's Witnesses. This book is a collection of personal interviews with survivors, detailing what they and their families and friends experienced. Other Books of Interest to the Reader and Index.

464. Fritsch, Debra M., and Ruth S. Hunter. **A Part of the Ribbon: A Time Travel Adventure Through the History of Korea**. Ken Cotrona, illustrator. Wethersfield, CT: Turtle Press, 1997. 216p. $5.95pa. ISBN 1-880336-11-1pa. 4-6

Although the way into fantasy is awkward, Jeffrey, thirteen, and his sister of six go with their *taekwondo* instructor back into Korea 2,000 years ago. They see the periods of history and the development of the sport.

465. Fritz, Jean. **Around the World in a Hundred Years: From Henry the Navigator to Magellan**. Anthony Bacon Venti, illustrator. New York: Putnam, 1994. 128p. $17.95. ISBN 0-399-22527-7. 4-7

In 1400, mapmakers named the space around the edge of the areas they had drawn as the Unknown. Later that century, explorers ventured into the Unknown searching for routes to the gold of China. The text discusses explorations, beginning with Prince Henry the Navigator (1394-1460) and ending with Magellan (1480?-1521), whose ship (after he had died in the Philippines) continued around the world. The explorers include Bartholomew Diaz exploring from 1487 to 1500, Christopher Columbus (1492-1504), Vasco da Gama (1497-1502), Pedro Álvares Cabral (1500-1501), John Cabot (1497-1498), Amerigo Vespucci (1499-1501), Juan Ponce de León (1513), and Vasco Núñez de Balboa (1513). Notes, Bibliography, and Index.

466. Fritz, Jean. **Can't You Make Them Behave, King George?** Tomie DePaola, illustrator. New York: Coward, 1982. 48p. $14.95; $5.95pa. ISBN 0-698-20315-1; 0-698-20542-1pa. 3-6

At age twenty-two, in 1760, George III (1738-1820) was crowned king of England. Before his coronation, he chose a bride from Germany whom he had not seen but who sounded as if she would make a good queen. He and Princess Charlotte of Mecklenburg raised a family, with George being as careful in his private life as he was in public. After he decided to tax the American colonists, he was surprised that they did not want to pay. He expected them to be dutiful children, and he did not want to fight, but their refusal left him no choice. When his government was ready for peace, he did not want to surrender, but he had to do what the parliament decreed. Notes from the Author.

467. Fritz, Jean. **Where Do You Think You're Going, Christopher Columbus?** Margot Tomes, illustrator. New York: Putnam, 1980. 80p. $13.95; $8.95pa. ISBN 0-399-20723-6; 0-399-20734-1pa. 3-6

Red-headed Christopher Columbus (1451-1506) nearly drowned off the coast of Portugal when he was twenty-five; after living through that experience, he seemed to think that he was blessed by God in whatever he did. He had read Marco Polo's book about his travels and that of Dr. Toscanelli, which claimed that Japan was 3,000 nautical miles to the west. He wanted to follow this route to the riches that Marco Polo had been able to carry over land before his route became inaccessible because the Turks denied safe transit. Eventually he convinced Isabelle of Castile that he would convert the people he met to Christianity, so she gave him money for the thirty-seven-day voyage from the Canary Islands to San Salvador. Although some of his friends, and certainly his enemies, believed that Columbus lacked leadership ability, he undertook more trips, still insisting that the island of Cuba was actually the mainland. After him, Amerigo Vespucci, John Cabot, and Vasco da Gama found the true mainland, but not Japan, which was actually 10,000 miles away. Notes and Index.

468. Fromer, Julie. **Jane Goodall: Living with the Chimps**. Antonio Castro, illustrator. New York: Twenty-First Century, 1992. 72p. $14.98. ISBN 0-8050-2115-7. 4-6

Jane Goodall has said that while she was a child, all she wanted to do was to be outdoors "watching and learning." When she was twenty-six, in 1960, she left England to go to the African jungle and study wild chimpanzees. To understand them, she had to understand their world and their society. She recorded every detail of their lives and discovered how much like humans they act. Many months passed before they let her get close enough to touch them, but she eventually won their trust. She is now concerned with using chimpanzees in scientific research because she thinks these animals suffer as much as humans would from such treatment. Glossary and Index.

469. Furlong, Monica. **Juniper**. New York: Knopf, 1991. 192p. $12.95. ISBN 0-394-83220-5. 5-8

This prequel to *Wise Child* tells how Juniper learned the secret teachings of the *dorans,* which she later imparted to Wise Child during the early Christian times. Euny teaches Juniper with a fierceness that Juniper refuses to use later in her life when she in turn imparts the knowledge of herbs, spells, and rituals to Wise Child.

470. Furlong, Monica. **Wise Child**. New York: Knopf, 1987. 228p. $11.95. ISBN 0-394-99105-2. 6-8

Juniper, an outcast, looks after Wise Child, age nine, after Wild Child's mother deserts her and her father does not return from sea. In early Christian times, the Scottish village mistrusts Juniper's powers of healing, and they need a scapegoat to blame for an outbreak of smallpox. Wise Child sees that Juniper's magic is nothing more than her close attention to detail, which helps her observe illnesses and remember the appropriate cures.

G

471. Gaffney, Timothy. **Edmund Hillary**. Chicago: Childrens Press, 1990. 128p. $28.20. ISBN 0-516-03052-3. (World's Great Explorers). 5-9

From New Zealand, where he learned to love snow, Edmund Hillary (b. 1919) traveled the globe attempting to go places no other human had been. In 1953, he reached the top of Mt. Everest in the Himalayas, at 29,028 feet (8,848 meters) the highest point on earth. In 1960, he went on an expedition in the Himalayas to search for the Abominable Snowman, or *yeti,* which he never found. By living at high altitude for a long time, he helped scientists study the effects of oxygen deficiency. His wife and a daughter died in an airplane crash on their way to be with him while he helped build a hospital in the Himalayas. Timeline of Events, Glossary, Bibliography, and Index.

472. Gaines, Ann. **Alexander von Humboldt: Colossus of Exploration**. New York: Chelsea House, 1990. 112p. $19.95. ISBN 0-7910-1313-8. (World Explorers). 5 up

Alexander von Humboldt (1769-1859) was a naturalist, botanist, mineralogist, marine biologist, volcanologist, anthropologist, explorer, geographer, philosopher, teacher, and writer. He was so interested in the natural world that he left Prussia when he was thirty to travel in South America exploring the rain forests and rivers. The rest of his life he devoted to publishing the data he had collected. His final publication, *Cosmos,* which he worked on for thirty years, appeared one year before he died; it was his attempt to say in plain language all that he had observed. Photographs, engravings, and reproductions enhance the text. Chronology, Further Reading, and Index.

473. Gallant, Roy. **The Day the Sky Split Apart: Investigating a Cosmic Mystery**. New York: Atheneum, 1995. 156p. $16. ISBN 0-689-80323-0. 6 up

On June 30, 1908, in the Tunguska wilderness of Siberia, a series of explosions occurred. Witnesses said that fire seemed to pour out of the sky, and seismographic instruments around the world registered impacts. In the 1920s, an anthropologist talked to natives and then began to investigate the event. Foreign researchers were kept from the area until 1992. Research there by Gallant and others indicates that this blast, which devastated an area half the size of Rhode Island, was probably an exploding meteorite. The question remains as to whether these kinds of destruction can be foreseen. The text looks at the initial investigations and asks questions about the future. Further Reading and Index.

474. Gallaz, Christophe. **Rose Blanche**. Roberto Innocenti, illustrator; Martha Coventry, translator. 1986. Mankato, MN: Creative Editions, Harcourt Brace, 1996. 28p. $17; $8pa. ISBN 0-15-200918-3; 0-15-200917-5pa. 6 up

One day during World War II, Rose Blanche follows an army truck through her German town, after she sees the mayor push a little boy inside it who did not want to go. When she discovers barbed wire with starving people behind it, she feeds the hungry prisoners her rations throughout the winter. One day she discovers the wire cut; in the fog, foreign soldiers see her and shoot her, thinking she is the enemy. She symbolizes the Germans who wanted to stop the war. *Mildred L. Batchelder Award* and *American Library Association Notable Books for Children.*

475. Galli, Letizia, author/illustrator. **Mona Lisa: The Secret of the Smile**. Nicholas B. A. Nicholson, translator. New York: Doubleday, 1996. 32p. $15.95. ISBN 0-385-32108-2. K-3

The text gives a brief overview of the life of Leonardo da Vinci. It looks at his interest in invention and his artistic endeavors and discusses his famous painting of the Mona Lisa at the end of the book. But it does not reveal the secret of the smile!

476. Galvin, Irene F. **The Maya of Central America**. Tarrytown, NY: Benchmark, 1996. 80p. $19.95. ISBN 0-7614-0091-5. 6-8

Galvin presents the Mayan culture through its art, poetry, religion, language, and way of life. Among the topics are hieroglyphs, the three separate Mayan calendars, and the study of astronomy, which the Mayans pursued. Illustrations aid the text. Bibliography, Chronology, Further Reading, Glossary, and Index.

477. Ganeri, Anita. **Benares**. New York: Dillon Press, 1993. 46p. $13.95. ISBN 0-87518-573-8. (Holy Cities). 4-6

From a religious viewpoint, Varanasi (formerly Benares), in India, is the spiritual center for the Hindus. The text focuses on the city and its 1,500 temples, palaces, and shrines. Over 1 million pilgrims visit the city annually to bathe in the sacred Ganges River. The most notable building, on the city's highest ground, is the mosque of Aurangzeb. Other topics include the history, culture, festivals and celebrations, art, and legends of Benares. Photographs enhance the text. Further Reading and Index.

478. Ganeri, Anita. **Exploration into India**. Englewood Cliffs, NJ: New Discovery, 1994. 48p. $15.95; $7.95pa. ISBN 0-02-718082-4; 0-382-24733-7pa. (Exploration Into). 4-6

The text looks at India from the time of the Indus Valley civilization, before the Aryans, and then the Greeks arrived. Other chapters cover India to A.D. 1001, with its new religions and the *guptas;* India under the Muslims and the Mogul Empire; the European presence in India; the British Raj, from 1756 to 1947; and modern India. Time Chart, Glossary, and Index.

479. Ganeri, Anita, and Rachel Wright. **India: Things to Make—Activities—Facts**. New York: Franklin Watts, 1994. 32p. $18. ISBN 0-531-14314-7. (Country Topics for Craft Projects). 4-6

India is a combination of very old traditions that still exist in contemporary culture. The topics include architecture, food, clothes, sports and leisure, religions, festivals, crafts, and history, with a brief look at some of India's many languages. Index.

480. Gardam, Jane. **A Long Way from Verona**. 1972. New York: Macmillan, 1988. 192p. $13.95. ISBN 0-02-735781-3. 6-9

At age nine, Jessica hears an author talk at her school, and she knows that she wants to write. When she is thirteen, during World War II, and her poem wins a *London Times* contest, all of the difficulties of the school year fade away. *Phoenix Award.*

481. Garfield, Leon. **Black Jack**. Antony Maitland, illustrator. New York: Random House, 1969. 192p. $4.50. ISBN 0-394-80713-8. 6-9

An orphaned boy and a hanged-man-come-back-to-life hold up a coach. After an insane girl on the coach escapes, she and the boy join a caravan, where she regains her sanity and they fall in love. After other events, the two stow away on the boy's uncle's ship and escape their eighteenth-century life in London.

482. Garfield, Leon. **The December Rose**. New York: Viking, 1987. 208p. $12.95. ISBN 0-670-81054-1. 6-9

Barnacle, a filthy sweep, is also a biter, a liar, and a thief in late-eighteenth-century London. After he steals a locket, the police come after him, but a barge owner pities him and takes him in. Further intrigues, espionage, and treason help to reveal information about a boat, *The December Rose*. Eventually, Barnacle reforms. *School Library Journal Best Book.*

483. Garfield, Leon. **Devil-in-the-Fog**. 1966. Magnolia, MA: Peter Smith, 1991. 205p. $15. ISBN 0-8446-6452-9. 5-8

George Treet, age fourteen, finds out that his family name is actually Dexter. He moves to Sir John Dexter's, but there he hears that Mr. Treet is a villain. After much confusion, George comes to understand that Mr. Treet has sold him to the Dexters to act as their heir. He fills the role well enough to irritate Sir John, but Lady Dexter likes him immensely. *Guardian Award for Children's Fiction.*

484. Garfield, Leon. **The Empty Sleeve**. New York: Delacorte, 1988. 207p. $14.95. ISBN 0-440-50049-4. 6-8

Peter and Paul are twins in eighteenth-century England. At age fourteen, Peter becomes a locksmith's apprentice in London; his angelic opposite, Paul, plans to stay at home. Before Peter leaves, an old man gives them two carved sailing ships encased in bottles, but Paul switches them so that he gets Peter's. As Peter becomes entangled in various difficulties in London, the ship that Paul has decays, and the old man cannot repair it. *School Library Journal Best Book.*

485. Garfield, Leon. **Footsteps**. 1980. New York: Yearling, 1988. 272p. $3.25pa. ISBN 0-440-40102-Xpa. 5-8

On his deathbed, William's father tells William, age twelve, that he cheated his business partner, Alfred Diamond. William rushes to London and searches for Diamond, or his son, at an address hidden inside his father's gold watch so that he can confess the deed. After several meetings with a man named John Robinson, William realizes that John Robinson is Diamond's son and that he is William's enemy. William saves John, however, when John almost dies in the fire he sets to destroy William's home. When all is resolved, William no longer hears the footsteps of his father's pacing as he has each night since his father's death. *Whitbread Book of the Year.*

486. Garfield, Leon. **Jack Holborn**. Antony Maitland, illustrator. New York: Random House, 1965. 250p. $5.99. ISBN 0-394-91323-X. 6-9

Abandoned as a baby, Jack Holborn stows away on the *Bristol* when he is thirteen. Pirates capture the ship, and the pirate captain tells Jack that he will identify Jack's mother if Jack saves him three times. Among the characters they meet as the result of shipwrecks and rescues are men who help make Jack rich and help him find his mother, in a variety of strange but believable ways.

487. Garfield, Leon. **The Night of the Comet**. New York: Delacorte, 1979. 149p. $8.95. ISBN 0-385-28753-4. 5-8

In the mid-eighteenth century, on April 6, Pigott's comet comes into the sky, and lovers prepare to have a party in its honor. Bostock tries to attract his friend's sister, but she ignores him. Others also have various difficulties with their partners during the celebration.

488. Garfield, Leon. **The Saracen Maid**. John O'Brien, illustrator. New York: Simon & Schuster, 1994. 26p. $14. ISBN 0-671-86646-X. 2-4

Set in the 1100s, this short book presents Gilbert, the forgetful son of a London merchant, who leaves for the East where pirates capture him, sell him into slavery, and cast him into a dungeon. His buyer plans to get a ransom for him, but Gilbert cannot remember his father's name or address. The buyer's daughter, a Saracen maid, pities Gilbert and helps him to escape.

489. Garfield, Leon. **Smith**. 1967. New York: Peter Smith, 1991. 218p. $16. ISBN 0-8446-6455-3. New York: Dell, 1987. 218p. $4.95pa. ISBN 0-440-48044-2pa. 6-9

Just before a man is murdered, Smith pickpockets the murderer and finds a document, which he cannot read. A blind man he meets has a daughter who will teach him to read, so Smith consents to live with the man and help him. After he learns how, he reads the document, but he refuses to give it up even though he is imprisoned for it. Smith and his blind benefactor eventually claim reward money for the document. *Carnegie Commendation* and *Phoenix Award*.

490. Garfield, Leon. **Young Nick and Jubilee**. New York: Delacorte, 1989. 137p. $13.95. ISBN 0-385-29777-7. 5-7

Nick, age ten, and Jubilee, age nine, survive in London during the eighteenth century as orphans living in parks and stealing their food. A thief, Mr. Owens, helps them get into a charity school by pretending to be their father. But part of the deal is that the schoolmaster makes surprise visits to the homes of his students. Thus, Nick and Jubilee have to live with Mr. Owens while waiting for the visit. Instead of throwing them out afterward, Mr. Owens finds he likes being their father, and he is a good one.

491. Garfunkel, Trudy. **On Wings of Joy: The Story of Ballet from the 16th Century to Today**. Boston: Little, Brown, 1994. 194p. $18.95. ISBN 0-316-30412-3. 6 up

Ballet began more than 400 years ago in the courts of Europe. In the seventeenth century, the English masque and the five positions of classical ballet were established. Although some changes occurred in the eighteenth century, Jean-Georges Noverre (1727-1810), the father of modern ballet, was the theorist of the times. Dancers received training commensurate with their body types. In the nineteenth century, Romanticism and Romantic ballet began. Famous dancers included Marie Taglioni, Jules Perrot, Carlotta Grisi, and Carlotta Brianza. During the twentieth century, modern dance arrived. Still, famous dancers preferred classical ballet. Names that dominate this century are Anna Pavlova and George Balanchine. Coda, Glossary, Bibliography, and Index.

492. Garland, Sherry. **Cabin 102**. San Diego, CA: Harcourt Brace, 1995. 243p. $11; $5pa. ISBN 0-15-238631-9; 0-15-200662-1pa. 5-9

Although set in the present, this historical fantasy couples the contemporary Dusty, twelve, with Tahni, an Arawak Indian girl who is in the cabin next door to Dusty's on a cruise ship. Through a series of inquiries and situations where people think he is crazy, Dusty finds out that Tahni drowned when the Spanish galleon *Estrella Vespertina* capsized in 1511. Now she is trying to return to her island of Bogati. With her story comes historical background on the Spanish conquest in the Caribbean and the end of the Arawak Indians.

493. Garrigue, Shelia. **The Eternal Spring of Mr. Ito**. 1985. New York: Aladdin, 1994. 163p. $3.95pa. ISBN 0-689-71809-8pa. 5-7

While living with Canadian relatives during World War II, after evacuation from England, Sara becomes friends with her uncle's gardener and World War I companion, Mr. Ito. He helps her start a bonsai plant, but the Japanese bomb Pearl Harbor in 1941, and the government interns Mr. Ito's family while he hides in a cave. Sara finds him and saves his bonsai tree, which has already been passed down through many generations, so that it can continue its long life.

494. Garza, Hedda. **Frida Kahlo**. New York: Chelsea House, 1994. 120p. $18.95; $7.95pa. ISBN 0-7910-1698-6; 0-7910-1699-4pa. (Hispanics of Achievement). 5 up

In 1925, Frida Kahlo (1907-1954) was one of the survivors of a bus crash in Mexico City in which several people died. She had a long recovery during which she began painting. She dreamed of becoming a doctor, but the crash kept her from walking without pain. She then married an artist, Diego Rivera, but continued struggling for recognition of the intensely personal paintings that she created. Although little known outside Mexico at her death, she is now known internationally for her unique style. Photographs and reproductions enhance the text. Chronology, Further Reading, and Index.

495.   Gay, Kathlyn. **Science in Ancient Greece**. New York: Franklin Watts, 1988. 95p. $16.60. ISBN 0-531-10487-7. (First Book). 4-6

An introduction to ancient Greece and its science precedes chapters on different developments from this culture. They include explanations of the universe, mathematicians and geometers, star gazers, geographers, physicians and anatomists, biologists and botanists, "purists" versus practical scientists, engineers and builders, and contemporary debt to the Greek culture for its discoveries. Photographs and drawings enhance the text. Glossary, Further Reading, and Index.

496.   Gee, Maurice. **The Champion**. New York: Simon & Schuster, 1993. 212p. $16. ISBN 0-671-86561-7. 6-9

Rex, aged twelve in 1943, anticipates the arrival of an American soldier who will stay with his family in New Zealand to recuperate. When the soldier arrives, Rex is shocked that he is black. Once Rex adjusts to Jack, Jack helps him become friends with other children who have had experiences like Jack's, a half-Maori boy and a Dalmatian immigrant. Then Rex and his friends in turn help Jack when white American soldiers recklessly pursue him.

497.   Gee, Maurice. **The Fire-Raiser**. Boston: Houghton Mifflin, 1992. 172p. $14.95. ISBN 0-395-62428-2. 5-9

In 1915, someone sets a fire in Kitty's New Zealand town. No one knows the culprit, but the children suspect one man of the deed. Although the adults disagree, the children also find benzene cans and rags near his home. When he repeats the arson, the children prove to be correct.

498.   Gehrts, Barbara. **Don't Say a Word**. New York: Macmillan, 1986. 170p. $11.95. ISBN 0-689-50412-8. 6-10

At the beginning of World War II, Anna lives with her family outside Berlin. But as the war progresses, the Gestapo arrests her father, a Luftwaffe officer, for giving information to the Allies. Anna's best friend, a Jew, commits suicide. Her boyfriend dies on the Russian front, and during military training her brother gets an infection that kills him. Her home is bombed, and her mother ages prematurely. Hitler's regime destroys families regardless of race and background. *American Library Association Notable Books for Children* and *International Board on Books for Young People*.

499.   **Georgia**. Minneapolis, MN: Lerner, 1992. 56p. $19.95. ISBN 0-8225-2807-X. (Then and Now). 5-9

Georgia, on the coast of the Black Sea, has a known history dating from the fourth century B.C., and it reached the height of its power during the twelfth and thirteenth centuries. The text covers the history, economics, geography, politics, ethnography, and possible future of Georgia. Maps and photographs complement the text. Glossary and Index.

500.   Geras, Adèle. **Voyage**. New York: Atheneum, 1983. 194p. $12.95. ISBN 0-689-30955-4. 5-9

Mina, age fourteen, and her family leave Russia in the early twentieth century for America, to escape the pogroms against Jews. On board the ship, Mina uses her energy to help those on board who can barely survive from the seasickness, the hunger, and the filth that surrounds them. The omniscient point of view exposes the diverse responses of those on board ship to this difficult experience.

501.   Getz, David. **Frozen Man**. Peter McCarty, illustrator. New York: Redfeather, Henry Holt, 1994. 68p. $14.95. ISBN 0-8050-3261-4. 4-7

A body found in the Alps between Austria and Italy seemed unexceptional until an archaeologist examined it and discovered that the man had died more than 5,000 years ago. From his body, archaeologists have learned what life in Europe might have been like during that time, including the type of clothing worn, the food eaten, and what the people looked like. Glossary, Bibliography, and Index.

502.   Gherman, Beverly. **The Mysterious Rays of Dr. Röntgen**. Stephen Marchesi, illustrator. New York: Atheneum, 1994. 32p. $14.95. ISBN 0-689-31839-1. 2-4

In 1895, Dr. Röntgen discovered x-rays. Scientists, including Thomas Edison, were delighted with his findings, but they did not know the danger, and several suffered from overexposure. The text looks at Röntgen's discovery as a continuum from earlier research and as a basis for later experiments and technological advancement. Among the details are Röntgen's wife's distress at seeing an x-ray of her finger and the expansion of the use of x-rays to help search for weapons. Chronology and Bibliography.

503.   Gherman, Beverly. **Robert Louis Stevenson: Teller of Tales**. New York: Atheneum, 1996. 144p. $16. ISBN 0-689-31985-1. 3-7

Robert Louis Stevenson (1859-1894) lived in a strict Scottish household and studied law to please his father. But he wanted to write, and his love of adventure took him across France on a donkey and across America chasing his true love to California. He wrote books to entertain his stepson, and after the success of *Treasure Island* he wrote other adventure stories. His family then went to the South Pacific, where he spent his final years living on Samoa. Index.

504. Gibbons, Gail, author/illustrator. **Beacons of Light: Lighthouses**. New York: Morrow, 1990. Unpaged. $16. ISBN 0-688-07379-4. 2-4

Using watercolors of various lighthouses, Gibbons gives a history of them since the Pharos at Alexandria, Egypt. She shows the first American lighthouse, erected in 1716 in Boston; the evolution of lights up to the Fresnel (invented in 1822); and the various sounds to warn ships of danger in the fog.

505. Gibbons, Gail, author/illustrator. **The Great St. Lawrence Seaway**. New York: Morrow, 1992. 40p. $15. ISBN 0-688-06984-3. 2-6

Among the explorers who wanted to find a waterway across the continent were Jacques Cartier, who turned back in 1535, and Samuel de Champlain in 1603, who had his boats ported over Niagara Falls. In 1666, Robert Cavelier de La Salle also failed, but he realized that the area would be good for trapping and colonization. The text continues with the history of the seaway and the various improvements that allow ships to sail along it from the Atlantic through canals to the Great Lakes.

506. Gibbons, Gail. **Knights in Shining Armor**. Boston: Little, Brown, 1995. Unpaged. $14.95. ISBN 0-316-30948-6. K-3

Called *ritters* in Germany, *chevaliers* in France, and *caballeros* in Spain, knights fought in Europe during the Middle Ages, from A.D. 500-1500. Men trained for many years before they could reach the rank of knight, using specific tactics and weapons which are illustrated in the text. Also appearing are brief comments about King Arthur and his favorite knights and a brief recounting of three different dragon legends.

507. Gibbons, Gail, author/illustrator. **Pirates: Robbers of the High Seas**. Boston: Little, Brown, 1993. Unpaged. $15.95. ISBN 0-316-30975-3. K-2

In this brief history of pirates, the text mentions the Barbary pirates, who raided off the coast of Africa around 1300; pirates during times of Spanish exploration, who watched for galleons to enter vulnerable spots for attack; the buccaneers of the 1600s; and the robbers on the Atlantic Ocean in the 1700s. Although people considered pirates evil, queens and kings hired some men to rob the ships of other countries, and people saw these privateers as heroes. Famous Pirates and Treasures.

508. Giblin, James. **Be Seated: A Book About Chairs**. New York: HarperCollins, 1993. 136p. $15. ISBN 0-06-021537-2. 4-8

The text gives a history of chairs beginning with the three-legged stools and chairs of the Egyptians, which were mortise- and tenon-joined. It includes the thrones of kings such as Solomon and the *klismos* of the Greeks with their curved lines. Giblin also discusses the Sheridan chair and the Shaker rocker. The chair becomes a part of social custom, art, and politics in the society that uses it. Bibliography, Notes, and Index.

509. Giblin, James. **When Plague Strikes: The Black Death, Smallpox, AIDS**. New York: HarperCollins, 1995. 212p. $14.95. ISBN 0-06-025854-3. 5-9

Three major plagues have hit the known world in the past 1,000 years: the Black Death, smallpox, and AIDS. They have killed millions of people and have left social, economic, and political havoc. Although each plague has helped to increase knowledge about the human body, each new one must be researched and tested for a cure. The text first recounts the Plague of Athens that struck in the summer of 430 B.C. Those who lived had terrible scars or lost their eyesight or their memory. Today no one is sure what the disease might have been, although typhus, smallpox, and the bubonic plague are candidates. The sure thing is that doctors did not know how to treat it. Giblin continues with information about the three plagues that have ravaged the world since. Source Notes, Bibliography, and Index. *American Library Association Best Books for Young Adults, Notable Children's Trade Books in the Field of Social Studies*, and *American Library Association Notable Books for Children*.

510. Giblin, James Cross. **Chimney Sweeps: Yesterday and Today**. New York: Trophy, 1987. 64p. $6.95pa. ISBN 0-06-446061-4pa. 4-6

The text looks at the history and folklore surrounding the profession of chimney sweep in Europe and America from the fifteenth century to the present. *American Book Award Winner, American Library Association Notable Books for Children, Horn Book Fanfare Honor List, Booklist Children's Editors Choices*, and *Golden Kite Award*.

511. Giblin, James Cross. **The Riddle of the Rosetta Stone: Key to Ancient Egypt**. New York: Crowell, 1990. 85p. $15.89. ISBN 0-690-04799-1. New York: Trophy, 1993. 85p. $5.95pa. ISBN 0-06-446137-8pa. 5-7

In 1799, Napoleon's soldiers found a black stone in an old fort north of Alexandria, Egypt, and sent it to Cairo to be examined by scholars whom Napoleon had brought on his campaign. They could not decipher the three languages inscribed on the stone before the British routed Napoleon and claimed the stone for the British Museum. Several other scholars who worked on the problem discovered that the three languages on the stone were Greek (Alexander ruled during its creation), Demotic (of the people), and hieroglyphic (sacred). A few years later, a poor young French student, Champollion, met some of the men who had been with Napoleon. He dedicated himself to finding the connection among the languages. In 1824, his book showed that the hieroglyphs were both sound and symbol and he correlated the three segments of the stone. Afterword about the Demotic Translation, Bibliography, and Index. *Notable Children's Trade Books in the Field of Social Studies*, and *American Library Association Notable Books for Children*.

512.   Giblin, James Cross. **The Truth About Unicorns**. Michael McDermott, illustrator. New York: Harper-Collins, 1991. 113p. $15; $6.95pa. ISBN 0-06-022478-9; 0-06-446147-5pa. 5 up

Although the unicorn is a mythical animal, it has appeared throughout history. The Chinese saw it as representing nobility and virtue, and many Christians have seen it as a symbol of Jesus Christ. Some have thought that the unicorn possesses magical powers; that it was the swiftest of beasts, so that no other beast could catch it; and that only the purest female could tame it. Photographs of the Unicorn Tapestries complement the text, which looks at the myths and legends of this being. Bibliography, Reading List, and Index. *American Library Association Notable Books for Children* and *School Library Journal Best Book*.

513.   Gibson, Michael. **The War in Vietnam**. New York: Bookwright Press, Franklin Watts, 1992. 63p. $19.14. ISBN 0-531-18408-0. (Witness History). 5-8

The text traces the history of Vietnam from 1887 until the French left in 1954. It discusses the United States's entry into the conflict after it began in 1961 and the country's exit before the fighting ended in 1975, as well as the current situation within the country. Black-and-white and a few color photographs highlight the text. Chronology, Glossary, and Index.

514.   Giff, Patricia Reilly. **Mother Teresa: Sister to the Poor**. Ted Lewin, illustrator. New York: Puffin, 1987. 57p. $4.99pa. ISBN 0-14-032225-6pa. (Women of Our Time). 2-6

As a teenager in Albania, Mother Teresa (1910-1997) decided that she wanted to join a convent. After going to India and serving others, she realized that the poor and disinherited need love as much as anyone else, and her efforts to help them have generated worldwide support.

515.   Gilbert, Adrian. **The French Revolution**. New York: Thomson Learning, 1995. 48p. $22.78. ISBN 1-56847-390-7. (Revolution!). 4-6

The text discusses the causes of the French Revolution and gives information about the years after the formation of the National Assembly to the death of Louis XVI in 1793. It presents both sides of the conflict, with emphasis on the unjust taxation, failure in reforms, and unendurable food shortages. Further Reading, Glossary, and Index.

516.   Giles, Gail. **Breath of the Dragon**. Boston: Houghton Mifflin, 1997. 106p. $14.95. ISBN 0-395-76476-9. 4-6

Malila, five, faces ignominy after police shoot her father as a thief and her mother escapes to America, leaving her with her grandmother. But her grandmother teaches her how to face life and to observe the Thai traditions of her ancestors. After her father is pronounced *suay* (unlucky), Malila is considered an outcast, and she spends her time drawing and listening to her grandmother's wisdom. When her grandmother dies, Malila, then fourteen, has to go to America, and with her, she carries the lessons she has learned.

517.   Gleiter, Jan. **Benito Juárez**. Francis Balistreri, illustrator. Austin, TX: Raintree/Steck-Vaughn, 1993. 32p. $19.97; $4.95pa. ISBN 0-8172-3381-4; 0-8114-6759-7pa. (Hispanic Stories). 4-7

Born a Zapotec Indian in Oaxaca, with few of the rights of the Spanish, Benito Juárez (1806-1871) worked his way through school and finally became a lawyer who defended the poor. He became Mexico's president before the French invaded in the 1860s and returned when they left. Several times he overcame heavy opposition and passed laws that took power away from the church. Throughout his career, he tried to govern with compassion. Glossary. English and Spanish text.

518.   Gleiter, Jan, and Kathleen Thompson. **Christopher Columbus**. Rick Whipple, illustrator. Austin, TX: Raintree/Steck-Vaughn, 1995. 32p. $19.97; $4.95pa. ISBN 0-8114-8456-4; 0-8114-9351-2pa. (First Biographies). K-3

In this fictional biography, thirteen-year-old Ferdinand tells about his father, Christopher Columbus, on his fourth voyage to the New World. As he recounts the other voyages, the son tries to protect his father from the men who want to go ashore against his father's orders. Key Dates.

519.   Gleiter, Jan, and Kathleen Thompson. **Diego Rivera**. Yoshi Miyake, illustrator. Austin, TX: Raintree/Steck-Vaughn, 1993. 32p. $19.97; $4.95pa. ISBN 0-8172-2908-6; 0-8114-6764-3pa. (Hispanic Stories). 4-7

As a child, Diego Rivera (1886-1957) drew pictures on everything he could reach, so his father restricted him to drawing in his room, but allowed him to draw on anything. As a young man, he went from Mexico, his home, to Spain and then Paris and later Italy. Among his friends was Picasso. Rivera's style developed, and when he returned to Mexico, he wanted to create art that everyone could see. He painted murals that featured workers. As a Communist, he spoke actively against Hitler in World War II. Glossary.

154 Gleiter

520. Gleiter, Jan, and Kathleen Thompson. **José Martí**. Les Didier, illustrator. Austin, TX: Raintree/Steck-Vaughn, 1993. 32p. $19.97; $4.95pa. ISBN 0-8172-2906-X; 0-8114-6761-9pa. (Hispanic Stories). 4-7

José Martí (1853-1895) was born in Cuba while the Spanish controlled it. At age sixteen, he was imprisoned for an article he wrote agitating against the Spanish, and he was eventually deported to Spain. There he studied law, and the Spanish government allowed him to go to Mexico. From Mexico, Guatemala, Spain, and New York, he continued to fight for Cuban freedom through his writing. He led the revolution of 1895 but was killed as soon as it began. His colleagues did not see Cuban freedom until 1902. Glossary. English and Spanish text.

521. Gleiter, Jan, and Kathleen Thompson. **Junípero Serra**. Charles Shaw, illustrator. Austin, TX: Raintree/Steck-Vaughn, 1993. 32p. $13.98; $5.95pa. ISBN 0-8172-2909-4; 0-8114-6765-1pa. (Hispanic Stories). 4-7

As a Franciscan teacher and scholar in Spain, Junípero Serra (1713-1784) decided to go to the New World and help the natives. He and a friend went to California and began to build missions—San Diego, San Francisco, San Antonio, and San Luis Obispo. He wanted to make Spanish settlement in the area easier. He convinced the viceroy that soldiers protecting the missions needed to have their families join them, which created the towns surrounding the missions. Glossary.

522. Gleiter, Jan, and Kathleen Thompson. **Miguel Hidalgo y Costilla**. Rick Karpinski, illustrator. Austin, TX: Raintree/Steck-Vaughn, 1993. 32p. $19.97; $4.95pa. ISBN 0-8172-2905-1; 0-8114-6757-0pa. (Hispanic Stories). 4-7

Miguel Hidalgo y Costilla (1753-1811) has been called the "Father of Mexican Independence" for two reasons. First, he was a Catholic priest. Secondly, he led his Indian followers in battle against the Spanish for independence. Because he did not have the leadership skills for battle, he lost. After he was tried and shot, the fight continued for another ten years until Mexico became free. Glossary. English and Spanish text.

523. Gleiter, Jan, and Kathleen Thompson. **Simón Bolívar**. Tom Redman, illustrator. Austin, TX: Raintree/Steck-Vaughn, 1993. 32p. $19.97; $4.95pa. ISBN 0-8172-2902-7; 0-8114-6751-1pa. (Hispanic Stories). 4-7

Born of very rich parents in Venezuela, Simón Bolívar (1782-1830) became an orphan, and a tutor taught him the ideas of European thinkers, such as Jean-Jacques Rousseau, who believed in liberty and equality. In Rome, Bolívar dedicated himself to freeing Venezuela from Spain. After two revolutions and many years, he succeeded, but his other dreams were never totally realized. Glossary. English and Spanish text.

524. Glubok, Shirley. **Great Lives: Painting**. New York: Scribner's, 1994. 238p. $24.95. ISBN 0-684-19052-4. (Great Lives). 5-9

Places where they live and experiences they have influence the subjects that artists choose to paint. Biographical profiles of 23 major painters appear in the text: Mary Cassatt, American (1844-1926); Marc Chagall, Russian (1887-1985); Frederick E. Church, American (1826-1900); Jacques-Louis David, French (1748-1825); Edgar Degas, French (1834-1917); Albrecht Dürer, German (1471-1528); Thomas Gainsborough, English (1727-1788); Paul Gaugin, French (1848-1903); El Greco, Greek (1541-1614); Winslow Homer, American (1836-1910); Leonardo da Vinci, Italian (1452-1519); Michelangelo, Italian (1475-1564); Claude Monet, French (1840-1926); Georgia O'Keeffe, American (1889-1986); Pablo Picasso, Spanish (1881-1973); Rembrandt van Rijn, Dutch (1606-1669); Diego Rivera, Mexican (1886-1957); Peter Paul Rubens, Flemish (1577-1640); Titian, Venetian (?-1576); Vincent van Gogh, Dutch (1853-1890); Diego de Veláquez, Spanish (1599-1660); Johannes Vermeer, Dutch (1632-1675); and James McNeill Whistler, American (1834-1903). Further Reading and Index.

525. Gogol, Sara. **A Mien Family**. Minneapolis, MN: Lerner, 1997. 56p. $16.95. ISBN 0-8225-3407-X. (Journey Between Two Worlds). 3-6

The text includes the Mien history as background for discussing the underlying causes of the Mien family becoming refugees. Photographs and personal experiences explain the Mien social, political, and religious traditions and the difficulty of parting from these ways to adapt to a new culture. Further Reading.

526. Gold, Alison Leslie. **Memories of Anne Frank: Reflections of a Childhood Friend**. New York: Scholastic, 1997. 135p. $16.95. ISBN 0-590-90722-0. 6-9

Hannah Pick-Goslar was Anne Frank's childhood friend from the ages of four to thirteen. She was also incarcerated in Bergen-Belsen although a fence separated them, and they talked to each other through the barbed wire. But like many young people, they were developing in different ways as they matured, and the text looks at their experiences. Photographs.

527. Goldenstern, Joyce. **Albert Einstein: Physicist and Genius**. Springfield, NJ: Enslow, 1995. 128p. $17.95. ISBN 0-89490-480-9. (Great Minds of Science). 6-9

Albert Einstein (1879-1955) formulated one of the most important ideas of the twentieth century, the General Theory of Relativity. He won the 1921 Nobel Prize in Physics, and his genius became famous. It saved his life when Hitler began killing Jews in World War II. From his Princeton, New Jersey, home, Einstein helped others to flee Europe, but he refused to become president of Israel. He wanted to continue work on scientific questions, many of which remained unanswered at his death. Photographs, Chronology, Further Reading, Glossary, and Index.

528.   Goldin, Barbara Diamond. **The Passover Journey: A Seder Companion**. Neil Waldman, illustrator. New York: Viking, 1994. 56p. $15.99. ISBN 0-670-82421-6. 3-6

This two-part text covers a history of Passover, or the Seder, beginning with the Israelites as slaves in Egypt when Moses helped them escape. It contains a segment about the Warsaw (Poland) Ghetto uprising during World War II at Passover, along with stories from both Midrash and Torah. The second part describes Passover rituals and includes an historical explanation of symbols in the fourteen steps of Seder. Glossary and Notes.

529.   Gonen, Rivka. **Charge! Weapons and Warfare in Ancient Times**. Minneapolis, MN: Runestone Press, 1993. 72p. $22.95. ISBN 0-8225-3201-8. (Buried Worlds). 5 up

In documenting the development of armor and weapons, the text presents early artillery such as the ballista. It also describes other weapons, including spears, swords, bows and arrows, and catapults; their use in warfare; and protective helmets, body armor, and shields. Excellent photographs and drawings of artifacts enhance the information. Glossary and Index

530.   Gonen, Rivka. **Fired Up: Making Pottery in Ancient Times**. Minneapolis, MN: Runestone Press, 1993. 72p. $22.95. ISBN 0-8225-3202-6. (Buried Worlds). 5 up

In an explanation of theories about the origins of pottery, the text presents the development of the potter's wheel and methods of dating pottery, which help archaeologists decide how old a site might be. Designs on pottery also help to distinguish its origins. Glossary and Index.

531.   Gonzales, Doreen. **Diego Rivera: His Art, His Life**. Springfield, NJ: Enslow, 1996. 128p. $18.95. ISBN 0-89490-764-6. 6-9

Gonzales sees Diego Rivera as an egotistical man, absorbed in himself and letting his art interfere with his marriage to Frida Kahlo, another Mexican painter, his children, and his extramarital love affairs. The text also discusses his political beliefs and his pride in his Mexican heritage. Further Reading and Index.

532.   Goodall, John S., author/illustrator. **Great Days of a Country House**. New York: Margaret K. McElderry, 1992. 58p. $15.95. ISBN 0-689-50545-0. 3-5

The text presents an English country house through the centuries, with pictures of it at different times such as the Tudor, Edwardian, Georgian, and World War I periods. The illustrations show many aspects of the times, including the differences between quarters of nobility and servants, the food eaten, and the customs followed.

533.   Goode, Diane, author/illustrator. **Mama's Perfect Present**. New York: Dutton, 1996. Unpaged. $14.99. ISBN 0-525-45493-4. K-3

The two children from *Where's Our Mama?* need to get a birthday gift for their mother. They search several early-twentieth-century Paris shops with their dog Zaza, causing chaos wherever they go. The dog helps them find the best present, a set of paints, which they use to create a portrait of their mother.

534.   Goodman, Joan Elizabeth. **Songs from Home**. San Diego, CA: Harcourt Brace, 1994. 213p. $10.95; $4.95pa. ISBN 0-14-203590-7; 0-15-203591-5pa. 5-9

Anna, aged twelve in 1969, lives in Rome with her father in a *pensione* (a dilapidated boardinghouse) and sings with him in restaurants at night for pay. She hates it and lies to people at her school about her life. When a friend moves nearby, she has to tell the truth. She finally decides to leave her father in Europe, because he still cannot face her mother's tragic death, and go to his family in America, although she has never met any of them.

535.   Goodman, Joan Elizabeth. **The Winter Hare**. Boston: Houghton Mifflin, 1996. 255p. $15.95. ISBN 0-395-78569-3. 6-9

Will Belet, twelve, is small for his age after a bout with pox during the twelfth century in England. He has the nickname of Rabbit, and is happy to become a page to his uncle because he wants to emulate King Arthur and become a knight during England's civil war of 1140. He discovers, however, that war is almost unbearable as he bravely helps the Empress Matilda escape from Oxford Castle and finds himself in the middle of a fight between his father and his uncle.

536.   Goodnough, David. **José Martí: Cuban Patriot and Poet**. Springfield, NJ: Enslow, 1996. 128p. $17.95. ISBN 0-89490-761-1. (Hispanic Biographies). 5-9

José Martí (1853-1895) promoted Cuban independence and kept the United States from dominating politics and economics in the Caribbean. The text also looks at Martí's cultural legacy; he wrote the song "Guantanamera" and founded the modernist literary movement in Latin America. The Spanish killed Martí when he returned to Cuba after years in exile. Chronology, Further Reading, Notes, and Index.

537. Gordon, Matthew S. **Ayatollah Khomeini**. New York: Chelsea House, 1986. 120p. $18.95. ISBN 0-87754-559-6. (World Leaders Past and Present). 5 up

For many of his Iranian countrymen, Ayatollah Khomeini (1902-1989) restored his nation's pride and independence, although many Westerners saw him as a fanatical tyrant. In 1941, he published a book that attacked the regime of Reza Pahlavi, the Shah of Iran. Khomeini hated the idea of modernization and detested the corruption of the shah's regime. Khomeini was arrested and exiled but continued to lead the millions who wanted to overthrow the shah. In 1979, he returned and established himself as the leader of Iran, with a government based on Islamic principles. His ideals give an insight into the Middle Eastern psyche. Photographs enhance the text. Chronology, Further Reading, and Index.

538. Gordon, Matthew S. **The Gemayels**. New York: Chelsea House, 1988. 112p. $18.95. ISBN 1-55546-834-9. (World Leaders Past and Present). 5 up

The Gemayel family members have been leaders in Lebanon since the 1930s. Pierre Gemayel, who gained recognition at the 1936 Berlin Olympics, wanted to form an orderly political organization like that of the Nazis in Germany. He formed Kataib, a fascist military organization that eventually became a legitimate political party. His son, Bashir (1947-1982), became the Kataib commander and then the head of the Lebanese forces in 1976. In August 1982, Bashir was elected president, but a month later he was assassinated. Bashir's older brother, Amin, became president. He has been moderate, but he still has problems maintaining peace in his country. Photographs and reproductions enhance the text. Chronology, Further Reading, and Index.

539. Gordon, Shelia. **The Middle of Somewhere**. New York: Jackson, Orchard, 1990. 154p. $13.95. ISBN 0-531-05908-1. 5-7

The stories of forced removals in South Africa, at a time before Nelson Mandela was freed from prison, are important slices of history. Rebecca and Noni, both age nine, keep hearing about Pofadderkloof, a place supposedly nicer than their current home. However, the government has lied to their people before, and the adults try to stay where they are. Noni's family leaves, and Rebecca must adjust to the loss of her friend while waiting for her mother's biweekly visits and for Papa's release from prison. The story ends in 1990, when the government releases both Rebecca's papa and Mandela.

540. Gorrell, Gena K. **North Star to Freedom: The Story of the Underground Railroad**. New York: Delacorte, 1997. 168p. $17.95. ISBN 0-385-32319-0. 6-8

The focus of this book, unlike other texts on the Underground Railroad, is Canada. Many of the slaves who took the railroad ended their journey in Canada with the help of abolitionists and Quakers along the way. Individual accounts from slaves who settled in Canada add new insights about this ordeal of American history. Reproductions, Bibliography, Further Reading, Notes, and Index.

541. Gosnell, Kelvin. **Belarus, Ukraine, and Moldova**. Brookfield, CT: Millbrook Press, 1992. 32p. $15.90. ISBN 1-56294-306-5. (Former Soviet States). 4-7

The text discusses the cultural background, politics, economics, and histories of the former Soviet republics of Belarus, Ukraine, and Moldova. Originally inhabited by Slavs, Belarus lies east of Poland and north of Ukraine. Ukraine has had human inhabitants at least since 6000 B.C., because it sits on a major trade route; Moldova is more closely connected to Romania through its language and culture. Glossary and Index.

542. Gourley, Catherine. **Beryl Markham: Never Turn Back**. Berkeley, CA: Conari Press, 1997. 224p. $6.95. ISBN 1-57324-073-7. (Barnard Biography). 6-10

Beryl Markham (1903-1986) spent most of her life in Kenya although born in England. She became a pilot in the early days of aviation, setting a record with her transatlantic flight; was a horse trainer; and spent time in Hollywood after publishing a book. The text examines her life and the risks that she took without regard to being female. Bibliography and Index.

543. Graham, Harriet. **A Boy and His Bear**. New York: Simon & Schuster, Margaret K. McElderry, 1996. 196p. $16. ISBN 0-689-80943-3. 6-9

Dickon becomes apprenticed to a tanner after his widowed mother remarries in medieval England. He hates having to work on the skins of animals that he loves, and when he goes on an errand to the bear pits where bears fight dogs, he rescues a cub and flees. He sails to France with entertainers, and the Bear Catcher follows him. In some scenes, the bear cub gives its view of the situation, and eventually, Dickon does what he must, which is set the bear free.

544. Graham, Ian. **Spacecraft**. Roger Stewart, illustrator. Austin, TX: Raintree/Steck-Vaughn, 1995. 32p. $13.98. ISBN 0-8114-6193-9. (Pointers). 3-6

Two-page discussions on each type of spacecraft place it within its twentieth-century historical context. The first spacecraft, launched by the Russians, were *Sputnik I* and *II* in 1957. The United States followed in 1958 with *Explorer V*. After these were the space capsules, *Gemini, Apollo, Soyuz,* the space shuttle, modern satellites, deep space probes, the *Viking* lander, *Salyut, Skylab,* and *Mir*. Illustrations enhance the information. Glossary and Index.

545. Granfield, Linda. **In Flanders Fields: The Story of the Poem by John McCrae**. Janet Wilson, illustrator. New York: Doubleday, 1996. Unpaged. $15.95. ISBN 0-385-32228-3. 5 up

Using the poem *In Flanders Fields* as a base, the text discusses the poem, gives an overview of World War I, and briefly capsulizes the life of the Canadian poet, John McCrae. Sketches, photographs, and memorabilia add to the illustrations.

546. Grant, Neil. **The Egyptians**. New York: Oxford University Press, 1996. 46p. $9.95. ISBN 0-19-521239-8. (Spotlights). 4-6

The text looks at the Egyptians in double-page spreads. The topics include the cultural and social life, the government, religion, and warfare. Architecture and artifacts related to the topics from museums or historical sites enhance the material. Since the overview has little depth, it merely introduces the Egyptians.

547. Graves, Charles. **Marco Polo**. Ray Keane, illustrator. New York: Chelsea Juniors, 1991. 100p. $14.95. ISBN 0-7910-1505-X. (Discovery Biography). 3-6

This fictional biography of Marco Polo (1524-1324) tells of Polo's experiences as he traveled with his father to the court of the Kublai Khan in Cathay. It is based on Polo's own book about the journey.

548. Gravett, Chris. **Arms and Armor**. Richard Hook, Chris Rothero, and Peter Sarson, illustrators. Austin, TX: Raintree/Steck-Vaughn, 1995. 32p. $13.98. ISBN 0-8114-6190-4. (Pointers). 3-7

Two-page spreads on types of arms and armor explain their effectiveness and give historical information as well as illustrations. The periods and items covered include Early Bronze weapons (through 612 B.C.), Chinese crossbowmen (1500-500 B.C.), armies of iron (500 B.C.-A.D. 100), the age of mail armor (A.D. 300-1300), Eastern warriors (A.D. 1200-1500), medieval foot soldiers (A.D. 1300-1500), steel plates for soldiers (A.D. 1100-1600), Japanese samurai (A.D. 400-1600), muskets and powder (A.D. 1700-1900), firearms (A.D. 1800s), and today's armor made of Kevlar. Glossary and Index.

549. Gravett, Christopher. **Castle**. Geoff Dann, illustrator. New York: Knopf, 1994. 63p. $19. ISBN 0-679-86000-2. (Eyewitness). 4-6

Clear photographs of artifacts and buildings tell the story of castles through the centuries. The text looks at what constitutes a castle; in doing so it covers castles on the Loire River in France and some in Spain and Germany. Other castles included are in Japan and from the Crusades. The parts of a castle may include the chapel, garrison, prison, hall, and kitchen; the book also discusses defenses, entertainment, and the fields and animals around castles. Metalworkers, woodworkers, and other builders kept the castles functioning. Index.

550. Gravett, Christopher. **Knight**. Geoff Dann, photographs. New York: Knopf, 1993. 63p. $19. ISBN 0-679-83882-1. (Eyewitness). 4-8

Text and photographs give detailed information about the history of knights, the ritual of knighthood, their training, and their armor. Two-page spreads include such topics as the first knights, the Normans, armor, arms, horses, castles at war and under siege, battle, castles in peace, lords and ladies of the manor, chivalry, tournaments and jousts, foot combat, heraldry, hunting and hawking, faith and pilgrimage, the Crusades, Knights of Christ, Knights of the Rising Sun, professional knights, and the decline of chivalry by the seventeenth century. Index.

551. Gravett, Christopher. **The Knight's Handbook: How to Become a Champion in Shining Armor**. New York: Cobblehill, Dutton, 1997. 36p. $12.99. ISBN 0-525-65241-8. 3-6

Intriguing information fills the pages of this book about medieval knights and ideas about how to become one. Clothes of the jousting knights, instructions for making a personal helmet and sword, living in a castle, and plans for turrets and drawbridges are some of the topics. Items to make include a siege catapult, a board game, and a shield. They will help readers understand the medieval period.

552. Gravett, Christopher. **The World of the Medieval Knight**. Brett Breckon, illustrator. New York: Peter Bedrick, 1997. 64p. $19.95. ISBN 0-87226-277-4. 5-10

Among the topics covered in double-page spreads are horses, weapons, castle life, hunting, and jousting. For each main topic, Gravett includes more specific information in subsequent pages. Glossary and Index.

553. Gray, Charlotte. **Bob Geldof: Champion of Africa's Hungry People**. Milwaukee, WI: Gareth Stevens, 1990. 68p. $16.95. ISBN 0-8368-0391-4. (People Who Made a Difference). 3-6

Bob Geldof organized a group of rock singers to record an album and contribute their earnings to the starving children in Ethiopia. Then he arranged a series of concerts called Live Aid as a way to collect more money. During 1985, Geldof collected $92 million for the cause. Organizations, Books, List of New Words, Important Dates, and Index.

554.   Green, Robert. **Alexander the Great**. New York: Franklin Watts, 1996. 63p. $20.95; ISBN 0-531-20230-5. (Ancient Biography First Book). 4-6

Alexander (356-323 B.C.) conquered most of the known world before his death at 33. The text introduces his life and his achievements. Photographs, illustrations, and reproductions enhance the text. Index.

555.   Green, Robert. **Cleopatra**. New York: Franklin Watts, 1996. 63p. $20.95. ISBN 0-531-20231-3. (Ancient Biography First Book). 4-6

This biography of Cleopatra (69-30 B.C.) will serve as an introduction to the woman who conquered two Roman emperors before facing destruction by a third. Photographs, illustrations, and reproductions enhance the text. Index.

556.   Green, Robert. **Herod the Great**. New York: Franklin Watts, 1996. 63p. $20.95. ISBN 0-531-20232-1. (Ancient Biography First Book). 4-6

Herod the Great (73-4 B.C.) made the decision to kill all of the boy babies in Palestine in an attempt to destroy Jesus. However, the complexity of the political situation will take careful reading. Photographs, illustrations, and reproductions enhance the text. Index.

557.   Green, Robert. **Julius Caesar**. New York: Franklin Watts, 1996. 63p. $20.95. ISBN 0-531-20241-0. (Ancient Biography First Book). 4-6

Julius Caesar (100-44 B.C.) was a major figure in the Roman world. The text introduces Caesar and describes some of his contributions to his people. Photographs, illustrations, and reproductions enhance the text. Index.

558.   Green, Robert. **Tutankhamun**. New York: Franklin Watts, 1996. 64p. $20.95; $5.95pa. ISBN 0-531-20233-X; 0-531-15802-0pa. (First Books—Ancient Biographies). 5-7

The text looks at Howard Carter's exciting discovery of King Tut's tomb in 1922 and gives a biography of this young pharaoh (c. 1358 B.C.) culled from information about artifacts found in the tomb. It also includes a list of Internet sources with other information on King Tutankhamun. Chronology and Index.

559.   Greenberg, Keith E. **An Armenian Family**. Minneapolis, MN: Lerner, 1997. 56p. $16.95. ISBN 0-8225-3409-6. (Journey Between Two Worlds). 3-6

The text includes the history of the Armenians as a background for understanding the reasons that Armenian families have become refugees. Photographs and personal experiences explain the Armenian social, political, and religious traditions and how the people have had to adapt to a new culture in exile. Further Reading.

560.   Greenberg, Keith Elliot. **A Haitian Family**. Minneapolis, MN: Lerner, 1997. 56p. $16.95. ISBN 0-8225-3410-X. (Journey Between Two Worlds). 3-6

The history of the Haitians is a background for understanding the reasons that Haitian families have had to leave their country in recent years. Photographs and personal experiences explain the Haitian social, political, and religious traditions and how difficult keeping them in a new country can be. Further Reading.

561.   Greene, Carol. **Albert Schweitzer: Friend of All Life**. Chicago: Childrens Press, 1993. 45p. $4.95pa. ISBN 0-516-04258-9pa. (Rookie Biography). 2-3

Albert Schweitzer (1875-1965) was a humanitarian who became a physician and pursued medical missionary work in the jungles of Africa. He was also an accomplished musician. Most importantly, he realized the spiritual value of life and tried to infuse this knowledge into everything he did. Index.

562.   Greene, Carol. **Marco Polo: Voyager to the Orient**. Chicago: Childrens Press, 1987. 112p. $19.30. ISBN 0-516-03229-1. (People of Distinction). 4-6

Marco Polo (1254-1324) was fifteen before he first saw his father, who had been traveling in the East. The text places Polo within the history of his times and describes his trip to the court of the Mongol ruler, Kublai Khan; Greene bases her information on the book Polo wrote while in prison, after he returned from the East and lost political favor in Genoa. Chronology and Index.

563.   Greene, Carol. **Marie Curie: Pioneer Physicist**. Chicago: Childrens Press, 1984. 112p. $19.30. ISBN 0-516-03203-8. (People of Distinction). 4 up

Marie Curie (1867-1934) grew up in Poland and wanted to go to Paris to continue her studies, because women could not pursue higher education in Poland. She worked so that her sister could go and then she followed. In Paris, she met her husband when she used his laboratory. After his death, she experienced difficulties but continued to work. Her discoveries about radium allowed radiology to become important as a method of discovering shrapnel in soldiers during World War I. What she did not know was that radiology could cause cancer, and she suffered the consequences. Time Line and Index.

564. Greene, Carol. **Robert Louis Stevenson: Author of** *A Child's Garden of Verses*. Chicago: Childrens Press, 1994. 47p. $17.70; $4.95pa. ISBN 0-516-04265-3; 0-516-44265-1pa. (Rookie Biography). 2-3

Robert Louis Stevenson (1850-1894) wrote adventure books and poetry. He was sickly as a child, but later went to the University of Edinburgh, Scotland, in the city where he grew up. After he married, he traveled to find a place where he would feel better. He and his stepson created *Treasure Island* and its hero, Long John Silver. Its publication in 1883 earned money for Stevenson, who wanted only to be a writer. After he wrote more, someone financed a journey to Samoa for him and his family on the condition that he write letters about the trip. He got better in the South Seas, but died in Samoa while still relatively young. Important Dates and Index.

565. Greene, Carol. **Rudyard Kipling: Author of the** *Jungle Books*. Chicago: Childrens Press, 1994. 47p. $17.70; $4.95pa. ISBN 0-516-04266-1; 0-516-44266-Xpa. (Rookie Biography). 2-3

Rudyard Kipling (1865-1936) grew up in Bombay, India, son of British parents. When he was five, his parents took him back to England for school, and he and his sister were mistreated by their caregivers. Kipling survived this five-year ordeal by reading as much as possible, although he suffered from bad eyesight. He returned to India at age seventeen to work for a newspaper. When his first book of poems was published, he became famous throughout India. He married an American and kept writing. They lived in Vermont, England, and wintered in South Africa. When Kipling's daughter died, he became very distressed; when his son was killed in World War I, he became bitter. For his writing, he received the 1907 Nobel Prize for Literature. Important Dates and Index.

566. Greene, Carol. **Símon Bolívar: South American Liberator**. Chicago: Childrens Press, 1989. 115p. $19.30. ISBN 0-516-03267-4. (People of Distinction). 4-6

Born in Caracas, Venezuela, Símon Bolívar (1783-1830) was not particularly strong as a child, but he later led others to revolt against their oppressors. Before he did, he went to Spain to study and develop his revolutionary ideas. When he returned to Venezuela, he helped to liberate Bolivia, Colombia, Ecuador, Peru, and Venezuela from the domination of Spain. Time Line and Index.

567. Greene, Carol. **Wolfgang Amadeus Mozart: Musician**. Chicago: Childrens Press, 1987. 126p. $19.30. ISBN 0-516-03261-5. (People of Distinction). 4-6

As a young child, Wolfgang Amadeus Mozart (1756-1791) seemed to know everything that his father, a musician, could teach him. At seven, he could compose as he played, without writing down the notes. He went on tour in Europe, first with his father and later, at age twenty-one, without his father. He incurred many debts, however, and spent much of his life writing music on commission so that he could pay his bills. He is one of the greatest musicians who ever lived. Time Line and Index.

568. Greene, Jacqueline D. **Marie: Mystery at the Paris Ballet, Paris, 1775**. Lyn Durham, illustrator. New York: Simon & Schuster, Aladdin, 1997. 71p. $5.99pa. ISBN 0-689-80989-1pa. (Girlhood Journeys). 3-5

Marie desires to be a ballerina in eighteenth-century Paris, but she faces dismissal from the Paris Opera after an accusation that she has ruined someone's wig and stolen her shoe.

569. Greene, Jacqueline Dembar. **One Foot Ashore**. New York: Walker, 1994. 196p. $16.95. ISBN 0-8027-8281-7. 5-8

When she is ten in 1648, during the Portuguese Inquisition, Maria Ben Lazar and her sister Isobel (age six) are taken from their Jewish parents to Brazil, where they are made to work as slaves and learn the Catholic religion. Maria escapes in 1654 and stows away on a ship to Amsterdam, in search of her parents and her sister from whom she has been separated. In Amsterdam, the Dutch painter, Rembrandt, who lives in the Jewish quarter, keeps her in his house until she has the unexpected happiness of being reunited with her parents and later finding that her sister is in New Amsterdam. Isobel's story appears in *Out of Many Waters* (Walker, 1988).

570. Greene, Jacqueline, Dembar. **Out of Many Waters**. New York: Walker, 1988. 200p. $16.95; $8.95pa. ISBN 0-8027-6811-3; 0-8027-7401-6pa. 5-8

After being kidnapped by Portuguese Catholics during the Portuguese Inquisition in 1548, Isobel (age twelve) and Maria (age sixteen) try to escape from Brazil during 1654 by stowing away on different ships. Isobel reaches New Amsterdam rather than Amsterdam, as she had hoped and where she thinks her parents and Maria might be. After enduring storms and pirates, she becomes one of the twenty-three immigrants to be New Amsterdam's first Jewish refugees. *One Foot Ashore* (Walker, 1994) tells Maria's story. *Sydney Taylor Honor Book* and *New York Public Library Book for the Teen Age*.

571. Greene, Laura Offenhartz. **Child Labor: Then and Now**. New York: Franklin Watts, 1992. 144p. $20.60. ISBN 0-531-13008-8. (Impact). 5-10

Ever since the British, with their chimney sweeps in the 1700s, and the Industrial Revolution, with children working in factories, child labor has been a serious problem. In the early twentieth century, Lewis Hine photographed children, especially immigrants, working in the terrible conditions of mines, mills, factories, sweat-shops, and farms. A change in the laws has helped the United States, but child labor still exists in countries from which America gets many goods. Engravings enhance the text. Selected Bibliography and Index.

572. Greenfeld, Howard. **The Hidden Children**. New York: Ticknor & Fields, 1993. 118p. $15.95. ISBN 0-395-66074-2. 4 up

Many children in the Holocaust lived with strangers who risked their lives to protect the children. All Jewish children learned to lie and conceal their true identities. They learned when they could laugh or cry and when they must be silent. Among the places they hid were attics, basements, haylofts, underground passages, orphanages, and convents. All lost their childhood years. For Further Reading and Index.

573. Gregory, Tony. **The Dark Ages**. New York: Facts on File, 1993. 78p. $17.95. ISBN 0-8160-2787-0. (Il-lustrated History of the World). 4-7

When Roman dominance ended, new cultures and tribes, such as the Anglo-Saxons, Celts, and Vikings, ap-peared. Charlemagne gained power in France. New empires and cultures rose to power with the Byzantines and Islam. Part of the text discusses the eastern world of the Silk Road, the Americas, the Mayan culture, and the Pa-cific. Beautiful illustrations highlight the text. Glossary, Further Reading, and Index.

574. Griese, Arnold A. **At the Mouth of the Luckiest River**. Glo Coalson, illustrator. 1978. Honesdale, PA: Boyds Mills Press, 1996. 128p. $7.95pa. ISBN 1-56397-563-7pa. 2-5

Tatlek has a crippled foot, and the people in his early-nineteenth-century Athabaskan tribe wonder what he can ever become. The medicine man fears that Tatlek might take away his job, because Tatlek's *yega* (spirit) may be a good rather than bad thing. The medicine man tries to control his tribe with lies, so Tatlek has to catch him lying and prove to the people that the Eskimos are friends, rather than enemies as the medicine man would have them believe.

575. Griese, Arnold A. **The Wind Is Not a River**. Glo Coalson, illustrator. 1978. Honesdale, PA: Boyds Mills Press, 1996. 128p. $7.95pa. ISBN 1-56397-564-5pa. 2-5

On the island of Attu in 1942, as they are going to church, Sasan and her younger brother, Sidak, see Japa-nese soldiers arrive to take over their island. They escape from their village and the invaders into the hills, where they must forage for food as their Aleut ancestors once did. When they find a wounded Japanese soldier on the beach, they have to decide if they will help him or leave him to die. They decide that they must do what they can for him, but when Japanese soldiers seem to be trying to find him, they have to make further decisions. *Notable Children's Trade Book in the Field of Social Studies.*

576. Grosjean, Didier, and Claudine Roland. **Rousseau: Still Voyages**. Francine De Boeck, illustrator; John Good-man, translator. New York: Chelsea House, 1995. 60p. $14.95. ISBN 0-7910-2816-X. (Art for Children). 3-7

An eleven-year-old boy becomes interested in pictures, supposedly painted by a customs officer, that show jungles and wild animals. He begins reading a boring book and finds out that Henri Rousseau (1844-1910), called "Le Douanier," was a "Sunday" painter who had a full-time job during the week. The boy goes with his parents to Paris to investigate some of the information he discovered in the book, and their explorations reveal many interesting facts about Rousseau, his life, and the influences on his paintings. Reproductions, Glossary, and Chronology.

577. Guiberson, Brenda Z., author/illustrator. **Lighthouses: Watchers at Sea**. New York: Henry Holt, Red-feather, 1995. 70p. $15.95. ISBN 0-8050-3170-7. 3-6

In 280 B.C., the Egyptian lighthouse known as the Pharos helped guard the Mediterranean. Since then, light-houses have sometimes been the only beacon to guide ships lost at sea. Lighthouse keepers have risked their lives to keep lights burning before electricity was discovered, and even afterward, when high winds have destroyed lines. The text relates tales of shipwrecks and near-shipwrecks stopped by the lighthouse signal as well as the lonely life of the lighthouse keeper. It includes technical information such as the design of the lighthouses, the lenses, and the modern methods that replace lighthouses. Other elements give a sense of the role that lighthouses have played in history.

578. Guittard, Charles. **The Romans: Life in the Empire**. Mary Kae LaRose, translator; Annie-Calude Martin, illustrator. Brookfield, CT: Millbrook Press, 1992. 64p. $16.40; $7.95pa. ISBN 1-56294-200-X; 0-7613-0097-Xpa. (Peoples of the Past). 5-8

The Romans constructed buildings, roads, and bridges so that they would endure; because of this, archaeolo-gists and historians have been able to trace and reveal Roman culture. The text looks at the formation of the Ro-man Empire, Roman cities, the provinces, a child's life, dress, food and drink, entertainment, arts and sciences, and the Roman gods. Dates to Remember, Map, Find Out More, Glossary, and Index.

579.   Gurko, Miriam. **Theodor Herzl: The Road to Israel**. Erika Weihs, illustrator. Philadelphia, PA: Jewish Publication Society, 1988. 89p. $14.95. ISBN 0-8276-0312-6. 3-7

When he was growing up in Vienna, Theodor Herzl (1860-1904) was not particularly interested in Jewish matters, as his family was rather erratic in its practice of the religion. But he became increasingly aware of the anti-Semitic atmosphere of late-nineteenth-century Europe. The trial of Alfred Dreyfus, the Jewish army officer unjustly accused of treason in France, disturbed him. He realized that Jews needed their own homeland. His ceaseless efforts led to the foundation of the World Zionist Organization, but he sometimes neglected his own family because of his social concerns. He was unable to see a Jewish state established during his lifetime, but without his work, Israel might never have come into being. Important Dates and Index.

580.   Guzzetti, Paula. **A Family Called Brontë**. New York: Dillon Press, 1994. 128p. $13.95. ISBN 0-87518-592-4. (People in Focus). 6-9

The text looks at the lives of the Brontës—Charlotte, Emily, Anne, and Branwell—as they grew up in rural nineteenth-century England. They made tiny hand-stitched books, about the size of postage stamps, from scraps of paper and wrote in them. They spent early years caring for children, but they failed as governesses and teachers and began writing instead. In 1847, the three sisters published *Jane Eyre, Wuthering Heights*, and *Agnes Grey* under male pen names (Currer Bell, Ellis Bell, and Acton Bell) so that the novels would be more readily received in literary circles. Their lives were shadowed by tuberculosis and the failed career of their brother, who died at age thirty-one. Chronology, Bibliography, and Index.

H

581.   Haas, Gerda. **Tracking the Holocaust**. Minneapolis, MN: Runestone Press, 1995. 176p. $22.95. ISBN 0-8225-3257-7. 5 up

When Gerda Haas's American-born children did not understand why some things that happened were important to her, Haas decided that she must recount her own youth, so that her children would know what she had experienced by the age of twenty-three. She traces the stories of eight persons caught in the Holocaust, six of whom survived. The text gives a history from the beginning of Nazi rule in Germany in the 1930s. Haas covers Germany, Poland, Denmark, Norway, Holland, Belgium, Luxembourg, France, Italy, Hungary, and the Balkan countries. In most of these countries, she places one of the story subjects and describes that person's experiences. Sentencing, Sources, Documentary Material, Map Citation, The Testimonies of Survivors and Victims, and Index.

582.   Halliburton, Warren. **The West Indian-American Experience**. Brookfield, CT: Millbrook Press, 1994. 64p. $16.40. ISBN 1-56294-340-5. (Coming to America). 4-8

European settlers eradicated the Arawaks, original inhabitants of the Caribbean, but traces of the culture remain. In the centuries after Columbus, many of the inhabitants died from diseases or became slaves to their conquerors. Between 1640 and 1713 more than seven slave revolts occurred in the British islands. In 1760, Tacky's Rebellion broke out in Jamaica, and in 1831 another revolt led to the abolishment of slavers in 1833. More recent inhabitants of the islands have immigrated to the United States, looking for economic opportunities. They found them, along with racial discrimination, unlike any they had experienced in the West Indies. Between 1952 and the 1960s, few islanders were admitted to the country, but after that the laws changed. More About West Indian Americans and Index.

583.   Halliburton, Warren J., and Kathilyn Solomon Probosz. **Africa's Struggle for Independence**. New York: Crestwood House, 1992. 48p. $13.95. ISBN 0-89686-679-3. (Africa Today). 5-10

Africa as a continent has struggled with the slave trade and colonialism. The text examines the history of the independence movement in Africa from the European colonization of the continent to the present, with photographs to complement the text. Index.

584.   Hancock, Lyn. **Nunavut**. Minneapolis, MN: Lerner, 1995. 76p. $14.21. ISBN 0-8225-2758-8. 3-6

Although not technically a history book, more than half the text deals with the history of this Canadian province. Charts, maps, photographs, and prints illustrate the uniqueness of this area, whose first inhabitants were the distant ancestors of the Inuit who made their way to North America via the Bering Strait from Asia into Alaska around 10,000 years ago. Among the famous people associated with Nunavut and briefly described here are Roald Amundsen, an explorer (1872-1928), and James Houston, a writer (b. 1921). Fast Facts, Glossary, Pronunciation Guide, and Index.

585.   Handler, Andrew, and Susan V. Meschel. **Young People Speak: Surviving the Holocaust in Hungary**. New York: Franklin Watts, 1993. 160p. $13.40. ISBN 0-531-11044-3. 6-9

Eleven Jews who survived their childhoods in Hungary during World War II tell their stories. None seemed to realize that death was a possibility, even though they lost homes, friends, and family members. One commented that injecting spinach under Hitler's skin after the war would be a good way to punish him. Another tells of a grandmother who stole his birthday candy and blamed a servant; the servant subsequently reported the grandmother to the Nazis. Photographs, Bibliography, and Index.

586.   Hanmer, Trudy J. **Leningrad**. New York: New Discovery, 1992. 96p. $14.95. ISBN 0-02-742615-7. (Cities at War). 6-9

The Russian city of Leningrad refused to submit to the German invasion in World War II. The Germans decided to surround the city in the winter of 1941 and keep any supplies from reaching the people, in hopes of starving and freezing them into submission. For nearly three years (900 days), no fuel or food reached the people, while Nazi bombers patrolled the skies. Two million people died during the siege. Photographs, Notes, Further Reading, and Index.

587.   Hansen, Joyce. **The Captive**. New York: Scholastic, 1994. 195p. $13.95; $3.50pa. ISBN 0-590-41625-1; 0-590-41624-3pa. 5-8

Slavers capture Kofi, 12, when a family servant betrays him, and take him from his African home to America in 1788. There he works for a New England family of somber Puritans. Then he meets Paul Cuffe, an African American shipbuilder who wants to take Africans back to their homeland. He becomes a first mate on Cuffe's ship, which gives him a chance to go home. *Coretta Scott King Honor* and *Notable Children's Trade Books in the Field of Social Studies*.

588. Harbor, Bernard. **Conflict in Eastern Europe**. New York: New Discovery, 1993. 48p. $13.95. ISBN 0-02-742626-2. (Conflicts). 6-9

The text looks at the revolutions that occurred in Eastern Europe in 1989, after which Communism fell. Included is information about the fall of the Berlin Wall; the role of Gorbachev; the death of Romania's Ceauescu; and the changes in Czechoslovakia, Hungary, Poland, and Albania. Economics and privatization, ethnic conflicts, the differences between East and West, and religion all come into the discussion. Glossary, Further Information, and Index.

589. Hargrove, Jim. **Diego Rivera: Mexican Muralist**. Chicago: Childrens Press, 1990. 127p. $11.95. ISBN 0-5160-3268-2. (People of Distinction). 4-6

Diego Rivera (1886-1957) decided that he needed to bring art to the masses, and he did so by painting murals on exterior walls for all to see. He became a Communist because he hated the extreme division between rich and poor, but the Communists made him leave their party. Other flamboyant aspects of his life included four wives and innumerable lovers. Chronology and Index.

590. Hargrove, Jim. **Pablo Casals: Cellist of Conscience**. Chicago: Childrens Press, 1991. 127p. $19.30; $5.95pa. ISBN 0-516-03272-0; 0-516-43272-9pa. (People of Distinction). 6-9

Pablo Casals (1876-1973) became an extraordinary cellist during his life, playing around the world. The text looks at his childhood, after his birth in Catalonia; his struggle to take music lessons; his subsequent fame; the difficulties of war in Spain and World War II, which shattered the dreams of so many; and his exile from Spain during the rise of Franco. Quotes from Casals help to validate the information. Photographs, Notes, and Index.

591. Hargrove, Jim. **René-Robert Cavelier Sieur de La Salle**. Chicago: Childrens Press, 1990. 128p. $17.95. ISBN 0-516-03054-X. (World's Great Explorers). 4-8

La Salle (1643-1687) traveled along the Illinois River to the mouth of the Mississippi River during winter, when he had to carry his canoes along the frozen water rather than ride in them. He planned to follow all 4,300 miles of the river, building forts for the French soldiers. He acquired for France and Louis XIV all of the land that France later sold to Thomas Jefferson in the Louisiana Purchase. Timeline, Glossary, Bibliography, and Index.

592. Harnett, Cynthia, author/illustrator. **The Cargo of the Madalena**. 1959. Minneapolis, MN: Lerner, 1984. 236p. $13.50. ISBN 0-8225-0890-7. 5 up

In 1482, William Caxton brings the printing press to England and hires Bendy to help him produce a manuscript of King Arthur's tales. Because scribes will lose their jobs to this machine, which prints a hundred copies to their one, they plot to keep away from Caxton the one thing he needs. Bendy discovers that his brothers, both scriveners, have hidden Caxton's paper, which disappeared from the cargo of the *Madalena*. Oddly, Bendy's father, also a scrivener, looks forward to the progress signaled by the printing press and disapproves of his sons' deceit because it also supports the Red Rose Henry Tudor's plan to dethrone Edward IV. *Carnegie Commendation.*

593. Harnett, Cynthia, author/illustrator. **The Great House**. 1949. Minneapolis, MN: Lerner, 1984. 180p. $9.95. ISBN 0-8225-0893-1. 5 up

Geoffrey's father, a friend of Sir Christopher Wren in London, moves Geoffrey and his sister Barbara to the country in 1690. Although Elizabeth is happy that the country client has a daughter, no one will let them play together, though they meet by accident. Geoffrey thinks that the house should be repositioned to overlook the river, and the adults eventually realize that he has the best idea. The client decides to send Geoffrey to Oxford.

594. Harnett, Cynthia, author/illustrator. **The Merchant's Mark**. 1951. Minneapolis, MN: Lerner, 1984. 192p. $9.95. ISBN 0-8225-0891-5. 5 up

Nicholas, age fifteen, trains to take over the Fetterlock wool business from his father. In 1493, their wool has a high reputation with foreign buyers. At the same time, he has to plan for his arranged marriage to Cecily, a girl whom he has never met. Fortunately, when they meet, they become friends, and they help to stop the distribution of mysterious inferior wool with a counterfeit Fetterlock mark on it. *Carnegie Medal.*

595. Harnett, Cynthia, author/illustrator. **The Sign of the Green Falcon**. 1953. Minneapolis, MN: Lerner, 1984. 219p. $9.95. ISBN 0-8225-0888-5. 5 up

In 1415, Dickon finds out that he will be apprenticed to his godfather, Richard Whittington, a London mercer. He knows that it is a great honor, but he wanted to be a grocer like his father and brother. He and his other brother find themselves involved with the Lollards in a plot against Henry V when other mercer apprentices trap them. Because they are honest and Adam tries to help others at Agincourt, the two escape charges.

596. Harnett, Cynthia, author/illustrator. **Stars of Fortune**. 1956. Minneapolis, MN: Lerner, 1984. 288p. $9.95. ISBN 0-8225-0892-3. 5 up

Four of the Washington children in Sulgrave Manor become involved in a plot to help the young Princess Elizabeth flee from England to Italy. She lives nearby in Woodstock, held prisoner by her elder sister, Mary Tudor. A subplot reveals how the priests survived while Henry VIII tried to annihilate all of the Catholics and their property. Fortunately, Elizabeth did not escape; if she had, she probably would have lost her chance at the throne.

597. Harnett, Cynthia. **The Writing on the Hearth**. Gareth Floyd, illustrator. 1971. Minneapolis, MN: Lerner, 1984. 300p. $13.50. ISBN 0-8225-0889-3. 5 up

Stephen and his sister, Lys, are orphans who live with their stepfather in rural England during the fifteenth century. Because Stephen's father died in service to the earl, Stephen will be allowed to learn to read and write. If he does well, he might even be sent to Oxford for study. One day during a storm, Stephen takes shelter with Meg, a woman some people accuse of being a witch. Meg has a visitor, and when Stephen listens to the conversation, he begins to think the rumors are true. After encountering a series of problems, including the plague in London, Henry VI's accusations, and William Caxton's concerns, Stephen realizes that he has made a mistake. His honesty gains him the position at Oxford that he so badly wants.

598. Harris, Christie. **Raven's Cry**. Bill Reid, illustrator. 1966. Seattle, WA: University of Washington Press, 1992. 193p. $14.95pa. ISBN 0-295-97221-1pa. 5-10

When the white men find the Haida people in 1775, they decimate the sea otter which is the Haida's livelihood. In addition to greed, the invading hunters bring smallpox, consumption, death, and vile treatment. By 1884, only 600 of the tribe remained, having suffered horribly from the outsiders who destroyed their culture and defiled their religion.

599. Harris, Geraldine. **Ancient Egypt**. New York: Facts on File, 1990. 96p. $17.95. ISBN 0-8160-1971-1. (Cultural Atlas for Young People). 6-9

This oversize book groups its topics into two segments, one on Egypt before the pharaohs and one going down the Nile. Illustrations augment the history with cartouches of pharaoh's names, human forms of Egyptian deities, maps, and photographs. The text concentrates on archaeological information gleaned from ancient Egyptian sites in Karnak and Abu Simbel. It discusses mummy preparation, the construction of the pyramids, and many other topics that reveal the lives of the ancient Egyptians. Chronology, Glossary, Gazetteer, and Index.

600. Harris, Jacqueline L. **Science in Ancient Rome**. New York: Franklin Watts, 1988. 72p. $16.10. ISBN 0-531-10595-4. (First Book). 5-8

An introduction to ancient Rome and its science precedes chapters on different developments from this culture. Subjects include Roman builders of arches, concrete, and homes; Roman miners of brass and gold; Roman physicians; public health through sewers and aqueducts; the Roman calendar; and contemporary debt to the culture for its discoveries. Photographs supplement the text. Glossary, Further Reading, and Index.

601. Harris, Nathaniel. **Everyday Life in Ancient Egypt**. Keith Maddison, illustrator. New York: Franklin Watts, 1995. 32p. $12.25. ISBN 0-531-14309-0. (Clues to the Past). 3-6

Two-page spreads cover such topics as food, clothing, housing, education, religion, and architecture. Illustrations of artifacts such as pottery and jewelry complement and clarify the text as it presents the social life and customs of ancient Egyptians. Index.

602. Harris, Nathaniel. **Mummies: A Very Peculiar History**. David Salariya, illustrator. New York: Franklin Watts, 1995. 48p. $21.40; $5.95pa. ISBN 0-531-14354-6; 0-531-15271-5pa. (Very Peculiar History). 4-8

Drawings and text tell the story of mummies, from Egyptian times to the present, in two-page spreads. Using the definition of *mummy* as a corpse that has been preserved to keep it from decaying, the text notes that preservation may be either planned or a fluke of nature. The mummies here include Egyptians, English sailors, Danes, Inuits, Incas, Scythians, Sicilians, a Chinese court lady, and an Alpine traveler. Oliver Cromwell, Lord Nelson, Jeremy Bentham, Eva Perón, and Lenin are some of the famous figures whose bodies or body parts have been kept for posterity. Glossary and Index.

603. Hart, George. **Ancient Egypt**. New York: Knopf, 1990. 64p. $19. ISBN 0-679-90742-X. (Eyewitness Books). 4-7

Although very "busy," with from two to ten carefully labeled photographs on each page and some general text, Hart's book covers many topics. The contents include Egypt before the pharaohs, practices in life and afterlife, gods and goddesses, religion, writing, war, the Nile, various trades, daily habits, leisure activities, and a brief look at Egypt after the pharaohs. Index.

604.   Hart, Tony. **Toulouse-Lautrec**. Susan Hellard, illustrator. Hauppauge, NY: Barron's, 1994. Unpaged. $5.95pa. ISBN 0-8120-1825-7pa. (Famous Children). 3-5

By focusing on the childhood of the noted artist Toulouse-Lautrec (1864-1901), the text tries to give insight as to why he became an artist and how he chose his subject matter.

605.   Härtling, Peter. **Crutches**. New York: Lothrop, Lee & Shepard, 1988. 163p. $12. ISBN 0-688-07991-1. 5-8

Thomas, age twelve, becomes separated from his mother on a transport from Koln, Germany, to Vienna, Austria. After he discovers that his aunt is gone and her house has been bombed, he attaches himself to a one-legged man on crutches, who stays with him until they locate his mother. The man tries to avoid relationships, but he begins to care about Thomas and does not want to tell him when the Red Cross locates Thomas's mother. The man's integrity, his growing love for Thomas, and his concern for Thomas's well-being, however, force him to take Thomas back to Germany. *Mildred L. Batchelder Award* and *American Library Association Notable Books for Children.*

606.   Haslam, Andrew, and Alexandra Parsons. **Ancient Egypt**. New York: Thomson Learning, 1995. 64p. $18.95. ISBN 1-56847-140-8. (Make It Work!). 3-7

The text presents information on ancient Egypt interspersed with suggestions about creating various projects, from clothing to dioramas to food. Topics include clothes, landscape, beliefs, artwork, boats, and pyramids. Glossary and Index.

607.   Haugaard, Erik. **The Boy and the Samurai**. Boston: Houghton Mifflin, 1991. 221p. $14.95. ISBN 0-395-56398-4. 6-9

The orphan Saru, or "monkey," is both homeless and friendless, surviving by begging and living near a temple shrine. Saru becomes friends with a kind samurai and helps him rescue his wife from the warlord's castle in sixteenth-century Japan. His plan saves the three of them plus a priest who has acted as his mentor. Saru realizes that he must always tell the truth, because it will keep him free. *Parents' Choice.*

608.   Haugaard, Erik. **A Boy's Will**. 1983. Boston: Houghton Mifflin, 1990. $5.95pa. ISBN 0-395-54962-0pa. 4-7

Patrick overhears a British navy captain say that he plans to capture John Paul Jones off the southern coast of Ireland in 1779. From the island of Skellig Michael, a place that St. Patrick made famous, Patrick sails to meet Jones and warn him of the plot.

609.   Haugaard, Erik. **Chase Me, Catch Nobody**. Boston: Houghton Mifflin, 1980. 209p. $7.95. ISBN 0-395-29208-5. 6-9

Erik, age fourteen, goes with a school group from Denmark to Germany during his spring vacation in 1937. When a man asks Erik to take a package off the ferry for him, Erik agrees, but realizes that he must also deliver the package when the Gestapo meet the man and escort him from the ferry. After Erik delivers the passports in the package, he becomes involved in helping a Jewish girl get to Denmark after hiding in an attic for a year. Before any of the plot resolves, Erik and his one friend have to escape on a leaky little boat.

610.   Haugaard, Erik. **A Messenger for Parliament**. Boston: Houghton Mifflin, 1976. 218p. $6.95. ISBN 0-395-24392-0. 6-9

Oliver, named for Oliver Cromwell when he was only a plowman in 1630, spends time with his father as a camp follower of the Parliamentary Army after his mother dies in 1641. Oliver meets a variety of people and becomes a messenger for Cromwell himself during the English civil war. Oliver tells this story as an old man who has lived in America for many years.

611.   Haugaard, Erik Christian. **The Revenge of the Forty-Seven Samurai**. Boston: Houghton Mifflin, 1995. 240p. $14.95. ISBN 0-395-70809-5. 6-9

Jiro, a lowly servant in a deceased samurai's household during the fourteenth year of Genroku (1701) under the shogun Tokugawa Tsunayoshi, observes the plans for revenge against Lord Kira, the man whose demands on Lord Asano caused him to commit ritual suicide. Jiro assists in preparing for the final fight against Lord Kira, although he wonders why the samurai retainers want to sacrifice themselves. Because he is not a samurai, he can question their values and be glad that he does not have to make a life-and-death decision on such a seemingly insignificant point. *American Library Association Notable Books for Children* and *American Library Association Notable Books for Young Adults.*

612.   Hautzig, Esther. **Riches**. Donna Diamond, illustrator. New York: HarperCollins, 1992. 44p. $14. ISBN 0-06-022260-3. 4-8

When a couple from a small European town retire from their hard work, in the nineteenth century, the husband asks a rabbi what to do in his leisure time. The rabbi suggests that he drive a cart around the countryside for three months while his wife stays at home studying as she wants. After he does, he realizes that many things in life are more important than material objects. *Notable Children's Trade Books in the Field of Social Studies* and *Jewish Book Award Finalist.*

613. Haywood, John. **The Romans**. New York: Oxford University Press, 1996. 46p. $9.95. ISBN 0-19-521240-1. (Spotlights). 4-6

The text looks at the Romans in double-page spreads. The topics include the cultural and social life, government, religion, and warfare. Architecture and artifacts related to the topics in museums or historical sites enhance the material. The overview, however, has little depth.

614. Hazell, Rebecca, author/illustrator. **Heroes: Great Men Through the Ages**. New York: Abbeville, 1997. 80p. $19.95. ISBN 0-7892-0289-1. 5-8

In this collective biography, Hazell chooses twelve men whose contributions to society made changes in politics, art, or daily life. Among the men she includes are Mohandas Gandhi (1869-1948), Indian leader; Mansa Kankan Musa, a Muslim leader in West Africa during the 1300s; Leonardo da Vinci (1452-1519), Renaissance artist; William Shakespeare (1564-1616), Elizabethan dramatist; and Jorge Luis Borges (1899-1986), Argentinian author. Further Reading.

615. Hazell, Rebecca, author/illustrator. **Heroines: Great Women Through the Ages**. New York: Abbeville, 1996. 79p. $19.95. ISBN 0-7892-0289-1. 5-8

The text covers twelve women in three or four pages each from ancient Greece to contemporary times. Additional to the information about each life is background on the culture and the history of the times in which she lived. Among those included are Lady Murasaki Shikibu (973?-1025?), Sacagawea (1787?-1812), Agnodice of ancient Greece (3rd Century B.C.), Anna Akhmatova (1888-1966), Madame Sun Yat-Sen (1893-1931), Frida Kahlo (1907-1954), Eleanor of Aquitaine (1122-1202), Joan of Arc (1412?-1431), Queen Elizabeth I (1533-1603), Harriet Tubman (1820?-1913), Marie Curie (1867-1934), and Amelia Earhart ((1897-1937). Further Reading.

616. Head, Judith. **Culebra Cut**. Minneapolis, MN: Carolrhoda, 1995. 153p. $14.96. ISBN 0-87614-878-X. (Adventures in Time). 4-7

William, age eleven, lives in Panama with his father, a physician, during 1911, when workers are constructing the Panama Canal. He learns as much as possible about the canal and loves living close to it, so that he can visit the most difficult portion of the project, Culebra Cut. He gets a friend, Victoria, however, who gives him a different perspective on the canal. He learns about the jungle and a Jamaican healer, and sees the work of a racist bully, Bud. More About the Panama Canal.

617. Hendry, Frances Mary. **Quest for a Maid**. New York: Farrar, Straus & Giroux, 1992. 273p. $14.95; $4.95pa. ISBN 0-374-36162-2; 0-374-46155-4pa. 5 up

Meg, age nine, thinks that her sister killed King Alexander of Scotland with witchcraft to help a woman who wanted to claim the throne for her son. As a helper in the home of Sir Patrick Spens in the thirteenth century, Meg gets to accompany Sir Spens to Norway to return with Margaret, the rightful heir to the throne. Meg discovers that her sister should not be accused of this crime because she did not commit it. *Bulletin Blue Ribbon Book* and *American Library Association Notable Books for Children.*

618. Heneghan, James. **Wish Me Luck**. New York: Farrar, Straus & Giroux, 1997. 196p. $16. ISBN 0-374-38453-3. 5-8

Jamie Monaghan wonders about his new classmate, Tom Bleeker, instead of being concerned for the German bombs that might fall on Liverpool. When the bombing begins, however, he has to leave home for Canada on the *City of Benares*. Bleeker and his sister are also on the ship, and when torpedoes cause it to begin sinking in the mid-Atlantic, Bleeker saves both the wounded Jamie and his sister. Bleeker is swept away in the water after saving them, and Jamie thinks he is dead although he knows that Bleeker is resilient. Bleeker does survive, and they become friends involved in several adventures.

619. Hersom, Kathleen. **The Half Child**. New York: Simon & Schuster, 1991. 176p. $13.95. ISBN 0-671-74225-6. 5-9

Lucy, age ten, has a flashback to 1650, when her four-year-old sister disappeared in the moors near Durham, England, after the birth of another child. Sarah seemed to be dim-witted, and the family thought she was a changeling who would return to the fairies one day. Lucy kept searching for her sister, knowing that Sarah understood the hostility toward her. Lucy says that she married the man who found Sarah and placed her in a foster home during the difficult times of the English civil war and Cromwell's cause.

620. Heslewood, Juliet. **Introducing Picasso**. Boston: Little, Brown, 1993. 32p. $15.95. ISBN 0-316-35017-3. 4-6

Pablo Picasso's (1881-1973) career spanned most of the twentieth century. Along with other painters, he started the Cubist movement, and went through definitive periods in his own evolution as an artist. Reproductions of his paintings and sculptures and those of other artists who influenced him highlight the text. Timeline and Index.

621. Hesse, Karen. **Letters from Rifka**. New York: Holt, 1992. 148p. $14.95. ISBN 0-8050-1964-2. New York: Puffin, 1993. 148p. $3.99pa. ISBN 0-14-036391-2pa. 5-9

Rifka, age twelve in 1919, flees Russia with her family to escape the Jewish pogroms. She carries with her a beloved volume of poetry by Alexander Pushkin. In the book, she writes letters to her cousin, Tovah, to tell about her experiences on the journey. Rifka has to endure the humiliation of doctors' examinations, typhus, ringworm treatment in Belgium (during which she loses her hair), and being detained at Ellis Island because of her baldness. Her ability to speak other languages allows her to help a young Russian peasant (her enemy) and an orphaned Polish baby at Ellis Island.

622. Hetfield, Jamie. **The Asante of West Africa**. New York: Rosen, Power Kids Press, 1997. 24p. $13.95. ISBN 0-8239-2329-0. (Celebrating the Peoples and Civilizations of Africa). K-2

This simple introduction to a people from West Africa includes ten one-page chapters telling where and how the Asante live, customs, government, food, and religion.

623. Hetfield, Jamie. **The Yoruba of West Africa**. New York: Rosen, Power Kids Press, 1996. 24p. $13.95. ISBN 0-8239-2332-0. (Celebrating the Peoples and Civilizations of Africa). K-2

This simple introduction to a people from West Africa includes ten one-page chapters telling where and how the Yoruba live, customs, government, food, and religion.

624. Hetfield, Jamie, and Marianne Johnston. **Maasai**. New York: Rosen, Power Kids Press, 1997. 24p. $13.95. ISBN 0-8239-2330-4. (Celebrating the Peoples and Civilizations of Africa). K-2

The Maasai have lived mainly as East African nomads. The text includes ten one-page chapters telling where and how they live, their customs, government, food, and religion.

625. Heuck, Sigrid. **The Hideout**. Rika Lesser, translator. New York: Dutton, 1988. 183p. $5pa. ISBN 0-525-44343-6pa. 4-7

An old woman finds Rebecca, age nine, in a bombed air raid shelter during 1944, but Rebecca does not remember her own identity. The woman registers her with a Missing Persons Bureau and sends her to an orphanage. There she makes friends with a boy hiding in a nearby cornfield, and he tells her fantastic stories. When she hears an enemy air raid, she suddenly remembers her name, and at the end of the war, she is able to reunite with her parents.

626. Hicks, Peter. **The Aztecs**. New York: Thompson Learning, 1993. 32p. $14.95. ISBN 1-56847-058-4. (Look into the Past). 4-6

Hicks presents the Aztecs and their lives through both text and color photographs of archaeological sites as they exist today. Details of politics, wars, travel, and the arts appear in the work, which draws heavily on early Spanish records. Glossary, Important Dates, Books to Read, and Index.

627. Hicks, Peter. **The Romans**. New York: Thompson Learning, 1994. 32p. $14.95. ISBN 1-56847-063-0. (Look into the Past). 4-6

From its founding until its fall, the Roman Empire incorporated much diversity. The text highlights life in town and country, what people looked like, military life, religion, and rituals practiced by the people. The idea that life was expendable contrasts with the enormous engineering contributions the Romans made to civilization through the centuries. Photographs highlight the text. Glossary, Important Dates, Books to Read, and Index.

628. Hill, Anthony. **The Burnt Stick**. Mark Sofilas, illustrator. Boston: Houghton Mifflin, 1995. 54p. $12.95. ISBN 0-395-73974-8. 3-5

When he was five, government authorities took John Jagamarra away from his aborigine mother in Australia, because his father was white. They raised him at a mission school without consideration for his or his mother's loss. Twice she fooled the authorities who came for him by rubbing ashes into his skin, so that he looked dark, but they unexpectedly returned a third time. The boy was never reunited with his mother, as was the practice in Australia through the 1960s.

629. Hill, Susan. **The Glass Angels**. Valerie Littlewood, illustrator. Cambridge, MA: Candlewick, 1992. 93p. $17.95; $9.99pa. ISBN 1-56402-111-4; 1-56402-516-0pa. 3-6

In England after World War II, Tilly and her widowed mother try to survive. A seamstress, Tilly's mother gets a commission to make a wedding gown, but water leaking through the roof ruins the dress while she is ill. Tilly goes for help and solves her mother's problem.

630. Hirsch, Charles. **Taxation: Paying for Government**. Austin, TX: Blackbirch/Steck-Vaughn, 1993. 48p. $15.49. ISBN 0-8114-7356-2. (Good Citizenship). 5-9

After defining what taxes are, the text tells what the government uses taxes for and the kinds of taxes. A history shows that taxes were first mentioned in 3500 B.C. in Sumer (currently Iraq). Egyptians, Greeks, and Romans all paid taxes. Spanish taxes financed Columbus's trip to the New World. However, many have complained about unfair taxes, one of the major reasons that the American Revolution began. A final presentation on the Internal Revenue Service completes the information. Photographs and drawings supplement the text. Further Reading, Glossary, and Index.

631. Ho, Minfong. **The Clay Marble**. New York: Farrar, Straus & Giroux, 1991. 163p. $13.95. ISBN 0-374-31340-7. 6-9

Dara, age twelve, and her family have to leave their Cambodian farm in 1980 after Communists kill her father in the war. Dara's brother, Sarun, becomes militaristic and shoots her friend by mistake. They finally reach a Thai border refugee camp where they find food and shelter; there they also get rice plants to start over at the war's end, to reform their "clay marble."

632. Hoare, Stephen. **The Modern World**. New York: Facts on File, 1993. 78p. $17.95. ISBN 0-8160-2792-7. (Illustrated History of the World). 4-7

A history of the twentieth century must discuss the decline of European colonial empires and give a background for World War I, which in turn led to World War II. The postwar world, with the cold war between East and West, stayed in the forefront until the end of the 1980s. Human rights, religious struggles, and space travel continued to be important to societies. Illustrations highlight the text. Glossary, Further Reading, and Index.

633. Hoestlandt, Jo. **Star of Fear, Star of Hope**. Johanna King, illustrator; Mark Polizzotti, translator. New York: Walker, 1995. Unpaged. $16.85. ISBN 0-8027-8373-2. 2-5

An old woman tells the story of her friend, Lydia, who came to spend the night on her ninth birthday in 1942. Lydia had to wear a star on her sleeve, and when someone in fear, who also wears a star, knocks on the door while Lydia is at the narrator's apartment, Lydia wants to go home. The narrator is angry, but Lydia leaves her a present, and the narrator never sees her again. She does not know what happened to her; she only knows that no one in Lydia's family was at home the next day or ever again. *Mildred Batchelder Honor Award, Sydney Taylor Book Award, IRA Teachers' Choice,* and *American Library Association Notable Books for Children.*

634. Holeman, Linda. **Promise Song**. Plattsburg, NY: Tundra, 1997. 260p. $7.95. ISBN 0-88776-387-1. 6-9

Rosetta and her sister Flora lose everything when their parents die, including their country, when they are sent to Canada in 1900. They arrive in Nova Scotia, and different families adopt them. Rosetta becomes an indentured servant, and her master steals her money, but she eventually forms a bond with his wife, and they both escape his harshness to find Flora.

635. Holland, Gini. **Diego Rivera**. Gary Rees, illustrator. Austin, TX: Raintree/Steck-Vaughn, 1997. 32p. $21.40. ISBN 0-8172-4453-0. (First Biographies). K-3

Diego Rivera (1886-1957) was a Mexican mural painter who refused to compromise his subject matter for anyone. This brief biography gives a balanced view of Rivera and his political beliefs as well as his artistic concerns that people of all social and economic strata should be able to enjoy art. Key Dates.

636. Holland, Gini. **Nelson Mandela**. Mike White, illustrator. Austin, TX: Raintree/Steck-Vaughn, 1997. 32p. $21.40. ISBN 0-8172-4454-9. (First Biographies). K-3

Nelson Mandela (b. 1918) was the son of a Thembu chief who advocated civil rights for his people in South Africa. After obtaining a law degree and serving twenty-seven years in prison when he challenged the government's laws, he emerged and was elected president of South Africa. This biography is a good introduction to the problems of apartheid. Key Dates.

637. Holm, Ann. **North to Freedom**. L. W. Kingsland, translator. 1965. New York: Peter Smith, 1984. 190p. $17.55. ISBN 0-8446-6156-2. San Diego, CA: Harcourt Brace, 1990. 239p. $4.95pa. ISBN 0-15-257553-7pa. 3-7

David, age twelve, escapes from a camp somewhere in the Soviet Union by jumping over a fence during a thirty-second electricity interruption. He travels via Salonika through Italy on his way to Denmark. He has been in the camp most of his life, but a man befriended him and taught him several languages. He can converse, but he does not remember laughter, colors, or oranges. Music amazes him. He eventually reaches Denmark and re-unites with his mother. *Gyldendal Prize for Best Scandinavian Children's Book, American Library Association Notable Books for Children, Gold Medal Winner of Boys' Club of America, Junior Book Award,* and *Lewis Carroll Shelf Award.*

638.   Holman, Felice. **The Wild Children**. New York: Scribners, 1983. 160p. $13.95. ISBN 0-684-17970-9. New York: Puffin, 1985. 160p. $4.99pa. ISBN 0-14-031930-1pa. 6-9

Alex, age twelve, walks over 100 miles to Moscow after the Russian Revolution ends, and he is the only member of his family not arrested. During the 1920s, he becomes one of the homeless *bezprizoni*, a band of children who search for food and shelter. They travel illegally on trains to the south in hopes of finding better provisions. Alex makes a contact that helps them reach Finland on their way to America. *American Library Association Notable Books for Young Adults.*

639.   Hong, Lily Toy, author/illustrator. **The Empress and the Silkworm**. Niles, IL: Albert Whitman, 1995. 32p. $16.95. ISBN 0-8075-2009-8. 1-4

When a silkworm falls into the tea of the Empress Si Ling-Chi, she takes it out and notices a long, shiny thread unwinding from its body. Supposedly this event led her husband, the Yellow Emperor Huang-Ti, to be-gin manufacturing silk fabric. The story includes background on silk science and the silk trade.

640.   Hoobler, Dorothy, and Thomas Hoobler. **African Portraits**. John Gampert, illustrator. Austin, TX: Raintree/Steck-Vaughn, 1993. 96p. $16.98. ISBN 0-8114-6378-8. (Images Across the Ages). 6 up

The text gives short biographical profiles of persons from the possible birthplace of the human race, Af-rica. The sub-Saharan figures are: Piankhy, King of Kush who invaded Egypt (751?-716 B.C.); King Ezana (fourth century A.D.) of ancient Ethiopia; King Lalibela (twelfth century) of Zagwe; King Mansa Musa, Mali Muslim leader (d. 1332); Ahmed Baba, Timbuktu scholar (1556-1627); Euware the Great, mighty warrior (d. 1473); Ann Nzinga, warrior-queen of Angola (1583-1663); Cinque, slave from Sierra Leone (c. 1811-1879); Menelik II, king of Shoa in Ethiopia (1844-1913) and Taitu, his wife (d. 1918); Kwame Nkrumah, who freed Ghana (1909-1972); Wole Soy-inka, writer (b. 1934); Kipchoge Keino, Olympic runner (b. 1940); and Miriam Makeba (b. 1932) and Joseph Shabalala (c. 1945), South African musicians. Glossary, Bibliography, Sources, and Index.

641.   Hoobler, Dorothy, and Thomas Hoobler. **Chinese Portraits**. Victoria Bruck, illustrator. Austin, TX: Raintree/Steck-Vaughn, 1993. 96p. $16.98. ISBN 0-8114-6375-3. (Images Across the Ages). 6 up

The text gives short biographical profiles of prominent persons in Chinese civilization for the past 3,000 years. They are: Confucius, the hidden orchid (551-479 B.C.); Shi Huang Di, the first emperor (259-210 B.C.); the Ban Family, the tigers (640-604? B.C.); Empress Wu, only female son of heaven (A.D. 625-705); Li Bo, vagabond (701-762); Du Fu, candidate (712-770); Ma Yuan, one-corner Ma (twelfth century); Zheng He, ad-miral of the western seas (1371-1433?); Yuan Mei, the poetic gourmet (1716-1796?); Lin Xezu, anti-drug cru-sader (1785-1850); Soong Family, makers of a new China (twentieth century). Spelling of Chinese Names in English, Glossary, Bibliography, Sources, and Index.

642.   Hoobler, Dorothy, and Thomas Hoobler. **Cleopatra**. New York: Chelsea House, 1985. 115p. $18.95. ISBN 0-87754-589-8. (World Leaders Past and Present). 5 up

Cleopatra (69-30 B.C.) knew that she had to protect herself, so she made liaisons—first with her brother, then with Caesar, and finally with Mark Antony—in order to keep her position. She had skill and courage and the will to survive. The text looks at this woman whom historians have represented in various lights through the centuries: seductive, cunning, clever, manipulative, and malevolent. Photographs and reproductions enhance the text. Chronology, Further Reading, and Index.

643.   Hoobler, Dorothy, and Thomas Hoobler. **French Portraits**. Bill Farnsworth, illustrator. Austin, TX: Raintree/Steck-Vaughn, 1994. 96p. $16.98. ISBN 0-8114-6382-6. (Images Across the Ages). 6 up

The text gives short biographical profiles of persons who helped to shape the history of France. They are: Charlemagne, king and emperor (742?-814); Joan of Arc, woman warrior (1412?-1431); Jacques Cartier, ex-plorer (1491-1557); Molière, playwright (1622-1673); Madame Geoffrin, *salon* hostess (1699-1777); Maxi-milien Robespierre, revolutionary zealot (1758-1794); Antonin Carême, French chef (1784-1833); George Sand, author (1804-1876); Pierre Auguste Renoir, painter (1841-1919); Charles de Gaulle, French leader (1890-1970); and Catherine Deneuve, actress (b. 1943). Glossary, Bibliography, Sources, and Index.

644.   Hoobler, Dorothy, and Thomas Hoobler. **Italian Portraits**. Kim Fujiwari, illustrator. Austin, TX: Rain-tree/Steck-Vaughn, 1993. 96p. $16.98. ISBN 0-8114-6377-X. (Images Across the Ages). 6 up

The text gives short biographical profiles of figures from Italy's history. They are: Julius Caesar, con-queror (100-44 B.C.); Suetonius, Roman gossip (A.D. 69-140); St. Francis of Assisi, contemplative leader (1182-1226); Dante, writer (1265-1321); Isabella (1474-1539) and Beatrice d'Este (1475-1497), feminists;

Leonardo da Vinci (1452-1519) and Michelangelo Buonarroti (1475-1564), artists; Galileo Galilei, astronomer and physicist (1564-1642); Alessandro di Cagliostro, magician and alchemist (1743-1795); Giuseppe Verdi, musician and composer (1813-1901); and Maria Montessori, educator (1870-1952). Glossary, Bibliography, Sources, and Index.

645.   Hoobler, Dorothy, and Thomas Hoobler. **Japanese Portraits**. Victoria Bruck, illustrator. Austin, TX: Raintree/Steck-Vaughn, 1993. 96p. $16.98. ISBN 0-8114-6381-8. (Images Across the Ages). 6 up

The text gives short biographical profiles of prominent persons from both ancient and modern Japanese civilization. They are: Shotoku Taichi, the prince of sacred virtue (574-623); Murasaki Shikibu (978?-1031?) and Sei Shonagon (962?-1013), writers; Yoritomo (1147-1199) and Yoshitsune (1159-1189), the tragic Minamoto brothers; Nichiren, "the pillar of Japan" (1222-1282); Sen No Rikyu, the tea master (1522-1591); Okuni, female founder of kabuki (1571-1610?); Mitsui Shuho, businesswoman (1590-1676); Bash, poet (1644-1694); Hokusai, artist (1760-1849); Saigo Takemori, the last samurai (1827-1877); Hani Motoko, woman reporter and school founder (1873-1957); and Ako Morita, salesman to the world (b. 1921). Glossary, Bibliography, Sources, and Index.

646.   Hoobler, Dorothy, and Thomas Hoobler. **Mexican Portraits**. Robert Kuester, illustrator. Austin, TX: Raintree/Steck-Vaughn, 1993. 96p. $16.98. ISBN 0-8114-6376-1. (Images Across the Ages). 6 up

The text gives short biographical profiles of figures from Mexico's ancient and modern, as well as religious, cultures. They are: King Nezahualcoyotl, poet and engineer of Texcoco (1402-1472); Moctezuma II, Aztec leader (1467-1520); Malinche, translator to Cortés (1501-1550); Juan Diego, religious visionary (1474-1548); Diego de la Cruz, slave (mid-1700s); Juana Inés de la Cruz, poet (1651-1695); Miguel Hidalgo y Costilla, priest (1753-1811); Benito Juárez, political leader (1806-1872); Pancho Villa (1877-1923) and Emiliano Zapata (1879-1919), revolutionaries; Diego Rivera (1886-1957) and Frida Kahlo (1907-1954), painters; and Amalia Hernández, dancer (b. 1919?). Glossary, Bibliography, Sources, and Index.

647.   Hoobler, Dorothy, and Thomas Hoobler. **Russian Portraits**. John Edens, illustrator. Austin, TX: Raintree/Steck-Vaughn, 1994. 96p. $16.98. ISBN 0-8114-6380-X. (Images Across the Ages). 6 up

The text gives short biographical profiles of persons important throughout the history of Russia. They are: Alexander Nevsky, repeller of Mongol and Swedish invaders (1220?-1263); Yermak, Cossack leader (d. 1584); Avvakum, Russian Orthodox priest (1620-1682); Feodosia Morozova, noble woman (1630-1675); Peter the Great, founder of St. Petersburg (1672-1725); Catherine the Great, empress (1729-1796); Alexander Pushkin, poet (1799-1837); Leo Tolstoy, novelist (1828-1910); Peter Tchaikovsky, composer and musician (1840-1893); Anna Pavlova, ballet dancer (1882-1931); Vera Zasulich, revolutionary (1849-1919); Sergei Eisenstein, movie maker (1898-1948); and Andrei Sakharov, scientist and human rights activist (1921-1989) and his wife, Elena Bonner, nurse and human rights activist (b. 1923). Glossary, Bibliography, Sources, and Index.

648.   Hoobler, Dorothy, and Thomas Hoobler. **Showa: The Age of Hirohito**. New York: Walker, 1990. 176p. $15.95. ISBN 0-8027-6966-7. 6-12

As the 124th emperor of Japan, Hirohito of the Showa reign supposedly declared war on the United States and then decided to surrender. Whether he actually had any choice in the matter is unclear; through the centuries, the emperor of Japan has been the titular head of state, descended from the gods, but not the real decision maker. The Hooblers begin the story in 1853 when Admiral Perry entered Edo Bay to ask for admittance to Japanese ports. They note that although the emperor's signature was on the treaty agreement, the shogun was the person with the real power who made the decision. Since 1600, the members of the Tokugawa family had been the shoguns, but after the treaty, the *daimyo*, other families, took power from the Tokugawa family in 1868. A new emperor was enthroned, and the samurai class's rights and privileges were abolished. In 1877, Saigo, a former samurai, led a rebellion but was defeated. Finally a constitution was written in 1889. Hirohito was born in 1901 and trained by a former samurai who knew calligraphy, bonsai, ikebana (flower arranging), and the tea ceremony. Hirohito learned many things but especially loved marine biology. Always frustrated by the isolation of his role, he said before his death in 1989 that the favorite time in his life was his visit to Great Britain when he was a young man. This book, very informative and very interesting, gives insights into rarely discussed areas of Japanese culture.

649.   Hoobler, Dorothy, and Thomas Hoobler. **South American Portraits**. Stephen Marchesi, illustrator. Austin, TX: Raintree/Steck-Vaughn, 1994. 96p. $16.98. ISBN 0-8114-6383-4. (Images Across the Ages). 6 up

The text gives short biographical profiles of persons who helped to shape the history of South America. They are: Garcilaso de la Vega, Peruvian-born Spanish soldier, historian, and translator (1539?-1616); Rose of Lima, saint from Lima, Peru (1586-1617); Antônio Francisco Lisboa, architect and sculptor (1738-1814); Simón Bolívar (1783-1830) and José de San Martín (1778-1850), liberators; Maria Antônio Muniz, head of a Brazilian family with a tragic cycle (1762-1870); Domingo Faustino Sarmiento, Argentinian president (1811-1888); Simón I. Patiño, Bolivian tin mine owner (1865-1947); Gabriela Mistral, Chilean author, (1889-1957); Heitor Villa-Lobos, Brazilian musician (1887-1959); Evita Perón, Argentinian leader (1919-1952); Pelé, soccer star (b. 1940); and Gabriel García Márquez, Columbian novelist (b. 1928). Glossary, Bibliography, Sources, and Index.

650. Hoobler, Thomas, and Dorothy Hoobler. **Toussaint L'Ouverture**. New York: Chelsea House, 1989. 111p. $18.95. ISBN 1-55546-818-7. (World Leaders Past and Present). 5 up

Toussaint L'Ouverture (1744-1803) led the one rebellion in which slaves succeeded in overthrowing their masters and assuming leadership of their own country. A slave for forty-seven years, he had read widely and become a medic, and he used his knowledge to become a general, a diplomat, and a leader uniting his people into a nation after the slaves rebelled in 1791. The slaves claimed victories over armies from France, Spain, and Britain so that St. Domingue could eventually transform itself into Haiti, the second independent nation in the Western Hemisphere. Engravings and illustrations enhance the text. Chronology, Further Reading, and Index.

651. Hook, Jason. **The Vikings**. New York: Thompson-Learning, 1993. 32p. $14.95. ISBN 1-56847-060-6. (Look into the Past). 4-6

More than 1,000 years ago, the Vikings swarmed through Europe. Though they retreated later, their influence has remained. The text, highlighted with photographs of artifacts and sites, emphasizes their culture, language, religion, and daily life. Glossary, Important Dates, Books to Read, and Index.

652. Hooper, Maureen Brett. **The Violin Man**. Gary Undercuffler, illustrator. Honesdale, PA: Caroline House, 1991. 70p. $12.95. ISBN 1-878093-79-7. 3-6

Antonio, age ten, helps the violin man who comes to his Italian town in the 1880s to search for a Stradivarius violin. The man uses a clue in a diary he found in Milan to search for the unique instrument, which disappeared over 100 years earlier. When they finally find the instrument, the owner is happy to get the money from selling it, and the buyer is ecstatic to have the valuable violin.

653. Howard, Ellen. **A Different Kind of Courage**. New York: Atheneum, 1996. 176p. $15. ISBN 0-689-80774-0. 4-6

Zina, age eleven, and the younger Bertrand meet as they are both coming to America in June 1940. Bertrand, his sister, and his mother fled Paris as the Germans arrived; Zina's Russian father cannot find work after living in the south of France for twenty years. They and other children leave their families and their homes under the sponsorship of an American woman, and when they meet each other, they find hope despite their fears.

654. Howard, Ellen. **When Daylight Comes**. New York: Atheneum, 1985. 192p. $14.95. ISBN 0-689-31133-8. 5-9

Helena, the daughter of a wealthy St. Jan (John)'s plantation owner in the Caribbean, watches slaves revolt on the island in 1733. They capture her, make her work in the fields, and demand that she serve a former slave who was once an African queen. She learns how to accept responsibility and to understand real love while in this unexpectedly difficult situation.

655. Howarth, Sarah. **Medieval People**. Brookfield, CT: Millbrook Press, 1992. 47p. $15.40. ISBN 1-56294-153-4. (People and Places). 4-6

The text describes the everyday lives of thirteen people during the Middle Ages through the use of quotations, case studies, and illustrations of the time. It notes how they lived and worked as well as where they fit into the general social structure. The people include a knight, a lady, a monk, a pilgrim, a merchant, a doctor, and a bishop. Bibliography and Index. *Child Study Association Children's Books of the Year.*

656. Howarth, Sarah. **Medieval Places**. Brookfield, CT: Millbrook Press, 1992. 47p. $15.40. ISBN 1-56294-152-6. (People and Places). 4-6

The places of the Middle Ages help to put into perspective where people went during the day and what functions were appropriate to each place. Some of the places covered here are the village, the castle, and the church. Illustrations augment the text. Further Reading, Glossary, and Index. *Child Study Association Children's Books of the Year.*

657. Howarth, Sarah. **Renaissance People**. Brookfield, CT: Millbrook Press, 1992. 47p. $15.40. ISBN 1-56294-088-0. (People and Places). 4-6

The text describes the everyday lives of thirteen people during the fifteenth and sixteenth centuries through the use of quotations, case studies, and illustrations of the time. It notes how they lived and worked as well as where they fit into the general social structure. The people featured include a witch, a banker, a beggar, an actor, and a merchant. Bibliography and Index.

658. Howarth, Sarah. **Renaissance Places**. Brookfield, CT: Millbrook Press, 1992. 47p. $15.40. ISBN 1-56294-089-9. (People and Places). 4-6

The text presents places that one would have had to visit during the Renaissance to understand the life of the people; it is complemented by paintings, reproductions, drawings, and photographs. The places are the city, the sculptor's workshop, the chapel, the printer's workshop, the theater, the palace, the library, the Parliament, the New World, the observatory, the monastery, the home, and the deserted village. Glossary, Further Reading, and Index.

659. Howarth, Sarah. **Roman People**. Brookfield, CT: Millbrook Press, 1995. 48p. $15.40. ISBN 0-56294-650-1. (People and Places). 4-6

This investigation of the people who lived in Rome reveals what they were supposed to do in their jobs and how they were to act in society. Among the people covered are the emperor, the centurion, the tax collector, the hostage, the surveyor, and the mother. Further Reading, Glossary, and Index.

660. Howarth, Sarah. **Roman Places**. Brookfield, CT: Millbrook Press, 1995. 48p. $14.90. ISBN 0-56294-651-X. (People and Places). 4-6

Knowledge of Roman places helps to put into perspective where the people went during the day and what functions were appropriate to each place. Some of the places covered here are the forum, the baths, the vineyard, the hospital, and the colony. Illustrations augment the text. Further Reading, Glossary, and Index.

661. Hoyt-Goldsmith, Diane. **Day of the Dead: A Mexican-American Celebration**. New York: Holiday House, 1994. 30p. $15.95; $6.95pa. ISBN 0-8234-0194-3; 0-8234-1200-8pa. 3-6

For the Aztecs, the way a person died indicated the type of afterlife he or she would have. When the Spanish came to the Mexican peninsula, they brought All Saints' Day, which was then combined with the Aztec acknowledgment of the dead. The text gives the history of and details on the preparation for the modern celebration each November 1 and 2. The author notes that Frida Kahlo, the Mexican artist, collected *Día de Muertos* objects that keep Aztecs beliefs as part of the present as well as the past. Glossary and Index.

662. Hudson, Jan. **Dawn Rider**. New York: Philomel/Putnam, 1990. 175p. $14.95. ISBN 0-399-22178-6. 6 up

In 1750, Kit Fox, age sixteen, does not feel special until she sees a horse. She knows that she wants to ride this powerful animal, but her Blackfeet tribe does not think that women should be involved in horse training. She sneaks away from home every morning and earns the confidence of the horse. When the Snakes invade the tribe and the men have to leave to fight them, she proves her value by racing to a nearby tribe for guns. *Writer's Guild of Alberta Awards for Excellence* (Canada).

663. Hudson, Jan. **Sweetgrass**. New York: Philomel, 1989. 160p. $13.95. ISBN 0-399-21721-5. 6-9

Sweetgrass, age fifteen, a Blackfoot in the nineteenth century, worries about not being married when most of the younger girls have already become wives. She also worries about whether the boy she loves will have enough horses for her father to approve him and whether her stepmother will decide that Sweetgrass is responsible enough to be a wife. Her people struggle in their lives on the Canadian prairie, and after she nurses both her brother and her stepmother through smallpox by feeding them fish (a forbidden food), her father decides that she may marry. *Canadian Library Association Book of the Year, Governor General's Literary Awards, International Board of Books for Young People, American Library Association Notable Books for Children, School Library Journal Best Book,* and *Canada Council Children's Literature Prize.*

664. Hughes, Libby. **Madam Prime Minister: A Biography of Margaret Thatcher**. New York: Dillon Press, 1989. 144p. $13.95. ISBN 0-87518-410-3. (People in Focus). 6-9

Although she pursued chemistry at Oxford University, Margaret Thatcher (b. 1925) decided to study law after graduation because of her interest in politics. She showed that she was willing to work as a child of eleven. She won a speech contest, asserting to someone that she was not "lucky" to win because she had carefully prepared the speech and deserved the credit. She first ran to become a member of Parliament and then became the head of her Conservative Party. Several years later, the people elected her as the first woman Prime Minister. During the ten years she served, Britons nicknamed her the "Iron Lady." Selected Bibliography and Index.

665. Hughes, Libby. **Nelson Mandela: Voice of Freedom**. New York: Dillon Press, 1992. 144p. $12.95. ISBN 0-87518-484-7. 6-9

Nelson Mandela (b. 1918) has had a major impact on race relations in South Africa, partly by suffering personal deprivation. He helped to establish the African National Congress and the anti-apartheid movements that struggled to give blacks their rights, but he was incarcerated as a political prisoner for twenty-seven years. He became president of South Africa after the period covered in this book ends. Bibliography and Index.

666. Hull, Mary. **The Travels of Marco Polo**. San Diego, CA: Lucent, 1995. 96p. $14.95. ISBN 1-56006-238-X. (World History). 6-10

After giving background on the world politics at the time of Marco Polo (1254-1323?), Hull then tells of the Polo family's two journeys to the East. On the second, Marco Polo went; he related this journey, beginning in 1271, in his diaries. During Polo's experiences, he became a favorite of the Great Khan in Khan-Balik, the city now known as Beijing. After much time and money, the family decided to leave, and after 15,000 miles, they returned to Venice in 1295. There they had to face the cultural changes that had occurred during their absence. Reproductions enhance the text. Further Reading, Notes, and Index.

667. Humble, Richard. **The Age of Leif Eriksson**. Richard Hook, illustrator. New York: Franklin Watts, 1989. 32p. $11.90. ISBN 0-531-10741-8. (Exploration Through the Ages). 3-6

After a brief introduction to the Vikings, the text looks specifically at Leif Eriksson's father, Erik the Red, and Eriksson's own exploits. While exiled in Greenland, Erik fathered Leif, and Leif eventually traveled west to the coast of Labrador. He and his men won a battle with the Skraelings, but they had too few people for a viable settlement. The text adds much information about Eriksson. Glossary, Time Chart, and Index.

668. Humble, Richard. **Ships**. Peter Cornwall, illustrator. Austin, TX: Raintree/Steck-Vaughn, 1994. 32p. $21.40. ISBN 0-8114-6158-0. (Pointers). 3-7

Two-page spreads on each type of ship tell its structure and give historical information and an illustration. The types of ships presented are Egyptian warships, Greek triremes, Viking long ships, man-of-war ships, ships of the Line, early steamships, clipper ships, ironclads, turret rams, submarines, aircraft carriers, and ocean liners. Glossary and Index.

669. Humble, Richard. **The Travels of Marco Polo**. Richard Hook, illustrator. New York: Franklin Watts, 1990. 32p. $11.90. ISBN 0-531-14022-9. (Exploration Through the Ages). 3-6

The text discusses the journey of Marco Polo (1254-1323?) to the court of the Mongol emperor, Kublai Khan, in the thirteenth century, and describes many of the places that Polo visited. Illustrations enhance the brief text. Index.

670. Humble, Richard. **U-Boat**. New York: Franklin Watts, 1990. 32p. $17.71. ISBN 0-531-14023-7. (Fighting Ships). 3-5

"U-Boat" stands for *Unterseeboot*, German for "submarine." These boats fought in both World War I and World War II, with the most desperate battles occurring between the summer of 1940 and the spring of 1943. Of the twenty-six different types of submarines that led the German attack, the most successful was the Type VIIC. Diagrams augment the text, which discusses the crews, life on board (one toilet for forty-four men), and their foes. Glossary, Time Chart, and Index.

671. Humble, Richard. **A World War Two Submarine**. Mark Bergin, illustrator. New York: Peter Bedrick, 1991. 48p. $18.95. ISBN 0-87226-351-7. (Inside Story). 4-7

The very first submarine used in the United States was in 1776, when the *Turtle* was put to service to explode British ammunition. It failed, but it caused engineers to began searching for a submarine that would work. The text looks at submarine warfare during the World Wars and how they were designed and built. Diagrams and drawings show the midships, bow tubes, sleeping and eating arrangements, sonar, torpedoes and guns, and uniforms worn by the crew. A brief discussion of the Battle of the Atlantic from 1940 to 1943 describes subs in action. Chronology, Glossary, and Index.

672. Humphrey, Judy. **Genghis Khan**. New York: Chelsea House, 1987. 112p. $18.95. ISBN 0-87754-527-8. (World Leaders Past and Present). 5 up

Genghis Khan (1162-1227) established the world's largest empire by using intimidation to supplement his political and military strategies. He spent his childhood traveling with his father's nomads, but when he was thirteen, his father died and the clan deserted. His people eventually recognized the resourceful Genghis as their leader, or khan, in 1183. He began raiding, which consolidated his local power, but then he began attacking the neighbors to add to his wealth. In 1227, his empire crossed the Asian continent. He established trade routes and laws that remained long after his death. Photographs and reproductions enhance the text. Chronology, Further Reading, and Index.

673. Hunt, Jonathan, author/illustrator. **Leif's Saga: A Viking Tale**. New York: Simon & Schuster, 1996. 40p. $16. ISBN 0-689-80492-X. 2-4

Sigrid's father, Asgrim, tells her, as he builds his knörr, that he got the oak wood for the boat from Leif Eriksson, another man from Greenland, who had sailed further than anyone else and brought the logs back to him. Eriksson had reached Helluland, Markland, and Vinland. Information about Leif and the Norsemen appears in the endnote.

674. Hunter, Erica C. D. **First Civilizations: Cultural Atlas for Young People**. New York: Facts on File, 1994. 96p. $19.95. ISBN 0-8160-2976-8. 6 up

In this book, text and photographs of artifacts and ruins complement one another as they give an overview of history from its beginnings to 323 B.C. in the Middle East. The broad categories are: early peoples to 11,000 B.C.; the first farmers (11,000-9300 B.C.); movement toward civilization (7000-4000 B.C.); states in conflict (3000-2350 B.C.); kings of Agade (2350-2000 B.C.); rival kingdoms (2000-1500 B.C.); the Kassite empire (1600-1200 B.C.); changing kingdoms (1200-900 B.C.); the late Assyrian empire (1000-750 B.C.);

Assyria triumphant (750-626 B.C.); Babylonian revival (626-560 B.C.); the rise of the Persian empire (560-521 B.C.); the empire of Darius (521-486 B.C.); and the end of the ancient Near East (486-323 B.C.). Glossary, Further Reading, Gazetteer, and Index.

675. Hunter, Mollie. **The Ghosts of Glencoe**. 1969. Edinburgh, Scotland: Canongate, 1995. 191p. $7.95pa. ISBN 0-86241-467-9pa. 6-9

In 1692, Ensign Stewart finds out that some of the Scottish-born officers in the British army are in sympathy with the British cause and plan to massacre Scots at Glencoe. He decides to warn the rebels that the army will attack. His warning is too late to save the Macdonalds, but he escapes from his situation as a traitor.

676. Hunter, Mollie. **The Lothian Run**. 1970. Edinburgh, Scotland: Canongate, 1990. 221p. $4.95pa. ISBN 0-86241-069-Xpa. 5-8

In 1736, Sandy, age sixteen, discovers a Scottish smuggling gang. They take documents to Jacobites in France who plan to overthrow the ruling Hanoverians. The lawyer who employs Sandy is delighted with the investigation because it enables him to capture several people who are part of the plot.

677. Hunter, Mollie. **The Spanish Letters**. Elizabeth Grant, illustrator. 1964. Edinburgh, Scotland: Canongate, 1990. 173p. $6.95pa. ISBN 0-86241-057-6pa. 5-8

Jamie is a "caddie," or guide, in Edinburgh during 1589. At age fifteen, he helps discover a Spanish plot to capture Scotland and England when he overhears various conversations in his job. After his report reaches Queen Elizabeth, and King James escapes capture, he earns the chance for a better job.

678. Hunter, Mollie. **The 13th Member**. 1971. Magnolia, MA: Peter Smith, 1988. 214p. $19.55. ISBN 0-8446-6362-X. 6-9

In 1590, Adam Lawrie, age sixteen, follows Gilly, the kitchen maid, after she leaves the house. She goes into the dark of a Scottish night to participate in a thirteen-member witches' coven from which she is trying to free herself. After Adam and Gilly, with the help of a trusted scholar, discover the plot to murder James I, they walk to England, where they hope to start new lives using Gilly's ability to heal people and Adam's innate intelligence.

679. Hunter, Nigel. **Einstein**. New York: Bookwright Press, Franklin Watts, 1987. 32p. $11.90. ISBN 0-531-18092-1. (Great Lives). 3-6

Nine years old before he could speak fluently, teachers thought Albert Einstein (1879-1955) was a slow learner. He learned to play the violin, but he would not wear socks. His family and he moved often, and he renounced his German citizenship twice to live in Switzerland and the United States. In 1922, he received the Nobel Prize for Physics for his theory of general relativity. He worked on this idea while he served as a patents office clerk. Afterward, he became a university professor in Prague. His immense knowledge showed him that an atomic bomb was possible, and he was very concerned that the Germans would create it first during World War II. However, he was against the Americans using the power they had harnessed because he was a pacifist, except against the atrocities of Hitler. Important Dates, Glossary, Books to Read, and Index.

680. Hurwitz, Johanna. **Anne Frank: Life in Hiding**. Vera Rosenberry, illustrator. Philadelphia, PA: Jewish Publication Society, 1988. 62p. $12.95. ISBN 0-8276-0311-8. 2-5

Anne Frank (1929-1945) was born in Germany, but her family moved to Amsterdam in 1933, because her father had business ties there and hoped to raise his family in a more tolerant political environment. The family was Jewish, and Hitler and the German government were passing laws that denied Jews certain freedoms. Anne's sixteen-year-old sister received a summons to report to the Nazi government, just after Anne's thirteenth birthday, and the family went into hiding, hoping to survive the war. They did not, and the text follows Anne to Auschwitz and to Bergen-Belsen, where first her sister and then Anne died of typhus three months before Anne's sixteenth birthday. Important Dates, Author's Note, and Index. *Texas Blue Bonnet Award* and *Notable Children's Trade Book in the Field of Social Studies.*

681. Hurwitz, Johanna. **Astrid Lindgren: Storyteller to the World**. Michael Dooling, illustrator. New York: Viking, 1989. 54p. $10.95; $3.95pa. ISBN 0-670-82207-8; 0-14-032692-8pa. (Women of Our Time). 2-6

With much background information on life in Sweden intertwined with information on Lindgren (b. 1907) in this fictional biography, the reader gets a strong sense of the influences on her life. She first began writing by telling her ill daughter stories about Pippi Longstocking, a name her daughter created.

682. Husain, Shahrukh. **Mecca**. New York: Dillon Press, 1993. 46p. $13.95. ISBN 0-87518-572-X. (Holy Cities). 5-9

Mecca, Islam's most sacred city, has been important to the Middle East since Ibrahim discovered the Zamzam spring there. Muhammad, born in the city in approximately A.D. 570, had a revelation from God that followers of Islam should pray toward *Kaaba*, the most sacred Islamic sanctuary inside the Great Mosque, the Haram.

Contemporary Muslims look forward to their *hajj* or pilgrimage to the city as an affirmation of their faith. Non-Muslims may not enter the city. The text looks at the religion and the people who follow it. Photographs enhance the text. Timeline, Further Reading, and Index.

683. Husain, Shahrukh. **What Do We Know About Islam?** New York: Peter Bedrick, 1997. 40p. $18.95. ISBN 0-87226-388-6. (What Do We Know About). 4-7

After summarizing a history of Islam, Hussein discusses holidays, the pilgrimage to Mecca, dietary restrictions, art, and other topics. In the timeline, modern leaders receive acknowledgment. Chronology, Glossary, and Index.

684. Huynh Quang Nhuong. **The Land I Lost: Adventures of a Boy in Vietnam**. Vo-dinh Mai, illustrator. 1982. Magnolia, MA: Peter Smith, 1992. 115p. $17.75. ISBN 0-8446-6586-X. New York: Trophy, 1986. 115p. $3.95pa. ISBN 0-06-440183-9pa. 4-7

Huynh Quang Nhuong grew up in Vietnam during the 1960s and was drafted into the army. A gunshot paralyzed him, and he came to the United States for treatment and further schooling in chemistry. In this book he tells the story of his childhood and the things he remembers. On the list are his beautiful grandmother, crocodiles, horse snakes, killer wild hogs, a 200-pound catfish, taming pythons, fishing in flooded rice fields, and his pet water buffalo. *American Library Association Notable Books for Children, Notable Children's Trade Books in the Field of Social Studies, NCTE Teachers' Choices,* and *Booklist Editors' Choices.*

685. Hyndley, Kate. **The Voyage of the Beagle (Darwin)**. Peter T. Bull, illustrator. New York: Bookwright Press, Franklin Watts, 1989. 32p. $11.90. ISBN 0-531-18272-X. (Great Journeys). 5-9

Charles Darwin (1809-1882) went aboard the HMS *Beagle* for a voyage that lasted for five years, from 1831 to 1836. During this trip, he observed natural habitats not available in England, which gave him additional information on which to base his theory of the evolution of species expressed in *On the Origin of Species* and *The Descent of Man.* The text covers this experience in two-page chapters. Illustrations augment the text. Bibliography and Index.

I

686.   Ibazebo, Isimeme. **Exploration into Africa**. Englewood Cliffs, NJ: New Discovery, 1994. 48p. $7.95pa. ISBN 0-382-24732-9pa. (Exploration Into . . .). 4-6

Chapters illustrated with photographs and drawings give an overview of African settlement and discovery. They cover Africa to the 1400s and Great Zimbabwe; the traders and visitors from Islamic countries and Europe; the 1500s to the 1800s and the kingdoms of the Guinea Coast and Rozvi; the changing times from slave trade to European exploration searching for the Nile, the Niger, Timbuktu, and routes to the coast; colonization of Africa; and Africa today. Time Chart, Glossary, and Index.

687.   Ireland, Karin. **Albert Einstein**. Englewood Cliffs, NJ: Silver Burdett, 1989. 109p. $13.98. ISBN 0-382-09523-5. (Pioneers in Change). 5-9

Albert Einstein (1879-1955) refused to talk until he was three years old, and many thought that he might be retarded. He hated the discipline in German schools and would not study as required, preferring to investigate the laws of physics. He transferred to schools in Switzerland and discovered that not all schools were as mindless as the German schools, where questions were discouraged and rote memory applauded. He renounced his German citizenship, but as an adult, he was considered Jewish first and had to endure the difficulties of this background. He became an American citizen, warned President Roosevelt about the possibility of a German atomic bomb, and spent the last years of his life at Princeton. He was distraught when the American atomic bomb killed people in Japan, and he was disturbed that his son had to remain in a mental hospital. He did not have enough time to complete his unified field theory, but otherwise he lived a full and happy life. Photographs, Bibliography, and Index.

688.   Isadora, Rachel, author/illustrator. **Young Mozart**. New York: Viking, 1997. 32p. $14.99. ISBN 0-670-87120-6. K-3

When he was only five, Wolfgang Amadeus Mozart (1756-1791) was performing for the royalty of Europe. During the next sixteen years, he composed more than 300 works. This book introduces Mozart and his musical accomplishments to young readers.

689.   Italia, Robert. **Courageous Crimefighters**. Minneapolis, MN: Oliver Press, 1995. 160p. $14.95. ISBN 1-881508-21-8. (Profiles). 6-9

People who lived the adventures that make mystery and detective books so appealing risk their lives to catch criminals. The text looks at eight of these people: Sir Robert Peel (1788-1850) of Scotland Yard in England; Allan Pinkerton (1819-1884), the original private eye in America; Samuel Steele (1851-1919), a Canadian mountie; Leander H. McNelly (1844-1877), captain of the Texas Rangers; Melvin Purvis (1903-1960) and Eliot Ness (1902-1957), top agents in the Federal Bureau of Investigation; Estes Kefauver (1903-1963), a crusader in Congress; and Simon Wiesenthal (b. 1908), hunter of Nazis. Bibliography and Index.

690.   Iverson, Peter. **Carlos Montezuma**. Kim Fujiwara, illustrator. Austin, TX: Raintree/Steck-Vaughn, 1993. 32p. $19.97; $4.95pa. ISBN 0-8172-3408-X; 0-8114-4092-3pa. (Native American Stories). 3-5

Pima Indians captured Wassaja or Carlos Montezuma (1867-1923) and sold him to a man who gave him a different name. Then he was adopted by someone else who supported his college and medical school education. He returned to Arizona to learn about his family and the Yavapai Indians. In 1911, he started the Society of American Indians and continued to help his tribe members.

691. Jackson, Ellen. **The Winter Solstice**. Jan Davey Ellis, illustrator. Brookfield, CT: Millbrook Press, 1994. Unpaged. $15.40. ISBN 1-56294-400-2. 3-4

The winter solstice was a time of ritual and tradition for the Celts, the Romans, and the Native Americans. Its magic has had an influence throughout history and is reflected in the present with the celebration of Hallow-een and All Souls' Day. A Cherokee legend ends the presentation.

692. Jackson, Lawrence. **Newfoundland & Labrador**. Minneapolis, MN: Lerner, 1995. 76p. $14.21. ISBN 0-8225-2757-X. 3-6

Although not technically a history book, over half the text reveals the history of these areas. Charts, maps, photographs, and prints illustrate the individuality of this area, whose first inhabitants were the Maritime-Archaic Indians around 8,000 years ago. Among the famous persons briefly described are Robert Bartlett (1875-1945), who explored the North Pole with Robert Peary, and Shanawdithit (1801-1829), considered to be the last Beothuk; British settlers captured her in 1823. Fast Facts, Glossary, Pronunciation Guide, and Index.

693. Jacobs, Francine. **A Passion for Danger: Nansen's Arctic Adventures**. New York: Putnam, 1994. 160p. $17.95. ISBN 0-399-22674-5. 5-9

Fridtjof Nansen (1861-1930) of Norway was an explorer, statesman, scientist, and humanitarian. In 1882, he took a sealer into the seas of Greenland and began explorations in the area. In 1893, he spent seventeen months attempting to cross the Arctic Ocean to find the North Pole. The text looks at his journeys as he related them in his memoirs and presents the numerous dangers he encountered. He was unsuccessful in reaching the Pole, but his information on oceanography, meteorology, and diet helped those who came after him. In 1906, he became Norway's first minister to England. That Nansen received the Nobel Prize in 1922 for his work with World War I refugees shows his interest in helping others. Photographs, Bibliography, Notes, and Index.

694. Jacobs, Francine. **The Tainos: The People Who Welcomed Columbus**. Patrick Collins, illustrator. New York: Putnam, 1992. 103p. $15.95. ISBN 0-399-22116-6. 5-9

The Indians who met Christopher Columbus and his crews in 1492 were called Tainos. They had no writ-ten language, so all that survives about them are the writings made during the time of Columbus and picto-graphs discovered in caves on the islands. They were peaceful farming people whose ancestors had come from South America hundreds of years before. Although the Tainos welcomed Columbus and his men, the visitors called them Indians because they thought they were in India. Then they destroyed the Taino culture in their greed for gold. In fifty years, the Tainos became extinct. Notes, Museums, Bibliography, and Index.

695. Jacobs, William. **Champlain: A Life of Courage**. New York: Franklin Watts, 1994. 63p. $19.90. ISBN 0-531-20112-0. (First Books). 4-6

Samuel de Champlain (1567-1635) was known as "the Father of New France." He risked his life to map the Canadian interior from the eastern coastline of North America along the Saint Lawrence River to Cape Cod and wrote four books about the land. He understood that Canada's wealth was furs, fish, timber, and farmland rather than gold. He also worked for over thirty years to spread the Catholic religion among the Indians. Finally, he founded the city of Quebec and made its survival possible. Important Dates, Note on Sources, and Index.

696. Jacobs, William. **Pizarro: Conqueror of Peru**. New York: Franklin Watts, 1994. 63p. $19.90. ISBN 0-531-20107-4. (First Books). 4-6

Francisco Pizarro (c. 1475-1541), born to poor parents who never married, could neither read nor write at his death. But he and those who were with him believed that God had led them to find the gold of Peru for the Spanish government. Thus, their victory over the Incas, no matter how brutal, had a holy mandate. Pizarro's tri-umph over the Incan leader, Atahualpa, shaped the future of both South America and, to a lesser extent, North America. His methods of achieving victory, however, were less than admirable. Important Dates, For Further Reading, and Index.

697. Jacobs, William. **War with Mexico**. Brookfield, CT: Millbrook Press, 1994. 64p. $15.90; $5.95pa. ISBN 1-56294-366-9; 1-56294-776-1pa. (Spotlight on American History). 5-8

War between Mexico and the United States started in 1846 over territories that both claimed. Battles occurred at Monterey and Buena Vista as the United States drove toward Mexico City. When the United States won the war, many thought the boundaries of the country would extend with the Treaty of Guadalupe Hidalgo. What ensued after 1848 was anything but peaceful because of the bills in Congress to keep slavery from being legal in the new territories. The text discusses these various aspects of this war. Chronology, Fur-ther Reading, Bibliography, and Index.

698. Jacobs, William Jay. **Coronado: Dreamer in Golden Armor**. New York: Franklin Watts, 1994. 64p. $19.90; $5.95pa. ISBN 0-531-20140-6; 0-531-15722-9pa. (First Book Explorer). 3-6

Coronado (1510-1554) set out from New Spain, now Mexico, in 1540, at the head of his army on a quest for gold in the legendary Seven Cities of Gold. After seeing what Cortés took from the Aztecs and Pizarro collected from the Incas, he had reason to believe that he would be successful. He was well-educated and aggressive, but ten years later he returned with neither gold nor glory. But he did record his travels throughout the southwestern area of the current United States, and those journals reveal what life was like at that time. Photographs and reproductions enhance the text. Important Dates, For Further Reading, and Index.

699. Jacobs, William Jay. **Cortés: Conqueror of Mexico**. New York: Franklin Watts, 1994. 64p. $19.90; $5.95pa. ISBN 0-531-20138-4; 0-531-15723-7pa. (First Book Explorer). 3-6

The Aztec Indians, deeply religious, saw Hernando Cortés (1485-1547) as a god, and they welcomed him. Ironically, he had only a few hundred soldiers, but because of the mistaken identity, he and his soldiers were able to conquer the Aztec civilization, though it was hundreds of years old and protected by thousands of warriors. The text looks at this ambitious and lucky man. Reproductions, Important Dates, For Further Reading, and Index.

700. Jacobs, William Jay. **Great Lives: Human Rights**. New York: Scribners, 1990. 278p. $22.95. ISBN 0-684-19036-2. 4-7

People concerned with the rights of all humans have been expressing their beliefs throughout history. The text uses a chronological organization to profile some of these people who have spoken out for others. In the New World setting, human rights advocates included Anne Hutchinson and Roger Williams. In the nineteenth century, such people as Dorothea Dix and Frederick Douglass professed their beliefs. In the industrial age, Susan B. Anthony and Andrew Carnegie are examples; in the twentieth century are such figures as Emma Goldman, Jacob Riis, Cesar Chavez, and Martin Luther King, Jr. For Further Reading and Index.

701. Jacobs, William Jay. **Great Lives**: **World Religions**. New York: Atheneum, 1996. 280p. $23. ISBN 0-689-80486-5. 4-7

The text covers religions and religious leaders throughout world history. Beginning with the religions of ancient Egypt and Persia, it continues with Asian religions, Judaism, Christianity, and Islam. Among the figures presented are Amenhotep IV, Zarathustra, Confucius, Buddha, Muhammad, Mahavira, Gandhi, Jesus, Khomeini, Moses, Jeremiah, Meir, Erasmus, Thomas Aquinas, John Calvin, John Wesley, George Fox, Roger Williams, Anne Hutchinson, Martin Luther King, Jr., Mother Teresa, and Joseph Smith. If appropriate, a brief interpretation of a person's theology also appears. Further Reading and Index.

702. Jacobs, William Jay. **Magellan: Voyager with a Dream**. New York: Franklin Watts, 1994. 64p. $19.90. ISBN 0-531-20139-2. (First Book). 4-6

Ferdinand Magellan (1480?-1521) wanted to find a way to circumnavigate the earth, but his Portuguese king was not interested. Magellan thus renounced his Portugese citizenship and offered his services to Charles of Spain, who offered patronage and funding. After Magellan's ships left in 1519, he had to overcome a mutiny before he found the Pacific Ocean. He died, however, as he fought a warring tribe on one of the Pacific islands. Important Dates, For Further Reading, and Index.

703. Jacobs, William Jay. **Mother Teresa**. Brookfield, CT: Millbrook Press, 1991. 48p. $13.99; $6.95pa. ISBN 1-56294-020-1; 1-87884-157-2pa. (Gateway Biography). 3-5

Mother Teresa, born in Albania in 1910, decided at age eighteen that she wanted to become a nun and dedicate her life to helping others. She taught in Calcutta before she began to help others who suffered from loneliness and poverty. The results of her work have spread to homes around the globe, and she received the Nobel Peace Prize in 1979. She died in 1997. Chronology and Index.

704. Jacobsen, Karen L. **Egypt**. Chicago: Children's Press, 1990. 48p. $5.50pa. ISBN 0-516-41184-5pa. (A New True Book). K-4

This overview of Egypt, essentially a young reader's introduction to the country, includes information on ancient Egypt illustrated with color photographs. The list of rulers incorporates Queen Hatshepsut, who came to power in 1520 B.C., Alexander the Great, Ptolemy (Alexander's general), and the last of the Ptolemy family rulers, Cleopatra. Later rulers include Saladin in 1171, Napoleon (briefly), and Muhammed Ali. Discussion of the Suez Canal and the peace treaty with Israel under Anwar Sadat in 1979 end the text. Words You Should Know and Index.

705. James, Simon. **Ancient Rome**. New York: Viking, 1992. 48p. $15. ISBN 0-670-84493-4. (See Through History). 4-6

The text looks at the Augustan era at the height of the early Roman Empire. Four cross-sections show the insides of various places. The two-page topic treatments include family life, food and festivals, houses, government, work, public life, science and philosophy, sports, and games. Chronology, Glossary, and Index.

706. Jenkins, Earnestine. **A Glorious Past: Ancient Egypt, Ethiopia, and Nubia**. New York: Chelsea House, 1994. 118p. $19.95; $7.95pa. ISBN 0-7910-2258-7; 0-7910-2684-1pa. (Milestones in Black American History). 5 up

The past of African-Americans can be traced to the African civilizations of Egypt, Nubia, and Ethiopia. Older than Egypt, which began in approximately 3100 B.C., Nubia, starting in about 3800 B.C., lasted longer than 5,000 years and possessed uncountable wealth. The Nubians were builders and creators of beautiful artifacts in gold, ebony, bronze, glass, and silver, and they developed their own alphabet. In the first century A.D., Ethiopia, originally known as Axum or Abyssinia, began a thousand-year history during which it controlled much of northern Africa and the wealthy Red Sea trade. Ezana, a strong king of the third century A.D., established Christianity and increased the kingdom's wealth. Among the Axumite literature is the story of the queen of Sheba and her visit to Solomon. Index.

707. Jessop, Joanne. **Big Buildings of the Ancient World**. New York: Franklin Watts, 1994. 48p. $21.40; $8.95pa. ISBN 0-531-14286-8; 0-531-15709-1pa. (X-Ray Picture Books). 3-6

Chapters on ten ancient buildings constructed before the seventeenth century show illustrations of both insides and outsides and discuss how the structures were built. Additional information about the culture in which the buildings were assembled surrounds the main text. The buildings introduced are the Great Pyramid (Egypt, 2660-2640 B.C.), Abu Simbel (Egypt, c. 1250-c. 1224 B.C.), the Parthenon (Athens, 447-432 B.C.), the Colosseum (Rome, A.D. 72-80), the cathedral at Notre Dame (Paris, 1163-1270), Bodiam Castle (England, 1385-c. 1483), the monastery of Mont St. Michel (France, thirteenth-century), the Basilica of St. Peter (Rome, 1506-1626), the Taj Mahal (India, 1631-1642), and the Forbidden City (Peking, China, started 1273). Glossary and Index.

708. Jiang, Ji-Li. **Red Scarf Girl: A Memoir of the Cultural Revolution**. New York: HarperCollins, 1997. 285p. $14.95. ISBN 0-06-027585-5. 6-10

When Ji-Li Jiang was twelve in 1966, she was intelligent and a leader, but the Cultural Revolution changed her life. No longer were intelligence, talent, or wealth respected. She had always believed that the Communist Party was kind and that Chairman Mao was dearer than her parents. When her father is detained, she must decide whether to renounce him or the Party.

709. Johnson, Dolores, author/illustrator. **Now Let Me Fly: The Story of a Slave Family**. New York: Macmillan, 1993. Unpaged. $14.95; $5.99pa. ISBN 0-02-747699-5; 0-689-80966-2pa. 1-4

Minna hears drums on the African savanna and thinks there will be dancing and stories. Instead, a member of her own tribe kidnaps her and marches her toward slavery. She travels for three months on a ship to a place called America, where she is sold at auction to a plantation owner. She and Amadi, the boy she meets on the ship, eventually marry and have children, but they have no chance of freedom.

710. Joosse, Barbara M. **The Morning Chair**. Marcia Sewall, illustrator. New York: Clarion, 1995. 32p. $14.95. ISBN 0-395-62337-5. K-2

In 1950, Bram and his family leave Holland for America, where his father hopes to get a job. When he was in Holland, he sat in his mother's lap in the morning chair to have tea. Not until the furniture arrives in their New York apartment and the morning chair reappears does Bram feel comfortable.

K

711. Kamen, Gloria, author/illustrator. **Edward Lear: King of Nonsense**. New York: Atheneum, 1990. 74p. $15. ISBN 0-689-31419-1. 3-6

Although his family was wealthy at his birth in 1812, Edward Lear's family lost its money, and in 1825, the family was forever separated. Lear suffered from epilepsy and asthma, but he loved art and enjoyed drawing subjects in nature. He liked to use puns when he wrote to his friends, and children loved the playfulness in the stories Lear told them. In the 1830s, Lear bemoaned the fact that no books had pictures that made people laugh before his books were published. He had to spend much of his later life in Italy, because the English climate was too severe for his health conditions, but he continued to entertain any children in his presence. Bibliography.

712. Kamen, Gloria. **Hidden Music: The Life of Fanny Mendelssohn**. New York: Atheneum, 1996. 82p. $15. ISBN 0-689-31714-X. 5-8

Fanny Mendelssohn's (1805-1847) father told her that her music could be only an ornament; unlike her brother, Felix, she could not have a career in music. Yet, she composed more than 400 scores, and she had the chance to direct an orchestra in her home on one occasion. She supposedly did not even complain when her brother played some of her compositions and claimed them as his own. The text looks at her life and that of her family in the context of the times. Glossary, Bibliography, and Index.

713. Kamen, Gloria, author/illustrator. **Kipling: Storyteller of East and West**. New York: Atheneum, 1985. 74p. $15. ISBN 0-689-31195-8. 4-6

As a young child, Rudyard Kipling (1865-1936) lived happily in India, speaking Hindi with the family's servants. His parents sent him to England to live with a couple who had advertised their availability in the newspaper, and he was very unhappy with them. In isolation from people he loved, Kipling began to write, and in boarding school he blossomed as an author. Based on his experiences living in India, England, and Vermont, and those of others he met, he wrote *Mowgli*, *Captains Courageous*, *Kim*, and other stories and won the Nobel Prize. Bibliography and Glossary.

714. Kaplan, Zoë Coralnik. **Eleanor of Aquitaine**. New York: Chelsea House, 1986. 114p. $18.95. ISBN 0-87754-552-7. (World Leaders Past and Present). 5 up

Eleanor of Aquitaine (1122-1204) was wife of two kings and mother of two others. She married her first husband, Louis Capet (Louis VII of France), when she was fifteen. She divorced him in 1152 to marry Henry Plantagenet, who became king of England two years later. She returned to France after this marriage soured to establish the court of love. In 1174, Henry disbanded her court and had her jailed for causing her children to rise against him. He held her captive for fifteen years until her favorite son, Richard the Lionheart, came to power at Henry's death. She went on a crusade with her first husband, and she continued to travel well into her seventies when she crossed the Alps. Photographs and reproductions enhance the text. Chronology, Further Reading, and Index.

715. Katz, Welwyn Wilton. **Out of the Dark**. New York: Margaret K. McElderry, 1996. 192p. $16. ISBN 0-689-80947-6. 6-9

Ben Elliot and his younger brother, Keith, have to move to their father's boyhood home in a tiny Newfoundland village after their mother dies. Ben hates leaving all his friends, and the children in the new town resent his attitude toward them. As he spends time in a nearby Viking settlement, Ben imagines that he is Tor, a Viking shipbuilder. His pretenses become reality in this historical fantasy when Ben finds himself inside the Viking world.

716. Kaye, Tony. **Lech Walesa**. New York: Chelsea House, 1989. 112p. $18.95; $7.95pa. ISBN 1-55546-856-X; 0-7910-0689-1pa. (World Leaders Past and Present). 5 up

Although not able to go to college, Lech Walesa (b. 1943) showed his intelligence and capability in his jobs, and his disgust at labor conditions in Poland made him organize workers to complain. He was fired from three jobs for his social agitations, beginning in 1968. In 1980, he began the Solidarity movement, and for his efforts he won the Nobel Peace Prize in 1983. When Communism failed in 1990, the people of Poland elected him to be their first president. Photographs enhance the text. Further Reading, Glossary, and Index.

717. **Kazakhstan**. Minneapolis, MN: Lerner, 1993. 56p. $19.95. ISBN 0-8225-2815-0. (Then and Now). 5-9

The Mongolian hordes invaded and influenced Kazakhstan for centuries. This text discusses this history and other problems the country now faces in its struggle for success since becoming independent in 1991. Photographs and maps enhance additional information about economics, geography, politics, and ethnography. Glossary and Index.

718. Kellner, Douglas. **Kwame Nkrumah**. New York: Chelsea House, 1987. 112p. $18.95. ISBN 0-87754-546-4. (World Leaders Past and Present). 5 up

Kwame Nkrumah (1909-1972) founded modern Ghana and was a leader in the pan-African movement to promote African unity and overthrow colonial rule. He studied in the United States and England but returned to his country to serve in 1947. He sponsored nonviolent protests which led to his imprisonment, but he was freed in 1951. The Gold Coast obtained sovereignty from the British in 1957 and was renamed Ghana. Nkrumah transformed Ghana into a modern nation, but could not quell its different factions. His programs fought tribalism, but the poor economy and corruption kept many groups from supporting him, and he eventually left office in 1966. He lived in Guinea and died in Rumania. Photographs enhance the text. Chronology, Further Reading, and Index.

719. Kemp, Gene. **The Well**. Chantal Fouracre, illustrator. New York: Faber, 1984. 90p. $11.95. ISBN 0-571-13284-7. 4-6

When Annie's older brother, Tom, tells her that a dragon lives in their well and is invisible to everyone but him, Annie believes him. When she has to start wearing glasses and her sister runs away to London in 1935, Annie feels lonely, and she realizes that Tom's fantasy world satisfies his imagination. As soon as Annie gets her own kitten, however, she enjoys playing with it and Tom and his friends.

720. Kendra, Judith. **Tibetans**. New York: Thomson Learning, 1994. 48p. $24.21. ISBN 1-56847-152-1. (Threatened Cultures). 5-8

Cultures with traditional ways of life unlike anything in the modern world are threatened with extinction when they come face to face with newer, more powerful societies. In 1950, the Chinese invaded Tibet. Since then the Tibetans have struggled to maintain their identity. The text integrates the past and the present as it shows Tibetan customs. A major concern is the continued exile of the greatest Buddhist leader, the Dalai Lama. Glossary, Further Reading, Further Information, and Index.

721. Kent, Deborah. **The Titanic**. Chicago: Childrens Press, 1993. 31p. $17.30; $4.95pa. ISBN 0-516-06672-2; 0-516-06672-2pa. (Cornerstones of Freedom). 3-5

The "nonsinkable" ocean liner *Titanic* sank after sailing in the Atlantic for four days because on April 14, 1912, she collided with an iceberg. The text recounts this situation and tells about some of those involved. Photographs and reproductions appear throughout the text. Index.

722. Kent, Peter, author/illustrator. **A Slice Through a City**. Brookfield, CT: Millbrook Press, 1996. 32p. $16.90. ISBN 0-7613-0039-2. 4-8

The text presents a European city, which resembles London and other places in England, as it might have evolved during the ages. Cross-sections show the site during the times of the Stone Age, the Romans, and later times in history with eleven two-page spreads.

723. Kent, Zachary. **Christopher Columbus**. Chicago: Childrens Press, 1991. 128p. $28.20. ISBN 0-516-03064-7. (The World's Great Explorers). 3-6

With photographs and reproductions, the text presents Columbus's life and his departure from Genoa with three ships on his way to the East. Appendix, Timeline of Events in Columbus's Lifetime, Glossary, Bibliography, and Index.

724. Kent, Zachary. **James Cook**. Chicago: Childrens Press, 1991. 128p. $28.20. ISBN 0-516-03066-3. (The World's Great Explorers). 3-6

James Cook (1728-1779) used the chronometer to help him explore the Pacific Ocean and claim Australia for the British government. He surveyed the coast of Newfoundland and Labrador, watched the Transit of Venus from Tahiti, and explored New Zealand's coast. He left Hawaii from Kealakekua Bay, but a storm forced his return. The natives, disturbed about having to give him more gifts, killed him, and his crew returned to England. Photographs and reproductions augment the text. Timeline, Glossary, Bibliography, and Index.

725. Kent, Zachary. **Marco Polo: Traveler to Central and Eastern Asia**. Chicago: Childrens Press, 1992. 128p. $28.20. ISBN 0-516-43070-X. (The World's Great Explorers). 5-6

Marco Polo (1254-1323) grew up in Venice and left in 1271 to travel with his father to the court of Kubla Khan. They reached the court in present-day Beijing in 1275. Marco Polo became a favorite of the Khan and did not return to his home until 1295. He wrote about his travels and influenced many explorers in the fifteenth and sixteenth centuries.

726.   Kent, Zachary. **World War I: "The War to End Wars."** Springfield, NJ: Enslow, 1994. 128p. $17.95. ISBN 0-89490-523-6. (American War). 6 up

Starting with the sinking of the *Lusitania* in 1915, the text relates the progress of World War, I from its beginning in Sarajevo in August 1914 until its end in November 1918. It presents the major battles starting with the Hindenburg Line marked by the Germans, Belleau Wood, the Marne, Saint-Mihiel, and the Meuse-Argonne offensive. Among the leaders on both sides were Captain Baron Manfred von Richthofen, "The Red Baron"; Sergeant York; General Douglas MacArthur; and General John J. (Black Jack) Pershing. During the war, more than 116,000 American soldiers died, and 4 million more from other nations. Afterward, President Woodrow Wilson tried to start the League of Nations, but American isolationism defeated his plan. Photographs complement the text. Chronology, Notes, Further Reading, and Index.

727.   Kerr, Daisy. **Keeping Clean**. New York: Franklin Watts, 1995. 48p. $14.42. ISBN 0-531-15353-8. 4-7

This text relates a history of bathing, plumbing, and waste removal. Each two-page spread deals with a different time or region as they cover such topics as the ancient world, the Middle Ages, Roman baths, spaceship hygiene, and lavatories on board ships. Illustrations augment the text. Glossary and Index.

728.   Kerr, Judith, author/illustrator. **When Hitler Stole Pink Rabbit**. New York: Putnam, 1972. 192p. $14.95. ISBN 0-698-20182-5. New York: Yearling, 1974. 192p. $3.99pa. ISBN 0-440-49017-0pa. 4-7

Anna's Jewish family leaves Berlin for Switzerland in 1933 after her father disappears. At the border, she has to leave her pink rabbit, her favorite stuffed animal. The family joins her father and goes to France, but as the war comes to France, they escape to England. Anna, age nine when she leaves Berlin, has to learn new languages and attend new schools while her family runs from the war.

729.   Killeen, Richard. **The Easter Rising**. New York: Thomson Learning, 1995. 48p. $22.78. ISBN 1-56847-391-5. (Revolution!). 4-6

In 1916, Ireland's people, led by the Fenians, revolted against British rule. The text tells about this violent bid for freedom after several hundred years of British occupation. Further Reading, Glossary, and Index.

730.   King, Celia. **Seven Ancient Wonders of the World**. San Francisco: Chronicle, 1990. Unpaged. $9.95. ISBN 0-87701-707-7. 3 up

The seven ancient wonders of the world pop up in this book. They are the Pyramids of Egypt, the Pharos lighthouse at Alexandria, the Hanging Gardens of Babylon, the Temple of Diana at Ephesus, the Colossus of Rhodes, the Statue of Zeus at Olympia, and the Mausoleum at Halicarnassus.

731.   King, John. **The Gulf War**. New York: Dillon Press, Macmillan, 1991. 48p. $13.95. ISBN 0-87518-514-2. 5-10

Questions arise as to why the United States fought the Gulf War in 1991. The text looks at geography in the area, history, the role of oil, and Saddam Hussein's Iraq as it asks why Hussein initially invaded Kuwait. The crisis began in August 1990 and escalated to the attack in January 1991. Glossary, Key Events, Further Reading, and Index.

732.   King, John. **Kurds**. New York: Thomson Learning, 1994. 48p. $15.95. ISBN 1-56847-149-1. (Threatened Cultures). 5-8

The text presents three people—one in Turkey, one in Iraq, and one in Iran—who have no homeland. They are Kurds who have been displaced. By addressing the history and politics of these people, the text illustrates the problems they face. Photographs and maps enhance the text. Further Reading, Glossary, and Index.

733.   King, Perry Scott. **Pericles**. New York: Chelsea House, 1988. 112p. $18.95. ISBN 0-87754-547-2. (World Leaders Past and Present). 5 up

Pericles (499-429 B.C.), a general, was such an influential member of the governing council of Athens that his time is called the "age of Pericles." He was the son of Xanthippus, a Greek war hero, and Agariste, a descendent of Cleisthemes, the founder of Athenian democracy. Pericles entered public life when he sponsored the chorus for performances of *The Persians*. He was an orator who advocated democracy and additional rights for the lower classes. In his attempt to establish the Athenian empire, he led Athens into frequent wars against rivals who were unwilling to accept Athenian dominance, and defeated them with naval power. He built the temples on the Acropolis, such as the Parthenon, as monuments to Athenian glory. Photographs and reproductions enhance the text. Chronology, Further Reading, and Index.

734. Kinsey-Warnock, Natalie. **Wilderness Cat**. Mark Graham, illustrator. New York: Dutton, 1992. 32p. $14. ISBN 0-525-65068-7. K-3

When Serena's father tells her that Moses, the cat, cannot move with the family from Vermont to Canada in the late 1700s, she is disappointed. In the Canadian wilderness, they have a hard life trying to find food, but the Indians sometimes supply them. Finally, Serena's father and brother have to go to town to get work so they will have money to survive. Serena and her mother hear a cry at the door while they are gone, and Moses awaits them, hauling a rabbit in his mouth.

735. Kirwan, Anna. **Juliet: A Dream Takes Flight, England, 1339**. Lynne Marshall, illustrator. New York: Simon & Schuster, 1996. 72p. $13; $5.99pa. ISBN 0-689-81137-3; 0-689-80983-2pa. (Girlhood Journeys). 2-6

Juliet, age ten, is the daughter of a gameskeeper in 1339; her best friend Marguerite, age twelve, is the daughter of the lord of the manor. When a stranger arrives in their small English town, Marguerite's father arranges a marriage with him against Marguerite's will, and Juliet helps her devise a plan to break the contract.

736. Kirwan, Anna. **Juliet: Rescue at Marlehead Manor, England, 1340**. Lynne Marshall, illustrator. New York: Simon & Schuster, Aladdin. 1997. 71p. $5.99pa. ISBN 0-689-80987-5pa. (Girlhood Journeys). 3-5

As a maid-in-waiting to a lady in the fourteenth century, Juliet tries to get a message to a woman whose husband has been wrongly imprisoned.

737. Kisling, Lee. **The Fool's War**. New York: HarperCollins, 1992. 166p. $14. ISBN 0-06-020836-8. 5-8

Clemmy, age fifteen, must take charge of the family farm in the Middle Ages after his father dies. The farm, although successful, does not challenge his capabilities, and he becomes involved in various other endeavors. He saves the village idiot from his father's abuse and learns to read Latin with a monk's help. He leaves to serve the king and keeps him from having to fight against "the Turk," Suleiman the Magnificent. A touch of fantasy saves them from the Turks, but the history of the mid-sixteenth century is apparent throughout the tale.

738. Kittredge, Mary. **Marc Antony**. New York: Chelsea House, 1988. 112p. $18.95; $7.95pa. ISBN 0-87754-505-7; 0-7910-0610-7pa. (World Leaders Past and Present). 5 up

Marc Antony (83?-30 B.C.) rose briefly above the political tumult in Rome to become its leader in 44 B.C. He first served in Syria and Egypt and acquired riches enough to buy influence and win election to his first public office in 52 B.C. He took Julius Caesar's position in 44 B.C., and after appropriating Caesar's fortune, gained control of the army and drove Caesar's assassins into exile. Soon, however, he had to share power with Octavian and Lepidus in the Second Triumvirate. In 41 B.C., he met and fell in love with Cleopatra of Alexandria and married her. In 32 B.C., Rome declared war on them, and when Octavian won control in 30 B.C., Antony committed suicide. Reproductions highlight the text. Further Reading, Chronology, and Index.

739. Klein, Robin. **All in the Blue Unclouded Weather**. New York: Viking, 1991. 162p. $11.95. ISBN 0-670-83909-4. 5-9

In rural Australia, after World War II, four sisters, the Melling girls, have individual interests and goals, but have to cope collectively with their cousin's troublemaking. Grace wants to leave home; Heather, age thirteen, acts superior to the others; Cathy wants approval from a wealthy girl in school; and Vivienne, the youngest, hates the hand-me-downs that she must wear. Vivienne decides to spend all her money in a secondhand store on a china plate that matches her mother's wedding plate, and her mother is very pleased with her sacrifice.

740. Klein, Robin. **Dresses of Red and Gold**. New York: Viking 1992. 177p. $12.50. ISBN 0-670-84733-X. 5-9

This sequel to *All in the Blue Unclouded Weather* takes place in the autumn after World War II has ended. The Melling girls continue living in their small Australian town while their father looks for work. One sister has gone to the city to study dressmaking, but Heather, age fourteen, and the younger girls have various experiences; Cathy brags about a large birthday party, which she has to stage when guests show up, and Vivienne stays in the hospital with a tonsillectomy after her elderly roommate dies. Grace comes to visit but looks forward to leaving. Their snobbish cousin comes to visit often without an invitation.

741. Klein, Robin. **The Sky in Silver Lace**. New York: Viking, 1996. 178p. $13.99. ISBN 0-670-86692-X. 5-8

The Melling sisters (Vivienne, Heather, Cathy, and Grace) and their mother, from *All in the Blue Unclouded Weather* and *Dresses of Red and Gold,* have to find a place to live because their father has left home in the midst of marital problems. During this time in the 1940s, they move three times in the suburb of an Australian city. But the dreams of each girl seem a little closer to coming true, and their annoying cousin, Isobel, has an experience that somewhat chastens her irritating attitude.

742. Knight, Theodore. **The Olympic Games**. San Diego, CA: Lucent, 1991. 112p. $12.95. ISBN 1-56006-119-7. (Overview). 3-5

The text gives a history of the Olympic Games, from the first games in Greece through the games in 1988. It highlights some of the records achieved as well as humorous and tragic moments. Because the games have sometimes been a place for political statements, the text also discusses boycotts and terrorism. Bibliography, Glossary, and Index.

743. Kodama, Tatsuharu. **Shin's Tricycle**. Kazuko Hokumen-Jones, translator; Noriyuki Ando, illustrator. New York: Walker, 1995. 34p. $15.95. ISBN 0-8027-8375-9. 2-5

Every August, a father visualizes his son, Shin, riding a red tricycle. But his son, age three, and two other children died when the bomb fell on Hiroshima in August 1945. Shin and his friend were buried with the red tricycle that Shin had just received as an early birthday gift from his uncle. Years later, the children were buried properly and the tricycle was placed on display in the Hiroshima Peace Museum. The illustrations are impressionistic, and the beginning of the book gives the historical background for the subject. The father notes that Shin died so that others could find peace. *IRA Children's Choices* and *Notable Children's Trade Books in the Field of Social Studies*.

744. Koenig, Viviane. **The Ancient Egyptians: Life in the Nile Valley**. Mary Kae LaRose, translator; Veronique Ageorges, illustrator. 1992. Brookfield, CT: Millbrook Press, 1996. 64p. $7.95pa. ISBN 0-7613-0099-6pa. (Peoples of the Past). 5-8

Over 5,000 years ago, the Egyptian culture, which lasted for 2,000 years, began to form. Only in the past two or three centuries has information about this civilization begun to materialize. Archaeologists have found artifacts that have helped them learn something about the towns, the temples, and the tombs of these people. The text discusses the importance of the Nile, daily life, craftsmen and artists, scribes and scholars, and pharaohs. Find Out More, Glossary, and Index.

745. Kogawa, Joy. **Naomi's Road**. Matt Gould, illustrator. New York: Oxford University Press, 1988. 82p. $8.95pa. ISBN 0-19-540547-1pa. 3-6

In the 1940s, while Canada and Japan are at war, Naomi and her older brother are taken from their Vancouver home to an internment camp in British Columbia. Although she endures much hardship and faces prejudice, Naomi keeps hoping that life will soon be different. To escape, she plays with her dolls while her brother plays his flute.

746. Konigsburg, E. L. **A Proud Taste for Scarlet and Miniver**. New York: Atheneum, 1973. 202p. $14.95. ISBN 0-689-30111-1. New York: Dell, 1989. 202p. $3.99pa. ISBN 0-440-47201-6pa. 6 up

As she waits for Henry II to arrive in heaven, Eleanor of Aquitaine (c. 1122-1204) and her companions remember her life. They recall incidents from the twelfth century in France and England in which she was involved. She was the mother of two kings, King Richard the Lionheart and King John, and the wife of two kings, Henry II of England and Louis VII of France. *Phoenix Honor Book*.

747. Koral, April. **An Album of War Refugees**. New York: Franklin Watts, 1989. 96p. $13.90. ISBN 0-531-10765-5. (Picture Album). 6-9

The text presents refugees from different countries who have come to the United States since the Armenians arrived in 1915. The latest refugees have come from Central America. Personal stories bring immediacy to situations in which people have had to leave their homes, usually having lost all material items, in order to save their lives. In their land of exile, they have faced new political, social, and economic problems. Bibliography and Index.

748. Kordon, Klaus. **Brothers Like Friends**. Elizabeth D. Crawford, translator. New York: Philomel, 1992. 206p. $14.95. ISBN 0-399-22137-9. 5 up

Frank, age seven, lives in Berlin, Germany, in the Russian sector during 1950. His two favorite things are his half-brother, Burkie the soccer star, and his own dream world. His life changes, however, when his mother decides to marry a man who has little interest in the children and his brother dies from an unusual injury in a soccer game. Fortunately, he has kindly neighbors who try to support him. *German Youth Literature Award Runner-up*.

749. Koslow, Philip. **Ancient Ghana: The Land of Gold**. New York: Chelsea House, 1995. 63p. $14.95; $7.95pa. ISBN 0-7910-3126-8; 0-7910-2941-7pa. (The Kingdoms of Africa). 3-6

The civilization in ancient Ghana flourished between the eighth and twelfth centuries; modern archaeologists and historians obtained information about it through archaeological digs and from *griot* stories. The gold trade and the spread of Islam had great influence on the society. Photographs and maps augment the text. Chronology, Further Reading, Glossary, and Index.

750. Koslow, Philip. **Asante**. New York: Chelsea House, 1996. 64p. $14.95; $7.95pa. ISBN 0-7910-3140-3; 0-7910-3139-Xpa. (The Kingdoms of Africa). 3-6

The Asante people lived on the west coast of Africa for thousands of years as traders, first with other African tribes and then with Europeans who dealt in glass, iron, weapons, and slaves. They advanced through slave labor, and by the eighteenth century, Kumase was a major city in the world. In the nineteenth century, the Asante were unable to organize other African nations in trying to stop European colonization, although the Asante in Ghana led the fight for African independence in the twentieth century. The text looks at these people and their achievements. Photographs, Chronology, Further Reading, Glossary, and Index.

751. Koslow, Philip. **Centuries of Greatness: The West African Kingdoms 750–1900**. New York: Chelsea House, 1995. 118p. $14.95; $7.95pa. ISBN 0-7910-2266-8; 0-7910-2692-2pa. (Milestones in Black American History). 5 up

Covering over 1,000 years of history in Africa, the text presents information from the Ghanian Empire through the slave trade. Military, economic, and political background helps clarify the history of Africa's groups, and several first-person accounts give an immediacy to some of the information. Black-and-white photographs show the area. Further Reading, Chronology, and Index.

752. Koslow, Philip. **Dahomey: The Warrior Kings**. New York: Chelsea House, 1996. 63p. $15.95; $8.95pa. ISBN 0-7910-3137-3; 0-7910-3138-1pa. (The Kingdoms of Africa). 5-8

In the seventeenth and eighteenth centuries, Dahomey was a powerful West African kingdom. The five chapters cover its history from the establishment of the empire; the rule of the warring kings; the kingdom's political and soical structure; to its culture, religion, art, and technology. The rulers of Dahomey prospered by trading slaves, and the text covers this aspect of the history. Photographs, Chronology, Further Reading, Glossary, and Index.

753. Koslow, Philip. **El Cid**. New York: Chelsea House, 1993. 111p. $18.95. ISBN 0-7910-1239-5. (Hispanics of Achievement). 5 up

As Spain's national hero, Rodrigo Díaz (d. 1099) was given the name "El Cid" (derived from the Arabic word for "lord") for his exploits. In the eleventh century, at age seventeen, he took command of the Castilian army. Later, King Alfonso VI banished him, but during fifteen years of exile, he led a private army to victories over Christians and Muslims alike. In 1094, he captured Valencia and became its ruler. Then he crushed a Muslim army on the plains of Cuarte, the beginning of the "Reconquest" to reclaim land from Muslims. Photographs and reproductions enhance the text. Chronology, Further Reading, and Index.

754. Koslow, Philip. **Yorubaland: The Flowering of Genius**. New York: Chelsea House, 1996. 64p. $14.95; $7.95pa. ISBN 0-7910-3131-4; 0-7910-3132-2pa. (The Kingdoms of Africa). 3-6

Around the fourth century A.D., the Yoruba people began to settle in what is now southwestern Nigeria, and Ile Ife emerged as the spiritual center. Before the sixteenth century, Yoruban sculpture in terra-cotta and bronze was well developed. In the late sixteenth century, Oyo began to emerge as the dominant state, and it later began to trade with the Europeans, including slaves. In 1730, the Dahomey rulers began to pay tribute. By the early nineteenth century, a holy war had begun with the Fulani Muslims. From 1878 to 1893, a war among the Yorubaland states led to British occupation, and they became part of the colony of Nigeria, which did not achieve its independence until 1960. Pictures of Yoruban artwork complement the text. Chronology, Further Reading, Glossary, and Index.

755. Kossman, Nina. **Behind the Border**. New York: Lothrop, Lee & Shepard, 1994. 96p. $14. ISBN 0-688-13494-7. 4-7

Nina's family decides to leave Russia in the 1960s, but her teacher hears about it before they get permission and calls Nina's father a traitor. Nina has been taught to love Lenin and to fear foreign tourists who might put a small bomb in candy or chewing gum. When she loses her beach ball on the Black Sea, it floats behind the border where she cannot go to retrieve it. When the teacher says that Nina's father will die of a heart attack on the plane, Nina realizes that the teacher spreads lies. Notes.

756. Kramer, Ann, and Simon Adams. **Exploration and Empire: Empire-Builders, European Expansion and the Development of Science**. New York: Warwick Press, Franklin Watts, 1990. 48p. $13.90. ISBN 0-531-19074-9. (Historical Atlas). 3-8

The text looks at world history from the Renaissance to the Industrial Revolution in five chapters, the first establishing the world situation in 1450 and the others presenting different regions of the world. Topics include the development of printing, the roles of women, slavery, the end of the Aztec and Incan empires, growth of worldwide trade, early settlement of the Americas, the rise of the Chinese and Japanese empires, European expansion, and the growth of science. Illustrations enhance the text. Index.

757. Kramer, Stephen. **Theodoric's Rainbow**. New York: W. H. Freeman, 1995. 32p. $17.95. ISBN 0-7267-6603-5. K-4

Rainbows fascinated Theodoric of Freiburg (1250-c. 1310), a medieval friar. The story looks at his scientific investigations as he attempted to discover what caused rainbows. *Notable Children's Trade Books in the Field of Social Studies*.

758. Krensky, Stephen. **Breaking into Print: Before and After the Invention of the Printing Press**. Bonnie Christensen, illustrator. Boston: Little, Brown, 1996. 32p. $15.95. ISBN 0-316-50376-2. 2-5

The arrival of the printing press transformed society. Before its invention, people could write little more than their names, and they had to memorize information because books were too expensive for most people to own. Monks hand-lettered the books, and one book took many months to copy. The text looks at the changes that occurred in society because of the printing press. The History of Printing.

759. Kristy, Davida. **Coubertin's Olympics: How the Games Began**. Minneapolis, MN: Lerner, 1995. 128p. $17.21. ISBN 0-8225-3327-8. 5 up

Baron Pierre de Coubertin (1863-1937) decided to reestablish the Olympics, last held in A.D. 388 in Greece, more than 1,500 years later. He was successful in 1896. He gave speeches, arranged alliances, and organized an international conference on amateur sports where he slyly changed the topic to the Olympics. Not given recognition in 1896, he was eventually named President for Life of the Olympic Games. The torch ritual began in 1936, and it took twelve days to transport the torch from Olympia, Greece, to Berlin, Germany. De Coubertin seems to have sacrificed his personal life for this dream that he made into reality. Sources of Information and Index. *New York Public Library Books for the Teen Age*.

760. Kristy, Davida. **George Balanchine: American Ballet Master**. Minneapolis, MN: Lerner, 1996. 128p. $17.21. ISBN 0-8225-4951-4. (Lerner Biographies). 5 up

Gyorgy Balanchivadze (1904-1983) never wanted to be a dancer, and after his mother enrolled him in ballet school, he ran away. Yet he returned and discovered that the rigorous training gave him ideas for new movements and new stories to tell through dance. Later he traveled throughout Europe, where he met an American who thought that Americans would like ballet. He changed his Russian name to George Balanchine and created popular dances for Broadway, film, and the circus before forming his own ballet company. The text looks at his life and his accomplishments. Sources, Bibliography, and Index.

761. Krull, Kathleen. **Lives of the Artists: Masterpieces, Messes (and What the Neighbors Thought)**. Kathryn Hewitt, illustrator. San Diego, CA: Harcourt Brace, 1995. 96p. $19. ISBN 0-15-200103-4. 4-8

Vignettes on artists, arranged chronologically, give interesting insights into their lives and sometimes their relationships to each other. The artists are Leonardo da Vinci (Italy, 1452-1519), Michelangelo Buonarroti (Italy, 1475-1564), Peter Bruegel (Netherlands, 1525-1569), Sofonisba Anguissola who served King Philip II of Spain although Italian (1532-1625), Rembrandt van Rijn (Holland, 1606-1669), Katsushika Hokusai (Japan, 1760-1849), Mary Cassatt (American relocated in France, 1845-1926), Vincent van Gogh (Holland, 1853-1890), Käthe Kollwitz (Germany, 1867-1945), Henri Matisse (France, 1869-1954), Pablo Picasso (Spain 1881-1973), Marc Chagall (Russia, 1887-1985), Marcel Duchamp (France, 1887-1968), Georgia O'Keeffe (United States, 1887-1986), William H. Johnson (United States, 1901-1970), Salvador Dali (Spain, 1904-1989), Isamu Noguchi (United States, 1904-1988), Diego Rivera (Mexico, 1886-1957), Frida Kahlo (Mexico, 1907-1954), and Andy Warhol (United States, 1928-1987). Artistic Terms, Index of Artists, and For Further Reading and Looking. *IRA Teachers' Choices*, *American Bookseller Pick of the Lists*, and *New York Public Library Books for the Teen Age*.

762. Krull, Kathleen. **Lives of the Athletes: Thrills, Spills (and What the Neighbors Thought)**. Kathryn Hewitt, illustrator. San Diego, CA: Harcourt Brace, 1997. 96p. $19. ISBN 0-15-200806-3. 4-7

In capsule biographies, Krull tells a little about the lives of some international athletes. She includes commentary on Jim Thorpe (1888-1953), Duke Kahanamoku (1890-1968), Babe Ruth (1895-1948), Red Grange (1903-1991), Johnny Weissmuller (1903-1984), Gertrude Ederle (b. 1906), Babe Didrikson Zaharias (1911-1956), Sonja Henie (1912-1969), Jesse Owens (1913-1980), Jackie Robinson (1919-1972), Sir Edmund Hillary (b. 1919), Maurice Richard (b. 1921), Maureen Connolly (1934-1969), Roberto Clemente (1934-1972), Wilma Rudolph (1940-1994), Arthur Ashe (1943-1993), Pete Maravich (1947-1988), Bruce Lee (1940-1973), Pelé (b. 1940), and Flo Hyman (1954-1986). Selected Bibliography.

763. Krull, Kathleen. **Lives of the Musicians: Good Times, Bad Times (and What the Neighbors Thought)**. Kathryn Hewitt, illustrator. San Diego, CA: Harcourt Brace, 1993. 96p. $18.95. ISBN 0-15-248010-2. 4-8

Vignettes on musicians, arranged chronologically, give interesting insights into their lives and sometimes their relationships to each other. The musicians included are Antonio Vivaldi (Italy, 1876-1741), Johann Sebastian Bach (Germany, 1685-1750), Wolfgang Amadeus Mozart (Austria, 1756-1791), Ludwig van Beethoven (Germany, 1770-1827), Frédéric Chopin (Poland, 1810-1849), Giuseppe Verdi (Italy, 1813-1901), Clara Schumann (Germany, 1819-1896),

Stephen Foster (America, 1826-1864), Johannes Brahms (Germany, 1833-1897), Peter Ilich Tchaikovsky (Russia, 1840-1893), William Gilbert (England, 1836-1911) and Arthur Sullivan (England, 1842-1900), Erik Satie (France, 1866-1925), Scott Joplin (America, 1868-1917), Charles Ives (1874-1954), Igor Stravinsky (Russia, 1882-1971), Nadia Boulanger (France, 1887-1979), Sergei Prokofiev (Ukraine, 1891-1953), George Gershwin (America, 1898-1937), and Woody Guthrie (America, 1912-1967). Musical Terms, Index of Composers, and For Further Reading and Listening. *Boston Globe-Horn Book Honor, American Library Association Notable Books for Children, Notable Children's Trade Books in the Field of Social Studies, PEN Center USA West Literary Award, IRA Teachers' Choices, New York Public Library's Books for the Teen Age*, and *Golden Kite Honor*.

764.   Krull, Kathleen. **Lives of the Writers: Comedies, Tragedies (and What the Neighbors Thought)**. Kathryn Hewitt, illustrator. San Diego, CA: Harcourt Brace, 1994. 96p. $19. ISBN 0-15-248009-9. 4 up

Vignettes on writers, arranged chronologically, give interesting insights into their lives and sometimes their relationships to each other. Writers covered are Murasaki Shikibu (Japan, 973?-1025?), Miguel de Cervantes (Spain, 1547-1616), William Shakespeare (England, 1564-1616), Jane Austen (England, 1775-1817), Hans Christian Anderson (Denmark, 1805-1875), Edgar Allan Poe (America, 1809-1849), Charles Dickens (England, 1812-1870), Charlotte Brontë (England, 1816-1855) and Emily Brontë (England, 1818-1848), Emily Dickinson (America, 1830-1886), Louisa May Alcott (America, 1832-1888), Mark Twain (America, 1835-1910), Frances Hodgson Burnett (England, 1849-1924), Robert Louis Stevenson (Scotland, 1850-1894), Jack London (America, 1876-1916), Carl Sandburg (America, 1878-1967), E. B. White (America, 1899-1985), Zora Neale Hurston (America, 1901?-1960), Langston Hughes (1902-1967), and Isaac Bashevis Singer (Poland and America, 1904-1991). Literary Terms, Index of Writers, and For Further Reading and Writing. *American Bookseller Pick of the Lists, NCTE Notable Children's Trade Books in the Language Arts*, and *IRA Teachers' Choices*.

765.   Krupp, Robin Rector, author/illustrator. **Let's Go Traveling**. New York: Morrow, 1992. Unpaged. $15. ISBN 0-688-08989-5. 3-5

With illustrations of postcards, diary entries, word lists, photographs, and maps, the text presents sites of ancient civilization. They include the prehistoric caves of France at Lascaux, Avebury and Stonehenge in England, the pyramids of Egypt, the Mayan temples of Mexico, Machu Picchu in Peru, and the Great Wall of China.

766.   Kuckreja, Madhavi. **Prince Norodom Sihanouk**. New York: Chelsea House, 1990. 110p. $18.95. ISBN 1-55546-851-9. (World Leaders Past and Present). 5 up

The leader of the Southeast Asian nation of Cambodia, who freed it from France without war, is Prince Norodom Sihanouk (b. 1922). He tried to keep Cambodia on a neutral course, but the war in Vietnam moved into his country, and Pol Pot's Khmer Rouge rebels overthrew him in 1970. He watched from abroad as war tore his nation, but he had no power to stop the rebels as they killed over 2 million people through execution or overwork. In 1979, Vietnam drove out the Khmer Rouge, and for ten years, Sihanouk allied with Pol Pot's murderers. Photographs enhance the text. Chronology, Further Reading, and Index.

767.   Kudlinski, Kathleen V. **Marie: An Invitation to Dance, Paris, 1775**. Lyn Durham, illustrator. New York: Simon & Schuster, 1996. 72p. $13; $5.99pa. ISBN 0-689-81139-X; 0-689-80985-9pa. (Girlhood Journeys). 2-6

Marie lives in Paris during 1775 where she wants to become a ballerina. Because her family has little money, she has no choice but to attend a convent school, get married, and have children. She has a chance to change her situation when a person who could support her as a patron sees her dance.

768.   **Kyrgyzstan**. Minneapolis, MN: Lerner, 1993. 56p. $19.95. ISBN 0-8225-2814-2. (Then and Now). 5-9

The Kyrgyz (or Kirghiz), a nomadic, Turkic-speaking, Sunni Muslim people with Mongol strains, comprise a little over half the population of Kyrgyzstan. Their huge differences from their twentieth-century captors, the Soviet Union communists, along with other problems, are the focus of this text covering the history, economics, geography, and politics of the country. Maps and photographs complement the text. Glossary and Index.

L

769. Lafferty, Peter. **Archimedes**. New York: Bookwright Press, Franklin Watts, 1991. 48p. $17.71. ISBN 0-531-18403-X. (Pioneers of Science). 4-6

Archimedes (287?-212 B.C.), a Greek mathematician and scientist, discovered formulas for the area and volume of several geometric figures, applied geometry to hydrostatics and mechanics, devised various mechanisms (such as the Archimedean screw), and discovered the principle of buoyancy. The text looks at his life from a historical context, with illustrations and diagrams. Chronology, Glossary, Bibliography, and Index.

770. Lampton, Christopher. **Epidemic**. Brookfield, CT: Millbrook Press, 1992. 64p. $13.40. ISBN 1-56294-126-7. (Disaster Book). 4-6

In a discussion about the start of epidemics and how they spread, the text recounts some of the most serious epidemics, with emphasis on the bubonic plague of the mid-fourteenth century. Although the text mentions AIDS, it does not dwell on it as a modern-day plague. Bibliography and Index.

771. Landau, Elaine. **The Curse of Tutankhamen**. Brookfield, CT: Millbrook Press, 1996. 48p. $14.90. ISBN 0-7613-0014-7. (Mysteries of Science). 4-7

Landau offers a variety of causes for the so-called "curse" on those who went into Tutankhamen's Egyptian tomb. Although Lord Carnarvon and at least six other people suffered tragedies afterward, others did not. The possibilities that Landau offers make this speculative subject more intriguing. Glossary, Notes, and Index.

772. Landau, Elaine. **Yeti: Abominable Snowman of the Himalayas**. Brookfield, CT: Millbrook Press, 1993. 47p. $14.40. ISBN 1-56294-349-9. (Mysteries of Science). 3-6

The first account of the *yeti,* or Abominable Snowman of the Himalayas, was published in 1832. Then, in 1938, a British explorer reported that a *yeti* had rescued him from certain death. In 1951, Erick Shipton took photographs of footprints in the snow. The existence of the *yeti* is still unproven, but the possibility continues to intrigue. Photographs enhance the text. For Further Reading, Glossary, and Index.

773. Langley, Andrew. **Discovering the New World: The Voyages of Christopher Columbus**. Paul Crompton, illustrator. New York: Chelsea House, 1994. 32p. $14.95. ISBN 0-7910-2821-6. (Great Explorers). 4-8

The text presents Columbus's life and his desire to go east. It describes the process of setting out from Spain and what life would have been like aboard the Santa Maria. It also covers Columbus's second and third voyages. Glossary and Index.

774. Langley, Andrew. **Exploring the Pacific: The Expeditions of James Cook**. David McAllister, illustrator. New York: Chelsea House, 1994. 32p. $14.95. ISBN 0-7910-2819-4. (Great Explorers). 4-8

As a boy, James Cook (1728-1779) wanted to be a sailor, but his father discouraged him and urged him to become a shopkeeper. He left, learned about the sea, joined the Royal Navy, and was determined to be a success. In 1758, he first commanded a warship. He made important trips in the Pacific Ocean, was the father of Antarctic exploration, and mapped coastlines and islands. He tried to be honorable to the native peoples he met, and he became distressed that Europeans had brought diseases that destroyed many of the natives. He claimed Australia as a British colony. Glossary and Index.

775. Langley, Andrew. **The Industrial Revolution**. New York: Viking, 1994. 48p. $15.99. ISBN 0-670-85835-8. 6-8

In two-page spreads, Langley discusses some of the many subjects constituting the Industrial Revolution. In addition to typical illustrations are four transparent overlays which, when lifted, reveal the inside of a coal miner's home, a railroad station, a cotton factory, and the crew's quarters on an immigrant ship. Beginning with the world in 1700, Langley continues with other topics: the need to grow more food, machines on land, spinning and weaving, cotton, iron, coal, steam, inventions, canals, railroads, the joining of continents, country life, town life, factories, health and disease, social reform, riots and hunger, immigrants, art and architecture, and electric power. Key Dates, Glossary, and Index.

776. Langley, Andrew. **Medieval Life**. Geoff Dann and Geoff Brightling, photographs. New York: Knopf, 1996. 63p. $19. ISBN 0-679-98077-6. (Eyewitness Books). 5-8

The profuse illustrations augmenting the text give an overview of medieval life. Topics covered in double-page spreads include the structure of society, daily life in different societal levels, the role and influence of religion, health and disease, jobs, and culture and the arts. Index.

777.   Langley, Andrew, and Philip de Souza. **The Roman News**. New York: Candlewick, 1996. 32p. $15.99. ISBN 0-7636-0055-5. 5 up

The approach to the Romans through newspaper style highlights fashion, sports, trade, food, and the military. Each page has headlines, sometimes with classifieds advertising such things as reusable wax tablets. Highly readable and slightly sensational, the news under a headline such as "Caesar Stabbed" seems much more accessible than in a textbook. Maps and Index.

778.   Langone, John. **In the Shogun's Shadow: Understanding a Changing Japan**. Steve Parton, illustrator. Boston: Little, Brown, 1994. 202p. $16.95. ISBN 0-316-51409-8. 6-9

For Americans, understanding a culture as different as Japanese society takes a change in mindset. Langone gives pointers in his text, divided into three main parts: Japan's geography and history, modern Japanese society, and United States-Japanese relations. Within these general areas, he discusses religion, daily life, sex and sex roles, work, youth, and cultural expectations. An appendix gives information on spoken and unspoken language. Notes and Index.

779.   Langstaff, John, selector and editor. **"I Have a Song to Sing O!": An Introduction to the Songs of Gilbert and Sullivan**. Emma Chichester Clark, illustrator. New York: Margaret K. McElderry, 1994. 74p. $17.95. ISBN 0-689-50591-4. 4 up

This collection of songs includes both piano and vocal scores for ten songs from Gilbert and Sullivan musicals, including *The Mikado* and *The Pirates of Penzance*.

780.   Lankford, Mary. **Quinceañera: A Latina's Journey to Womanhood**. Brookfield, CT: Millbrook Press, 1994. 47p. $15.40. ISBN 1-56294-363-4. 4-7

Although the text describes the celebration of *quinceañera* in the life of a modern girl, the ritual is ages old, tracing back to the ancient native American cultures of Central and Latin America, particularly Mexico. After the Spanish conquered the Aztecs in 1521, the traditions of the Spaniards' Catholic religion meshed with the initiation rites of the Aztecs. At fifteen, a young woman had to choose between a lifetime of service to the church or marriage. The quinceañera marks the passage from childhood to adulthood and affirms religious faith. Photographs illustrate the text. Further Reading and Index. *New York Public Library Books for the Teen Age.*

781.   Lantier, Patricia, and James Bentley. **Albert Schweitzer: The Doctor Who Devoted His Life to Africa's Sick.** Milwaukee, WI: Gareth Stevens, 1991. 68p. $16.95. ISBN 0-8368-0457-0. (People Who Made a Difference). 3-6

Albert Schweitzer (1875-1965) was an accomplished organist (and organ builder), theologian, philosopher, and physician. He became a minister, but decided that he wanted to become a missionary in Africa, so he retrained as a doctor. He lived in Lambaréné, the Republic of Gabon, for fifty years, and built a hospital there. By the end of his service, the hospital had grown to seventy rows of huts and treated up to 600 people each day. In 1952, Schweitzer won the Nobel Peace Prize and used the money to build a hospital section for leprosy patients. To Find Out More, List of New Words, Important Dates, and Index.

782.   Lantier, Patricia, and David Winner. **Desmond Tutu: Religious Leader Devoted to Freedom**. Milwaukee, WI: Gareth Stevens, 1991. 68p. $16.95. ISBN 0-8368-0459-7. (People Who Made a Difference). 3-6

Desmond Tutu (b. 1931) grew up in South Africa. He was smart enough to get into medical school but did not have the money to attend. A priest who had helped him influenced him to become an Episcopal priest. When he went to England, he saw that people of all races could live together without one having power over the other, and he began working to promote equality in South Africa. He had to let the rest of the world know what was happening, and in 1984 he won the Nobel Peace Prize for his efforts. Organizations, Books, List of New Words, Important Dates, and Index.

783.   Larroche, Caroline. **Corot from A to Z**. Claudia Bedrick, translator. New York: Peter Bedrick, 1996. 59p. $14.95. ISBN 0-87226-477-7. 4-10

Jean-Baptiste-Camille Corot's life (1796-1875) and work in chapters titled with thematic words in alphabetical order describe him in an artistic context as well as a historical setting. The table of contents exhibits miniature reproductions of Corot's paintings which show his style.

784.   Lasker, Joe, author/illustrator. **The Great Alexander the Great**. New York: Puffin, 1990. Unpaged. $13.95. ISBN 0-670-34841-4. 1-4

The horse Bucephalus would not allow anyone to ride him, and no one believed that Alexander (356-323 B.C.) would be any more successful than others who had tried. Alexander's father, Philip of Macedonia, said he would give the horse to Alexander if he could ride it. Alexander did because he turned the horse around so it would not fear its own shadow. From the age of twenty, Alexander led his men as king of Macedonia throughout the known world and into the unknown country of India. He united all of Greece and swept into Persia. When seventy cities were named Alexandria, few nations remained to be conquered. Alexander, although young, became ill and died.

785. Lasker, Joe, author/illustrator. **A Tournament of Knights**. New York: Crowell, 1986. 32p. $12.95. ISBN 0-690-04541-7. 1-3

The text describes a medieval tournament where the knights test themselves against each other. It shows the tent raising and the gatherings where knights who lost often had to sacrifice horse or armor or land. The story follows a young knight who must defend himself and his father's title against an older and more experienced combatant. He wins only because the other knight's armor overheats in the sun. *IRA Children's Choices, IRA Teachers' Choices,* and *Redbook Picture Book Award.*

786. Lasky, Kathryn. **Days of the Dead**. Christopher G. Knight, photographs. New York: Hyperion, 1994. 48p. $15.95. ISBN 0-7868-2018-7. 3-6

In Mexico, the days of the dead go from October 31 to November 3. Photographs show the various parts of the ritual in Mexico. At the end of the text, other cultures and their celebrations of the dead are listed. Glossary.

787. Lasky, Kathryn. **The Librarian Who Measured the Earth**. Kevin Hawkes, illustrator. Boston: Little, Brown, 1994. 48p. $16.95. ISBN 0-316-51526-4. 2-5

Over 2,000 years ago, the Greek Eratosthenes, from Cyrene on the coast of Africa, measured the earth. His calculation was only 200 miles off that of recent measurements made with highly technical instruments, though he used only camels, plumb lines, and angles of shadows. He studied in Athens, made lists of events, and wrote a comedy, a history, and a book on the constellations. Then he went to Alexandria to serve as tutor to Ptolemy III's son, Philopator. Soon after he arrived, Eratosthenes became the head librarian of the greatest library in the world. Bibliography.

788. Lasky, Kathryn. **The Night Journey**. Trina S. Hynam, illustrator. New York: Viking, 1986. 152p. $12.95. ISBN 0-670-80935-7. New York: Penguin, 1986. 152p. $4.99pa. ISBN 0-14-032048-2pa. 5-9

Not until she is thirteen does Rache hear the story of Jewish pogroms and her grandmother's escape from Russia with her family in 1900. Her grandmother hid under chicken crates, paraded as a Purim player, and crossed the border with her cookies. The cookies held the family's gold. *National Jewish Awards, American Library Association Notable Books for Children, Association of Jewish Libraries Award,* and *Sydney Taylor Book Award.*

789. Lattimore, Deborah Nourse, author/illustrator. **The Dragon's Robe**. New York: Trophy, 1993. 32p. $4.95pa. ISBN 0-06-443321-8pa. K-3

A poor young weaver in twelfth-century China, Kwan Yin, stops to help the keeper of the Royal Dragon's shrine while she is on her way to the Emperor's Palace to see if he has work for her. She follows two lords, one who has been given rice and another who has been given a sword, and watches them disobey the keeper's orders. She weaves a robe for the dragon, as the keeper has asked. When the Tartar khan tries to take it from her, the dragon destroys him instead. The keeper reveals himself to be the Emperor and acknowledges her loyalty.

790. Lattimore, Deborah Nourse, author/illustrator. **The Sailor Who Captured the Sea: A Story of the Book of Kells**. New York: HarperCollins, 1991. 32p. $15.95. ISBN 0-06-023710-4. K-3

In 804, three brothers in different trades leave Dublin because of Viking raiders. They take refuge in the monastery of St. Columba, where the older two men toil over the Book of Kells until warring kings make them stop and work for them instead. The youngest remains, and because he saves a Viking boy from drowning, the Vikings allow him to finish the book. The illustrations give a sense of the illuminations in the Book of Kells.

791. **Latvia**. Minneapolis, MN: Lerner, 1992. 56p. $19.95. ISBN 0-8225-2802-9. (Then and Now). 5-9

The text covers the history, economics, geography, politics, ethnography, and possible future of Latvia, a Baltic country that the Soviet Union annexed in 1940. Latvia gained its freedom in 1991. Maps and photographs complement the text. Glossary and Index.

792. Layton, George. **The Swap**. New York: Putnam, 1997. 192p. $16.95. ISBN 0-399-23148-X. 5-8

The narrator, a boy of eleven living in northern England during the 1950s, undergoes the difficulties of growing up from being taunted by his classmates for his beliefs. After spending a week in London on an exchange with a wealthy family, he regrets his working-class background but eventually realizes that he is happy with his mother and his aunt in their town.

793. Lazo, Caroline. **Elie Wiesel**. New York: Dillon Press, 1994. 64p. $13.95. ISBN 0-87518-636-X. (Peacemakers). 4-8

When Elie Wiesel (b. 1928) lived in Sighet, Rumania, after the Nazis started rounding people up and taking them away, a man returned to town and said that the Nazis had killed everyone. He had been shot in the leg and had pretended to be dead when he fell into the pit with the others, but he escaped after the Nazis left. No one believed the man's stories, even after the Nazis returned. Wiesel went into a concentration camp as a young man with his father and helplessly watched his father die, a situation he wrote about in *Night*. His father's last questions were "Where is God? Where is Man?" The text gives a brief overview of anti-Semitism before telling Wiesel's story. He survived, but 6 million Jews did not, and Wiesel continues to write about them. He received the Nobel Peace Prize in 1986. For Further Reading and Index.

794. Lazo, Caroline. **Lech Walesa**. New York: Dillon Press, 1993. 64p. $13.95. ISBN 0-87518-525-8. (Peacemakers). 4-8

Lech Walesa (b. 1943) risked his job and his life by organizing workers in the Gdansk, Poland, shipyards. In 1980, he called the workers to join in the Solidarity movement, an effort to gain better working conditions in their Communist country. When he won the Nobel Peace Prize, he could not go to accept it for fear that he would not be allowed to reenter Poland. After the fall of communism in 1989, Walesa was elected the first president of Poland. For Further Reading and Index.

795. Lazo, Caroline. **Mother Teresa**. New York: Dillon Press, 1993. 64p. $13.95. ISBN 0-87518-559-2. (Peacemakers). 4-8

Mother Teresa (1910-1997) founded the Missionaries of Charity after she left her Albanian home as a teenager to join a convent and teach the poor. Her work, which continues today, led to the Nobel Peace Prize in 1979. Photographs, For Further Reading, and Index.

796. Lazo, Caroline. **Rigoberta Menchú**. New York: Dillon Press, 1994. 64p. $13.95. ISBN 0-87518-619-X. (Peacemakers). 4 up

Rigoberta Menchú realized the power of the spoken word as a young girl of Mayan ancestry in Guatemala during the 1970s. She saw that the Indian dialects allowed the people to talk without the Spanish-speaking minority of wealthy landowners and military leaders understanding them. However, the poor could not understand the Spanish either. She taught herself Spanish and began to try to secure human rights for the Indians of Guatemala. Her parents were murdered when she was a teenager, and she went into exile in Mexico in 1981 to keep herself alive. From there she worked, and she won the Nobel Peace Prize for her efforts in 1992. For Further Reading and Index.

797. Lazo, Caroline. **The Terra Cotta Army of Emperor Qin**. New York: New Discovery, Macmillan, 1993. 80p. $14.95. ISBN 0-02-754631-4. (Timestop). 5-9

In 1974, men digging near the city of Xian in China unearthed the life-size figure of an ancient warrior. What they subsequently discovered was a field of over 7,500 warriors made of terra-cotta, each one individually created. Some held spears, others knelt with their bows and arrows, and still others rode horseback. They had been in the same spot for over 2,000 years, guarding the tomb of China's first emperor, Qin. The text looks at the story of Qin and the creation of this army. For Further Reading and Index.

798. Lazo, Caroline Evensen. **Mahatma Gandhi**. New York: Dillon Press, 1993. 64p. $13.95. ISBN 0-87518-526-6. (Peacemakers). 4 up

Mahatma Gandhi (1869-1948) returned to India after education abroad and eventually became its leader. His policy of nonviolent resistance helped to free his country from British rule. He was assassinated by one of his countrymen. Bibliography and Index.

799. Leder, Jane Mersky. **A Russian Jewish Family**. Alan Leder, photographs. Minneapolis, MN: Lerner, 1996. 64p. $21.50; $8.95pa. ISBN 0-8225-3401-0; 0-8225-9744-6pa. (Journey Between Two Worlds). 3-6

Although not a history book, the text includes the history of the Jewish people in Russia as a background for understanding the reasons that Jewish families have chosen to immigrate. Photographs and personal experiences explain Jewish social and religious traditions and how Jews have had to adapt to a new culture in order to survive as immigrants in a new world. Further Reading.

800. Lee, Kathleen. **Tracing Our Italian Roots**. Santa Fe, NM: John Muir, 1993. 46p. $12.95. ISBN 1-56261-148-8. 1-5

The text looks at the reasons people left Italy in the early part of the twentieth century to come to the United States. The book's two parts, the Old World and the New World, give an overview with two-page looks at topics such as crossing the Atlantic, Ellis Island, family life, prejudices faced, achievements in America, and famous people of Italian descent who have contributed to American culture. Archival photographs highlight the text. Index.

801. Leitner, Isabella, with Irving A. Leitner. **The Big Lie: A True Story**. Judy Pedersen, illustrator. New York: Scholastic, 1992. 79p. $13.95. ISBN 0-590-45569-9. 3-6

In a straightforward, nonsensational account, Leitner tells how she, her mother, her brother, and her four sisters were herded into a ghetto and then taken to Auschwitz in 1944. Her mother and youngest sister go to the left (to be gassed) and the others go to the right to be stripped and shaved. They escape during a forced march and take shelter with Russian troops, but another sister dies in Bergen-Belsen. The rest finally get to America where their father waits, having failed to get papers for all before they were originally deported. Afterword. *Notable Children's Trade Books in the Field of Social Studies.*

802. Leitner, Isabella, and Irving A. Leitner. **Isabella: From Auschwitz to Freedom**. 1978. New York: Anchor, 1994. 240p. $12.95pa. ISBN 0-385-47318-4pa. 6 up

In the text, Leitner describes the deportation of her family to Auschwitz where they were imprisoned for a year. Her sister and mother went to their deaths as soon as they arrived, and the rest of the family of four sisters had to struggle to survive. They also were sent to the concentration camp at Birnbaumel. The Russians rescued them, and they emigrated to New York. What one finds is that in the despair perhaps the only saving emotion can be love.

803. Lessem, Don. **The Iceman**. New York: Crown, 1994. 32p. $15. ISBN 0-517-59596-6. 3-6

In 1991, two hikers found a human body sticking out of the ice in the mountains between Austria and Italy. Archaeologists discovered that the frozen man was over 5,000 years old. The examination of his body has helped reveal what life was like during the Age of Copper in the area where he was found. The text, with photographs, records the results of the find. Index.

804. Levin, Betty. **Brother Moose**. New York: Greenwillow, 1990. 214p. $12.95. ISBN 0-688-09266-7. 5-9

Louisa and Nell meet in a Canadian orphanage, which they leave in the 1870 to live with people who have offered to take them. Various problems erupt after they separate. Louisa goes with an old Indian and his grandson to search for Nell's benefactor.

805. Levine, Arthur A. **All the Lights in the Night**. James E. Ransome, illustrator. New York: Tambourine, 1991. 32p. $16. ISBN 0-688-10107-0. K-3

An older brother sends Moses and another brother money for travel from Russia to Palestine to join him. They leave behind the conflicts with the tsar's soldiers, who blame the Jews for all their problems, and sail toward their new home. They take a small lamp with enough oil for one night of Hanukkah, but they have to give it to the ship's captain as extra fare. They look in the sky and see that all the stars can become their lamps.

806. Levine, Ellen. **Anna Pavlova: Genius of the Dance**. New York: Scholastic, 1995. 132p. $14.95. ISBN 0-590-44304-6. 6-9

Anna Pavlova, born the daughter of a laundress in 1881, saw a ballet when she was eight and knew from then on that she must dance. Not able to enter the ballet school in St. Petersburg, Russia, until she was ten, she quickly learned and excelled. Throughout her life she wanted to dance for everyone, not just the wealthy who could afford the front-row seats. She traveled extensively, usually accompanied by a troupe that performed with her. During the second half of her life, she spent much time abroad teaching students and trying to make her dance a gift. She even danced when ill. When she could no longer go on stage, her friends knew that her illness was serious, and she died in 1931. Glossary, Selected Bibliography, and Index.

807. Levinson, Nancy Smiler. **Christopher Columbus: Voyager to the Unknown**. New York: Lodestar, Dutton, 1990. 118p. $17. ISBN 0-525-67292-3. 5-9

Illustrated with reproductions of paintings and manuscripts from museums throughout the world, Levinson presents Columbus, noting the influence of his reading—Toscanelli and Marco Polo—on his decision to find a route to the riches of the east. Levinson shows the relationships of Columbus to Isabel and her cold husband, Ferdinand, and to the people with whom he sailed, in the well-documented text. Clear maps of the four voyages show exactly where Columbus's logs indicate that he stopped. Chronology, Articles of Capitulation, Letter of Introduction, Crew on First Voyage, Suggested Reading, and Index.

808. Levitin, Sonia. **Journey to America**. Charles Robinson, illustrator. 1970. New York: Atheneum, 1993. 160p. $13.95. ISBN 0-689-31829-4. New York: Macmillan, 1986. 160p. $3.95pa. ISBN 0-689-71130-1pa. 3-7

In 1938, Lisa's father goes on a "vacation" to Switzerland from their home in Berlin. He then leaves for America, and Lisa, her two sisters, and her mother wait for him to send for them. Because the Nazis will not allow them to take any of their belongings when they hear from Lisa's father, they leave for Switzerland carrying nothing. Then they have to remain in Zurich for almost a year before they can arrange passage to America and reunite. *National Jewish Awards.*

809. Levitin, Sonia. **A Piece of Home**. Juan Wijngaard, illustrator. New York: Dial, 1996. Unpaged. $14.99. ISBN 0-8037-1625-7. K-3

When Gregor's family leaves Russia, each person chooses one thing to bring. His mother chooses the samovar and his father, the small accordion called a *garmoshka*. Gregor wants the blanket that his Great-Grandmother made for him. On the journey, he realizes that his American cousin might laugh at him for such a silly item, but when he arrives, the blanket unites the two.

810. Lewis, Hilda. **The Ship That Flew**. 1939. Chatam, NY: S. G. Phillips, 1958. 246p. $22.95. ISBN 0-87599-067-3. 5-7

When Peter sees a six-inch ship in a shop, he spends all his money to buy it. The ship magically enlarges and carries Peter and his three siblings through time. They have experiences in Asgard, Robin Hood's England, Egypt during the reign of Amenemhot the First, and the time of William the Conqueror. In this historical fantasy, as the children grow up, they travel less frequently; finally, Peter returns the ship and becomes a writer, using his words on which to travel.

811. Lincoln, Margarette. **The Pirate's Handbook: How to Become a Rogue of the High Seas**. New York: Cobblehill, 1995. 29p. $12.99. ISBN 0-525-65209-4. 3-6

Interspersed with ways to make costumes and food related to pirates, the text includes photographs and drawings along with specific information about different kinds of pirates. Among those included are the Muslim corsairs of the sixteenth century, the buccaneers of the seventeenth century, the pirates in East and West Africa of the early eighteenth century, and pirates from the Philippines in the nineteenth century. Additional topics are clothing, provisions, codes of conduct, charts and maps, types of ships such as the schooner and galley, flags, attacks, treasure, punishment, and language. Rogue's Gallery.

812. Linnéa, Sharon. **Raoul Wallenberg: The Man Who Stopped Death**. Philadelphia, PA: Jewish Publication Society, 1993. 151p. $17.95; $9.95pa. ISBN 0-8276-0440-8; 0-8276-0448-3pa. 6 up

Raoul Wallenberg was a Swedish diplomat who went to Budapest, Hungary, during World War II to try to help free the Jews there. He issued passports which he said the Swedish government had authorized for Jews so that they could leave. He also offered diplomatic immunity under the Swedish flag and dared the Nazis to defy him. He disappeared soon after the Soviets came into the city, and stories about his last days are contradictory and uncertain. He was in a prison, but it is uncertain whether he died when the Russians said he did. Index.

813. Liptak, Karen. **Endangered Peoples**. New York: Franklin Watts, 1993. 160p. $13.40. ISBN 0-531-10987-9. (Impact). 6-9

The text examines five ethnic groups around the world who maintain tribal existences and have been studied in the twentieth century. These tribes are the Yanomani of the Amazon rain forest, the San (Bushmen) of the Kalahari Desert, the Bambuti (pygmies) of the Ituri Forest, the Aborigines of Australia, and the Inuits (Eskimos) of the Arctic. Their histories and habits, and the things that threaten them, complete the information. Photographs and drawings enhance the text. Further Reading, Glossary, Notes, and Index.

814. **Lithuania**. Minneapolis, MN: Lerner, 1992. 56p. $19.95. ISBN 0-8225-2804-5. (Then and Now). 5-9

The text covers the history, economics, geography, politics, ethnography, and possible future of Lithuania, including its environmental problems. Maps and photographs complement the text. Glossary and Index.

815. Litowinsky, Olga. **The High Voyage: The Final Crossing of Christopher Columbus**. New York: Delacorte, 1991. 147p. $14.95. ISBN 0-385-30304-1. 5-8

In 1502, Fernando, thirteen, joins his father on another voyage trying to find India. They reach Jamaica instead. Several crew members mutiny against Columbus, but the others defeat them. Columbus eventually gets a ship to sail back to Spain. Fernando decides that he wants to stay in Spain rather than explore the world.

816. Little, Jean. **From Anna**. Joan Sandin, illustrator. New York: HarperCollins, 1972. 208p. $14.89; $3.95pa. ISBN 0-06-023912-3; 0-06-440044-1pa. 4-6

Anna, age nine, has to move from Germany with her family in 1933, and she is concerned about her awkwardness. A doctor in Canada examines her and finds that she has poor eyesight. When she gets glasses, Anna blossoms into a happy young girl.

817. Little, Mimi. **Yoshiko and the Foreigner**. New York: Farrar, Straus & Giroux, 1996. 40p. $16. ISBN 0-374-32448-4. 2-5

Although she knows that she should not speak to foreigners, Yoshiko cannot resist helping a lost American Air Force officer when he tries to ask her a question in Japanese. She begins a friendship with him without telling her family, but they are separated when he receives orders to return to America. He writes to ask her to marry him and also sends her father a letter requesting to marry her. When she tells her father that the Japanese gifts he appreciates came from the American, her father gives his consent. The two marry in 1960.

818. Littlefield, Holly. **Colors of Germany**. Minneapolis, MN: Carolrhoda, 1998. 24p. $14.21; $5.95pa. ISBN 0-87614-887-9; 1-57505-214-8pa. (Colors of the World). K-3

Chapters titled with color names introduce traditions, history, legends, cars, and the fall of the Berlin Wall in 1989. Index.

819.   Littlefield, Holly. **Colors of Japan**. Minneapolis, MN: Carolrhoda, 1997. 24p. $14.21; $5.95pa. ISBN 0-87614-885-2; 1-57505-215-6pa. (Colors of the World). K-3
   Colors become the controlling idea for information about Japan's trains, cities, customs, and history. Index.

820.   Littlesugar, Amy. **Marie in Fourth Position: The Story of Degas' the Little Dancer**. Ian Schoenherr, illustrator. New York: Philomel, 1996. Unpaged. $15.95. ISBN 0-399-22794-6. 1-3
   Marie van Goethem modeled for Edgar Degas's sculpture called *The Little Dancer* so that she could earn money to support her parents. What she finds is that by modeling, she improves her dancing and advances beyond "rat" girl in the Paris Opera chorus.

821.   Llorente, Pilar Molina. **The Apprentice**. Juan Ramon Alonso, translator. New York: Farrar, Straus & Giroux, 1993. 101p. $4.95pa. ISBN 0-374-40432-1pa. 6-9
   Arduino wants to become a painter's apprentice in Florence, Italy, during the Renaissance. He gets the chance, but finds that his dream of painting frescoes does not match the reality of cleaning and mixing pigments. He also finds that the Maestro is keeping the previous apprentice chained in the attic because his talent promised to be greater than the Maestro's. When the Maestro becomes sick, Arduino convinces him to free Donato from the attic and let him complete an important commission. He does, and Donato and Arduino save the Maestro's reputation. A serving woman, also annoyed by various situations, and a duchess show the female point of view and demonstrate that women never had a chance to be apprentices in the Renaissance. *Mildred L. Batchelder Award.*

822.   Lloyd, Dana Ohlmeyer. **Ho Chi Minh**. New York: Chelsea House, 1986. 112p. $18.95. ISBN 0-87754-571-5. (World Leaders Past and Present). 5 up
   Ho Chi Minh (1890-1968) was head of the long struggle to liberate Vietnam from foreign control. He led an army against the French and became president of communist North Vietnam. He traveled to Europe as a young man to request independence from the French at the Versailles Peace conference, but after he was denied, he traveled to the Soviet Union in 1923 to study their revolution and the developing communist system. He returned and defeated the French, with settlement made at the 1954 Geneva Convention. Some think him great; others think of him as betraying his country to communism. Photographs enhance the text. Chronology, Further Reading, and Index.

823.   Llywelyn, Morgan. **Brian Boru: Emperor of the Irish**. Chester Springs, PA: O'Brien Press, Dufor Editions, 1991. 160p. $8.95pa. ISBN 0-86278-230-9pa. 6-9
   In the tenth century, Brian Boru becomes determined to free and rule Ireland by either overcoming or contenting the Viking raiders. As a child, Boru watches the Vikings as they raid his Munster home and kill his mother, brothers, and servants. At Clonmacnois, while studying with the monks, Boru reviews battle plans of Alexander the Great and Julius Caesar and learns ways to build, make music, and do mathematics so that he will be prepared to conquer and rule. His honesty and his commitment earn the respect of thousands who follow him and help him achieve his goal. *Irish Children's Book Trust Book of the Year.*

824.   Llywelyn, Morgan. **Xerxes**. New York: Chelsea House, 1987. 112p. $18.95. ISBN 0-87754-447-6. (World Leaders Past and Present). 5 up
   Xerxes (c. 519-465 B.C.), king of Persia, thought that his empire was the center of civilization. The accounts of his life conflict. Some show that he was easily manipulated and an indecisive coward, and others portray him as a sensitive ruler, reformer, and strong warrior. When he ascended the throne in 486 B.C., he suppressed revolts in Egypt and Marathon. Then he started to invade Greece. Xerxes beat the quickly consolidated Greek city-states at Thermopylae, but mistakenly engaged the Greek fleet at Salamis, where it defeated and disgraced him. As he grew older, he became more involved in court intrigue, annoying his wives and children and irritating his generals enough so that someone murdered him in his chambers. Oddly, Xerxes is probably responsible for the rise of Greek civilization, because his encroachment upon Greek lands seemed to be the only cause that could unite the city-states. Photographs and engravings enhance the text. Chronology, Further Reading, and Index.

825.   Loewen, Nancy. **Beethoven**. Vero Beach, FL: Rourke, 1989. 111p. $22.60. ISBN 0-86592-609-3. (Profiles in Music). 4-7
   When he was only four, Ludwig van Beethoven (1770-1827) began composing his own songs. From that time on, he had a stunning career in music composition and performance. He premiered the ninth of his symphonies, conducting while deaf before an appreciative Viennese audience in 1824. Photographs highlight the text. Glossary, Index, and Listening Choices.

826.   Long, Cathryn. **The Middle East in Search of Peace**. Brookfield, CT: Millbrook Press, 1996. 64p. $16.90. ISBN 0-761-30105-4. (Headliners). 4-8
   The text explores the origins of the Israeli-Arab conflict; previous peace plans; and the peace plan initiated in 1993 between Yitzhak Rabin, then prime minister of Israel, and Yasir Arafat, Palestine Liberation Organization chairman. It includes the peace plan provisions; secret meetings; the *Intifada,* begun in 1987; and *Hamas.* Chronology, For Further Reading, and Index.

827. Lorbiecki, Marybeth. **From My Palace of Leaves in Sarajevo**. Herbert Tauss, illustrator. New York: Dial, 1997. 64p. $14.99. ISBN 0-8037-2033-5. 5-8

Nadja, ten, writes letters to her American cousin Alex before the war begins in Sarajevo, Bosnia. After the war, her letters become more desperate as she begins to hear bombs and guns instead of the music she loves. She has to live without electricity, and the availability of enough food or water is never certain. She keeps hoping that things will be better, and this emotion also fills her letters.

828. Loumaye, Jacqueline. **Chagall: My Sad and Joyous Village**. Veronique Boiry, illustrator; John Goodman, translator. New York: Chelsea House, 1994. 57p. $14.95. ISBN 0-7910-2807-0. (Art for Children). 4-8

Marc Chagall (1887-1985) was born in Russia in Vitebsk, where he began creating his unusual paintings with their dreamlike style. The text, with a story line of two persons discussing Chagall's paintings and his life, gives insight into the man, who had to leave his country, and into his work. He spent the latter half of his life in Nice, France, where the light influenced his work, including stained-glass designs. Color reproductions augment the text. Glossary and Chronology.

829. Loumaye, Jacqueline. **Degas: The Painted Gesture**. Nadine Massart, illustrator; John Goodman, translator. New York: Chelsea House, 1994. 57p. $14.95. ISBN 0-7910-2809-7. (Art for Children). 4-8

Students look at and discuss the life and work of Edgar Degas (1834-1917). By examining his paintings almost as if they were characters themselves, the text reveals the man and his time. Chronology and Glossary.

830. Loumaye, Jacqueline. **Van Gogh: The Touch of Yellow**. Claudine Roucha, illustrator; John Goodman, translator. New York: Chelsea House, 1994. 57p. $14.95. ISBN 0-7910-2817-8. (Art for Children). 4-8

When a child visits Uncle Paul, his uncle introduces him to van Gogh, and they visit places where the paintings are displayed. Reproductions show the variety in van Gogh's work, and information about his life complements the discussion of his paintings and their depictions of the places where he lived. Glossary and Chronology.

831. Loverance, Rowena, and Tim Wood. **Ancient Greece**. New York: Viking, 1993. 48p. $14.99. ISBN 0-670-84754-2. (See Through History). 5-8

See-through illustrations of a town house, public buildings in the Athenian marketplace, an open-air theater, and a warship reveal aspects of ancient Greece. Two-page spreads give information on topics concerning the origin of the Greeks and their land and sea, family life, food and festivals, houses, city-states and government, work, public life, science and philosophy, sports and games, the theater, gods and goddesses, temples and oracles, death and burial, ships, war, and the Greek legacy. Key Dates, Glossary, and Index.

832. Lowry, Lois. **Number the Stars.** Boston: Houghton Mifflin, 1989. 169p. $14.95. ISBN 0-395-51060-0. New York: Dell, 1989. 169p. $4.50pa. ISBN 0-440-40327-8pa. 4-7

Annemarie and her friend Ellen pretend to be sisters one night when the Nazis come to Ellen's Copenhagen home to arrest her parents, who have already gone into hiding. Ellen's family and others get to Annemarie's uncle's fishing boat, and Annemarie saves them all from the Nazis by taking a handkerchief covered with blood and cocaine to the boat after it was accidentally left behind. The handkerchief deadens the Nazis' search dogs' sense of smell and saves the Jews from being discovered under a vat of fish. *Newbery Medal, National Jewish Awards, Association of Jewish Libraries Award, Sydney Taylor Book Award, American Library Association Notable Books for Children,* and *School Library Journal Best Book.*

833. Lucas, Eileen. **Vincent van Gogh**. New York: Franklin Watts, 1991. 63p. $18.43. ISBN 0-531-20024-8. (First Books). 4-8

Vincent van Gogh (1853-1890) tried several professions before he decided that he wanted to be a painter. He moved to France, and the pictures he saw in Paris greatly influenced him. He lived mainly in the Provence area of France, where he painted many of his pictures. Six months after van Gogh died, his brother, Theo, to whom he was very close, also died. Theo's wife had them buried side by side. Van Gogh had a mental disease for which he was hospitalized, although doctors have never been sure what it was. Reproductions of van Gogh's paintings complement the text. Masterpieces of Vincent van Gogh, For Further Reading, and Index.

834. Lunn, Janet. **Shadow in Hawthorn Bay**. New York: Scribners, 1987. 192p. $13.95. ISBN 0-684-18843-0. New York: Penguin, 1988. 192p. $3.95pa. ISBN 0-14-032436-4pa. 5-9

Mairi, who lives in Scotland around 1800, has *an dà shelladh* or the "second sight." She hears her cousin Duncan calling to her from Canada to tell her to come where he has emigrated. She goes and finds that he has recently drowned. Instead of letting the experience disturb her, she decides to marry and begin a new life. *Canada Council Children's Literature Prize, Canada Children's Book of the Year Award,* and *International Board on Books for Young People.*

835.   Lynch, Anne. **Great Buildings**. Alexandria, VA: Time-Life, 1996. 64p. $16. ISBN 0-8094-9371-3. 5-8
        Chronological coverage of twenty-six buildings thoughout history display their construction and unusual aspects. Photographs and drawings, some with cross-sectional views, add to the value of the text. Buildings include a Trobriand woven hut, a Mayan pyramid in Mexico, Ishtar's Gate in Babylon, the Baths of Caracalla in Rome, a Hindu temple in India, a Buddhist shrine in Indonesia, the hall of Supreme Harmony in Beijing, the Horyuji Temple Complex in Japan, the Hagia Sophia in Istanbul, the Alhambra in Granada, Notre Dame in Paris, St. Peter's in Rome, Versailles, Casa Milá in Barcelona, the Toronto SkyDome, and the Sydney Opera House. Photographs, Glossary, and Index.

836. Macaulay, David, author/illustrator. **Castle**. Boston: Houghton Mifflin, 1977. 80p. $16.95; $7.95pa. ISBN 0-395-25784-0; 0-395-32920-5pa. 5 up

The castle that Macaulay builds is imaginary, but is based on the concept, structural process, and physical appearance of several castles constructed to help the English conquer Wales between 1277 and 1305. These castles and the towns around them were the culmination of over two centuries of development, in Europe and the Holy Land, of the castle as a way to keep military forces together. Glossary. *Caldecott Honor Book.*

837. Macaulay, David, author/illustrator. **Cathedral: The Story of Its Construction**. Boston: Houghton Mifflin, 1973. 77p. $16.95. ISBN 0-395-17513-5. 3 up

Macaulay builds an imaginary cathedral based on the French cathedral at Reims. The text discusses the people's reasons for wanting a cathedral, how they got the money to build it, and how long it took them to complete such a huge building in the twelfth century. Illustrations and diagrams reveal what an enormous accomplishment building a cathedral was and also the prestige that it brought to the village in which it was constructed.

838. Macaulay, David, author/illustrator. **Ship**. Boston: Houghton Mifflin, 1993. 96p. $19.95. ISBN 0-395-52439-3. 6 up

The space shuttles of the fifteenth century were small ships called caravels. No drawings remain to show what these ships looked like or how they were built. The text looks at a caravel recovered by archaeologists from the Caribbean waters and recreates it piece by piece. Then it uses a diary format to tell of the ship's last voyage from Seville to its sinking.

839. MacDonald, Fiona. **Cities: Citizens and Civilizations**. New York: Franklin Watts, 1992. 48p. $13.95; $7.95pa. ISBN 0-531-15247-2; 0-531-15287-1pa. (Timelines). 5-8

In two-page topic spreads, the text covers many cities, with detailed illustrations showing each city's character. The sites covered are the first cities (Sumer, ancient Egypt, and Thebes); Greek city-states (Athens and Sparta); Rome; the Viking Hedeby in Denmark; early American Mesa Verde; Córdoba, Spain; Paris; Venice; Florence; Nurenberg; Constantinople; Amsterdam; Vienna; St. Petersburg, Russia; New York; industrial cities like Pittsburgh and Leeds, England; and London. It also discusses suburbs; inner cities; cityscapes of Paris, France, and Sydney, Australia; and what future cities might resemble. Timeline, Glossary, and Index.

840. MacDonald, Fiona. **First Facts About the Ancient Greeks**. Mark Bergin, illustrator. New York: Peter Bedrick, 1997. 32p. $14.95. ISBN 0-87226-552-3. (First Facts). 4-6

Information about women, clothing, athletes, and other topics introduce the reader to the Greeks. Glossary and Index.

841. MacDonald, Fiona. **A Greek Temple**. Mark Bergin, illustrator. New York: Peter Bedrick, 1992. 48p. $18.95. ISBN 0-87226-351-4. (Inside Story). 4-8

This survey illustrates the construction and history of the Parthenon in ancient Greece, as well as including other information. Two-page topics and diagrams discuss homes for the gods, prayers and sacrifices, festival games, temple design, proportions of buildings, site preparation, citizens and workers, columns and walls, roofs, Parthenon sculptures, the craftsman's day, inside the Parthenon and on the Acropolis, Athena's birthday, memorials, the past and the present, and contemporary Greek influence. Glossary and Index.

842. MacDonald, Fiona. **I Wonder Why Greeks Built Temples and Other Questions About Ancient Greece**. New York: Kingfisher, 1997. $9.95. 32p. ISBN 0-7534-5056-9. (I Wonder Why). 2-4

With double-page spreads, the story of the Greeks unfolds through questions and answers. Among the sections are everyday life, customs, religion, government, famous people, and military life. Index.

843. MacDonald, Fiona. **I Wonder Why Romans Wore Togas and Other Questions About Ancient Rome**. New York: Kingfisher, 1997. $9.95. 32p. ISBN 0-7534-5057-7. (I Wonder Why). 2-4

The double-page spreads recount Roman life with pertinent questions and answers. Among the sections are everyday life, customs, religion, government, famous people, and military life. Index.

844. MacDonald, Fiona. **A Medieval Castle**. Mark Bergin, illustrator. New York: Peter Bedrick, 1990. 48p. $16.95. ISBN 0-87226-340-1. (Inside Story). 5-7

With text and cutaway illustrations, the author and illustrator reveal the civilization and expectations of people who lived and worked in castles during the Middle Ages. Index.

845. MacDonald, Fiona. **A Medieval Cathedral**. John James, illustrator. New York: Peter Bedrick, 1991. 48p. $18.95; $8.95pa. ISBN 0-87226-350-9; 0-87226-266-9pa. (Inside Story). 5-8

Most cathedrals were built during the Middle Ages, between 550 and 1450. With detailed and informative illustrations accompanying the text, topics covered are choice of site, cathedral architecture, stone quarrying, the foundation, craftsmen, stone tracery, the worker's day, wall building, types of drains, gargoyles and roofs, floors and vaults, bell towers and spires, priests and people, pilgrims, miracle plays, monasteries, and other facts. Glossary and Index.

846. MacDonald, Fiona. **The Middle Ages**. New York: Facts on File, 1993. 78p. $17.95. ISBN 0-8160-2788-9. (Illustrated History of the World). 4-7

In the western world, during the Middle Ages, life focused on government, religion, chivalry, and survival. More people began to live in towns as trade developed. The crises of the Black Death, the Mongol advance, and the Ottomans touched many, with exploration and foreign voyages signaling the end of the Middle Ages and the beginning of the Renaissance. Outside of the western world, other orders prevailed. Islamic government and society ruled the Near East, and in the Far East, China's Sing empire was in power. Illustrations highlight the text. Glossary, Further Reading, and Index.

847. MacDonald, Fiona. **A 19th Century Railway Station**. John James, illustrator. New York: Peter Bedrick, 1990. 48p. $16.95. ISBN 0-87226-341-X. (Inside Story). 5-7

The text explains how nineteenth-century railway stations were financed, built, decorated, and managed. Detailed pictures augment the text and give information about the people who worked in the stations and the activities undertaken there. Glossary and Index.

848. MacDonald, Fiona. **A Roman Fort**. Gerald Wood, illustrator. New York: Peter Bedrick, 1983. 48p. $18.95; $8.95pa. ISBN 0-87226-370-3; 0-87226-259-6pa. (Inside Story). 6-8

Two-page spreads present various topics related to a Roman fort. The discussions include army legions and organization, Roman roads and construction, camps, searching for sites to build forts, the expansion of a fort into a village, food and water, illness and injury, gods and spirits, soldiers on parade and off-duty, and types of warfare. Clear drawings, diagrams, and maps highlight the text. Glossary and Index.

849. MacDonald, Fiona. **A Samurai Castle**. John James and David Antram, illustrators. New York: Peter Bedrick, 1995. 48p. $18.95. ISBN 0-87226-381-9. (Inside Story). 5-8

The text covers samurai castles of the seventeenth and eighteenth centuries in Japan. It gives information on their construction, history, and inhabitants. The double-page spreads offer diverse topics such as women's lives, interiors, towns around the castles, methods of entertaining visitors, and arms. Glossary and Index.

850. MacDonald, Fiona. **A 16th Century Mosque**. Mark Bergin, illustrator. New York: Peter Bedrick, 1994. 48p. $18.95. ISBN 0-87226-310-X. 5 up

In two-page spreads, text and vivid illustrations cover such topics as the spread of Islam and the faith, the first mosque, various styles of mosques, the lives of the workers who built them, the Ottoman Empire, Suleyman the Magnificent and his mosque, the domed roofs, the call to prayer, mihrab and minbar, woodwork and tiles, carpets and rugs, light and color, the people of the mosque, schools and colleges, and medicine and charity, as well as mosques around the world. Glossary, Dates in This Book, and Index.

851. MacDonald, Fiona, and Gerald Wood. **Exploring the World**. New York: Peter Bedrick, 1996. 48p. $18.95. ISBN 0-87226-648-4. (Voyages of Discovery). 3-6

The text tells of well-known navigators such as Magellan and Drake. The detailed illustrations expand the text and include cross sections of ships as well as maps in the short chapters. Glossary and Index.

852. MacDonald, Robert. **Maori**. New York: Thomson Learning, 1994. 48p. $24.21. ISBN 1-56847-151-3. (Threatened Cultures). 4-8

Cultures such as that of the Maori in New Zealand, which maintain traditional ways of life unlike anything in the modern world, are threatened with extinction when they come face to face with technology. The text shows how the Maoris have tried to integrate their ancient traditions into contemporary situations through looking at both the past and the present of the Maori tribe. Glossary of Maori Words, Glossary of English Words, Further Reading, Further Information, and Index.

853. MacGrory, Yvonne. **The Secret of the Ruby Ring**. Terry Myler, illustrator. Dublin, Ireland, and Minneapolis, MN: Milkweed Press, 1994. 192p. $14.95; $6.95pa. ISBN 0-915943-88-3; 0-915943-92-1pa. 4-6

In this historical fantasy, Lucy's grandmother gives her a star ruby ring just before her eleventh birthday. A grateful rajah gave it to a family member who saved his life, and the ring has passed to the family's daughters since 1880. Lucy discovers a message in the box, which says the ring will grant two wishes. Suddenly she finds herself in Langley Castle during 1885, where the servants think she is a new maid. Her experiences change her views of the present, to which she finally returns after a difficult adventure during which the lady of the house accuses her of stealing the ruby ring. After she wakes up in the present, her family goes on a visit to nearby Dunard Castle, which she finds was previously named "Langley." There she sees portraits and hears things that she already knew from her experience.

854. Macht, Norman L. **Christopher Columbus**. New York: Chelsea House, 1992. 80p. $14.95; $4.95pa. ISBN 0-7910-1752-4; 0-7910-1953-5pa. (Junior World Biographies). 4-6

The text examines the life of Christopher Columbus (1451-1506), including his voyages and discoveries in the New World which he dedicated to Queen Isabella of Portugal. Bibliography and Index.

855. MacMillan, Dianne M. **Chinese New Year**. Springfield, NJ: Enslow, 1994. 48p. $15.95. ISBN 0-89490-500-7. (Best Holiday Books). 2-5

Although Chinese people live all over the world, they observe their New Year as they have for thousands of years. The text presents the history of the holiday as well as the way it is currently celebrated. Glossary and Index.

856. MacMillan, Dianne M. **Diwali: Hindu Festival of Lights**. Springfield, NJ: Enslow, 1977. 48p. $16.95. ISBN 0-89490-817-0. 4-8

Hindu beliefs become apparent in this description of an important festival as well as a presentation of the important books, legends, and other traditions associated with the religion. Glossary and Index.

857. MacMillan, Dianne M. **Jewish Holidays in the Spring**. Springfield, NJ: Enslow, 1994. 48p. $15.95. ISBN 0-89490-503-1. (Best Holiday Books). 2-5

After a brief introduction to the Jewish religion, the text presents the history and current rituals of five Jewish holidays celebrated in the spring: Purim, Passover, Yom Ha-Azma'ut, Lag B'Omer, and Shavuot. Glossary and Index.

858. MacMillan, Dianne M. **Ramadan and Id Al-Fitr**. Springfield, NJ: Enslow, 1994. 48p. $15.95. ISBN 0-89490-502-3. (Best Holiday Books). 2-5

A brief look at Muhammad's life, the pillars of Islam, and the role of the mosque in the life of Muslims precedes the discussion of Ramadan, the holiday during the ninth month of the Islamic lunar calendar. Ramadan ends on the first day of the tenth month with Id Al-Fitr, a celebration that lasts for a day. Glossary and Index.

859. MacMillan, Dianne M. **Tet: Vietnamese New Year**. Springfield, NJ: Enslow, 1994. 48p. $15.95. ISBN 0-89490-501-5. (Best Holiday Books). 2-5

For the Vietnamese, Tet is like a birthday, Thanksgiving, Christmas, and New Year's all in one holiday that lasts for three days. It begins on the first day of the new lunar year, as it has for centuries. The text traces its history and the way it is currently celebrated. Glossary and Index.

860. Maestro, Betsy. **The Discovery of the Americas**. Giulio Maestro, illustrator. New York: Lothrop, Lee & Shepard, 1991. 48p. $16. ISBN 0-688-06837-5. 2-5

Beginning with the migration of peoples into North and South America more than 20,000 years ago, the text presents theories and facts about the settlements discovered on the two continents. Cultures and explorers before Columbus include the Mayans, possibly Saint Brendan from Ireland in the sixth century, the Vikings Bjarni Herjolfsson in the tenth century and Leif Ericsson in the eleventh, possibly Prince Madoc of Wales in the twelfth, and the Hopewell mound builders. Those explorers after Columbus mentioned in the text are Italians John Cabot in 1497 and Amerigo Vespucci in 1499, Vasco Nuñez de Balboa from Spain in 1513, and Ferdinand Magellan from Portugal in 1519. Additional Information, Some People of the Ancient and Early Americas, The Age of Discovery, How the Americas Got Their Name, and Other Interesting Voyages.

861. Maestro, Betsy. **Exploration and Conquest: The Americas After Columbus: 1500-1620**. Giulio Maestro, illustrator. New York: Lothrop, Lee & Shepard, 1994. 48p. $16. ISBN 0-688-09267-5. 4-6

Noting that Spanish discovery of the New World ignored or exploited the people who had lived there for years, the authors describe the feats and effects of explorers after Columbus. Balboa (1513) saw the Pacific. Ponce de León (1513) found Florida. Magellan began his voyage around the world in 1519, while Cortés overpowered the Aztecs. Pizarro and deSoto (1532) conquered the Incas in Peru when Cabez de Vaca was in Texas. DeSoto went to Florida in 1539, and Coronado left Mexico in search of the Seven Cities of Gold in 1540. After Spain lost interest in America, European explorers arrived. John Cabot, Giovanni da Verrazano, Jacques Cartier, and John Hawkins (who began the slave trade) came. Britain's Francis Drake, Martin Frobisher, Humphrey Gilbert, John Davis, Walter Raleigh (at Roanoke), John White, and Virginia Dare added their names to history. After 1600, famous arrivals were John Smith, John Rolfe, Champlain, and Henry Hudson. Where these people arrived on shore, the indigenous cultures disappeared. Additional Information, Table of Dates, Some Other Explorers, North America—1500-1620, Contacts Between Native Americans and European Explorers, Impact of the European Arrival in the Americas, Native American Contributions to the World, and European Colonies and Settlements in the New World.

862. Maestro, Betsy. **The Story of Money**. Giulio Maestro, illustrator. New York: Clarion, 1993. 48p. $15.95. ISBN 0-395-56242-2. 3-5

Among the objects used for money throughout history are tea leaves, shells, feathers, animal teeth, tobacco, blankets, barley, salt, feathers, and metal balls. When the Sumerians used metal bars of the same weight and stamped the amount on the bar, they invented the first known metal money. The text has other interesting information about money through the centuries and short chapters on American money, unusual money, and currencies of other countries. Illustrations complement the text.

863. Major, John S. **The Silk Route: 7000 Miles of History**. Stephen Fieser, illustrator. New York: HarperCollins, 1995. 32p. $14.95. ISBN 0-06-022924-1. 4-7

Silk has long been a symbol of riches and luxury, and a 7,000-mile-long trade route flourished for centuries by which silk traveled from China throughout the East. The story begins in A.D. 700 with the Tang Dynasty. The trade journey began in Chang'an (city), with traders stopping to pray at Dunhuang (monastery), crossing the Taklamakan (desert), stopping at Kashgar (oasis), traveling over Pamirs (mountains), stopping in Tashkent (market), going through Transoxiana (wild country with nomads), and visiting Herat (Persian city), Baghdad (greatest Islamic city), Damascus, Tyre, and Byzantium. *American Booksellers' Pick of the Lists*.

864. Malone, Michael, author/photographer. **A Guatemalan Family**. Minneapolis, MN: Lerner, 1996. 64p. $21.50; $8.95pa. ISBN 0-8225-3400-2; 0-8225-9742-Xpa. (Journey Between Two Worlds). 3-6

Although not a history book, this text includes the history of Guatemala as a background for understanding the reasons why families from the country have had to leave. Photographs and personal experiences explain the social and religious traditions of Guatemalans and how they have had to adapt to a new culture to survive as refugees from a home they loved. Further Reading.

865. Malone, Michael. **A Nicaraguan Family**. Minneapolis, MN: Lerner, 1998. 56p. $16.95. ISBN 0-8225-9779-9. (Journey Between Two Worlds). 3-6

The text relates the history of the Nicaraguans as a background for understanding the reasons for the social unrest and physical dangers for Nicaraguans in the past decades. Families whose members have become refugees share their personal experiences and explain how difficult being parted from their social, political, and religious traditions can be. Further Reading.

866. Malterre, Elona. **The Last Wolf of Ireland**. New York: Clarion, 1990. 127p. $13.95. ISBN 0-395-54381-9. 5-7

Around 1786 in Ireland, Devin and his friend, Katey, see the Squire kill a mother wolf, and they save the litter. They feed them until a village boy tells what they are doing. Devin saves one male, but the society hates wolves, and when the wolf is grown, someone mortally wounds it. Devin has cared for it and it returns to Devin before dying.

867. Mann, Elizabeth. **The Great Pyramid: The Story of the Farmers, the God-King & the Most Astounding Structure Ever Built**. Laura Lo Turco, illustrator. New York: Mikaya Press, 1996. 48p. $18.95. ISBN 0-9650493-1-0. (The Wonders of the World). 4-6

Mann looks at the Great Pyramid in Giza through the eyes of the farmers and the Pharaoh Khufu who would have been living at the time it was constructed. Complementing the text are photographs, archival reproductions, and paintings. A four-page foldout helps give a sense of the size of this fifty-story structure. Index.

868. Mann, Kenny. **Egypt, Kush, Aksum: Northeast Africa**. New York: Dillon Press, 1996. 105p. $15.95; $7.95pa. ISBN 0-87518-655-6; 0-382-39657-Xpa. (African Kingdoms of the Past). 4-6

Egypt's influence through the centuries has been well documented elsewhere. Kush was the southern part of Nubia in which the Egyptian occupation as well as the African peoples left their influence in the fifteenth century B.C. with Kush rising to power in the eighth century B.C. Aksum was a powerful kingdom in the area of northern Ethiopia in the early Christian period. These three countries were important African places, and the photographs and text reveal their achievements and contributions to African history. Chronology, Further Reading, and Index.

869.   Mann, Kenny. **Oyo, Benin, Ashanti: The Guinea Coast**. New York: Dillon Press, 1996. 105p. $15.95; $7.95pa. ISBN 0-87518-657-2; 0-382-39177-2pa. (African Kingdoms of the Past). 6-10

In this text, African legends become part of the history of the area. The text covers environment, kingdom building, and the slave trade in Oyo, Benin, and Ashanti. Information on the history of each area, along with the individual cultures found there, gives each an identity. An epilogue covers the areas' history from colonization to the present. Photographs, Chronology, Further Reading, and Index.

870.   Mann, Kenny. **Zenj, Buganda: East Africa**. New York: Dillon Press, 1996. 105p. $15.95; $7.95pa. ISBN 0-87518-660-2; 0-382-39658-8pa. (African Kingdoms of the Past). 4-6

Buganda, along the shore of Lake Victoria in the present republic of Uganda, was a powerful kingdom during the nineteenth century as was Zenj. Bibliography, Chronology, Further Reading, Glossary, and Index.

871.   Manson, Christopher. **Two Travelers**. New York: Holt, 1990. 32p. $14.95. ISBN 0-8050-1214-1. 2-6

When Charlemagne's servant, Isaac, travels to Baghdad from France in 787, he returns with a gift from the caliph, an elephant named Abulabaz. Isaac and the elephant distrust each other until they have to cross stormy seas and high mountains. Then they begin to rely on each other's help. When Isaac leaves the elephant with Charlemagne, it begins to pine after him. Charlemagne recalls Isaac to care for Abulabaz until the elephant's death in 810.

872.   Margeson, Susan M. **Viking**. Peter Anderson, illustrator. New York: Dorling Kindersley, Knopf, 1994. 63p. $19. ISBN 0-679-86002-9. (Eyewitness). 4-6

The two-page spreads, illustrated with photographs and drawings on the Vikings, cover who they were; their warships, warriors, and weapons; how they terrorized both West and East as they went into Russia; their forts; their kings and freemen, women and children; games; gods, legends, and burials; runes; and the Jelling stone. Index.

873.   Margolies, Barbara A. **Warriors, Wigmen, and the Crocodile People: Journeys in Papua New Guinea**. New York: Four Winds Press, 1993. 40p. $14.95. ISBN 0-02-762283-5. 3-5

People in Papua New Guinea have been following the same traditions for centuries. The text and photographs give insight into two groups (the Hulis and the people of the Sepik River) and their rituals.

874.   Markham, Lois. **Inventions That Changed Modern Life**. Austin, TX: Raintree/Steck-Vaughn, 1994. 48p. $15.96. ISBN 0-8114-4930-0. (20 Events Series). 6 up

In the late eighteenth century, James Watt's steam engine was produced for sale, Nicolas Appert began working with food preservation, and Eli Whitney designed interchangeable parts for guns. In the nineteenth century, Richard Trevithick and George Stephenson worked with locomotives. Photography began with experiments in France and England by Josiah Wedgwood, Joseph-Nicéphore Niepce, Louis Daguerre, and W. H. Fox Talbot. Cyrus McCormick began work on the combine harvester, and Isaac Singer patented the sewing machine begun by Elias Howe. Work on refrigeration, plastics, the telephone, electric light, and the automobile ended the century. In 1901, Marconi's radio worked. Also in the twentieth century, the airplane, assembly line, rocket, nuclear fission, television, computers, and lasers have changed the way people live. Each topic covers two pages. Glossary, Suggested Readings, and Index.

875.   Marko, Katherine. **Away to Fundy Bay**. New York: Walker, 1985. 145p. $11.95. ISBN 0-8027-6594-7. 5-9

During 1775, Doone, age thirteen, tries to escape the British press gangs in Halifax, Nova Scotia, by going to his mother's friends' farm near Fundy Bay. After a time, his uncle dies, and he is able to rescue his mother and sister, who had had to remain as servants to the man. When he saves the farm owner's son from hanging after the son is accused of treason, the owner gives Doone land for his family.

876.   Marrin, Albert. **The Airman's War: World War II in the Sky**. New York: Atheneum, 1982. 213p. $11.95. ISBN 0-689-30907-4. 5 up

In 1939, German Reichsmarshal Hermann Goering boasted that no one would ever bomb Germany. He thought that Germany controlled the skies. He was wrong. The text looks at the importance of air power in World War II after many leaders of the American armed services had ignored the value of an air force in the early 1930s. Three men, "Hap" Arnold, "Tooey" Spaatz, and Ira Eaker, fulfilled "Billy" Mitchell's goal for a strong air fleet. The text tells their stories; the stories of pilots in the war flying bombers and fighter planes; the stories of the planes they flew, such as the B-17s, the Liberators, the Spitfires, and the Messerschmitts; and the battles they fought, some of them bombing raids that lasted around the clock. Photographs, Maps, Some More Books, and Index.

877. Marrin, Albert. **Aztecs and Spaniards: Cortés and the Conquest of Mexico**. New York: Atheneum, 1986. 212p. $12.95. ISBN 0-689-31176-1. 5-8

The legend goes that in 1168 a god commanded the Aztecs to move south in search of a better home. They did, and they settled in the valley of Mexico, where they built their city on islands in a large lake. They grew, in less than two centuries, to a vast empire. In 1519, when Cortés arrived, no city in Europe could match the size of Tenochtitlán. The Spaniards had come to get wealth and they decided to take it from the Aztecs. When Cortés marched on the city, the final Aztec uprising led to the Night of Tears, when so many died by Spanish swords. Some More Books and Index.

878. Marrin, Albert. **The Sea King: Sir Francis Drake and His Times**. New York: Atheneum, 1995. 168p. $18. ISBN 0-689-31887-1. 6-10

Instead of telling Francis Drake (1540?-1596) that she planned to knight him, Queen Elizabeth I implied that she was going to use the sword she had laid on his neck to cut off his head. She knighted him, though, because she was indebted to this man, who had gained a position for England in the New World after Spain and Portugal had seemed to control it. He was a great mariner and navigator as well as commander. He was a leader, a preacher, and a lover of children. He usually freed his prisoners and gave them gifts. But he was also demanding, insistent on obedience, and ruthless when necessary. The text covers his life and the times, including the Spanish Inquisition and the Spanish Armada, and the difficulties of life at sea. Some More Books, Notes, and Index. *School Library Journal Starred Review*.

879. Marrin, Albert. **The Sea Rovers: Pirates, Privateers, and Buccaneers**. New York: Atheneum, 1984. 173p. $15.95. ISBN 0-689-31029-3. 5 up

In the early history of Europeans coming to American shores, pirates rode the seas in search of other peoples' wealth. English sea dogs such as Jack Hawkins and Francis Drake helped Queen Elizabeth declare war on Spain. Henry Morgan, Blackbeard, and Captain Kidd looked for booty on all the ships sailing the Atlantic. On the Mediterranean, the Barbary pirates patrolled the northern coast of Africa, but the U.S. Navy proved itself by thwarting their progress. The text looks at these pirates as well as women who also sailed under the pirate flag, the Jolly Roger. Some More Books and Index.

880. Marrin, Albert. **The Secret Armies: Spies, Counterspies, and Saboteurs in World War II**. New York: Atheneum, 1985. 239p. $13.95. ISBN 0-689-31165-6. 5 up

Spies and counterspies worked in Europe during World War II under code names, such as Hedgehog, Zigzag, and Tricycle, to gather information behind German lines and pass misinformation to Nazi intelligence. People participated in the Resistance movement, in the Maquis in France, in the Netherlands, and in other conquered countries where people risked their lives. These undercover agents cracked the German secret code with the Enigma machine and helped ensure an Allied victory. The text looks at all aspects of these important participants in the war. Photographs, More Books, and Index.

881. Marston, Elsa. **The Ancient Egyptians**. Freeport, NY: Marshall Cavendish, 1996. 80p. $19.95. ISBN 0-7614-0073-7. (Cultures of the Past). 5-8

The text looks at the artifacts, monuments, domestic scenes, and historical aspects of ancient Egypt while telling about the evolution of the Egyptian dynasties. It also presents a competent explanation of the complex Egyptian religious beliefs. Photographs, Drawings, Bibliography, Chronology, Further Reading, Glossary, and Index.

882. Martell, Hazel. **What Do We Know About the Celts?** New York: Peter Bedrick, 1993. 45p. $18.95. ISBN 0-87226-363-0. (What Do We Know About . . .). 3 up

With illustrations or photographs of ancient sites and artifacts on each page, the text tells about Celtic life in the times before the Romans in Ireland and England—the history, daily routine, social structure, and culture. Holidays, getting food, clothing, and travels are part of the information. Glossary and Index.

883. Martell, Hazel Mary. **The Age of Discovery**. New York: Facts on File, 1993. 78p. $17.95. ISBN 0-8160-2789-7. (Illustrated History of the World). 4-7

The Reformation changed the western world. Also during this time, printing was developed, another stunning shift. Russia emerged as a power under Peter the Great, Japan flourished with its shoguns, and the Spanish and Portuguese colonized the Americas. Illustrations highlight the text. Glossary, Further Reading, and Index.

884. Martell, Hazel Mary. **The Ancient Chinese**. New York: New Discovery, Macmillan, 1993. 64p. $14.95. ISBN 0-02-730653-4. (Worlds of the Past). 4-8

The double-page topics on ancient China include government, social structure, everyday life, food, arts and crafts, and brief dynastic histories. Photographs and color reproductions augment the text. Chronology, Glossary, and Index.

885. Martell, Hazel Mary. **The Celts**. New York: Viking, 1996. 48p. $16.99. ISBN 0-670-86558-3. (See Through History). 5-8

The text gives information about the Celts, people who inhabited Ireland and England before the Romans came. It looks at their daily lives, government, foods, weapons, and houses with full illustrations and see-through overlays of fortress interiors, homes, and burial sites. Chronology, Glossary, and Index.

886. Martell, Hazel Mary. **Food and Feasts with the Vikings**. New York: New Discovery, 1995. 32p. $14.95. ISBN 0-02-726317-7. 4-7

The text looks at the ways food was grown and prepared during Viking times, from approximately A.D. 700 to 1000, by focusing on the crops in the countryside and the types of food that had to be shipped to the towns. One had to eat when traveling, so the text covers food that travelers ate, especially aboard ship. Additional information about cooking utensils and recipes from the Viking period give a good sense of the times. Photographs and reproductions enhance the text. Glossary, Further Reading, and Index.

887. Martell, Hazel Mary. **Over 6,000 Years Ago: In the Stone Age**. New York: Crestwood House, 1992. 32p. $13.95. ISBN 0-02-762429-3. (History Detective). 4-6

By referring to the archaeological digs in Europe, Martell shows the cultural and technological developments during the Stone Age. The New Stone Age lasted from 8000 to 6000 B.C., and people during that time lived in settled villages where they grew crops and domesticated animals. They also created pottery and wove artistically as well as for practical clothing. Chronology, Glossary, For Further Reading, and Index.

888. Martell, Hazel Mary. **The Vikings and Jorvik**. New York: Dillon Press, Macmillan, 1993. 32p. $13.95. ISBN 0-87518-541-X. (Hidden Worlds). 4-7

One record of the Vikings' first arrival in England, in the *Anglo-Saxon Chronicle*, says that they came in A.D. 789. In A.D. 793, they raided the monastery at Lindisfarne on the coast of Northumberland, stealing the monastery's treasures and killing some of the monks. Recently archaeologists have found information that shows Vikings' skills in shipbuilding and metalworking and their endeavors as traders and farmers. They captured the English town of Eoforwic (York) in A.D. 867 and established a major trading center there, which flourished until the Norman Conquest in 1066. The text, with photographs, illustrations, and maps, tells about these people. Glossary and Index.

889. Martell, Hazel Mary, and Paul G. Bahn. **The Kingfisher Book of the Ancient World: From the Ice Age to the Roman Empire**. New York: Kingfisher, 1995. 160p. $19.95. ISBN 1-85697-565-7. 5-7

After telling how archaeologists discover information about prehistoric cultures, the text then summarizes the major cultures between 10,000 B.C. and A.D. 600. They include the Fertile Crescent, Egypt to Asia, Greece and Rome, Europe, Africa, the Americas, and the Pacific Islands. Maps, Photographs, Chronology, Glossary, and Index.

890. Martell, Helen M. **What Do We Know About the Vikings?** New York: Peter Bedrick, 1992. 40p. $18.95. ISBN 0-87226-355-X. (What Do We Know About . . .). 4-6

With illustrations or photographs of ancient sites and artifacts on each page, the text tells about Viking life during the eleventh and twelfth centuries: the history, daily routine, social structure, and culture. Holidays, getting food, clothing, and travels are part of the information. Glossary and Index.

891. Martin, Christopher. **H. G. Wells: Life & Works**. Vero Beach, FL: Rourke, 1988. 112p. $22.60. ISBN 0-86592-297-7. 5-9

H. G. Wells (1866-1946) described himself as the ugly duckling who found out he was a swan. Born into the Victorian lower middle class, he had to struggle for the science education he wanted. He wanted to live in a utopia, and he created these worlds in his work. In his realistic science fiction writing, he exposed what he saw as the horrors of the twentieth century. Glossary, List of Dates, Further Reading, and Index.

892. Martin, Marvin. **The Beatles: The Music Was Never the Same**. New York: Franklin Watts, 1996. 207p. $22.70. ISBN 0-531-11307-8. 6 up

In this collective biography, Martin recalls the role of the Beatles in changing popular music. He includes details from history, from their careers, and their influence on the present. Discography and Index.

893. Martinez, Elizabeth Coonrod. **Sor Juana: A Trailblazing Thinker**. Brookfield, CT: Millbrook Press, 1994. 32p. $13.90. ISBN 1-56294-406-1. 2-4

Born Juana Ines de Asbaje y Ramirez near Mexico City on November 12, 1648, Sor Juana learned to read at three and heard about the University of Mexico when she was six. She wanted to go there, but women were not allowed. Her mother sent her to live with an aunt and uncle in Mexico City when she was ten, and a tutor helped her with languages. She learned Latin, Nahuatl (the Aztec language), Portuguese, and Basque. When she was fifteen, professors from the university tested her and found that she knew an enormous amount. During this same time, she was writing poems and plays. Because she had no dowry, and thus could not marry, she became a nun at the age of nineteen so that she could study as she wished. She had friends from all over the world who were amazed at her knowledge, and they visited her until the archbishop declared that she would suffer the Inquisition if she wrote any more. She died of plague in 1695. Important Dates in the Life, Find Out More, and Index.

894. Marton, Jirina, author/illustrator. **You Can Go Home Again**. New York: Annick, 1994. Unpaged. $15.95; $5.95pa. ISBN 1-55037-991-7; 1-55037-990-9pa. K-3

When Annie asks her mother about her mother's childhood, she tells Annie about two black elephant statues that she used to play with in the home of her uncle, a concert pianist. When the war started, she had to leave the city. Annie suggests that they return to her mother's home. They all go to Prague and find that everything is different, but they discover the elephants in a restaurant across the street, where Uncle Billy had left them for Annie's mother if she ever returned.

895. Maruki, Toshi, author/illustrator. **Hiroshima, No Pika**. New York: Lothrop, Lee & Shepard, 1982. 48p. $16. ISBN 0-688-01297-3. 4-7

In 1945, Mii is seven. She and her parents experience the chaos following the blast of the atomic bomb dropped by the American airplane, the *Enola Gay*. In shock, Mii carries her chopsticks for several days before she realizes that they are still in her hand. After some time, her father dies, and Mii never gets any larger than she was when the bomb fell. The expressionist illustrations heighten the fury of the scene without overly realistic gore. *Mildred L. Batchelder Award, Jane Addams Children's Book Award,* and *American Library Association Notable Books for Children.*

896. Marvin, Isabel R. **Bridge to Freedom**. Philadelphia, PA: Jewish Publication Society, 1991. 136p. $14.95. ISBN 0-8276-0377-0. 5-9

In March 1945, Kurt, age fifteen and German, has deserted his army unit and fears capture by the retreating Germans as well as by the advancing Americans. He enters a cave where Rachel, age sixteen and Jewish, hides after escaping from Berlin. They have to trust each other in order to cross a bridge over the Rhine River into Belgium. Aided by American soldiers and Belgian farmers, they both reach Liège, and find each other again on May 8, Victory in Europe Day.

897. Marx, Trish. **Echoes of World War II**. Minneapolis, MN: Lerner, 1994. 96p. $14.96. ISBN 0-8225-4898-4. 5-8

In pictures of war, one often sees soldiers. The children are less visible, but what happens to the children during a war has a huge impact on the future. Marx follows the paths of six children, four in Europe and two in Asia, through World War II. Some left their parents and others had parents leave them. These six survived, which is why their stories can be told. Photographs augment the text. Index.

898. Marzollo, Jean. **My First Book of Biographies: Great Men and Women Every Child Should Know**. Irene Trivas, illustrator. New York: Cartwheel, Scholastic, 1994. 80p. $14.95. ISBN 0-590-45014-X. 2-3

The text highlights the reasons for fame in the lives of the 45 people presented. The capsule biographies cover two columns of one page opposite a portrait of the person. Included here are Neil Armstrong and Edwin Aldrin, Jr. (both 1930-), Rachel Carson (1907-1964), George Washington Carver (1864-1943), Cesar Chavez (1927-1993), Winston Churchill (1874-1965), Cleopatra (69-30 B.C.), Christopher Columbus (1451-1506), Marie Curie (1867-1934), Pierre Curie (1859-1906), Walt Disney (1901-1966), Amelia Earhart (1897-1937), Thomas Alva Edison (1847-1931), Albert Einstein (1879-1955), Elizabeth I (1533-1603), Duke Ellington (1899-1974), Benjamin Franklin (1706-1790), Mohandas Gandhi (1869-1948), Katsushika Hokusai (1760-1849), Thomas Jefferson (1743-1826), Helen Keller (1880-1968), Anne Sullivan (1866-1936), Martin Luther King, Jr. (1929-1968), Rosa Parks (1913-), Leonardo da Vinci (1452-1519), Abraham Lincoln (1809-1865), Yo-Yo Ma (1955-), Gabriela Mistral (1889-1957), Wolfgang Amadeus Mozart (1756-1791), Jesse Owens (1913-1980), Peter the Great (1672-1725), Beatrix Potter (1866-1943), Eleanor Roosevelt (1884-1962), Franklin Roosevelt (1882-1945), Sequoyah (c. 1760-1843), William Shakespeare (1564-1616), Elizabeth Cady Stanton (1815-1902), Lucretia Mott (1793-1880), Susan B. Anthony (1820-1906), Maria Tallchief (1925-); George Balanchine (1904-1983), Harriet Tubman (1820-1913), Frederick Douglass (1818-1895), George Washington (1732-1799), and Babe Didrikson Zaharias (1914-1956).

899. Mason, Antony. **Cézanne: An Introduction to the Artist's Life and Work**. Hauppauge, NY: Barron's, 1994. 32p. $14.95; $8.50pa. ISBN 0-8120-6459-3; 0-8120-1293-3pa. (Famous Artists). 5 up

Born in the south of France, Cézanne (1839-1906) left the area as a young man to attend art school in Paris, where he met Pissarro, Renoir, Monet, Sisley, and other Impressionists. He exhibited with them, and after his father died and left him money, he never had to worry about selling his paintings. He continued to investigate the form, color, and structure of objects and their relationships to each other. Beautifully clear reproductions highlight the text, which has helpful comments about composition. Chronology, Art History, Museums, Glossary, and Indexes.

900. Mason, Antony. **If You Were There in Biblical Times**. Michael Welpy, illustrator. New York: Simon & Schuster, 1996. 32p. $16.95. ISBN 0-689-80953-0. 3-6

The text looks at the groups of people who lived during the times in which the Bible was recorded. It notes the differences between wealthy Egyptians and poor Israelites. A game takes players across Egypt and Mesopotamia searching for sacred scrolls during this period of history, about 3,000 years ago.

901. Mason, Antony. **If You Were There in Medieval Times**. Richard Berridge, illustrator. New York: Simon & Schuster, 1996. 32p. $16.95. ISBN 0-689-80952-2. 3-6

In Europe during the thirteenth century, people who lived in castles could be either wealthy or poor. The nobles, with their wealth, supported many servants who were expected to answer the nobles' every need. All saw lavish banquets, and some traveled on the seas. The text looks at the medieval period from the fall of the Roman Empire to the Dark Ages. A mystery maze invites readers to search for secrets.

902. Mason, Antony. **Leonardo da Vinci: An Introduction to the Artist's Life and Work**. Hauppauge, NY: Barron's, 1994. 32p. $14.95; $8.50pa. ISBN 0-8120-6460-7; 0-8120-1997-0pa. (Famous Artists). 5 up

As one of Italy's most gifted painters, Leonardo da Vinci (1452-1519) was famous while he lived. He made detailed studies of almost everything, including the human body, animals, and mechanical movement. His notebook sketches, written backwards so that they can be read only with a mirror, show that he conceived of military tanks, helicopters, airplanes, and other machines that were not invented until more than 400 years later. He apprenticed himself to Verrocchio in Florence and then worked in Milan at the court of Duke Ludovico Sforza, during which time he painted the *Mona Lisa*. Clear reproductions highlight the text, which includes helpful comments about composition. Chronology, Art History, Museums, Glossary, and Indexes.

903. Mason, Antony. **Matisse: An Introduction to the Artist's Life and Work**. Hauppauge, NY: Barron's, 1995. 32p. $14.95; $8.50pa. ISBN 0-8120-6534-4; 0-8120-9426-3pa. (Famous Artists). 5 up

One of the most inventive of twentieth-century artists was Henri Matisse (1869-1954), born in France. He worked in a group with other artists called "Fauves." He worked to achieve a sense of movement, and his bold use of color and simplicity of design made him famous. Some of the influences on his artistic career include Morocco, odalisques, dance themes, jazz, and the Vence Chapel. Beautifully clear reproductions highlight the text, which includes helpful comments about composition. Chronology, Art History, Museums, Glossary, and Indexes.

904. Mason, Antony. **Michelangelo: An Introduction to the Artist's Life and Work**. Hauppauge, NY: Barron's, 1994. 32p. $14.95; $8.50pa. ISBN 0-8120-6461-5; 0-8120-1998-9pa. (Famous Artists). 5 up

Michelangelo Buonarroti, born near Florence, Italy, in 1475, died in Rome in 1564. His works, especially the frescoes painted on the Sistine Chapel ceiling in Rome's Vatican and the sculpture *David*, are some of the finest art treasures in the world. He was one of the first artists to be admired for his genius and creativity rather than being considered merely a servant to a patron. Clear reproductions highlight the text, which includes helpful comments about composition. Chronology, Art History, Museums, Glossary, and Indexes.

905. Mason, Antony. **Monet: An Introduction to the Artist's Life and Work**. Hauppauge, NY: Barron's, 1994. 32p. $14.95; $8.50pa. ISBN 0-8120-6494-1; 0-8120-9174-4pa. (Famous Artists). 5 up

Claude Monet (1840-1926), today one of the most famous French artists, as a young man refused to use traditional methods of painting. He wanted his pictures to capture the mood of his surroundings by showing the reflection of the light; he and other artists who thought as he did became the Impressionists. He lived by the sea as a young boy, moved to Paris, almost starved while he tried to paint, enjoyed Giverny outside Paris, and developed series of paintings on various subjects, such as Rouen Cathedral and water lilies. Clear reproductions highlight the text, which includes helpful comments about composition. Chronology, Art History, Museums, Glossary, and Indexes.

906. Mason, Antony. **Picasso: An Introduction to the Artist's Life and Work**. Hauppauge, NY: Barron's, 1994. 32p. $14.95; $8.50pa. ISBN 0-8120-6496-8; 0-8120-9175-2pa. (Famous Artists). 5 up

Pablo Picasso (1881-1973) may be the greatest artist of the twentieth century. He helped found the Cubist movement and brought new ideas to art. After growing up in Spain, he went through several distinct periods in his artistic development, known as the Blue Period, the Rose Period, Analytical Cubism, Synthetic Cubism, World War I, Guernica, World War II, and the final years. Clear reproductions highlight the text, which includes helpful comments about composition. Chronology, Art History, Museums, Glossary, and Indexes.

907. Mason, Antony. **Van Gogh: An Introduction to the Artist's Life and Work**. Hauppauge, NY: Barron's, 1994. 32p. $14.95; $8.50pa. ISBN 0-8120-6462-3; 0-8120-1997-7pa. (Famous Artists). 5 up

As a young man from a middle class family in the Netherlands, Vincent van Gogh (1853-1890) painted but became interested in religion and becoming a minister. After little success, he began painting seriously, but never made much money. He was often hungry and ill, and these physical problems may have strongly influenced his colorful, bold, passionate paintings. What may seem at first to be pure globs of paint are actually carefully conceived brush strokes in such famous paintings as *The Sunflowers* and *The Starry Night*. Clear reproductions highlight the text, which includes helpful comments about composition. Chronology, Art History, Museums, Glossary, and Indexes.

908.   Matas, Carol. **After the War**. New York: Simon & Schuster, 1996. 128p. $16. ISBN 0-689-80350-8. 6-9

Ruth, age fifteen, survives the Ostroviec ghetto, Auschwitz, Buchenwald, and anti-Semitic pogroms in Poland after the end of World War II, unlike eighty members of her family. She joins a Zionist group preparing to travel via ship and illegally enter Israel. The British attack the ship and take her and the others to Cyprus. In the refugee camp there, she finds her brother and eventually escapes with her boyfriend into Israel.

909.   Matas, Carol. **The Burning Time**. New York: Delacorte, 1994. 113p. $15.95. ISBN 0-385-32097-3. 6-10

Rose Rives, aged fifteen in 1600, helps her mother with herbs and midwifery in France. When her father falls off a horse and dies, her life changes. Her mother saves the life of the wife and child of their chateau owner, but the doctor says that her mother must be evil to be able to do things he cannot. This attitude extends into the village, and Rose's mother and other women are accused of witchcraft by the priest and other men. Rose sees her mother scalded in torture, and she gives her herbs in secret to save her from further suffering before escaping herself. Not for five years are the innocent women cleared, but by then, almost all of them have been burned.

910.   Matas, Carol. **Daniel's Story**. New York: Scholastic, 1993. 136p. $13.95. ISBN 0-590-46920-7. 4-7

In 1941, Daniel, age fourteen, takes a train with his family from Frankfurt, Germany, to the Jewish ghetto in Lodz, Poland. Although his family has lived in Frankfurt for more than 600 years, they have to leave. At Auschwitz and Buchenwald, he recalls photographs from his younger life and contrasts what they meant to him then with his current situation. He and his father survive; other family members do not. *Notable Children's Trade Books in the Field of Social Studies*.

911.   Matas, Carol. **Sworn Enemies**. New York: Bantam, 1993. 132p. $16. ISBN 0-553-08326-0. 6-9

Aaron, a sixteen-year-old yeshiva student whose father has paid to keep him from serving in the Russian army of 1840, suffers the jealousy of Zev, a boy who loves the same girl. Zev gets the military to kidnap Aaron in order to fill their quota, but the recruiters also capture Zev. The two must go on a forced march together; even after they conspire to escape, their dislike of each other continues because of their differing backgrounds and personalities.

912.   Mathews, Sally Schofer, author/illustrator. **The Sad Night: The Story of an Aztec Victory and a Spanish Loss**. New York: Clarion, 1994. Unpaged. $16.95. ISBN 0-395-63035-5. 4-6

Mathews has based her artwork on the twenty Aztec codes and codex fragments remaining from the Spanish destruction of the Aztecs, which she tells about in the book. The Aztecs had built a strong empire, beginning with Tenochtitlán, in fewer than 200 years, and their King Moctezuma was the most powerful man in Mexico. Aztec troubles began in the year of 1 Reed (1519), when they expected the return of their feathered serpent god, Quetzalcoatl, in the guise of a man. Instead, Hernán Cortés arrived, and they mistook him for the god. They bestowed gifts of gold on Cortés, but the Spanish took Montezuma prisoner instead of thanking him. Other events led to Montezuma's death, the defeat of the Spaniards, and the last battle the Aztecs would ever win. Cortés returned with more men the next year to end the Aztec domination. Today the area is Mexico City, where people recently found some of the Aztec gold the Spaniards melted and then lost when they were trying to escape their first defeat. More about Aztecs and Cortés.

913.   Matthews, Rupert. **The First People**. Jonathan Heap, illustrator. New York: Bookwright Press, Franklin Watts, 1990. 32p. $11.40. ISBN 0-531-18298-3. (Prehistoric Life). 4-6

The text defines the characteristics of human beings that make them different from their ancestors. It traces the evolution of humans through fossil records and current anthropological theory in a comparison of Neanderthals and their culture with humans of today. Two-page spreads discuss a variety of topics. Photographs and maps highlight the text. Bibliography, Glossary, and Index.

914.   Matthews, Rupert. **The First Settlements**. Bernard Long, illustrator. New York: Bookwright Press, Franklin Watts, 1990. 32p. $11.40. ISBN 0-531-18299-1. (Prehistoric Life). 4-6

Two-page topic spreads present the changes in migration, culture, and settlement that occurred when humans shifted from being hunter-gatherers to farmers. The text also covers the development of metals and the establishment of the first cities. Photographs and maps enhance the text. Bibliography, Glossary, and Index.

915. Maurer, Richard. **Airborne: The Search for the Secret of Flight**. New York: Aladdin, 1990. 48p. $5.95pa. ISBN 0-671-69423-5pa. (NOVA). 5-8

A history of flight, the text begins with experiments and designs for various types of aircraft, gliders, and hot-air balloons from the 1600s. It continues through the history of experimentation until the Wright brothers flew their heavier-than-air craft in 1903. Drawings, photographs, and diagrams illustrate the principles of flight that had to be understood before flying became possible. When such terms as *aileron*, *elevator*, *rudder*, and *throttle* became attached to the principles, human flight began. Index.

916. Mayerson, Evelyn Wilde. **The Cat Who Escaped from Steerage**. New York: Scribners, 1990. 64p. $15. ISBN 0-684-19209-8. 4-6

While Chanah, age nine, travels with her cat on the ship from Poland via France to America in 1910, her cat disappears. She knows that the cat has ventured into other areas of the ship, but the guards will not allow her to search. When the ship reaches Ellis Island, Chanah finds her cat with a Polish woman who has taken care of it during the journey, but returns it.

917. Mayne, William. **Low Tide**. New York: Delacorte, 1993. 198p. $14. ISBN 0-385-30904-X. 4-7

While Charlie, his sister Elisabeth, and his Maori friend, Wiremu, fish early one morning in Jade Bay on the coast of New Zealand, an especially low tide reveals a rock in the distance, with a wrecked ship thought to have treasure aboard perched on top. They go to examine the ship, and while they are on it a huge tidal wave sweeps them and the ship into the mountains where the Koroua, a legendary mountain man, lives. He assuages their fears and helps them return home while revealing the truth about himself and the ship.

918. McAuley, Karen. **Golda Meir**. New York: Chelsea House, 1985. 110p. $18.95. ISBN 0-87754-568-5. (World Leaders Past and Present). 5 up

Golda Meir (1898-1978), born into a Russian family that immigrated to Wisconsin, experienced anti-Semitism as a child. As a young adult, she became committed to Zionism and socialism, and in 1921, she moved to Palestine. Finally, in 1948, her dream for the State of Israel came true. She was a kibbutz worker, a social activist, a politician, an ambassador, and finally a prime minister for her country. Photographs enhance the text. Chronology, Further Reading, and Index.

919. McCaughrean, Geraldine. **El Cid**. Victor G. Ambrus, illustrator. New York: Oxford University Press, 1989. 126p. $17.95. ISBN 0-19-276077-7. 6 up

El Cid, or Rodrigo Diaz de Vivar (1040-1099), was a soldier-hero who won glory when he helped to conquer the Moors at Valencia after they had taken much of Spain. He violated all of the conditions of surrender by burning the leader, cadi ibn Djahhaff, at the stake and slaughtering citizens. He then ruled most of Valencia and Murcia. The text includes this and other stories of El Cid's exploits.

920. McCaughrean, Geraldine. **A Little Lower Than the Angels**. New York: Oxford University Press, 1987. 133p. $15. ISBN 0-19-271561-5. 6-9

Gabriel is a bound apprentice to a stonemason, but he escapes and joins a group performing mystery and miracle plays in fourteenth-century England. He thinks that he is healing townspeople who declare that the plays have healed them until he discovers that the troupe's leader pays townspeople to pretend. Although disappointed, he thinks that the plays are important for people to see, and he helps his two friends, a father and daughter, record the words for players in the future. *Whitbread Book of the Year*.

921. McCully, Emily Arnold. **The Amazing Felix**. New York: Putnam, 1993. Unpaged. $14.95. ISBN 0-399-22428-9. 2-4

In the 1920s, Felix tries to practice the piano as his father has instructed him, but he does not like it. His father is a famous concert pianist who wants his children to play the piano well. When Felix crosses the ocean by ship to join his father in England, he meets a magician and starts to practice magic instead. When he joins his father at a castle, both the music and the magic help.

922. McCully, Emily Arnold, author/illustrator. **Mirette on the Highwire**. New York: Putnam, 1992. 32p. $15.95. ISBN 0-399-22130-1. K-4

After Bellini comes to live at her mother's boardinghouse in Paris in the late nineteenth century, Mirette sees him walking on a high wire in the backyard. She wants to learn and starts practicing. She finds out that the man is a famous high-wire artist who no longer has the nerve to perform. Someone persuades him to try again, but he freezes until he sees Mirette waiting for him on the other end of the wire.

923. McCully, Emily Arnold, author/illustrator. **The Pirate Queen**. New York: Putnam, 1995. 32p. $16.95. ISBN 0-399-22657-5. 3-5

Grania O'Malley, born into a pirating family, had married by age sixteen and taken charge of her husband's family's fleet of ships. She saw two husbands and a son die, fought in battles, was imprisoned, and suffered British confiscation of her riches. She appealed to Queen Elizabeth I about her loss. O'Malley was a woman of contrasts who had a singleness of purpose.

924. McCully, Emily Arnold, author/illustrator. **Starring Mirette & Bellini**. New York: Putnam, 1997. Unpaged. $15.95. ISBN 0-399-22636-2. K-4

During the late nineteenth century, Mirette learns how to walk a tightrope from Monsieur Bellini, a performer who has lost his nerve. Bellini lives at Mirette's mother's boardinghouse in Paris, and to please Mirette, he walks from one rooftop to another. He freezes, however, until Mirette walks on the wire toward him and helps him finish his walk.

925. McCurdy, Michael, author/illustrator. **Trapped by the Ice!: Shackleton's Amazing Antarctic Adventure**. New York: Walker, 1997. 41p. $16.95. ISBN 0-8027-8438-0. 4-7

In 1915, Sir Ernest Shackleton tried to cross the Antarctic, but ice stopped and soon sank his ship. Since rescue planes were nonexistent, the crew had to survive without the ship until the ice broke. Their journals tell how they did it without losing a man. Bibliography and Index.

926. McCutcheon, Elsie. **Summer of the Zeppelin**. New York: Farrar, Straus & Giroux, 1985. 168p. $11.95. ISBN 0-374-37294-2. 5-9

When Elvira is twelve, in 1918, a German zeppelin bombs a small English village near her home. She and her friend then meet a German prisoner working nearby who speaks English. Although his people have hurt her nation, she tries to help him return to Germany to find his sister, because she knows that her father, away fighting for three years, would want her to be kind.

927. McGowen, Tom. **The Time of the Forest**. Boston: Houghton Mifflin, 1988. 110p. $12.95. ISBN 0-395-44471-3. 5-8

When Wolf and his tribe see strangers in the forest, they are not surprised, but they have difficulty coping with a tribe living only five days of travel away that keeps its animals in pens and plows the ground. The two tribes fight each other, but Wolf saves a girl from the farming tribe. After he helps her, each of their tribes ostracizes them, and they have to leave to form their own group.

928. McGraw, Eloise. **The Golden Goblet**. 1961. Magnolia, MA: Peter Smith, 1988. 248p. $17. ISBN 0-8446-6342-5. New York: Viking, 1990. 248p. $4.99pa. ISBN 0-14-030335-9pa. 5-9

Ranofer, age twelve, begins to watch his brother's disgusting friend and determines that he is stealing gold from his employer in ancient Egypt. Ranofer's brother not only takes Ranofer's inheritance and refuses to buy Ranofer an apprenticeship, but also is a thief; he steals from a queen's tomb. When Ranofer realizes what is happening, he reports it to the palace, and the guards finally believe him when he identifies the objects. As a result of his loyalty, he becomes a goldsmith's apprentice. *Newbery Honor.*

929. McGraw, Eloise. **Mara, Daughter of the Nile**. 1953. Magnolia, MA: Peter Smith, 1991. 280p. $16.50. ISBN 0-8446-6536-3. 5-9

Mara, age seventeen, has blue eyes, an unusual characteristic in Egypt during 1550 B.C. Although a slave, she speaks and reads Babylonian. This ability enables her to translate for the wife of Hatshepsut's brother, Thutmose, and to become a spy for evil brothers who are trying to destroy Thutmose. Then she begins to spy on the brothers for Thutmose's brother, Sheftu. After proving her loyalty to Sheftu, she marries him when the evil brothers are apprehended.

930. McGraw, Eloise. **Master Cornhill**. 1973. New York: Penguin, 1987. 218p. $4.95pa. ISBN 0-14-032255-8pa. 5 up

Michael, aged eleven in 1666, returns to London after having been evacuated because of the plague and finds that all the members of his adoptive family have died. While he hides from press gangs, he begins working for Mr. Maas, the best mapmaker in London. After living through the Great Fire, Michael realizes that to be an artist as he desires, he must take creative risks.

931. McNeese, Tim. **The Great Wall of China**. San Diego, CA: Lucent, 1997. 96p. $16.95. ISBN 1-56006-428-5. (Building History). 6-8

The text and photographs cover the building techniques of the Great Wall and give the historical background leading to its construction. Chronology, Bibliography, Further Reading, and Index.

932. McNeill, Sarah. **Ancient Egyptian People**. Brookfield, CT: Millbrook Press, 1997. 48p. $15.90. ISBN 0-7613-0056-2. (People and Places). 5-8

Among the thirteen ancient Egyptian classes discussed in this text are peasants, priests, pharaohs, women, mummy-makers, and servants. For each group, McNeill discusses their rank, roles in society, and their community responsibilities. Illustrations of artifacts and landscape highlight the text. Further Reading, Glossary, and Index.

933. McNeill, Sarah. **Ancient Egyptian Places**. Brookfield, CT: Millbrook Press, 1997. 48p. $15.90. ISBN 0-7613-0057-0. (People and Places). 5-8

McNeill highlights thirteen different places important in Egyptian life. They include the factory, the pyramid, the tomb, the Nile, and the desert. Illustrations of artifacts and landscape highlight the text. Further Reading, Glossary, and Index.

934. McPherson, Stephanie Sammartino. **Ordinary Genius: The Story of Albert Einstein**. Minneapolis, MN: Carolrhoda, 1995. 95p. $17.50. ISBN 0-87614-788-0. (Trailblazers). 5-8

Albert Einstein (1879-1955) developed theories of relativity that changed the way people perceive space and time. He hated violence and wanted world peace. He was also proud to be Jewish, and he worked to help Jews have a better life. Black-and-white photographs supplement the text. Bibliography and Index. *Outstanding Science Trade Books for Children.*

935. McSwigan, Marie. **Snow Treasure**. Andre LeBlanc, illustrator. 1942. New York: Scholastic, 1986. 156p. $3.50pa. ISBN 0-590-42537-4pa. 3-7

In 1940, Peter Lundstrom and the other children of the village fool the Nazis who parachute into their Norwegian village and hold it hostage. Peter's uncle tells him that the children can save the country's gold, hidden in the town, by riding their sleds with the gold bullion under them to the shore of the fjord. There they can bury the gold under snowmen until men working with his uncle can retrieve it for loading onto a camouflaged boat nearby.

936. McTavish, Douglas. **Galileo**. New York: Bookwright Press, Franklin Watts, 1991. 48p. $12.40. ISBN 0-531-18405-6. (Pioneers of Science). 4-6

Galileo (1564-1642) lived in a time when the Catholic Church refused to accept any information that countered its beliefs. Galileo suffered because he taught that the earth was not the center of the universe. Questioned by the Inquisition, he lived under house arrest at the end of his life. The text looks more at his relationship to the Church than at his many discoveries, such as four of the moons of Jupiter which he saw through the telescope he invented. Illustrations enhance the text. Chronology, Glossary, and Index.

937. McTavish, Douglas. **Isaac Newton**. New York: Bookwright Press, Franklin Watts, 1990. 48p. $17.71. ISBN 0-531-18351-3. (Pioneers of Science). 5-8

Isaac Newton (1642-1727) made important discoveries that have affected history. The text looks at his life growing up in England and the scientists and thinkers who influenced him. He invented differential calculus and formulated the theories of universal gravitation, terrestrial mechanics, and color. Anecdotal information says that the sight of a falling apple led to his treatise on gravitation, which he presented in his work, *Principia Mathematica* (1687). Chronology, Glossary, Bibliography, and Index.

938. Mead, Alice. **Adem's Cross**. New York: Farrar, Straus & Giroux, 1996. 144p. $15. ISBN 0-374-30057-7. 5 up

In 1993, Adem, age fourteen and of Albanian descent, lives in Kosovo, the poorest province of the former Yugoslavia, which the Serbs occupy. While his sister, Fatmira, stands on a bridge reading a poem, the Serbs shoot her. Adem's family undergoes further suffering for his sister's passive resistance, and three soldiers grab Adem on a lonely road, tear off his shirt, and carve the Serb insignia on his chest. He decides to escape so that the nightmare for his family can end. A Serbian man, supposedly his enemy, and a gypsy, Fikel, help him to cross the border into Albania. *American Library Association Notable Books for Young Adults.*

939. Meadows, Matthew, author/illustrator. **Pablo Picasso**. New York: Sterling, 1996. 32p. $14.95. ISBN 0-8069-6160-0. (Art for Young People). 3-5

Two-page spreads present Picasso's works and give an elementary understanding of the ideas that inspired him. The text places him in context of the twentieth century. Glossary and Index.

940. Medearis, Angela Shelf. **Come This Far to Freedom: A History of African Americans**. New York: Atheneum, 1993. 148p. $14.95. ISBN 0-689-31522-8. 5 up

Medearis divides the history of African Americans into five parts: coming from Africa to the hardships of slavery, the fight for freedom, the fresh start during Reconstruction after the Civil War, the movement for equality, and the people who have continued to break down the barriers in politics, the military, the sciences, and other fields. Important Dates, Bibliography, and Index.

941.   Medearis, Angela Shelf. **Our People**. Michael Bryant, illustrator. New York: Atheneum, 1994. 32p. $14.95. ISBN 0-689-31826-X. K-3

This brief overview lists some of the many accomplishments of African Americans throughout history, from the construction of the pyramids in Egypt to contemporary scientists. Among the professions included are royalty, mathematicians, artists, explorers, Underground Railroad conductors, cowboys, businesspeople, doctors, farmers, politicians, and inventors. The narrator has her father's assurance that she can do anything she wants.

942.   Mellecker, Judith. **The Fox and the Kingfisher**. Robert Andrew Parker, illustrator. New York: Knopf, 1990. 40p. $14.95. ISBN 0-679-80539-7. K-3

In 1902, not wanting their widowed father to remarry, two children use a golden key given to them by the new stableboy to turn themselves into a fox and a kingfisher from Christmas until spring. By then they are ready to accept their father's decision. In this historical fantasy, they discover that they would rather be their father's children, even if he is married, than lonely animals.

943.   Mellecker, Judith. **Randolph's Dream**. Robert Andrew Parker, illustrator. New York: Knopf, 1991. 40p. $14.95. ISBN 0-679-81115-X. K-3

During the Blitz of World War II, Randolph has to leave London for the countryside to stay with relatives. During the day, he helps in the garden and collects moths, stamps, and string. At night, he dreams of flying around the countryside. Then he begins to dream of flying to North Africa, where his father serves in the military. One of his dreams in this historical fantasy tells him that his father is lost in the desert, and Randolph saves him. When he wakes up the next morning, he still has an orange in his pocket from this trip.

944.   Meltzer, Milton. **Columbus and the World Around Him**. New York: Franklin Watts, 1990. 192p. $23.40. ISBN 0-531-10899-6. 6 up

Meltzer draws upon Columbus's journal and other contemporary records to understand the man. Meltzer presents the European culture in which Columbus matured as it moved from medievalism to the early Renaissance. Columbus saw people in the New World as inferior and deserving of enslavement, with their lands as prizes for the explorers and Queen Isabella. A Note on Sources and Index.

945.   Meltzer, Milton. **Gold: The True Story of Why People Search for It, Mine It, Trade It, Steal It, Mint It, Hoard It**. New York: HarperCollins, 1993. 167p. $15. ISBN 0-06-022983-7. 4-8

Photographs complement the text, which tells of humankind's 5,000-year quest for gold. Included are such topics as shekels, bezants, florins, ducats, and guineas. Other chapters look at where to get gold in the mines and the slaves who mined it, African empires built on gold, the gold rush in California, the search from Australia to South Africa, and what people endured when others came to their lands looking for gold. Bibliography and Index.

946.   Meyer, Carolyn, and Charles Gallenkamp. **The Mystery of the Ancient Maya**. 1975. New York: Margaret K. McElderry, 1995. 178p. $15. ISBN 0-689-50619-8. 6-9

Since the mid-1800s, explorers have uncovered evidence showing that the Mayan civilization, which covered 125,000 square miles over parts of modern Mexico, Guatemala, Belize, Honduras, and El Salvador, was very advanced. Archaeologists have found ruins filled with jade, pottery, sculptures, wall paintings, and other beautiful artifacts. The text includes much new and recently discovered information on the Maya, such as advances in the reading of hieroglyphic inscriptions, new interpretations of images in the art, and much about all aspects of the society. In four parts, the text tries to address such points as how the ruins were discovered, what the explorers found, who these people were, and what happened to their civilization. Glossary and Index.

947.   Michaelson, Carol. **Ancient China**. New York: Time, 1996. 64p. $15. ISBN 0-80949-248-2. (Nature Company Discoveries). 6 up

Among the topics covered in the text are mythology, Confucian and Daoist philosophies, Buddhism, views about death, justification of the ruler's right to govern, living in ancient China, and the creative aspects of the times. Included is information on the social order, peasants, land, clothing, celebrations, medical practices, printing, silk, and writing. A four-page foldout of the Great Wall highlights the text. Chronology, Glossary, and Index.

948.   Micklethwait, Lucy. **A Child's Book of Art: Great Pictures, First Words**. New York: Dorling Kindersley, 1996. 64p. $16.95. ISBN 0-7894-1003-6. K-3

Famous paintings throughout history are divided according to topics that a child would understand. Several subject-related paintings illustrate each topic. The topics are the family, at home (van Gogh's *Bedroom at Arles*), in the garden (Monet's *A Girl with a Watering Can*), pets (Dürer's *Hare),* animals on the farm, wild animals, birds, fruit, things to do, action words, counting, colors, shapes, opposites, seasons, weather, the sea, faces, five senses, travel playing, working, eating, sleeping, and others. Picture List.

949. Millar, Heather. **China's Tang Dynasty**. Freeport, NY: Marshall Cavendish, 1996. 80p. $19.95. ISBN 0-7614-0074-5. (Cultures of the Past). 6-10

The text examines the artifacts, monuments, domestic scenes, and historical aspects of China's Tang Dynasty, which lasted from 618 to 907, as it discusses the religion, art, education, and customs of the time. Included is an explanation of Confucian and Buddhist ideals and their legacy. During this era, some of China's most famous poets were working, including Tu Fu, Wang Wei, and Li Po. Photographs, Drawings, Bibliography, Chronology, Further Reading, Glossary, and Index.

950. Millar, Heather. **The Kingdom of Benin West Africa**. Tarrytown, NY: Benchmark, 1996. 80p. $19.95. ISBN 0-7614-0088-5. 6-8

Benin was one of the most important kingdoms in West Africa 500 years ago. The text includes an overview of its history and information about the slavery practiced there before the Europeans ever landed on the coast. Belief systems with witches, ghosts, magic, and sacrificial rites were important then, but the text also includes information about life there during contemporary times.

951. Millard, Anne. **Pyramids**. New York: Kingfisher Books, 1996. 63p. $14.95. ISBN 1-85697-674-2. Brookfield, CT: Copper Beach, 1996. 64p. $6.95pa. ISBN 1-56294-194-1pa. 4 up

The text looks at different types of pyramids, including those built in Egypt at different times and those built by other civilizations. It looks at the process of building an Egyptian pyramid, from cutting the huge stones to moving them onto the pyramid, and discusses how important the pyramids were to Egyptian lifestyle and religion. Among the other pyramids covered are some in North America, South and Central America, the Louvre in Paris, and the Transamerica pyramid in San Francisco. Glossary and Index.

952. Milton, Nancy. **The Giraffe That Walked to Paris**. Roger Roth, illustrator. New York: Crown, 1992. 32p. $15.95. ISBN 0-517-58133-7. K-4

The King of Egypt sends a gift to King Charles X of France in 1826, hoping to ease tension between the two countries. His gift is a giraffe, which travels first by ship and then by land from Marseilles, where the ship was rerouted because of bad weather. It takes the entourage forty-one days to reach Paris, while the king waits anxiously for the giraffe's arrival.

953. Minks, Benton, and Louise Minks. **The French and Indian War**. San Diego, CA: Lucent, 1995. 112p. $16.95. ISBN 1-56006-236-3. (World History Series). 6 up

In 1754, the French and Indian War began the battle between France and England over control of the New World. John Cabot arrived on the coast of Canada in 1497 and returned to England with positive reports. In 1614, John Smith charted the Atlantic coast from Virginia to Maine. Although other explorers also visited, at the beginning of the eighteenth century only France and England remained interested in owning the land. This absorbing history of the French and British tactics uses sources written during the period, the research of recognized scholars, and recent archaeological evidence. King George's War, begun in 1744, ended with the Treaty of Aix-la-Chapelle in 1748, in which Louisbourg was returned to France. In 1755, the French defeated the British in the Battle of the Wilderness, and in 1756, the formal war began. In 1757, the Marquis de Montcalm destroyed Forts Oswego and William Henry. In England, William Pitt decided to converge on Quebec, where General Jeffrey Amherst took Louisbourg in 1758, but Montcalm defended Fort Ticonderoga. The British began building Fort Pitt on the site of the burned Fort Duquesne. In 1759, the English captured Quebec, and the French surrendered in 1760. In 1763, Chief Pontiac led the Northwest Territory Indian nations against the English, and when the war officially ended that year, with the Peace of Paris, the British were unable to expand into the Indian territories as they desired. The British also needed money to pay for the war, so they began to tax the American colonists. These and other events led to the next war, the War of Independence. Notes, Glossary, For Further Reading, Additional Works Consulted, Research Bibliography, and Index.

954. Mochizuki, Ken. **Passage to Freedom: The Sugihara Story**. New York: Lee & Low, 1997. 32p. $15.95. ISBN 1-880000-49-0. 3-6

Hiroki Sugihara is five in 1940, living at the Japanese consulate in Lithuania. When hundreds of Jewish refugees arrive at the gate wanting visas to Japan, his father decides to disobey the Japanese goverment and help these people fleeing from the Nazis. Sugihara tells his story as an adult reflecting on his family's involvement in history.

955. Moktefi, Mokhtar. **The Arabs in the Golden Age**. Veronique Ageorges, illustrator; Mary Kae LaRose, translator. Brookfield, CT: Millbrook Press, 1992. 64p. $16.40. ISBN 1-56294-201-8. (Peoples of the Past). 4-8

The Golden Age of the Arabs began in the early eighth century, when Muhammad's teachings began to spread, and lasted into the thirteenth century. Islam was the creative force behind the military, religious, and cultural prominence that the Arabs achieved during this time. Islam was and is a set of laws guiding all aspects of the lives of its believers. During this period, many beautiful artworks, including calligraphic manuscripts, were produced; many people learned to read; and many advances occurred in technology, science, medicine, and mathematics. The text looks at the Islamic world, the caliph's rule, the empire, city and country life, Arab society, and the sharing of knowledge. Dates to Remember, Map, Find Out More, Glossary, and Index.

956. **Moldova**. Minneapolis, MN: Lerner, 1993. 56p. $19.95. ISBN 0-8225-2809-6. (Then and Now). 5-9

With a Romanian culture and language, Moldova has been separate from other former Soviet Union countries. The text covers the history, economics, geography, politics, ethnography, and possible future of Moldova as it continues to assert its freedom. Maps and photographs complement the text. Glossary and Index.

957. Monjo, F. N. **Letters to Horseface: Young Mozart's Travels in Italy**. Don Bolognese and Elaine Raphael, illustrators. New York: Viking, 1976. 92p. $10.95. ISBN 0-670-42738-1. 4-7

During 1769, when he was fourteen, Mozart traveled in Italy for a year with his father. He wrote letters to his sister, Nannerl, affectionately called "Horseface." The text, done as fictionalized letters, tells about his music (including the composition of his first opera), the people he met, and what he did during that time. About This Story and Bibliography.

958. Montgomery, Mary. **Marie Curie**. Severino Baraldi, illustrator. Englewood Cliffs, NJ: Silver Burdett, 1990. 104p. $12.95. ISBN 0-382-09981-8. (What Made Them Great). 5-8

Marie Curie (1867-1934), known as Manya, grew up in Poland before attending school in Paris, where she finished first in her class. She met and married Pierre Curie, and they spent a life together doing scientific research that won her two Nobel Prizes. Appendix, Books for Further Reading, and Index.

959. Mooney, Bel. **The Stove Haunting**. Boston: Houghton Mifflin, 1988. 126p. $12.95. ISBN 0-395-46764-0. 5-8

Daniel and his parents find an ugly old stove behind a wall in the old rectory they renovate after moving from London to the West country. When Daniel, age eleven, looks inside the stove, he finds himself in the rectory during 1835. In this historical fantasy, he assumes the work of a kitchen boy who blacks the stove. He sees the privileged wealthy begin to weaken when faced with agricultural unions and Methodism. Daniel's best friend is one of the secret organizers in these groups against the upper class. Daniel watches the choices that these people make in order to live more fulfilled and purposeful lives.

960. Mooney, Bel. **The Voices of Silence**. New York: Delacorte, 1997. 144p. $14.95. ISBN 0-385-32326-3. 3-6

Flora Popescu, thirteen, knows that no one can criticize the head of her country of Romania in 1989. But one day, everything changes, including her daily routine, her family, and her best friend. She thinks it all relates to the new boy in her class named Daniel who is wealthy enough to own blue jeans and who has meat for lunch while everyone else stays hungry. Daniel helps her to realize that her father might be in danger because of his beliefs, and she has to find a way to save him.

961. Morgan, Nina. **Guglielmo Marconi**. New York: Bookwright Press, Franklin Watts, 1991. 48p. $12.40. ISBN 0-531-18417-X. (Pioneers of Science). 5-7

When Guglielmo Marconi (1874-1937) was born, a servant remarked that he had large ears. His mother supposedly responded, "He will be able to hear the still small voice of the air." Whether or not she really said it, Marconi did exactly that. His life paralleled the development of wireless communication, and he worked hard to improve it. He patented the wireless telegraph, set up a company, and was the first person to send telegraph messages without wires. His experimentation with radio waves led to the radio and a worldwide system of wireless communication. Photographs, Illustrations, Date Chart, Books to Read, Glossary, and Index.

962. Morgan, Nina. **Louis Pasteur**. New York: Bookwright Press, Franklin Watts, 1992. 48p. $12.40. ISBN 0-531-18459-5. (Pioneers of Science). 5-9

The text looks at the life of Louis Pasteur (1822-1895) as well as the world before and after him. He worked with chemicals and crystals before he became interested in microbes or germs, which he thought were the possible cause of much disease but also the possible cure for others. He saved the silkworm industry and helped makers of wine and milk with his pasteurization process. His belief was that one should use one's knowledge, share it, and serve one's country. Photographs and Illustrations, Date Chart, Glossary, Books to Read, and Index.

963. Morimoto, Junko, author/illustrator. **My Hiroshima**. New York: Viking, 1987. Unpaged. $13.95. ISBN 0-670-83181-6. 3-6

The author remembers the years during World War II when she had to begin wearing military clothes and practicing drills. Then one day she stayed home sick from school. She heard an airplane far off, and then everything went black as the atomic bomb exploded over Hiroshima on August 6, 1945. The bomb destroyed her family's home, but although everyone was wounded, they were alive. She describes the scene afterward and the long recovery.

964. Morley, Jacqueline. **Clothes: For Work, Play and Display**. Vanda Baginskia, Mark Bergin, John James, Carolyn Scrace, and Gerald Wood, illustrators. New York: Franklin Watts, 1992. 48p. $7.95pa. ISBN 0-531-15740-7pa. (Timelines). 5-8

Two-page spreads divide the text into minichapters with many illustrations to show clothes throughout history. The time periods covered are the first clothes people wore; classical clothes of the Minoans, Greeks, and Romans; the Dark Ages; armor and tournament gear; medieval and Renaissance Italy; farthingales with Spanish influence in the sixteenth century; seventeenth-century Cavaliers and Puritans in England; court clothes and politics of France; crinoline petticoats introduced in 1857; folk costumes; dress reforms like bloomers; sportswear; between the World Wars; work clothes; clothes today; and clothes of the future. Time-line, Glossary, and Index.

965. Morley, Jacqueline. **An Egyptian Pyramid**. John James and Mark Bergin, illustrators. New York: Peter Bedrick, 1991. 48p. $18.95. ISBN 0-87226-346-0. (Inside Story). 4-6

Two-page spreads and illustrations cover topics about the pyramids. Those discussed are the meaning of the pyramid, laying the foundation, quarrying the stone, building the structure, the laborer's year, the craftsman's day, the towns around the pyramids, the people and their lives, the festivities, the pharaoh and his life, the priests and scribes, death and mummification, and other burial practices. Glossary and Index.

966. Morley, Jacqueline. **Exploring North America**. David Antram, illustrator. New York: Peter Bedrick, 1996. 48p. $18.95. ISBN 0-87226-488-2. (Voyages of Discovery). 3-6

The text covers the four centuries of exploration beginning with Columbus, Cabot, and the Conquistadores and continues through Cartier, Champlain, Lewis and Clark, Mackenzie, and Fremont. The entries, which give an overview of the topic, cover double-page spreads and contain illustrations. Maps, Glossary, and Index.

967. Morley, Jacqueline. **A Roman Villa**. John James, illustrator. New York: Peter Bedrick, 1992. 48p. $18.95. ISBN 0-87226-360-6. (Inside Story). 4-6

Villas in ancient Rome during the first century A.D. belonged to the wealthy, and they tell what life in Rome was like for the upper class. With these people lived servants, farmers, carpenters, stonemasons, and cooks. Two-page spreads offer information on the Roman house, including rooms, baths, and lands; the people who lived there; the crops, including olives and wine; and what might have happened on a rainy day. Roman Facts, Glossary, and Index.

968. Morpurgo, Michael. **Butterfly Lion**. New York: Viking, 1997. 96p. $14.99. ISBN 0-670-87461-2. 4-7

When Bertie lives in South Africa at the turn of the century, he rescues a rare white lion cub from hyenas and begins a friendship with the animal. He goes to boarding school in England, and tells the white lion that they will meet again. The lion becomes part of a French circus, but years later, during World War I, Bertie sees the white lion's picture on a circus poster and begins his quest to see him again.

969. Morpurgo, Michael. **King of the Cloud Forests**. New York: Viking, 1988. 146p. $12.95. ISBN 0-670-82069-5. 5 up

In 1937, the Japanese bomb China, and Ashley, age fourteen, must leave his missionary father for India in the company of a family friend, pretending to be his son. In Tibet, the two become separated when they are trapped by a blizzard, and Ashley awakens to find huge creatures nursing him. He goes with them and realizes that they are the legendary Yetis of the mountains. When he finally reunites with Uncle Sung, he hesitates to relate the experience, but in England he finds the man whose photograph the Yetis gave him and knows that he did not dream his experience.

970. Morpurgo, Michael. **Mr. Nobody's Eyes**. New York: Viking, 1990. 138p. $12.95. ISBN 0-670-83022-4. 5-8

Harry, age ten, wants to return to the time when he and his mother were the only family members; Harry's father died when he was shot down over the English Channel in World War II. But by 1947, Harry's mother has remarried and had another baby. Harry hides in the basement of the bombed-out house next door and looks after a chimpanzee, Ocky, who has run away from the circus. The two leave London for Bournemouth. When his stepfather rescues him, Harry realizes that he does care.

971. Morpurgo, Michael. **Twist of Gold**. New York: Viking, 1993. 246p. $14.99. ISBN 0-670-84851-4. 5-9

When Sean O'Brien's mother is too sick from hunger to travel during the 1850s, he and his sister leave Ireland to join their father in America. They carry with them the symbol of their clan: the golden torc (necklace) of their ancestors. Thieves who know of their possession try to steal it, and twice they lose it. But twice they find it again as they travel from Boston to California to meet their father, and surprisingly, their mother, who has been able to make a quicker, safer journey.

972. Morpurgo, Michael. **Waiting for Anya**. New York: Viking, 1991. 172p. $12.95. ISBN 0-670-83735-0. 5-8

Jo, age twelve and a shepherd on the border between Spain and France, helps to save Jewish children in World War II by smuggling them over the border. With Germans patrolling and infiltrating the town, several people realize that if the children pretend to be shepherds, they will be able to roam over the mountains without suspicion to escape. *School Library Journal Best Book.*

973. Morpurgo, Michael. **The War of Jenkins' Ear**. New York: Philomel, 1995. 178p. $16.95. ISBN 0-399-22735-0. 6-9

In 1952, Toby Jenkins begins the year at Redlands Prep in Sussex, England. A new boy, Christopher, refuses to bow to the headmaster's demands, and tells Toby that he is Jesus Christ reincarnated and plans to save the world. Toby doubts, but a miracle occurs that makes Toby Christopher's first disciple. In a fight between the village boys and the school boys, Christopher advocates peace and tolerance. When authorities find out about Christopher's claims, they expel him and threaten Toby with expulsion unless he recants his support. Although he still believes in Christopher, Toby acquiesces rather than embarrass his parents. *American Library Association Notable Books for Young Adults.*

974. Morpurgo, Michael. **Why the Whales Came**. 1987. New York: Apple, Scholastic, 1990. 141p. $2.75pa. ISBN 0-590-42912-4pa. 5-7

Gracie's parents have told her to avoid the Birdman, who lives on the Isles of Sicily, because he is mad. In 1914, Gracie finds herself at his home and discovers that he is merely deaf. He carves lovely birds and knows why the people in Gracie's neighborhood think the nearby island is cursed. One day a whale beaches itself nearby, and he begs the townspeople to help it return to the water. Because the Birdman has given Gracie's mother food while her husband serves in the navy, she understands that he needs their aid. Although she is only ten, Gracie helps the others see the value in this remarkable man.

975. Morris, Gilbert. **The Dangerous Voyage**. Minneapolis, MN: Bethany House, 1995. 104p. $5.99pa. ISBN 1-55661-395-4pa. (Time Navigators, 1). 4-6

Time travelers Danny and Dixie Fortune find themselves in seventeenth-century London boarding the *Mayflower*. Because one of their shipmates steals the Recall Unit that will return them home, they must stay on the ship for its entire journey to the colonies. They meet figures known through history, such as John Alden, as well as those who seek freedom to worship, known as the "saints," and those who want a better life, the "strangers." The Fortunes' Christian values become clear during the plot development.

976. Morrison, Ian A. **Middle East**. Austin, TX: Raintree/Steck-Vaughn, 1991. 96p. $16.98. ISBN 0-8114-2440-5. 5-9

This survey of the Middle East gives information on its geography, languages, religions, history, occupations, family life, food, cities, and education. It emphasizes that knowing the history of the area helps one to understand past and present conflicts among the peoples who live there. Index.

977. Morrison, Taylor, author/illustrator. **Antonio's Apprenticeship: Painting a Fresco in Renaissance Italy**. New York: Holiday House, 1996. Unpaged. $15.95. ISBN 0-8234-1213-X. 3-5

As an apprentice learning how to paint frescoes in Florence during 1478, Antonio learns how to prepare the brushes and charcoal sticks, mix plaster, grind pigments, and transfer the master artist's drawing onto the moistened plaster. After he works carefully, Antonio gets to add finishing brushstrokes to the fresco. Glossary.

978. Morrison, Taylor, author/illustrator. **Neptune's Fountain: A Young Sculptor in Renaissance Italy**. New York: Holiday House, 1997. 32p. $15.95. ISBN 0-8234-1293-8. 3-6

Marco goes to Luigi Borghini's studio in seventeenth-century Rome, shows the great sculptor his wax figure, and asks to become apprenticed. Borghini takes him in. Only after sketching cadavers, copying drawings, and molding wax and mud does Marco get to cut stone. He visits a quarry where he finds the white marble for Borghini's masterpiece, the "Neptune Fountain," organizes its transportation by boat, and is allowed to carve a waterspout on the finished product.

979. Moscinski, Sharon. **Tracing Our Irish Roots**. Santa Fe, NM: John Muir, 1993. 46p. $12.95. ISBN 1-56261-148-8. 3-6

The text looks at life in Ireland for people who decided to emigrate to the United States. Many had to leave after the potato famine because they had no way to support themselves, but they have contributed much to American culture. The two parts of the text, the Old World and the New World, give an overview, with two-page spreads on such topics as crossing the Atlantic, Ellis Island, family life, prejudices faced, achievements in America, and famous people of Irish descent. Archival photographs highlight the text. Index.

980. Moser, Barry. **Fly! A Brief History of Flight Illustrated**. New York: Willa Perlman, HarperCollins, 1993. Unpaged. $16. ISBN 0-06-022893-8. 2-6

This brief history of flight has illustrations of airplanes and their famous pilots who have contributed to the history of flight in the nineteenth and twentieth centuries. Bibliography.

981. Moss, Carol. **Science in Ancient Mesopotamia**. New York: Franklin Watts, 1988. 72p. $16.60. ISBN 0-531-10594-6. (First Book). 5-8

An introduction to ancient Mesopotamia and its science precedes chapters on different developments from this culture. They include writing, medicine, mathematics, exploration of the skies, surveys of nature, everyday technology, and the contemporary debt to the culture for its discoveries. Photographs supplement the text. Glossary, Further Reading, and Index.

982. Moss, Miriam. **Forts and Castles**. Chris Forsey, illustrator. Austin, TX: Raintree/Steck-Vaughn, 1994. 32p. $21.40. ISBN 0-8114-6157-2. (Pointers). 3-6

The brief text and labeled illustrations on two-page spreads discuss the history and architecture of several forts and castles, focusing on their ability to protect themselves in times of siege. The various types are a Bronze Age citadel, an Iron Age hill fort, Herod's fort, a Norman keep, a Crusader castle, a medieval castle, a fourteenth-century castle, a French château, a Japanese castle, an Indian fortress, a Civil War fort, and a romantic castle, Neuschwanstein. Glossary and Index.

983. Muhlberger, Richard. **What Makes a Bruegel a Bruegel?** New York: Viking, 1993. 48p. $11.99. ISBN 0-670-85203-1. 5-9

Pieter Bruegel the Elder (c. 1525-1569) drew everyday scenes. The stress of living in Belgium under the foreign domination of Spain underlies but is not overt in his work. His subjects reveal themselves in their poses rather than through facial expressions, and he filled his paintings with many details. Paintings reproduced and discussed are *The Fall of Icarus, Children's Games, The Fall of the Rebel Angels, Two Monkeys, The Tower of Babel, The Adoration of the Kings, The Harvesters, Hunters in the Snow, The Land of Cockaigne, The Wedding Banquet, The Peasant Dance*, and *The Parable of the Blind*.

984. Muhlberger, Richard. **What Makes a Degas a Degas?** New York: Viking, 1993. 48p. $11.99. ISBN 0-670-85205-8. 5-9

Hilaire-Germain-Edgar Degas (1834-1917) was born in Paris to parents who exposed him to music and art. After a rift with his father over becoming a painter, Degas pursued the traditional route of traveling to Italy to study the masters. He returned to Paris and joined the Impressionists, but he preferred to paint inside, plan his paintings, and base them on strong drawing, unlike his friends. He thus bridged the new and the old in the art of his time. In his work, he cut figures off at the edge of the canvas for a candid effect, tipped the stage upward as if viewed from above, painted patches of brilliant color to augment movement, and opened large spaces in the background to take the eye into the depths. Works reproduced and discussed are *The Bellelli Family, A Woman Seated Beside a Vase of Flowers, Carriage at the Races, The Orchestra at the Opéra, Race Horses at Longchamp, Portraits in an Office (New Orleans), The Dance Class, Miss La La at the Cirque Fernando, Woman Ironing, The Singer in Green, The Millinery Shop*, and *Dancers, Pink and Green*.

985. Muhlberger, Richard. **What Makes a Goya a Goya?** New York: Viking, 1994. 48p. $11.99. ISBN 0-670-85743-2. 5-9

Francisco José de Goya y Lucientes (1746-1828) moved with his family to Saragossa, Spain, where he became an apprentice in 1760. In Madrid by 1763, he worked with Francisco Bayeu at the royal court and viewed the royal art collection, becoming most inspired by Diego Velázquez from the previous century. Goya's images are simultaneously realistic and fantastic and dreamlike. He blamed injustice and superstition for the wars around him, and he preferred the reason of the Enlightenment in which he lived. As the text discusses Goya's life, it comments on his painting and its evolution. He used quick, loose brushstrokes and black, roughly indicated backgrounds, and liked women dressed in the traditional Spanish costume of a *maja*. Works included are *The Crockery Vendor, Don Manuel Osorio Manrique de Zuñiga, Goya in His Studio, The Duchess of Alba, The Family of Charles IV, Bullfight in a Village, The Burial of the Sardine, The Colossus, The Third of May, 1808, The Forge, Self-Portrait with Doctor Arrieta,* and *The Witches' Sabbath*.

986. Muhlberger, Richard. **What Makes a Leonardo a Leonardo?** New York: Viking, 1994. 48p. $11.99. ISBN 0-670-85744-0. 5-9

Leonardo da Vinci (1452-1519) became famous during his lifetime; in fact, someone published a biography about him the year before he died. Another biographer, Vasari, wrote about him in 1550 and again in 1568, after interviewing people who had known Leonardo. Leonardo's parents never married, and apparently he spent his childhood with grandparents who willed him their estate. He moved to Florence with his father as a teenager and became apprenticed to Verrocchio, with whom he worked for approximately thirteen years.

Leonardo's diaries show his many interests—music, biology, botany, engineering, and invention. He finished few of his paintings, probably because he was a perfectionist. The twelve paintings reproduced and discussed here are *The Baptism of Christ, The Annunciation, Ginevra de' Benci, The Adoration of the Magi, Lady with an Ermine, The Virgin of the Rocks, The Last Supper, The Virgin and Child with Saints Anne and John the Baptist, The Battle of Anghiari, Mona Lisa, The Virgin and Child with Saint Anne,* and *Saint John the Baptist.* Leonardo used deep shadows to show three dimensions with gestures conveying real-life emotions. His aerial or atmospheric perspective make his backgrounds look blurry, pale, and far away.

987. Muhlberger, Richard. **What Makes a Monet a Monet?** New York: Viking, 1994. 48p. $11.99. ISBN 0-670-85742-4. 5-9

Monet (1840-1926) tried to capture a special moment in each painting by paying more attention to the overall subject than to specific detail. He started his art by doing caricatures of people on the beach at Honfleur. When he began painting seriously, he returned to his studio, but he saw Eugene Boudin's paintings and went with him to paint outside, rather than remaining in the studio where traditional painters thought one should stay. Paintings discussed in the text are *Garden at Sainte-Adresse, The Luncheon, La Grenouillère, Poppy Field, Argenteuil, Gare Saint-Lazare, Bouquet of Sunflowers, Haystacks, Poplars, Rouen Cathedral, Bridge over a Pool of Water Lilies, The Houses of Parliament,* and *Water Lilies.*

988. Muhlberger, Richard. **What Makes a Picasso a Picasso?** New York: Viking, 1994. 48p. $11.99. ISBN 0-670-85741-6. 5-9

Pablo Ruiz Picasso (1881-1973) almost single-handedly created modern art with his thousands of works—painting, sculpture, prints, and ceramics. He was a superb draftsman, able to accurately capture almost anything with his pencil. In 1900, he moved from Barcelona, Spain, to Paris, France, and eventually settled there. The color in his early paintings reflects his own emotional life. In his styles, he showed several viewpoints at once, and exaggerated and distorted shapes and colors for emotion while simplifying things into basic shapes (such as circles and triangles) with bold black or color outlines. His works reproduced and discussed are *Harlequin, The Blind Man's Meal, Family of the Saltimbanques, Gertrude Stein, Les Demoiselles d'Avignon, Daniel-Henry Kahnweiler, Violin and Fruit, Three Musicians, Three Women at the Spring, Guernica, Night Fishing at Antibes,* and *First Steps.*

989. Mulvihill, Margaret. **The French Revolution**. Gerald Wood, illustrator. New York: Gloucester Press, Franklin Watts, 1989. 32p. $11.90. ISBN 0-531-17167-1. (History Highlights). 3-6

The brief text and accompanying watercolors give an introduction to the causes of the French Revolution in 1789, the events from the Bastille to the guillotines, and the results of the revolution. Chronology and Index.

990. Mulvihill, Margaret. **Roman Forts**. Gerald Wood, illustrator. New York: Franklin Watts, 1990. 32p. $11.90. ISBN 0-531-17201-5. (History Highlights). 3-5

The text examines the structure and defenses of ancient Roman forts as it overviews military life and how the army influenced both the growth and decline of the Roman Empire. The military helped to establish outposts and built roads to reach them after they gained control of an area. Color illustrations and photographs enhance the text. Chronology, Glossary, and Index.

991. Munro, Bob. **Aircraft**. Ian Moores, illustrator. Austin, TX: Raintree/Steck-Vaughn, 1994. 32p. $21.40. ISBN 0-8114-6161-0. (Pointers). 3-6

The two-page spreads of brief text and labeled illustrations describe different types of aircraft. They include a long-range airliner, commuter airline, medium-range airline, supersonic airliner, helicopter, tilt-rotor aircraft, jump jet, supersonic fighter, swing-wing interceptor, stealth fighter, aerobatic airplane, and glider. Glossary and Index.

992. Murphy, Nora. **A Hmong Family**. Minneapolis, MN: Lerner, 1997. 64p. $16.13; $8.95pa. ISBN 0-8225-3406-1; 0-614-28837-1pa. (Journey Between Two Worlds). 5-7

At eleven, Xiong Pao Vang has to cope with a new culture after he and his family have escaped from Laos and the wars there. Further Reading and Index.

993. Murray, Jocelyn. **Africa**. New York: Facts on File, 1990. 96p. $17.95. ISBN 0-8160-2209-7. (Cultural Atlas for Young People). 6-9

The text examines as many facets of Africa as possible, using full-color illustrations and maps. Chronology, Glossary, Gazetteer, and Index.

994. Myers, Walter Dean. **Toussaint L'Ouverture: The Fight for Haiti's Freedom**. Jacob Lawrence, illustrator. New York: Simon & Schuster, 1996. 40p. $16. ISBN 0-689-80126-2. 3-7

Toussaint L'Ouverture (1743?-1803), a freed slave who became general of a Haitian slave army, helped to defeat Haiti's French conquerors in 1791. His leadership liberated the island. The text looks at L'Ouverture's early life and how it inspired Jacob Lawrence's artwork in the 1930s and 1940s. *American Library Association Notable Books for Children.*

N

995. Nardo, Don. **The Age of Augustus**. San Diego, CA: Lucent, 1996. 112p. $16.95. ISBN 1-56006-306-8. (World History). 5-8

Nardo discusses the rise of Augustus Caesar (63 B.C.-A.D. 14) as emperor of Rome and his accomplishments made by consolidating Rome's power. He also includes commentary about people who were living and working at the time such as the writers Livy, Horace, and Virgil. Photographs, maps, and reproductions augment the text. Bibliography, Chronology, Further Reading, and Index.

996. Nardo, Don. **Chernobyl**. Brian McGovern, illustrator. San Diego, CA: Lucent, 1990. 64p. $12.95. ISBN 1-56006-008-5. (World Disasters). 5 up

On April 27, 1986, in Pripyat, Ukraine (then the Soviet Union), the nuclear reactor malfunctioned, and the ensuing nuclear accident affected the town and those nearby forever. The Soviet authorities refused to announce the disaster, but Swedish scientists detected the radiation in the air. Although safeguards are supposedly followed at all nuclear plants, the situation showed that the worst can happen when humans err. Photographs, diagrams, and drawings accent the text. Further Reading, Glossary, Works Consulted, and Index.

997. Nardo, Don. **Krakatoa**. San Diego, CA: Lucent, 1990. 64p. $12.95. ISBN 1-56006-001-5. (World Disasters). 5-8

The 1883 eruption of Krakatoa, in Indonesia, killed 36,000 people with the resulting tidal waves. It influenced weather and sunsets across the globe for months afterward. The cultural, historical, and geographic contexts of this disaster and how it affected both people and environment appear in the text, with supporting illustrations, diagrams, and maps. Glossary, Further Reading, and Index.

998. Nardo, Don. **Traditional Japan**. San Diego, CA: Lucent, 1995. 112p. $16.95. ISBN 1-56006-244-4. (World History Series). 6-10

The strong feeling of group solidarity that defines Japan as a nation is rooted in its political and cultural history, extending from ancient times to its opening to the West in 1854. The Japanese psyche seems to see itself as part of the nation rather than as an individual; the Japanese have always been adept at borrowing from other cultures but making the material distinctly their own. Sources written during the periods presented and research of renowned historians helps to interpret traditional Japan. Shotoku, the first Japanese statesman, came to power in 590. During and after his reign, the Taika Reform and the Taiho Code were instituted, and Nara was declared the capital in 710. In 794, Kyoto became the new capital. By 858, the Fijiwara family firmly controlled the state. During their leadership, Lady Murasaki wrote *The Tale of Genji*. The Taira and Minamoto fought the Genpei War between 1180 and 1185, with Minamoto Yoritomo establishing a military government and becoming shogun in 1192. The Mongols invaded twice during the thirteenth century, but the Emperor Go-Daigo ascended the throne in 1318. His power led to civil war between the north and the south from 1336 until 1392. From 1467 to 1477, the Onin war almost destroyed Kyoto. The Portuguese arrived in 1542, and in 1592, Japan invaded Korea. In 1635, a Japanese edict forbade all foreign travel and isolated the country until 1853, when Commodore Perry arrived; Japan signed the Treaty of Kanagawa in 1854. In the next decade, the Meiji Restoration began as the period of isolation ended. Notes, For Further Reading, Works Consulted, and Index.

999. Nash, Amy K. **North Korea**. New York: Chelsea House, 1991. 128p. $15.95. ISBN 0-7910-0157-1. (Places and People of the World). 6-8

The text relates both the history of and the present situation in North Korea. A timeline indicates that the Chinese recognized the walled town-state of Old Choson (the present-day Pyongyang) in 300 B.C. In A.D. 58-668, during the Period of the Three Kingdoms of Koguryo, Paekche, and Silla, someone began recording Korean history. During this time, Buddhism and Confucianism became religions. Around the eleventh and twelfth centuries, the Mongols invaded, and Kublai Khan enlisted Korean men to fight Japan. In 1785, the Koreans banned all forms of Western learning. In 1948, Syngman Rhee became the president of the Republic of (South) Korea, and Kim Il Sung became premier of the Democratic People's Republic of Korea. The Korean War began on June 25, 1950, when the North Koreans attacked across the Thirty-Eighth Parallel; it ended in 1953. In the late 1980s, peace talks began once more. Photographs and reproductions enhance the text. Glossary and Index.

1000. Needham, Kate. **The Time Trekkers Visit the Middle Ages**. Sheena Vickers and Dave Burroughs, illustrators. Brookfield, CT: Copper Beach, 1996. 32p. $14.90; $5.95pa. ISBN 0-7613-0481-9; 1-56294-196-8pa. 3-4

Four trekkers, Lucy, Jools, Sam, and Eddie, travel through Lucy's grandfather's time machine to the Middle Ages. Each child holds a "gizmo" that gives information on science, places and people, history and arts, cross-sections, and terms. At the end of the text is a brief overview of the history of the Middle Ages. Index.

1001. Neimark, Anne E. **Diego Rivera: Artist of the People**. New York: HarperCollins, 1992. 116p. $16.89. ISBN 0-06-021784-7. 3-7

Diego Rivera (1886-1957) expressed his concerns for human dignity in his art. In this fictional biography, Neimark has invented some scenes that she cannot verify, just as Rivera himself fictionalized life with his tales about various experiences as he lived and traveled in Spain, France, the U.S.S.R., the United States, and Mexico. He caused controversy, refusing to compromise his beliefs in his work or his life. Reproductions, Murals, Books for Further Reading, and Index.

1002. Nerlove, Miriam, author/illustrator. **Flowers on the Wall**. New York: Margaret K. McElderry, 1996. 32p. $16. ISBN 0-689-50614-7. K-3

Rachel spends the cold winter of 1938 in Warsaw, Poland, painting flowers on the walls inside her apartment, because she has no shoes to wear outside. Although her family brings her little gifts periodically, the war continues, and she and her family suffer both before and after the Nazis deport them to Treblinka in 1942. Whatever Rachel's dreams, World War II did not allow them to come to fruition.

1003. Neuberger, Anne E. **The Girl-Son**. Minneapolis, MN: Carolrhoda, 1994. 131p. $14.96. ISBN 0-87614-846-1. 4-6

Induk's mother, a widow in late-nineteenth-century Korea, refuses to live with either her husband's or her own family, and thus Induk has no chance for a decent life. She does not understand her mother, who decides that Induk will go to school to become a scholar like her father; when Induk is seven years old, she dresses Induk like a boy and sends her to school, where Induk plays as a boy and loves the learning. Then her mother hears of a school for girls. Induk continues her schooling through the help of others, even people in the United States, until she graduates from college and becomes a teacher. For her belief in freedom for Koreans during the Japanese occupation beginning in 1910, and her public protesting, she goes to jail. After she is freed in 1919, she travels and eventually fulfills her dream of establishing a school in Korea to help others, in honor of those who helped her. This story is based on the life of Induk Pahk, who died in 1980. *Notable Children's Trade Books in the Field of Social Studies* and *Society of School Librarians International Outstanding Book.*

1004. Newfield, Marcia. **The Life of Louis Pasteur**. Antonio Castro, illustrator. New York: Twenty-First Century, 1991. 80p. $13.98. ISBN 0-941477-67-3. (Pioneers in Health and Medicine). 4-7

When Louis Pasteur (1822-1895) found a treatment for rabies, he was hesitant to try it on a human until he realized that it was the last chance for the man to survive. It worked, but Pasteur worried throughout the course of the treatment about the results. He was a successful teacher who shared his knowledge with his students. His motto was "Onward!" but he made his students challenge any belief that would not stand up to scientific inquiry. On his seventieth birthday, he still asked people to question what they had done with their teaching and if they had served their country. He is the father of microbiology. For Further Reading and Index.

1005. Newman, Robert. **The Case of the Baker Street Irregular**. 1978. Magnolia, MA: Peter Smith, 1984. 200p. $18.75. ISBN 0-8446-6762-5. 3-7

After Andrew's aunt dies, he goes from Cornwall to London with his tutor. The tutor disappears, but Andrew meets Sherlock Holmes, who helps him to find the man and also to reunite with his mother. At age fourteen in the 1890s, Andrew realizes that his mother has not enjoyed their separation and that they will try to stay together while she follows her stage career.

1006. Newman, Robert. **The Case of the Etruscan Treasure**. New York: Atheneum, 1983. 173p. $10.95. ISBN 0-689-30992-9. 3-7

Andrew's mother stars in a New York play in the 1890s, and Andrew and Sara come with her. Inspector Wyatt joins them and they become involved with a crime boss who wants them to help him find files that were removed from a building before arsonists destroyed it.

1007. Newman, Robert. **The Case of the Frightened Friend**. New York: Atheneum, 1984. 168p. $11.95. ISBN 0-689-31018-8. 3-7

When Andrew's school friend fears that someone is trying to kill him at home, Andrew tells his friend from Scotland Yard. They investigate the school friend's late-nineteenth-century London home and stepmother and discover a spy working in an important government office.

1008. Newman, Robert. **The Case of the Indian Curse**. New York: Atheneum, 1986. 168p. $11.95. ISBN 0-689-31177-X. 3-7

Beasley, the friend of Andrew's new stepfather, becomes ill, and Andrew and Sara show concern. After they are both kidnapped, they discover that Thugs from India are trying to kill the person who could reveal their activities to others. They have been drugging Beasley so that he will tell them what he knows. After several serious encounters, they discover and reveal the Thug leader to Scotland Yard.

1009. Newman, Robert. **The Case of the Somerville Secret**. New York: Atheneum, 1981. 184p. $12.95. ISBN 0-689-30825-6. 3-7

Inspector Wyatt needs Andrew and Sara's help to solve the London murder of a former military man in the 1890s. They find a sixteen-year-old child who looks like a monster with six toes and no intelligence. The people who killed Inspector Wyatt's friend are also trying to kill the deformed child for their own personal gain.

1010. Newman, Robert. **The Case of the Threatened King**. New York: Atheneum, 1982. 212p. $10.95. ISBN 0-689-30887-6. 3-7

Someone kidnaps Sara, Andrew's friend, along with the daughter of the Serbian ambassador to England. Inspector Wyatt soon finds out that someone wants to kill the King of Serbia during his visit to London in the late nineteenth century.

1011. Newman, Robert. **The Case of the Vanishing Corpse**. 1980. New York: Atheneum, 1990. 221p. $4.95pa. ISBN 0-689-30755-1pa. 3-7

Because Andrew's mother is an actress, he meets George Bernard Shaw as they dine in London during his summer vacation. On one of his walks with his friend, Sara, he meets the local constable, Peter Wyatt. When Andrew's mother's diamonds disappear, Wyatt helps with the investigation. Then Andrew is drawn into the search for the murderer of a man on their street. A strange priest of an Egyptian religion lives nearby and may be involved with the case.

1012. Newman, Robert. **The Case of the Watching Boy**. New York: Atheneum, 1987. 171p. $13.95. ISBN 0-689-31317-9. 3-7

Andrew and Markham, who met at school, decide to help a woman get her child back, only to find out that the boy is not hers. They discover in the 1890s that the boy is the heir to the Rumanian throne and that the woman is an accomplice plotting with people to get the boy's father to abdicate. Andrew realizes that such situations make the history that used to bore him in school.

1013. Newton, David E. **James Watson & Francis Crick: Discovery of the Double Helix**. New York: Facts on File, 1992. 130p. $17.95. ISBN 0-8160-2558-4. 6 up

Two scientists, one working in England and the other in America, began to work together to discover how molecules in living bodies could determine biological traits. In 1953, in one of the greatest accomplishments in the history of science, Francis Crick (b. 1916) and James Watson (b. 1928) discovered the DNA molecule. The text looks at their lives, the search, and what the discovery means to science. Glossary, Further Reading, and Index.

1014. Newton, David E. **Tokyo**. New York: New Discovery, 1992. 96p. $14.95. ISBN 0-02-768235-8. (Cities at War). 6-9

In World War II, many Japanese young people enlisted in the military because they wanted to bring honor to their families. When the Allies continued to threaten invasion as the war progressed, people became fearful of the result, and pride was rarely the issue. Bombing of Tokyo began in 1944, but it was spared from the atomic bomb. Photographs, Notes, Further Reading, and Index.

1015. Nichol, Barbara. **Beethoven Lives Upstairs**. Scott Cameron, illustrator. New York: Orchard, 1994. Unpaged. $15.95. ISBN 0-531-06828-5. 3-5

In 1822, when Christoph is ten years old, he writes letters to his uncle to tell him about the man who has moved into the upstairs of Christoph's Vienna home. Because Christoph's father is dead, he thinks that his uncle should come and help them with the situation. The man upstairs happens to be Beethoven, a famous musician who has gone deaf. Eventually Christoph accepts the situation, and after he is given tickets to a performance of Beethoven's Ninth Symphony, he realizes that the man still has much joy. *Book Links* and *Booklist Editors' Choices*.

1016. Nickelson, Harry. **Vietnam**. San Diego, CA: Lucent, 1989. 96p. $22.59. ISBN 1-56006-110-3. (Overview). 5-12

The text begins with Vietnam's status as French Indochina during the 1950s and ends with the current situation in the country. It shows the tragedy for all in both words and photographs from news sources and describes how the aftermath of the Vietnam War affected American foreign policy. Bibliography and Index.

1017. Nicolle, David. **Medieval Knights**. New York: Viking, 1997. 48p. $16.99. ISBN 0-670-87463-9. (See Through History). 5-7

The world of medieval knights appears in this text, which includes see-through pages of a knight's chainmail suit of armor, a fortified manor house, a cliffside fortress of the Crusaders, and the ships of the seabound knights. Key Dates, Glossary, and Index.

1018.   Nivola, Claire A., author/illustrator. **Elisabeth**. New York: Farrar, Straus & Giroux, 1997. 32p. $16. ISBN 0-374-32085-3. 5-7

When a Jewish child has to leave everything at her home in Nazi Germany, including her beloved doll Elisabeth, and cannot return for her, she does not understand. She is lonely without the doll, but based on the author's mother's story, she is estastic when one day in an antique shop, she finds Elisabeth.

1019.   Noblet, Martine, and Chantal Deltenre. **The Amazon and the Americas**. Maureen Walker, translator. Hauppauge, NY: Barron's, 1995. 77p. $11.95; $6.95pa. ISBN 0-8120-6489-5; 0-8120-9160-4pa. (Tintin's Travel Diaries). 5 up

The text asks thirty questions about the Amazon and the Americas, covering a variety of topics such as what is the "Igapo" and the "Green Hell," who are the Indians, where is the carnival, who were the filibusters, and where did the Caribs live. Illustrations and photographs complement the simple text that appears on the lefthand page and the more scholarly answers on the righthand pages. Glossary, Chronological Chart, Map, Bibliography, and Index.

1020.   Nolan, Dennis. **Wolf Child**. New York: Macmillan, 1989. 40p. $14.95. ISBN 0-02-768141-6. 1-5

When he is too old to help the women and too young to hunt, Teo, age nine, begins to make obsidian tools for his tribe. He also finds a wolf cub, which he tames, but the chief makes him take the wolf into the forest after the first snow. When the tribe leaves, the wolf follows and saves Teo and the chief from being killed by a mammoth.

1021.   Noonan, Jon. **Captain Cook**. Yoshi Miyake, illustrator. New York: Crestwood House, 1993. 48p. $12.95. ISBN 0-89686-709-9. (Explorers). 4-8

Captain James Cook (1728-1779) made three voyages to the South Seas. He went to Tahiti and Australia on the *Endeavor*, to the Antarctic circle on a second voyage, and to Alaska and Hawaii on his last voyage. When he returned to Hawaii after having been given many gifts upon his first departure, he irritated the islanders, and they attacked him. If Cook had been able to swim, he might have escaped, but he could not, and the islanders killed him. Glossary and Index.

1022.   Noonan, Jon. **Ferdinand Magellan**. Yoshi Miyake, illustrator. New York: Crestwood House, 1993. 48p. $12.95. ISBN 0-89686-706-4. (Explorers). 4-8

Ferdinand Magellan (1480?-1521) was always brave as a child and even saved his cousin's life. His character served him well as he sailed from Spain, lost his command, and then found South America. He survived mutiny only to die after reaching the Philippines, but his ship and crew continued the journey around the world. Glossary and Index.

1023.   Noonan, Jon. **Marco Polo**. New York: Crestwood House, 1993. 48p. $12.95. ISBN 0-89686-704-8. (Explorers). 4-8

Marco Polo (1254-1324) grew up in Venice while his father, whom he had never met, traveled in the East. After his father returned to Venice, he decided to take Marco with him on the next trip to the East. The text tells of their problems en route to the City of Peace before Polo met the Great Khan in 1275. Polo became an honored member of the household, followed the Mongol customs, and learned to write in four of the languages that the 12,000 members of the household spoke. At that time, China's Great Wall was nearly 1,200 miles long. Polo served the Khan for seventeen years, visiting all areas of Cathay. Glossary and Index.

$$\boxed{\text{O}}$$

1024.   Oakes, Catherine. **The Middle Ages**. Stephen Biesty, illustrator. San Diego, CA: Gulliver, Harcourt Brace, 1989. 28p. $14.95. ISBN 0-15-200451-3. (Exploring the Past). 3-7

Striking color illustrations reveal life during the Middle Ages. The text covers such topics as education and universities; religion and pilgrimages; the life of the nobility with feasts and tournaments; life in the country with the lord and his peasants; life in the towns with people and their homes, clothes, and health; and what was happening in navigation and exploration. Time Chart and Index.

1025.   O'Callahan, Jay. **Tulips**. Deborah Santini, illustrator. 1992. Atlanta, GA: Peachtree, 1996. 28p. $19.95. ISBN 1-56145-134-7. K-3

Grand Ma Mere has one of the most beautiful gardens in Paris, and she loves her flowers. She also loves her grandson, Pierre, but he is not the best of all children. He is a trickster who irritates the servants when he comes to visit around 1900. They decide that they will trick him instead.

1026.   O'Connor, Barbara. **Mammolina: A Story About Maria Montessori**. Sara Campitelli, illustrator. Minneapolis, MN: Carolrhoda, 1993. 64p. $11.21; $5.95pa. ISBN 0-87614-743-0; 0-87614-602-7pa. 3-5

Because she thought school was boring, Maria Montessori (1870-1952) tried to change the situation for future children. She became the first female doctor in Italy and decided, after having a baby as a result of a love affair, that she would give up the child in order to have a career. She worked with disabled children and had successes previously not seen in that population. She had to dissect cadavers at night because men and women seeing naked bodies together was not permissible. The text looks at most aspects of her life and at her achievements in making education an exciting topic. Bibliography.

1027.   O'Connor, Barbara. **The World at His Fingertips: A Story About Louis Braille**. Minneapolis, MN: Lerner, 1997. 64p. $14.21. ISBN 1-57505-052-8. (Creative Minds). 3-6

Louis Braille (1809-1852), blind from age three when he poked an awl in one eye and the ensuing infection spread to the other, helped other blind people to "see." When he attended school in Paris, he created the Braille alphabet, which made sense to him and to others who wanted to read more rapidly with their fingertips. Bibliography and Index.

1028.   O'Connor, Karen. **A Kurdish Family**. Rick Moncauskas, photographer. Minneapolis, MN: Lerner, 1996. 64p. $21.50; $8.95pa. ISBN 0-8225-3402-9; 0-8225-9743-8pa. (Journey Between Two Worlds). 3-6

Although not a history book, the text includes the history of the Kurdish people as a background for understanding the reasons why families from Kurdish areas have had to leave their homes. Photographs and personal experiences explain Kurdish social and religious traditions and how the Kurds have had to adapt to a new culture to survive as refugees. Further Reading.

1029.   O'Dell, Scott. **The Hawk That Dare Not Hunt by Day**. 1975. Greenville, SC: Bob Jones University Press, 1986. 182p. $6.49pa. ISBN 0-89084-368-6pa. 4-7

Tom and his Uncle Jack smuggle goods into England from Europe. When Tom sells William Tyndale an illegal manuscript of the Bible written by Martin Luther in 1524, Tyndale only wants to translate it and let the common people have copies. Tom takes Tyndale to Antwerp to have the translation printed, but another man betrays Tyndale, who is then hung for his crime. After Tyndale's death, the traitor ironically loses everything for his self-serving action.

1030.   O'Dell, Scott. **My Name Is Not Angelica**. Boston: Houghton Mifflin, 1989. 130p. $14.95. ISBN 0-395-51061-9. New York: Yearling, Dell, 1990. 130p. $3.99pa. ISBN 0-440-40379-0pa. 5-9

When one of their African tribespeople betrays them, Raisha and her betrothed are captured and taken to St. John's in the Caribbean to be sold into slavery. Her owner gives Raisha the name Angelica, but Raisha hates the name as well as the servitude. In 1733, she joins the slave revolt but refuses to jump off a cliff as the others, including her husband, do when the plantation owners stop the revolt, because she does not want to kill the child growing within her.

1031.   Odijk, Pamela. **The Aztecs**. Englewood Cliffs, NJ: Silver Burdett, 1990. 47p. $14.95. ISBN 0-382-09887-0. 5-7

As a wandering people, the Aztecs settled Tenocha and the Mexica in the Basin of Mexico around 1168; by the fifteenth and sixteenth centuries, they ruled a large empire in southern Mexico from their capital of Tenochtitlán. Most of the information about them comes from Spanish accounts of Aztec books. The Spanish, however, destroyed any of the documents dealing with the Aztec civilization. Among the topics are the environment, how families lived, food and medicine, clothes, religion and ritual, laws, writing, legends and literature, music and dancing, travel and exploration, wars and battles, inventions and special skills, and the end of the Aztec era. Photographs and reproductions enhance the text. Glossary and Index.

1032. Odijk, Pamela. **The Chinese**. Englewood Cliffs, NJ: Silver Burdett, 1991. 47p. $14.95. ISBN 0-382-09894-3. 5-7

China had one of the most long-lasting and stable civilizations in the world before it changed to Communism in the twentieth century. The Shang and Zhou dynasties, beginning in 1400 B.C., established China's basic characteristics. Inventions and special skills associated with the culture include silk making, astronomy, metalworking, porcelain, paper, printing, gunpowder, the compass, and the wheelbarrow. Other topics presented include food and medicine, clothes, religion and rituals, law, writing, legends and literature, art and architecture, transportation and communication, and wars and battles. Photographs and reproductions enhance the text. Glossary and Index.

1033. Odijk, Pamela. **The Japanese**. Englewood Cliffs, NJ: Silver Burdett, 1991. 47p. $14.95. ISBN 0-382-09898-6. 5-7

Before the Chinese writing system reached Japan in the fifth century A.D., the Japanese had no written historical records. Information from previous times comes from anthropologists, archaeologists, and legends; the earliest known inhabitants were the Jomon culture in 11,000 B.C. This text looks at life and culture in Japan before it opened to the West in A.D. 1854. Among the topics are the environment, how families lived, food and medicine, clothes, religion and ritual, laws, writing, legends and literature, music and dancing, travel and exploration, wars and battles, inventions and special skills, and the end of this era. Photographs and reproductions enhance the text. Glossary and Index.

1034. Odijk, Pamela. **The Mayas**. Englewood Cliffs, NJ: Silver Burdett, 1990. 48p. $14.95. ISBN 0-382-09890-0. (Ancient World). 5-7

Ancient Mayans lived in what is presently southern Mexico, Belize, Guatemala, Honduras, and western El Salvador. The ancient Mayans were farmers, architects who built pyramids, and artists and goldsmiths. Their social system harmonized with the environment and they believed in and respected the eternity of time. They also had their own calendar. Their formative period occurred from c. 2000 B.C. to A.D. 250 and their classic period from A.D. 250 to A.D. 900. They entered a decline around A.D. 900 and had been in decline for 600 years by the time the Spanish arrived and took power. The text covers a variety of topics about Mayan culture; among them are the environment, how families lived, food and medicine, clothes, religion and ritual, laws, writing, legends and literature, music and dancing, travel and exploration, wars and battles, inventions and special skills, and the end of the civilization. Photographs and reproductions enhance the text. Glossary and Index.

1035. Odijk, Pamela. **The Phoenicians**. Englewood Cliffs, NJ: Silver Burdett, 1989. 47p. $14.95. ISBN 0-382-09891-9. (Ancient World). 5-8

The Phoenicians lived in what is currently Lebanon, parts of Syria, and Israel; their main city was Tyre. The text discusses their civilization, including their land, food, law, arts and architecture, hunting, medicine, clothing, religion, laws, legends, and recreation. Phoenician refugees founded Carthage and fought in the Punic Wars against Rome. Glossary and Index.

1036. Odijk, Pamela. **The Romans**. Englewood Cliffs, NJ: Silver Burdett, 1989. 47p. $14.95. ISBN 0-382-09885-4. (Ancient World). 5-8

The text discusses the civilization of ancient Rome, including hunting, medicine, clothing, religion, laws, legends, recreation, transportation, music, dancing, inventions and special skills, and why the civilization declined. Photographs, diagrams, maps, and reproductions accent the text. Glossary and Index.

1037. Odijk, Pamela. **The Sumerians**. Englewood Cliffs, NJ: Silver Burdett, 1990. 48p. $14.95. ISBN 0-382-09892-7. (Ancient World). 5-7

The Sumerians, who inhabited the land which today is Iraq, have a history from the beginning of the fourth millennium B.C., the date of the oldest inscribed tablet found at Uruk. This advanced society had much that is still part of civilization today, including libraries. Among the topics in the text are land, flora and fauna of the time, agriculture, how families lived, food and medicine, clothing, religion, laws, writing, legends, art and architecture, transportation and communication, music, wars, and inventions and special skills. Names and places associated with the Sumerians are Ur, Nippur, King Gudea, Ur-Nammu, Girsu, Lugal-Zaggisi, Enheduanna, and Eridu. Photographs and reproductions enhance the text. Glossary and Index.

1038. O'Hara, Elizabeth (Eilís Ní Dhuibhne). **The Hiring Fair**. Chester Springs, PA: Poolbeg, DuFour Editions, 1994. 159p. $8.95pa. ISBN 1-85371-275-2pa. 5-8

In 1890, Sally is twelve and the oldest and most scatterbrained of three children. Her father drowns while fishing, as the rest of the family is enjoying a party. After his death, the family has no income with which to pay the rent on their land in Donegal, Ireland. The mother takes Sally and her sister to a hiring fair where two men hire them to work for six months. Although their situation is unexpected and difficult, their masters generally treat them well, and they save their land. *Bisto Book of the Year Merit Award* and *Irish Children's Book Trust.*

1039. Olawsky, Lynn A. **Colors of Australia**. Minneapolis, MN: Carolrhoda, 1998. 24p. $14.21; $5.95pa. ISBN 0-87614-884-4; 1-57505-213-Xpa. (Colors of the World). K-3

With colors indigenous to Australia controlling chapter content, the text discusses the history, topography, and special symbols of the country. Topics include the gold rush, Aborigines, sheep, Botany Bay, Sydney Opera House, eucalyptus, koalas, and kangaroos. Index.

1040. Olawsky, Lynn A. **Colors of Mexico**. Minneapolis, MN: Carolrhoda, 1997. 24p. $5.95pa. ISBN 1-57505-216-4pa. (Colors of the World). K-3

The main colors of Mexico serve as introductions into Mexican customs, traditions, history, and main cities. Index.

1041. Oliphant, Margaret. **The Earliest Civilizations**. New York: Facts on File, 1993. 78p. $17.95. ISBN 0-8160-2785-4. (Illustrated History of the World). 4-7

The earliest civilizations of the world included the nomadic hunters of the Stone Age, the Golden Age of Egypt, Troy, and the Mycenaean world, as well as the Minoan society on Crete. The Aryan Indians, further inside Asia, also developed a system of writing. Beautiful illustrations highlight the text. Glossary, Further Reading, and Index.

1042. O'Neal, Michael. **King Arthur: Opposing Viewpoints**. San Diego, CA: Greenhaven, 1992. 112p. $14.95. ISBN 0-89908-095-2. (Great Mysteries—Opposing Viewpoints). 6-9

The earliest reference to King Arthur occurs around 600. The question remains as to whether he was real or legendary. The text examines the conflicting evidence about the existence and historical basis of this man. Bibliography and Index.

1043. O'Neal, Michael. **Pyramids: Opposing Viewpoints**. San Diego, CA: Greenhaven, 1995. 96p. $16.95. ISBN 1-56510-216-9. (Great Mysteries—Opposing Viewpoints). 6-9

The first known expedition to explore the Great Pyramid at Giza was that of Al Mamun from the Persian city of Baghdad in A.D. 820. The Great Pyramid, which King Khufu ("Cheops" to the Greeks) had built in the twenty-fifth century B.C., is one of three at this location. Khafre ("Khephren" to the Greeks), Khufu's successor, built a second, and Menkaure ("Mycerinus" to the Greeks) built the third, along with three smaller pyramids for his queens. Topics covered in the text give the various views of scholars and archaeologists about why the pyramids were built—as tombs, public works projects, or scientific instruments. Another curiosity is how they were built. A third concern is the dangers encountered by those who enter them. Many different theories have arisen through the centuries about these immense structures.

1044. Oppenheim, Shulamith Levey. **The Lily Cupboard**. Ronald Himler, illustrator. New York: HarperCollins, 1992. 32p. $15. ISBN 0-06-024669-3. K-3

During World War II in 1940, Miriam has to stay with a Dutch farm family because she is Jewish. The family gives her a rabbit, which she names after her father, and she hides with the rabbit in the secret lily cupboard when the Nazis come to search the farmhouse. *Notable Children's Trade Books in the Field of Social Studies.*

1045. Orgel, Doris. **The Devil in Vienna**. 1978. Magnolia, MA: Peter Smith, 1995. $18.05. ISBN 0-8446-6797-8. New York: Viking, 1988. $4.99pa. ISBN 0-14-032500-Xpa. 6-8

When Inge is thirteen, in 1938, she misses her best friend, who has recently moved to Munich with her Nazi storm trooper father. When Inge's letters are returned, she does not understand why. Then, when Liselotte comes back to Vienna, after Hitler gains power over the Austrian leader, Schuschnigg, she lets Inge know how serious the situation is for the Jews. Inge begins to see other signs while her mother furtively plans for them to leave the country. *Child Study Children's Book Committee at Bank Street College Award, Association of Jewish Libraries Award, Golden Kite Honor Book,* and *Sydney Taylor Book Award.*

1046. Orlev, Uri. **The Island on Bird Street**. Hillel Halkin, translator. Boston: Houghton Mifflin, 1984. 162p. $14.95; $5.95pa. ISBN 0-395-33887-5; 0-395-61623-9pa. 5 up

Alex, age eleven, hides in the ruins of the Warsaw ghetto after police take his father away during World War II. He has to use his ingenuity to stay alive by searching for food and supplies in empty apartments, and he survives until his father returns almost a year later. *Sydney Taylor Book Award, American Library Association Notable Books for Children,* and *Association of Jewish Libraries Award.*

1047.   Orlev, Uri. **The Lady with the Hat**. Hillel Halkin, translator. Boston: Houghton Mifflin, 1995. 183p. $14.95. ISBN 0-395-69957-6. 6 up

Yulek, aged seventeen in 1947, survives in an Italian Zionist training camp, although the rest of his family dies in concentration camps during World War II. Yulek decides to return to his former home in Poland, but when he arrives, he discovers that anti-Semitism still pervades the town. He also hears that an English woman has inquired about his family. He thinks that his Aunt Malka, who left years before to marry a Christian, must be searching for him. He knows neither her married name nor her location. After he tries to find her, he ends up in Palestine running the British blockade. Among the characters who flesh out the novel are residents of the kibbutz where Yulek goes and a Jewish girl who, after hiding in a convent during the war, decides that she wants to become a nun in Jerusalem. *American Library Association Notable Books for Children, American Library Association Notable Books for Young Adults,* and *Mildred Batchelder Award.*

1048.   Orlev, Uri. **Lydia, Queen of Palestine**. Hillel Halkin, translator. Boston: Houghton Mifflin, 1993. 170p. $13.95. ISBN 0-395-65660-5. New York: Puffin, 1995. 170p. $3.99pa. ISBN 0-14-037089-7pa. 4-8

During World War II, Lydia, age ten, goes from her mother's home in Bucharest, Romania, to Palestine to join her father, after he sends a message to let them know that he has arrived safely. Although the Nazi threat is real, Lydia is more upset that her father has remarried. She has to adjust to her new status with him as well as to life on the kibbutz. When her mother finally arrives safely via Turkey, Lydia has to face her mother's new husband as well. By 1944, Lydia realizes that her situation is unpleasant but not the worst that could happen.

1049.   Osborn, Kevin. **The Peoples of the Arctic**. New York: Chelsea House, 1990. 111p. $15.95. ISBN 0-87754-875-5. (Peoples of North America). 5 up

Starting with the past, the text and accompanying photographs present information about the Inuits, their lives, and their history as the first Americans. By seeing their landscape, one gains a feeling for the culture and its timelessness. Further Reading and Index.

1050.   Overton, Jenny. **The Ship from Simnel Street**. New York: Greenwillow, 1986. 144p. $10.25. ISBN 0-688-06182-6. 6-9

Polly runs away from her English home during the Peninsula War to find the soldier she loves. Her father goes after her, and her mother and another person have to keep the family bakery working while they are gone. Everything that happens connects to the cakes that the family bakes, such as hot cross buns for Easter, cradle cake for babies, and simnel cake for mother's day. All return safely, with Polly married to her soldier.

P

1051. Palacios, Argentina. **!Viva Mexico!: A Story of Benito Juárez and Cinco de Mayo**. Howard Berelson, illustrator. Austin, TX: Raintree/Steck-Vaughn, 1993. 32p. $21.40; $4.95pa. ISBN 0-8114-7214-0; 0-8114-8054-2pa. (Stories of America—Holidays). 2-5

A Zapotec Indian in Mexico, Juárez (1806-1872) was eleven before an uncle began to teach him to read during spare time from farming and sheepherding. Because his state had no public schools, Juárez soon went to Oaxaca, forty miles away, to study. By working to pay for his schooling, he eventually became a lawyer in 1831. After he ran for governor of his state and won, he established schools throughout the area and became president of Mexico in 1861. The French, however, soon arrived to conquer Mexico. On the *Cinco de Mayo* in 1862, the Mexicans beat the French at the battle of Puebla, but the French imported reinforcements and governed for five more years until Juárez and his underground finally defeated them.

1052. Parker, Steve. **Aristotle and Scientific Thought**. New York: Chelsea House, 1995. 32p. $14.95. ISBN 0-7910-3004-0. (Science Discoveries). 4-8

In a presentation of Aristotle's life, the text first notes the Greek philosophers who came before Aristotle (384-322 B.C.). Aristotle studied at Plato's academy and became interested in many things, including nature. He was the first naturalist to categorize living things as vertebrates or invertebrates. He studied the sea animals and characterized aspects of human anatomy. He also began his own school at the Lyceum in 334 B.C. The final topic is Aristotle's legacy and the timeline of his world. Photographs and reproductions enhance the text. Glossary and Index.

1053. Parker, Steve. **Charles Darwin and Evolution**. New York: Chelsea House, 1995. 32p. $14.95. ISBN 0-7910-3007-5. (Science Discoveries). 5-9

The text, with complementary photographs and reproductions, looks at the life of Charles Darwin (1809-1882). His early years, spent collecting things in nature, and his five-year trip on the *Beagle* helped him to develop his theory that all things survive because of natural selection. *The Origin of Species* shocked many because it denied the stories in the Bible. Others, however, realized that his research was reasonable, and in ensuing years, his theory became a practical basis for scientists who began to ask about the purpose of everything and how these things might help survival and reproduction. World in Darwin's Time, Glossary, and Index.

1054. Parker, Steve. **Galileo and the Universe**. Tony Smith, illustrator. New York: Chelsea House, 1995. 32p. $14.95. ISBN 0-7910-3008-3. (Science Discoveries). 4-8

When he was seventeen, Galileo thought that he might become a doctor. One day, as he watched a lamp swing back and forth, he realized that whether it swung a long way or only slightly, it took the same amount of time. He then became interested in physics and mathematics and gave up medicine. When he concluded that the sun was not the center of the universe, and refused to stop writing about this discovery, the powerful Church imprisoned him. The text looks at Galileo in the context of his times and at his legacy to astronomy. The World in Galileo's Time, Glossary, and Index.

1055. Parker, Steve. **Guglielmo Marconi and Radio**. New York: Chelsea House, 1995. 32p. $14.95. ISBN 0-791-03009-1. (Science Discoveries). 3-7

Guglielmo Marconi (1874-1937) began experimenting with radio waves in 1890; by 1895, he could send signals with a directional antenna several kilometers away. Because the radio waves traveled through air, the system became known as "wireless communication." Marconi made his equipment more and more powerful, so that by 1920 radio messages could circle the globe. Without his tests of radio waves in the attic of the Bologna, Italy, villa in which his family lived, the development of television and radar might have been delayed. When he died, radio stations around the world went silent for two minutes. The World in Marconi's Time, Glossary, and Index.

1056. Parker, Steve. **Isaac Newton and Gravity**. New York: Chelsea House, 1995. 32p. $14.95. ISBN 0-7910-3010-5. (Science Discoveries). 3-7

Isaac Newton (1642-1727) made revolutionary advances in gravity, forces, motion, mechanics, astronomy, and mathematics. He drew together many theories that had appeared in science and showed that seemingly different events and processes had the same underlying causes. His basic framework for the physical sciences lasted for 200 years. He has been called "the culminating fighter in the Scientific Revolution of the seventeenth century." Glossary and Index.

1057. Parker, Steve. **Louis Pasteur and Germs**. New York: Chelsea House, 1995. 32p. $14.95. ISBN 0-7910-3002-4. (Science Discoveries). 3-7

Louis Pasteur (1822-1895) founded the science of microbiology, which is the study of living things, such as bacteria and viruses, that are visible only with the aid of a microscope. His research made advances possible in medicine, public health, and hygiene; he initiated vaccinations and invented the pasteurization of milk. The text looks at Pasteur in terms of his times and of his work. Glossary and Index.

1058. Parker, Steve. **Marie Curie and Radium**. New York: Chelsea House, 1995. 32p. $14.95. ISBN 0-7910-3011-3. (Science Discoveries). 3-7

Marie Curie (1867-1934) helped to start the atomic age with her work on radioactive elements. She discovered radium while struggling against a lack of money and recognition, illness, and those who believed that women could not be real scientists. The winner of two Nobel Prizes, she is one of the pioneers of science. Photographs and reproductions complement the text. The World in Marie Curie's Time, Glossary, and Index.

1059. Parris, Ronald. **Rendille**. New York: Rosen, 1994. 64p. $15.95. ISBN 0-8239-1763-0. (Heritage Library of African Peoples). 5-8

As a small group of desert dwellers in Kenya, the Rendille have a reputation for being able to survive in harsh conditions. They divide into two distinct groups, cattle herders or farmers, with each group having its own customs. The text looks at the people, their society, their daily life, customs and rituals, European contact, and social change. Photographs, boxed sidebar information, and maps enhance the text. Glossary, Further Reading, and Index.

1060. Parsons, Tom, author/illustrator. **Pierre Auguste Renoir**. New York: Sterling, 1996. 32p. $14.95. ISBN 0-8069-6162-7. (Art for Young People). 3-5

Two-page spreads present Renoir's works and give an elementary understanding of the ideas that inspired him. The text places him in the context of the nineteenth century. Glossary and Index.

1061. Paterson, Katherine. **Of Nightingales That Weep**. Haru Wells, illustrator. 1974. New York: Trophy, HarperCollins, 1989. 172p. $4.50pa. ISBN 0-06-440282-7pa. 5 up

Taiko, age eleven, likes to remember her samurai father instead of the ugly potter that her mother married after her father's death. She is happy to serve the child emperor at the Heike imperial court with her beauty and her lovely singing voice. After several years, her talents intrigue Hideo, an enemy Genji spy, and she refuses to come home to help her pregnant mother and stepfather. When she does return, her mother and brother have died, and an accident scars her face. She can no longer expect to return to Hideo, and she begins to see the inner beauty of the potter. *Phoenix Award* and *American Library Association Notable Children's Books of 1971-1975.*

1062. Paton Walsh, Jill. **A Chance Child**. 1978. New York: Sunburst, Farrar, Straus & Giroux, 1991. $3.95pa. ISBN 0-374-41174-3pa. 5 up

In alternating chapters, Creep's life is contrasted with that of Christopher and his sister, Pauline. Creep lives in the 1820s in the sordid mining community, and Christopher, living in the present, thinks that Creep is his half-brother. This view of the 1820s would not be so real to Christopher if his sister Pauline did not also know Creep.

1063. Paton Walsh, Jill. **Fireweed**. 1970. New York: Farrar, Straus & Giroux, 1988. 144p. $3.50pa. ISBN 0-374-42316-4pa. 6 up

Bill, age fifteen, hates being evacuated to Wales during World War II, so he returns to London. His aunt's house has been bombed, and it is off limits. He meets Julie, a girl whose family thinks she is dead because Germans sank the ship on which she supposedly sailed to Canada. The two sleep in bomb shelters and do odd jobs before setting up house in a bombed area looking after a young orphan boy.

1064. Pearson, Anne. **Ancient Greece**. New York: Knopf, 1992. 63p. $20. ISBN 0-679-81682-8. (Eyewitness). 6-9

To give an understanding of Greek art, architecture, and artifacts, illustrations accompany the text. Topics covered in double-page spreads include Minoan and Mycenaean civilization, Athenian politics, mythology, religion, women's lives, childhood, games, food and drink, theater, hygiene, clothing, sports, art, agriculture, trade, crafts, warfare, science and medicine, philosophy, death and the afterlife, Alexander the Great, and Hellenism. Index.

1065. Pearson, Anne. **Everyday Life in Ancient Greece**. New York: Franklin Watts, 1995. 32p. $18. ISBN 0-531-14310-4. (Clues to the Past). 3-6

Two-page spreads augmented by photographs and drawings discuss various facets of Greek life. Some of the topics covered are farming and fishing, homes, women's rooms, clothes and jewelry, school, childhood, craftsmen, markets, sports and games, theater, the army, religion, death, and burial. Index.

1066. Pearson, Anne. **The Vikings**. New York: Viking, 1994. 48p. $15.99. ISBN 0-670-85834-X. 6-8

Two-page discussions present many subjects that reveal Viking life. In addition to the normal illustrations are four transparent overlays which, when lifted, reveal the inside of a house, a ship, a church, and the location of items in the Oseberg ship find. The topics covered are fame, kings, freemen and slaves, farming and food, hunting and fishing, families, holidays, clothes, arts and crafts, ships, trade, weapons and warfare, death and burial, law, settlers, gods, the coming of Christianity, sagas and runes, and the end of the Viking era. Key Dates, Glossary, and Index.

1067. Pearson, Anne. **What Do We Know About the Greeks?** New York: Peter Bedrick, 1992. 45p. $16.95. ISBN 0-87226-356-8. (What Do We Know About . . .). 3-6

Through information gleaned from archaeological searches and artifacts collected, the text looks at the Greek culture. It discusses the eating habits, education, housing, recreation, religion, art, and other concepts of Greek life until 146 B.C. Photographs and drawings enhance the text. Glossary and Index.

1068. Pearson, Kit. **The Lights Go On Again**. New York: Viking, 1994. 201p. $13.99. ISBN 0-670-84919-7. 5-8

In this sequel to *The Sky Is Falling* and *Looking at the Moon*, as the end of World War II nears, Norah, age fifteen, and Gavin, age ten, are preparing to return to England from Toronto when they receive word that their parents have been killed by a bomb. Their grandfather comes to Canada to get them, but Gavin decides that he wants to stay with his Aunt Florence, the woman who has cared for him throughout the war and of whom he has grown very fond. When Gavin begins to remember facets of his childhood, though, he changes his mind and returns to England. He finds a country in need, unlike the wealthy Canadian home he has left, but he tries to adjust.

1069. Pearson, Kit. **Looking at the Moon**. New York: Viking, 1992. 212p. $12.95. ISBN 0-670-84097-1. 5-9

In the sequel to *The Sky Is Falling,* Norah and her Canadian "family" spend the summer of 1944 at their lake cottage. She becomes moody and difficult in her third Canadian summer, but she does not realize that her feelings relate to the changes in her body. Otherwise, she has adjusted to this different environment.

1070. Pearson, Kit. **The Sky Is Falling**. New York: Viking, 1990. 248p. $12.95. ISBN 0-670-82849-1. 4-6

When she does not know that she is being sent away, Norah, age ten, enjoys the dangers of the bombing raids in England as World War II begins. But she has to go to Canada with her five-year-old brother. The voyage, the new school, and the house where the two adults seem to care more about Gavin upsets her. She ignores Gavin, but she finally comes to understand that she is jealous of his loving manner and ability to attract both children and adults. *Geoffrey Bilson Award for Historical Fiction for Young People* (Canada)*, Mr. Christie's Book Awards* (Canada), and *Canadian Children's Book of the Year Award.*

1071. Peffer-Engels, John. **The Benin Kingdom of West Africa**. New York: Rosen, Power Kids Press, 1996. 24p. $13.95. ISBN 0-8239-2334-7. K-2

This simple text introduces youngsters to the Edo people of West Africa, one of the groups from which many of the slaves in America are descendants. Their lives today with culture, royalty, trade, and art give a basic understanding of age-old traditions. Photographs, Glossary, and Index.

1072. Pelgrom, Els. **The Winter When Time Was Frozen**. Maryka Rudnik and Raphel Rudnik, translators. New York: Morrow, 1980. 253p. $12.88. ISBN 0-688-32247-6. 6-10

During the winter of 1944-1945, Noortje, age eleven, and her father stay on a Dutch farm with several other people. The food disappears more rapidly than it should for the number of people in the house who are eating it, and Noortje finds out that the farm's owner is feeding a Jewish family hiding in a nearby cave. When a baby is born in the cave, they take it inside before the Nazis discover the family. When the war ends, after a horrible period with V-1 bombs exploding, the baby's uncle says that all of the family died in a concentration camp. *Mildred L. Batchelder Award.*

1073. Pelta, Kathy. **Discovering Christopher Columbus: How History Is Invented**. Minneapolis, MN: Lerner, 1991. 112p. $19.95. ISBN 0-8225-4899-2. 6-9

The text looks at the life of Christopher Columbus and his voyages beginning in 1492 and ending in 1506. Additional chapters examine the historical response to his discovery in the subsequent centuries. An ending chapter titled "You, the Historian" shows how information can be disseminated, even when it is wrong, because historians copy what another historian has written without trying to get the information from as original a source as possible. Sometimes even primary sources are unreliable. Pelta comments about a letter from Columbus that washed ashore in a barrel. It would have been interesting, except that it was written in modern English, a language that was not even spoken during Columbus's lifetime. Sources and Information. *Notable Children's Trade Books in the Field of Social Studies* and *American Library Association Notable Books for Children.*

1074. Perdrizet, Marie-Pierre. **The Cathedral Builders**. Eddy Krähenbühl, illustrator; Mary Beth Raycraft, translator. Brookfield, CT: Millbrook Press, 1992. 64p. $16.40. ISBN 1-56294-162-3. (Peoples of the Past). 5-8

Gothic cathedrals were planned and constructed in the eleventh and twelfth centuries when almost everyone in the area was Christian. The text looks at the building of the cathedral from stone; architectural details such as buttresses; the stained-glass windows; why the cathedrals were built; what celebrations took place in them; and the legacy of the builders. An interesting addition is the guide on how to experience a cathedral. Illustrations enhance the text. Dates to Remember, Find Out More, Glossary, and Index. *New York Public Library Books for the Teen Age.*

1075. Perez, Louis G. **The Dalai Lama**. Vero Beach, FL: Rourke, 1993. 112p. $22.60. ISBN 0-86625-480-3. (Biographies of World Leaders). 5-8

A child found in the Tibetan wilderness became the spiritual leader of his people. Tibetan monks believe that babies must be treated in special ways; a baby, reincarnated from a life that helped others, had to be nurtured to ascertain if he were destined to be the next Dalai Lama. This child, Tenzin Gyatso, passed the tests. As an adult, he won the Nobel Peace Prize for his attempts to help free his people from Chinese oppression through nonviolent means. He has been exiled from Tibet since 1959 but continues to press for an end to Chinese aggression. The text, with photographs, examines Buddhist beliefs and the Dalai Lama's life. Time Line, Glossary, Bibliography, Media Resources, and Index.

1076. Perl, Lila. **From Top Hats to Baseball Caps, from Bustles to Blue Jeans: Why We Dress the Way We Do**. New York: Clarion, 1990. 118p. $14.95. ISBN 0-899-19872-4. 5-9

Perl thinks that through the years in Western Europe and the United States such things as social class, women's liberation, war, and technology have influenced styles of clothing. She includes chapters on pants, skirts, shoes, and hats. The text is complemented with photographs and drawings. Bibliography and Index.

1077. Perl, Lila. **Isaac Bashevis Singer: The Life of a Storyteller**. Donna Ruff, illustrator. Philadelphia, PA: Jewish Publication Society, 1995. 95p. $12.95. ISBN 0-8276-0512-9. 5-7

In 1904, Icek-Hersz Zynger was born in Poland, where his first stories written in Yiddish were published. In 1935, Isaac Bashevis Singer came to the United States, where he continued writing. Singer has won many awards for his work, including a Newbery Honor, a National Book Award, and the Nobel Prize for Literature. At his death in 1991, he received the acclaim worthy of his body of work. Important Dates, Bibliography, Works, and Index.

1078. Perl, Lila, and Marion Blumenthal Lazan. **Four Perfect Pebbles: A Holocaust Story**. New York: Morrow, 1996. 130p. $15. ISBN 0-688-14294-X. 5-8

Before experiencing the Holocaust in Bergen-Belsen, Marion Blumenthal Lazan had a happy, secure family life in prewar Germany. Her grandparents had run a business since 1894, but Hitler's decrees gradually decreased their rights until they were forced to move from Hoya to Hanover and then to Holland. Before they could leave for America, the Nazis invaded and deported them to Westerbork, then to Bergen-Belsen, and onto a death train to Auschwitz before the Russians liberated them. Marion's father died of typhus after liberation, however, and she, her mother, and her brother had to spend three years as displaced persons before they eventually arrived in the United States. Photographs and Bibliography. *American Library Association Notable Books for Children.*

1079. Pernoud, Régine. **A Day with a Medieval Troubadour**. Giorgio Bacchin, illustrator. Dominique Clift, translator. Minneapolis, MN: Runestone, 1997. 64p. $16.95. ISBN 0-8225-1915-1. (A Day With). 5-7

A medieval troubadour was a person who either wrote or composed anything, and their tradition began in the Provence region of France at the end of the eleventh century. After background about troubadours and their part in pilgrimages to places such as Santiago, the text describes a day with a twelfth-century troubadour named Peire Vidal. Glossary, Further Reading, and Index. *Andersen Prize Europe.*

1080. Pernoud, Régine. **A Day with a Miller**. Giorgio Bacchin, illustrator. Dominique Clift, translator. Minneapolis, MN: Runestone, 1997. 64p. $16.95. ISBN 0-8225-1914-3. (A Day With). 5-7

The text gives a brief history of the importance of milling for food and follows with the description of a day in the life of a miller in twelfth-century France. Illustrations enhance his story. Glossary, Further Reading, and Index. *Andersen Prize Europe.*

1081. Pernoud, Régine. **A Day with a Noblewoman**. Giorgio Bacchin, illustrator. Dominique Clift, translator. Minneapolis, MN: Runestone, 1997. 64p. $16.95. ISBN 0-8225-1916-X. (A Day With). 5-7.

A brief description of the nobility in France during the thirteenth century and a discussion of the Crusades precedes the details of a day in the life of the widow Blanche, a thirteenth-century noblewoman who must manage her large land holdings by herself. Glossary, Further Reading, and Index. *Andersen Prize Europe.*

1082.   Pernoud, Régine. **A Day with a Stonecutter**. Giorgio Bacchin, illustrator. Dominique Clift, translator. Minneapolis, MN: Runestone, 1997. 64p. $16.95. ISBN 0-8225-1913-5. (A Day With). 5-7

The text begins with a description of the various parts of medieval cathedrals, especially Chartres, and the roles that stonecutters played in their creation. It then tells the story of one day in the life of Yves, a stonecutter who works at the Abbey of St. George in Normandy during the twelfth century. Glossary, Further Reading, and Index. *Andersen Prize Europe*.

1083.   Pettit, Jayne. **My Name Is San Ho**. New York: Scholastic, 1992. 149p. $13.95. ISBN 0-590-44172-8. 5-8

San Ho, age ten, goes from his small Vietnamese village with his mother to a friend's home in Saigon in 1972. She does not come back for three years, and when she returns, she is married to an American. San Ho travels to America with them, where he has to adjust to both his father and his new culture, while trying to learn English and struggling to understand what happened to his country.

1084.   Pfeifer, Kathryn. **The 761st Tank Battalion**. New York: Twenty-First Century Books, 1994. 80p. $14.98. ISBN 0-8050-3057-3. (African-American Soldiers). 4-6

The 761st Tank Battalion went to Europe during World War II and began serving in October 1944. It was the first African American armored unit to be committed to combat in the war. When the average life of a separate tank battalion on the front lines was approximately 10 to 12 days, the 761st stayed in combat for 183 and 83 consecutive days. As members continued to serve under General George Patton, they exhibited courage as they faced some of Germany's elite troops. When they returned to their homes, they faced racism and segregation until 33 years later, when the surviving members received the Presidential Unit Citation from the Carter administration. Chronology of African Americans in the U.S. Armed Forces, Index, and Bibliography.

1085.   Pflaum, Rosalynd. **Marie Curie and Her Daughter Irene**. Minneapolis, MN: Lerner, 1993. 144p. $15.95. ISBN 0-8225-4915-8. 4-6

Marie Curie (1867-1934) and Irene Joliot-Curie (1897-1956) were mother and daughter pioneer scientists who both won the Nobel Prize. Marie Curie was the discoverer of radium, polonium, and natural radiation. Her daughter Irene discovered artificial radiation. Black-and-white photographs supplement the text. Bibliography and Index. *Outstanding Science Trade Book for Children, SSLI Outstanding Secondary Science Book*.

1086.   Phillips, Ann. **The Peace Child**. New York: Oxford University Press, 1988. 150p. $15. ISBN 0-19-271560-7. 5 up

In 1380, Alys, age ten, finds out that she was born into another family. When she was born, the families traded babies as a way to settle a blood feud. She has to devote her energy to keeping the peace between the two groups, and two years later, during the plague, she travels between them and helps them survive. At her own marriage, she plans for all of her children to be "peace children."

1087.   Pico, Fernando. **The Red Comb**. Argentina Palacios, translator; María Antonio Ordóñez, illustrator. Mahwah, NJ: Bridgewater, 1994. Unpaged. $14.95; $4.95pa. ISBN 0-8167-3539-5; 0-8167-3540-9pa. 2-4

The story of Pedro Calderón in Puerto Rico in the nineteenth century tells that he became wealthy by capturing runaway slaves from nearby sugar-cane plantations. Some people detest his way of earning money, and Rosa and Vitita thwart him when they successfully hide one of the runaways by pretending that she is a relative.

1088.   Pierre, Michel. **Good Day, Mister Gauguin**. New York: Chelsea House, 1995. 60p. $14.95. ISBN 0-7910-2811-9. (Art for Children). 3-6

The text combines a straightforward account of Paul Gauguin's (1848-1903) life with a fictional story of a child pursuing information about this man at various museums in Paris where Gauguin's paintings hang. Also included are reproductions of the paintings. Glossary and Chronology.

1089.   Pietrusza, David. **The Battle of Waterloo**. San Diego, CA: Lucent, 1996. 96p. $26.59. ISBN 1-56006-423-4. (Battles of the Nineteenth Century). 6-9

The battle of Waterloo in 1815 set a combination of British, Dutch, and Belgian forces totaling 67,000 against Napoleon's forces of 74,000 French. When Gebhard von Blücher arrived with the Prussian army, Napoleon met defeat. The text looks at this battle as well as at Napoleon's ambitions to control Europe, which drove him to fight so often. One segment also looks at Napoleon's achievement in establishing his Code. Bibliography, Chronology, Further Reading, and Index.

1090.   Pimlott, John. **Middle East: A Background to the Conflicts**. New York: Gloucester, Franklin Watts, 1991. 36p. $11.90. ISBN 0-531-17329-1. (Hotspots). 3-5

The text starts with a brief summary of the 1991 Gulf War, and then examines the nineteenth-century conflicts leading to this war. Additional information about the Arab-Israeli difficulties shows that the peace process in this area has a history of violence and discord to overcome. Photographs supplement the text. Chronology, Glossary, and Index.

1091.   Pinguilly, Yves. **Da Vinci: The Painter Who Spoke with Birds**. John Goodman, translator. New York: Chelsea House, 1993. 62p. $14.95. ISBN 0-7910-2808-9. (Art for Children). 3-6

Letters between an uncle and niece introduce the life and work of Leonardo da Vinci in Italy during the Renaissance. Reproductions and drawings highlight the text. Chronology and Glossary.

1092.   Pirotta, Saviour. **Jerusalem**. New York: Dillon Press, 1993. 46p. $13.95. ISBN 0-87518-569-X. (Holy Cities). 4-6

From a religious viewpoint, Jerusalem is the holy city of Christians, Muslims, and Jews. The text focuses on the history of these groups and how Jerusalem became so important to each of them. Other topics include important places of worship, culture, festivals and celebrations, art, and legends. Photographs enhance the text. Further Reading and Index.

1093.   Pirotta, Saviour. **Rome**. New York: Dillon Press, 1993. 46p. $13.95. ISBN 0-87518-570-3. (Holy Cities). 4-6

From a religious viewpoint, Rome is the spiritual center of the Catholic Church. The text focuses on the Vatican and its ceremonies, including papal audiences, and the traditions of Catholicism. Other topics include its history, important places of worship, culture, festivals and celebrations, art, and legends. Photographs enhance the text. Further Reading and Index.

1094.   Pitt, Nancy. **Beyond the High White Wall**. New York: Scribners, 1986. 135p. $11.95. ISBN 0-684-18663-2. 6-9

After Libby sees a foreman on her family's property in the Ukraine murder an innocent Jewish man in 1903, she begins to understand why her family plans to leave the home they love for America. Someone burns their home before they can leave, and other incidents make life uncomfortable. However, the fact that they have decided to take control of their lives by leaving pleases her.

1095.   Platt, Richard. **Castle**. Stephen Biesty, illustrator. New York: Dorling Kindersley, 1994. 27p. $16.95. ISBN 1-56458-467-4. (Stephen Biesty's Cross-Sections). 5-10

Platt and Biesty show what happens both inside and outside a castle by examining it layer by layer and including intriguing bits of information. Lords, for example, needed to get a license to crenellate or they would be accused of having an adulterine castle. Subject segments are defense and siege, garrison and prisoners, building a castle, trades and skills, lifestyles of the lords, food and feasting, entertainment, livestock and produce, weapons, and punishments. Glossary and Index.

1096.   Platt, Richard. **Pirate**. Tina Chambers, illustrator. New York: Knopf, 1995. 64p. $19. ISBN 0-679-87255-8. (Eyewitness). 5-8

Photographs of artifacts and drawings complement the text, presented in two-page spreads that cover different topics. They include the pirates of ancient Greece and Rome, the raiders of the north, the Barbary Coast in the eleventh century, the corsairs of Malta during the sixteenth and seventeenth centuries, and the privateers, buccaneers, and pirates of the Caribbean. Other topics are women pirates like Mary Read, the Jolly Roger flag, pirate life, pirates in the Indian Ocean, American privateers, the French corsairs, and pirates of the China Sea. Index.

1097.   Platt, Richard. **The Smithsonian Visual Timeline of Inventions**. New York: Dorling Kindersley, 1994. 64p. $16.95. ISBN 1-56458-675-8. 5-9

Each segment contains an overview of the period followed by a timeline presenting inventions helpful to counting and communication, daily life and health, agriculture and industry, and travel and conquest. A brief list of world events correlates to the inventions. For example, the closed-eye needle appeared in 1450. Time segments are 600,000 B.C. (Fire, etc.) to A.D. 1299 for the first inventions; 1300-1779 for inventions motivated by printing and the spread of ideas; 1780-1869 and the rise of steam power and the Industrial Revolution; 1870-1939 and the use of electric power in the modern world; and 1940-2000, when transistors and information seem most important. Index of Inventions and Index of Inventors.

1098.   Pollard, Michael. **The Nineteenth Century**. New York: Facts on File, 1993. 78p. $17.95. ISBN 0-8160-2791-9. (Illustrated History of the World). 4-7.

In the nineteenth century, towns and the cities showed changes from the old way of life. The British went into India and Americans went west in attempts to build empires. The slave trade led to the Civil War in the United States. Other changes affected Europe, Africa, Australia, and New Zealand as steamships reshaped travel, the oil age began, and the communication revolution started. Illustrations highlight the text. Glossary, Further Reading, and Index.

1099. Pollard, Michael. **The Red Cross and the Red Crescent**. New York: New Discovery, 1994. 64p. $7.95. ISBN 0-02-774720-4. (Organizations That Help the World). 4-8

The Red Cross and the Red Crescent are two organizations created in the nineteenth century to help soldiers on the battlefield receive help more quickly. Neutral emergency units became available that could offer medical aid without threatening the enemy. In Europe, Jean-Herni Dunant watched the Battle of Solferino in 1859. In 1862, he wrote a book about it in which he suggested ways to alleviate some of the deaths. At the same time, Clara Barton in America had become interested in helping prisoners and the wounded. In 1863, an international conference to launch the Red Cross movement opened in Geneva with representatives from 16 countries. On August 22, 1964, the first Geneva Convention had signatures from 12 countries. During the Franco-Prussian war of 1870-1871, the Red Cross helped trace and report on prisoners of war, and Clara Barton provided relief on the battlefields. In 1873, Barton returned to the United States to begin setting up the Red Cross in America. Various other treaties and disagreements continued to refine the process. Since then, the Red Cross (Red Crescent in Islamic countries) has been a major relief organization. Glossary, Important Dates, How You Can Help, and Index.

1100. Pope, Elizabeth Marie. **The Perilous Gard**. Richard Cuffari, illustrator. Boston: Houghton Mifflin, 1974. 272p. $16.95. ISBN 0-395-18512-2. New York: Puffin, Penguin, 1992. 272p. $5.99pa. ISBN 0-14-034912-Xpa. 6 up

In 1558, Queen Mary sends Kate from Hatfield House to Sir Geoffrey's Elvenwood Hall in Derbyshire, the place known as the "perilous gard." The people are fearful of fairy folk who live in the caves and think that Kate is one of them. She shows that she is not by saving a boy during a flash flood. But when Sir Geoffrey's young daughter disappears, Kate realizes that the fairy folk have kidnapped her for their All Hallows' Eve sacrifice. Kate follows them and tells her friend Christopher where to go to trade places as the sacrifice. Because she learns their rules, Kate claims Christopher before the sacrifice, and the fairy folk must free him. *Newbery Honor.*

1101. Pople, Maureen. **The Other Side of the Family**. New York: Henry Holt, 1988. 167p. $13.95. ISBN 0-8050-0758-X. 5-9

Kate, age fifteen, journeys to Australia during World War II to stay with relatives on both sides of the family. Her mother's parents make no decisions without consulting Kate's grandfather's bowling club, and her father's mother has not spoken to Kate's parents for twenty years. Yet she finds that her father's mother, although deaf and poor rather than glamorous as Kate had heard, has much respect from the neighbors. Kate quickly learns to admire her integrity and intelligence.

1102. Posell, Elsa. **Homecoming**. San Diego, CA: Harcourt Brace, 1987. 230p. $14.95. ISBN 0-15-235160-4. 6-9

Olya and her wealthy family face opposition after the government of Tsar Nicholas falls in 1918, because their Jewish family supported the tsar. Her father escapes to America, but before the others can join him, Olya's mother dies. The children, with financial aid and other help from people they meet, finally arrive in Antwerp where they can take a ship to America.

1103. Poulton, Michael. **Life in the Time of Augustus and the Ancient Romans**. Christine Molan, illustrator. Austin, TX: Raintree/Steck-Vaughn, 1993. 63p. $16.98. ISBN 0-8114-3350-1. (Life in the Time of). 4-8

After members of Julius Caesar's senate murdered him in 44 B.C., Octavian began his rise to power; he completed it with the defeat of Antonius and Cleopatra. The text focuses on religion, the Roman army, ships and trade, life in Rome and the countryside, and the architecture and building of the period. Each chapter covers specifics of the topics with illustrations to clarify. Glossary and Index.

1104. Poulton, Michael. **Life in the Time of Pericles and the Ancient Greeks**. John James, illustrator. Austin, TX: Raintree/Steck-Vaughn, 1993. 63p. $16.98. ISBN 0-8114-3352-8. (Life in the Time of). 4-8

Pericles (499-429 B.C.) rose to power after the Greeks fought the Persians and survived the battles at Marathon, Thermopylae, and Salamis. He ascended to leadership during a time when Athenian culture was flourishing—the theater, religious rites, and the Olympic games. Pericles seemed to become too proud as he grew older and the Athenian battle with Sparta became more open. When the plague broke out, many citizens blamed Pericles, but Pericles died of it himself before Sparta became the victor. Each chapter covers specifics of the topics with illustrations to clarify. Glossary and Index.

1105. Powell, Anton. **Ancient Greece**. New York: Facts on File, 1989. 96p. $17.95. ISBN 0-8160-1972-X. (Cultural Atlas for Young People). 6-9

As much as possible about ancient Greece appears in this text, complemented by full-color illustrations. Topics that help one to understand the life of the ancient Greeks include the Minoan, Cretan, and Mycenaen civilizations of the fifteenth and fourteenth centuries B.C.; the Trojan War, about which Homer wrote, from 900-700 B.C.; Homer's primitive Greece; Athens and its dramatists, historians, and philosophers; the growth of Athens; the Olympic games, and much more. Chronology, Glossary, Gazetteer, and Index.

1106.   Powell, Anton, and Philip Steele. **The Greek News**. New York: Candlewick, 1996. 32p. $15.99. ISBN 1-56402-874-7. 4-9

The approach to the Greeks through newspaper style highlights fashion, sports, trade, food, and the military. Each page has headlines, sometimes with classifieds advertising such things as "instruments for sale." Highly readable and slightly sensational, the news under a headline such as "Olympic Games Spoiled" seems much more accessible than in a textbook. Maps and Index.

1107.   Poynter, Margaret. **Marie Curie: Discoverer of Radium**. Springfield, NJ: Enslow, 1994. 128p. $17.95. ISBN 0-89490-477-9. (Great Minds of Science). 4-6

Marie Curie (1867-1934) grew up in Poland, saved money to send her sister to school in Paris, and then followed herself. In Paris, she learned a new language and managed to graduate at the top of her class. Her excellence in scientific research led to a Nobel Prize for chemistry and another one for physics. Photographs, Chronology, Notes, Glossary, Further Reading, and Index.

1108.   Prince, Alison. **How's Business**. New York: Four Winds, 1988. 176p. $12.95. ISBN 0-02-775202-X. 4-6

Howard (How) goes to live with his aunt and uncle in Lincolnshire in 1944. Although he has hated sleeping in the London bomb shelters, he has enjoyed wandering around the city selling or trading items that he has collected. He continues his activities in his new locale, but his friendship with a girl whose mother is German causes the local gang to jeer at him more than they would a mere evacuee. His bravery wins respect for him and acceptance for his friend, Anna, and when his parents announce that they are moving to Lincolnshire, he can continue his business, brought with him from London.

1109.   Prior, Katherine. **Initiation Customs**. New York: Thomson Learning, 1993. 32p. $13.95. ISBN 1-56847-035-5. (Comparing Religions). 4-8

Six major religions—Buddhism, Christianity, Hinduism, Judaism, Islam, and Sikhism—have specific ideas about the introduction to adulthood. The text examines the age for initiation ceremonies, how much study and preparation each requires, the special clothing worn, and the symbols that represent the religion. Topics such as baptism and confirmation for Christians, bar mitzvah for Jews, *uanayana* for Hindus, *anint* for Sikhs, and *pravrajya* for Buddhists show these rituals.

1110.   Prior, Katherine. **Pilgrimages and Journeys**. New York: Thomson Learning, 1993. 32p. $13.95. ISBN 1-56847-032-0. (Comparing Religions). 4-8

Six major religions—Buddhism, Christianity, Hinduism, Judaism, Islam, and Sikhism—have used pilgrimages and journeys as part of their faith. The text looks at why people go on pilgrimages, where they go, how they behave and dress, and what journeys they took in the past. Photographs of holy sites such as Jerusalem augment the text. Glossary, Books to Read, and Index.

1111.   Provensen, Alice, and Martin Provensen, authors/illustrators. **The Glorious Flight: Across the Channel with Louis Bleriot, July 25, 1909**. New York: Viking, 1983. Unpaged. $5.99pa. ISBN 0-14-050729-9pa. K-3

After many attempts to fly across the English Channel, Louis Bleriot (1872-1936) finally succeeded on July 25, 1909. The text looks at his trials and the support of his large family from the point of view of one of his children, who describes the various injuries he sustained on each of his attempts.

1112.   Provensen, Alice, and Martin Provensen. **Leonardo da Vinci: The Artist, Inventor, Scientist in Three-Dimensional Movable Pictures**. New York: Viking, 1984. 12p. $15.95. ISBN 0-670-42384-X. K-2

This exciting overview of Leonardo da Vinci's (1452-1519) accomplishments uses facsimiles of several of his inventions, both successful and not. Pull-tabs reveal samples of his diaries, which he wrote backward so that they could be read only with a mirror; a copy of the *Mona Lisa* pops up on its easel at the end of the text.

1113.   Pruneti, Luigi. **Viking Explorers**. Paul Clark, translator. New York: Peter Bedrick, 1996. 48p. $18.95. ISBN 0-87226-486-6. (Voyages of Discovery). 3-6

The text covers the ships and homes of the Vikings as well as their raids into England, Iceland, Greenland, Europe, the New World, and the Byzantine Empire. The entries, which give an overview of the topic, cover double-page spreads and contain illustrations. Maps, Glossary, and Index.

1114.   Pryor, Bonnie. **Seth of the Lion People**. New York: Morrow, 1988. 118p. $11.95; $4.95pa. ISBN 0-688-07327-1; 0-688-13624-9pa. 3-7

At age thirteen, Seth has to endure the hostility of his peers because of his disability; a falling rock that killed his mother also shattered his leg and crippled him. But Seth has other interests, and learning the tribe's stories from his dying father, the Teller-of-Tales, is one of them. When the leader of the tribe, a hunter, threatens him, he leaves and finds a place for the tribe to move so that its hunters can find food more easily.

1115.   Pullman, Philip. **Spring-Heeled Jack: A Story of Bravery and Evil**. David Mostyn, illustrator. New York: Knopf, 1991. 112p. $10.99. ISBN 0-679-91057-3. 4-8

With their mother dead and their father disappeared at sea, three orphans run away, intending to sail to America. Mack the Knife, however, grabs them. Spring-Heeled Jack, with springs in his shoes and clothes like the devil, comes to rescue them. One of the stories proceeds in cartoons, whereas the other occurs in regular text in this historical fantasy set in the nineteenth century. In the end, their father reappears on the ship sailing to America. *School Library Journal Best Book.*

1116.   Putnam, James. **Mummy**. Peter Hayman, illustrator. New York: Knopf, 1993. 63p. $19. ISBN 0-679-83881-3. (Eyewitness). 4 up

Two-page spreads on mummies include a large Egyptian section, which covers Egyptian mummies, how to wrap mummies, mummy masks, Egyptian mythology, Tutankhamun's treasures, and the mummy's curse. Other mummies discussed are those of Greeks, Romans, Sicilians, animals, people in the Andes, the iceman, and the Bog Man. Archaeologists have located still other mummies in several additional places. Photographs and Index.

R

1117.   Reed, Don C. **The Kraken**. Honesdale, PA: Boyds Mills Press, 1995. 217p. $15.95. ISBN 1-56397-216-6. 5-8

When Tom is twelve years old, in Newfoundland during 1872, he has to help his father, recently blinded by his own gun, to support their fishing family. The merchant who buys the yearly catch begins to cheat the fishers, and Tom has to work harder for the money. In the plot is a battle with a huge squid, called the *kraken,* and also with human evil in the guise of the dishonest merchant. Afterword.

1118.   Reef, Catherine. **Albert Einstein, Scientist of the 20th Century**. New York: Dillon Press, 1991. 62p. $13.95. ISBN 0-87518-462-6. (Taking Part). 3-6

Albert Einstein (1879-1955) did not talk until he was three years old, but when he did, he wanted to know where his baby sister's "wheels" were—all toys had wheels. One time, when he lay in bed ill, his father gave him a compass. Noticing that the needle always pointed to the north, Einstein began to realize that all things were controlled by something hidden. This was a basis of his approach to life. He loved music, especially that of the mathematically exact Mozart, and he loved thinking. His experiments could not be performed in a laboratory because he had to think them through. In 1905, he published articles on light, time, and mass, and his theory of relativity changed the way scientists perceived the universe. The text looks at his ideas about Zionism, his unified field theory, and his life. Glossary and Index.

1119.   Rees, David. **The Exeter Blitz**. New York: Dutton, 1980. 126p. $7.95. ISBN 0-525-66683-4. 5-9

While Colin Lockwood stands on the cathedral tower, he sees the German bombers blitz the town of Exeter in 1942 during a Baedeker raid. He begins to worry about other members of his family—his sister at the cinema, his mother at a local fashion show, and his father and other sister. Their home destroyed but their lives intact, they help to reconstruct the town. The omniscient point of view allows each family member to share emotions and thoughts about the situation. *Carnegie Medal.*

1120.   Rees, Rosemary. **The Ancient Egyptians**. New York: Heinemann, 1997. 64p. $14.95. ISBN 0-431-07803-3. (Understanding People in the Past). 3-4

Each topic fills a double-page spread of color photographs, maps, museum artifacts, and drawings. Among the subjects covered are the social life, the economics, the political arena, the cultural life, and the religion of the Egyptians along with pharaohs and pyramids. Chronology, Glossary, and Index.

1121.   Rees, Rosemary. **The Ancient Greeks**. New York: Heinemann, 1997. 64p. $14.95. ISBN 0-431-07790-8. (Understanding People in the Past). 3-4

Information about the social and cultural life, the economics, the political aspects, and the religion of the Greeks fills double-page spreads of color photographs, maps, museum artifacts, and drawings. Special topics concern the Olympics and the theater. Chronology, Glossary, and Index.

1122.   Reeves, Nicholas. **Into the Mummy's Tomb: The Real-life Discovery of Tutankhamun's Treasures**. New York: Scholastic, 1992. 64p. $16.95. ISBN 0-590-45752-7. (Time Quest). 4-6

In 1922, Howard Carter finally discovered what he had been seeking for years. With the financial help of Lord Carnarvon, he found the tomb of King Tutankhamun. Reeves, an Egyptologist, went to Carter's patron's home in 1988, where he opened two locked cupboards containing many ancient Egyptian treasures hidden there after the tomb was excavated. The text looks at some of these treasures, but, more importantly, it describes the process Carter went through to save every tiny item in the tomb and to reach the mummy buried inside several coffins. Photographs, Glossary, How Mummies Were Made, and Further Reading. *American Library Association Quick Picks for Reluctant Young Adult Readers, School Library Journal Best Book,* and *American Library Association Booklist Editors' Choices.*

1123.   Reiss, Johanna. **The Journey Back**. 1976. New York: HarperCollins, 1992. 212p. $17.89; $3.95pa. ISBN 0-06-021457-0; 0-06-447042-3pa. 5 up

Annie and her sister return to their Dutch home after World War II ends in 1945, in this sequel to *The Upstairs Room*. Annie misses the couple who kept them, but at the same time, she wants her new stepmother to like her. She finds that life cannot return to the way it was before the war changed everything. *Notable Children's Trade Books in the Field of Social Studies, Newbery Honor, National Jewish Awards,* and *New York Public Library Books for the Teen Age.*

1124. Reiss, Johanna. **The Upstairs Room**. New York: HarperCollins, 1972. 196p. $15; $4.50pa. ISBN 0-690-85127-8; 0-06-440370-Xpa. 5 up

In 1942, Annie, age ten, and her sister leave their parents and older sister to hide in the upstairs room of a farmhouse in Holland. They expect to be free to leave any day, but the war lasts two more years during which they, as Jews, cannot be seen by anyone without endangering their lives as well as the lives of the generous couple who hides them. The story tells of their two years in the room, including the day when Annie goes outside and hides in the tall wheat, only to be marooned in the hot sun while Nazi soldiers examine the house. *Newbery Honor, American Library Association Notable Children's Books of 1971-1975, New York Times Outstanding Children's Books, Jane Addams Honor Book, Buxtehude Bulla Prize of Germany,* and *Jewish Book Council Children's Book Award.*

1125. Resnick, Abraham. **The Holocaust**. San Diego, CA: Lucent, 1991. 128p. $12.95. ISBN 1-56006-124-3. (Overview). 4-7

The text discusses the Holocaust, from its beginning with *Kristallnacht* through its terrors during World War II as the Nazis imprisoned and executed millions of Jews in concentration camps. It also covers the establishment of the Jewish state of Israel in Palestine after the end of the war. Quotes personalize the text, and photographs and drawings augment it. Further Reading, Glossary, and Index.

1126. Resnick, Abraham. **Lenin: Founder of the Soviet Union**. Chicago: Childrens Press, 1987. 131p. $17.27. ISBN 0-516-03260-7. (People of Distinction). 4-8

Vladimir Lenin (1870-1924) grew up in tsarist Russia and was shocked when he discovered that his older brother had been arrested for being involved in a plot to assassinate Tsar Alexander III. His brother was hanged, and Lenin seemed to think that he must take his brother's place in ridding the country of a rotten system of government. He and his colleagues overthrew the government of Nicholas II in 1917 to begin the Russian Revolution. As Lenin took power and oversaw the beginning of the communist state, people observed that he could be either ruthless or kind, depending on his mood. Timeline and Index.

1127. Reynoldson, Fiona. **Conflict and Change**. New York: Facts on File, 1993. 78p. $17.95. ISBN 0-8160-2790-0. (Illustrated History of the World). 4-7

The text looks at the changes in European town and country life after 1650. It examines absolute rulers, such as Peter the Great, along with the rise of science, industry, and the arts. It was an era of revolution in the American colonies and in France. In China, the Manchu ruled, and in Japan, the Tokugawa Shogunate. The Moguls had power in Russia, and in Africa the slave trade was beginning. The Dutch entered South Africa; the aborigines were in Australia and the Maori in New Zealand. Illustrations highlight the text. Glossary, Further Reading, and Index.

1128. Reynoldson, Fiona. **Women and War**. New York: Thomson Learning, 1994. 48p. $14.95. ISBN 1-56847-082-7. (World War II). 5-8

Women participated in various ways during World War II. The text looks at their importance, using eyewitness accounts as sources. Among the topics included are food and supply rationing, jobs, evacuations, resistance, forced labor, imprisonment, and combat. It tells all aspects of women's situations, including the brutality of concentration camps and condescension from males. Photographs and Index.

1129. Ricciuti, Edward R. **Somalia: A Crisis of Famine and War**. Brookfield, CT: Millbrook Press, 1993. 64p. $16.90. ISBN 1-56294-376-6. (Headliners). 6-10

This history of Somalia shows that it emerged in the late nineteenth century as a colonial state under various European countries. As the home of clans, the people remained separate, and in 1967 a revolution began. In the latter half of the twentieth century, Somalia has been the seat of widespread famine and conflict. Photographs augment the text. Chronology, Further Reading, and Index.

1130. Rice, Bebe Faas. **The Year the Wolves Came**. New York: Dutton, 1994. 148p. $14.99. ISBN 0-525-45209-5. 5-9

Wolves frighten Therese, age ten, and her family when they enter their Canadian prairie home during a 1906 snowstorm. A Russian worker realizes that the wolves have come to find their leader, left in the village thirteen years before. Their leader happens to be Therese's mother. The story is a combination of history, fantasy, and folklore.

1131. Rice, Earle, Jr. **The Cuban Revolution**. San Diego, CA: Lucent, 1995. 112p. $16.95. ISBN 1-56006-275-4. (World History Series). 6-9

Fidel Castro believes that he was born to change history, and he has attempted to do so in Cuba since the early 1950s. He seized control of the Cuban government in 1959 and became *el líder máximo* (maximum leader). Castro's opportunity to oust the government rulers began when Batista overthrew the democratic government in 1952. Castro was probably successful in 1959 because of political repression, economic imbalance and depression, and a perceived threat of "Yankee imperialism" that resulted from uneven policies begun in 1898. In 1960, Castro reestablished relations with the Soviet Union and nationalized United States holdings on the island. These actions led the United States to sever ties in 1961 and attempt an invasion at the Bay of Pigs in April of that year—an invasion that was a miserable failure. The Cuban missile crisis occurred from October 24 through 29, 1962, when the Soviets attempted to place missiles capable of firing on the United States in Cuba. Castro continues to rule Cuba. The island's future remains uncertain. Notes, Glossary, For Further Reading, Works Consulted, and Index.

1132.   Richardson, Gillian. **Saskatchewan**. Minneapolis, MN: Lerner, 1995. 76p. $14.21. ISBN 0-8225-2760-X. 3-6
Although not technically a history book, over half the text reveals the history of this Canadian province. Charts, maps, photographs, and prints illustrate the individuality of this area, whose first inhabitants were Indians who used stone weapons to kill game animals (such as giant sloths and mammoths) around 12,000 years ago. Many Native American tribes are indigenous to the Saskatchewan area. Among the famous people from Saskatchewan briefly described are John G. Diefenbaker, a prime minister of Canada (1895-1979), and Violet McNaughton, a champion of women's rights (1879-1968). Fast Facts, Glossary, Pronunciation Guide, and Index.

1133.   Richmond, Robin. **Introducing Michelangelo**. Boston: Little, Brown, 1992. 32p. $14.95. ISBN 0-316-74440-9. 3-6
Michelangelo (1475-1564), one of the world's greatest artists, always wanted to draw. He had many arguments with his father before he was allowed to become apprenticed to another artist. To become even better, he studied cadavers, cutting them apart so that he could understand how the muscles and bones fit together. The text looks at the works of Michelangelo and shows four photographs of different stages in the recent cleaning of the Sistine Chapel ceiling, which reveal the lovely colors he originally used. This discovery has revised the idea that Michelangelo preferred dark paintings. Some Key Dates and Index.

1134.   Richter, Hans. **Friedrich**. 1970. Magnolia, MA: Peter Smith, 1992. 149p. $18.25. ISBN 0-8446-6573-8. New York: Penguin, 1987. 149p. $4.99pa. ISBN 0-14-032205-1pa. 5-9
Beginning in 1925, Friedrich's prosperous German family begins to lose its money as the narrator's poor family begins to rise in society. Hitler's propaganda about Jews affects Friedrich because of his Jewish family, and the narrator's father becomes a Nazi supporter. Friedrich eventually dies from shrapnel, which hits him outside a bomb shelter. His only "crime" is that he is Jewish. *Mildred L. Batchelder Award*.

1135.   Ridd, Stephen, ed. **Julius Caesar in Gaul and Britain**. Austin, TX: Raintree/Steck-Vaughn. 1995. 48p. $22.83. ISBN 0-8114-8283-9. (History Eyewitness). 6 up
Taken from the Latin work *De Bello Gallico* (*About the Gallic War*), the text relates the story of Caesar's first expeditions into Britain in 55 and 54 B.C. Caesar wrote seven of the eight chapters, and these commentaries (as Caesar called his writings) are the only written source of information extant about the lives and deaths of the Gauls at this time. The idea that the British tribes painted their faces for war with blue paint originated here. This work is one of the major sources for current historical fiction. Glossary and Index.

1136.   Ringgold, Faith, author/illustrator. **Bonjour, Lonnie**. New York: Hyperion. Unpaged. $15.95. ISBN 0-7868-0076-3. 2-4
In this fantasy which reveals a historical past, Lonnie, a red-haired and green-eyed orphan, is in Paris where he follows a "Love Bird," which leads him to a place where he learns his family's history. He discovers an African-American grandfather in Paris since the 1920s, a French grandmother, a father killed in World War II, and a Jewish mother who died in the Holocaust. He wants to stay, but his family convinces him that he would be happier back in the United States with his adoptive family.

1137.   Roberts, Elizabeth. **Georgia, Armenia, and Azerbaijan**. Brookfield, CT: Millbrook Press, 1992. 32p. $15.90. ISBN 1-56294-309-X. (Former Soviet States). 4-7
The text discusses the cultural background, politics, economics, and histories of the former Soviet republics of Georgia, Armenia, and Azerbaijan. Georgia borders the Black Sea and was the home of Stalin. Armenia borders Turkey, and Turks have often invaded it and persecuted its citizens. Azerbaijan borders both Iraq and the Caspian Sea. Glossary and Index.

1138.   Roberts, Jack L. **Nelson Mandela: Determined to Be Free**. Brookfield, CT: Millbrook Press, 1995. 48p. $13.90. ISBN 1-56294-558-0. 2-4
The text starts with the story of Nelson Mandela's father, a chief of the Tembu tribe in South Africa, as he was dying. He requested that his son receive a good education. Rolihlahla did receive an education, although he had to work for it, and his background prepared him to become a force in the struggle for justice and freedom in his country even though he stayed in prison for twenty-seven years. Photographs, Important Dates, Further Reading, and Index.

1139. Robles, Harold E. **Albert Schweitzer: An Adventurer for Humanity**. Brookfield, CT: Millbrook Press, 1994. 64p. $15.40. ISBN 1-56294-352-9. 4-6

Albert Schweitzer (1875-1965) was one of the rare human beings who strongly advocated human and animal rights, health care, world peace, arms reduction, and protection of the environment. He was also an accomplished musician. He and his family went to Africa where he worked with the natives. He made their lives better by building a hospital that became larger as his cures and his caring became known. Photographs enhance the text. Further Reading and Index.

1140. Rockwell, Anne, author/illustrator. **Romulus and Remus**. New York: Simon & Schuster, 1997. 40p. $15; $3.99pa. ISBN 0-689-81291-4; 0-689-81290-6pa. (Ready-to-Read). 1-2

A female wolf raises the twins Romulus and Remus with Remus especially enjoying hunting expeditions with her children. Romulus builds a city called Rome on seven hills and becomes its king.

1141. Roe, Elaine Corbeil. **Circle of Light**. New York: HarperCollins, 1989. 248p. $13.95. ISBN 0-06-025079-8. 5-8

Lucy, age thirteen, decides that she will apply for a scholarship to a Catholic high school in Ontario after she sees the boy on whom she has a crush skating with a girl who goes to that school. As she studies for the scholarship competition, she feels isolated because she wants to be with her friends instead. She does not win, but she learns about her self and her relationships.

1142. Rogasky, Barbara. **Smoke and Ashes**. New York: Holiday House, 1988. 187p. $16.95. ISBN 0-8234-0697-0. 5 up

The text gives a brief history of the roots of Nazi anti-Semitism and some of the reasons for Hitler's rise to power. Then it follows the development of the plan to exterminate the Jews. Quotations from both major and minor Nazi leaders show how they built the ghettos and concentration camps, why they built them, and who built them. Other chapters look at life in the camps for the Jews, their armed resistance in Warsaw, and what the United States and Britain did and did not do about their situation. A final chapter lists the Nazis tried at Nuremberg and what happened to them. Bibliography and Index.

1143. Rogerson, John. **Cultural Atlas of the Bible**. New York: Facts on File, 1993. 96p. $17.95. ISBN 0-8160-2903-3. (Cultural Atlas for Young People). 6-9

Much of the Christian book called the Bible is history, and this text tells what portions of the book have been verified through archaeological evidence. Additionally, the text tries to present the forces that caused these stories to be perpetuated through the centuries, from oral tradition down to their first written form during the Babylonian Exile beginning in 597 B.C. Illustrations of sites highlight the text. Chronology, Glossary, Gazetteer, and Index.

1144. Romei, Francesca. **Leonardo da Vinci: Artist, Inventor, and Scientist of the Renaissance**. Andrea Ricciardi and Sergio Ricciardi, illustrators. New York: Peter Bedrick, 1994. 64p. $19.95. ISBN 0-87226-313-4. (Masters of Art). 4 up

Leonardo da Vinci (1452-1519), one of the world's greatest artists, was also interested in many other things. The double-page spreads in the text cover his life in Florence, his contemporaries, his concept of perspective in painting, Verrocchio's workshop where he apprenticed, his painting, machines, bronze casting, his equestrian monument, the Medicis, his life in Milan, anatomy, mathematics, hydraulics, flight, and architecture. His works include *The Annunciation, The Adoration of the Magi, The Virgin of the Rocks, The Last Supper,* and *The Mona Lisa*. Index.

1145. Roop, Peter, and Connie Roop, eds. **I, Columbus: My Journal—1492-3**. Peter E. Hanson, illustrator. New York: Walker, 1990. 58p. $13.95. ISBN 0-8027-6977-2. 4-8

With a beginning in which he addresses the Christian queen and king of Spain, Columbus tells of preparing three vessels for his voyage to India to see the Great Khan, and announces that he plans to record the events of the journey. The text recaps this journal, in which Columbus noted the number of miles traveled each day and the encounters with Native Americans when he reached land. He presented the log to the queen and king when he returned.

1146. Roper, Robert. **In Caverns of Blue Ice**. Boston: Little, Brown, 1991. 188p. $14.95. ISBN 0-316-75606-7. 4-7

When Louise DeMaistre is only twelve years old in her French Alp village during the early 1950s, she guides her older brother out of a tough spot on a sheer mountain face, showing that she is a mountain climber like the rest of her family. She works first as a porter with Edouard Bruzel, a senior guide, and then she makes ascents on some of the most dangerous peaks. She passes difficult exams to become the first woman Alpine guide and eventually climbs the Himalayas in Nepal, where she almost loses her life.

1147.   Rosen, Billi. **Andi's War**. 1989. New York: Puffin, 1991. 144p. $3.95pa. ISBN 0-14-034404-7pa. 6-9

While Andi and her brother live with their grandparents in a small village, their Communist guerrilla parents fight in the Greek Civil War to gain control over the Monarchists after World War II. Andi, age eleven, fears nothing, but Paul is younger, and the Monarchists lure him into a trap that will help them capture his mother. Paul suffers intensely and eventually dies because he refuses to reveal what he knows.

1148.   Rosenberg, Maxine B. **Hiding to Survive: Stories of Jewish Children Rescued from the Holocaust**. New York: Clarion, 1994. 166p. $15.95. ISBN 0-395-65014-3. 6 up

In the text, fourteen people who remember hiding as children during the Holocaust tell their stories. They come from Greece, Belgium, Poland, Holland, Hungary, Lithuania, and France. A farm dog protected one from a German shepherd that was searching a hayloft. Another lay in a tiny hole waiting for her uncle to return and lift the trap door. Some of the survivors have kept up with those who saved them, though others have never seen their rescuers again. They found that those who helped them had a variety of reasons, some perhaps political, but others humane. Glossary and Further Reading. *Bulletin Blue Ribbon Book*.

1149.   Ross, Lillian Hammer. **Sarah, Also Known as Hannah**. Helen Cogancherry, illustrator. Morton Grove, IL: Albert Whitman, 1994. 63p. $11.95. ISBN 0-8075-7237-3. 3-6

In 1910, after their father's death, Sarah's sister, Hannah, is set to leave their East European *shtetl* for America, where they have relatives. Then their mother decides that she needs Hannah to help raise the other children. Sarah, age twelve, goes instead, using Hannah's papers. She makes friends on her journey, but unexpected twists and turns enliven the separation from home and the ocean voyage.

1150.   Ross, Nicholas. **Miró**. Hauppauge, NY: Barron's, 1995. 32p. $14.95; $8.50pa. ISBN 0-8120-6535-2; 0-8120-9427-1pa. (Famous Artists). 5 up

Joan Miró (1893-1983), often described as a Spanish surrealist, worked in a variety of media: sculpture, textiles, pottery, theater, public monuments, and painting. The text discusses the influences on Miró's life, such as his Catalonian ancestry, his life in Paris, the Spanish Civil and World Wars, theater, tapestry, and other artists such as Salvador Dali, Pablo Picasso, and Antoni Gaudí, who came from his hometown of Barcelona. Clear reproductions highlight the text. Chronology, Art History, Museums, Glossary, and Indexes.

1151.   Ross, Stewart. **Bandits & Outlaws**. Brookfield, CT: Copper Beach, Millbrook Press, 1995. 48p. $15.90; $5.95pa. ISBN 1-56294-649-8; 1-56294-189-5pa. (Fact or Fiction). 4-6

The text includes historical facts about 20 individuals or groups who have been considered bandits and outlaws. Among them are Spartacus, Ali Baba, Robin Hood, Rob Roy, Jesse James, Zapata, and Bonnie Parker. It describes the acts these people committed and the unpleasant ways that many of them died. Chronology and Index.

1152.   Ross, Stewart. **Conquerors & Explorers**. Brookfield, CT: Copper Beech, 1996. 48p. $17.90; 6.95pa. ISBN 0-7613-0532-7; 0-7613-0509-2pa. (Fact or Fiction). 4-6

Many illustrations complement the text of historical information and other topics about explorers and conquerors from the Greek period through the exploration into space. Index.

1153.   Ross, Stewart. **Knights**. Brookfield, CT: Copper Beach, 1996. 48p. $16.90; $6.95pa. ISBN 0-7613-0453-3; 0-7613-0468-1pa. (Fact or Fiction). 3-6

The text looks at the roles of knights throughout history. Among the knights included are ancient chariot riders, Hannibal, the Roman cavalry, Charlemagne, King Arthur, samurai warriors, Mongols, and twentieth-century "knights" such as World War I pilots and the Canadian Mounties. Short chapters on chivalry, arms and armor, castles, and feudalism, along with brief profiles of famous and legendary knights, also appear. Diverse illustrations highlight the text. Chronology and Index.

1154.   Roth, Susan. **Marco Polo: His Notebook**. New York: Doubleday, 1991. Unpaged. $14.95. ISBN 0-385-26495-X. 4-6

In diary format, Marco Polo (1254-1323?) tells about his travels from the time he sailed from Venice in 1271 until he returned twenty-four years later. He describes Persia, China, the Gobi Desert, India, and Ceylon as he might have for people who had never imagined such places. The tinted pages of the book seem antique, adding to the mystique of its content. Maps and reproductions illustrate the text.

1155.   Roth, Susan L., author/illustrator. **Buddha**. New York: Doubleday, 1994. Unpaged. $15.95. ISBN 0-385-31072-2. 2-4

To document her text on Siddhartha, the man who relinquished his riches to become a holy man, Roth consulted more than 100 sources and visited Buddhist shrines. Born to Maya and Shuddhodana, Siddhartha's father tried to shield him from his fate, but when Siddhartha went outside the gates of the palace and saw the poor and hungry, he worried about them. On the day that his son Rahula was born, Siddhartha left his wife Yashodhara. Buddha delivered his famous Deer Park sermon, in which he presented the Noble Eightfold Path and the Doctrine of the Four Truths, near Benares, India.

1156. Roth-Hano, Renée. **Touch Wood: A Girlhood in Occupied France**. New York: Four Winds, 1988. 297p. $16.95. ISBN 0-02-777340-X. New York: Penguin, 1989. 297p. $5.99pa. ISBN 0-14-034085-8pa. 5-9

On August 22, 1940, Renée Roth's parents send her and her two sisters to a convent in Normandy, where they will stay while the Nazis are in France. They had already escaped from Alsace when Renée was nine. The diary form of the novel tells about the interactions between the sisters, other friends in the convent, and the nuns in charge. They remain safe until the bombing at the front of the Allied invasion, and the family eventually reunites in Paris. *American Library Association Notable Books for Children.*

1157. Rowland-Warne, L. **Costume**. New York: Knopf, 1992. 64p. $19. ISBN 0-679-81680-1. 4-6

The topics here cover all aspects of clothes from shoes to hats. The illustrations and photographs give a good sense of dress in the eighteenth through twentieth centuries, although references to prehistory, Roman times, and the Viking era are included. Index.

1158. Rowlands, Avril. **Milk and Honey**. New York: Oxford University Press, 1990. 143p. $15. ISBN 0-19-271627-1. 4-7

In 1958, after Nelson, age twelve, and his family arrive in England, he soon becomes homesick for the sunshine and color of his Jamaican homeland. As some of the first immigrants, they find out that British citizens do not welcome them. Nelson, however, makes friends with old Mrs. Waterman, who helps him adjust to this new and hostile place by treating him respectfully and requesting his help with weeding her garden.

1159. Rubalcaba, Jill. **A Place in the Sun**. New York: Clarion, 1997. 86p. $13.95. ISBN 0-395-82645-4. 3-6

During the Egypt of Ramses II more than 3,000 years ago, Senmut, nine, worries about his stonecutter father's life after a cobra bites him. Then Senmut accidently kills a dove, a serious crime, and is banished to the gold mines in Nubia. He carves an amulet in hope of saving his father, and an overseer, pleased with his work, sends Senmut and the amulet back to Thebes where the plague rages. When the Pharaoh's son Merneptah survives as does Senmut's father, the Pharoah seems to attribute it to Senmut and rewards him with a place in the court.

1160. Rumford, James, author/illustrator. **The Cloudmakers**. Boston: Houghton Mifflin, 1996. Unpaged. $15.95. ISBN 0-395-76505-6. 1-4

In 751, Arab troops win a battle in Turkestan and capture Young Wu and his grandfather. To keep from being sold into slavery, Young Wu tells the Sultan of Samarkand that his grandfather makes clouds. For seven days, Grandfather makes paper with hemp and lye, as the Chinese did beginning in A.D. 105. Although the paper is not a cloud, the Sultan realizes that he has a prize, and keeps the two with him.

1161. Rupert, Janet E. **The African Mask**. New York: Clarion, 1994. 125p. $13.95. ISBN 0-395-67295-3. 6-9

In eleventh-century Africa, Layo, age twelve, goes to the city of Ife to meet her Yoruban husband and learn what job she will have as his wife. Instead of making the pottery for which her grandmother is famous, she finds that she will have to help with bronzes, a medium she does not yet appreciate. She tries to have the agreement broken, but realizes almost too late that her grandmother knows better than she what is best.

1162. Rushton, Lucy. **Birth Customs**. New York: Thomson Learning, 1993. 32p. $13.95; $5.95pa. ISBN 1-56847-034-7; 1-56847-502-0pa. (Comparing Religions). 4-8

Six major religions—Buddhism, Christianity, Hinduism, Judaism, Islam, and Sikhism—have customs surrounding the birth of a child. The text looks at the choosing of a name, the prayers said over the child, the ceremonies, and gifts to the child and family. Photographs enhance the information. Glossary, Books to Read, and Index.

1163. Rushton, Lucy. **Death Customs**. New York: Thomson Learning, 1993. 32p. $13.95; $5.95pa. ISBN 1-56847-031-2; 1-56847-503-9pa. (Comparing Religions). 4-8

Six major religions—Buddhism, Christianity, Hinduism, Judaism, Islam, and Sikhism—have specific rituals for approaching death. The text looks at the practices, the attitudes toward death, mourning customs, and ways to remember the dead. Glossary, Books to Read, and Index.

1164. Russell, Ching Yeung. **First Apple**. Christopher Zhong and Yuan Zhang, illustrators. Honesdale, PA: Boyds Mills Press, 1994. 127p. $13.95. ISBN 1-56397-206-9. 3-5

Ying, age nine, hears that her grandmother has never had an apple. In the town of Tai Kong, China, where Ying lives, she decides to earn money to buy an apple for her grandmother's seventy-first birthday. Although she earns the money to buy the apple, a bully takes half of it from her and she loses the rest. When someone else helps her, she is able to give her grandmother the "rich man's food." Glossary.

1165.   Russell, Christina. **Lichee Tree**. Honesdale, PA: Boyds Mills Press, 1997. 128p. $14.95. ISBN 1-56397-629-3. 4-6

In the 1940s, Ying, ten, looks forward to selling the lichees on her tree when they ripen. She expects to use the proceeds for a trip to Canton where she can buy glass beads and watch the foreigners. When the village thief robs the family, Ying knows that she will have to help her family. Although she lives with a backdrop of confusion in the Chinese world, she focuses on getting her profit from the lichees.

1166.   **Russia**. Minneapolis, MN: Lerner, 1992. 56p. $19.95. ISBN 0-8225-2805-3. (Then and Now). 5-9

As the largest of the countries to gain its freedom in 1991, Russia continues to have severe problems. The text looks at its history, beginning with the arrival of the Mongol hordes through Peter the Great, Ivan, and its other rulers. It also examines the economics, geography, politics, and ethnography of the country. Maps and photographs complement the text. Glossary and Index.

1167.   Ryan, Peter. **Explorers and Mapmakers**. Chris Molan, illustrator. New York: Lodestar, 1990. 48p. $14.95. ISBN 0-525-67285-0. (Time Detective). 4-6

Before a place can be mapped, someone needs to explore it to find where it is and what is in it. The text looks at a variety of explorers, including Ptolemy (d. 283 B.C.), Christopher Columbus (1451-1506), Marco Polo (1254-1324), Francisco de Orellana (c. 1490-1546, discoverer of the Amazon), Cheng Ho (c. 1371-c. 1433, saw the east coast of Africa 70 years before Vasco da Gama arrived), and Meriwether Lewis (1774-1809) and William Clark (c. 1771-c. 1833), as well as the maps their travels helped them create.

S

1168. Sabuda, Robert, author/illustrator. **Tutankhamen's Gift**. New York: Atheneum, 1994. Unpaged. $16. ISBN 0-689-31818-9. 3-5

Pictures painted on papyrus authenticate this fictionalized account of Tutankhamen, the youngest son of an Egyptian queen and Amenhotep III. Tutankhamen, a frail ten-year-old, came to the throne at his brother Amenhotep IV's death. Notes on the text elaborate the story of a king who died young, with no heirs, but was remembered kindly by his subjects.

1169. Sacks, Margaret. **Beyond Safe Boundaries**. New York: Dutton, 1989. 160p. $13.95. ISBN 0-525-67281-1. 5 up

Elizabeth Levin, age fifteen, has every imaginable comfort in her South African home in 1962, even though, as Jews, the family has not had full rights. Then her sister goes to college in Johannesburg, becomes involved with student leaders of mixed race, and begins opposing apartheid. Because of her actions and the family's beliefs, their safe world changes. *School Library Journal Best Book.*

1170. San Souci, Robert D. **Young Arthur**. Jan-Michael Henterly, illustrator. New York: Doubleday, 1997. Unpaged. $15.95. ISBN 0-385-32268-2. 2-5

Arthur grows up and becomes king of his people in medieval England when he finds his sword Excalibur. His destiny is foretold at his birth.

1171. Sandin, Joan, author/illustrator. **The Long Way to a New Land**. New York: HarperCollins, 1981. 64p. $14.89; $3.75pa. ISBN 0-06-025194-8; 0-06-444100-8pa. (An I Can Read Book). K-3

Carl Erik's family leaves Sweden in 1868 during a famine to come to America. They sail to America via England and find that Carl Erik's father has a job for the winter. *American Library Association Notable Books for Children, Booklist Children's Editor's Choices, Notable Children's Trade Books in the Field of Social Studies*, and *American Library Association USA Children's Books of International Interest.*

1172. Sattler, Helen Roney. **Hominids: A Look Back at Our Ancestors**. Christopher Santoro, illustrator. New York: Lothrop, Lee & Shepard, 1988. 125p. $15.95. ISBN 0-688-06061-7. 4-8

Drawings of early fossil remains decorate this story of our early ancestors: the Australopithecines, Genus Homo, Homo Habilis, Homo Erectus, Homo Sapiens Neanderthalensis, and modern humans (Homo Sapiens). Time Chart, Species Chart, Bibliography, and Index.

1173. Sauvain, Philip. **El Alamein**. Harry Clow, illustrator. New York: New Discovery, 1992. 32p. $13.95. ISBN 0-02-781081-X. (Great Battles and Sieges). 5-9

During World War II, one of the great battles was the Battle of El Alamein in Egypt during 1942, in which the British overcame the Germans. The text looks at the events leading to the battle, the battle itself, and the aftermath. Maps, photographs, and drawings supplement the text. Further Reading, Glossary, and Index.

1174. Sauvain, Philip. **Hastings**. Christopher Rothero, illustrator. New York: New Discovery-Macmillan, 1992. 32p. $13.95. ISBN 0-02-781079-8. (Great Battles and Sieges). 5 up

The text presents the background of William of Normandy's claim to the throne of England and discusses the battle that allowed him to become England's king in 1066 at Hastings. This battle was the beginning of the Norman conquest, and Sauvain adds other interesting bits of information about William and the Normans. Maps, photographs, and drawings supplement the text. Further Reading, Glossary, and Index.

1175. Sauvain, Philip. **Waterloo**. Tony Gibbons and Fred Anderson, illustrators. New York: New Discovery, 1993. 32p. $13.95. ISBN 0-02-781096-8. (Great Battles and Sieges). 5 up

The Battle of Waterloo in 1815 caused Napoleon's demise as a world leader after fifteen years of conquests. The text looks at the events leading to the battle, the battle itself, and the aftermath. Maps, photographs, and drawings supplement the text. Further Reading, Glossary, and Index.

1176. Say, Allen, author/illustrator. **El Chino**. Boston: Houghton Mifflin, 1990. 32p. $14.95. ISBN 0-395-52023-1. 2-5

Bill Wong, a Chinese American, became a famous bullfighter in Spain. Say tells his story using first person to give a sense of immediacy to Wong's experiences as he won over the Spanish crowd through his exploits with the bull. *Bulletin Blue Ribbon Book.*

1177. Say, Allen, author/illustrator. **Grandfather's Journey**. Boston: Houghton Mifflin, 1993. 32p. $16.95. ISBN 0-395-57035-2. K-3

The narrator's grandfather leaves Japan as a young man to see America in the early twentieth century. He travels around the country wearing western clothes. After he returns to Japan, he marries. Then he brings his bride to San Francisco and raises his daughter. They go to Japan to live, with the grandfather planning to return for a visit. But World War II destroys his plans as well as his home and his city. The narrator carries on his grandfather's dream by living in America and raising his own daughter there. *Bulletin Blue Ribbon Book* and *Caldecott Medal*.

1178. Scheller, William. **Amazing Archaeologists and Their Finds**. Minneapolis, MN: Oliver Press, 1994. 160p. $14.95. ISBN 1-881508-17-X. (Profiles). 6 up

Because of the ceaseless work of people who are intrigued with the past, some of the secrets to history have been unlocked through archaeology. The people and their finds discussed in this book are: Austen Henry Layard (1817-1884) and Hormuzd Rassam (1826-1910), who found Assyria; Henri Mouhot (1826-1861), discoverer of the Temple of Angkor in present-day Cambodia; Heinrich Schliemann (1822-1890), finder of Troy; Sir Arthur Evans (1851-1941), Knossos; Edward Thompson (1840-1935), the sacred well at Chichén Itzá; Hiram Bingham (1875-1956), the Inca hideaway at Machu Picchu; Howard Carter (1874-1939), the tomb of Tutankhamen in Egypt; and Kathleen Kenyon (1906-1978), the biblical city of Jericho. Time Line of Ancient Civilizations, Bibliography, and Index.

1179. Schlein, Miriam. **I Sailed with Columbus**. Tom Newsom, illustrator. New York: HarperCollins, 1991. 136p. $14.95. ISBN 0-06-022513-0. 3-7

Julio, twelve, leaves the monastery in which he was raised and sails with Christopher Columbus (Cristóbal Colón) in 1492 on the *Santa Maria*. As the monks had requested, he keeps a diary in which he records events and facts about the voyage. He never loses faith in Columbus, but he looks forward to returning to Spain and becoming a farmer with money earned on the voyage.

1180. Schneider, Mical. **Between the Dragon and the Eagle**. Minneapolis, MN: Carolrhoda, 1997. 151p. $14.96. ISBN 0-87614-649-3. (Adventures in Time). 4-6

Schneider traces a length of blue silk as it travels along the Silk Road from Changan, China, to Rome in A.D. 100. Among the adventures of the traders who carry the silk are a mud slide, a suspicious border guard, and a sandstorm.

1181. Schomp, Virginia. **The Ancient Greeks**. Freeport, NY: Marshall Cavendish, 1996. 79p. $19.95. ISBN 0-7614-0070-2. (Cultures of the Past). 5-8

The text presents the artifacts, monuments, domestic habits, and historical aspects of ancient Greece as it examines the lifestyle of the people. It covers the chronological and cultural history; the Greek belief system, defined through the twelve Olympian gods and goddesses; the societal mores; and the Greek legacy. To the Greeks, the gods and goddesses were an important part of daily life, and the text develops this idea. Photographs, Drawings, Bibliography, Chronology, Further Reading, Glossary, and Index.

1182. Schur, Maxine. **The Circlemaker**. New York: Dial, 1994. 192p. $14.99. ISBN 0-8037-1354-1. New York: Puffin, 1996. 192p. $4.99pa. ISBN 0-14-037997-5pa. 5-7

One day in 1852, a sign appears in Mendel's village of Molovsk, Russia, announcing that all Jewish boys over the age of twelve will be conscripted for twenty-five years into the czar's army. Mendel runs to his friend Zalman's hut, but his family has left. Mendel escapes so that his own family will not have to pay a bribe for him to stay out of the army. A man sees him at a train station and guides him to the border. Ironically, the person with whom he must find the border is the boy he has hated throughout his school years. They do succeed, and Mendel journeys to Germany and sails to America via steerage class.

1183. Schur, Maxine. **Day of Delight: A Jewish Sabbath in Ethiopia**. Brian Pinkney, illustrator. New York: Dial, 1994. Unpaged. $15.99. ISBN 0-8037-1413-0. 2-5

Although not technically historical, the story tells of Menelik's Ethiopian Jewish family as the members prepare for the Sabbath. For over a thousand years, Jews have lived in the mountains of Ethiopia, making their livings as blacksmiths and calling themselves *Beta Israel*. Because of civil war and famine, many have now immigrated to Israel, and the way of life described in the story is coming to an end. Author's Note, Pronunciation Guide, and Glossary.

1184.   Schur, Maxine. **When I Left My Village**. J. Brian Pinkney, illustrator. New York: Dial, 1996. 64p. $14.99. ISBN 0-8037-1561-7. 4-6

This sequel to *Day of Delight* shows Menelik, age twelve, and his family leaving Ethiopia because of famine and heightened persecution of his people, the *Beta Israel* or Ethiopian Jews. To get to the Sudan, the family has to endure fear of detection, hunger, and concern about being caught at the border crossing. They eventually reach Israel to resettle near Jerusalem.

1185.   **Scrawl! Writing in Ancient Times**. Minneapolis, MN: Runestone Press, 1994. 72p. $22.95. ISBN 0-8225-3209-3. (Buried Worlds). 6 up

Paleography, the study of writing, gives insights into what ancient civilizations achieved in communication and what they thought was important. The text looks at various ancient scripts and what they reveal. Glossary and Index.

1186.   Segal, Jerry. **The Place Where Nobody Stopped**. Dav Pilkey, illustrator. New York: Orchard, 1991. 154p. $14.95. ISBN 0-531-05897-2. 5 up

For the years between 1895 and 1906, Yosif the baker never has anyone stop at his place located on the road from Vitebsk to Smolensk. When someone does stop, it is the Cossack sergeant major, and he mistreats Yosif. Others who stop need to be supported or hidden, including Mordecai ben Yahbahbai, who becomes a boarder. Yosif's kindness gains more respect than the Cossack's bullying. *Bulletin Blue Ribbon Book*.

1187.   Semel, Nava. **Becoming Gershona**. Seymour Simckes, translator. New York: Viking, 1990. 128p. $11.95. ISBN 0-670-83105-0. 6-8

As a *sabra* (Israeli born), Gershona, age twelve, is the only child of a mother who survived Auschwitz and a father whose own father abandoned him as a young child to go to the United States. When her grandfather returns to Tel Aviv in 1958 and remarries her grandmother, Gershona must acquaint herself with him while reconciling his decisions. She must also deal with her first love for a new boy who recently arrived from Poland, and she must gain acceptance from peers in her neighborhood.

1188.   Semel, Nava. **Flying Lessons**. Hillel Halkin, translator. New York: Simon & Schuster, 1995. $14. ISBN 0-689-80161-0. 5-7

Monsieur Maurice, a concentration camp survivor, a cobbler, and an Israeli neighbor, tells Hadara that anything is possible. Hadara believes him and jumps from the tallest tree in her father's citrus grove in an attempt to fly. She may be too old to believe him, but she may also want to escape from the various situations around her, such as her grieving widower father, the woman who wants to end his grief and become Hadara's stepmother, and a kind boy who stutters.

1189.   Service, Pamela F. **The Reluctant God**. New York: Atheneum, 1988. 211p. $13.95. ISBN 0-689-31404-3. 6-9

Lorna, in England, wants to be back in Egypt with her widowed father at his archaeological dig. This historical fantasy also tells about Ameni, training to be a priest in 2000 B.C. while his twin brother prepares to become the pharaoh, Senusert III. After Lorna returns to Egypt, she and Ameni meet in a tomb where Ameni is searching for eternity. She takes him back to England with her to find a relic that he needs to fulfill his destiny.

1190.   Severance, John B. **Gandhi, Great Soul**. New York: Clarion, 1997. 144p. $15.95. ISBN 0-395-77179-X. 6-9

Mohandas K. Gandhi (1869-1947) helped to free India from British colonialism. Severance gives a balanced account of Gandhi's life from his privileged upbringing and attendance at British schools, his unhappy arranged marriage when he was thirteen, his experiences in South Africa that influenced his concerns for the rights of individuals, through his contributions to the concept of *satyagraha*, or peaceful resistance. Severance also gives the context of Indian politics that became the focus of Gandhi's protest. Photographs, Bibliography, and Index.

1191.   Seymour-Jones, Carole. **Refugees**. New York: New Discovery, 1992. 48p. $12.95. ISBN 0-02-735402-4. (Past and Present). 5-7

People have had to flee their homes because of war, poverty, starvation, or government persecution. Among the historical flights of people included in the text are the dispersions under Genghis Khan and the Mongols around 1214, the Trail of Tears in 1838 when the Cherokees had to leave their homes, the boat people fleeing to Thailand following the fall of Saigon in 1975, and the escape of the Israelites from Egypt around 1280 B.C. The text looks at the way these people coped and how other societies have tried to help. Key Dates, Glossary, and Index.

1192. Shea, Pegi Deitz. **The Whispering Cloth: A Refugee's Story**. Anita Riggio, illustrator; You Yang, stitcher. Honesdale, PA: Boyds Mills Press, 1996. $14.95; $7.95pa. ISBN 1-56397-134-8; 1-56397-623-5pa. K-3

When Mai learns to embroider, her grandmother sells the *pa'ndau* (story cloths) on which she works to traders who come to their Thai refugee camp in the early 1970s. Mai wants to make her own story cloth, but her grandmother tells her that she must first have a story. Mai tells the story of her parents' deaths and escaping with her grandmother to the camp. Her grandmother tells her she cannot sell the cloth until she finishes her story. When Mai decides on an ending, she chooses to keep the cloth. *Notable Children's Trade Books in the Field of Social Studies.*

1193. Shemin, Margaretha. **The Little Riders**. 1963. Peter Spier, illustrator. New York: Beech Tree, 1993. 76p. ISBN 0-688-12499-2. 4-6

Johanna's father took her to Holland to stay with her grandparents while he and her mother went on a trip. After they left, the Germans invaded Holland, and Johanna could not return to America. During the last year of the war, a German officer is billeted in Johanna's room, an imposition that infuriates and frightens the family, except that he plays his flute at night. Of most concern to them are the "little riders," the mechanical lead figures that circled the church tower clock at noon each day, which Johanna's grandfather had kept working. When the Germans started taking lead for ammunition, he disassembled the riders, planning to hide them. The Germans arrived before he finished his task, but Johanna and the German officer living in the house achieve the goal.

1194. Sherrow, Victoria. **Amsterdam**. New York: New Discovery, 1992. 96p. $14.95. ISBN 0-02-782465-9. (Cities at War). 6 up

The text looks at the effects of World War II on the people who lived in Amsterdam. Eyewitnesses, diaries, and other primary sources tell about the Dutch fascists (NSB), the Nazi invasion, the Resistance, protection of the Jews, and the response to the end of the war. Sherrow also uses quotes from Anne Frank and Ida Vos. Documentary photographs focus and accentuate the text. Bibliography and Index.

1195. Sherrow, Victoria. **The Maya Indians**. New York: Chelsea House, 1993. 79p. $14.95. ISBN 0-7910-1666-8. (The Junior Library of American Indians). 3-6

The Mayan civilization, when combined with the Olmec society that joined with them at the end of the Classic period around A.D. 800, spanned more than 3,000 years. The text looks at history and culture, daily routine, and descendants. When Cortés came, he conquered the Maya in Guatemala around 1520. Photographs and reproductions enhance the text. Glossary, Chronology, and Index.

1196. Shiefman, Vicki. **Good-bye to the Trees**. New York: Atheneum, 1993. 150p. $14.95. ISBN 0-689-31806-5. 4-8

Fagel, aged thirteen in 1907, leaves her widowed mother and family in Slonim, Russia, to go to Chelsea, Massachusetts. She says good-bye to all of the trees, though she is actually saying good-bye to her family. In America, she plans to work enough to pay for the rest of the family to join her. What she finds are new customs and opportunities, but she knows that she will not be happy until the family reunites.

1197. Silverman, Robin. **A Bosnian Family**. Minneapolis, MN: Lerner, 1997. 64p. $21.50; $5.95pa. ISBN 0-8225-3429-0; 0-8225-9743-8pa. (Journey Between Two Worlds). 3-6

Although not a history book, the text includes the history of the Bosnian people as a background for understanding the reasons why families from Bosnia and the former Yugoslavia have had to leave their homes. Photographs and personal experiences explain Bosnian social and religious traditions and how the people have had to adapt to a new culture to survive as refugees. Further Reading.

1198. Sim, Dorrith M. **In My Pocket**. Gerald Fitzgerald, illustrator. San Diego, CA: Harcourt Brace, 1996. 32p. $16. ISBN 0-15-201357-1. K-3

When a young Jewish girl leaves her parents in Germany, she takes a ship and a train to Scotland where she stays with a couple during the war. She only knows one English phrase, "I have a handkerchief in my pocket." As she learns new words, she puts them "in her pocket" where she keeps the letter she gets from her parents while waiting to rejoin them after World War II ends.

1198a. Simms, George Otto. **St. Patrick: The Real Story of Patrick**. David Rooney, illustrator. Chester Springs, PA: Dufour, 1992. 93p. $13.95. ISBN 0-86278-270-8. 5-9

In a book divided into two parts, Simms first looks at the words Patrick (389?–461?) wrote about his experiences and beliefs. The second part presents the legends and stories that have arisen about his life. Simms discusses St. Patrick's struggles to establish the Christian faith in Ireland. Reproductions and illustrations augment the text.

1199. Simon, Charnant. **Explorers of the Ancient World**. Chicago: Childrens Press, 1990. 128p. $26.20. ISBN 0-516-03053-1. (The World's Great Explorers). 4-8

The text looks at the voyages and discoveries of explorers in the ancient world. They include Hanno of Carthage (c. 500 B.C.), Hensi of Egypt (c. 1500 B.C.), Eudoxus of Greece (c. 120 B.C.), Pytheas of Greece (c. 330 B.C.), and Alexander the Great (356-323 B.C.). Timeline, Glossary, Bibliography, and Index.

1200. Singer, Donna. **Structures That Changed the Way the World Looked**. Austin, TX: Raintree/Steck-Vaughn, 1995. 48p. $15.96. ISBN 0-8114-4937-8. (20 Events Series). 6 up

Humans in recorded history have built structures that have survived to tell something about the people who built them. The structures identified here and discussed in two-page spreads are the Great Pyramid (Cairo, Egypt), the Parthenon (Athens, Greece), the Great Wall of China, the Colosseum (Rome, Italy), Palenque (Chiapas, Mexico), Angkor (near Siem Reap, Cambodia), Great Zimbabwe (near Harare, Zimbabwe), Tower of London (England), Anasazi Cliff Dwellings (Mesa Verda, Colorado), Chartres Cathedral (France), Dikes of the Netherlands, Alhambra (Granada, Spain), Taj Mahal (Agra, India), Suez Canal (between Egypt and Israel), Statue of Liberty (New York), Eiffel Tower (Paris, France), Hoover Dam (near Las Vegas, Nevada), Golden Gate Bridge (San Francisco), Sears Tower (Chicago), and the English Channel Tunnel (between France and England). Glossary, Suggested Readings, and Index.

1201. Sis, Peter, author/illustrator. **Starry Messenger**. New York: Farrar, Straus & Giroux, 1996. 40p. $16. ISBN 0-374-379191-1. 1-5

When Galileo Galilei (1564-1642) said that the earth is not the fixed center of the universe, he was basing his decision on discoveries he had made by using his telescope to map the heavens. Galileo was a scientist, mathematician, astronomer, philosopher, and a physicist. When his ideas became too popular, the Catholic Church leaders decided that his ideas conflicted with the Bible, and they imprisoned him in his home. A simplified text accompanies script notes and illustrations about Galileo's life and discoveries.

1202. Skurzynski, Gloria. **The Minstrel in the Tower**. Julek Heller, illustrator. New York: Random House, 1988. 64p. $6.99; $3.99pa. ISBN 0-394-99598-8; 0-394-89598-3pa. (Stepping Stone Book). 2-4

In 1195, when their mother is sick, Alice, age eight, and Roger, age eleven, go to find an uncle of whom they have just become aware. Scoundrels kidnap them, but Alice escapes and finds her uncle. He tells her that her father has died in the Crusades at Acre, and then he goes with the two to help their mother.

1203. Skurzynski, Gloria. **What Happened in Hamelin**. 1979. New York: Random House, 1993. $3.99pa. ISBN 0-679-83645-3pa. 5-9

Gast frees the town of Hamelin from its rat infestation, but the town does not give him his final payment. In retribution, he feeds 130 Hamelin children bread containing purple rye. The rye keeps them from sleeping, and on July 26, 1284, he leads the children away from Hamelin while their parents pray in the church for them to sleep. He plans to sell the children, each for a piece of silver, as his payment. *Christopher Award, Booklist Reviewers' Choice,* and *Horn Book Fanfare Honor List.*

1204. Slaughter, Charles H. **The Dirty War**. New York: Walker, 1994. 166p. $15.95. ISBN 0-8027-8312-0. 5-8

In Buenos Aires, Argentina, in 1976, thousands of people disappeared from the streets when the military took over the government from President Isabel Perón. Slaughter starts each chapter with a brief segment from the Buenos Aires newspaper as he describes the effects of this coup on innocent people. Atre, age fourteen, his friend Chino, and his family try to survive by ignoring the situation, but they cannot. The army takes Atre's father, and he and Chino find him. Chino and Atre get Atre's father's story published in the newspaper, which keeps him alive and eventually leads to his freedom. But the army also takes Chino, and he is not as fortunate. The "dirty war" ended in 1983 after the military realized that some parents will fight for their children's rights. Glossary of Spanish Words and Phrases.

1205. Sloan, Frank. **Bismarck!** New York: Franklin Watts, 1991. 63p. $18.43. ISBN 0-531-20002-7. (First Books). 4-6

On June 8, 1989, the search for the *Bismarck* ended when the tiny submarine *Argo* found it under the Atlantic Ocean. The *Bismarck*, launched on February 14, 1939, was one of Hitler's U-boats pitted against the British. It was one-sixth of a mile long and suited for battle, weighing 7,000 tons more than the World War I peace treaty allowed. The text, with photographs and illustrations, talks about the building of the ship, the chase and battle with the *Hood*, and the sinking of the *Bismarck* in May 1941. Glossary, Finding Out More, and Index.

1206. Smith, Brenda. **Egypt of the Pharaohs**. San Diego, CA: Lucent, 1996. 112p. $16.95. ISBN 1-56006-241-X. (World History Series). 6-9

The text looks at Egypt and the creation of the pyramids in great depth, using quotes as available from both primary and secondary sources. A final chapter examines the significance of the Egyptian culture to world history. Bibliography, Chronology, Further Reading, Notes, and Index.

1207.   Smith, Carter, ed. **The Korean War**. Englewood Cliffs, NJ: Silver Burdett, 1990. 64p. $14.98; $7.95pa. ISBN 0-382-09953-2; 0-382-09949-4pa. (Turning Points in American History). 4-8

The text gives the background as to why the United States was involved in the Korean War and the surprise of the Chinese joining on the side of the North Koreans. It focuses on the battles and the strategy of the war, which lasted from 1950 to 1953. Photographs highlight the text. Bibliography and Index.

1208.   Smucker, Barbara. **Incredible Jumbo**. New York: Viking, 1991. 177p. $12.95. ISBN 0-670-82970-6. 4-6

In 1865, Tod, ten, gets a job as assistant elephant keeper at the London Zoo. He becomes attached to Jumbo, but P. T. Barnum purchases Jumbo to take to America as a performer in his circus. Tod stows away so that he can follow Jumbo to the United States.

1209.   Snyder, Zilpha Keatley. **Song of the Gargoyle**. New York: Delacorte, 1991. 224p. $14.95. ISBN 0-385-30301-7. 5-8

In this medieval setting, Tymmon sees a helmeted knight kidnap his father. He leaves the castle and encounters outlaws, peasants, and greedy lords on his journey with his faithful dog, Troff. Troff is so ugly that he resembles a gargoyle, but Tymmon thinks he is magical and converses with him. Various adventures occur, and at the conclusion, Tymmon knows he would prefer to be a court jester rather than a knight.

1210.   **Sold! The Origins of Money and Trade**. Minneapolis, MN: Runestone Press, 1994. 64p. $22.95. ISBN 0-8225-3206-9. (Buried Worlds). 6 up

When archaeologists find ruins of ancient civilizations, they also find the types of coins that people used before 500 B.C. Additionally, they may find items that the ancients sold, and through them create some understanding of ancient commerce. Glossary and Index.

1211.   Speed, Peter. **Life in the Time of Harald Hardrada and the Vikings**. Richard Hook, illustrator. Austin, TX: Raintree/Steck-Vaughn, 1993. 63p. $16.98. ISBN 0-8114-3353-6. (Life in the Time of). 4-8

Harald III Harsrasi (1015-1066), half-brother of Olaf, King of Norway, became king himself after he returned from Byzantium and service in the Varangian guard. His nickname "Hardrada" denoted his ruthlessness. During his lifetime, the Vikings continued to live as traders and warriors, believing in Valhalla and Ragnarok. They invaded England, Ireland, France, and Italy before they went into Russia, America, and Byzantium. Harald went back to invade England in 1066 and captured York, but at the ensuing Battle of Stamford Bridge, he died. Although the Saxons defeated these Vikings, the Saxons soon faced defeat with the arrival of William the Conqueror. Each chapter covers specifics of the topics, with illustrations to clarify. Glossary and Index.

1212.   Sperry, Armstrong. **Call It Courage.** 1940. New York: Macmillan, 1968. $16. ISBN 0-02-786030-2. New York: Aladdin, 1990. $3.95pa. ISBN 0-689-71391-6pa. 5-7

Matufu knows that facing the thing he fears most, the sea, is the only way to escape the derision of his Polynesian island people, who call him "Boy Who Was Afraid." Almost drowned as a child with his mother, who saved him as she died, he has not recovered from the fear. He takes his dog into a canoe, and they leave. An albatross guides them through a storm toward land, and Matufu saves himself and the dog by killing a tiger shark, octopus, and wild boar. When they see savages on the island, he and the dog sail away in the canoe he built. As he arrives home and his father declares his pride in his son, he dies. His new name, however, is the tribal name by which he is remembered, "Stout Heart." *Newbery Medal.*

1213.   Spier, Peter. **Father, May I Come?** New York: Doubleday, 1993. 24p. $13.95. ISBN 0-385-30935-X. 3-6

The text contrasts the times of 1687 and 1987, when two different Dutch men with the same name, Sietze Hemme, run back from the Dutch coast with the news that a ship is in trouble. In 1687, the village hauls a wooden lifeboat to the shore of the North Sea with the help of horses. In 1987, a motorized lifeboat awaits the men who will board it on the edge of the sea.

1214.   Spivak, Dawnine. **Grass Sandals**. Demi, illustrator. New York: Simon & Schuster, 1997. 40p. $16. ISBN 0-689-80776-7. 1-4

Basho was one of the greatest Japanese haiku poets. He loved Japan and spent much of his later life walking through the land and writing his haiku to describe its beauty. On each spread of the book appears a Japanese character for a word in both a haiku and the story.

1215.   Spyri, Johanna, and Loretta Krupinski, retellers. **Heidi**. Loretta Krupinski, illustrator. New York: Harper-Collins, 1996. Unpaged. $14.95. ISBN 0-06-023438-5. K-3

This version of *Heidi* simples the story of the little girl who goes to the Swiss mountains to live with her grandfather during the nineteenth century. The people in the village help her to understand the values of life, which have no relationship to money.

1216. Stacey, Tom. **The Titanic**. Maurie Manning and Michael Spackman, illustrators. San Diego, CA: Lucent, 1990. 64p. $22.95. ISBN 1-56006-006-9. (World Disasters). 5-7

The *Titanic* was advertised as the ship that could not sink, but a few days into its maiden voyage, on April 14, 1914, icebergs sank it. The text recounts the story as it has been pieced together by rescue teams and survivors. In 1985, Robert Ballard and his submarine *Jason* discovered the wreckage of the *Titanic*, thereby allowing new information to become available. Diagrams and drawings augment the text. Further Reading, Glossary, Other Works, and Index.

1217. Stanley, Diane. **Elena**. New York: Hyperion, 1996. 56p. $13.95. ISBN 0-7868-0256-1. 4-7

Elena (a character based on a friend of Stanley's mother) was a widow whose husband died when Pancho Villa's army raided their village. She fled from Mexico to California during the Mexican Revolution in the early 1900s. The text covers her decision to leave with her son so that he would not be drafted into the army and her concern that her other three children escape problems in the war-ravaged country.

1218. Stanley, Diane, author/illustrator. **Leonardo Da Vinci**. New York: Morrow, 1996. 48p. $16. ISBN 0-688-10437-1. 4-7

In addition to presenting the known facts about Leonardo da Vinci (1452-1519), Stanley also recreates the time in Florence during which he lived. She describes the preliminary steps for painting and sculpting and the various problems da Vinci had in getting materials and investigating his ideas. She uses da Vinci's own writing to show his intelligence and his inquisitiveness. Bibliography. *Bulletin Blue Ribbon Book, American Library Association Notable Books for Children, Orbis Pictus Award for Outstanding Nonfiction for Children,* and *School Library Journal Best Book.*

1218a. Stanley, Diane, and Peter Vennema. **Cleopatra**. Diane Stanley, illustrator. New York: Morrow, 1994. Unpaged. $15. ISBN 0-688-10413-4. 3-6

Almost all information available about Cleopatra, the woman descended from the Macedonian Greek royal line of Alexander the Great and who became queen of Egypt at age eighteen in 51 B.C., comes from her enemies or from Plutarch who lived one hundred years later. The text discusses her joint reign with her brother Ptolemy XIII, ten, also nominally her husband until she defected to Julius Caesar upon his arrival to capture Alexandria for the Romans. She and Caesar had a son, but after Caesar was murdered, Cleopatra captivated Marc Antony. They lived as husband and wife and had three children. Their defeat by Octavian, Caesar's grand-nephew and adopted son, led to Antony's death and Cleopatra's suicide. The drawings and maps reflect the Egyptian style and clarify that Cleopatra lived long after the pyramids were constructed. Bibliography and Pronunciation Guide.

1219. Steedman, Scott. **The Egyptian News**. New York: Candlewick, 1997. 32p. $15.99. ISBN 0-56402-873-0. 4-9

The approach to the Egyptians through the style of a newspaper highlights fashion, sports, trade, food, and the military. Each page has headlines, sometimes with classifieds advertising such things as used papyrus. Highly readable and slightly sensational, the news under a headline such as "Boy-King Murdered?" seems much more accessible than in a textbook. Maps and Index.

1220. Steele, Philip. **The Aztec News**. New York: Candlewick, 1997. 32p. $15.99. ISBN 0-7636-0115-2. 4-9

The approach to the Aztecs through the style of a newspaper highlights fashion, sports, trade, food, and the military. Each page has headlines, sometimes with classifieds advertising a variety of items that the Aztecs used. Highly readable and slightly sensational, the news under a headline such as "Spanish Flee City" seems much more accessible than in a textbook. Maps and Index.

1221. Steele, Philip, author/illustrator. **Castles**. New York: Kingfisher, 1995. 63p. $14.95. ISBN 1-8567-547-9. 3-7

This presentation of castles includes fold-out illustrations showing cross-sections of a castle's interior. The various chapters include information on the age during which castles were built, the towns surrounding a castle, castle defenses, castle life of all dimensions (food, kitchens, fashions, hunting and hawking, jousting, heraldry), and what happens when a castle is besieged. Castles In History, Glossary, and Index.

1222. Steele, Philip. **Censorship**. New York: New Discovery, 1992. 48p. $12.95. ISBN 0-02-735404-0. (Past and Present). 5-7

The text looks at the history of censorship, including the Chinese emperor who burned books in 213 B.C., Roman censors, religion and the printing press, revolution, and private censorship. It examines the reasons stated for censorship and assesses freedom or control as a motive. Key Dates, Glossary, and Index.

1223. Steele, Philip. **The Egyptians and the Valley of the Kings**. New York: Dillon Press, 1994. 32p. $13.95. ISBN 0-87518-539-8. (Hidden Worlds). 4-7

Photographs and maps give an overview of Egypt. Topics included are the pharaohs, pyramids and tombs, the archaeologists' search for Thebes, the attempts to break the language barrier of hieroglyphics, the mask of Tutankhamen, the rulers and the gods, and other bits of information. Glossary and Index.

1224.　Steele, Philip. **I Wonder Why Castles Had Moats: And Other Questions About Long Ago**. Tony Kenyon, illustrator. New York: Kingfisher, 1994. 32p. $8.95. ISBN 1-85697-879-6. (I Wonder Why). 4-6

With questions and answers, the text and illustrations look at the Middle Ages, using a humorous tone. Diagrams, Maps, and Index.

1225.　Steele, Philip. **I Wonder Why Pyramids Were Built: And Other Questions About Ancient Egypt**. Tony Kenyon, illustrator. New York: Kingfisher, 1995. 32p. $8.95. ISBN 1-85697-550-9. (I Wonder Why). 4-6

With questions and answers, the text and illustrations look at ancient Egypt, using a humorous tone. Diagrams, Maps, and Index.

1226.　Steele, Philip. **The Incas and Machu Picchu**. New York: Dillon Press, 1993. 32p. $13.95. ISBN 0-87518-536-3. (Hidden Worlds). 6-8

The Incan civilization began in ancient Peru about 3,500 years ago. The Incas settled in the Cuzco region, in the Andes, about 900 years ago. In 1438, the ruler, Pachacuti Inca Yupanqui, built a powerful state. His brother, Atahualpa, overthrew him, but then Pizarro came and destroyed Atahualpa. One of the major temples of the area was Machu Picchu. In 1911, Hiram Bingham led an expedition in search of the lost city of the Incas. The text talks about the archaeologists who found these ruins and who reconstructed information about this civilization from the finds they made at the site. Photographs, maps, and illustrations augment the text. Glossary and Index.

1227.　Steele, Philip. **Kidnapping**. New York: New Discovery, 1992. 48p. $12.95 ISBN 0-02-735403-2. (Past and Present). 5-7

The text looks at the history of kidnapping, including the hostages of the Greeks and Romans, Joseph in the Bible, the Children's Crusade, and ransoms for kings. It tries to account for the reasons behind kidnappings and abductions and ways to overcome or avoid them. Key Dates, Glossary, and Index.

1228.　Steele, Philip. **Pirates**. New York: Kingfisher, 1997. 64p. $15.95. ISBN 0-7534-5052-6. 3-5

Steele looks at the lives of pirates from Roman times through the 1990s. He tells about pirates in the Caribbean and in northern America, China, the Middle East, Spain, and Britain. The illustrations decorating the capsule biographies of fifty rogues make his version especially attractive. Glossary and Index.

1229.　Steele, Philip. **The Romans and Pompeii**. New York: Dillon Press, 1994. 32p. $13.95. ISBN 0-87518-538-X. (Hidden Worlds). 4-7

On August 24, A.D. 79, the wealthy city of Pompeii met a "terrible end," destroyed not by armies but by the mysterious forces of nature in the form of lava spewing from Mount Vesuvius, which most people had believed was extinct. Seventeen years prior, an earthquake had damaged some of the buildings; on the morning of the volcanic eruption, dogs started howling and springs dried up. The eruption blasted material twelve miles into the air. The text looks at this event and what archaeologists have found out about the society it destroyed. Glossary and Index.

1230.　Steele, Philip. **Smuggling**. New York: New Discovery, 1993. 48p. $12.95. ISBN 0-02-786884-2. (Past and Present). 5-7

Smugglers have been working for centuries. One of the first documented smuggling operations was the Trojan Horse that the Greeks took into Troy. Other accounts describe Chinese silk smuggling and illegal trading on the seas. The text discusses the history of smuggling, money as the main motive, drugs today, contraband, and how to detect and deter smugglers. Key Dates, Glossary, and Index.

1231.　Steele, Philip. **Thermopylae**. Roger Payne, illustrator. New York: New Discovery, 1992. 32p. $13.95. ISBN 0-02-786887-7. (Great Battle and Sieges). 5 up

For more than two days in 480 B.C., 300 Greek soldiers from Sparta and Thespiae held back the Persian army, the largest force ever seen in the world, but every Greek eventually died. The text looks at the events that led to the battle and gives background on the two armies that fought in it. Topics include the Immortals of Persia, the hoplites of Greece under Leonidas, the march itself, the battle in the pass, the treachery of the Greek Ephialtes to Xerxes, and then the revenge and conquest when the Greek navy defeated the Persians in a battle at Salamis. Glossary, For Further Reading, and Index.

1232.　Steele, Philip. **Thor Heyerdahl and the Kon-Tiki Voyage**. New York: Dillion Press, 1993. 32p. $13.95. ISBN 0-87518-533-9. (Great 20th Century Expeditions). 4-6

After describing the fright of a huge storm at sea in 1947, while Thor Heyerdahl and his crew were trying to sail their raft across the Pacific, Steele tells why they made this journey and the preparation they needed. Heyerdahl wanted to see if he could sail a raft from Peru to the Polynesian Islands. If he could, it would show that an ancient connection could have existed between cultures that seemed strikingly similar, those of the Americas and the South Pacific. As he and his crew built the raft, they chose materials that would have been available to the ancient Peruvians. Heyerdahl's theories that the South Americans settled the Polynesian Islands might not be correct, but at least he proved it was possible. Photographs, Glossary, Further Reading, and Index.

1233.   Steffens, Bradley. **The Children's Crusade**. San Diego, CA: Lucent, 1991. 64p. $11.95. ISBN 1-56006-019-0. (World Disasters). 4-7

In 1212, hundreds of children marched into France and boarded ships to go to Palestine, where they expected to help regain the city of Jerusalem from the Moslems. They never reached their intended destination. Some died from starvation or exhaustion, and others were taken into the slave trade when they went ashore. The text looks at their lives in their villages during the thirteenth century, the wars that beckoned them, and the legacy of the Crusades. Glossary, Further Reading, Works Consulted, and Index.

1234.   Stefoff, Rebecca. **The Viking Explorers**. New York: Chelsea House, 1993. 111p. $19.95. ISBN 0-7910-1295-6. (World Explorers). 5 up

In A.D. 793, men from the north, whom their victims called "Norsemen," landed on the peaceful island of Lindisfarne in the North Sea, raided the abbey, and killed the monks who lived there. Survivors watched from hiding places as the plunderers took relics and enslaved clerics before sailing their striped-sail ships into the wind. For the next 300 years, the Viking age flourished as these men terrorized other areas of northern Europe. They went as far as Russia and to the coasts of Greenland and Iceland, and probably visited the coast of North America five centuries before Columbus. Photographs and reproductions highlight the text. Chronology, Further Reading, and Index.

1235.   Stein, R. Conrad. **The Aztec Empire**. Freeport, NY: Marshall Cavendish, 1996. 80p. $19.95. ISBN 0-7614-0072-9. (Cultures of the Past). 5-8

The text examines the artifacts, monuments, domestic scenes, and historical aspects of the Aztecs as it looks at the history, beliefs, and lifestyles of the people. It also notes the influence of the Aztecs on modern Mexico and discusses the discovery of the ruins of Tenochtitlán. Photographs, Drawings, Bibliography, Chronology, Further Reading, Glossary, and Index.

1236.   Stein, R. Conrad. **Christopher Columbus**. Chicago: Childrens Press, 1992. 32p. ISBN 0-516-04851-1. (Cornerstones of Freedom). 3-5

The text looks at the influences on Christopher Columbus (1451-1506) that piqued his interest in the East, especially Marco Polo's journal of his own trip. It then follows Columbus on his voyage to Cuba, which he thought was Japan, and where he watched people "drinking the smoke" of a tobacco plant. He returned to Spain and later made other journeys to the New World; his son wrote a biography about him in which he said that his father liked Seneca and quoted him about revealing "a vast continent." Index.

1237.   Stein, R. Conrad. **Francisco de Coronado**. Chicago: Childrens Press, 1992. 128p. $17.27. ISBN 0-516-03068-X. (The World's Great Explorers). 3 up

Coronado (1510-1554) left for New Spain in 1535 to make his home in Mexico City. He married and had daughters, and Viceroy Mendoza named him governor of New Galicia. Then Mendoza sent Marcos de Niza and the slave Estéban on an expedition to locate the Seven Cities of Cíbola, and de Niza returned to tell Coronado about the trip. Coronado went to find the gold in 1540. When he returned empty-handed, Mendoza put him on trial in 1545 for mishandling the expedition, although he had done no wrong. Reproductions and photographs help to tell his story. Timeline, Glossary, Bibliography, and Index.

1238.   Stein, R. Conrad. **Hernando Cortés**. Chicago: Childrens Press, 1991. 128p. $15.27. ISBN 0-516-03059-0. (The World's Great Explorers). 3 up

In looking at the life of Hernando Cortés (1485-1547), Stein complements stunning photographs and reproductions with information about the conquests Cortés made in the New World. He conquered first the Aztecs, at Tenochtitlán, and then all of Mexico. He created New Spain by his battles. What the contemporary world thinks about his conquests ends the text. Appendices, Timeline, Glossary, Bibliography, and Index.

1239.   Stein, R. Conrad. **The Iran Hostage Crisis**. Chicago: Childrens Press, 1994. 32p. $15.27. ISBN 0-516-06681-1. (Cornerstones of Freedom). 5 up

On November 4, 1979, Iranian students seized 60 employees in the U.S. embassy in Tehran. They kept most of the hostages for 444 days in various places separated from each other. After Jimmy Carter lost the presidential election, Ronald Reagan took office on the same day the hostages were released, January 20, 1981. People displayed yellow ribbons everywhere so that others would not forget the hostages before the Iranians freed them. Index.

1240.   Stein, R. Conrad. **The Korean War: "The Forgotten War."** Hillside, NJ: Enslow, 1994. 128p. ISBN 0-89490-526-0. (American War). 6-9

Although 54,000 Americans died in the Korean War, fought from 1950 to 1953, many Americans at home lost interest because they did not understand the threat of Communist control spreading when the North Koreans invaded South Korea. This war did not have the media coverage common today, and no major event such as Pearl Harbor caused it to start. The text, with photographs, looks at the war and its effects on those who fought and on their families. Chronology, Further Reading, and Index.

1241. Stein, R. Conrad. **World War II in Europe: "America Goes to War."** Hillside, NJ: Enslow, 1994. 128p. $17.95. ISBN 0-89490-525-2. (American War). 6 up

Stein begins the text on World War II with the story of "Canned Goods." The Germans dressed convicts in Polish army uniforms, then killed them and announced that they were Polish invaders whom they had caught before they infiltrated Germany. Adolf Hitler used this farce to justify his invasion of Poland in 1939. Even though the German people were against war, Hitler declared it anyway. Many Germans were shocked that France and Great Britain supported Poland because they had refused to do anything when Hitler had previously broken the Treaty of Versailles. The other chapters follow the war across Europe. Chronology, Notes, Further Reading, and Index.

1242. Stein, Wendy. **Witches: Opposing Viewpoints**. San Diego, CA: Greenhaven, 1995. 112p. $19.95. ISBN 1-56510-240-1. (Great Mysteries—Opposing Viewpoints). 6-9

In an attempt to define "witch," the author asserts that witches either destroy or heal, depending upon intent. Some researchers trace the etymology of "witch" to *witan* (to know) in Old English, and others select *wiccian* (to cast a spell). The text presents a history of witches from the Western world, mentioning the Inquisition; a trial in Arras, France, from 1459 to 1460; witchcraft in England, especially Chelmsford in Essex; witch covens in sixteenth-century Scotland (1591); and the Salem witch hunt in the American colonies from 1620 to 1725. Some believe that misogyny (hatred of women) is a leading cause of witch hunts because more than 80 percent of the people persecuted as witches have been female. Contemporary witches worship a goddess that is said to have been worshipped more than 35,000 years ago. In history, the most overt worship of the goddess occurred in Greece from approximately 1500 B.C. to 900 B.C. with Diana, Selene, and Hecate. But sources also indicate other pockets of goddess worship. For Further Exploration, Additional Works Consulted, and Index.

1243. Steins, Richard. **The Allies Against the Axis: World War II (1940-1950)**. New York: Twenty-First Century Books, 1994. 64p. $15.95. ISBN 0-8050-2586-3. (First Person America). 5-8

America entered World War II after the Japanese bombed Pearl Harbor in 1941, thus ending its isolationist policy. Steins looks at the war on both oceans and notes such situations as the challenges of army segregation, the fear and paranoia of the county according to a nisei (second-generation Japanese American), the women working in factories, soldiers returning to peacetime, and the descent of the Iron Curtain. Photographs enhance the text. Timeline, For Further Reading, and Index.

1244. Sterckx, Pierre. **Brueghel: A Gift for Telling Stories**. John Goodman, translator; Claudine Roucha, illustrator. New York: Chelsea House, 1995. 56p. $14.95. ISBN 0-7910-2806-2. (Art for Children). 5-9

The text, complemented with beautiful reproductions, presents children visiting a Brussels art museum where they see Brueghel's paintings. As they examine the paintings, they discuss what they know of his life and how the pictures reveal the times in which he lived (1526-1569). He created fifty masterpieces while he was between the ages of thirty and forty. Index.

1245. Sterling, Shirley. **My Name Is Seepeetza**. Buffalo, NY: Douglas & McIntyre, Groundwood, 1997. 128p. $14.95. ISBN 0-88899-290-4. 5-8

Seepeetza, better known as Martha at the Indian residential school in British Columbia where she has to live, wets the bed and day dreams about her family ranch on the reservation before the government forced her to attend school. The nuns make her wear the wet bed sheet over her head, and the children taunt her for having green eyes and looking white. The journal format presents Seepeetza in the sixth grade during the 1950s feeling helpless, afraid, and homesick. The nuns, however, are not always bad, nor are Seepeetza's parents always perfect. *Sheila A. Egoff Children's Book Prize*.

1246. Stevens, Bryna. **Handel and the Famous Sword Swallower of Halle**. Ruth Tietjen, illustrator. New York: Philomel, 1990. Unpaged. $14.95. ISBN 0-399-21548-4. K-3

Handel (1685-1759) was allowed to take music lessons after Duke Johann Adolph I summoned his father, who hated music, to the castle; Handel's father was famous as a surgeon and healer of a sword swallower. At the castle, the duke heard Handel, then age eight, play, and he insisted that Handel be trained. The text looks at Handel's music in light of anecdotes such as this one.

1247. Stewart, Whitney. **Aung San Suu Kyi: Fearless Voice of Burma**. Minneapolis, MN: Lerner, 1997. 128p. $17.96. ISBN 0-8225-4931-X. (Newsmakers). 5 up

Aung San Suu Kyi is a quiet woman who became the leader of Burma's renewed struggle for democracy. In 1989, the government placed her under house arrest, and from her home she led Burma's National League for Democracy in victory at the polls; however, the military government refused to recognize the election. In 1992, she won the Nobel Prize for Peace, still under house arrest. Stewart interviewed her for this biography. Sources, Bibliography, and Index.

1248.   Stewart, Whitney. **The 14th Dalai Lama: Spiritual Leader of Tibet**. Minneapolis, MN: Lerner, 1996. 128p. $17.96. ISBN 0-8225-4926-3. (Newsmakers). 5 up

The fourteenth Dalai Lama, chosen as a small child to lead the people of Tibet, lived a life of isolation in the palace and then had to negotiate with the Chinese Communist leader, Mao, before Mao exiled him to India. While outside his country, he has promoted nonviolence and the importance of human rights, stances that won him a Nobel Prize for Peace in 1989. He remains a beloved and respected spiritual leader. Photographs, Bibliography, and Index.

1249.   Stewart, Whitney. **Sir Edmund Hillary: To Everest and Beyond**. Minneapolis, MN: Lerner, 1996. 128p. $17.96. ISBN 0-8225-4927-1. (Newsmakers). 5 up

In 1953, Sir Edmund Hillary (b. 1919), with Tenzing Norgay, became the first human to reach the summit of Mount Everest. Growing up in New Zealand, Hillary had learned that careful planning and preparation allow success. Later he led an expedition across Antarctica and another to the mouth of India's Ganges River, high in the Himalayan Mountains. Hillary has helped the Sherpas have better lives through improved schools and medical help. In more recent years, he has been working to keep an environmental balance in the Himalayas between their natural resources and the tourists who pay to climb them. Photographs, Bibliography, and Index.

1250.   Stolz, Mary. **Bartholomew Fair**. New York: Greenwillow, 1990. 152p. $12.95. ISBN 0-688-09522-4. 5-8

In 1597, six people wake up one August morning looking forward to the last day of the Bartholomew Fair. Elizabeth I, a student, a cloth merchant, an aristocrat, a maid, and an apprentice each face mortality in some way—either to think that they are just beginning to enjoy life or to muse that they have already experienced most of their life on earth. The day's events meet the expectations of some of the characters and deflate the hopes of others, but all help to recreate Elizabethan England.

1251.   Stolz, Mary. **Zekmet the Stone Carver: A Tale of Ancient Egypt**. Deborah Nourse Lattimore, illustrator. San Diego, CA: Harcourt Brace, 1988. 32p. $13.95. ISBN 0-15-299961-2. 2-4

Kafre, the Pharaoh, wants to have a monument that will last forever to complement his pyramid. He asks his vizier Ho-tep to think of the perfect shape. Ho-tep asks a stone carver, Zekmet; when Zekmet sees a lion in the moonlight, he realizes that the lion's body with the pharaoh's face will be the best. Though both the stone carver and the Pharaoh die before the monument can be completed, the stone carver's son finishes it.

1252.   Stolz, Mary Slattery. **Ivy Larkin**. 1986. New York: Yearling, 1989. 226p. $3.25pa. ISBN 0-440-40175-5pa. 5-7

Ivy, age fourteen, resents the feelings of inadequacy that the other students in her private school make her suffer as a scholarship student in the early 1930s during the Depression. She cannot understand why her mother demands that she continue going to school when extra expenses strain the family's resources, especially as her father does not have a job. Her close family and the changes that occur in her sister when she looks after a puppy help the year seem more positive as it passes.

1253.   **Stones and Bones: How Archaeologists Trace Human Origins**. Minneapolis, MN: Runestone Press, 1994. 64p. $11.95. ISBN 0-8225-3207-7. (Buried Worlds). 4-9

Archaeology as a science is only a century old. During that time, scientists have learned a lot about prehistoric humans and ancient civilizations. The text explains the methodology of archaeology and gives theories that have sprung from this research. Glossary and Index.

1254.   **The Story of Flight** New York: Scholastic, 1995. 45p. $19.95. ISBN 0-590-47643-2. (Voyages of Discovery). 4-6

The text discusses the dreams of flying that humans have had as it presents information on kites, gliders, balloons, and dirigibles. Discussions of modern flight include an introduction to the Wright brothers, the early flyers, flying aces, warplanes, and the functions of navigational systems. The text also contains a cross-section of an airship, a fold-out page showing the interior of the Wright brothers' workshop, and tracing-paper design sketches to place over the finished planes. Chronology and Index.

1255.   Strahinich, Helen. **The Holocaust: Understanding and Remembering**. Springfield, NJ: Enslow, 1996. 112p. $18.95. ISBN 0-89490-725-5. (Issues in Focus). 6 up

The text follows Hitler's rise to power, his annihilation of the Jews, and the aftermath of the Holocaust. It examines the difficult questions as to why so many Jews remained in Germany, why the Germans neglected to save the Jews, and where anti-Semitism arose. The text also looks at Jews in Italy and the Netherlands as well as other persecuted groups including Gypsies, homosexuals, and the Polish elite. Further Reading, Glossary, and Index.

1256. **Street Smart! Cities of the Ancient World**. Minneapolis, MN: Runestone Press, 1994. 80p. $22.95. ISBN 0-8225-3208-5. (Buried Worlds). 5-8

The text presents cities and their components. Archaeologists designate their finds as "cities" only when at least several thousand people lived there and had control of an area outside the walls where they could grow food. Cities developed for economic reasons, near military outposts for safety reasons, or for religious reasons. The world's first city was probably Uruk in southern Mesopotamia, around 4000 B.C. Other Middle Eastern cities are Babylon (after 2000 B.C.), Zimbabwe (1000 B.C.), and Tell al-Amarna (1400 B.C.). Ancient cities of Asia along rivers include Mohenjo-Daro and Harappa (2400-1650 B.C.), Zhengzhou and An-Yang (1600 B.C.-1400 B.C.), and Changan (207 B.C.). Ancient cities of the Mediterranean were Athens, Sparta, Knossos, Pompeii, and Rome. In the Americas, cities are still being discovered. The group that established the Olmec civilization's major city has not yet been identified. The Mayan Teotihuacán, destroyed in A.D. 750, was the first true urban center in the Americas. The largest Aztec city was Tenochtitlán, lasting from 1325 until approximately 1521. For the Incas, Cuzco was the great city, but thieves looted it in 1532. Pronunciation Guide, Glossary, and Index.

1257. Streissguth, Thomas. **France**. Minneapolis, MN: Carolrhoda, 1997. 48p. $14.95. ISBN 1-57505-128-1. (A Ticket To...). K-2

The geography of France along with its people, topography, cities, foods, schools, religions, and leisure activities appear in the text. Glossary, New Words to Say, Bibliography, and Index.

1258. Streissguth, Thomas. **France**. Minneapolis, MN: Carolrhoda, 1998. 48p. $14.95. ISBN 1-57505-103-6. (Globetrotters). 3-5

France's location on the western side of Europe makes it a place to cultivate grapes for wines and create hundreds of cheeses. The text looks at aspects of French life and history with additional facts included in boxed text. Glossary, Pronunciation Guide, Further Reading, and Index.

1259. Streissguth, Thomas. **Japan**. Minneapolis, MN: Carolrhoda, 1997. 48p. $14.95. ISBN 1-57505-127-3. (A Ticket To...). K-2

Japan's people, history, location, schools, sports, entertainment, and traditions appear in the text. Glossary, New Words to Say, Bibliography, and Index.

1260. Streissguth, Thomas. **Japan**. Minneapolis, MN: Carolrhoda, 1998. 48p. $14.95. ISBN 1-57505-102-8. (Globetrotters). 3-5

To reach Japan's 4,000 islands, one must travel by boat or plane, but many of its people live crowded in its cities. The text looks at the history, topography, cultures, homes, schools, foods, arts, and holidays. Glossary, Pronunciation Guide, Further Reading, and Index.

1261. Streissguth, Thomas. **Mexico**. Minneapolis, MN: Carolrhoda, 1997. 48p. $14.95. ISBN 1-57505-125-7. (A Ticket To...). K-2

Mexico has an even longer history than the United States, and the text looks briefly at it, customs, traditions, foods, cities, and people. Glossary, New Words to Say, Bibliography, and Index.

1262. Streissguth, Thomas. **Mexico**. Minneapolis, MN: Carolrhoda, 1998. 48p. $14.95. ISBN 1-57505-100-1. (Globetrotters). 3-5

A brief overview of Mexico's history precedes information about its people, location, values, neighborhoods, foods, markets, holidays, games, and music. Boxed text includes additional information. Glossary, Pronunciation Guide, Further Reading, and Index.

1263. Streissguth, Thomas. **Russia**. Minneapolis, MN: Carolrhoda, 1997. 48p. $14.95. ISBN 1-57505-126-5. (A Ticket To...). K-2

The topics covered include Russia's geography, people, homes, food, alphabet, school, sports, and history with color photographs. Glossary, New Words to Say, Bibliography, and Index.

1264. Streissguth, Thomas. **Russia**. Minneapolis, MN: Carolrhoda, 1998. 48p. $14.95. ISBN 1-57505-101-X. (Globetrotters). 3-5

Russia covers parts of both Europe and Asia, and its people follow traditions and customs of their continent, their culture, or their country. The text examines Russia's people, history, foods, leisure time, and the major changes in the past decade. Glossary, Pronunciation Guide, Further Reading, and Index.

1265. Strom, Yale. **Uncertain Roads: Searching for the Gypsies**. New York: Four Winds Press, 1993. 111p. $19.95. ISBN 0-02-788531-3. 5 up

Historical summaries, interviews, first-person narratives, and photographs describe the lives of the Rom (gypsy). Gypsies in both urban and rural areas of Sweden, Romania, Hungary, and the Ukraine tell about their experiences and their ways of life. A musical score appears at the end of each of the four chapters, with lyrics in both English and Romani. The Roms, as they prefer to be called, face continued prejudice in Europe with its new boundaries, as they try to escape attack and find housing. Bibliography.

1266. Sturgis, Alexander. **Introducing Rembrandt**. Boston: Little, Brown, 1994. 32p. $15.95. ISBN 0-316-82022-9. (Introducing the Artist). 3-5

Filled with reproductions, the text tells the story of Rembrandt (1606-1669) and places him in his world of seventeenth-century Holland where, by age seventeen, he had become the leading portrait painter in Amsterdam. His unique applications of light and dark (chiaroscuro) allowed his paintings to show emotion and expression. He painted the rich merchants of the country and then added Bible legends and history paintings to his repertoire. A short section discusses his style. Key Dates and Index.

1267. Sullivan, George. **Slave Ship: The Story of the Henrietta Marie**. New York: Cobblehill, Dutton, 1994. 80p. $15.99. ISBN 0-525-65174-8. 5-8

In 1972, divers found the remains of a sunken ship in the Gulf of Mexico. One of the first items found was a pair of shackles, which indicated that the ship had been a slave ship. On the ship's bell was engraved the name *Henrietta Marie* and the date 1699. Records show that the ship had unloaded its human cargo in Jamaica and had sunk in a storm while returning to London. Background information about slavers and photographs of the items discovered in the ship give an insight into what the people on board might have endured. This ship is the only slaver to have been scientifically studied. Bibliography and Index.

1268. Sumption, Christine, and Kathleen Thompson. **Carlos Finlay**. Les Didier, illustrator. Austin, TX: Raintree/Steck-Vaughn, 1991. 32p. $19.97. ISBN 0-8172-3378-4. (Hispanic Stories). 4-7

After Carlos Finlay (1833-1915) was born in Cuba, he studied abroad in France and Germany before he attended medical school in the United States. In Cuba, he began studying the disease yellow fever, which gave people fever, headaches, and backaches. After their skin became yellowish, they began to bleed inside, became unconscious, and often died. Finlay finally determined that mosquitoes transmitted the disease, but doctors would not believe him. When Walter Reed went to Cuba to study the disease, he did not believe Finlay either. But after nothing else showed promise, Reed went to Finlay and found that what he said was true. Reed, however, did not give Finlay credit in his paper, and not until the middle of the twentieth century did Finlay receive acclaim for his accomplishment. Glossary. English and Spanish text.

1269. **Sunk! Exploring Underwater Archaeology**. Minneapolis, MN: Runestone Press, 1994. 72p. $22.95. ISBN 0-8225-3205-0. (Buried Worlds). 5 up

Underwater excavation reveals amazing amounts of information about the past. Archaeologists searching underwater require special implements and diving equipment. Even though underwater, they must also make exact measurements and use careful retrieval methods for artifacts, as if they were on land. Their efforts have recovered cities and ships buried in the water. The text looks at the past hiding underneath the Mediterranean, the scientific value of shipwrecks, and harbors ruined by the rising sea. The first scientific excavation of a 3,000-year-old shipwreck, led by Peter Throckmorton and George Bass, occurred in the 1960s near Cape Gelidonya, off the coast of Turkey. Pronunciation Guide, Glossary, and Index.

1270. Sutcliff, Rosemary. **Flame-Colored Taffeta**. New York: Farrar, Straus & Giroux, 1986. 120p. $14; $4.95pa. ISBN 0-374-32344-5; 0-374-42341-5pa. 6-8

When Damaris is twelve and Peter is thirteen, in the mid-eighteenth century, they help a wounded man on the Sussex coast of England. Because smugglers fill the area, they suspect that he may be escaping from trouble, and they discover that he is an emissary for Bonnie Prince Charlie. The Wise Woman, a healer, hides and cares for him. Damaris admits that she wants to have a petticoat of flame-colored taffeta. Tom sends her one for her wedding four years after he escapes.

1271. Sutcliff, Rosemary. **The Shining Company**. New York: Farrar, Straus & Giroux, 1990. 304p. $14.95; $6.95pa. ISBN 0-374-36807-4; 0-374-46616-5pa. 6-10

Around A.D. 600, Prosper, age twelve, dreams of becoming Prince Gorthyn's shield bearer; two years later, near Edinburgh, he does. Gorthyn is one of King Mynyddog's 300 men training for battle. In the Saxon battle near York, only Prosper and one other survive. To escape their loneliness, they follow the source of a merchant's tales to Constantinople. *American Library Association Notable Books for Children*.

1272. Sutcliff, Rosemary. **Warrior Scarlet**. Charles Keeping, illustrator. 1958. New York: Random House, 1977. 240p. $6.95. ISBN 0-8098-3024-8. New York: Sunburst; Farrar, Straus & Giroux, 1995. 207p. $5.95pa. ISBN 0-374-48244-6pa. 5-9

In the Bronze Age, Drem looks forward to wearing the scarlet cloak that will identify him as a tribal warrior. But he must first kill a wolf. Because he has only one good arm, he fails in his attempt to kill the wolf, and he is cast out of the tribe. Later, he kills three wolves while trying to protect another outcast, and tribal leaders reconsider their law. They recognize that Drem has more than earned the right to wear a scarlet cloak. *International Board of Books for Young People* and *Carnegie Commendation*.

1273. Sutcliff, Rosemary. **The Witch's Brat**. Robert Micklewright, illustrator. New York: Henry Z. Walck, 1970. 143p. $7.95. ISBN 0-8098-3095-7. 5-9

Lovel is cast out from his village after being blamed for the death of a cow. He walks to the monastery, and the brothers take him in. He learns about herbs and healing and meets the king's jongleur, Rahere. Several years later, Rahere returns and asks Lovel to go to London with him to start a hospital. They begin building St. Bartholomew's, and Lovel's gifts help the wounded even before the hospital opens.

1274. Swinimer, Ciarunja Chesaina. **Pokot**. New York: Rosen, 1994. 64p. $15.95. ISBN 0-8239-1756-8. (Heritage Library of African Peoples). 5-8

Tracing their origin to the Nile River valley, the Pokots have been cattle herders or farmers throughout their history. They have lived in the Upper Rift Valley of western Kenya in thirty different clans, each identified by a totem animal. The text looks at politics and history, European contact and colonial rule, culture, daily life, and a view of the future, with enhancing photographs and reproductions. Glossary, Further Reading, and Index.

1275. Swisher, Clarice. **Pablo Picasso**. San Diego, CA: Lucent, 1995. 112p. $16.95. ISBN 1-56006-062-X. (The Importance of). 5 up

Pablo Picasso (1881-1973) lived through most of the twentieth century, during which he saw wars and changes in all the arts. The chapters look at his childhood and education from 1881 to 1898; his maturation as an artist from 1898 to 1905; his role in Cubism from 1905 to 1912; his influence on collages and ballet and his turning point from 1912 to 1922; the era of post-Cubism, covering 1922 to 1936; the Spanish civil war and *Guernica* during 1936 to 1945; his fame and wealth from 1945 to 1954; and his old age to 1973. It ends with a discussion of his influence on the art world. Notes, For Further Reading, Additional Works Consulted, and Index.

1276. Switzer, Ellen. **The Magic of Mozart: Mozart, *The Magic Flute,* and the Salzburg Marionettes**. Costas, photographs. New York: Atheneum, 1995. 90p. $19.95. ISBN 0-689-31851-0. 4-8

Beginning with the winter weather in Salzburg when Mozart (1756-1791) was born, Switzer surmises that the neighborhood women who attended the birth wore heavy gloves and much clothing, because the house had only one fireplace. She continues with a biography of Mozart ending with his writing of *The Magic Flute*. Photographs of marionettes performing the action complement the discussion of the story behind this opera. A third section tells about the Salzburg Marionette Theater and the types of puppets used through the years in its performances. Bibliography.

1277. Szablya, Helen M., and Peggy King Anderson. **The Fall of the Red Star. Sherman, CT: Boyds Mills Press, 1996. 166p. $15.95. ISBN 1-56397-419-3**. 5-8

Stephen, age fourteen, becomes a freedom fighter in Budapest, Hungary, during the revolution in 1956, after the Soviet Union tries to invade and occupy the country. Eight years before, the Communists had taken his father, but Stephen still hopes that his father is alive. Stephen fights in street battles, makes and throws Molotov cocktails, kills someone, and helps his sister deliver her baby. When the Communists win, he, his sister, and his mother flee, but their journey becomes especially perilous when they try to save other people in the swamp they are crossing by boat to the Austrian border.

T

1278. **Tajikistan**. Minneapolis, MN: Lerner, 1993. 56p. $19.95. ISBN 0-8225-2816-9. (Then and Now). 5-9

This country of west-central Asia borders on Afghanistan and China. The Tajik settled it in the tenth century, and the Mongols conquered it in the thirteenth century. The text covers Tajikistan's history, economics, geography, politics, and ethnography. Maps and photographs complement the text. Glossary and Index.

1279. Tames, Richard. **Anne Frank: 1929-1945**. New York: Franklin Watts, 1989. 32p. $18.50. ISBN 0-531-10763-9. (Lifetimes). 3-6

Anne Frank only lived to her teen years, but her diary made her famous throughout the world after her death in a concentration camp during World War II. This text, with photographs, tells how she and her family and the others with them lived in the cramped rooms where they hid before the Nazis found them. It also explains what a concentration camp was and gives some of the background of the Holocaust. Find Out More, Glossary, and Index.

1280. Tames, Richard. **Florence Nightingale: 1820-1910**. New York: Franklin Watts, 1989. 32p. $18.50. ISBN 0-531-10848-1. (Lifetimes). 3-6

Although Florence Nightingale (1820-1910) grew up in a wealthy household, she was dissatisfied with society life. She was more interested in reading and asked permission to study mathematics, but her parents refused. She then turned to the one thing she could do which they would condone: helping the sick. She became a nurse, and after she served the British soldiers in the Crimean War, she devoted her life to reforming the methods used to help the sick and injured. Find Out More, Important Dates, Glossary, and Index.

1281. Tames, Richard. **Marie Curie**. New York: Franklin Watts, 1989. 32p. $18.50. ISBN 0-531-10850-3. (Lifetimes). 3-6

Marie Curie (1867-1934) helped her family and then helped herself. Although she wanted to go to France to study in Paris, she worked so that her sister could go first. After she had enough money, Marie joined her sister. Curie had to learn French at the same time she was studying other subjects, and she still earned the top grades in her class. She met and married Pierre Curie. Together they made major discoveries about radium. Marie Curie won two Nobel Prizes, one in physics and one in chemistry, an amazing feat. She suffered throughout her life from radiation sickness, a disease that had no name during her lifetime but was caused by the materials with which she worked. Find Out More, Important Dates, Glossary, and Index.

1282. Tames, Richard. **Mother Teresa**. New York: Franklin Watts, 1989. 32p. $18.50. ISBN 0-531-10847-3. (Lifetimes). 3-6

Agnes Gonxha Bojaxhiu (1910-1997) was wealthy as a child until her father died suddenly when she was eight. He had always given people food and helped the old and the poor, practical activities that his little daughter had observed. Agnes followed his philosophy when she decided to become a nun and begin teaching poor children. She eventually founded the Missionary Sisters in Calcutta, a group that has spread around the world in an effort to help the underprivileged. Find Out More, Important Dates, Glossary, and Index.

1283. Tames, Richard. **Nelson Mandela**. New York: Franklin Watts, 1991. 32p. $18.50. ISBN 0-531-14124-1. (Lifetimes). 3-6

Nelson Mandela (b. 1918) was imprisoned for twenty-seven years for trying to help the South African blacks gain freedom through the African National Congress. He was a member of the royal family of his tribe, though this meant nothing to the South Afrikaaners. He was finally freed and then, after this book was published, became the president of South Africa. Photographs enhance the text. Bibliography, Glossary, and Index.

1284. Tanaka, Shelly. **I Was There: Discovering the Iceman**. New York: Hyperion, 1997. 48p. $16.95. ISBN 0-7868-0284-7. 3-6

Tanaka documents the discovery in the Italian Alps of a mummy more than 5,000 years old in 1991. She recreates the last days of the man using known facts about the time period and artifacts that were found with him. Photographs enhance the text. Chronology, Further Reading, and Glossary.

1285. Tanaka, Shelley, and Hugh Brewster, eds. **Anastasia's Album**. New York: Hyperion, 1996. 64p. $17.95. ISBN 0-7868-0292-8. 6 up

Using quotes from letters and diaries of family members and close friends, the text tells the story of Anastasia, the youngest Romanov daughter who died during the Russian Revolution by firing squad. The photographs of family and palaces recreates the time in which she lived. Glossary.

1286. Taylor, Theodore. **The Cay**. 1969. New York: Doubleday, 1989. 138p. $15.95. ISBN 0-385-07906-0. New York: Flare, 1995. 138p. $4.50pa. ISBN 0-380-01003-8pa. 6-9

In 1942, Phillip, eleven, sails with his mother from Curaçao to Norfolk after German submarines begin torpedoing ships in the harbor. After Germans sink their ship, an old Black man, Timothy, saves Phillip and a cat. On the raft, Phillip finds that he is blind from a head injury sustained during the ship's explosion. On the island where they wash up, Timothy teaches Phillip how to be independent in spite of his disability so that Phillip can survive if Timothy dies. *Jane Addams Book Award*.

1287. Temple, Frances. **The Beduins' Gazelle**. New York: Jackson, Orchard, 1996. 160p. $15.95. ISBN 0-531-09519-3. 6-9

Halima and Atiyah, betrothed since birth, look forward to a desert wedding in the Middle East in 1302. Uncle Saladeen, however, decides that Atiyah should study the Koran in Fez. Then Halima and her camel become separated from their tribal caravan during a sandstorm as they migrate toward water. An enemy sheikh sees her and decides that she will become one of his wives. In this book, the same Etienne presented in *The Ramsay Scallop* meets Atiyah at the university in Fez and helps him rescue Halima from the greedy sheikh.

1288. Thomas, Dawn C. **Kai: A Mission for Her Village**. Vanessa Holley, illustrator. New York: Simon & Schuster, 1996. 72p. $13; $5.99pa. ISBN 0-689-81140-3; 0-689-80986-7pa. (Girlhood Journeys). 2-6

Kai lives in a Yoruba village during 1440. Famine threatens, and the king chooses Kai and her sister to go north to seek help from other Yoruba tribe members. They must walk through the forest and across the savanna on their journey. Their experience in the land now known as Nigeria teaches them about themselves.

1289. Thomas, Paul. **The Central Asian States**. Brookfield, CT: Millbrook Press, 1992. 32p. $15.90. ISBN 1-56294-307-3. (Former Soviet States). 4-7

On the southern border of Kazakhstan lie the central Asian states of Uzbekistan, Kyrgyzstan, Tajikistan, and Turkmenistan. The text discusses the cultural background, politics, economics, and history of these former Soviet republics. Uzbekistan, with its cities of Bukhara and Samarqand, borders Afghanistan on the south. Turkmenistan, the most western of the states, borders Afghanistan and the Caspian Sea. Tajikistan has both Afghanistan and Pakistan on its southern border, while Kyrgyzstan lies next to China. Glossary and Index.

1290. Thompson, Alexa. **Nova Scotia**. Minneapolis, MN: Lerner, 1995. 76p. $14.21. ISBN 0-8225-2759-6. 3-6

Although not technically a history book, over half the text reveals the history of this Canadian province. Charts, maps, photographs, and prints illustrate the individuality of this area, whose first inhabitants were the Paleo-Indians around 11,000 years ago. Among the famous Nova Scotians briefly described are Samuel Cunard (1797-1865) and Thomas Haliburton (1796-1865). Fast Facts, Glossary, Pronunciation Guide, and Index.

1291. Thompson, Kathleen. **Pedro Menéndez de Avilés**. Charles Shaw, illustrator. Austin, TX: Raintree/Steck-Vaughn, 1991. 32p. $19.97. ISBN 0-8172-3383-0. (Hispanic Stories). 4-7

Pedro Menéndez de Avilés (1519-1574), born in Spain, became a sailor who loved his job. He decided that he would drive the French out of the Spanish colony of Florida, first discovered by Ponce de Léon. In 1565, he entered Florida and forcibly removed the settled French. Glossary. English and Spanish text.

1292. Thompson, Kathleen. **Sor Juana Inés de la Cruz**. Rick Karpinski, illustrator. Austin, TX: Raintree/Steck-Vaughn, 1993. 32p. $19.97. ISBN 0-8172-3377-6. (Hispanic Stories). 4-7

Born near the volcano Popocatépetl in about 1648, Inés de la Cruz was probably the greatest poet born in Mexico. She taught herself by studying wherever she could find books, but she could not marry because, as an orphan, she had no dowry. Someone paid for her to enter the convent, and she went there with her books. She entertained the greatest thinkers and scientists of the times. Throughout her life she wrote poetry in various languages, but the archbishop hated women, especially intelligent ones, and he finally found a way to trick her into not being allowed to write any more. Glossary. English and Spanish text.

1293. Thomson, Ruth. **Aztecs: Facts—Things to Make—Activities**. New York: Franklin Watts, 1993. 32p. $11.90. ISBN 0-531-14245-0. (Craft Topics). 4-6

The text and illustrations give facts about the social, religious, and political aspects of the Aztec civilization in thirteen two-page spreads. Projects with directions for making items directly related to the Aztecs, from simple to difficult, give further insight. Glossary and Index.

1294. Time-Life. **What Life Was Like on the Banks of the Nile: Egypt 3050-30 B.C.** Alexandria, VA: Time-Life, 1996. 192p. $19.95. ISBN 0-8094-9378-0. 6 up

Using primary documents from the lives of Egyptian citizens, the text recreates their times. A farmer who wrote to his family while away on administrative duties shows some of the domestic problems. The thoughts and concerns of pharaohs, warriors, and commoners also appear as well as the roles of women. This insight into Egyptian times is unusual because of the human emotions that so clearly speak through the text. Photographs, Reproductions, Bibliography, Glossary, and Index.

1295.   Tolan, Mary, and Pam Brown. **Florence Nightingale: The Founder of Modern Nursing**. Milwaukee, WI: Gareth Stevens, 1991. 68p. $16.95. ISBN 0-8368-0456-2. (People Who Made a Difference). 3-6

The daughter of a wealthy British family, Florence Nightingale (b. 1820) believed that God would tell her what to do with her life. In 1844, she decided not to marry but to work in a hospital. Her parents refused because of the low status of hospitals, and Florence soon had a nervous breakdown. She discovered a place in Kaiserswerth, Germany, where she could train to be a nurse, and she finally went, accompanied by her sister and mother who used the trip as a pretense for going on vacation. Sixteen years later, Florence reorganized and ran a hospital in London so that it functioned efficiently. In 1854, people begged her to take her knowledge to the Crimean war front in Turkey. She remained for two years, organizing the military's poor and inefficient medical service. Afterwards, she reorganized the military's peacetime facilities, though military physicians resented her intrusion and her success. Her tireless work eventually exhausted her, but she kept trying to help others. Not until her father and then her mother died, when Florence was sixty, was she able to make her own decisions and help others receive the best medical care possible. To Find Out More, List of New Words, Important Dates, and Index.

1296.   Toll, Nelly S. **Behind the Secret Window: A Memoir of a Hidden Childhood During World War II**. New York: Dial, 1993. 176p. $17. ISBN 0-8037-1362-2. 6 up

The Nazis began to occupy the town where Nelly Toll lived in 1941. When she was eight years old, in 1943, Nelly Toll and her mother went into hiding in a Gentile family's Lwów, Poland, home. She kept a journal and made vividly colored paintings to forget her world. Her art and the captions she gave the pictures give a sense of the experience. Other members of the family did not return, but Nelly and her mother survived this difficult time. Color plates of the drawings give insight to the times.

1297.   Trease, Geoffrey. **A Flight of Angels**. Minneapolis, MN: Lerner, 1989. 117p. $9.95. ISBN 0-8225-0731-5. 4-7

Sheila and her friends decide to search the underground caves in their city of Nottingham when they have to do a local history project for school. When a development planned for the area threatens to close the wine shop over the caves, the children have to work fast. What they discover reveals life in their town during 1550. In the caves they find alabaster statues of great artistic value, which had been hidden for over 400 years. They are also able to save jobs as a result of their investigation.

1298.   Treece, Henry. **Men of the Hills**. Christine Price, illustrator. New York: S. G. Phillips, 1958. 182p. $22.95. ISBN 0-87599-115-7. 6-9

Over 4,000 years ago in prehistoric England, Lalo, son of the chief of the Men of the Hills, has to kill a wolf to become a man. On the same day, the nomadic conquerors arrive, and he also has to kill humans. Although the nomads kill his father and others, Lalo escapes. He has to learn to live on his own, so he befriends Cradoc, the boy who would one day be the chief of the wild nomads. Because they are only interested in survival, they realize that helping each other is the best way.

1299.   Treece, Henry. **The Road to Miklagard**. Christine Price, illustrator. New York: S. G. Phillips, 1957. 254p. $22.95. ISBN 0-87599-118-1. 6-10

Harald, the Viking hero of *Viking's Dawn*, wants more excitement, so he joins Prince Arkil of Denmark, and they sail to Ireland to take the treasure guarded by the giant Grummoch. They enslave the giant in A.D. 785, but Turkish slavers capture them and sell them to Abu Mazur of Spain. Arkil dies, but Harald rescues Abu Mazur from a traitorous gardener, and Abu Mazur asks Harald to take his daughter to Miklagard (Istanbul). In Miklagard, Marriba and Irene, Constantine's mother, disagree, and Harald sends Marriba back to Spain while he and Grummoch return home.

1300.   Treseder, Terry Walton. **Hear O Israel: A Story of the Warsaw Ghetto**. Lloyd Bloom, illustrator. New York: Atheneum, 1990. 41p. $13.95. ISBN 0-689-31456-6. 6 up

The Gestapo transports Isaac, his older brother, and his father to the Treblinka death camp from the Warsaw ghetto after Isaac's mother, other brothers, and sister have died of typhus. Even as Isaac, who is only twelve years old, and his father walk toward the gas chamber, Isaac keeps his faith.

1301.   Triggs, Tony D. **Viking Warriors**. John James, illustrator. New York: Bookwright Press, Franklin Watts, 1991. 24p. $10.40. ISBN 0-531-18356-4. (Beginning History). 2-4

Photographs and illustrations highlight the information presented in two-page topic spreads. The text looks at Viking weapons, forts, religious beliefs, and settlements during the tenth and eleventh centuries. Glossary and Index.

1302. **Turkmenistan**. Minneapolis, MN: Lerner, 1993. 56p. $19.95. ISBN 0-8225-2813-4. (Then and Now). 5-9

As part of the Persian Empire on the border of Afghanistan, Turkmenistan was ruled by such powers as Genghis Khan and Timur. The text covers the history, economics, geography, politics, and ethnography of this recently freed country. Maps and photographs complement the text. Glossary and Index.

1303. Turnbull, Ann. **No Friend of Mine**. Cambridge, MA: Candlewick Press, 1995. 127p. $15.95. ISBN 1-56402-565-9. 3-6

Lennie Dyer, age eleven and brother of Mary Dyer from *Speedwell*, has to face the class bully every day in his coal-mining hometown of Culverton, England, prior to World War II. His father has black dust on his lungs, and Lennie has to work to help the family. After he becomes friends with Ralph, the son of the mine owner, Ralph's family accuses him of stealing from their house, and Ralph's fear of his own father keeps him from defending his friend. Lennie's innocence and his disgust at Ralph's behavior keep Lennie from responding to Ralph's apology and renewed pleas for friendship.

1304. Turnbull, Ann. **Room for a Stranger**. Bergenfield, NJ: Candlewick Press, 1996. 112p. $15.99. ISBN 1-56402-868-2. 5-7

Doreen Dyer, age twelve, after appearances in *Speedwell* and *No Friend of Mine*, is unhappy with an evacuee who comes to live with the family. Rhoda can do everything better than Doreen and she is also attractive. After an official invites Rhoda to perform in a town concert, Doreen can no longer contain her jealousy. She expresses her antagonism, and Rhoda runs away to the mines, where a cave-in injures her. When Doreen meets Rhoda's actress mother, she realizes that Rhoda's life has not been as happy as she has advertised.

1305. Turnbull, Ann. **Speedwell**. Cambridge, MA: Candlewick Press, 1992. 119p. $14.95. ISBN 1-56402-112-2. 5-9

In 1930, Mary's father is away from their English home, looking for work, and Mary's mother has no patience with her dreaming. Mary, however, thinks that the only way she can achieve something is to train the homing pigeon Speedwell. She continues to train that pigeon and the others during her father's absence. When he returns, they are ready for him.

1306. Turner, Ann. **Time of the Bison**. Beth Peck, illustrator. New York: Macmillan, 1987. 54p. $12.95. ISBN 0-02-789300-6. 3-5

Scar Boy, eleven, wants an adult name, but he has done nothing to earn one. He loves to draw, paint, and sculpt figures, although his tribe forbids such activity because they think the figures contain power over which they have no control. After Scar Boy makes a mud horse, his father takes him to a clan gathering, where he meets a painter who shows him drawings inside of caves. The artist promises to teach Scar Boy enough so that he can earn the name of "Animal Shaper."

1307. Turner, Bonnie. **The Haunted Igloo**. Boston: Houghton Mifflin, 1991. 152p. $13.95. ISBN 0-395-57037-7. 4-7

In the early 1930s, Jean-Paul, age ten, has difficulty adjusting to his new life in the Canadian Northwest Territories where his father, a geologist, searches for radium in pitchblende. He fears that the Inuit boys may tease him about his limp. The boys enclose him in an igloo as an initiation, but after he raises a runt into a good sled dog and helps deliver his mother's baby, after getting aid from one of the boys' mothers, he earns their respect.

1308. Turner, Robyn Montana. **Frida Kahlo**. Boston: Little, Brown, 1993. 32p. $16.95. ISBN 0-316-85651-8. (Portraits of Women Artists for Children). 3-6

Frida Kahlo (1907-1954) said, "The only thing I know is that I paint because I need to, and I paint always whatever passes through my head, without any other consideration." During her lifetime in Mexico, she had only two solo art shows. Today her paintings hang in museums and galleries around the world, and Mexico considers her one of its greatest artists. She suffered during her life both physically, after being hit by a bus, and mentally, during her tempestuous marriage to Diego Rivera, another major Mexican artist.

1309. Turner, Robyn Montana. **Rosa Bonheur**. Boston: Little, Brown, 1991. 32p. $16.95. ISBN 0-316-85648-7. (Portraits of Women Artists for Children). 3-6

Rosa Bonheur (1822-1899) lived in France during a time when women were not allowed to attend the best art schools, because they were not permitted to look at nude models. After her mother died, Rosa caused enough trouble in schools that her father permitted her to stay with him in his artist's studio. There she began her training as an artist. She went to the Louvre to copy the old masters and learn new techniques. As she continued her work, she began to prefer painting horses, dogs, cows and bulls, wild beasts, deer, landscapes with animals, and studies of Native Americans, whom she sketched when she studied them close up during the Buffalo Bill show's stay outside Paris for seven months. Queen Victoria requested that one of Bonheur's paintings of horses be shown in England.

1310. Turvey, Peter. **Inventions: Inventors and Ingenious Ideas**. New York: Franklin Watts, 1992. 48p. $13.95. ISBN 0-531-14308-2. (Timelines). 5-8

The text and illustrations combine to give the history of inventions, from the making of fire to the space stations of the future. Included are inventors and ingenious ideas during the classical period of the Greeks and Romans, the Middle Ages, the Renaissance, and the present. Chronology, Glossary, and Index.

1311. Twist, Clint. **Charles Darwin: On the Trail of Evolution**. Austin, TX: Raintree/Steck-Vaughn, 1994. 46p. $15.96. ISBN 0-8114-7255-8. (Beyond the Horizons). 5-8

Charles Darwin (1809-1882) gained fame for the publication of *The Origin of Species* in 1859. The text looks at the historical background of his times; the means of transportation that were available to him, such as the HMS *Beagle* on which he sailed for five years observing the natural world; his theory of evolution that he developed from what he saw; the effect of his theory of evolution and what happened after that theory shocked the world. Photographs highlight the text. Glossary, Further Reading and Index.

1312. Twist, Clint. **Christopher Columbus**. Austin, TX: Raintree/Steck-Vaughn, 1994. 46p. $15.96. ISBN 0-8114-7253-1. (Beyond the Horizons). 5-8

The text presents the historical background of Columbus's voyage in 1492 by describing the times in which he lived, including the Renaissance, the Reformation, and the Inquisition. It presents the modes of transportation available, his voyages, the discoveries he made, the Native Americans who lived in the New World, and what happened as a result of his trips. Photographs, paintings, drawings, and maps augment the text. Glossary, Further Reading, and Index.

1313. Twist, Clint. **Gagarin and Armstrong: The First Steps in Space**. Austin, TX: Raintree/Steck-Vaughn, 1995. 46p. $15.96. ISBN 0-8114-3978-X. (Beyond the Horizons). 5-8

Two men were part of two different races in space. In 1961, the Russian Yuri Gagarin became the first person to travel through space. In 1969, Neil Armstrong became the first person to step on the surface of the moon. The text gives historical background, the technology of transportation, the two actual journeys, the discoveries and achievements of the expeditions, information on space and the lunar environment, and information on what happened as a result of the expeditions. Photographs, paintings, drawings, and maps augment the text. Glossary, Further Reading, and Index.

1314. Twist, Clint. **James Cook: Across the Pacific to Australia**. Austin, TX: Raintree/Steck-Vaughn, 1995. 46p. $15.96. ISBN 0-8114-3975-5. (Beyond the Horizons). 5-8

James Cook (1728-1799) sailed as far north and as far south as ships could go in his time. He tried to find the Southern continent, but explorers did not find Antarctica until 100 years later. His voyages were for scientific exploration, not for political conquest. He always recognized the local powers of the places he visited, but irritated the Hawaiians so badly that they killed him. Along with historical background, transportation available, and the technology of the time, the text discusses native peoples of the Pacific, such as the Maoris, Kooris, Melanesians, and Easter Islanders. Also included is what happened as a result of Cook's explorations. Photographs, paintings, drawings, and maps augment the text. Glossary, Further Reading, and Index.

1315. Twist, Clint. **Stanley and Livingstone: Expeditions Through Africa**. Austin, TX: Raintree/Steck-Vaughn, 1995. 46p. $15.96. ISBN 0-8114-3976-3. (Beyond the Horizons). 5-8

Henry Stanley (1841-1904) and David Livingstone (1813-1873) both explored in Africa. Livingstone went to Africa as a medical missionary, but disliked being a doctor. He loved travel, and went as many miles as he could. He wanted to get rid of the slavers and establish a trade center near the middle of the continent, but the slavers were too ruthless for him to succeed. He met Stanley, a newspaperman, and they visited for several months. Stanley's trips to Africa were motivated by self-improvement. He had little regard for the men who helped him carve out the Congo for the Belgian ruler. The text discusses the historical background, the transportation methods and equipment, the people of Africa, and what happened as a result of these explorations. Photographs, paintings, drawings, and maps augment the text. Glossary, Further Reading, and Index.

U

1316. **Ukraine**. Minneapolis, MN: Lerner, 1993. 56p. $19.95. ISBN 0-8225-2808-8. (Then and Now). 5-9

This area of the former Soviet Union has known human inhabitants at least since 6000 B.C. As a major trade crossroads, it has been a spot that other countries have tried to control for centuries. In the late sixteenth century, a Cossack state formed in it. These and other concerns appear in the text as it discusses the history, economics, geography, politics, and ethnography of the area. Maps and photographs complement the text. Glossary and Index.

1317. Ullstein, Susan, and Charlotte Gray. **Mother Teresa: Servant to the World's Suffering People**. Milwaukee, WI: Gareth Stevens, 1990. 68p. $16.95. ISBN 0-8368-0393-0. (People Who Made a Difference). 3-6

Agnes Gonxha Bojaxhiu (1910-1997) grew up in Skopje, Albania, and decided when she was eighteen that she wanted to be a nun. She went to India and chose the name "Teresa." In Calcutta, she taught for twenty years before she decided that she wanted to help the poor. She believed that "being unwanted is the worst disease any man or woman can have," and throughout her life she has tried to help those whom others have discarded. Her Missionary Sisters of Charity have spread around the world, and she earned the Nobel Peace Prize in 1979. Map of World Sites, Organizations, Books, List of New Words, Important Dates, and Index.

1318. **Uzbekistan**. Minneapolis, MN: Lerner, 1993. 56p. $19.95. ISBN 0-8225-2812-6. (Then and Now). 5-9

A country of west-central Asia, Uzbekistan was settled in ancient times, before Alexander the Great, Genghis Khan, and Tamerlane, in turn, conquered it. The Uzbek peoples finally overran it in the early sixteenth century. Russia conquered the area in the nineteenth century. The text covers this history as well as economics, geography, politics, and ethnography. Maps and photographs complement the text. Glossary and Index.

V

1319.   Vá, Leong, author/illustrator. **A Letter to the King**. James Anderson, translator. New York: Harper-Collins, 1991. 32p. $14.95. ISBN 0-06-020079-0. K-3

Because her father has been unjustly imprisoned, little Ti Ying brings a letter to the king. No one, not even a boy, has had the nerve to act as she does. She goes to the Forbidden City, around the first century, and offers to take her father's place so that he can continue saving his patients in their village near the Great Wall. The king likes her bravery and decides to free her father instead.

1320.   Van der Linde, Laurel. **The White Stallions: The Story of the Dancing Horses of Lipizza**. New York: New Discovery, 1994. 72p. $14.95. ISBN 0-02-759055-0. (Timestop). 5-9

In 1580, Archduke Charles II started a horse farm in the town of Lipizza near the Adriatic Sea. His horses, carefully trained and known as the Lipizzaners, were used by the Hapsburgs and trained at the Spanish Riding School, the court stables. They have been threatened with extinction several times—during the time of Napoleon as he advanced on Austria, during World War I when they became the property of the Italian government, and in World War II when Hitler's Nazis almost destroyed them. The text tells their story and discusses the dancelike movements of dressage. Glossary and Index.

1321.   Van Steenwyk, Elizabeth. **The California Gold Rush: West with the Forty-Niners**. New York: Franklin Watts, 1991. 63p. $19.90. ISBN 0-531-20032-9. (First Books). 5-7

The California Gold Rush around 1846-1850 was an important event in the nineteenth century. It changed more people's lives than any other episode except the Civil War. It opened new routes of transportation and changed the face of California and the West. These topics and the lives of the miners before, during, and after the event appear in the text, which is enhanced with photographs and reproductions. Glossary, Further Reading, and Index.

1322.   Vander Els, Betty. **The Bomber's Moon**. New York: Farrar, Straus & Giroux, 1985. 168p. $14. ISBN 0-374-30864-0. 5-7

In 1942, Ruth and her brother separate from their missionary parents, leaving them in China. They go first to another part of the country but then continue to India, where they have to read letters filled with censored text and try to figure out what their parents are telling them. After many problems and four years, they reunite in Shanghai, but the children have changed during this crucial period of their lives.

1323.   Vander Els, Betty. **Leaving Point**. New York: Farrar, Straus & Giroux, 1987. 212p. $15. ISBN 0-374-34376-4. 5-7

In the sequel to *The Bomber's Moon*, Ruth is fourteen and living in Kwangchen, China, with her parents. A new Communist regime under Mao Tze-Tung has taken control of the government, and its soldiers are mistreating foreign families. While they wait in 1950 for permission to leave the country, Ruth becomes friends with a Chinese girl. Their relationship threatens the safety of the Chinese girl's family, but Ruth's departure reduces the chance of retaliation for fraternizing with a foreigner.

1324.   Várdy, Steven Béla. **Attila**. New York: Chelsea House, 1991. 112p. $18.95. ISBN 1-55546-803-9. (World Leaders Past and Present). 5 up

Attila (d. 453) led the Huns out of the eastern steppes to conquer Romans, barbarians, and anyone else in their path. Questions remain about Attila's character as to whether he was bloodthirsty or the one to bring a new feudal order to a decaying Europe. Some also see him as the grandfather of the Hungarian people. The text, with photographs and reproductions, looks at the career and legacy of this man. Further Reading, Chronology, and Index.

1325.   Venezia, Mike, author/illustrator. **Botticelli**. Chicago: Childrens Press, 1991. 32p. $5.95pa. ISBN 0-516-42291-Xpa. (Getting to Know the World's Great Artists). K-3

Sandro Botticelli (1444?-1510) was an important Italian painter during the Renaissance. His *Birth of Venus* is one of the paintings showing his love of mythological subjects. Illustrations enhance the text.

1326.   Venezia, Mike, author/illustrator. **Da Vinci**. Chicago: Childrens Press, 1989. 32p. $5.95pa. ISBN 0-516-42275-8pa. (Getting to Know the World's Great Artists). K-3

Leonardo da Vinci (1452-1519) was one of the greatest artists in history. His *Mona Lisa* and *The Last Supper* are two of his few paintings. He was also greatly interested in why things happen, and he filled his notebooks with investigative drawings. Illustrations highlight the text.

1327. Venezia, Mike, author/illustrator. **Diego Rivera**. Chicago: Childrens Press, 1993. 32p. $5.95pa. ISBN 0-516-42299-5pa. (Getting to Know the World's Great Artists). K-3

Diego Rivera (1886-1957), a Mexican painter, wanted his art to be accessible to all the people. He began to paint murals of everyday life in Mexico on walls outside for everyone to enjoy. Illustrations highlight the text.

1328. Venezia, Mike, author/illustrator. **Francisco Goya**. Chicago: Childrens Press, 1993. 32p. $5.95pa. ISBN 0-516-42292-8pa. (Getting to Know the World's Great Artists). K-3

Francisco Goya (1746-1828), a Spanish artist, was known for his work showing the political and social influences of his time. Illustrations enhance the text.

1329. Venezia, Mike, author/illustrator. **Henri Toulouse-Lautrec**. Chicago: Childrens Press, 1995. 32p. $5.95pa. ISBN 0-516-42283-9pa. (Getting to Know the World's Great Artists). K-3

Henri Toulouse-Lautrec (1864-1901) was a French painter known for the scenes he painted of Parisian theaters and dance halls in the late nineteenth century. His growth was stunted because of a childhood accident, but his paintings do not reflect his personal life. Illustrations supplement the text.

1330. Venezia, Mike, author/illustrator. **Ludwig van Beethoven**. Chicago: Childrens Press, 1995. 32p. $19.50. ISBN 0-516-44541-3. (Getting to Know the World's Great Artists). 3-4

Ludwig van Beethoven (1770-1827) is recognized today as one of the greatest composers who ever lived, and he was deaf in his later years. He had a somewhat tumultuous life, and Venezia illustrates it with facts and humorous cartoons.

1331. Venezia, Mike, author/illustrator. **Michelangelo**. Chicago: Childrens Press, 1991. 32p. $5.95pa. ISBN 0-516-42293-6pa. (Getting to Know the World's Great Artists). K-3

Michelangelo Buonarroti (1475-1564) was one of the world's greatest artists. He is known for painting the Sistine Chapel murals in Rome's Vatican and his sculptures such as *David,* now located in Florence, Italy. Illustrations highlight the text.

1332. Venezia, Mike, author/illustrator. **Monet**. Chicago: Childrens Press, 1989. 32p. $5.95pa. ISBN 0-516-02276-8. (Getting to Know the World's Great Artists). K-3

Claude Monet (1840-1926) especially liked the way colors reflect in water and the way water makes the clouds and sky look. These preferences he put into his work, and he even set up a studio in a boat so that he could sail on a river and stop and paint wherever he pleased. The text tells his story with reproductions of his work in the Impressionist style that he helped to create.

1333. Venezia, Mike, author/illustrator. **Pieter Bruegel**. Chicago: Childrens Press, 1992. 32p. $5.95pa. ISBN 0-516-42279-0pa. (Getting to Know the World's Great Artists). K-3

Pieter Bruegel (c. 1525-1569) was a Flemish painter known for his scenes of everyday life. The text describes the times and shows illustrations of his art.

1334. Venezia, Mike, author/illustrator. **Peter Tchaikovsky**. Chicago: Childrens Press, 1994. 32p. $18.60. ISBN 0-516-04537-7. (Getting to Know the World's Greatest Composers). K-4

Peter Tchaikovsky (1840-1893) was a great Russian composer who lived in St. Petersburg just as Russians were beginning to want to listen to Russian music. Cartoons complement and comment about the text on alternate pages. The author mentions Tchaikovsky's patron and notes that he was unhappy much of the time because he never found someone with whom he could fall in love. (The text does not mention Tchaikovsky's sexual preference.) Because Tchaikovsky wrote *The Nutcracker*, he is a composer of whom many children may have heard. More advanced listeners may also have heard the *1812 Overture*.

1335. Venezia, Mike, author/illustrator. **Picasso**. Chicago: Childrens Press, 1988. 32p. $5.95pa. ISBN 0-516-42271-5pa. (Getting to Know the World's Great Artists). K-3

Pablo Picasso (1881-1973), a renowned twentieth-century artist, created a new art style called Cubism. He evolved from it into other styles and periods in his art. His *Guernica* shows his response to the horrors of the Spanish Civil War in 1937, and his other periods also sometimes reflect his emotions. Illustrations enhance the text.

1336. Venezia, Mike, author/illustrator. **Pierre Auguste Renoir**. Chicago: Childrens Press, 1996. 32p. $19.50; $5.95pa. ISBN 0-516-02225-3; 0-516-20068-2pa. (Getting to Know the World's Great Artists). K-4

Pierre Auguste Renoir (1841-1919), a renowned Impressionist artist, was an important painter of people during the latter half of the nineteenth century, although he sometimes chose to paint landscapes or work on still lifes. His paintings such as *Luncheon at the Boating Party* and *Au Moulin de la Galette* show his style. Illustrations enhance the text.

1337. Venezia, Mike, author/illustrator. **Rembrandt**. Chicago: Childrens Press, 1988. 32p. $5.95pa. ISBN 0-516-42272-3pa. (Getting to Know the World's Great Artists). K-3

Considered one of the greatest painters of all times, Rembrandt Harmenszoon van Rijn, (1606-1669) lived in Holland. His paintings, often dark because brightly colored paints cost a lot of money, have their own brilliance. *The Night Watch*, a huge painting with faces of many people Rembrandt knew, is perhaps his most famous. Illustrations enhance the text.

1338. Venezia, Mike, author/illustrator. **Salvador Dali**. Chicago: Childrens Press, 1993. 32p. $5.95pa. ISBN 0-516-42296-0pa. (Getting to Know the World's Great Artists). K-3

Salvador Dali (1904-1989) was a Spanish surrealist painter who combined unexpected objects or figures in his paintings. His flamboyant personality is well documented. Illustrations augment the text.

1339. Venezia, Mike, author/illustrator. **Vincent van Gogh**. Chicago: Childrens Press, 1988. 29p. $5.95pa. ISBN 0-516-02274-Xpa. (Getting to Know the World's Great Artists). K-3

Using a combination of cartoons and reproductions, the text gives an overview of the life of Vincent van Gogh (1853-1890). Although van Gogh lived a rather unhappy life, Venezia gives a positive view of what he accomplished by using the bright colors that van Gogh adapted from Japanese painting. A good mix of humor, information, and reproductions of van Gogh's paintings makes this a good introduction to his life and work.

1340. Venezia, Mike, author/illustrator. **Wolfgang Amadeus Mozart**. Chicago: Childrens Press, 1995. 32p. $19.50. ISBN 0-516-44541-3. (Getting to Know the World's Great Artists). 3-4

Wolfgang Amadeus Mozart (1756-1791) learned to play the violin when he was four, and when he was six, he wrote his first concerto. The text introduces Mozart and his career as a child managed by his father. Illustrations enhance the text.

1341. Ventura, Piero, author/illustrator. **Clothing**. Boston: Houghton Mifflin, 1993. 64p. $16.95. ISBN 0-395-66791-7. 4-8

The text, with illustrations, gives a history of clothing. The periods and topics covered are prehistory, Egypt, the Ancient East, tanning leather, Crete, Greek styles, Rome, classical society, Byzantium, the barbarians, from sheep to cloth, pyramidal societies, late Middle Ages, thirteenth and fourteenth centuries, merchants and tailors in the 1400s, end of the Middle Ages, society in the 1500s, sixteenth century, the early 1600s, the style of the Sun King, the early 1700s and getting dressed in the noble ranks, the French revolution, the early 1800s, nineteenth-century society, a tailor's shop in the early 1900s, and the mid-twentieth century. Glossary.

1342. Ventura, Piero, author/illustrator. **Darwin: Nature Reinterpreted**. Boston: Houghton Mifflin, 1995. 76p. $16.95. ISBN 0-395-70738-2. 5-6

Charles Darwin's theory of evolution, published in his book *The Origin of Species* in 1859, changed some of the ways in which humans viewed nature. Ventura looks at some of these changes in double-page topic spreads that include Linneas, Humboldt, Darwin's theory and his *Beagle* voyage, the Brazilian rain forest, mass extinctions, Patagonia, the Andes, the Galápagos Islands, corals, Australia, and Monet's garden. Index.

1343. Ventura, Piero, author/illustrator. **Food: Its Evolution Through the Ages**. Boston: Houghton Mifflin, 1994. 64p. $16.95. ISBN 0-395-66790-9. 4-8

Illustrations and text tell the story of food through the centuries. Included are hunting with pits and snares, bows and arrows, and traps; fishing; gatherers; agriculture in ancient Egypt and Rome; making bread; grain transportation; beekeeping, spices, and cured meats; animals and vegetables in the New World; harvesters; steam engines; freezing; canning; cattle raising and breed selection; pasteurization and sterilization; diet; factory ships; and new foods and products. Glossary.

1344. Ventura, Piero, author/illustrator. **1492: The Year of the New World**. New York: Putnam, 1992. 96p. $19.95. ISBN 0-399-22332-0. 4 up

Illustrations and text present what was happening in the Old World during 1492 in Germany, Flanders, England, France, the Ottoman Empire, Genoa, Portugal, and Spain. It looks at Columbus's voyage and those people found in this world: the Tainos, Aztecs, Maya, and Inca. Other important voyages of discovery after 1492 were to the Orient. Some Important Dates in European History 1493-1558, Important Dates in Italian Renaissance Art, Native North and South Americans, Five Hundred Years Later, and Index.

1345. Ventura, Piero, author/illustrator. **Great Composers**. New York: Putnam, 1989. 124p. $20.95. ISBN 0-399-21746-0. 5-8

The text covers several centuries of music by giving a short synopsis on each composer included, and illustrations to highlight the area of the world in which each composer lived and worked. Other topics, such as "troubadours" and "operetta," also appear. Modern composers incorporated are Benny Goodman, Louis Armstrong, and the Beatles. Index.

1346. Ventura, Piero, author/illustrator. **Michelangelo's World**. New York: Putnam, 1988. 38p. $13.95. ISBN 0-399-21593-X. 3-6

Michelangelo Buonarroti (1475-1564), one of the greatest artists who ever lived, was a sculptor, painter, poet, and architect who worked during the Italian Renaissance. The text and its illustrations give a sense of his life and the times.

1347. Ventura, Piero, author/illustrator. **Venice: Birth of a City**. New York: Putnam, 1988. Unpaged. $13.95. ISBN 0-399-21531-X. K-3

In A.D. 452, the city of Venice came into being on the Adriatic Sea. By the 1400s, it had become a political and economic power as well as a cultural center. This lasted until Napoleon conquered it in 1797. His soldiers looted the city and burned the ceremonial gallery of the doges, who had ruled for over 600 years. For the next fifty years, the city remained in Austrian hands. Then and thereafter, the city has had to cope with pollution and subsidence, because it is slowly sinking into the sea. Illustrations clarify the text.

1348. Verhoeven, Rian, and Ruud Van Der Rol. **Anne Frank: Beyond the Diary, A Photographic Remembrance**. Tony Langham and Plym Peters, translators. New York: Viking, 1993. 112p. $17. ISBN 0-670-84932-4. 5 up

Text and accompanying photographs or illustrations describe Anne Frank's (1929-1945) life before her family went into hiding when the Nazis arrived in Amsterdam, Holland. Her father, an amateur photographer, reveals her happy childhood while the political life around her continued to deteriorate without her knowledge. The text includes excerpts from the diary she wrote while confined in the back rooms during the Nazi occupation, and it continues with explanations of what happened to the family after the Nazis took them to the concentration camps. (This information is available at the Anne Frank House in Amsterdam.) Maps, Chronology, Notes, Sources, and Index of People and Places. *Christopher Award, American Library Association Notable Books for Children, A Publishers Weekly Nonfiction Book of the Year, Booklist Editor's Choice, Mildred L. Batchelder Honor,* and *Bulletin Blue Ribbon Book.*

1349. Vernon, Roland. **Introducing Bach**. Englewood Cliffs, NJ: Silver Burdett, 1996. 32p. $13.95; $6.95pa. ISBN 0-382-39157-8; 0-382-39155-1pa. (Famous Composers Series). 5-7

Johann Sebastian Bach (1685-1750) wrote music to the glory of God, but people in his own time knew him best as an organist. Tradition, important to Bach, became his way of expressing himself, because he took the styles of the past to new heights. The text places Bach in the context of his family, in his times, as an organ virtuoso, in the Weimar court, in Cöthen, as cantor of Leipzig, and as a church musician. Stunning color photographs and reproductions augment the text. Time Chart, Glossary, and Index.

1350. Vernon, Roland. **Introducing Beethoven**. Englewood Cliffs, NJ: Silver Burdett, 1996. 32p. $13.95; $6.95pa. ISBN 0-382-39154-3; 0-382-39153-5pa. 3-7

Ludwig van Beethoven (1770-1827), born at a time of change in Europe, wrote his music during the transition from the Classical to the Romantic period. The text looks at his life in double-page topic spreads that include his time at court, his classical training, life in Vienna, the *Eroica* symphony, his opera *Fidelio*, the new order after Napoleon's exile, and his difficulties with his deafness. Photographs and reproductions highlight the text. Time Chart, Glossary, and Index.

1351. Vernon, Roland. **Introducing Mozart**. Parsippany, NY: Silver Burdett, 1996. 32p. $14.95. ISBN 0-382-39159-4. (Famous Composers Series). 5-7

This brief overview of Wolfgang Amadeus Mozart (1756-1791) includes full-color drawings, photographs, and engravings as well as sidebar information on events, artistic movements, and people of his time. Although short, the text is sophisticated and places Mozart in his times. Glossary and Index.

1352. Vining, Elizabeth Gray. **Adam of the Road**. Robert Lawson, illustrator. New York: Viking, 1942. 320p. $17.99. ISBN 0-670-10435-3. New York: Puffin, 1987. 320p. $5.99pa. ISBN 0-14-032464-Xpa. 4-8

After Adam's minstrel father returns from France, the two walk from place to place in England, but they become separated at a large fair in Winchester, England. Adam falls off a wall and knocks himself unconscious; while he slowly recovers, he and his father do not know where the other is. When he is well enough, Adam goes to London to search for Roger. He does not find him until the following spring when they both return to St. Alban's. *Newbery Medal.*

1353. Vos, Ida. **Anna Is Still Here**. Terese Edelstein and Inez Smidt, translators. Boston: Houghton Mifflin, 1993. 139p. $13.95. ISBN 0-395-65368-1. 3-7

Although World War II has ended, Anna still shudders at the years she spent hidden from the Nazis in Holland and thinks that danger lurks everywhere. As the year continues, she and her parents begin to talk about their experiences apart, and Anna makes friends with a Jewish woman who lost her family. When the woman discovers that her daughter has been adopted by another family, she has to look at life differently. Anna realizes that she must do the same, in this sequel to *Hide and Seek*.

1354.   Vos, Ida. **Dancing on the Bridge at Avignon**. Terese Edelstein and Inez Smidt, translators. Boston: Houghton Mifflin, 1995. 183p. $14.95. ISBN 0-395-72039-7. 5-9

Rosa de Jong, age ten, is a talented violinist living in Holland during World War II. Her family hopes that a German general, once rescued by Rosa's uncle, will sign papers that will save them from deportation to Poland. A depressed Rosa remembers when she could go to school and play in the streets without fear. She takes lessons from a Jewish concertmaster until he is arrested, and her playing of his son's composition finally saves her life, but not the lives of her family.

1355.   Vos, Ida. **Hide and Seek**. Terese Edelstein and Inez Smidt, translators. Boston: Houghton Mifflin, 1991. 133p. $13.95. ISBN 0-395-56470-0. 4-8

Rachel, age eight, tells various incidents from her life during five years after the Nazis arrive in Holland in 1940. She has to give up her bicycle, stay off the tram, not play games, and wear a yellow star on her sleeve. She feels as if she is in a cage, and after the liberation, her sister refuses to go into the street right away because it is not yet dark. Among the unexpected emotions after the war is the guilt felt by Jews without tattoos. Then Rachel and her family have to part from the people who hid and protected them. Perhaps worst is the delayed grief about all that happened.

W

1356. Waldman, Neil. **The Never-Ending Greenness**. New York: Morrow, 1997. 40p. $16. ISBN 0-688-14479-9. 2-6

An old man remembers his family's escape from the ghetto in Vilna, Poland, during World War II and their subsequent hiding in the forests around the town. After he immigrates to Israel, he helps to plant trees so that his new country can resemble the "never-ending greenness" of his childhood. His attempts correlate with celebrations of Tu b'Shvat, the Jewish New Year of the Trees.

1357. Wallace, Barbara Brooks. **Cousins in the Castle**. New York: Atheneum, 1996. 152p. $15. ISBN 0-689-80637-X. 4-6

Amelia, age eleven, lives with her widower father in London in the late nineteenth century. When he dies on a business trip, she has to go to America to live with relatives. Her cousin Charlotte, an unpleasant woman, accompanies her on the journey, but Amelia also meets an orphaned singer named Primrose, who is on her way to New York to perform in musical comedy. At the dock, Cousin Charlotte abandons Amelia, and Mrs. Dobbins takes Amelia into her basement, only to disappear the next morning. Amelia realizes that she is a prisoner, but she escapes and finds Primrose (actually a boy), and together they locate Amelia's relatives. Fortunately, her father is alive, and Cousin Charlotte is actually Amelia's grandmother.

1358. Walsh, Jill Paton. **Pepi and the Secret Names**. Fiona French, illustrator. New York: Lothrop, Lee & Shepard, 1995. Unpaged. $15. ISBN 0-688-13438-9. 2-5

In this historical fantasy, Pepi supplies the models for his father to paint on the walls of the tomb prepared for Prince Dhutmose (whose whip was found in his nephew Tutankhamen's tomb, according to the notes at the end). Pepi tells the lion, the crocodile, and the hawk that he knows their secret names. They accompany him, but the cobra comes to Pepi and demands to be included, even telling Pepi his secret name. Hieroglyphics and Egyptian-style illustrations decorate the text.

1359. Walworth, Nancy Zinsser. **Augustus Caesar**. New York: Chelsea House, 1988. 112p. $18.95; $7.95pa. ISBN 1-55546-804-7; 0-7910-0617-4pa. (World Leaders Past and Present). 5 up

Augustus Caesar (63 B.C.-A.D. 14), adopted son of Julius Caesar, became the first emperor of Rome. He was frail and sickly as a boy, but had great determination and intelligence. These qualities led him to join forces with Mark Antony in 43 B.C. to destroy Caesar's assassins. Later he fought against Antony at the Battle of Actium in 31 B.C. to become the single supreme ruler. He retained all necessary powers of office while staying within the limits of tradition. He streamlined the army, funded roads, and began an imperial administration. All of his achievements and his character developments appear in this text, enhanced by photographs and reproductions. Chronology, Further Reading, and Index.

1360. Walworth, Nancy Zinsser. **Constantine**. New York: Chelsea House, 1989. 112p. $18.95. ISBN 1-55546-805-5. (World Leaders Past and Present). 5 up

Constantine (d. 337) dreamed that he was visited by Jesus Christ. This dream changed the world when he decided that he would convert to Christianity. His decision ended Roman paganism and began the rise of Christianity. He had a vision of greatness for the Roman world which his father helped to instill in him. He was able to inspire the masses, calm the pagans, and return financial strength to the Roman Empire. He changed the public image of Christianity by establishing it as a complex organization. Photographs and reproductions enhance the text. Chronology, Further Reading, and Index.

1361. Wangari, Esther. **Ameru**. New York: Rosen, 1995. 64p. $15.95. ISBN 0-8239-1766-5. (Heritage Library of African Peoples, East Africa). 5-8

Various traditions disagree on the origin of the Ameru, but in one story they had to escape Egypt; in a tradition paralleling the Israelites' leaving Egypt, the Ameru eventually reached Kenya. In Kenya, the Ameru district lies on the equator around the slopes of Mt. Kenya. History about this group, along with information about its social structure, its customs and rituals, colonialism, and its future, appear in the text. Photographs, boxed information, and maps enhance the text. Glossary, Further Reading, and Index.

1362. Warburton, Lois. **Aztec Civilization**. San Diego, CA: Lucent, 1995. 127p. $16.95. ISBN 1-56006-277-0. (World History). 6 up

The information on the Aztecs begins with a description of the current ruins in Mexico City, where the ruins of an ancient Aztec temple are all that remains of the sophisticated city of Tenochititlán, a Toltec construction. The Aztecs overran the Toltecs in the twelfth century. Daily life, religion (including human sacrifice), political views, and wealth are among the topics covered in this book. The Aztec empire ended when Cortés came because Moctezuma probably thought that Cortés was the god Quetzlcoatl returned to save the people. Instead, in 1521, Cortés killed them. Photographs and reproductions enhance the text. Maps, Timeline, Works Consulted, Further Reading, and Index.

1363. Warburton, Lois. **The Beginning of Writing**. San Diego, CA: Lucent, 1990. 128p. $16.95. ISBN 1-56006-113-8. 6-10

Before people had writing, they had to communicate. The text looks at their attempts and how these cultures began to form alphabets in order to write. The text highlights the Egyptian, Mayan, Chinese, and American Indian societies. Photographs enhance the text. Bibliography, Glossary, and Index.

1364. Warburton, Lois. **Railroads: Bridging the Continents**. San Diego, CA: Lucent, 1991. 96p. $16.95. ISBN 1-56006-216-9. 6-9

In the text, period paintings, prints, and photographs from Library of Congress collections illustrate two-page spreads that present various topics. They include the major western trails, early railroads, and the inland and ocean waterways. The text examines the history, development, and technology of the steam engine and railroads; discusses the decline of rail transport in the United States; and describes the growth of railroads in Europe and Japan, focusing on their high-speed trains and magnetic levitation. Chronology and Index.

1365. Waterlow, Julia. **The Ancient Chinese**. New York: Thompson Learning, 1995. 32p. $14.95. ISBN 1-56847-169-6. (Look into the Past). 4-6

The text gives an overview of China's early civilization and the Chinese philosophies. Two-page spreads cover rulers, travel, beliefs, farming, trading, arts, and daily life. Illustrations augment the text. Glossary, Important Dates, Books to Read, and Index.

1366. Watkins, Richard R., author/illustrator. **Gladiator**. Boston: Houghton Mifflin, 1997. 87p. $17. ISBN 0-395-82656-X. 5-8

Gladiators served as the entertainment for all levels of Roman society. The text examines their history and the training that they had to undergo before they shed the shame of slavery for the confidence of combat. Illustrations show the cruelty of these games and the bloodthirsty spectators who demanded them.

1367. Watkins, Yoko Kawashima. **My Brother, My Sister, and I**. New York: Macmillan, 1994. 275p. $16.95. ISBN 0-02-792526-9. 5 up

In this sequel to *So Far from the Bamboo Grove*, Watkins continues the fictionalized account of her life as the thirteen-year-old Yoko, with her sister Ko and brother Hideyo, after their escape from Korea into Japan after World War II. When the warehouse where they live burns in a fire, they live with Yo in the hospital, who was severely wounded in the fire while trying to retrieve the ashes of their mother and the money she gave them before her death. The warehouse owners' heir accuses them of arson and murder, so they must disprove those charges. Additionally, they are trying to find their father, who the Soviets have captured. Yoko hates her school and her horrid treatment by the other girls, who laugh at her poverty. That a child can survive in such adverse circumstances shows the importance of character and love. A few of the adults they meet help them cope until they eventually find their father, aged from years in a Siberian prison camp. *American Library Association Notable Books for Young Adults, Parenting Magazine Best Book, New York Times Notable Book,* and *Publishers Weekly Best Book.*

1368. Weil, Lisl, author/illustrator. **Wolferl: The First Six Years in the Life of Wolfgang Amadeus Mozart, 1756-1762**. New York: Holiday House, 1991. Unpaged. $14.95. ISBN 0-8234-0876-0. K-3

Mozart (1756-1791) was the second of his parents' seven children to live in Salzburg, Austria. They gave him such a long name that his sister started calling him "Wolferl." When he was only three, he could hear a piece of music and play it by ear. His father took Wolferl and his sister to perform in Vienna after Wolferl started composing at age five; one of the young princesses he met was Marie Antoinette. As the winter worsened, they returned to Salzburg, where he continued to compose and play. At his death, he had composed 600 pieces. Glossary.

1369. Weisberg, Barbara. **Coronado's Golden Quest**. Mike Eagle, illustrator. Austin, TX: Raintree/Steck-Vaughn, 1993. 79p. $24.26; $5.95pa. ISBN 0-8114-7232-9; 0-8114-8072-0pa. (Stories of America—Personal Challenge). 5-9

Viceroy Mendoza of Spain spent his personal fortune to send Coronado (1510-1554) and an army to find the seven cities of gold that they had heard so much about. They left in 1540, but after more than a year of searching and treachery, they realized that gold was not to be located in the southwest above Mexico. Coronado was wounded when he fell from a horse, and other incidents doomed the journey. A slave named Turk convinced the party that Quivera, his home, had gold and that he would lead them from Cicuye to their rewards. They discovered that he was lying because he thought this was the only way he could escape his captors. Epilogue, Afterword, and Notes.

1370. Weitzman, David. **Great Lives: Human Culture**. New York: Scribner's, 1994. 294p. $22.95. ISBN 0-684-19438-4. (Great Lives). 5-9

Biographical profiles of 27 anthropologists and archaeologists describe their work and their motivations. They are Ruth Benedict (American, 1887-1948); Franz Boas (American, 1858-1942); James Henry Breasted (American, 1865-1935); Howard Carter (English, 1873-1939); Herbert, Fifth Earl of Carnarvon (English, 1866-1923); Jean-François Champollion (French, 1790-1832); Arthur Evans (English, 1851-1941); Alice Cunningham Fletcher (American, 1838-1923); Jane Goodall (English, b. 1934); Georg Fredrich Grotefend (German, 1775-1883); Zora Neale Hurston (American, 1891-1960); Alfred Kroeber (English, 1876-1960); Austen Henry Layard (French, 1817-1894); Louis S. B. Leakey (English, 1903-1972); Mary Nicol Leakey (English, b. 1913); Richard Leakey (Kenyan, b. 1944); Robert Harry Lowie (American, 1883-1957); Max Mallowan (English, 1904-1978); Margaret Mead (American, 1901-1978); Elsie Clews Parsons (American, 1875-1941); Hortense Powder-maker (American, 1900-1970); Mary Kawena Pukui (Hawaiian, 1895-1986); Heinrich Schliemann (German, 1822-1890); Michael Ventris (English, 1922-1956); Robert Eric Mortimer Wheeler (English, 1890-1976); Charles Leonard Woolley (English, 1880-1960); and Yigael Yadin (Israeli, 1917-1984). Further Reading and Index.

1371. Wepman, Dennis. **Alexander the Great**. New York: Chelsea House, 1986. 112p. $18.95. ISBN 0-87754-594-4. (World Leaders Past and Present). 5 up

Alexander succeeded to the Macedonian throne in 336 B.C. and quickly secured military and political su-premacy over the states of the Greek peninsula. Between 334 and 323 B.C., he established a reputation as one of the greatest leaders the world has ever seen. His empire included the Balkans, parts of northern Africa, the eastern Mediter-ranean, southwestern Asia, and much of India. He believed that East and West could be united under a single system of government and grow accustomed to one way of life. He may have been bloodthirsty, or he may have been trying to create peace. Photographs and reproductions enhance the text. Glossary, Chronology, and Index.

1372. Wepman, Dennis. **Jomo Kenyatta**. New York: Chelsea House, 1985. 112p. $18.95. ISBN 0-87754-575-8. (World Leaders Past and Present). 5 up

Jomo Kenyatta (b. 1894) resolved to free the Kenyan people from British subjugation. He went to London in 1929 and furthered his political education by watching the British at home. He realized then that the British thought their civilization was the best model for everyone. Kenyatta returned to Kenya in 1946 and united the Kenyan tribes. The British imprisoned him, but he regained his freedom in 1961 to become a respected leader of the country. Photographs enhance the text. Chronology, Further Reading, and Index.

1373. West, Alan. **José Martí: Man of Poetry, Soldier of Freedom**. Brookfield, CT: Millbrook Press, 1994. 32p. $13.90. ISBN 1-56294-408-8. (Hispanic Heritage). 5-8

José Martí (1853-1895), son of Spanish parents who lived in poverty, had a teacher, Mendive, near his Cu-ban home who recognized his abilities and paid for his schooling. Martí wrote his first poem for Mendive's wife upon the death of her child. He continued to compose poetry even as he went to prison at age seventeen for writ-ing a letter against the government, and as he was exiled in Spain, and as he returned to Mexico and other South American countries to work for freedom for Cuba. His poem "La Guantanamera" was set to music and sung throughout Cuba and the rest of the world. He died while leading an uprising against Spain in Cuba at Dos Ríos. Important Dates, Find Out More, and Index.

1374. West, Delno C., and Jean M. West. **Braving the North Atlantic: The Vikings, the Cabots, and Jacques Cartier Voyage to America**. New York: Atheneum, 1996. 86p. $16. ISBN 0-689-31822-7. 5-9

The text details the explorations of John Cabot, a Genoese sailor, and his son, Sebastian, in the New World as they tried to find the Northwest Passage to the Orient. The British king sponsored their explorations, and fifteenth-century sources reveal their journey. France also sent an explorer, Jacques Cartier. He found the St. Lawrence River, and his claim made Canada a colony of France. Index.

1375. Westall, Robert. **The Kingdom by the Sea**. New York: Farrar, Straus & Giroux, 1990. 176p. $15. ISBN 0-374-34205-9. 6-9

Harry escapes a bomb in 1942, but his family does not reach the bomb shelter, and his house is destroyed. Not knowing if his family is dead, Harry leaves. On the English coast, people help him, but one man suggests that he go home to officially say good-bye to the memory of his family. When he returns, he finds his family, relo-cated and frustrated at his disappearance. *Guardian Award for Children's Fiction.*

1376. Westall, Robert. **The Promise**. New York: Scholastic, 1991. 176p. $13.95. ISBN 0-590-43760-7. 6-9

During the early part of World War II, Bob, age fourteen, has a crush on Valerie, a sickly girl who stays home as much as she goes to school. When she asks Bob to come and find her if she ever gets lost, he readily agrees. She dies and begins to haunt him, reminding him of his promise. Bob recalls that time and how he became more interested in the war effort and thought less of Valerie, not expecting her to demand solace from the grave.

1377.   Westerfeld, Scott. **The Berlin Airlift**. Englewood Cliffs, NJ: Silver Burdett, 1989. 64p. $16.98. ISBN 0-382-09833-1. (Turning Points). 5 up

Although the title indicates that the text covers the Berlin airlift in 1948 and 1949, it also discusses several other points important to the history of the time. It includes background on the Iron Curtain and on the Marshall Plan, with a biographical commentary on George Marshall, "Operation Vittles," and the rise of the Berlin Wall. Index and Suggested Reading.

1378.   Wheatley, Nadia, and Donna Rawlins. **My Place**. Brooklyn, NY: Kane, Miller, 1992. Unpaged. $14.95; $7.95pa. ISBN 0-916291-42-1; 0-916291-54-5pa. 3-6

Laura, age ten, describes her home in Australia in 1988, shows a map of the neighborhood, and tells what she and her friends did for her birthday. Mike, age ten, describes his place in 1978, before it changed and Laura moved in. Children tell about their homes, all on the same plot of land, every ten years back in time from 1968 to 1788. Before 1788, the ground was free from buildings.

1379.   Whitelaw, Nancy. **Joseph Stalin: From Peasant to Premier**. New York: Dillon Press, 1992. 149p. $12.95. ISBN 0-87518-557-6. (People in Focus). 5 up

At age fifteen, Iosif Dzhugashvili (1879-1953) won a scholarship to a seminary school. Three decades later, he was one of the most powerful and most feared men in the world. He always hated authority and fought against it; this characteristic got him expelled from the seminary. One of the difficulties in writing accurately about Stalin is that he ordered systematic alterations of some records and destruction of others, so the true picture can never be known entirely. The text tries to tell as much truth as possible about Stalin's life. Time Line, Selected Bibliography, and Index.

1380.   Whitman, Sylvia. **Hernando de Soto and the Explorers of the American South**. New York: Chelsea House, 1991. 112p. $19.95. ISBN 0-7910-1301-4. (World Explorers). 5 up

Hernando de Soto (1500-1542) returned to the New World, landing on Florida's coast, to find gold in 1539. He had gained much wealth when Pizarro conquered the Incas in Peru, and he expected the same in experience. He roamed through the American South looking for gold, silver, and pearls, but his expedition deteriorated as the men raped, pillaged, and plundered the Indians. On this horrendous journey, he discovered the Mississippi River. Engravings and reproductions enhance the text. Chronology, Further Reading, and Index.

1381.   Whittock, Martyn J. **The Roman Empire**. New York: Peter Bedrick, 1996. 64p. $17.95. ISBN 0-87226-118-2. 4-6

The text covers the rise of the Roman Empire and the lifestyles during the Republic. Biographical sketches of emperors and barbarians as well as information from primary and secondary sources in sidebars help to establish that historical period. Photographs, reproductions, and maps enhance the text. Index.

1382.   Wilcox, Charlotte, author/illustrator. **Mummies and Their Mysteries**. Minneapolis, MN: Carolrhoda, 1993. 64p. $22.95; $7.95pa. ISBN 0-87614-767-8; 0-87614-643-4pa. 4-6

The most famous mummies come from Egypt, but the Incan empire also had millions. America's mummies have been found in caves and preserved in ice; some mummies have been found in the Far East. Europe's mysterious mummies include the Bog people. Photographs enhance the text. Glossary and Where to See Mummies.

1383.   Wildsmith, Brian. **Saint Francis**. Grand Rapids, MI: William B. Eerdman, 1996. 34p. $20. ISBN 0-8028-5123-1. 1-4

As a young man of the thirteenth century, Francis (of Assisi) was wealthy and thoughtless, but he gave up his social class and privileges to help others. The text looks at his love of nature and the legends that have evolved about him as he gave his time and effort to those who needed them. *American Bookseller's Pick of the Lists.*

1384.   Wilkinson, Philip. **Amazing Buildings**. Paolo Donati, illustrator. New York: Dorling Kindersley, 1993. 48p. $16.95. ISBN 1-56458-234-5. (Amazing). 3-7

The text presents illustrations of cross-sections, as well as drawings and photographs, of twenty-one buildings throughout the world. Included are the palace of Minos in ancient Crete; the Colosseum in Rome; the Mayan Temple of the Inscriptions; Krak des Chevaliers, built in Syria during the Crusades; the Alhambra in Granada, Spain (thirteenth century); Chartres Cathedral, built during the Middle Ages in France; the Imperial Palace of Beijing (1368-1644); Teatro Olimpico, the sixteenth-century replica of an ancient Roman theater in Vicenza, Italy; Himeji Castle in Japan, built in the seventeenth century; the Taj Mahal in India; Versailles of the French King Louis XIV; Brighton Pavilion in nineteenth-century England; the Houses of Parliament in London; the Paris Opera during the reign of Napoleon III (1852-1870); Germany's Neuschwanstein Castle (1864-1886); the Statue of Liberty in New York; the Van Eetvelde House in Brussels; the Notre-Dame-du-Haut, designed by Le Corbusier, in eastern France; the Guggenheim Museum of Frank Lloyd Wright; the Sydney, Australia, Opera House; and the Toronto Sky Dome, built for the Olympics. Index.

1385. Wilkinson, Philip. **Building**. Dave King and Geoff Dann, illustrators. New York: Knopf, 1995. 61p. $16.95. ISBN 0-679-97256-0. (Eyewitness). 4-12

Photographs and drawings give clear pictures of the various aspects of building. Topics covered in two-page spreads are structural engineering, house construction, and building materials. These include wood, earth, bricks, stone, timber frames, the roof, thatching, columns and arches, vaults, staircases, fireplaces and chimneys, doors and doorways, windows, stained glass, balconies, and building on unusual topography. Index.

1386. Wilkinson, Philip, and Jacqueline Dineen. **The Lands of the Bible**. Robert R. Ingpen, illustrator. New York: Chelsea House, 1994. 92p. $19.95. ISBN 0-7910-2752-X. (Mysterious Places). 6 up

Illustrations and text give background information on ten places noted in the Bible. The places are Ur (Iraq, c. 4000-2000 B.C.), Saqqara (Egypt, c. 2680 B.C.), Babylon (Iraq c. 1792-1750 B.C. and c. 625-540 B.C.), Boghazköy (Turkey, c. 1700-1200 B.C.), Karnak (Egypt, c. 1480-1080 B.C.), Abu Simbel (Egypt, c. 1305-1200 B.C.), Khorsabad (Iraq, 720-705 B.C.), Persepolis (Iran, c. 520-330 B.C.), Petra (Jordan, c. 170 B.C.-A.D. 100), and Alexandria (Egypt, c. 320 B.C.-A.D. 391). Further Reading and Index.

1387. Wilkinson, Philip, and Jacqueline Dineen. **The Mediterranean**. Robert R. Ingpen, illustrator. New York: Chelsea House, 1994. 92p. $19.95. ISBN 0-7910-2751-1. (Mysterious Places). 5 up

The illustrations and maps, along with the text, tell about places in past history. The places are Tarxien on Malta (3600-2500 B.C.); Knossos on Crete (2000-1450 B.C.); Mycenae in Greece (1600-1100 B.C.); Delphi in Greece (650 B.C.- A.D. 150); Epidaurus in Greece (320 B.C.-A.D.150); Rhodes, an island of Greece (280-226 B.C.); Leptis Magna in Libya (46 B.C.-A.D. 211); Hagia Sophia in Istanbul, Turkey (A.D. 360-537); Mistra in Greece (A.D. 1262-1460); and the Topkapi in Istanbul, Turkey (A.D.1465-1853). Further Reading and Index.

1388. Wilkinson, Philip, and Jacqueline Dineen. **People Who Changed the World**. Robert Ingpen, illustrator. New York: Chelsea House, 1994. 93p. $19.95. ISBN 0-7910-2764-3. (Turning Points in History). 5-10

Religious leaders, philosophers, and explorers have changed the world. Those presented in the text include Confucius (c. 551-479 B.C.), Gautama Buddha (c. 563-480 B.C.), Pericles (c. 495-429 B.C.), Jesus Christ (c. 6 B.C.-c. A.D. 30), Muhammad (c. A.D. 570-632), St. Benedict of Nursia (c. A.D. 480-550), Marco Polo (1215-1294), Lorenzo de Medici (1449-1492), Christopher Columbus (1451-1506), Martin Luther (1483-1546), Ferdinand Magellan (1480-1521), James Cook (1728-1779), Karl Marx (1818-1883), Henri Dunant (1828-1910), Sigmund Freud (1856-1939), Leopold II of Belgium (1835-1909) who colonized Africa, and Martin Luther King, Jr. (1929-1968). Events included are the Black Plague, the Irish Famine, and the Wall Street stock market crash. Further Reading and Index.

1389. Wilkinson, Philip, and Jacqueline Dineen. **Statesmen Who Changed the World**. Robert Ingpen, illustrator. New York: Chelsea House, 1994. 93p. $19.95. ISBN 0-7910-2762-7. (Turning Points in History). 5-10

Using the definition that a statesperson is someone who influences people around the world rather than only in their own country or neighborhood, the text looks at people who have had a vision of changes whether good or bad. Included are Asoka, the Buddhist emperor (270-232 B.C.); Shih Huang Ti, Emperor of China (259-210 B.C.); Julius Caesar, Consul of Rome (100-44 B.C.); Constantine of Byzantium (A.D. 285-337); King John and the Magna Carta (1167-1216); Isabella of Castille (1451-1504) and Ferdinand II of Aragon (1452-1516); Cortés and the Aztec Empire (1485-1547); Ivan IV of Russia (1530-1584); the Manchu Empire of China under Prince Dorgon (1612-1650); Prague's Frederick V (1596-1632); the fall of the Bastille in 1789 under Louis XVI (1754-1793) and Marie Antoinette of Austria (1755-1793); Simón Bolívar (1783-1830) in South America; Emperor Meiji (1852-1912) opening up Japan; Palmerston (1784-1865) and the opening of India; Bismarck (1815-1898) and German unity; Lenin (1870-1924) and the Russian Revolution; Gandhi (1869-1948) and Indian independence; Mao (1893-1976) and the Chinese Long March; Eleanor Roosevelt (1884-1962) and the United Nations; and Gorbachev (b. 1931) and the Berlin Wall. Further Reading and Index.

1390. Wilkinson, Philip and Michael Pollard. **Generals Who Changed the World**. Robert Ingpen, illustrator. New York: Chelsea House, 1994. 93p. $19.95. ISBN 0-7910-2761-9. (Turning Points in History). 5-10

Generals have changed the map of the Earth through the battles they have won or lost. The generals discussed in the text cover many centuries. They are Alexander of Macedonia (356-323 B.C.); the Vandals, Huns, and Visigoths under Alaric (c. A.D. 370-410); Viking raiders beginning in the eighth century; William I (c. 1027-1087) conquered England in 1066; Abu Bakr, leader of the Almoravids, who overcame Ghana in 1056; the first crusade in 1095 called by Urban II; Genghis Khan (c. 1162-1227) and the Mongols; Sultan Mehmet II (1432-1481) who overtook Byzantium; Babur (1483-1530), conqueror of India; the revolt of the Netherlands toward Spain under William the Silent (1533-1584); Drake and the defeat of the Spanish Armada in 1588 (1540-1596); John III Sobieski (1624-1696) saving Vienna from the Turks; James Wolfe (1727-1759) capturing Quebec; Washington (1732-1799) after Lexington; Napoleon (1769-1821) attacking Moscow; Robert E. Lee (1807-1870) and Sharpsburg; Paul Kruger's Boers (1825-1904) against Great Britain; the beginning of World War I under Kaiser Wilhelm II (1859-1941); Japan's bombing of Pearl Harbor with Hideki Tojo as prime minister (1884-1948); and Dwight Eisenhower (1890-1969) and D-Day. Further Reading and Index.

1391. Wilkinson, Philip, and Michael Pollard. **The Magical East**. Robert R. Ingpen, illustrator. New York: Chelsea House, 1994. 92p. $19.95. ISBN 0-7910-2754-6. (Mysterious Places). 6 up

Illustrations along with text tell about places of the East that are important to past and present civilizations. They are Mohenjo-Daro (India, c. 2400-1800 B.C.); the Great Wall (China, c. 300 B.C.-A.D. 40); Yoshinogari (Japan, c. 300 B.C.-A.D. 300); Ellora (India, c. A.D. 600-900); Nara (Japan c. A.D. 710-795); Angkor (Kampuchea, c. A.D. 900-1150); Easter Island (Oceania, c. A.D. 100-1680); Great Zimbabwe (Zimbabwe, c. A.D. 1200-1450); the Forbidden City (Beijing, China, c. A.D. 1404-1450); and the Taj Mahal (Agra, India, c. A.D. 1632-1643). Further Reading and Index.

1392. Wilkinson, Philip, and Michael Pollard. **Scientists Who Changed the World**. Robert R. Ingpen, illustrator. New York: Chelsea House, 1994. 93p. $19.95. ISBN 0-7910-2763-5. (Turning Points in History). 4-6

People who have had an interest in why and how things happen have helped shape the world. Brief profiles of some of those scientists or groups appear in the text. They are Kaifung, Johannes Gutenberg (fifteenth century), Galileo Galilei (1564-1642), Isaac Newton (1642-1727), James Watt (1736-1819), Donkin and Hall (early nineteenth-century cannery), Louis Daguerre (1789-1851), Charles Darwin (1809-1882), Joseph Lister (1827-1912), Alexander Graham Bell (1847-1922), Marie Curie (1867-1934), the Wright brothers (early twentieth century), Henry Ford (1863-1947), Albert Einstein (1879-1955), John Logie Baird (1888-1946), Alan Turing (1912-1954), the Manhattan Project (early 1940s), Crick and Watson (twentieth century), Wilkins and Franklin (twentieth century), the launch of Sputnik I in 1957, and astronauts Aldrin, Armstrong, and Collins. Photographs enhance the text. Timeline and Index.

1393. Willard, Nancy. **Gutenberg's Gift: A Book Lover's Pop-Up Book**. San Diego, CA: Harcourt Brace, 1995. Unpaged. $20. ISBN 0-15-200783-0. 3-6

Looking at the life of Johann Gutenberg (1397?-1468), Willard creates a narrative poem in which Gutenberg works hard to complete his first printed Bible in time to give it to his wife for Christmas. Pop-ups and moving parts augment the text and other illustrations. An afterword notes that the Bible was finally printed in 1455, but that Gutenberg no longer owned the printing shop—and as far as anyone knows, he never had a wife.

1394. Williams, A. Susan. **The Greeks**. New York: Thompson Learning, 1993. 32p. $14.95. ISBN 1-56847-059-2. (Look into the Past). 4-6

The text especially emphasizes the religion, theaters, scientific theory, politics, and travel of the Greeks. Photographs complement the text. Glossary, Important Dates, Books to Read, and Index.

1395. Williams, Barbara. **Titanic Crossing**. New York: Dial Press, 1995. 149p. $14. 99. ISBN 0-8037-1790-3. 4-8

Albert Trask, age thirteen, has the chance to travel from England to America on the *Titanic* in 1912. He roams the deck with Emily, a friend on the ship who notes that third-class passengers have few lifeboats. When the ship sinks, Albert has to save his six-year-old sister. He does, but his mother dies. He and his sister then have to face their dead father's mother in their new home, and Albert learns to assert himself appropriately.

1396. Williams, Brian. **Ancient China**. New York: Viking, 1996. 48p. $16.99. ISBN 0-670-87157-5. (See Through History). 6-9

The topics in this look at China, with overlays to show the insides of a typical Chinese house, include farming, religion, architecture, clothing, and other aspects of daily life. The history covers the beginnings of Chinese history through the massacre in Tiananmen Square in 1989. Illustrations highlight the text. Chronology, Glossary, and Index.

1397. Williams, Brian. **Forts and Castles**. New York: Viking, 1994. 48p. $15.99. ISBN 0-670-85898-6. (See Through History). 6-9

People began building forts and castles in prehistoric times when walled towns were important, and they continued through the Middle Ages. They helped kings control lands, protect their subjects, and impress their enemies. Armies tried to capture them and developed complex weapons to achieve their goals. See-through cutaways of a Mycenaean citadel in Greece, a besieged castle in the Middle Ages, the castle of a Japanese warlord, and a U.S. Army frontier fort highlight the text. Two-page topics cover information on Hattusas, Tiryns, the siege of Lachish, hill forts, the Great Wall of China, Roman forts, Masada, the Normans, Crusader castles, the Moors in Spain, the Renaissance, Japanese castles, Sacsayhuaman, Golconda, Vauban fortresses, cavalry fort, Fort Sumter, and the end of the age. Key Dates and Glossary and Index.

1398. Williams, Brian, and Brenda Williams. **The Age of Discovery: From the Renaissance to American Independence**. James Field, illustrator. New York: Peter Bedrick, 1994. 64p. $18.95. ISBN 0-87226-311-8. (Timelink). 5-8

The text presents history in 50-year segments and depicts discoveries from all cultures. Various aids such as comparative time charts, maps, charts, and graphs show the major historical events from 1491 to 1789 in the Americas, Asia, and Africa. Illustrations complement the text.

1399. Wilson, Anthony. **Visual Timeline of Transportation**. New York: Dorling Kindersley, 1995. 48p. $16.95. ISBN 1-56458-880-7. 3-5

Brief essays introduce the four time periods identified as changes in modes of transportation. Following is a timeline divided into air and space, land, and water, with photographs of the different vehicles or animals that people used for travel. An additional category notes important milestones, such as the 1970 explosion of Apollo 13. The four segments are 10,000 B.C. to A.D. 1779, when humans could only go as fast as the fastest domesticated animal; 1780-1879, the age of steam; 1880-1959, the rise of powered flight and the automobile; and 1960 to 2000, the time of space travel. Future Trends and Index.

1400. Winter, Jeanette, author/illustrator. **Klara's New World**. New York: Knopf, 1992. 41p. $15.99. ISBN 0-679-90626-6. 2-7

In 1852, Klara, age eight, and her family have to leave Sweden during a famine; they head for America where they hope to grow crops. They sail on an ocean, a river, and a lake as well as riding a train, during the three months that it takes them to reach Minnesota.

1401. Winter, Jonah. **Diego**. Amy Prince, translator; Jeannette Winter, illustrator. New York: Knopf, 1991. Unpaged. $15. ISBN 0-679-81987-8. 1-4

In Spanish and English, the text tells the story of Diego Rivera (1886-1957). As a child, he became ill after his twin brother died, and his parents sent him to live with a healer. When he came home, his father gave him some chalk, and thereafter all he wanted to do was draw. His studies took him to Paris; in Italy, he got the idea to paint murals. When he returned to Mexico, he painted murals about everything he saw, because he wanted to share art and his concept of life with the people. *Bulletin Blue Ribbon Book*.

1402. Wisniewski, David, author/illustrator. **Sundiata: Lion King of Mali**. New York: Clarion, 1992. Unpaged. $15.95. ISBN 0-395-61302-7. 2-4

Sundiata (c. 1200), son of the second wife of the king of Mali, could neither speak nor walk when he was a boy. His father nevertheless chose Sundiata as the heir, and his *griot* (the man who told him the history of his people) helped him to both talk and walk. When he seemed powerful enough to take the throne, he left Mali so that he could stay alive. When he was eighteen, he returned to his homeland to defeat the evil usurper king and claim the throne. His rule returned peace to the people.

1403. Wood, Marion. **Ancient America**. New York: Facts on File, 1990. 96p. $17.95. ISBN 0-8160-2210-0. (Cultural Atlas for Young People). 6-9

Wood covers the Americas, from the Inuit in the north to the Inca living in the empire that extended as far south as Chile. With as much information as possible, the text gives a picture of conditions in the Americas before the explorers came from Europe to change everything. Chronology, Glossary, Gazetteer, and Index. *New York Public Library Books for the Teen Age*.

1404. Wood, Tim. **Ancient Wonders**. New York: Viking, 1997. 48p. $16.99. ISBN 0-670-87468-X. (See Through History). 5-7

The text looks at the ancient wonders of the world, and the see-through pages show the insides of the Egyptian pharoahs' tombs, Minoan temples on the island of Knossos, the cliff tombs and temples of Petra in Egypt, and the church of Hagia Sophia in Constantinople. Key Dates, Glossary, and Index.

1405. Wood, Tim. **The Aztecs**. New York: Viking, 1992. 48p. $14.99. ISBN 0-670-84492-6. (See Through History). 4-7

When a small band of Spanish explorers arrived in Mexico, they found the militaristic Aztec empire, which stretched from the Atlantic to the Pacific with over 15 million people living in 500 cities and towns. See-through cutaways of a typical Aztec house, an Aztec knight temple, Montezuma's palace and its hidden gold treasures, and the Great Temple of Tenochtitlán (where human sacrifices occurred) highlight the text. The topics presented in two-page spreads include the people, the empire, Tenochtitlán, the Great Temple, the army, warfare, trade, writing, the emperor, arts and crafts, food and farming, growing up, homes, the calendar, gods, and the end of the empire. Key Dates and Glossary and Index.

1406.   Wood, Tim. **The Incas**. New York: Viking, 1996. 48p. $16.99. ISBN 0-670-87037-4. (See Through History). 6-9

The topics in this look at the Incas and Peru, with overlays to show the insides of an Incan temple, include farming, religion, architecture, clothing, and other aspects of daily life. The history covers what is known about the Incan Empire and devotes the final two chapters to the Spanish conquest. Illustrations highlight the text. Chronology, Glossary, and Index.

1407.   Wood, Tim. **The Renaissance**. New York: Viking, 1993. 48p. $14.99. ISBN 0-670-85149-3. (See Through History). 6-9

For a thousand years after the fall of the Romans, many of their achievements were forgotten, but in the fifteenth and sixteenth centuries scholars rediscovered many ancient Greek and Roman writings. Artists and scientists, including Michelangelo and Galileo, began to build their own work on the classical base previously established. See-through cutaways of a Florentine town house, Columbus's ship the *Santa Maria*, St. Peter's in Rome, and a printer's workshop highlight the text. The two-page topical spreads include information on the re-birth of learning, city-states, government, trade, exploration, ships, architecture, patrons, palaces, women at court, alchemy and science, technology, printing, astronomy, medical advances, warfare, churches and cathedrals, and the Reformation. Key Dates, Glossary, and Index.

1408.   Wooding, Sharon, author/illustrator. **The Painter's Cat**. New York: Putnam, 1994. Unpaged. $14.95. ISBN 0-399-22414-9. 2-4

Lorenzo Lotto (1480?-1556), a Renaissance artist, becomes so involved in painting his canvas that he forgets to feed his cat. The cat, Micio, goes into the streets of Venice looking for his dinner.

1409.   Woodruff, Elvira. **The Disappearing Bike Shop**. New York: Yearling, Dell, 1994. 169p. $13.95. ISBN 0-8234-0933-3. 4 up

When Freckle and Tyler, fifth graders, meet an unusual bicycle salesman and inventor, they find out through their adventures that he is Leonardo da Vinci traveling through time from his life in 1452 through 1519.

1410.   Woodruff, Elvira. **The Orphan of Ellis Island: A Time-Travel Adventure**. New York: Scholastic, 1997. 181p. $14.95. ISBN 0-590-48245-9. 4-6

In this historical fantasy, Dominic is a fifth-grader who is embarrassed on a class trip to Ellis Island because he has no family of his own as an orphan and foster child. He hides in a closet at the site and goes to sleep. He awakens in Italy of 1908, meets three orphaned brothers, and goes with two of them to the United States after the untimely death of the third. He discovers a sense of family and returns to the present where he wakes with more confidence.

1411.   Woods, Geraldine. **Science in Ancient Egypt**. New York: Franklin Watts, 1988. 92p. $16.10. ISBN 0-531-10486-9. (First Book). 5-8

An introduction to Egypt and its science precedes chapters on different developments from this culture. They include the pyramids, mathematics, astronomy and timekeeping, medicine, writing and agriculture, crafts and technology, and contemporary debt to the culture for its discoveries. Photographs and drawings enhance the text. Glossary, Further Reading, and Index.

1412.   Woolf, Felicity. **Picture This: A First Introduction to Paintings**. New York: Doubleday, 1990. 40p. $14.95. ISBN 0-385-41135-9. 4-8

The text looks at the history of painting, from the illuminated manuscript to the twentieth-century action painting of Jackson Pollock. The topics include early oil painting, frescoes, mythological subjects, self-portraits, Dutch painting, eighteenth-century French, Turner, two versions of the Ophelia story, Impressionists, van Gogh, Expressionism, and Surrealism. Glossary, Gallery List, and Index.

1413.   Wright, Rachel. **Egyptians**. New York: Franklin Watts, 1993. 32p. $11.90. ISBN 0-531-14209-4. (Craft Topics). 4-6

The text and illustrations give facts about the social, religious, and political aspects of the Egyptian civilization in thirteen two-page spreads. Projects with directions for making items directly related to the Egyptians, from simple to difficult, give further insight. Glossary and Index.

1414.   Wulffson, Don L. **The Upside-Down Ship**. Niles, IL: Albert Whitman, 1986. 136p. $9.75. ISBN 0-8075-8346-4. 5-8

When Bruce returns to Aberdeen, Scotland, in the 1760s after being shipwrecked for six years in Iceland, he has difficulty accepting the attitudes of civilization. His whaling vessel had become lodged in an iceberg, and he had survived on whale meat and stored supplies while drowned sailors lay frozen in another area of the ship. A polar bear that he had befriended as a cub caught fish for him. Bruce's brother becomes angry at his return because his mother died thinking that Bruce was dead.

X

1415. Xydes, Georgia. **Alexander Mackenzie and the Explorers of Canada**. New York: Chelsea House, 1992. 110p. $19.95. ISBN 0-7910-1314-6. (World Explorers). 5 up

Alexander Mackenzie (c. 1764-1820) was a man of contradictions. He hated the wilderness, but he conquered western Canada. He wanted to be an aristocrat, but he spent many years freezing in wooden structures. Although a loner, he was forced to keep close company with voyagers and Indians. As a fur trader, he sacrificed his health while revolutionizing the Canadian trade system. During his 1789 and 1793 expeditions, he explored Canada to the Pacific and to the Arctic Ocean. One river, a mountain range, and a place in western Canada bear his name. Photographs, engravings, and reproductions enhance the text. Chronology, Further Reading, and Index.

1416.   Yancey, Diane. **Life in the Elizabethan Theater**. San Diego, CA: Lucent, 1996. 112p. $16.95. ISBN 1-56006-343-2. (The Way People Live). 6-9

Yancey recreates the times of Shakespeare and Elizabeth I in this history. She quotes scholars and gives specific details such as how blood and livers from butcher shops were used as stage props. Such items enliven the subject and make it accessible. Bibliography, Chronology, Further Reading, and Index.

1417.   Yarbro, Chelsea Quinn. **Floating Illusions**. New York: HarperCollins, 1986. 215p. $12.95. ISBN 0-06-026643-0. 6-8

While Millicent, fourteen, crosses the Atlantic on an ocean liner in 1910, several people are murdered. Among the friends she makes during her investigation are a magician, a militant feminist, and Anton, a noble. When the magician's life is threatened, he can no longer be a suspect, and Millicent identifies the criminal.

1418.   Yates, Sarah. **Alberta**. Minneapolis, MN: Lerner, 1995. 76p. $14.21. ISBN 0-8225-2763-4. 3-6

Although not technically a history book, over half the text reveals the history of this Canadian province. Charts, maps, photographs, and prints illustrate the individuality of this area, whose first inhabitants probably came across the land bridge from Asia at least 10,000 years ago. These aboriginals recorded their lives by drawing picture on cliffs and other stone surfaces in places like Writing-on-Stone Provincial Park. Among the famous Albertans briefly described are Crowfoot (1830?-1890) and Red Crow (1830?-1900). Fast Facts, Glossary, Pronunciation Guide, and Index.

1419.   Yolen, Jane. **The Ballad of the Pirate Queens**. David Shannon, illustrator. San Diego, CA: Harcourt Brace, 1995. Unpaged. $15. ISBN 0-15-200710-5. 3-6

This story, in ballad form, tells about two famous pirate queens, Anne and Mary, who try to save their ship in 1720 when the governor's men climb aboard in Port Maria Bay; their pirate husbands and other crew members stay below drinking and gambling. The women stand trial along with the men, but they are set free because they are pregnant. The men hang on the gallows. Author's Note. *Bulletin Blue Ribbon Book, IRA Children's Choices,* and *American Library Association Notable Books for Children.*

1420.   Yolen, Jane H. **The Seeing Stick**. Remy Charlip and Demetra Maraslis, illustrators. New York: HarperCollins, 1977. 32p. $14.89. ISBN 0-690-00596-2. K-3

The only child of the Emperor in fifteenth-century Peking, Hwei Ming is blind. Everyone tries to help her, but no one can earn the reward her father offers for curing her. An old man with a stick tells her stories and lets her feel the carvings that he makes on the stick so that she "sees" the characters. As she begins to feel the faces of those around her, she "sees" each one of them for the first time. The old man, however, refuses the Emperor's monetary reward because of his pleasure in helping Hwei Ming.

1421.   Yount, Lisa. **Antoni Van Leeuwenhoek: First to See Microscopic Life**. Springfield, NJ: Enslow, 1996. 128p. $18.95. ISBN 0-89490-680-1. (Great Minds of Science). 4-8

Antoni Van Leeuwenhoek (1632-1723) lacked formal scientific training, but his interest in a variety of things led him from his profession as a cloth merchant to making his own microscopes. When he first saw the lice living on his leg multiply via the microscope, he was rather disturbed. Other aspects of his life appear in the text along with some diagrams and illustrations. Photographs, Further Reading, Glossary, Notes, and Index.

1422.   Yount, Lisa. **Louis Pasteur**. San Diego, CA: Lucent, 1994. 96p. $16.95. ISBN 1-56006-051-4. (The Importance of). 5-8

Louis Pasteur (1822-1895) stressed the importance of testing and experimentation in his science laboratory and devoted much of his time to the needs of farmers and factory owners. His work saved money for wine, beer, and vinegar makers as well as silkworm, chicken, sheep, and cattle raisers. He wanted to control living beings so that they could protect or help human beings. He was especially loyal to France, and his research was also an attempt to help his country. He was the first to realize that microorganisms could cause disease as well as cure it. He improved public health, made surgery safer, and prevented many deaths in war. People who remembered Pasteur after his death noted his kindness, his absorption in his thoughts, and his clear love for people. Photographs, Notes, For Further Reading, Works Consulted, and Index.

1423.   Yount, Lisa. **William Harvey: Discoverer of How Blood Circulates**. Springfield, NJ: Enslow, 1994. 128p. $17.95. ISBN 0-89490-481-7. (Great Minds of Science). 4-8

William Harvey (1578-1657) was the first of seven sons born in his Folkestone, England, family. After attending Cambridge, he went to Padua, Italy, for advanced medical training. He heard Fabricius, his anatomy teacher, talk about little flaps or doors on the blood vessels, and he remembered this later as he was trying to understand how blood moved through the body. In 1628, he published his book on the movement of the heart and the blood. During his life, he supported King Charles; when Cromwell defeated the king, Harvey lost everything, but he kept working on his ideas. Afterword: A New Kind of Science, Activities, Chronology, Notes, Glossary, and Index.

1424.   Yue, Charlotte, and David Yue. **Christopher Columbus: How He Did It**. David Yue, illustrator. Boston: Houghton Mifflin, 1992. 136p. $13.95. ISBN 0-395-52100-9. 5-8

The details in text and drawings carefully describe the ships that Columbus took with him on his voyage in 1492 and what happened aboard in the tiny living quarters. Descriptions of the people, the tools, the armor, and the strong nautical skills of Columbus give answers not found in other books. Illustrations, charts, maps, and drawings augment the text. Bibliography and Index.

1425. Zei, Alki. **Petros' War**. Edward Fenton, translator. New York: Dutton, 1972. 236p. $8.95. ISBN 0-525-36962-7. 4-9

After Greece declares war on Italy in 1940, Petros, age nine, sees his life change. Previously only interested in turtles, he begins to write slogans on Athenian walls about the lack of food. Then he becomes a member of the underground resistance fighting against the Italians and the Germans. Everyone in the family joins the resistance, and they carry messages, hide people, and distribute information. His uncle fights in the mountains and communicates with the family via British Broadcasting radio. *Mildred L. Batchelder Award.*

1426. Zei, Alki. **The Sound of Dragon's Feet**. Edward Fenton, translator. New York: Dutton, 1979. 113p. $8.50. ISBN 0-525-39712-4. 4-9

The daughter of a Russian physician in 1894, Sasha wants to know how one can hear dragon feet, and states her admiration for lion tamers. She asks her new tutor, a man who has served in prison for trying to gain more rights for workers, and he tells her that courage is more than sticking one's head into the mouth of a lion. He says that people have to jeopardize their own lives for others before they can be considered brave. *Mildred L. Batchelder Award.*

1427. Zei, Alki. **Wildcat Under Glass**. Edward Fenton, translator. New York: Henry Holt, 1968. 177p. $4.50. ISBN 0-03-068005-0. 5-9

Melia and her older sister, Myrto, see that the adults in their Greek home in 1936 have become more thoughtful and are having quiet discussions from which the children are excluded. Then their cousin, Niko, comes to the island where they have a summer home and hides in a deserted windmill. Spanish Fascist spies—"Black Shirts"—come looking for him, imprison a friend's father, and burn their grandfather's books. In Athens, a teacher asks Myrto to spy on her family as a leader of the Youth Organization. Such events show them that their situation is much more serious than they had thought. *Mildred L. Batchelder Award.*

1428. Zeifert, Harriet. **A New Coat for Anna**. Anita Lobel, illustrator. 1986. New York: Knopf, 1988. 30p. $5.99pa. ISBN 0-394-89861-3pa. K-2

After World War II, when Anna's coat becomes too small, her mother has no money to buy her a new one. Her mother begins to trade her heirlooms, including a necklace, a gold watch, and a lamp. One item buys wool; another item gets it spun into yarn. Then the yarn becomes cloth, and finally it is a lovely red coat. *American Library Association Notable Books for Children.*

1429.   **Adventure Canada**. CD-ROM. System requirements: IBM or compatible PC, 486/33 MHz or higher CPU, 8 MB RAM, Microsoft Windows 3.1 or later, CD-ROM drive, sound card, mouse, SVGA 256-color display, loudspeakers or headphones. Macintosh: 6 MB RAM, System 7.0, 13-inch monitor (256 colors), CD-ROM drive. Richmond, British Columbia, Canada: Virtual Reality Systems, 1994. $69.95. 5-12

This CD-ROM provides an overview of Canada's history, geography, and daily life. The program has three levels: national, provincial, and natural region. Slides, video, and maps give the information about each level.

1430.   **Air and Space Smithsonian Dreams of Flight**. CD-ROM. System requirements: IBM or compatible PC, 486/25 MHz or higher CPU, 4 MB RAM (8 MB recommended), Microsoft Windows 3.1 or later, CD-ROM drive, sound card, mouse, SVGA 256-color display, loudspeakers or headphones. Portland, OR: Creative Multimedia, 1995. $29.95. 5 up

The four areas to explore in this CD-ROM are "Aviation Pioneers," "Flying Machines," "Milestones," and "Culture." Each section includes multimedia resources, photographs, audio, personal interviews, and aerodynamic demonstrations. It includes the history of flight.

1431.   This number is not used.

1432.   **Art & Music: Impressionism**. CD-ROM. System requirements: IBM or compatible PC, 386/20 MHz or higher CPU, 4 MB RAM (8 MB recommended), Microsoft Windows 3.1 or later, CD-ROM drive, sound card, mouse, SVGA 256-color display, loudspeakers or headphones. Macintosh: 6 to 8 MB RAM, System 7.0, 13-inch monitor (256 colors), CD-ROM drive. Minneapolis, MN: Gareth Stevens, 1995. $80. 6 up

The modes available to study the paintings and music of the Impressionist period are the Feature Presentation, Text, View, Index, Question, and Quiz. The information focuses on the artists' use of light and color and how the composers worked to create similar effects with instrumentation. Attitudes toward nature, Oriental art, and traditional forms become clear.

1433.   **Art & Music: Romanticism**. CD-ROM. System requirements: IBM or compatible PC, 386/20 MHz or higher CPU, 4 MB RAM (8 MB recommended), Microsoft Windows 3.1 or later, CD-ROM drive, sound card, mouse, SVGA 256-color display, loudspeakers or headphones. Macintosh: 6 to 8 MB RAM, System 7.0, 13-inch monitor (256 colors), CD-ROM drive. Minneapolis, MN: Gareth Stevens, 1995. $80. 6 up

The modes available to study the paintings and music of the Romantic Period are the Feature Presentation, Text, View, Index, Question, and Quiz. Artists include Delacroix and music focuses on such works as Berlioz's *Requiem*.

1434.   **Art & Music: Surrealism**. CD-ROM. System requirements: IBM or compatible PC, 386/20 MHz or higher CPU, 4 MB RAM (8 MB recommended), Microsoft Windows 3.1 or later, CD-ROM drive, sound card, mouse, SVGA 256-color display, loudspeakers or headphones. Macintosh: 6 to 8 MB RAM, System 7.0, 13-inch monitor (256 colors), CD-ROM drive. Minneapolis, MN: Gareth Stevens, 1995. $80. 6 up

The modes available to study the paintings and music of the surrealist period are the Feature Presentation, Text, View, Index, Question, and Quiz. Freud, Einstein, the French Symbolists, Cubists, and Dadaists show their influence on the music and art of the 1920s.

1435.   **Art & Music: The Baroque**. CD-ROM. System requirements: IBM or compatible PC, 386/20 MHz or higher CPU, 4 MB RAM (8 MB recommended), Microsoft Windows 3.1 or later, CD-ROM drive, sound card, mouse, SVGA 256-color display, loudspeakers or headphones. Macintosh: 6 to 8 MB RAM, System 7.0, 13-inch monitor (256 colors), CD-ROM drive. Minneapolis, MN: Gareth Stevens, 1995. $80. 6 up

The modes available to study the paintings and music of the Baroque period are the Feature Presentation, Text, View, Index, Question, and Quiz. Artists range from Caravaggio to Rembrandt and the music from Frescobaldi to Handel; also included is the music and drama of opera.

1436. **Art & Music: The Eighteenth Century**. CD-ROM. System requirements: IBM or compatible PC, 386/20 MHz or higher CPU, 4 MB RAM (8 MB recommended), Microsoft Windows 3.1 or later, CD-ROM drive, sound card, mouse, SVGA 256-color display, loudspeakers or headphones. Macintosh: 6 to 8 MB RAM, System 7.0, 13-inch monitor (256 colors), CD-ROM drive. Minneapolis, MN: Gareth Stevens, 1995. $80. 6 up

The modes available to study the paintings and music of the eighteenth century are the Feature Presentation, Text, View, Index, Question, and Quiz. Developments in painting and sculpture parallel music's changes to comic opera and the Viennese classical style.

1437. **Art & Music: The Medieval Era**. CD-ROM. System requirements: IBM or compatible PC, 386/20 MHz or higher CPU, 4 MB RAM (8 MB recommended), Microsoft Windows 3.1 or later, CD-ROM drive, sound card, mouse, SVGA 256-color display, loudspeakers or headphones. Macintosh: 6 to 8 MB RAM, System 7.0, 13-inch monitor (256 colors), CD-ROM drive. Minneapolis, MN: Gareth Stevens, 1995. $80. 6 up

The modes available to study the evolution of art in the medieval period are the Feature Presentation, Text, View, Index, Question, and Quiz. Manuscript illumination, the cathedral, and the secularization of music and literature are the main topics of discussion.

1438. **Art & Music: The Renaissance**. CD-ROM. System requirements: IBM or compatible PC, 386/20 MHz or higher CPU, 4 MB RAM (8 MB recommended), Microsoft Windows 3.1 or later, CD-ROM drive, sound card, mouse, SVGA 256-color display, loudspeakers or headphones. Macintosh: 6 to 8 MB RAM, System 7.0, 13-inch monitor (256 colors), CD-ROM drive. Minneapolis, MN: Gareth Stevens, 1995. $80. 6 up

The modes available to study the paintings and music of the Renaissance are the Feature Presentation, Text, View, Index, Question, and Quiz. Humanistic philosophy led Renaissance artists and composers to develop new forms and techniques, including oil painting and four-part polyphony.

1439. **Art & Music: The Twentieth Century**. CD-ROM. System requirements: IBM or compatible PC, 386/20 MHz or higher CPU, 4 MB RAM (8 MB recommended), Microsoft Windows 3.1 or later, CD-ROM drive, sound card, mouse, SVGA 256-color display, loudspeakers or headphones. Macintosh: 6 to 8 MB RAM, System 7.0, 13-inch monitor (256 colors), CD-ROM drive. Minneapolis, MN: Gareth Stevens, 1995. $80. 6 up

The modes available to study the paintings and music of the twentieth century are the Feature Presentation, Text, View, Index, Question, and Quiz. Artists covered are Matisse, Picasso, Braque, Kandinsky, and Klee, and the musicians included are Schoenberg, Berg, and Webern.

1440. **Canadian Treasures**. CD-ROM. System requirements: IBM or compatible PC (MPC), 486/33 MHz or higher CPU, 8 MB RAM, Microsoft Windows 3.1 or later, CD-ROM drive, sound card, mouse, SVGA 256-color display, loudspeakers or headphones. Macintosh: 6 MB RAM, System 7.0, 13-inch monitor (256 colors), CD-ROM drive. Seattle, WA: VR Dida Tech, 1997. $49.95. 4-8

Material from the National Archives of Canada fills the five sections of the program, "Making a Nation," "Discovery," "Portraits," "Nation's Capitol," and "Archive Link." Each section contains three topics. The information covers Canada's history, its people, and its traditions.

1441. **Castle Explorer**. CD-ROM. System requirements: IBM or compatible PC, 486/33 MHz or higher CPU, 8 MB RAM, Microsoft Windows 3.1 or later, CD-ROM drive, sound card, mouse, SVGA 256-color display, loudspeakers or headphones. Macintosh: 6 MB RAM, System 7.0, 13-inch monitor (256 colors), CD-ROM drive. New York: DK Multimedia, 1996. $29.95. 5-12

Students become either a page or a spy as they enter a fourteenth-century manor and move around the castle in cross-sections. They see the various rooms from the garrison to the master's quarters and encounter both visitors and workers during their study of medieval life.

1442. **Daring to Fly! From Icarus to the Red Baron**. CD-ROM. System requirements: IBM or compatible PC, 386SX or higher CPU, 4 MB RAM, Microsoft Windows 3.1 or later, CD-ROM drive, sound card, mouse, SVGA 256-color display, loudspeakers or headphones. (Macintosh version available.) Sausalito, CA: Arnowitz Studios, 1994. $59.95. 6-12

In the main menu of this CD-ROM, eight topic icons lead to exhibits such as "Science of Flight," "Lighter than Air," "Wings of War," and "Women Aloft." The disc presents the history of flight from the dreams of myths through the post-World War I era of aviation.

1443. **Exploring Ancient Cities**. CD-ROM. System requirements: IBM or compatible PC, 486/33 MHz or higher CPU, 8 MB RAM, Microsoft Windows 3.1 or later, CD-ROM drive, sound card, mouse, SVGA 256-color display, loudspeakers or headphones. Macintosh: 6 MB RAM, System 7.0, 13-inch monitor (256 colors), CD-ROM drive. San Francisco: Sumeria, 1994. $59.95. 6-12

An overview of the art, culture, and history of Crete, Petra, Pompeii, and Teotihuacán. This CD-ROM's content comes from material in *Scientific American* from 1967 to 1985. A timeline from 3000 B.C. to A.D. 1000, interactive maps, an index of slide shows, and sections on each of the four cities help users to find information.

1444. **Exploring the Titanic**. CD-ROM. System requirements: Macintosh LC or better, 4 MB RAM, System 7.0, color monitor (256 colors minimum), hard drive with 2.5 MB free, CD-ROM drive. New York: Scholastic, 1994. $149. 4-8

This CD-ROM is the interactive version of Robert D. Ballard's book, which details the sinking of the *Titanic* in 1912 and its recovery in 1985 by the submarine *Alvin*. A timeline relates the event to other happenings in the world; still other avenues examine the ship, the technology used to locate it, and an exploration of the wreck itself. Twenty-nine synthesized voices give information. Pages from the book are printable, as are text and notes.

1445. **Eyewitness Encyclopedia of Science**. CD-ROM. System requirements: Macintosh or IBM or compatible PC, 386/33 MHz or higher CPU, Windows 3.1 or higher, 4 MB RAM, CD-ROM drive, sound card, mouse, SVGA 256-color display, loudspeakers or headphones. New York: Dorling Kindersley, 1994. $79.95. 5-8

Although the CD-ROM covers much more, it includes a Who's Who of scientists, their contributions, and information about their lives.

1446. **Great Artists**. CD-ROM. System requirements: MS-DOS/MPC, 386/12 MHz or higher CPU, 4 MB RAM, Windows 3.1 or higher, hard drive with 4 MB free, CD-ROM drive, sound card, mouse, SVGA 256-color monitor (minimum), loudspeakers or headphones. Chatsworth, CA: Cambrix Publishing, 1995. $59.95. 6-12

To introduce forty major European artists, the *Great Artists* uses paintings housed in the National Gallery of London. Six sections of interactive features—Artists, Paintings, Topics, Art Atlas, Timeline, and a Workshop—present biographies of the artists, analyses of segments of the paintings, and an overview of life at the time. Male artists included are Botticelli, Campin, Canaletto, Caravaggio, Cézanne, Chardin, Claude, Constable, David, Dégas, Duccio, van Dyck, van Eyck, Gainsborough, van Gogh, Goya, Hals, Hogarth, Holbein, Ingrés, Leonardo, Monet, Piero, Poussin, Raphael, Rembrandt, Renoir, Rousseau, Rubens, Seurat, Stubbs, Tintoretto, Titian, Turner, Uccello, Velazquez, Vermeer, Wright; females are Judith Leyster (Dutch c. 1630) and Berthe Morisot (French c. 1880).

1447. **History Through Art: Ancient Greece**. CD-ROM. System requirements: IBM or compatible PC, 386/20 MHz or higher CPU, 4 MB RAM (8 MB recommended), Microsoft Windows 3.1 or later, CD-ROM drive, sound card, mouse, SVGA 256-color display, loudspeakers or headphones. Macintosh: 6 to 8 MB RAM, System 7.0, 13-inch monitor (256 colors), CD-ROM drive. Minneapolis, MN: Gareth Stevens, 1995. $75. 6 up

The modes available to study the art of Greek antiquity are the Feature Presentation, Text, View, Index, Question, and Quiz. The humanistic spirit appears in the sculpture and architecture developed during this period, when religion, government, social life, and art were interdependent.

1448. **History Through Art: Baroque**. CD-ROM. System requirements: IBM or compatible PC, 386/20 MHz or higher CPU, 4 MB RAM (8 MB recommended), Microsoft Windows 3.1 or later, CD-ROM drive, sound card, mouse, SVGA 256-color display, loudspeakers or headphones. Macintosh: 6 to 8 MB RAM, System 7.0, 13-inch monitor (256 colors), CD-ROM drive. Minneapolis, MN: Gareth Stevens, 1995. $75. 6 up

The modes available to study the art of the Baroque period are the Feature Presentation, Text, View, Index, Question, and Quiz. The famous sculptors, painters, architects, and musicians of the Baroque show the turmoil of the late sixteenth and seventeenth centuries.

1449. **History Through Art: Pre-Modern Era**. CD-ROM. System requirements: IBM or compatible PC, 386/20 MHz or higher CPU, 4 MB RAM (8 MB recommended), Microsoft Windows 3.1 or later, CD-ROM drive, sound card, mouse, SVGA 256-color display, loudspeakers or headphones. Macintosh: 6 to 8 MB RAM, System 7.0, 13-inch monitor (256 colors), CD-ROM drive. Minneapolis, MN: Gareth Stevens, 1995. $75. 6 up

The modes available to study the art of the late nineteenth century are the Feature Presentation, Text, View, Index, Question, and Quiz. The emergence of Realism and then Impressionism show how artists began to change their views of life in the nineteenth century.

1450. **History Through Art: Renaissance**. CD-ROM. System requirements: IBM or compatible PC, 386/20 MHz or higher CPU, 4 MB RAM (8 MB recommended), Microsoft Windows 3.1 or later, CD-ROM drive, sound card, mouse, SVGA 256-color display, loudspeakers or headphones. Macintosh: 6 to 8 MB RAM, System 7.0, 13-inch monitor (256 colors), CD-ROM drive. Minneapolis, MN: Gareth Stevens, 1995. $75. 6 up

The modes available to study the art of the Renaissance are the Feature Presentation, Text, View, Index, Question, and Quiz. Over fifty Renaissance artists and their studies of nature, anatomy, medicine, and the sciences appear in this CD-ROM. What they created represented their values and beliefs and influenced those of contemporary times.

1451. **History Through Art: 20th Century**. CD-ROM. System requirements: IBM or compatible PC, 386/20 MHz or higher CPU, 4 MB RAM (8 MB recommended), Microsoft Windows 3.1 or later, CD-ROM drive, sound card, mouse, SVGA 256-color display, loudspeakers or headphones. Macintosh: 6 to 8 MB RAM, System 7.0, 13-inch monitor (256 colors), CD-ROM drive. Minneapolis, MN: Gareth Stevens, 1995. $75. 6 up

The modes available to study the art of the twentieth century are the Feature Presentation, Text, View, Index, Question, and Quiz. Urbanization changed artists' views in the twentieth century, and the development of photography reflects these changes.

1452. **Jerusalem: Interactive Pilgrimage to the Holy City**. CD-ROM. System requirements: IBM or compatible PC, 486/33 MHz or higher CPU, 4 MB RAM, Microsoft Windows 3.1 or later, CD-ROM drive, sound card, mouse, SVGA 256-color display, loudspeakers or headphones. Macintosh: 4 MB RAM, System 7.0, 13-inch monitor (256 colors), CD-ROM drive. New York: Simon & Schuster Interactive, 1996. $39.95. 6 up

Three thousand years of history, from Herod's time to the present, fill this look at Jerusalem. Maps, photographs, and video footage augment the thorough information on the disc.

1453. **Le Louvre: The Palace & Its Paintings**. CD-ROM. System requirements: IBM or compatible PC, 486/33 MHz or higher CPU, 8 MB RAM, Microsoft Windows 3.1 or later, CD-ROM drive, sound card, mouse, SVGA 256-color display, loudspeakers or headphones. Macintosh: 6 MB RAM, System 7.0, 13-inch monitor (256 colors), CD-ROM drive. New York: BMG Entertainment/Montparnasse Multimedia, 1995. $49.95. 6 up

This tour of the Louvre discusses 100 paintings from eight centuries of art history. Two hours of narration and twenty minutes of music accompany the artworks, which are accessed by title, artist, or time period.

1454. **Maya Quest**. CD-ROM. System requirements: IBM or compatible PC, 486/33 MHz or higher CPU, 8 MB RAM, Microsoft Windows 3.1 or later, CD-ROM drive, sound card, mouse, SVGA 256-color display, loudspeakers or headphones. Macintosh: 6 MB RAM, System 7.0, 13-inch monitor (256 colors), CD-ROM drive. Minneapolis, MN: MECC, 1995. $79. 6 up

Three-dimensional tours by bicycle help to take the viewer into the Mayan historical sites in Central America. Two games access artifacts and historical information; the Multimedia Resource Tool contains pictures, text, music, and sounds.

1455. **One Tribe**. CD-ROM. System requirements: Macintosh or MS-DOS/MPC, 486/33 MHz or higher CPU, 4 MB RAM, Windows 3.1 or higher, CD-ROM drive, sound card, mouse, SVGA 256-color display (minimum), loudspeakers or headphones. Los Angeles: Virgin Sound and Vision, 1994. $24. 6-12

The video explores diversity among humans. Twenty-five themed slide shows cover topics such as faces, rituals, and animals; each show includes historical information about the evolution of humans in the areas of North America, Latin America, Europe, Asia, Australia, Africa, and the Arctic/Antarctic.

1456. **Stowaway! Stephen Biesty's Incredible Cross-Sections**. CD-ROM. System requirements: IBM or compatible PC, 386SX or higher CPU, 4 MB RAM, CD-ROM drive, sound card, mouse, SVGA 256-color display, loudspeakers or headphones. New York: Dorling Kindersley, 1994. $59.95. 6-12

By clicking the mouse on any part of an eighteenth-century warship, or on one of its crew members, one gets information about the ship. After learning many details about life on the ship, the viewer eventually finds the stowaway.

1457. **Teach Your Kids World History**. CD-ROM. System requirements: IBM or compatible PC, 386SX or higher CPU, 4 MB RAM, CD-ROM drive, sound card, mouse, SVGA 256-color display, loudspeakers or headphones. New York: Chelsea House, 1995. $79.95. 4-12

This CD-ROM, the same as the one entitled *Multimedia World History*, provides information about books written throughout history by author or title. Other access points include Time Periods, Region, Themes, and the history of each day of the year, as well as other levels such as wars, technology, exploration, and maps. The disc provides slides and video clips of various events and keeps a record of all topics accessed during a session. An accompanying text lists the historical figures included and suggests ways to find information on topics of interest.

1458. **Total History**. 3 CD-ROMs. System requirements: IBM or compatible PC, 386SX or higher CPU, 4 MB RAM, CD-ROM drive, sound card, mouse, SVGA 256-color display, loudspeakers or headphones. New York: Bureau of Electronic Publishing-Chelsea House, 1995. $99.95. 4-12

Multimedia U.S. History, Multimedia World History (same as *Teach Your Kids World History*), and *Multimedia World Factbook,* all available separately, constitute this package. *World History* provides information about books written throughout history by author or title; other access points include Time Periods, Region, Themes, and a history of each day of the year, as well as other levels such as wars, technology, exploration, and maps. *U.S. History* presents American people, American places, the armed forces, exploring the continent, general history, science and technology, government, and wars and conflicts. Both programs provide slides and video clips. The *World Factbook* allows access to facts in several ways, such as searching topics, timelines, and glossaries. All keep a history of topics consulted during a session.

1459. **The Way Things Work**. CD-ROM. System requirements: IBM or compatible PC, 386SX or higher CPU, 4 MB RAM, Microsoft Windows 3.1 or later, CD-ROM drive, sound card, mouse, SVGA 256-color display, loudspeakers or headphones. (Macintosh version available.) New York: Dorling Kindersley, 1994. $79.95. 6-12

A history timeline, brief biographies of inventors, specifications for the inventions, and animations showing the scientific principles underlying the inventions make this CD-ROM especially informative.

Videotapes: An Annotated Bibliography

1460. Abubakari: The Explorer King of Mali. Videocassette. Color. 15 min. Jenison, MI: All Media, 1993. $99. 4-8

Abubakari II, king of Mali, sent explorers across the Atlantic almost two centuries before Columbus. He ruled an advanced society in which universities functioned and professions included lawyers, doctors, explorers, and philosophers.

1461. Africa. 4 Videocassettes. Color. 17-22 min. Chicago: Encyclopaedia Britannica, 1993. $99. 5-12

Four programs present Africa and its peoples interacting and coping with the environment. The individual titles are *Central and Eastern Regions, Northern Region, Southern Region,* and *Western Region.*

1462. Africa: History and Culture. Videocassette. Color. 19 min. Irwindale, CA: Barr Media, 1990. $100. (Africa). 6-9

With views of cave drawings and live-action shots, the video provides an overview of Africa's ancient kingdoms and cultural heritage. The narrator comments that scientists believe that the human race originated in the Olduvai Gorge, where they have found 3-million-year-old fossils. Additional commentary includes information about Africa's geographical exploration and colonization.

1463. Africa: Land and People. Videocassette. Color. 24 min. Irwindale, CA: Barr Media, 1990. $100. (Africa). 6-9

Covering Africa in general, this video presents an introduction to the physical features, natural resources, education, religions, agriculture, languages, industries, climate, and social customs.

1464. Albert Einstein: The Education of a Genius. Videocassette. Color. 13 min. Princeton, NJ: Films for the Humanities and Sciences, 1989. $29.95. (Against the Odds). 4 up

Documentary footage, interviews, and animation help present this profile of the genius Albert Einstein (1879-1955).

1465. Ancient Egypt: The Gift of the Nile (3000 BC-30 BC). Videocassette. Color. 28 min. Chariot Productions. Niles, IL: United Learning, 1997. $125. 5-8

The video examines the Egyptians and their creation of a written language, acceptance of government under one ruler, and worship of a specific pantheon of gods.

1466. Ancient Rome. Videocassette. Color. 14.5 min. Chicago: Encyclopedia Britannica, 1993. $99. ISBN 0-8347-9988-X. 6-12

By beginning with pictures of modern Rome and moving to a model of the ancient city, the video recreates daily life in Rome around A.D. 300. The importance of places such as the Palatine, the Forum, the public baths, the Capitol, and the amphitheaters becomes apparent.

1467. The Arab World. Videocassette. Color. 25 min. Madison, WI: Knowledge Unlimited, 1995. $59.95. 5 up

Anwar Sadat said that the Arabs were a people trying to use their ancient traditions as a basis for constructing a modern civilization. The video covers early civilization and the imperialism that fired the Arab desire for independence. It shows the wide variety among Arab peoples; sometimes their one common trait is their language. It looks at the Sumerian civilization, religions, and economic conflicts with the West and among the Arabs themselves.

1468. Art and Architecture of Precolumbian Mexico. Videocassette. Color. 50 min. Boulder, CO: Alarion Press, 1994. $124. (History Through Art and Architecture). 5 up

Through art and architecture, the history of Precolumbian Mexico, from 1500 B.C. to A.D. 1500, is revealed. The video includes two segments: "The Jaguar and the Feathered Serpent" examines the Olmec, Zapotec, and Teotihuacán cultures; and "War and Human Sacrifice" looks at the Mixtecs, Toltecs, and Aztecs.

1469. **The Art and Architecture of the Maya**. Videocassette. Color. 53 min. Boulder, CO: Alarion Press, 1995. $124. 5 up

The art and architecture of the Mayan civilization help to reveal Mayan history. Divided into two parts, the video looks first at the "Kings, Glyphs, Temples, and Ballcourts" and then at "The Rise and Mysterious Decline of the Maya Kingdoms." Among the topics are the right to the throne, games, religious sacrifices, gods, calendars, and myths.

1470. **The Baltic States: Finding Independence**. Videocassette. Color. 20.5 min. InterFilm Sweden. Irwindale, CA: Barr Media, 1991. $90. 4-9

The video acquaints viewers with the history and problems facing the Baltic peoples in Estonia, Latvia, and Lithuania. An Estonian family demonstrates the lack of products available since the country escaped Communist rule in 1991, but the video is dated; products are now readily available to anyone who has the money.

1471. **Barefoot Gen**. Videocassette. Color. 80 min. Madhouse Studios. Dist. San Rafael, CA: Tara Releasing, 1995. $99.95. 6 up

This animation, set in Hiroshima, Japan, during 1945, shows Gen surviving the day-to-day struggles of wartime with his family. After the horrifying atomic bomb explosion, he tries to rebuild his life according to his father's antiwar teachings.

1472. **The Beginning Is in the End**. Videocassette. Color. 30 min. Ontario, Canada: TVOntario, 1990. $499 series; $99 ea. (Ancient Civilizations). 6 up

Part of a series examining the origins of civilizations, the video investigates the human needs for food, security, and creativity. This video looks at the beginnings of civilization in China, India, Egypt, and Central America, by first focusing on Sumer, near the junction of the Tigris and Euphrates Rivers in Mesopotamia.

1473. **Branching Out: Tracing Your Jewish Roots**. Videocassette. Color. 30 min. Teaneck, NJ: Ergo Media, 1995. $39.95. 6 up

A Jewish genealogist, Arthur Kurzweil, goes to Ellis Island and other sites to explain how to trace Jewish roots.

1474. **The British Way of Life**. Videocassette. Color. 23 min. Chatsworth, CA: Aims Media, 1989. $395. 5 up

This overview of British history begins with the end of the Ice Age and continues through the Roman and Norman invasions, the Vikings, the Empire, the Industrial Revolution, and the World Wars and their aftermath. It also discusses the development of British democracy, beginning with the Magna Carta, which became the basis for American law.

1475. **Canada: People and Places**. Videocassette. Color. 20 min. N.C.S.U./Benchmark. Dist. Briarcliff Manor, NY: Benchmark, 1997. $395. 5-9

This video gives a geographical and historical overview of Canada and its provinces including background on the divisions between French- and English-speaking areas.

1476. **Canada's Maple Tree: The Story of the Country's Emblem**. Videocassette. Color. 30 min. Bellingham, WA: DEBEC Educational Video, 1995. $35. 5 up

Among the many topics, which include the process of making maple syrup and maple furniture building, is a look at Canadian settlement. The maple leaf first appeared on coinage; then, on July 1, 1867, when the confederation of Canada came into being, it became a part of the flag.

1477. **The Canadian Way of Life**. Videocassette. Color. 21 min. Century 21 Video. Chatsworth, CA: Aims Media, 1995. $99.95. 6 up

The video presents a broad overview of Canada, the world's second-largest country, with its rich natural resources and its desire to preserve its distinct national identity.

1478. **Cathedrals with a Project**. Videocassette. Color. 16 min. Cos Cob, CT: Double Diamond, 1993. $89. (Glory of the Middle Ages). 5-9

This video describes the structural elements of the cathedrals of Chartres, Bourges, and Notre Dame de Paris by defining terms and comparing the styles of Gothic, Romanesque, and High Gothic. It uses examples to show how to build a cathedral from folded paper.

1479. **Central America**. Videocassette. Color. 21 min. Chicago: Encyclopaedia Britannica, 1993. $99. 5-12

This video explores the history and political significance of Central America and the Panama Canal.

1480. **Central Americans**. Videocassette. Color. 30 min. Schlessinger Video. Dist. Bala Cynwyd, PA: Library Video, 1993. $39.95. (Multicultural Peoples of North America). 4-10

Based on the Chelsea House series called Peoples of North America, this video highlights Central American culture. It gives reasons for the immigration of Central Americans to America, explanations of customs and traditions, and a history of their transition; it also presents the important leaders from the culture. Historians and sociologists discuss these aspects, and a Central American family explains its cultural identity, shared memories, and reasons for immigration.

1481. **Charles Darwin: Species Evolution**. Videocassette. Color. 24 min. Irwindale, CA: Barr Media, 1989. $50. 4-7

This video is an animation of Charles Darwin and his theory of evolution with its concept of natural selection.

1482. **Child in Two Worlds**. Videocassette. Color. 60 min. AVA Productions. Dist. Teaneck, NJ: Ergo Media, 1995. $39.95. 6 up

Many European Jewish parents sent their children to hide in Christian foster homes during World War II. This video presents five Jewish war orphans who survived.

1483. **Children Remember the Holocaust**. Videocassette. Color. 46 min. SVE and Churchill Media. Dist. Chicago: Churchill Media, 1996. $150. 4-9

Excerpts from diaries and pictures of children who died or suffered during the Holocaust give a sense of immediacy to their situation. The documentary, narrated by Keanu Reeves, connects the history of that time with the present. *American Library Association Notable Children's Films and Videos.*

1484. **Children's Heroes from Christian History**. 3 Videocassettes. Color. 35 min. ea. Worcester, PA: Vision Video, 1997. $39.95 set. 1-4

Each of the videos contains stories of four heroes who have shown great valor. They include John Bunyan (1628-1688), David Livingstone (1813-1873), Mary "Mother" Jones (1830-1930), William Wilberforce (1759-1833); William Carey (1761-1834), Robert Raikes (1735-1811), Hans Egede (1686-1758), John Paton (d. 1684), Eric Liddell (1902-1945), Ludwing Nommensen (c. 1825), and Father Damien (1840-1889).

1485. **China: A History**. Videocassette. Color. 22 min. Irwindale, CA: Barr Media, 1988. $100. (China). 4 up

This video gives the history of China as it examines the dynasties, the Great Wall, and the contributions of China to the world.

1486. **China: From President Sun to Chairman Mao**. Videocassette. Color. 15 min. Signet Productions. Dist. Morris Plains, NJ: Lucerne Media, 1995. $195. (The Changing Face of Asia). 6-12

Sun Yat-sen became president of China in 1912, and the program follows Chinese history until Chairman Mao took over leadership of the country in 1949.

1487. **China: The Ancient Land**. Videocassette. Color. 15 min. Signet Productions. Dist. Morris Plains, NJ: Lucerne Media, 1995. $195. (The Changing Face of Asia). 6-12

This video traces the history of China from the Shang Dynasty, in 1766 B.C., to approximately A.D. 1912, when Sun Yat-sen became president of China.

1488. **China: The Fifth Millennium**. Videocassette. Color. 15 min. Signet Productions. Dist. Morris Plains, NJ: Lucerne Media, 1995. $195. (The Changing Face of Asia). 6-12

China after Mao has its own set of problems. This video addresses China and its situation.

1489. **China Festival Celebration of Ancient Traditions**. Videocassette. Color. 23 min. Arlington Heights, IL: J.M. Oriental Arts, 1997. 3-8

A celebration in Kaifeng, China, the capital of the Song dynasty, presents the ancient customs of the country.

1490. **Chinese Americans**. Videocassette. Color. 30 min. Schlessinger Video. Dist. Bala Cynwyd, PA: Library Video, 1993. $39.95. (Multicultural Peoples of North America). 4-10

Based on the Chelsea House series called Peoples of North America, this video highlights Chinese culture. It gives reasons for the Chinese immigration to America, explanations of customs and traditions, and a history of their transition; it also presents the important leaders from the culture. Historians and sociologists discuss these aspects, and a Chinese family explains its cultural identity, shared memories, and reasons for immigration.

1491. **Christmas**. Videocassette. Color. 30 min. Schlessinger Video. Dist. Bala Cynwyd, PA: Library Video, 1994. ISBN 1-57225-014-3. $395.40 set; $29.95 ea. (Holidays for Children Video). K-4

Children's artwork helps to introduce the history of this holiday, along with holiday symbols and customs. Going on-site to Bethlehem to the supposed birthplace of the Christ child shows the Christian basis for this celebration.

1492. **Christopher Columbus**. Videocassette. Color. 17 min. Los Angeles: Churchill, 1991. $205. 4-8
Through illustration and dramatization, the video presents Columbus's attempt to reach the New World—finding the money and the first voyage. It also addresses the discoveries he made, using actors to dramatize the situations.

1493. **The Columbian Way of Life**. Videocassette. Color. 24 min. Chatsworth, CA: Aims Media, 1993. $99.95. 5 up
In addition to information about modern Colombia, the video talks about Colombia's history and its relationship to the development of its government.

1494. **Diamonds in the Snow**. Videocassette. Color. 59 min. New York: Cinema Guild, 1994. $350. 6-12
Mira Reym Binford was one of only twelve Jewish children to survive the Nazi occupation of the Polish town of Bendzin; she did so by pretending to be a Christian. A factory owner helped some Jews by hiring them to work for him. Binford returned to the town to interview relatives of the families who supported her.

1495. **Egypt: Children of the Nile**. Videocassette. Color. 24 min. Irwindale, CA: Barr Media, 1994. $1,170 series, $395 ea. (Middle East). 4-6
In this overview of Egypt's influence on the world, the video traces the impact of hieroglyphics on the development of communication and investigates Egyptian architecture, which encompasses some of the wonders of the world. It also looks at modern-day Egypt, the poverty outside Cairo juxtaposed to with wealth inside, and how the people cope.

1496. **Egypt: The Nile River Kingdom**. Videocassette. Color. 20 min. Irwindale, CA: Barr Media, 1988. $75. 4 up
The video traces the history of Egypt from the time of the ancient pharaohs to today's modern cities.

1497. **The Enchanting Travels of Benjamin of Tudela**. Videocassette. Color. 9 min. Dist. Teaneck, NJ: Ergo Media, 1991. $24.95. 2 up
Around A.D. 1200, Benjamin of Tudela sailed from Tudela, Spain, to the Mediterranean countries and the Near East; he recorded his journeys in a "Book of Travels." He kept population and information records on Jews in the cities he visited, such as Barcelona, Rome, Constantinople, Baghdad, and Jerusalem.

1498. **The End Is the Beginning**. Videocassette. Color. 30 min. Ontario, Canada: TVOntario, 1990. $499 series; $99 ea. (Ancient Civilizations). 6 up
Part of a series examining the origins of civilizations, the video investigates the human needs for food, security, and creativity. This video looks at the reasons for the decline of civilizations and shows the cyclical movement of history, in which the ending of one is often the beginning of another civilization.

1499. **England's Historic Treasures**. 3 Videocassettes. Color. 60 min. ea. Tadpole Lane Productions. Dist. Bethesda, MD: Acorn Media, 1997. $59.85 set; $19.95 ea. 6 up
The three videos in this series, *Treasures of the Trust*, *The Spirit of England*, and *A Celebration of Old Roses*, present an overview of British history through its artifacts and ruins including King Arthur's castle, the former home of Winston Churchill, and a tribute to Old Roses.

1500. **Estevanico and the Seven Cities of Gold**. Videocassette. Color. 20 min. Jenison, MI: All Media, 1993. $99. 4-6
Estevanico was a slave who went with Andres Dorontes to Florida in the 1500s. He acted as a go-between to the Indians because they liked his flamboyant character and dress. In Texas, he met Indians who told him about cities of gold, and he later led an expedition to the city of Cibola, which he believed was one of the seven cities. Zuni Indians thought he was a spy, and they killed him, but he was the first non-Indian to go into New Mexico and Arizona.

1501. **Galileo**. Videocassette. Color. Warner-Nest Animation. Dist. Irving, TX: Nest Entertainment, 1997. $29.95. K-3
An animation presents Galileo (1564-1642) and discusses his decision not to renounce his beliefs when the Inquision was persecuting him and keeping him under house arrest.

1502. **Galileo: The Solar System**. Videocassette. Color. 24 min. Irwindale, CA: Barr Media, 1989. $50. 4-9
Galileo (1564-1642) was the first to use a telescope to study the stars, and his belief in Copernicus's theory that the earth revolved around the sun led the Inquisition leaders to punish him. The video features his discoveries and breakthroughs.

1503.   **The German Way of Life**. Videocassette. Color. 25 min. Chatsworth, CA: Aims Media, 1990. $99.95. 5 up

Natural landforms, invading neighbors, and nationalism have formed the German psyche. The video looks at the role of the German public during the two world wars, the effects of the wars, and the current attempt to reunite.

1504.   **Germany: From Partition to Reunification, 1945-1990**. Videocassette. Color. 22 min. Briarcliff Manor, NY: Benchmark Media, 1994. $395. (World Geography and History). 5-7

The video explains the reasons behind the separation of Germany into two countries following World War II. Explanations for the cold war, NATO, the Warsaw Pact, the Communist blockade of West Berlin in 1948, and the erection of the Berlin Wall clarify the difficulties that eventually led to the surprise fall of the Wall in 1989.

1505.   **Growing Up in Japan**. Videocassette. Color. 20 min. Evanston, IL: Journal, 1992. $275. 4-8

The video looks at the life of young people in Japan, from the extreme pressures of schooling to the dualization of western and eastern ways. By examining their religious roots in Shintoism and Buddhism and their values of politeness, respect, and recognition of beauty, the video helps to reveal modern Japanese culture. Part of the historical aspect is a journey to Hiroshima to see memorials and museums dedicated to the victims of the atomic bomb.

1506.   **Hiroshima Maiden**. Videocassette. Color. 58 min. Arnold Shapiro. Dist. Chicago: Public Media Video, 1990. $29.95. (Wonderworks Family Movie). 5 up

In this professionally acted video, Miyeko, a Japanese girl badly scarred by the bombing of Hiroshima in 1945, comes to Connecticut to live with a family while she has plastic surgery. The son, Johnny, is fearful of her, and neighbors think she can cause radiation sickness in others. She and Johnny have to talk face to face before he can understand her needs and respond to the misconceptions of his friends.

1507.   **Israel**. Videocassette. Color. 20 min. Irwindale, CA: Barr Media, 1994. $1,170 series; $395 ea. (Middle East). 4 up

Israel has distinct geographic regions from the coast of the Mediterranean to the Jordan River. The video visits Jerusalem and discusses the world's three largest religions, Judaism, Christianity, and Islam. The history of religious and ethnic tension underlies the explanation of Israel's world position.

1508.   **Japan: Japan Today**. Videocassette. Color. 15 min. Signet Productions. Dist. Morris Plains, NJ: Lucerne Media, 1995. $195. (The Changing Face of Asia). 6-12

The third in a series, this video explores Japan as it is today, after World War II.

1509.   **Japan: Nation Reborn**. Videocassette. Color. 15 min. Signet Productions. Dist. Morris Plains, NJ: Lucerne Media, 1995. $195. (The Changing Face of Asia). 6-12

The second in a series, this program looks at Japan when it opened to the West.

1510.   **Japan: The Sacred Islands**. Videocassette. Color. 15 min. Signet Productions. Dist. Morris Plains, NJ: Lucerne Media, 1995. $195. (The Changing Face of Asia). 6-12

This program, first in a series, gives the early history of Japan.

1511.   **The Life of Anne Frank**. Videocassette. Color. 25 min. Princeton, NJ: Films for the Humanities and Sciences, 1990. $49.95. 4-6

Using quotations from Anne Frank's diary, the video illustrates Frank's days in the attic room with pictures, photos from the Frank family album, and historical documentary footage. *Booklist, Voice of Youth Advocates,* and *Video Rating Guide for Librarians* recommendations; *Blue Ribbon, American Film and Video Festival;* and *Silver Medal, New York International Film and Video Festival.*

1512.   **Linnea in Monet's Garden**. Videocassette. Color. 30 min. New York: First Run/Icarus, 1994. $19.95. 5 up

This video helps viewers to understand Monet's work. Actual shots of Monet's garden today in differing lights, which are then blended into the oil painting, gives the sense of nature's importance to Monet and the other Impressionists. *Association for Library Service to Children Notable Film.*

1513.   **Look and Do: China Parts 1 and 2**. Videocassette. Color. 32 min. Boulder, CO: Alarion Press, 1997. $94. 2-4

Part 1, "Magic Animals and the Beginning of Civilization," presents Chinese history to the Tang Dynasty by introducing Buddhism, the historical beginnings of the Silk Road, the Great Wall of China, the tradition behind jade, and the game of polo. Part 2, "The Song Dynasty, Genghis Khan and Marco Polo in the Forbidden City," begins with the Song Dynasty and continues to the Qing Dynasty with commentary on silk, porcelain china, the Polos, and the Mongol invasion.

1514. **Marco Polo**. Videocassette. Color. 30 min. Warner-Nest Animation. Irving, TX: Nest Entertainment, 1997. $29.95. K-3

The animation presents Marco Polo's adventures while traveling in India and China during the thirteenth century.

1515. **Martin Luther: Beginning of the Reformation**. Videocassette. Color. 14.45 min. Chicago: Encyclopaedia Britannica, 1993. $99. ISBN 0-8347-9990-1. 6 up

Filmed on location in Germany, the program presents the main events in Martin Luther's life during the sixteenth century that led to his conflict with church doctrine. Pictures, letters, historical sketches, and shots of historical buildings and statues round out the information.

1516. **Martin Luther: Translating the Bible**. Videocassette. Color. 13.59 min. Chicago: Encyclopaedia Britannica, 1993. $99. ISBN 0-8347-9990-1. 6 up

After the Diet of Worms, Martin Luther took refuge in Wartburg, where he began to translate the Bible from Latin into German, the vernacular of the people. In the video, the second of two on Martin Luther, views of historical sketches, paintings, maps, and historical books, including Bibles, augment the production.

1517. **The Maya**. Videocassette. Color. 30 min. Schlessinger Video. Dist. Bala Cynwyd, PA: Library Video, 1993. $39.95. (Indians of North America). 4-10

This video tells the history and culture of the Maya, a civilization that reached its height around A.D. 300-900. It focuses on the unique history of the Maya, using photographs and film footage. It also discusses government, spiritual life, myths, and the role of women in that culture. The architecture and city planning, mathematics and calendar, and hieroglyphic writing system make the culture special.

1518. **The Mayans and Aztecs**. Videocassette. Color. 20 min. Chariot Productions. Dist. Niles, IL: United Learning, 1997. $99. 6-8

The video presents the history of the ancient civilizations of the Aztecs, who lived in Mexico before the Spanish explorers arrived, and Mayans who lived in the vicinity around 600.

1519. **Medieval Times: Life in the Middle Ages (A.D. 1000-1450)**. Videocassette. Color. 30 min. Niles, IL: United Learning, 1992. $136. 5-12

Historical reenactments and on-site filming at Penhow Castle in the British Isles help to illustrate life in the Middle Ages. It shows the lifestyles of the rich nobles, knights, soldiers, clergy, and serfs, and demonstrates how they interacted.

1520. **Medieval Women**. Videocassette. Color. 24 min. Chicago: International Film Bureau, 1989. $245. 6 up

This program shows the perception of women during the European Middle Ages and examines their daily lives.

1521. **Mexico: The Heritage**. Videocassette. Color. 20 min. Evanston, IL: Altschul Group, 1993. $275. 4-8

One of three in a series, this video divides the history of Mexico into three time periods: pre-Columbian, Spanish colonial (lasting three centuries), and political independence, which began in 1917. Then it covers the attitudes and directions that Mexico has taken as a nation.

1522. **Mexico: The People of the Sun**. Videocassette. Color. 18 min. Briarcliff Manor, NY: Benchmark Media, 1995. $395. (World Geography and History). 5-7

The video shows how the cultures in Mexico have intermingled and how this has affected the way people live.

1523. **Michael Arvaarluk Kusugak**. Videocassette. Color. 20 min. School Services of Canada. Dist. Old Greenwich, CT: Listening Library, 1995. $49.95. (Meet the Author/Illustrator). 2-6

An Inuit author, Kusugak incorporates traditional spirit creatures from the Inuit into his contemporary stories about the Arctic. He has lived in igloos and tents, and he writes about those timeless experiences.

1524. **Middle Ages School Kit**. 4 Videocassettes. Color. 29 min. ea. Alexandria, VA: PBS Video, 1989. $200. 5-10

David Macauley narrates these videos, which include animated productions of his books *Castle* and *Cathedral*. The live-action sequences show him visiting towers, spires, buttresses, roofs, and moats of castles in England and cathedrals in France. Extensive supportive material aids teachers.

1525. **Middle America: Mexico to Venezuela and the Caribbean Islands**. Videocassette. Color. 18 min. Briarcliff Manor, NY: Benchmark Media, 1995. $395. (World Geography and History). 5-7

The video demonstrates how physical geography affects the lives of people in Middle America, particularly as to how they make a living and the choices they have.

1526. **Middle East: History and Culture**. Videocassette. Color. 20 min. Irwindale, CA: Barr Media, 1994. $1,170 series; $395 ea. (Middle East). 4 up

From the Sumerians (who invented cuneiform writing) to the present, the Middle East encompasses an extraordinary history. The modern civilizations, including the Egyptians, Jews, Muslims, Romans, Persians, and Greeks, have close ties to the past. Warring tensions have oppressed various parts of the region for centuries, from the Romans to the oil trade, but the inhabitants of the area have made some attempts toward peace.

1527. **The Moon Woman's Sisters—Highland Guatemala Maya Weaving**. Videocassette. Color. 40 min. Thousand Oaks, CA: Conejo, 1993. $40. 6 up

A brief introduction to four pre-Columbian Maya sites leads to a demonstration of the ancient art of backstrap weaving. While weaving, women share their daily lives. *Honorable Mention, Columbus International Film & Video Festival* and *3rd Place, BVF.*

1528. **The Mystery of the Cave Paintings**. Videocassette. Color. 16.12 min. Morris Plains, NJ: Lucerne Media, 1996. $145. 3-8

This look at the French and Spanish caves where Ice Age artwork still exists reveals that a six-year-old found the cave in Spain and that teenagers found the Lescaux caves in France. Additionally, the computer graphics and examination of the way the paintings might have been done more than 30,000 years ago will interest young viewers.

1529. **Mystery of the Maya**. Videocassette. Color. 38 min. New York: National Film Board of Canada, 1996. $195. 6-9

The Maya lived in Southeast Mexico and South America, and this video discusses their lives through dramatizations and photographs of their ruins. Among their achievements were a system of mathematics, writing, and astronomical discoveries.

1530. **The Mystery of the Pyramids**. Videocassette. Color. 23 min. Irwindale, CA: Barr Media, 1990. $295. 4-9

The video examines several different explanations for the building of the pyramids around 4,000 years ago. It also visits the Pyramid of Cheops, examines likely methods of construction, and discusses mysteries associated with the pyramids through the centuries.

1531. **Nightmare: The Immigration of Joachim and Rachel**. Videocassette. Color. 24 min. Princeton, NJ: Films for the Humanities and Sciences, 1992. $34.95. 3-6

Two children must try to survive in the Warsaw ghetto after the Nazis take away their parents. They eventually reach America, but not before they have many moments of terror.

1532. **On the Town**. Videocassette. Color. 30 min. Ontario, Canada: TVOntario, 1990. $499 series; $99 ea. (Ancient Civilizations). 6 up

Part of a series examining the origins of civilizations, the video investigates the human needs for food, security, and creativity. This video looks at the cultural high points of civilizations, including art, literature, architecture, engineering, and technology.

1533. **Peru's Treasure Tombs**. Videocassette. Color. 11 min. Washington, DC: National Geographic, 1997. $49. 4-9

The Moche people lived in Peru 1,200 years before the Incas. They created adobe brick pyramids, ceramics and pottery, and gold and turquoise jewel. Looters have taken valuables from their tombs but a few items have been recovered.

1534. **Poland: A Proud Heritage**. Videocassette. Color. 55 min. Chicago: Clearvue, 1989. $30. (Video Visits). 6 up

By looking at several sites in Poland and discussing why they are considered worthy of visits, this video teaches about Poland's history. The video shows Warsaw; Cracow's Wawel Hill, the ancient seat of Polish kings; the Tatra mountains; Gdansk, the birthplace of Solidarity; and Auschwitz, now a memorial of the Holocaust.

1535. **Rendezvous Canada, 1606**. Videocassette. Color. 30 min. New York: National Film Board of Canada, 1989. $350. 5-10

Film from two living history museums presents life in Canada around 1606, when the French arrived to settle near the Indians already there. The oldest son of a Huron chief and the French governor of Acadia relate experiences through actors who speak either French, Huron, or Micmac, and give a sense of life at that time.

1536. **The Road to Wannsee: Eleven Million Sentenced to Death**. Videocassette. Color. 50 min. AVA Productions. Dist. Teaneck, NJ: Ergo Media, 1995. $39.95. 6 up
   The program traces Hitler's rise to political power, his political aims, and his obsession with eliminating the Jews.

1537. **The Roots of African Civilization**. Videocassette. Color. 25 min. Madison, WI: Knowledge Unlimited, 1996. $59.95. ISBN 1-55933-205-0. 5 up
   The civilization and history of ancient West Africa, as presented in this video, show the importance of the oral tradition, art objects, and the emergence of the slave trade in the precolonial era.

1538. **Safekeeping**. Videocassette. Color. 30 min. Ontario, Canada: TVOntario, 1990. $499 series; $99 ea. (Ancient Civilizations). 6 up
   Part of a series examining the origins of civilizations, the video investigates the human needs for food, security, and creativity. This video looks at the evolution of government from Athens into Sparta and to Republican Rome.

1539. **Shtetl**. Videocassette. Color. 23 min. New York: Cinema Guild, 1997. $99.95. ISBN 0-7815-0627-1. 6 up
   Folk artist Mayer Kirshenblatt bases his paintings on his childhood in a Polish *shtetl*.

1540. **Sight by Touch**. Videocassette. Color. 27 min. Conex. Dist. Falls Church, VA: Landmark Media, 1995. $195. 6 up
   Louis Braille (1809?-1852) developed a system of notation for the blind. At first his method was rejected, but it proved to be an effective way for the blind to interact with the printed word.

1541. **This Just In . . . Columbus Has Landed**. Videocassette. Color. 45 min. Creighton University & Mason Video. Dist. Englewood, CO: SelectVideo, 1991. $45. 6 up
   Costuming, news footage, and good sound contribute to the authenticity of this video network news show. Interviews with people who knew Columbus include his brother, a friar, King Ferdinand, Queen Isabella, one of his ship captains, and others. Animation and maps trace Columbus's voyage.

1542. **Tsiolkovski: The Space Age**. Videocassette. Color. 24 min. Irwindale, CA: Barr Media, 1989. $50. 4-9
   This animation explains how Konstantin Tsiolkovski (1857-1935) conducted the crucial research that led him to the invention of the rocket in 1929.

1543. **Turkey: Between Europe and Asia**. Videocassette. Color. 19 min. Camera Q. Dist. Irwindale, CA: Barr Media, 1990. $90. 4-9
   Byzantium, Constantinople, and Istanbul: The three names for one city through the centuries show that although the names have changed, the city has remained an important site in its location between Asia and Europe. The video presents the history, geography, religion, agriculture, economy, and culture of Turkey.

1544. **Ukraine: Kiev and Lvov**. Videocassette. Color. 25 min. Derry, NH: Chip Taylor Communications, 1992. $150. (Exploring the World). 6 up
   Three brief segments give an overview of the Ukraine. The first relates the history and culture of Kiev, a fifth-century city that is the site of the Cathedral of St. Vladimir. The second segment presents the folk traditions of the area, including the folk dancing that came from the Cossacks of the 1600s. The third part shows Lvov, the capital of West Ukraine, with its baroque architecture and collection of Ukrainian artifacts.

1545. **The Vikings: Seafarers and Explorers**. Videocassette. Color. 15 min. Chicago: Encyclopaedia Britannica, 1993. $99. ISBN 0-8347-9992-8. 6-12
   The video discusses the Vikings' culture, their expeditions into southern Europe and the West, and the communities they conquered. The four parts of the video are "Life," "Ship Building and Seafaring," "Voyages," and "Trade."

1546. **We Must Never Forget: The Story of the Holocaust**. Videocassette. Color. 25 min. Madison, WI: Knowledge Unlimited, 1995. $55. 6 up
   The video examines the historical context that allowed the Holocaust to occur, emphasizing anti-Semitic attitudes in Europe, the impact of World War I on Germany, and Hitler's rise to power. It includes interviews with survivors of the Warsaw ghetto and of Auschwitz. Film footage, political cartoons from the time, and color maps help show this period for what it was. *Council on Nontheatrical Events Golden Eagle, National Educational Media Silver Apple,* and *New York Festivals Finalist.*

1547. **Who Built the Pyramids?** Videocassette. Color. 16 min. Washington, DC: National Geographic, 1997. $69. 4-9
   In seventy years, men shaped 6 million limestone blocks into three pyramids, one of them forty stories high. Whether these men were slaves or skilled craftsmen is currently a debate, but the question remains as to what force kept these workmen on task, but the methods they used are not too different from those used today.

Author/Illustrator Index

Reference is to entry number.

Title Index

Reference is to entry number.

Subject Index

Reference is to entry number.